Darkest Truths of Black Gold

Darkest Truths of Black Gold

✦

An Oil Industry Executive Breaks the Industry's Code of Silence

Robert Palmer Smith

iUniverse, Inc.
New York Lincoln Shanghai

Darkest Truths of Black Gold
An Oil Industry Executive Breaks the Industry's Code of Silence

iUniverse books may be ordered through booksellers or by contacting:

iUniverse
2021 Pine Lake Road, Suite 100
Lincoln, NE 68512
www.iuniverse.com
1-800-Authors (1-800-288-4677)

Because of the dynamic nature of the Internet, any Web addresses or links contained in this book may have changed since publication and may no longer be valid.

The views expressed in this work are solely those of the author and do not necessarily reflect the views of the publisher, and the publisher hereby disclaims any responsibility for them.

ISBN: 978-0-595-42597-6 (pbk)
ISBN: 978-0-595-90114-2 (cloth)
ISBN: 978-0-595-86925-1 (ebk)

Printed in the United States of America

If assassination were a viable alternative, this book is dedicated to those who would be the aim of such assassination. Without them, it would never have been written.

Contents

PROLOGUE

In business, as in life itself, one acts accordingly to the beliefs that he or she holds. Whether those beliefs are real or unreal, true or untrue, moral or immoral makes no difference to the way one acts, because those beliefs are held to be real, true and moral by the individual who holds them. And so it is with this chronology of thirty four years in the international oil business.

In the narrating and retelling of many of the episodes over a number of years before they were finally committed to writing in this volume, the author is the first to admit that embellishment, self-aggrandizement and memory lapses about dates over a span of thirty-four years may have had an influence on a few of the peripheral details. Every effort has been made to verify and correct any possible memory breaches, but, obviously, over such an extended period, there may be some dates that require slight modification. However, such modifications would not change the thrust or the focus of the happenings.

There will be some readers who will immediately rush to a computerized, modern and up to date library, or to the American Bar Association to authenticate each and every statement made in this narrative to corroborate if the statements, the understandings or the dates are correct. No matter. The positions taken, the acts committed, the moral judgments made and stood by are history and were believed to be real, true and moral at the time. They were all based on what was understood to be the factual circumstances and what we were told at the time and believed to be the lawful situation by people whom we trusted.

The desire to seem less than gullible, in the face of insurmountable evidence that that is just what happened in many instances, may have had an influence on one or two of the marginal details also. Nevertheless, be that as it may, the narration, as it is written, represents a true portrayal of the international oil business and the life of an international oil executive as it was played out by one individual over those many tumultuous years after the Second World War.

In the case of acts committed on behalf of the United States Government, the author fervently hopes that he made some contribution to the always, present necessity to support his country. A support eternally necessary in the ongoing requirement to protect it against those who would make every attempt to undermine it, both citizens and non-citizens. There is no rationalization intended for the disclosure of them. Espionage is a way of life in this terror ridden world of ours. All nations indulge in the art. No damage is believed to have been done by recording these deeds. The chronicling of these acts is undertaken merely to show that an international oil executive's responsibility isn't always in the pursuit of maximizing the company's profit.

Many of the individuals to whom the writer has referred are, no doubt, still alive. A determined effort has been made to ensure, in every possible way, that no finger has been pointed by the author saying, 'You are less than I am,' or 'You are more guilty than I.' However, there are one or two rare instances where, in the opinion of the author, it was felt that the individual or individuals concerned were less than honest in their approach to the circumstances believed to be in existence at that time. In cases such as those, there has been no hesitation made in identifying the person or persons and recording the suspicions of the writer.

The suicides of two colleagues have not been recorded at all. It would only lend an engrossing moment of lurid detail about unsavory liaisons. Liaisons which would be more appropriately read about in some of the many magazines found at the check-out counters of our supermarkets. And so it is with a myriad of other similar events about which, at another time and another locality, would read like Peyton Place if the author were so inclined.

Over a period of almost three and a half decades, any international oil executive would have reported to many superiors. In turn, he would have had hundreds of employees report to him. There were three men to whom this writer reported directly over the span of thirty-four years, who, if any one of them had stated, "We must sail into the waters of Abaddon. Are you with me?", the response would have been immediate. "Sail on my Captain! I await your orders!" Or if one had to lead a charge into a hail of gunfire, there were many that the author would thank God to have at his side. One would be Stella. One would be George. One would be that Marine captain, who used his men to shield the author and his wife from stray bullets. And one would be a Russian descendent, who learned the value of life and personal sacrifice at the knee of his forebears. Forebears, who were born in that sad and unfortunate country.

As I finished writing this chronology in Paris and watched the news and read the headlines, I could only sadly reflect that it appears that old adage is being reinforced on a daily basis, 'the only thing we learn from history is that we learn nothing from history'.

1

Hong Kong—Early 1948

"Take these fifty one dollar bills. Hire a sampan. Bring them out to that freighter moored in front of the Peninsula Hotel and give them to the Chief Engineer."

Seventeen years of schooling, five years as an officer in the United States Navy, one in commercial life, one in the merchant marine, and I was now going to put all that schooling and experience to work for my new employer in Hong Kong, The California Texas Oil Company, Ltd., an international oil company. In the decades of the acronym to come, the company's name was shortened to Caltex. In the many Board Rooms of its competitors around the world, it was very often referred to apprehensively as 'CPC', Caltex Petroleum Corporation. It was known affectionately among its many indentured staff members as THE COMPANY.

When the corporate culture wished to massage the frequently bruised feelings of its employees, it was called 'The Caltex Family'. My patient and long suffering wife explained the meaning of that phrase to me at one time. She had been enduring weeks and weeks of having to wile away the lonely nights all by herself in a strange country, while waiting for me to return from the office each evening. I was spending the not unusual sixty and seventy hour work weeks that 'The Caltex Family' often extracted from many of its dedicated staff members. On my arrival home late one evening, she greeted me in exasperation with the very heartfelt statement, "I know now what's meant by 'The Caltex Family'. You're goddamn well married to it!"

I was to learn later also, much to my chagrin, that 'The Caltex Family' was the step-sister of two of 'The Seven Sisters', Chevron and Texaco. Enrico Mattei, the head of the Italian state owned oil company was the first to popularize the phrase, 'The Seven Sisters', Esso, Gulf, Texaco, Mobil, Chevron, BP and Shell[1]. They were the household names of the seven largest international oil companies in the world. That is, the seven largest international oil companies in the world, until Caltex appeared on the skyline. Within Caltex, the Two Sisters that owned THE

COMPANY were occasionally referred to respectfully as 'The Shareholders', or much more frequently, as 'the goddamn shareholders'.

"Why?" I wanted to know as I took the fifty one dollar bills. I still had an inquisitive mind in spite of all that education.

"Because we have an arrangement with all the Chief Engineers of that shipping company. If they order our lubricating oil instead of a competitor's, they get a US dollar a barrel for themselves for each barrel ordered. And this one just ordered fifty barrels," my new manager, Dave Rowsome, informed me in a tone of voice that seemed to say: 'Will wonders never cease? Can this new crop of employees be as naïve as they seem?'

My introduction to the international oil business. It was only the beginning.

The international oil business was to take me around the world a number of times. It was to result in three evacuations—thank God for the United States Marines. It was to put me in a position where I couldn't refuse to 'take orders' from United States Naval Attachés in American Embassies. It would cause guns with rifle bolts drawn to be shoved in my face and my wife's. It would result in my being placed under curfew a number of times—once for six months. It would endanger my marriage and give my wife and elder daughter malaria.

As the years passed, there was a constant, recurring, chain reaction of thought and action in connection with those senior officers of THE COMPANY who had interviewed me, when I had applied for the position of 'international oil executive'. A thought process that always ended with the same question of provocative action. The ultimate question directed towards those very same, senior individuals. It was they who had convinced me that the international oil business offered a wonderful opportunity to, 'see the world, enjoy a substantial income and live a life of comfort and ease'. That question was to arise many times and it was always the same.

"Is assassination a viable alternative?"

In the beginning there were other options considered besides the explicit one of assassination. As time wore on, however, only the finale question would arise. The only question and the only answer to that question that would offer me complete and absolute satisfaction regarding those senior officers of THE COMPANY. The ones that I was convinced were responsible for putting me in the predicaments in which I would find myself over the years. Predicaments, which were light years away from that 'life of comfort and ease', which they had so vividly described during my pre-employment interviews. The only question and the only answer to that question were, in reality, one and the same.

"Is assassination a viable alternative?"

Their faces were always very clear in my mind as I graphically recalled the meetings. The only time they appeared to fade into the background momentarily was when the cause of my immediate quandary was sitting in front of me. Quandaries over the years that caused my intestines to react in agonizing bouts of gut-wrenching fear and absolute dread. Then that individual's face who was sitting in front of me became much more prominent. It was towards him that my mind directed the question. However, the question was always identical, even with that particular person and always with those senior officers ever present in the background, and, again, always with the same intense desire to implement the action. It was really a rhetorical question. It didn't need an answer. Only action.

"IS ASSASSINATION A VIABLE ALTERNATIVE!"

The sampan wended its way across the breathtakingly, beautiful harbour of Hong Kong and bounced and tossed on the waves stirred up by the freshening breeze. The many Chinese junks with their huge, slatted sails glided by ghostlike without a sound as they headed towards the open seas and distant ports. They had their hidden and unknown cargo carefully stowed away below decks and out of sight. Little did I realize that I was, also, embarking on an exhilarating, fascinating and often times dangerous career that was to span the world and thirty-four years.

The engineer, who was a Scotsman as were almost all ship's engineers in those days, accepted his fifty one dollar bills. He should have been asked what idiosyncrasy in his arrangement with THE COMPANY required that the payment be made in one dollar bills. Maybe they aren't as easy to trace as fifty dollar bills? More likely, the Chinese exchange shop received a higher commission on fifty transactions than it would have made on one fifty dollar transaction. I never did inquire and to this day it has vexed me.

Unfortunately for this Chief Engineer, he was unaware of other standard operating procedures of THE COMPANY in addition to the one of the usual payment of one dollar a barrel to him for every barrel of lubricating oil that he ordered. He informed me over a cup of coffee that the ship intended to sail late the next Sunday afternoon. He requested that I make arrangements to have the vessel fueled early Sunday morning. This would allow him to sail with a full complement of fuel oil for the next long haul.

Hastening back to shore and the office as bearer of these important instructions, I stood at the prow of the sampan and threw back my shoulders. My chest swelled with pride at the thought that I was now really part of that efficient and well organized industry known as the 'international oil business'. I disembarked from the sampan on my way to Queens Road where the office was located.

Immediately as I stepped ashore from the sampan, I became part of a massive, undulating river of faceless humanity. A river that seemed to flow in all directions simultaneously. A faceless and unrecognizable humanity to Westerners on their initial encounter with the millions of the Oriental race, with their moon-like features and delicate, smooth skin characterized by its yellow tone. It takes Westerners a considerable period of time to recognize that all Orientals' eyes do not slant in the same manner nor are they all of the same delicate hue, particularly, the strikingly, beautiful women. The sing-song chant of their voices takes on a most easily, recognizable cadence to those Westerners that are determined to make their home and their living in this ageless society. And who are, in addition, willing to make the effort to distinguish the difference between Northerners and Southerners, Mandarin and Cantonese, Shanghaiese and Pekinese.

It was a strange failing of the early, white colonizers that they never took the trouble to make the determined effort to recognize that other members of the genus Homo sapiens have distinguishing and readily, discernable characteristics. To those white colonialists, who initially went out to secure the empire for 'The King', all non-whites looked alike. If they were to meet their servants on a chance encounter in town, they would have difficulty recognizing them. This difficulty of recognition was not confined only to the Oriental, but to the Indian and to the black races of Africa as well. Black may be black, but in reality there are different shades of black.

'Anton Rupert, the remarkable scientist who built up the Rembrandt tobacco company in South Africa preferred to discuss blacks—like his fellow Afrikaner Laurens van der Post, in terms of flora and fauna, or catalysts and chemicals rather than as ordinary people or a practical political problem'[2]. For the children of the expatriates, who were born abroad while their parents were 'exploiting the natives', this problem never existed. From the day that they were born, they knew that there was a profound difference. My elder daughter not only knew that there was a difference, but had the effrontery when she had just entered her teens to announce to the white South Africans in a school essay in Johannesburg, the industrial and mining center of that hated and inhumane system of apartheid, 'that their black brethren were indeed human beings and not just another animal to be yoked to the plow'.

'The European colonizers of Algeria were, until 1962, citizens of metropolitan France, although perhaps three out of five of them were descendants of Italian,

Spanish, Greek, Maltese and other immigrants from the Mediterranean basin. Some had been in Algeria for as many as four generations and, like the pioneers who opened the American West, developed the land at the expense of the indigenous population. Although in the mid-twentieth century there were only about one million *colons*, as these settlers were called, to eight million Moslems, the Europeans of Algeria—even so liberal-minded a one as Albert Camus–tended to see the country as predominately European, with the mass of Moslems somewhat faceless in the background. The more racist or more insecure among them subjected the Moslems to daily humiliations and referred to them as *ratons*, 'little rats'[3].

Strangely enough in like fashion, this failure of recognition of fellow Homo sapiens is not confined to the different species of the human race. Almost all race goers, who have not been brought up on farms, have difficulty distinguishing the difference between one horse and another. And for a surety the colonialists, who were members of the Royal Hong Kong Race Track, weren't brought up on farms. A visit to the incomparably, luxurious Royal Hong Kong Race Track built on some of the most expensive land in the entire world will tell you something about the empire builders who congregate there in the members' stand. As with the difficulty of recognition of the Orientals, the Browns and the Blacks, they could only make the distinction between one horse and another if the diminutive character astride its back was wearing the owner's gaudy colors of the stable; there was a large Arabic numeral inscribed on the saddle cloth, and they were reading the race sheet.

Perhaps, therefore, the original empire builders can be forgiven for the failure of not being able to differentiate between the subjects they were sent out to rule in the name of their Monarchs. But only if it were an initial failing. Unfortunately, not too many of them made the effort to overcome this difficulty. They continued to look at Orientals, Browns, Blacks and horses through the same blinders, or as Anton Rupert did, 'in terms of flora and fauna, or chemicals and catalysts rather than ordinary people or a practical political problem'.

On my arrival back in the office I met the manager who was just leaving for the day.

"Well, how did it go?" he enquired.

"Fine, fine," I replied. Then, with just a noticeable trace of self-importance, I advised him of the Chief Engineer's request regarding the time of fueling. "I'll call the operations department now, and they can make the necessary arrangements for Sunday," I finished off in a very efficient manner.

"Sunday?" he echoed. "That's impossible! The weather forecast is for a perfect day with no wind. That's the day of the company picnic. We'll be using the company tug. Didn't you see the announcement on the bulletin board?" he asked in a very definitely, accusing tone of voice. Of course, I had seen the news of the company picnic, but being such a newcomer to the trade I was, obviously, unaware of what the logistics of such an undertaking involved.

How was I to know that the picnic required the use of the company tug? A fast moving and powerful vessel which would take us to an outlying area where we would have the beach all to ourselves. While there were those who preferred to loll on the sand and sun themselves, apparently there were sport enthusiasts among the staff who wanted to aquaplane. The company tug would provide the motivating power for this pastime as well as transporting us. I was so new to the international oil business that I was naïve enough to believe that if a customer wanted to have his ship fueled on a Sunday, the employees' pleasure would have to take second place.

Dave Rowsome, the very competent and extremely well liked manager, was a prewar employee as were almost all of the more senior staff in the office. They had all been brought up under the old colonial order.

This was an attitude of mind that said, 'We're bearing the brunt of having to live under the unrivaled conditions of this idyllic, island haven in the South China Sea. We have had to leave our country, friends and families. In addition, we have to put up with the difficulty of having to manage a large staff of personal servants in our homes. Further more, and even more importantly, *we* are running the business, *not* the customer. The customer should consider himself lucky that he is able to do business with THE COMPANY; not everyone has that advantage. Consequently, no customer is going to interfere with our life style by forcing us to forego our weekend pleasure by requesting that his vessel be fueled on a Sunday, which would entail the use of the company tug. Besides, the champagne has been chilled, and if the tug is utilized by these intruders, known as customers, there will be no one to enjoy the pleasures of the vintage Môet & Chandon.'

This was the very same attitude exhibited by the Colonial French Army, when they brought their wine cellars, valets and dress whites to the jungle to fight that horribly difficult and uncomfortably inconvenient war in the blistering tropics of Vietnam. The Colonial French Army was never able to adapt to the new world conditions in existence at the time of their attempt to keep control of their pre-World War II empire. As a result, they were forced to beat an ignominious retreat from the battle lines between Saigon and Hanoi. Nothing had changed since '1914 when graduates of the French Military Academy had marched into battle wearing white gloves and pompoms[4]' Their General Staff was still imbued with the same Maginot Line mentality that left them aghast when the Germans simply went around the 'impregnable earth barriers' of the Maginot Line and 'approached it from the rear, cutting off its supplies[5]'. A Line that was, in reality, a pre-revolutionary concept of defense in the same class as The Great Wall of China.

Fortunately for Caltex, there were some of their pre-war employees that were able to adapt. Dave Rowsome, the Manager, was one of them, albeit, his change in attitude didn't extend to the company picnic. Just as it was so sad to see the French Army defeated by its inherited state of mind, it was almost just as sad to see the toll of early retirements, transfers back home and just plain firings that took place after the Japanese were defeated. The individuals concerned just couldn't break life long habits and attitudes. There were still just too many 'order takers' in the ranks of the post-war international oil companies and not enough salesmen.

Nowhere was this state of mind more evident than in the case of one of my British colleagues in the office. He was a very likable and friendly individual named Ernie Clements. He was many years my senior and had been engaged by THE COMPANY before the war as a salesman. In those pre World War II days, salesmen just 'kept the books'. They merely recorded orders. For many years they had been satisfied to continue to perform this duty. The tally was completed at the end of the month. If you had committed the unpardonable sin of taking more orders than your quota, it was simply 'pumped-over' and sold back to you by the competitor whom you had so ungraciously offended.

So that was what was meant by the term 'pump-overs? I had heard it initially discussed by the operations staff, but I had failed to grasp its meaning.

It wasn't until after the war that newcomers to the old established way of doing business, such as Caltex, became aggressive and forced the antiquated, ensconced companies and their salesmen to perform the duties normally envisaged in connection with the selling of oil. That is to say, 'they had to get out of the office and *sell* the company's products'. To this day I can hear Dave's questioning tone of voice as he was walking past Ernie's office on a rainy day. "What, no raincoat?"

Ernie's telephone would ring early in the afternoon just prior to four o'clock. Experience soon told me that it had better not be a customer; Ernie was on his way home for his afternoon tea. No interruption to this centuries old English habit was going to interfere with this ritual. Certainly nothing so gauche as a customer's request for service. Even worse, a customer that wanted to spend his hard earned money on purchasing the company's products, which would entail considerable paperwork at this late hour of the day.

Ernie informed me at one time, when I had been quartered in his company home because I had momentarily run out of hotel rooms, that I was a very difficult person for whom to cater. I was never quite sure who was enduring the difficulty. It certainly wasn't Ernie, inasmuch as it was his cook boy who made the tea, his house boy who served it, his room boy who cleared up the debris and his wash amah who returned every piece of linen used to its original, immaculate condition after the formal British ritual of afternoon tea.

His remark to me was occasioned by my constant inability to be home at four o'clock in the afternoon for tea. It certainly wasn't any dedication on my part to my office duties that prevented me from being there. On the lush tropical island of Hong Kong, it wasn't my idea of filial duty to my seniors to be at his beck and call for afternoon tea while there were many more inviting tastes to savour in this free-wheeling society, even in the afternoon.

Ernie's wife was still in England shopping and hadn't yet arrived back from their last home leave. I guess this was the basic difficulty to which he was referring. He felt lonely and had no one to whom he could talk without my being there for tea. In any event, I hadn't grown use to the idea of having afternoon tea. In fact, I didn't even like the stuff and only acquired a taste for it and became addicted to it after having lived in Ceylon for five years, the home of some of the greatest tea grown in the world. Then I could understand Ernie, but it was rather too late to make amends at that stage six years afterwards.

At the time of his rather caustic remark my mind traveled back to the, then, not too distant past when, as a United States Naval Officer in the Boston Navy yard during the war, we were building attack vessels for the British government. At the same time we were indoctrinating the English crews who were to man the vessels. Four o'clock in the afternoon would roll around. 'Down tools!' It was time for our British associates to have tea. The American workmen and officers would look on with dismay and frustration. No power on earth was going to deter the English from having their afternoon tea, in spite of a raging world war and a host of expensively paid American workmen standing by and looking on in disgust.

This particular engineer, to whom I had delivered the fifty one dollar bills, was instrumental in my learning rapidly the various normal marketing and operating practices used by the international oil companies. One of these normal practices, in addition to not fueling a customer's vessel on a Sunday, was to fill with sea water the loading line from the shore tanks to the floating barge that carried the line. As the buying public is aware, there are a large number of different grades of fuel oil. By having the line filled with sea water after fueling a particular vessel, a different grade of fuel oil could be introduced into the line at the terminal without fear of pumping the residual amount of the prior grade left in the line into the subsequent vessel's tanks or discharging it into the harbour. Naturally, the standard, operating procedure was to discharge the sea water prior to filling the line with the new fuel oil and pumping it into the receiving vessel's tanks.

Somehow or other on Monday morning, while the Chief Engineer was fuming about the delay to his vessel's sailing date, the member of the company's operations staff, who was responsible for discharging the sea water from the loading line, failed to 'discharge' his duties as well. Perhaps, he had consumed too much of that chilled, fabulous Môet & Chandon that we all had enjoyed so much on the beach at the company's expense. In any event, the sea water was not emptied from the line prior to filling the fuel tanks of the vessel. It was not possible for either the Chief Engineer or the staff of THE COMPANY to be aware of this minor oversight. That is, not until the vessel had cleared the harbour and was on its way. We did soon learn of this unfortunate omission, however, when to our surprise and embarrassment the vessel limped back into port unable to continue on its voyage. Apparently, the combustibility of sea water does not compare very favourably with that of fuel oil.

One advantage of being in the international oil business, versus the domestic oil business, is that you are quickly exposed to learning situations early in your career as I was beginning to understand very rapidly.

The assignment in Hong Kong didn't last very long. It was merely a matter of months when THE COMPANY flew me to Beijing to the prestigious Chinese language school, 'Wa Win Wai Shiao'. I was to take the place of an employee who had opted out of the language course, because he didn't feel it was necessary to learn to speak Chinese in order to sell oil. It seems he was under the mistaken impression that he had come to China simply to sell oil to the 'natives'.

An international oil company executive's main duties, unlike a salesman's, has absolutely nothing to do with selling oil. It has to do with government relations, public relations, press relations, employee relations, espionage and smuggling guns and guerrillas into territories ruled by despotic colonialists. And breaking embargoes imposed by the British Government with the help of the British oil companies (one of which had a majority interest in it owned by the British Government), or running a river transport company on the Zambezi River in the heart of Africa. It was, in fact, being an 'international oil company executive'.

It was just as well that the assignment in Hong Kong didn't last very long, inasmuch as I was running out of hotel rooms. On the day of my arrival at the hotel at which I had been informed I was booked, I was taken upstairs by the room boy. It appeared strange that he would knock on the door before entering an empty room. Perhaps he was just making sure that the former occupant had departed. How right he was. A voice called out in answer to the knock. "Come right in," was the reception.

I only entered to apologize, "Presumably the room boy must have been given the wrong room number, or perhaps I am too early." I started to back out of the room with the intention of remaining in the lobby while the present occupant finished packing his possessions and vacated the room. Alternatively, I would verify the correctness of the room number.

"You're the new oil chap, aren't you?" was the rejoinder given from the sitting position of the occupant on one of the two beds in a very smallish room. An occupant clad only in a pair of under shorts. His attire, or lack of it, was due to the sweltering Hong Kong weather and non-existent air conditioning, which is so taken for granted in these modern days. In fact, the room was only large enough to contain the two beds, a modest table with a chair at one end near the entrance door and a chest of drawers at the far wall. "No," he continued, "you haven't gotten the wrong room, and I'm not departing." To say that I was at a loss for words would be putting it mildly.

He went on to explain in very precise English tones that the room was his permanent room. He had been a resident in the hotel before the war and had been taken a prisoner of war when the Japanese invaded Hong Kong. Having survived the rigors of internment, he returned to Hong Kong to continue his business endeavours from the point at which he had been interrupted when the Japanese had arrived seven years ago, and he had been interned. The hotel, recognizing all its long term prior permanent residents, had 'grand-fathered' them in as a matter of courtesy. They were allowed to occupy the rooms on a permanent basis, but only on the condition that they share the room with transients.

He gestured towards the chest of drawers, where carefully arranged on the top was a neat row of bottles and drink mixes. As my profession was engineering, my mind automatically calculated that exactly only half of the top of the chest had been utilized. Of course, it was the half nearest his bed. "But I'm not a transient," I hastened to explain. "I'm here on a permanent assignment."

"Well, old boy," he continued, "somebody has failed to clue you in. You had better sit down and have a drink. It is my practice to offer the first drink to all new-comers. For everything after that, you will have to make your own arrangements. And, oh yes, as a matter of explanation you may be in Hong Kong on a permanent assignment, but as far as the hotel industry is concerned you are a transient. You are only allowed a three day stay at any hotel. No doubt after a dozen or so moves, you will be able to locate more fixed accommodations. That is up to you and how you operate."

He continued to explain the protocol. "Half of the top of the chest of drawers is yours," which justified the precise division my mind had noted, "and the bottom two drawers are yours." To be sure, the permanent resident had the two top drawers which eliminated bending over every time you wanted something.

Exposure to hotel room shortages was no new experience, but shortages such as existed in Hong Kong were beyond the realm of imagination. No one had told me it would be necessary to move every three days. No one had told me I would have to share a room with an unknown British gentleman and share the bath as well. His voice was penetrating my consciousness with the question as to my preference of showering in the morning or the evening. If the morning, at what time, inasmuch as it was his habit to shower in the morning.

The reason for the practice of the hotel industry of restricting newcomers to only a three day stay on their initial arrival was made absolutely clear to me the very next day. *There was no place to live in Hong Kong.*

All available accommodations had been secured by those who were fortunate enough to have arrived on the heels of the departing Japanese. Alternatively, they were returning residents who could prove that they were the owners of the residences dotting the landscape of the island. In the case of the 'taipans', the companies with deep pockets that had no bottoms laid out astronomical sums of 'key money' to ensure that their senior staff and their families had a place to live. None of these credentials applied to young, new arrivals like myself.

The many companies, which had flooded into Hong Kong after the war, had originally booked hotel rooms for their newly arrived employees with the understanding that those employees would look for permanent accommodations. When they couldn't find a place to live, they simply stayed in the hotel. It didn't take the hotel industry long to learn that they were rapidly becoming vast dormitories for the newly arrived businessmen who couldn't find permanent shelter on this island paradise. Hence, the cast iron rule of a stay of no longer than three days.

And so began a hotel rhapsody which, when it was finally played out, introduced me to every hotel in Hong Kong and the majority of the hotels in Kowloon on the mainland. It, also, established a number of contacts with hotel managers and various employees of those establishments which were to stand me in good stead a number of times. At one stage, when I was on my third round of the better known hostelries, I would never have been able to make the satisfactory emergency arrangements I did at two AM in the morning without the benefit of those contacts.

The telephone rang shrilly. Why is it always so shrill at two AM when you have only just retired? Fumbling in the dark for the receiver and getting it to my ear was a major achievement, only to be greeted with a call for help.

"This is Mother," the voice said. "I'm down at the water taxi pier. My date is just drunk enough to be dangerous. There is no way I'm going to get in a water taxi with him in that condition. There would be no place to hide, but to jump over the side. Can you put me up for the night?"

Westerners might think that with an appeal for help to the water taxi driver, the passenger about to be molested could expect some aid. Not so in this part of the world. It is none of their business what those crazy 'da bezes' do. He would simply look the other way.

There are two times when the ferries between Kowloon, the mainland, and the city of Victoria on the island of Hong Kong stop running. One was normally at midnight. All transport across the harbour after that hour was by water taxi. The other was when the red flag went up indicating that a typhoon was on its way. Understandably, there was no water transportation of any kind navigating with a typhoon expected. Woe betide those conscientious office staff of THE COMPANY, who either didn't see the red flag from their windows or ignored it momentarily, hoping to finish up their urgent task for the day before departing for the mainland. Invariably, they spent the evening on the floor of the American Club in The Shanghai and Hong Kong Bank building, somewhat shielded from the cold marble floor by the use of the many decorative pillows normally strewn around the premises.

The American Club was very accommodating in this respect. The Club often sheltered young and attractive employees of the various companies when a typhoon left them stranded on the island and unable to proceed to the mainland. As Doc Taylor, the company accountant, use to say, "That made it very difficult on your knees, as the pillows had a tendency to keep slipping away and separating."

"Yes, Mother. Certainly!" was my immediate response. I replaced the receiver only to have it dawn on me that the present hotel accommodations that were my immediate three day stay happened to be a very small room with a single bed which barely catered for my six foot bulk. Hastily re-donning my clothes, I descended to the lobby. One of my better known contacts was asleep on duty.

Waking him gently, I explained my dilemma. He eyed me rather suspiciously on hearing that I was going to have a female visitor in a few minutes who was going to occupy my room, while I was requesting him to make other arrangements for me to sleep elsewhere. You could almost read his mind. 'These mad foreigners. A female visitor and he wants to sleep elsewhere?'

After a bit of grumbling, which he knew would increase the amount of bucsheese he was going to receive, he informed me the only possibility was to install another cot in the bridal suite. There were already nine occupants in the suite, but he would arrange to make additional space available for me. By the time my visitor arrived, he would have the cot made up and ready for me to occupy.

Mother knocked on the door in less than ten minutes, kissed me gently on the cheek and explained that she had had misgivings about accepting this individual's invitation in the first instance. She had fully intended to take the ferry back to the mainland before midnight. However, he seemed perfectly capable of absorbing the large amount of alcohol he was consuming. It wasn't until they reached the water taxi pier that she realized that it was not safe to attempt the trip across the harbour in a water taxi with him. Hence, her call for help to me.

'Mother', whose name was actually Stella, was the executive secretary for Dave Rowsome, the manager of the international oil company for which we both worked. She was very much older; always very much older when you are in your twenties and the individual concerned is in her thirties. She had to be one of the most kind hearted people that anyone would ever have the privilege of knowing. She took every young American, who joined the company, under her wing. She advised them of all the pitfalls in the hedonistic city of Hong Kong. In the office, she made sure that all their paper work was in the correct order and sent to the right departments. When, and you frequently did, run afoul of her boss she always let you know in advance. At times she actually took a great risk by intervening on your behalf.

As a result of her kindness and interest she took on the part of all the young Americans, she received the lovable nickname of 'Mother', and mother us all she did. It can be appreciated, therefore, when there was a call for help from this inestimable lady, there was never any hesitation in answering it to the very best of your ability. Not only was she one of the kindest individuals with whom one could hope to become acquainted, but she was dazzlingly beautiful as well. Her mother was Japanese and her father had been a Swedish captain on a China coastal vessel. A combination that left you with a tendency to become breathless every time you looked at her. It was her Swedish father and the resultant Swedish passport that saved her from joining the many company employees, who became guests of the Japanese government when the japs invaded the island.

Her taking risks on your behalf in the office must have seemed like child's play to her after her undertakings on behalf of the company employees who had been interned by the Japanese. It was a well recognized fact that the Chinese abhorred the Japanese with a passion during the Japanese occupation. What is probably not so well known is that there were many Chinese who were convinced that the Japanese would not be successful in their pursuit of subjugation of the Asian continent. As a consequence, they made many attempts to help the Allies in what ever way they could and at very great risk to themselves.

The Japanese did not have the reputation of treating very kindly those whom they believed were frustrating their war efforts. In fact, the stories were legion about the diabolical and sadistic delight they took in torturing their prisoners. Stella took the same risk when by contacting those farmers who were sympathetic to the Allies' cause, she was able to obtain food for the interned employees. She had it smuggled into the prisoner of war camps, where her efforts may well have resulted in the difference between life and death for some of those internees.

When the telephone rang in my office in Sydney, Australia almost twenty-three years later and a never to be forgotten voice laughingly said, "I need help. Can you put me up?" half my life dissolved instantly. I was transported back to Hong Kong and to that morning at two AM as we renewed a deep rooted relationship. A relationship built on such a firm foundation that it seemed like only yesterday that that call had come through that morning in Hong Kong.

And, now, nostalgia overtakes me in Paris as I pen these words. I am within driving distance of Stella's home in Stockholm where she retired. The anticipation that grips me at the very thought that it will only be a matter of hours and forty-five years before I will be sitting at Mother's knee and laughing and crying over those wonderful, wonderful days of our youth is simply overwhelming.

2

Beijing—Autumn 1948

To dwell for a year in the cloistered, ivory tower of the prestigious Chinese language school, Wa Win Wai Shiao in Beijing, looking forward to the past, was an experience in living that would be impossible to duplicate. Not only was the Chinese language taught, but the required curriculum included many hours on how to understand the people and the culture of the country in which one was an honoured guest. None of this 'chip on the shoulder' mentality which is so prevalent in Africa where the white colonialists had held sway for so many years. The Chinese attitude? 'You white savages were running around in lion skins, when we had a civilization that was already several thousand years old.'

Refreshing. It wasn't long before the decision was made. China, and Beijing in particular, was the place that would become my retirement home. Strange thoughts indeed as I recall those feelings sitting here in Paris, where I have lived in retirement for the past twelve years.

It will be recalled that it was the autumn of 1948 that Mao Tze-tung was proving to be a better general than the West's friend and ally, General Chang Kai-shek. The Chinese Red Army was moving relentlessly southward. They had left their caves at Yenan in the North and were proceeding, as our 'striped pants liberals' in the State Department announced, 'to liberate the people'. But this was China, everybody and anybody was quite prepared to believe everything and anything, even down to believing the State Department.

The story is told of the two Chinese friends who met at the Shanghai airport; one embarking and the other disembarking. The one who had just arrived queried his friend as to his destination. "I'm off to Beijing. It is not safe here in Shanghai," he replied. "And you, my friend, from where have you come?" he asked.

"I've just come from Beijing to Shanghai where it is safe. It is not safe in Beijing."

15

Whether or not it was safe in Beijing depended entirely on your own personal outlook. The power station was some distance out of town. When the lights went out, the belief was strongly held that the Red Army had captured the power station. Indisputably, it wasn't safe in Beijing. When the lights came on again, we were convinced that Chang Kai-shek's Nationalists had recaptured the power station. We knew we were safe.

If ever there were a group of people that lived in fantasy land at that time, it was the expatriates and the companies for whom they worked in China. Whatever lands were more distant than fantasy land, that was where the staff of the State Department lived. The entire world was coming down around our ears. To listen to the State Department, the armies of the 'second coming' were arriving, led by a messiah called Mao Tze-tung.

With our noses buried in our school books, the weather hovering around zero degrees Fahrenheit, and the Red Army advancing on us, we certainly lived in another world. There were three of us sharing the company house, which was owned, staffed and furnished by THE COMPANY. It was bitter, bitter cold in the mornings—no central heating of course—why do you think the Chinese wear all those heavy robes?

In order for us to be able to greet the cold light of dawn, the house boy would bring in one or two kerosene heaters an hour before it was time to arise. He also brought in the time honoured 'bed tea', which is the da beze's substitute for an alarm clock. No alarm clock salesman could ever be successful in China. With house boys, room boys, tea boys, cook boys and garden boys, some wag once commented that the famous, mystical 'Call of the East', could be summed up in one word as expressed by the imperial, English rajah in that royal tone that only the British can employ as they called … "BOYYYY"!

'Bed tea' is an enshrined ritual without which no working foreigner can start his day, if for no other reason than that he would never wake up unless his house boy brought it to him. This ritual told him that it was time to start thinking about going out into the harsh, cruel world of commerce, to a working day starting at eight o'clock in the morning and finishing at one o'clock in the afternoon.

The entire working day in China, unlike Hong Kong where the terribly, proper, British mentality prevailed, consisted of five hours. This five hours included time out for morning coffee, a chat with your fellow sojourners and perhaps a drink before returning to the office to get ready to go to lunch.

Lunch necessitated making the difficult decision of where to eat. Should it be The Club in town and play liars dice all afternoon for drinks? Or the Country Club and do the same, except that you could have a swim in between the fifth and sixth drink? For those in better physical condition, eighteen holes of golf would help to ease the morning's stressful endeavors of watching your competent Chinese staff do all your work and thinking for you. For those who had delusions of grandeur, it meant four chukka's of polo.

The Caltex Head Office in Shanghai had informed us that we would be met at the airport in Beijing on our arrival. Commercial firms had acquired the delightful and imperial habit of the diplomats and flew their company flags on their automobiles. Hence, it was not difficult to recognize the company car.

We approached it with confidence only to be disconcerted by the fact that the chauffeur was gazing beyond us. He was smiling a welcome to a most attractive fellow passenger of the opposite sex. Nobody had told the office in Shanghai that their resident manager had a live-in maid, a habit which most bachelors acquired soon after arrival in this land of beautiful women. In any event, we were politely frozen out of our transportation. The chauffeur didn't want to incur the wrath of his taipan by exposing three salivating newcomers to his master's property. Accordingly, we were reduced to attempting to hire some other means of conveyance. As in all of China, every local knows everything about the da bezes. The taxi drivers not only knew who we were, but where we were going as well as whom the company driver was meeting.

There were no street signs in Beijing, and no numbers posted on the houses. You were suppose to know where you were going or you didn't get there. We arrived safe and sound with the guidance of the taxi driver and over tipped him as do all Americans. This always made life difficult for our fellow expatriates from other countries who do not enjoy the privileges and the income of the upstart Americans.

As with all houses in China of any substance, there was a high wall surrounding the compound. This served a dual purpose. It provided a psychological barrier to anybody who thought of breaking in. In addition, it camouflaged the degree of wealth that the house represented. The wall was never painted. It was deliberately kept in a dilapidated state of repair on the outside to hide the fact that there were residents of considerable, worldly possessions behind that nondescript enclosure.

There was a telephone call that evening from the resident manager welcoming us to Beijing. He apologized for the fact that he hadn't received notice from Shanghai of our exact time of arrival or he would have had us met at the airport. It was diplomatically possible to refrain from mentioning that we had seen the company car at the airport. We assured him that no difficulty had been experienced in finding our way to the company house. He notified us that school would not start until the following Monday. We were to report to his office to be indoctrinated into the procedural rites of living in Beijing.

Early the next morning we arrived at the office just in time to hear him berating the aviation operations manager over the telephone at the top of his lungs. It wasn't possible to determine if the level of his tone of voice was due to the usual basic fault of the telephone connection, which always left a lot to be desired in this part of the world, or whether it had to with the extent of his annoyance with the aviation manager. It took only a short time of listening to the conversation to realize that it was the latter.

It appeared that the Nationalist Army had, again, commandeered the Caltex aviation refueling truck at the airport. The company's name and trade mark had not been removed before the truck was busy pumping aviation fuel into the Nationalist's bombers.

"How many times have I told you," he shouted, "that you are to have someone sleeping in that truck twenty-four hours a day? Every time the Nationalists commandeer that truck, you must be sure he removes the company name and trade mark! Why do you think we had those quick release screws installed? Suppose some photographer from Life magazine is at the airport when the Nationalists are refueling their bombers with our refueller with the company's name in full view? These are bombers that will take off in minutes and head North to bomb innocent women and children." His concern for the innocent women and children was touching.

He continued in a quieter voice with an attempt to stress the importance of his instructions concerning the removal of the company name and trade mark. "Can't you just visualize our fuel truck with the Caltex name and trade mark on the front cover of Life Magazine and the caption?"

CALTEX, AN AMERICAN OIL COMPANY, FUELING NATIONALIST BOMBERS AS THEY PREPARE AGAIN TO DEVASTATE THE COUNTRYSIDE AND MURDER INNOCENT WOMEN AND CHILDREN IN A USELESS ATTEMPT TO STEM THE ONCOMING TIDE OF THE LIBERATORS.

Yes, our liberal friends in the press, as well as the State Department, kept telling us that the oncoming tidal wave of the Red Army were 'liberators'. It is difficult to recall if 'Tiananmen Square' was the name of the Square where we use to congregate on a Sunday morning before leaving for the countryside.

The manager hung up the telephone and turned his attention from 'affairs of state' to the everyday routine of surviving in Beijing. He proceeded to lay out the company rules on what could be done, and what could not be done.

"THE COMPANY will not tolerate anyone dealing on the currency black market," he emphatically declared. "Should you be apprehended by the police for dealing on the black market, it will be noted in your personnel file. Further more, you will not be allowed to put the cost of buying them off on your expense account."

In other words, use a reliable black market dealer. He then produced the names and addresses of dealers who could be trusted, and who would never embarrass anyone by having the police involved. Naturally, the exchange rate included a charge to allow for the bucsheese required to ensure that the police were accommodating.

"If you wish to go south to Tientsin over a weekend, be sure to call the office there and check for the latest report of the progress of the Red Army," he continued. "We have had several members of the prior class marooned there when the communists cut the rail line over the weekend when they were down in Tientsin. They couldn't get back in time for their Monday class. THE COMPANY is incurring a lot of expense to keep you guys in school. They frown on your missing class. Even more importantly, it reflects on me in that it appears that I'm not keeping a tight ship here. I have too many other things to do than to have to wet nurse a bunch of students."

Over the period of time that we were in Beijing, it became very difficult to determine exactly what was meant by the phrase, 'too many things to do'. He was never in the office when we needed advice, and he was never to be found at home when we were looking for company. As our experience in China broadened, we came to realize that this was the modus operandi of the expatriate who was blessed with a competent Chinese staff and whose only real function in the office was to sign official documents.

It must be said that he did perform his royal duties exceptionally well one evening. We were invited to his company home for a 'welcome to Beijing' dinner, part of an international oil executive's employee relations duties. The word 'royal' is used merely to indicate the extent of the accommodations, the impressive appearance of the staff, the furnishings, and the food—all provided at company expense. And lo and behold, our eyes literally leapt out of our heads. Who was the hostess sitting at the head of the table for the evening? None other than our traveling companion on the plane from Shanghai to Beijing. The very same one who had pre-empted our company transportation at the airport.

She was beautifully dressed, wearing an exquisite, high necked, Chinese black gown which was slit down the one side from her thigh to the hemline. The material was embroidered with tiny white pearls in the design of a swan. We were to learn in school during the cultural sessions that the design of a swan indicated a female, while the design of a dragon indicated a male. Because of the style, many of the Chinese jackets and coats were indistinguishable in shape between male and female. Accordingly, it was necessary to indicate by some visible design the sex of the wearer, as well as to indicate who was subservient to whom, mostly the latter in this land of male chauvinism.

Male chauvinism in the West, basically, revolves around woman's rights in the office, at home and pro-choice. It is a misnomer to label women's rights in China as being in opposition to male chauvinism if such comparison is based on Western perceptions. In China, it meant survival.

A female child born to a peasant family, a family which was at or below the subsistence level, was an economic catastrophe. It meant that the child had to be fed and clothed until adulthood. Then the family had to pay to get her out of the household. The age old system of dowry is not something that has left this world in the twentieth century. To a Chinese peasant family, the arrival of a female child added years of poverty and servitude to an already impoverished life. To many there was but one solution.

However, the child could not be buried in the family plot. There were no family plots for the poor and starving of China. If there were a plot, the family couldn't publicly acknowledge that its female child had died the day it was born. This would be a serious loss of face for the surviving family members.

Was the day old female baby that I actually saw on the refuse heap in a back alley in Beijing a still born infant? Or was it a result of a centuries old social system which has kept the Chinese peasant class in a perpetual state of starvation and privation, with infanticide as one of the solutions to alleviate the problem?

The Western world, particularly the Americans, are concerned with the horsepower of the latest model automobile. Their elected representatives are committed to keeping the price of gasoline down to ensure their re-election in order that their constituents can continue to drive these gas guzzlers. Perhaps we had better attempt to understand the Third World's problems today. Problems of a Third World which, even today, are not all that far removed from those of the lives of Chinese peasants which have existed for centuries.

What is it in man's mind that blinds him to the realities of the world? Realities which he actually sees within his very own range of vision. It would be very soul satisfying to say that having seen a real life example, or rather a real death example, of a situation which had only previously been read about in books and then rather skeptically, that you then embarked on a world struggle. A world struggle to right the infamy of a system that consigned a new born female child to the rubbish heap.

What is it in the ordinary, decent person's perception of the dignity of man, who has been made in God's image, that will allow him to make a wager on the duration of a beggar's life? The vision of the dead child did not result in my making an attempt to organize a world struggle to right such infamy. It did make it impossible for me, nonetheless, to engage in that rather common pastime in Shanghai of businessmen making wagers on the way to and from their offices in regard to the remaining life span of the innumerable beggars on the street.

Each beggar had his own personal turf and woe betide any intruders. As a result, many of the beggars became familiar faces on the route to and from the office. Also familiar was the obvious deterioration which would take place in their resistance to the elements when the weather turned sharply colder and the winter months approached.

"He won't last the day out," was the comment that could be overheard concerning a particularly old and frail, long time resident of the street. A beggar who had become too feeble to even continue to beg alms from the well-to-do Westerners.

"I'll give you five to one he not only lasts the day out, but I'll make it ten to one that he is here on Monday morning," was the retort from his colleague. A handshake and the wager was consummated.

Have we become totally and completely calloused by the everyday blood and carnage that we see around the world in front of our very eyes? And especially calloused today, bombarded as we are continuously by the fare on television, that we can no longer equate to our fellow human beings? What does it do to our sense of values? What does it do to that innate sense of our being? Did it result in the holocaust years ago? Did it result in the Mai Lai massacre? And today, does it result in some declaring that the holocaust did not occur?

Nostradamus sees the third anti-Christ in a blue turban. Osama ben Laden could well prove that Nostradamus was, indeed, prophetic again. If not Osama bin Laden, the third anti-Christ may well be as successful as the other two anti-Christs, Napoleon and Hitler, were in plunging the world into a blood bath if we fail to recognize the plight of our fellow man.

One of the remonstrations of the company's resident manager in Beijing was that under no condition should curfew be violated. This was not a warning to merely observe the law as promulgated by the nervous Nationalists, who could see *'Red'* better in the daytime than at night. It was a realistic appraisal of the fact that the rag-tag horde of the retreating Nationalists was a nervous army. They were not given to asking questions first and firing later. There was much talk of incidents during curfew where they fired first, and then asked for the names of the victims from the surviving kin or from a neighbour. In our case, it would be THE COMPANY who would supply the details.

Curfew was religiously observed until one evening when the champagne flowed copiously, and spirits were at their peak. The deadline for departure was passing. Curfew was descending on the darkened city of Beijing before we were ready to leave for our respective abodes. To leave or not to leave?

One of the very attractive local residents at the party, Edie Wang, prevailed upon me to ignore the manager's strict advice concerning observance of the curfew. She said it was only a short distance to the company house. She had been a frequent visitor there for various dinner parties. I was completely at her mercy as far as location was concerned. I acceded to her urging and stayed until the festivities ended. We left the party en route to the company house long after the commencement of curfew.

We found a rickshaw coolie waiting outside who was also willing to risk breaking curfew, because he knew there were foreigners at the party. If one of the foreigners engaged him, he would earn the equivalent of a month's wages for a brief period of infraction of the curfew restrictions. A month's wages is, in reality, a substantial portion of a wage earner's life time span of earning ability, particularly, when the wage earner is a rickshaw coolie. The life span of a rickshaw coolie in China is twenty-seven years. Not only is a rickshaw coolie's life span a mere twenty-seven years, but there are no medical plan benefits. When the owner of the rickshaws is asked why he doesn't use animals instead of coolies to haul his rickshaws, he looks rather quizzically at you. He finds it difficult to understand why you don't realize that if an animal becomes ill, the animal has to be administered to. If a coolie becomes ill, he is simply fired and replaced with a new employee. It makes for very simple labour relations policies.

We had only proceeded a few blocks on our homeward bound journey when a forbidding shadow appeared out of nowhere. A Nationalist soldier on guard duty with the express purpose of enforcing the curfew stepped out of the darkness. Although, it is many years since that apparition appeared on the shadowy and unfriendly streets of Beijing, my blood still curdles as I hear in my mind, that gut wrenching sound of a rifle bolt being drawn in preparation for carrying out a soldiers duty of enforcing the curfew.

Why did he hesitate? Perhaps he was young and inexperienced. Perhaps we were to be his first victims, and he wasn't sure of how to handle his baptism of fire. Whatever the reason, he did hesitate.

My companion whispered, "Do not speak any Chinese at all. Talk slowly in the usual lost tones of a tourist that doesn't know his way around. I will tell him that you insisted we go home, because you weren't aware of the seriousness of the curfew."

The soldier, having lost the initiative of not firing first and asking questions afterwards, was now at a loss on how to proceed. After listening to her explanation and realizing that he had a stupid foreigner on his hands, and even more exasperating a stupid American foreigner, he turned his attention to the rickshaw coolie.

The trend of the conversation was evident. He cursed the coolie for being out after curfew. In the usual tried and true Chinese fashion, he cursed not only the coolie, but his ancestors and their progeny as well. Having done so, he felt he had regained control of the situation. Since he had failed to impose his will on the stupid foreigner, he could certainly take out his frustration on his fellow countryman, the rickshaw coolie.

He lowered the rifle which had been pointing in our direction during the entire conversation with the rifle bolt drawn and his eager and itching finger on the trigger. He then reversed it so that the butt of the rifle was now pointing at the rickshaw coolie's knees. He drew the rifle up in a wide circle. I suddenly realized to my horror that he intended to smash the rickshaw coolie's knees. He brought the rifle down with a powerful thrust. You could almost hear the impact of the wood striking the bone. The coolie screamed in excruciating pain and terror. I reacted automatically by starting to leap out of the rickshaw in the direction of the coolie's tormentor.

My companion, who was familiar with the streak of cruelty often exhibited by her fellow countrymen, physically restrained me by an almost inhuman show of force. She instinctively realized that any attempt to deter the soldier from his efforts to impose his will and frustrations on the hapless coolie could well result in our enduring the same fate at best. At worst, he would return to his original instructions which were 'to shoot on sight' anybody guilty of breaking the curfew.

He continued to strike at the coolie's knees with the butt of his rifle. The coolie by this time was writhing in agony on the ground and attempting to parry the blows. With the soldier's attention riveted on his sadistic endeavours, my companion signaled me to alight from the rickshaw on the side away from the two antagonists. We slowly descended without making any sudden moves that might startle the soldier, crossed the street to the far side and took refuge in the shadows as we continued on our way.

The soldier was aware of our departure. Since he was wreaking his frustration and vengeance on the rickshaw coolie and was entirely at a loss as to how to continue the confrontation with us, he made no indication of his awareness that we had left the scene. No doubt, he was considerably relieved not to have to continue with a situation that, obviously, could have a very inconclusive ending from his point of view.

We arrived safe and sound at the company house, a short distance from the encounter with the Nationalist soldier. It was, unquestionably, a disturbing experience and certainly bolstered the manager's forceful instructions not to break the curfew under any circumstances. There were no means to determine what eventually had transpired after leaving the scene, but for a long period of time the plight of the hapless rickshaw coolie weighed heavily on my mind.

Classes started bright and early on Monday morning as promised. THE COMPANY had provided bicycles for us to navigate our way to school. Students were not senior enough to warrant an expensive means of transport such as an automobile and a driver. In addition, it was highly unlikely that a cyclist could cause a fatal accident. Driving a vehicle in China was strictly forbidden by THE COMPANY.

A driver, who caused a fatality in China, was faced with the age old principle of having 'broken the rice bowl' of the victim. This meant that having been responsible for depriving a man's family of the product of his labour, you then had to take on that responsibility for his entire family for the rest of their lives or until such time as other means of providing support could be found.

To most Chinese, this age old custom was observed more in the breach than in fact. To the wealthy, foreign companies, this was a constant source of concern. Every Chinese believed that all Western companies had deep pockets to which there were no bottoms. Needless to say, the companies had provided enough evidence of such an attitude in prior settlements involving fatalities. This was due to the companies' desire to stay in business in China rather than to face the bureaucratic nightmare of trying to convince the authorities that such a principle of 'breaking a man's rice bowl' did not apply to the civilized world of business.

'Do not forget your gloves.' Cold was a way of life in North China. To accidentally touch the metal handlebars of your bicycle with your bare hands, because you had been foolish enough to forget your gloves, invariably left parts of your tender flesh adhering to the metal. It was so intensely cold that the moisture of your hands acted as an instant means of adhesion, when it froze immediately on contacting the handle-bars. At least, it was an invigorating way to start your classes. Being prone to forgetfulness left me very often in a state of very painful reminders of the constant need to remember my gloves.

Where in the job description of an international oil executive does it say that he rides to school on a bicycle and has his hands frozen to the handlebars of his means of conveyance? Or where does it say in the same job description that cycling on the way to school he has to be careful to avoid obstacles on the streets? Obstacles, such as dead or dying beggars. One had noticeably died the previous night.

'Garbage' collection in Beijing was notorious for being late and inefficient. Ostensibly in order to make up for this lapse in civic duties, there was a squad detailed to look for such bodies and encircle them with lime. Coming from a country known for its obsession with cleanliness and armed with the knowledge that surrounding a dead body with lime was a useless endeavour, we immediately blessed the numbingly cold weather. Sub-freezing temperatures that only moments before we had been cursing with a vengeance.

All of the problems of everyday survival evaporated when you crossed the prestigious threshold of the Wha Win Wai Shiao language institute. It was, unquestionably, a fascinating experience to be exposed to a foreign language in such ageless surroundings. And even more fascinating exposed to a foreign language in the heart of the capital of one of the oldest civilizations on earth.

The headmaster was nicknamed 'Dear'. It was a well earned and captivating nickname. He was the quintessence of the venerable old Chinese gentleman in his flowing robes and a thin white wisp of a beard on his chin. Deferential, yes, but in full command. His demeanor alone was enough to show that he wielded absolute authority.

The system of teaching was so excellent that in one month, when there was an meeting in the main hall auditorium, 'Dear' gave the address and gave it entirely in Chinese. It was incredible that the majority of students came away from the meeting with a full knowledge of what had transpired.

What was not so remarkable, but also predictable, was that our friends from the southern part of the United States would find the Chinese language totally unintelligible. Not so strange when you think that even in their own country, they have difficulty making themselves understood outside their local area of habitation.

The American staff of BAT, The British American Tobacco Company, were the worst offenders. The Yankees could hardly understand any attempt they made to converse in Chinese, which were the standing instructions of the staff to the students when they were on the school grounds. Any language but Chinese was forbidden. It was not surprising that we couldn't understand their Chinese. We had great difficulty understanding their southern dialect which they applied to English. They hotly maintained that English was their first language.

The facility with which we absorbed the Chinese language continued to astound the class. It was, beyond doubt, due to the expertise and dedication of the teaching staff more than to the ability of the students. In addition, the three of us were determined to master this language so different from our own. We hired tutors that came to the company house three evenings a week for two hour sessions. These tutors forced the nuances of the Mandarin dialect down our throats with such force that it would literally have made nature's providers of pâté de foie gras gag.

Forays would be made into the countryside to practice our new found talent. If there were any difficulty because of a different dialect of which there are hundreds in China, it was only necessary to obtain the services of a school child.

Chang Kai-shek had declared that the language of the elite, Mandarin, would be the lingua franco of China. If China were to be united, there had to be a common language. It was too late for the older population to make the change, but all school children had to learn the Northern dialect known as 'Beijing Wha' in the familiar, or officially, 'Mandarin'. Accordingly, when encountering difficulties with any of the local populace that did not speak Mandarin, it was only necessary to enlist the aid of a school child who would interpret for you to their elders.

The Forbidden City, the Temple of Heaven, The Great Wall, the Seven Dragon Screen, The Center of the Universe, all the great treasures of China's fabulous history at our finger tips. Where in the employees' manual did it say that this was part of an international oil company executive's life?

Reality was not long in approaching. On our return from the countryside one Saturday afternoon, the house boy announced that the great white masters' office had telephoned with an urgent message. We were to proceed to the American Embassy at once. Surely there must be a matter of grave concern for the Embassy staff to elect to work on a Saturday afternoon. Only the Embassy staff outdid the commercial expatriates in the field of fewer working hours.

It probably isn't fair to criticize the American Embassy for working fewer hours than their commercial equivalents. In the first instance, everyone enjoyed all the Chinese holidays which were too numerous to count. Furthermore, all of the embassies had their own national holidays. The Fourth of July would strike a note with every member of the expatriate community, as would Bastille Day for the French Embassy. Sometimes embassies closed in sympathy with each other. Sometimes American companies just declared they too would observe a national holiday, such as The Fourth of July.

Under any circumstances with a working day from eight AM to one PM, plus the Chinese holidays, plus any holidays that THE COMPANY decided to observe, plus two weeks annual holiday and an accumulated two months per year leave, there wasn't too much grumbling coming from the under worked and overpaid (overpaid according to the home office staff only) expatriates. Expatriates who sheltered themselves under the umbrella of the Extra-territorial rights that the great powers had set up for themselves and their nationals.

Whatever had made the embassy decide to work on a Saturday afternoon?

Arriving at the Embassy to find the staff scurrying hither and yon in a most frantic and unusually energetic way gave us the first uneasy feeling. Approaching a door which had a sign stating 'Tickets Purchased Here' gave us the second uneasy feeling.

We inquired, "Tickets to where?"

The reply was, "Tickets to Shanghai."

Our uneasiness gave way to a much more sense of forbidding. "Who is going to Shanghai?"

"All the Americans. The embassy has charted a train to take you to Tientsin. The United States Navy will pick you up there in a LST, take you to Tsingtao, where you will trans-ship to more comfortable quarters on a larger US Navy ship and proceed to Shanghai."

What possibly could have provoked such an idea and such activity on the part of the United States Government? The information was soon forthcoming. It emerged that Chang Kai-shek had informed the American government, and presumably the other governments as well, that he was pulling the remnants of his army out of the hills of the Beijing area. He was retreating south to Tientsin leaving Beijing and the surrounding countryside to the communists.

The details of the 'evacuation', as it was now officially being called, were sketched out by the embassy staff. The fighting between the Nationalists and the Communists had come so close to the airport area that all commercial flights had been cancelled.

'By November the Communists had gained such force that they had encircled Beijing and were ranging well south of the ancient capital. On the Shantung peninsula, they had formed a great arc around the old treaty port of Tsingtao and were closing in to take its formidable naval base so strategically placed midway between Shanghai and Mukden. Here, since 1945, when the Japanese surrendered its modern docks and installations, the United States had maintained its Western Pacific fleet. But now, unless it too were to become engaged in the war in China, the time had come for it to give up the facilities'[6].

Hindsight always has 20/20 vision. But still a student immersed in his Chinese studies should have the right to ask of his government at this late stage a number of questions. How was it possible that up until the closing of the airport the United States Embassy and its score of highly paid and trained intelligence staff didn't have an inkling that the 'war of liberation' against Chang Kai-shek was going so badly? So badly that the first attempt to get American Nationals out of the area was through the means of an evacuation plan.

What were the American military advisors on Chang Kai-shek's staff telling their counterparts in the Pentagon? That the war was going well? Keep sending money and selling armaments on credit to a 'born loser'?

The rumour mills were already girding up with stories about Madame Chang Kai-shek. One story had her landing in Taipei in Taiwan with plane loads of bullion and other valuables, which only told even the most casual on-looker that the highest authority in the fight against Mao Tze-tung had already conceded victory.

And what were the subjects of discussion in the Board Room of Caltex (China) Ltd. in Shanghai? Had the directors put the future appointments of the students that they had assigned to Beijing twelve months down on the agenda pending their graduation in Chinese language studies? Did they ever discuss the possibility that maybe some consideration for the safety of these students should be on a continuing basis? Did any one of them look at a map of China and shade in the area in 'blood red' colour that the 'freedom loving liberators' had wrested from the Kuomintang over the dead bodies of thousands and thousands of Chinese citizens?

A few rapid calculations of Mao Tze Tung's rate of progress and even the most benighted pre-war 'order taker' of THE COMPANY, who had survived long enough to squirm his way onto the Caltex Board of Directors in Shanghai, could have reached the simple conclusion that our class should never have been entered as freshmen in Wha Win Wai Shiao in the autumn of '48.

"You will stay in your homes until you receive telephone notice that you will be picked up by embassy hired vehicles. Do not leave your quarters. We don't know the exact time that you will be picked up and, therefore, you will only receive twenty to thirty minutes notice of the arrival of your transportation. Get your tickets at that other office where the sign is posted. You will have to pay for them in United States dollars," was the added bit of off hand advice given.

Payable in US dollars? Only some government bureaucrat could have had a part in that decision. Everyone who had US dollars was suspected of buying them on the black market. In actuality, there were well authenticated stories that Chang Kai-shek's son, who had been given the job of cleaning up the black market in Shanghai, was hanging people from the lamp posts in Shanghai as an example, because they were buying US dollars on the black market.

We indignantly notified the embassy staff member, who had informed us of the need to pay for our transportation in United States dollars, that we would take our chances with Mao Tze-tung's forces, rather than risk running afoul of Chang Kai-shek's son. We didn't know how Mao Tze-tung would handle us. We were sure where we would end up in the hands of Chang's son; on a lamp post dangling from a rope., while the State Department exchanged angry notes with the Chinese government.

We also hastened to add, 'there was still time to call our congressman. We would let him know that the United States Government was not going to evacuate us unless we were able to pay our way. And what's more, pay our way in US dollars'.

Just mention your congressman to a staffer in the embassy. His antenna immediately starts to emit warning signals that there must be something wrong with the operation, particularly, if a citizen feels strongly enough not to want to be evacuated. In no time at all, the instructions came down from on high. It would not be necessary to pay in US dollars. In fact, it would not be necessary to pay at all.

That taken care of our attention was turned to a crowd of expatriates who were not Americans. It materialized that they were under the impression that the evacuation was for all nationalities, not just Americans. The dismay and sense of foreboding that prevailed over this group was thick enough to feel when they discovered that the greatest power on earth was going to exclude them from the life line out of Beijing.

After a few choice comments about how Life Magazine would handle the headlines showing the Americans departing in first class style while all the other nationals stayed to greet the guns of Mao Tze-tung, the embassy rescinded that decision with almost more alacrity than they rescinded the need to pay for the passage in US dollars. This decision gave us lots of company during our departure from Beijing.

'The best laid plans of mice and..... .' The twenty to thirty minute notice that was to be given to the evacuees before being picked up by the embassy hired vehicles went the way of all good intentions and planning. The notice consisted of a knock on the door with instructions to board the vehicle immediately. Fortunately in accordance with the embassy's advice, all 'allowable' clothing and personal belongings had been packed. They stood ready at the door for immediate loading. 'Allowable' consisted of one large suitcase and any other personal belongings that could be carried by hand in addition to the suitcase.

Lunch had just been served and was assembled on the table ready to eat when the knock on the door came. Without so much as a bite, the three of us rose from the table, said goodbye fondly to the house boy, the cook boy and the other assorted servants and went out the front door to board our means of transport. The fire was ablaze in the fire place, the stereo was playing, steam was arising from the hot rice, and the beautiful furniture that THE COMPANY had purchased was all in place. None of it was ever seen again by any of us, including all our personal belongings that did not fit the definition of 'allowable'.

If our bicycles had left something to be desired in the way of transport, so did the hired vehicle that met our eyes as we left the house. An old and decrepit produce van with boarded sides and no roof greeted us. However, the ride to the train station was of no great duration. Further more, riding a bicycle had already cushioned our egos to additional jolts of a like kind as well as the necessity to leave with all deliberate haste. We jumped up on the back of the vehicle and joined about a dozen other evacuees who had been picked up along the route to our house and were already ensconced in the van. We now constituted a full load. The vehicle headed for the train station.

Outside of the short notice given for boarding the vehicle, full credit must be given to the embassy for all the arrangements made that resulted in a very successful evacuation. There were no delays. There were no causalities. There were no problems other than that of a little overcrowding, which good humour could easily overcome.

We waved goodbye to an exciting effort to learn the Chinese language and to a Beijing which none of us were ever to see again. No doubt, when President Nixon later opened up China as he would liked to have thought in the same manner as Admiral Perry opened up Japan, we could have gone back. Certainly not back to the Beijing that we had known, but back to the city itself. Instinctively, we all knew that it would not be possible to recapture what we had experienced during our short stay there. Consequently none of us ever did make the effort.

The train actually left on time. On time for that part of the world, only one hour late. A number of close Chinese friends came down to see us off. As the train gathered speed, tears could be seen forming in their eyes. Life at that stage was not to be thought of as long range planning.

'Goodbyes' were said that often meant, 'goodbye forever'. Some of us would not live long enough to be united. Some of us would move to distant parts of the world. Some of us would be left under the jurisdiction of a government which did not brook establishing communications between two entirely different and opposing political entities.

On arrival in Tientsin, the United States Consulate had duplicated the excellent efforts of their compatriots in Beijing. We were met by hired transport to convey us to the dockside in preparation for boarding the US Navy vessel which was to take us to Tsingtao. The vehicles were all marked with the names of the evacuees and all carried United States flags to identify them. The US flags announced that the occupants were under the protection of the United States Government. This time there were no trucks or vans, and all rode in style in comfortable automobiles. It was to be our last bit of comfort, nonetheless.

The place of embarkation was considerably up river and, as a result, the river was quite shallow. This necessitated the Navy having to use their old LST's (Landing Ship Tanks) for the evacuation. War time comrades will well remember those vessels with fondness or horror depending on how prone they were to seasickness. They were very flat bottomed vessels with wide doors at the bow. The doors would be opened, a ramp laid down over which the tanks would roll up and fill the vessel. The doors would then be closed. They wouldn't be opened again until the vessel ran up on some far and distant shore under a hail of gun fire, and the tanks would rumble down the ramp prepared to do battle.

Of course, no such program was envisaged for this old war horse at this stage. It was only serving to evacuate some unfortunate individuals who had been caught up in the middle of a difference of opinion between Chang Kai-shek and Mao Tze-tung.

Americans may not usually be classified as a disciplined people either at home or during political rallies, when they are out electioneering for their favorite candidate. Notwithstanding, when being evacuated, they tend to conform to the rules laid down by those in charge of the evacuation. 'Allowable' baggage was what the embassy had said would be allowed. That is what the predominate number of Americans had brought with them.

Perchance in fairness to other nationalities that have been exposed to a much less stable existence in their own home countries, 'allowable', meant anything and everything that could possibly be of any value to them at their destination. Wherever and whatever that destination may be. Many of them did not work for foreign companies with deep pockets. Of necessity, they had to bring every thing of value that they could possible salvage in order to exist in their next haven.

To say that the Americans were astounded by this attitude merely emphasized the vast abyss that exists between the Americans and the different political cultures, as well as the difference in the worldly wealth of the citizens of the many powers represented in the nationalities of those being evacuated.

However, even the non-Americans raised an eyebrow at the enterprising young man, who with his horn blaring and head light flashing, rode his motorbike up the gangway and parked it on the main deck of the LST, alongside the many bags and steamer trunks of his colleagues. The captain of the vessel was not inclined to argue with his passenger or had not been informed of the restrictions that the embassy had placed on the evacuees in the way of 'allowable' baggage. At mid-night with lights darkened, the vessel crept down river. Soon it was headed out to sea with the motor bike serving as a beacon of initiative to the young and daring.

An LST is designed to sleep its ship's company and the passengers it takes on board as members of the tank crews. There is, noticeably, limited space for the number of tanks that such a vessel can carry. So then is the accommodation for the crews of those tanks limited in numbers to equal the number of tanks carried. To load a vessel of this kind with human beings, instead of tanks, meant that there were hundreds of people who had no place to sleep other than on the deck. It, also, meant that all of the vessels facilities were strained to the breaking point, inasmuch as the designers of the vessel had never envisaged that the vessel would carry human cargo, instead of Sherman tanks or their like.

The first announcement made over the ship's loudspeaker confirmed this glaring omission on the part of the designers. In true Navy parlance the speaker rang out, "Now hear this. Due to the lack of facilities and the shortage of provisions, there will be only two meals served during the voyage to Tsingtao. The honor system will apply. It is expected that every passenger will observe the restrictions. That is all."

What was an international oil company executive doing on an LST, sleeping on a hard, cold deck, eating only two meals a day for which he had to stand in line for hours and wondering if he were ever going to survive long enough to get back to what most people envisage as a sane and civilized way of living?

The time was ripe for that insidious thought to come creeping back from the subconscious to the conscious as visions of certain senior members of THE COMPANY flashed into view. A view, which told me that they had their feet up on their huge polished desks and their secretaries had just hung up the telephone after confirming their reservations at the Four Seasons in New York for lunch. That insidious thought, which would engender the same question many times in the years to come, was going to bear fruit at some time in the not too distant future I assured myself.

IS ASSASSINATION A VIABLE ALTERNATIVE!

The two meal honour system worked to the extent that there was only one group of people that exploited it. The prevalent belief that was held by most of us about that group was that they probably wouldn't have abused it, if the food had been of the same low and boring quality to which they were accustomed. Albeit, the reason for the abuse was assumed to be understood by us, we were just human enough to take the opportunity to get in the occasional verbal barb in recognition of their exploitation.

This usually happened when having gotten into line for the first meal of the day, it was noticed that the individual in front of you was quite familiar. He had announced well over an hour ago that he was going to have his breakfast. Obviously, he had already had his first serving. He was now going to obtain his second for the same nine o'clock service.

"Ah, good morning Father and how was the meal? Do you think it will taste as good the second time?"

Understandably, the missionary priests had never been exposed to United States Navy food. A quality of food that though the military might malign it as part of their daily routine, to Catholic missionaries out of the hills of China it would appear as if they were dining at Charles of the Ritz.

It must, also, be said of the priesthood that such remarks hardly penetrated their benign countenances. Their reply, typically, was to comment that 'they would have to wait and see', almost as if being the holy of the church they were entitled to special treatment.

Just as all good things come to end, so do the bad ones. The first leg of the voyage was over. We arrived at Tsingtao to find a United States Naval Transport vessel waiting for us. Luxury! The military might again denigrate these vessels by calling them cattle pens. To the passengers of an LST who had been sleeping on a cold, hard deck and eating two meals a day, for which they had had to stand in line for hours, the transport resembled nothing more than the Queen Mary without the white paint.

And so we traveled to Shanghai in style. No amount of explanation about the original accommodations elicited any sympathy from our colleagues who were waiting at the pier as our ocean liner sailed up the Yangtze River.

Thus ended our introduction to the Chinese language and culture under the auspices of the illustrious Wha Win Wai Shiao. We were informed that two of us were to be posted to Hong Kong. One was to remain in Shanghai. And the Red Army continued to toil relentlessly Southward.

3

Shanghai and Taiwan—Late 1948

When the King shaves a fraction of the metal off the gold coins of his realm and returns them to circulation with the same face value and he, then, creates identical coins of a correspondingly reduced gold content with the shavings, John A.Pugsley, the author of The Alpha Strategy states quite emphatically, "The King is a Thief."[7]. When your government prints money that is not backed by gold or something of equivalent value, it joins Pugsley's King in that vast den of thieves, who have robbed you of the fruits of your labour.

In Shanghai, the bartender of The Shanghai Club on hearing the order for a draught beer automatically drew two glasses. The majority of beer drinkers are never satisfied with their first glass. Invariably, they will order the second one to quench their thirst. In most countries, the bartender would have been reprimanded for drawing the second draught in advance of the drinker having quaffed his first one.

Not so in China. The bartender was anxiously looking after the economic well being of the club member. He knew that the price of the second glass would rise before the drinker had finished his first. The member acknowledged the perceptiveness of the bartender with a nod of his head; plus the unvoiced promise of the appropriate bucsheese that would be forthcoming at the end of the month in recognition of the bartender's solicitousness.

Every foreigner, and for that matter almost every Chinese, was a millionaire. The first checks that Carl Stuby, my fellow evacuee from Beijing, and I drew in payment of club dues for temporary membership at The Shanghai Club in Shanghai were in the amount of C$700,000.00. Caltex had an urgent need for two engineers to under-take a lubrication survey of the sugar mill plants in Taiwan. Arrangements had been made for Carl and myself to complete the survey before I was to proceed to Hong Kong and Carl was to take up his duties in

Shanghai. In the meantime, THE COMPANY had graciously arranged for us to obtain temporary membership at The Shanghai Club for the duration of the special assignment, while we were preparing the material for the survey in Taiwan and after our return. It was during our stay in Shanghai that Carl and I became fervent disciples of the principle of 'sound money'.

It is frightening. Nay! More! It is terrifying to see your life savings wiped out by that insidious method by which corrupt and spendthrift governments pay their bills.

INFLATION!

Peter F.Drucker, who has come to be recognized—in Kenneth Boulding's words—as a foremost philosopher of American society, stated quite succinctly in his volume on "Managing in Turbulent Times" that, '... inflation is the systematic destruction of wealth by government'[8].

There was no doubt how strongly James F.Byrnes felt about inflation, when he delivered his first speech as Director of Economic Stabilization to the New York Herald Tribune forum on November 16,1942. The speech dealt largely with the danger of inflation. It ended with these words:

"If anything like inflation happened, our people would not be ready to take the part which we are pledged to take to organize the world for peace. There could be no greater tragedy."[9]

If there is anyone today that imagines that inflation is not a sinister and deadly threat to the well being of a nation and its citizens, they have only to examine the '.... six-point menu of intelligence regarding the United States that circulated in the Japanese embassy in Madrid as early as February 1942' only weeks after the 'Day of Infamy'—the 7th of December 1941. The japs were looking for intelligence that would help them to annihilate the giant they had attacked at Pearl Harbor. In addition to the clandestine spying, which would be normally expected in time of war in regard to shipping movements, aid to England, troop movements and aid to the other allies, there was among the six-point menu the one of '.... .problems related to inflation.'[10]

John A.Pugsley, the best-selling author, economist and investment advisor who identified 'The King as a Thief' has said about inflation, 'Without question, inflation is the most deadly of economic evils. It knows no geographical boundaries. It respects neither sex, nor race, nor creed, nor state of health or wealth. It has a more destructive effect on the lives of individuals than all other forms of plunder put together'[11]

John Maynard Keynes may have argued that 'just a little *bit* of inflation' was a basic primer for an economy. He had never been 'just a little *bit* pregnant', or he would have known that there is no such thing as being 'just a little *bit* pregnant'. Either you are ... or you are not. Just as there is no such thing as having.... 'just a little *bit* of inflation'.

'The tragic death by suicide in May 1993 of the Socialist Prime Minister of France, Pierre Beregovoy, offers a sad occasion for noting the contributions he made toward giving France sound policies. One of Mr.Beregovoy's phrases: "Inflation, a tax which hits the poor," symbolizes his most important achievement as finance minister during the 1980's, the stabilization of the French currency'.[12]

So concise and descriptive are these simple words of Pierre Beregovoy that even the 'Parliament of Whores' in Washington D.C., as P.J.O'Rourke so aptly calls them*[1] in his book of that title[13], would have no difficulty understanding the meaning. But that is a naïve, hopeful and in fact a very wistful judgment. They do understand it very well. It is that very 'Parliament of Whores' who have been responsible for our past devastating periods of inflation and will be responsible for our future ones.

In addition in 1993, the 'Parliament of Whores' was joined by a 'Gang of Whores' who took up residence in the White House. They are, also, known as 'Clintonites'. Just after the Democrats won the White House, the Clintonites and their mentor and his wife slowly but steadily began to lean on the Chairman of the Federal Reserve, Alan Greenspan, to fire up the boilers of inflation. Should the Chairman of the Fed bend to their pressure and start shoveling on the coal, they knew that this would create a short term period of Keynesian, illusionary prosperity which would last just long enough to get their man elected again.

And it would ensure that they all retain their well paid and powerful positions for another four years. Just as it would inexorably ensure that the blood, sweat and tears and the hard earned savings of the American taxpayer would be insidiously sucked up into that enormous vortex of uncontrolled spending to which the 'Parliament of Whores' and the so called 'New Democrat' and his Co-President were lethally addicted.

Fortunately, Mr. Greenspan did not yield to the pressure, but in not yielding, he produced a fundamental and real prosperity that endured throughout the first term and well into the second term of the "New Democrat". He thus provided one of the means by which, for the first time in decades, a Democratic president was re-elected to a second term.

China was in the throes of a massive, relentless and runaway wave of deadly inflation. The rise in the price of the second glass of beer while the drinker was having his first was only a minor irritant for the foreigners in the everyday task of coping with the government's printing presses. Presses that were running twenty-four hours a day and churning out money at a prodigious and self-destroying rate. It was not uncommon to see shoppers with attaché cases, paper bags, or ordinary overnight valises going shopping with their containers stuffed to the brim with the paper money of the Chang Kai-shek government.

That liberal, Democratic thief and whore in The United States Congress who made the oft quoted statement of, "Tax and tax, spend and spend, elect and elect," left out the method by which he intended to pay for his vicious philosophy, *PRINT AND PRINT.* Paper money was a commodity of which no wage earner or shop keeper had any desire to retain ownership for more than twenty four hours. The entire urban population was in the process of playing musical chairs with the millions of dollars in their possession. As soon as the opening of the shops in the morning signaled that 'the music had started to play', the populace began their march around the city to find something on which to spend the money they had received the previous day. A wary eye was kept on the clock in order that when the music stopped playing and the shops closed, you were not the unfortunate member of the game to end up in the loser's seat of not having spent all your money.

Again, the da bezes were in an enviable position. They were able to exchange their hard currency at the current day's exchange rate at the time they had to meet their monthly, monetary commitments or when some trinket in the market place attracted their fancy. 'The rich get richer and the poor get poorer' the old saying goes. The foreigners were not exposed to the vagaries of the hideous inflation to which the Chinese were subjected. Hideous is the only word that fits a system so devastating to its citizens that it robs them of the means to house themselves and feed their families.

Not only weren't the da bezes exposed to it, but they were able to take a unique advantage of it. All activities that involved periodic payments such as club bills, electricity, overseas telephone calls to the family at home, gas and sometimes rent (if it could be arranged) were paid in arrears.

During the first few days of the month, the telephone lines hummed in the evening between Shanghai and the various countries represented by the expatriate staff of the firms from those hard currency areas. At the day's exchange rate for the Americans when a telephone call was made at the beginning of the month, the cost would be in the neighborhood of forty or fifty US dollars a call. It was not surprising that five and six calls were made in the early days of the month, because, naturally, the account was debited in Chinese dollars at the price in effect at the time of the call.

When the end of the month rolled around and you received your bill from the telephone company, a bill which you judiciously avoiding paying until close to the end of the month after which you had received it, the exchange rate had jumped in quantum leaps. The two hundred and fifty US dollar or three hundred US dollar telephone bill from the beginning of the month had been reduced to twenty or thirty dollars by the time you arranged to exchange your hard earned United States dollars at the then current exchange rate. And so it was with all monthly bills.

A shroff was the man most disliked by those debtors who quite often were unable to meet their monthly bills. Shanghai entrepreneurs did not depend on the postal service to deliver their bills and have their clients mail back the payments. Every day's delay in this normal mail delivery method, utilized by all vendors of real goods or services in hard currency areas, resulted in untold losses as the savage inflation eroded the value of their invoices at a spine chilling rate.

The 'shroff', as the professional bill collector was called, was polite and deferential on his first call at the premises of the current debtor. Less polite and certainly not deferential on his second. Hints of the start of a new Tong war could be heard in his mumblings under his breath on his third visit to an unrepentant debtor, with the recalcitrant payer to be the first victim at the initiation of the Tong.

It was a constant source of amazement to us newcomers that there was nothing in the city of Shanghai that could not be bought on credit, whether it was tangible property or intangible such as in the form of personal services. This availability of credit was always present, in spite of the horrendous inflation that Shanghai dwellers had been undergoing for many years.

There was one monthly commitment for 'personal services' that newly arrived young foreigners were quick to be made aware did not fall into the shroff's normal routine of repeat visits. When the shroff arrived at the office to collect his employer's just dues and was airily waved away by the recently arrived, somewhat arrogant young buck, he didn't return the next day as would be his usual custom under normal circumstances. It was an accepted practice to allow shroffs to conduct their business during office hours and on the firms' premises. After all, every member of the staff from the Managing Director down to the office boy bought on credit, whether it was a grand piano or some mundane object such as daily fare for the table.

In the case of 'personal services', the second visit to the office of the well known international oil companies was made not by the shroff, but by the shroff's employer and provider of the services. The visit invariably resulted in uproarious laughter by all in the vicinity of the confrontation. Uncontrolled hilarity by the onlookers arose, as the shroff's employer draped her shapely, slender legs over the edge of the young employee's desk, proceeded to lightly powder her nose and adjust her thigh high stockings. Payment materialized at a speed faster than light by the recalcitrant debtor. He produced her remuneration, ushered her to the door with most obvious, impolite dispatch, undoubtedly promising her that he would never again be delinquent when her monthly invoice arrived in the care of her shroff.

The government owned telephone system and utilities never changed their method of billing. They had only to ask their owners to crank up the presses to a faster clip in order to meet their apparent inability to match income with outgo. After garnering untold losses of staggering amounts, the private clubs and other members of the community of entrepreneurs who ran their organizations for a profit changed their billing system .

When the maitre d'hotel of The Shanghai Club handed us the new shiny menus at dinner one evening, it was astonishing to see that the prices of the various courses had been reduced from sums with a large number of zeros after the initial digits to what appeared to be give away prices. There was no doubt in our minds. The Club would be bankrupt before the last meal of the evening was served, if those were the prices which they were going to charge for their usual six course dinner. And the wine list? If that number were not a misprint, we wondered how it would be possible to get the club to deliver ten cases of Dom Perigon for only C$100.00 a case.

A hundred Chinese dollars had ceased to have any value whatsoever. Hundred dollar bills were accumulated in piles of fifty bills per stack and securely tied in bundles. All members of the Shanghai community knew that a bundle that showed a one hundred dollar bill on the top of the pile was actually counted as C$5000.00.

While there was no faith of the populace in the intrinsic value of each note churned out by Chang Kai-shek's regime, there was an uncanny and almost childlike trust in the ability of the myriad bundles of paper to buy anything and everything that had any material value. After all, the Chinese had been buying and selling commodities over a number of years using these bundles of paper. The only difference, as time passed, was that more bundles were needed to accomplish the same objective. It never ceased to amaze those of us from countries where our elected representatives resembled petty thieves in the art of printing money, compared to the Ministry of Finance in Chang Kai-shek's government, to see the continued belief that the Chinese citizen had in these bundles. Bundles which represented the out pouring of his government's printing presses.

To see this conviction shaken was a sad occurrence. It happened at the Shanghai fish market. A shopper had just parted with a large number of bundles of freshly printed notes in exchange for a half dozen fish heads, with which he apparently intended to produce a savory fish broth. There was one exception in the pile of neat and clean stacks of currency. A pile that had seen somewhat longer service than its fellow companions. Yet one that had apparently already changed hands several times in the market place that very day. Why the fish monger questioned the validity of the somewhat used pile was a mystery, but question it he did.

The fastenings of the stack were severed. Instead of fifty one hundred dollar bills, there were only two. The one on the top of the pile and the one on the bottom of the stack. All the rest were carefully matched in width and length to the two legitimate notes. The notes in between the two genuine ones had been carefully cut out and assembled from the Sunday newspaper supplement. It had to be the Sunday supplement, because that was the only newsprint that was of better quality than the paper used by the Ministry of Finance in meeting its printing requirements.

The shopper's lament was that the stack had been received by him in good faith, and by its appearance had been accepted and used by many vendors and shoppers. Why destroy the trust of a fellow citizen he wailed by examining what lay between the top and bottom notes? In a very short time the stack would have no value whatsoever as a monetary means of exchange with the exchange rate exploding in stratospheric leaps and bounds. When the face value of the bundles decreased below the actual value of the paper itself, the last holder of the stack would trade it to the coal and wood merchants as tinder for sale to their customers. Had the fish monger not questioned the contents of the stack it would have had a normal life span and would have ended up in the cook fire of some peasant possibly helping to produce that savory fish broth from the fish heads of the market. Just as only a mere seventy-five years ago, 'a German housewife burned mark notes in her kitchen stove, since it was cheaper to burn marks than to use them to buy fire wood'[14].

No! It was not a misprint. We had read the number as C$100.00, but closer examination showed that there was no Chinese dollar sign in front of the digits of 100.00. And what was this additional notation? The word 'units' had been inserted after every entry of the prices of the various offerings of gourmet cuisine served up for the discerning taste of the members of the prestigious Shanghai Club. "What is the meaning of this doggerel?" my English dinner companion demanded of the maitre d'hotel. He had been in the habit of dining at The Club three or four evenings a week. Like the rest of us he was a very tardy payer at the end of the month. This, in essence, meant that his monthly food bill, while astronomically high in numbers, was just as astronomically low in actual value when settled by him.

The explanation by the maitre d'hotel was quite simple. "The word 'units' represents equivalent United States dollars," he informed us. "The Government does not allow us to price in United States dollars so we use the word 'units' instead. When you receive your bill, and even more importantly when you make payment, it is only necessary to multiply the total number of 'units' on your bill by the then current exchange rate between US dollars and Chinese dollars. The resultant number of Chinese dollars is the amount of your monthly bill, assuming you pay it upon receipt. Any delay in payment will necessitate that the calculation be made at the exchange rate in effect when you do pay the bill. For those members of The Club who do not use US dollars, they need merely make the additional calculation of converting their own currency to US dollars and then to Chinese dollars." And so went the 'free lunch'.

To be an accountant in China with an accountant's precise mind and inherent nature of demanding that all numbers fit into a logical sequence, and for which they had to be all accounted when they were added up, must have been a soul destroying experience. The stories were legion about to what lengths accountants went to transplant their disciplined methods of keeping track of their firms income and outgo from a normal and stable market to the hectic, uncontrolled and chaotic environment of a market where price lists were issued on a daily basis. Not only on a daily basis, but the day's price list of THE COMPANY had limitations as well. These limitations were foot notes to the price list detailing the limits during which the day's prices could remain in effect. If the exchange rate varied during the day by more than the allowable limit, selling ceased immediately.

There was a battery of telephone callers in the company's office that kept the service stations informed of the current rate of exchange. With an abnormally wild swing in the exchange rate, generally caused by the news that Chang Kai-shek's army had been again defeated on the field of battle, all selling ceased. It was not commenced again until the rumor had been laid to rest, and the exchange rate settled down to normal fluctuations.

Alternatively, if the exchange rate did not retreat to its regularly progressive upward journey and would have bypassed the limits of the day's price for a period of time, the 'day' was merely advanced to the next day's date. The present day's price was moved ahead to the next day's price and the product was sold at a price that would normally not have been in effect until the commencement of business the following day. We in the marketing department had great compassion and empathy for our fellow employees in the accounting department. Unfortunately, there was nothing that we could do to assist them. The only offering we had to give them was our sympathy.

Carl and I did, however, make our life and paper work a little less demanding when we were in Taiwan. We were both individually keeping track of our daily disbursements in order to transfer them to our weekly expense accounts. We had similar tastes in food and beer. Consequently, Carl noticed that our expense accounts invariably numerically matched each other at the end of the week. To keep track of the various outpourings of paper bundles used to meet the needs of daily sustenance, inn keepers' bills and travel was a laborious and time consuming detailed application of one's valuable time. It was time that could have been put to much more productive use for THE COMPANY.

It was Carl's efficient suggestion that we take turns in keeping track of our expenditures. One week he would meticulously note all of our combined expenditures that he had undertaken and that he had paid. The following week the duty would become mine. At the end of each week the current 'bookkeeper' would report his findings. The total amount would then be divided by two (plus or minus a few hundred thousand dollars in order to show some variation) and the non-working member would merely have to fill in the columns on his expense account form with fifty percent of the value in which he had been advised the week's activities had culminated.

Routine is a bad habit for any individual into which to fall. The efficient method of utilizing our time in order to become more productive for THE COMPANY, by dividing the weeks expenditures by two, proved to be a major embarrassment for our immediate supervisor Bill Beiswinger, Chief Lubrication Engineer, at a later date when he visited us in Taipei. Unfortunately for him, he had the reputation of being the only employee in the entire organization who had his expense accounts audited on a regular basis. He was a discerning drinker. Chivas Regal and Remey Martin were major drains on anyone's expense account in China and his in particular. Like the rest of us, albeit ours was only Tsingtao beer, it always appeared on our expense accounts in one form or another. He was an excellent engineer and had a razor sharp mind, but that mind was not given to mundane things like keeping track of expenses.

Bill's first question to us on his arrival in Taipei was, "What is the level of your expenses here? I'm going to use the same number and not be bothered with keeping track of all this nonsense." Carl gave him the number. Even to our supervisor with his prodigious spending habits it sounded high. "Are you sure?" he inquired as he turned to query me.

"Very definitely," I replied in a positive tone of voice. "The numbers have been in that range, plus or minus several hundred thousand dollars, for the past few weeks with the addition of the normal inflation rate," was my affirmative response. "You may wish to add fifteen or twenty percent by the time you return to Shanghai," I suggested.

We were well aware of his propensity to cover a major part of his extravagant tastes with his expense account. In any event, we had often been the recipients of his largess. In addition, it appeared to be a particularly adroit suggestion to ingratiate ourselves with the boss. "By the time you return to Shanghai, the exchange rate will have varied so much that no one will bother to research or have the time or the inclination for that matter to analyze recent exchange fluctuations," I concluded.

It was no wonder that the majority of the expatriates working for THE COMPANY and living in an expense account environment banked almost one hundred percent of their salary in a very safe depository at home, like Marine Midland Bank at 250 Park Avenue, New York in my case. A bank, which by a perverse coincidence, was owned by the Shanghai and Hong Kong Banking Corporation. Most expatriates lived entirely on their High Cost of Living Allowance, or HCLA as the acronym is known to those who have been recipients of this welcome assist to their efforts to balance their daily budgets.

Woe betide enterprising young engineers who efficiently improvise methods of improving the productive use of their time for THE COMPANY. We were, individually, so in the habit of arriving at a weekly number, that we failed to inform Bill of the necessity of dividing it by two. His expense account to which he had added twenty percent, the higher of the suggested variation of fifteen or twenty percent as might have been expected, was audited in a routine manner on his return to Shanghai. It was compared to ours as part of the audit, even though we were very junior members of THE COMPANY. The glaring discrepancy of his expenses being twice ours plus twenty percent, although as a senior member of management he was allowed a lot more leeway than were two lowly engineers, caused a turmoil in the office. It was the subject of dinner conversations for many months afterwards.

THE COMPANY had been in business in China for a considerable number of years and had a large staff of loyal Chinese employees. Every effort was made by management to shield them as much as possible from the hardships imposed on them by their government in the form of the devastating inflation caused by the government's printing presses, but not with too much success. While paper money was used in the majority of transactions in urban life, there was still the centuries old barter system that hadn't been entirely replaced in the market. However, because of administrative necessity the staff of THE COMPANY was paid with the printing press money of the government.

At the end of the month, it was sometimes very difficult to have the banks supply sufficient amounts of currency because of the high demand for it by all the firms headquartered in Shanghai. As a consequence, the barter economy was coming back into much more frequent application wherever it was possible. Naturally, both the buyer and the seller had to have something of value if the principle of barter were to work successfully.

The manager of the payroll department suddenly realized that THE COMPANY had a product that would provide the employees with a constant value. It could be exchanged in the market place at any time during the month without a loss of value either on a barter basis, or at the day's rate of exchange without the employee having his wages eroded by the inflationary spiral.

At the end of that month when the employees were paid, they were all delighted to learn that they would receive the equivalent of their month's wages in kerosene. Kerosene was a product for which there was a constant market and demand. It's price varied in Chinese dollars as did everything in Shanghai, with the change in the exchange rate of the United States dollar. Thus, there was no need for the employee to rush out and spend his 'kerosene' while marching to that interminable beat of 'musical chairs'. He merely had to wait until there was a need in his household which could be met by the market place. He would take a portion of his 'kerosene wages', exchange it for Chinese dollars at the day's rate and make his purchases without fear that he would find his monthly salary eroded by the vicious inflation. Alternatively, he would go to the market and barter part of his kerosene for whatever article of value he and his family were in need.

'Imitation is the most sincere form of flattery.' Whoever made that world famous statement never envisioned the chaos that would result when all the other oil companies realized what an excellent way to protect their employees the inventiveness of the payroll manager of Caltex had provided. The following month after the introduction of kerosene wages by Caltex, all the oil companies headquartered in Shanghai paid their employees in kerosene.

The next day the wails of despair and frustration could be heard throughout the city, even above the din of Shanghai's deafening traffic. Perhaps the payroll managers of the various oil companies had forgotten their elementary studies in university on the theory of supply and demand. The oil companies were one of the largest employers of labor in the city. Combined, the staff of the oil companies' employees numbered in the many thousands, and they all had kerosene to spend. The price dropped precipitously in the market.

A delegation met with the company's personnel manager before the opening of business the next day. Both sides recognized that an equitable solution had to be devised to compensate the employees for the loss in value of their wages. Considerable research was done to gauge the actual amount of reimbursement needed to keep the employees whole. Consultations were held with the other oil companies. A plan was worked out whereby only one oil company each month would pay their staff in kerosene. This would maintain the purchasing power of that particular company's employees who received their wages in kerosene. Our hearts went out to the accountants charged with the need to balance the loss one month in the employees' wages, and the necessity to make up that loss in future months without again endangering their purchasing power. We couldn't envisage what the payroll ledgers must have resembled in the way of pluses and minuses in the salary columns.

When the exchange rate of the current Chinese dollar reached the ludicrous and totally unwieldy rate of several millions of Chinese dollars for one US dollar, the Ministry of Finance recognized that it had a very practical problem on its hands. The life span of the bundles of paper money was reduced to such a short period that the ink was hardly dry on them before they were arriving at the coal and wood merchants as candidates for tinder, as the printing presses rolled on and on in an interminable cycle.

The company's payroll manager was in the midst of the massive undertaking of compensating the employees for the erosion in their earnings caused by the flooding of the market with kerosene wages, when the Ministry of Finance announced that the woes of its citizens were going to be settled by the issuance of a new currency. This currency was going to be metallic. The value of the coins would be represented by the value of the metal contained in the coins.

With great fanfare the Ministry of Finance issued the first coins and the central bank immediately undertook the gigantic task of exchanging the new coins for the all but worthless Chinese dollars presently in circulation.

Considerable artistic effort had gone into the design of the new coins. That is, if the reproduction of the likeness of Chang Kai-shek can be considered artistic. What quirk in the mentality of the artist led him to produce two different renditions of the same profile of the great leader will never be known. What is known, however, is that although the coins with the different profiles contained the same metallic content and were stamped as identical in value, one of the profiles occupied a larger part of the face of one of the coins than did the other. 'Big Heads' and 'Little Heads' they were immediately dubbed.

Almost every Westerner is secure in the knowledge that he understands how important 'face' is to the Chinese, or so he believes. The artist must have been a Westerner. No Oriental would ever create two items that were suppose to have identical metallic value and have one with a 'face' value of more than the other. The 'Big Heads' immediately commanded a higher value in the market place than did the 'Little Heads'.

Perhaps the difference in value could have been handled in the market place without too much of a strain being put on the unsung heroes of the accounting staff except for one enterprising member of the payroll staff of THE COMPANY. The new coins had been in circulation for several months. The relative value of the Big Heads and the Little Heads was well established. Generally, the staff was paid in equal number of each of the new coins. The payroll ledger was debited meticulously with the exact value of the sum of the number of the Big Heads and the Little Heads that had been distributed to each member of the staff.

The payroll department was still buried in its books trying to balance out the erosion in the kerosene wages of the previous fiasco, when they were greeted by an irate delegation the third monthly pay day after the issuance of the new coins. "You have paid us entirely in Little Heads," the leader of the delegation announced. "That represents a substantial reduction in our pay scale," he continued, "and we wish you to take immediate steps to compensate us for the discrepancy."

"That's impossible," the payroll manager exclaimed. "I personally just balanced the monthly bank statement. On the contrary, it shows that we bought all

Big Heads from the bank this month. In fact, the purchase was made by the Chief Clerk. We will summon him to verify that all employees were paid in Big Heads." The chief clerk? No where to be found.

Apparently he had purchased all Big Heads from the bank, the cost of which was debited to THE COMPANY. He then exchanged them in the market for Little Heads. A quick calculation using the difference in value of the Big Heads and the Little Heads times the hundreds and hundreds of employees on the pay-roll of THE COMPANY, and it became quickly evident that the chief clerk had retired early and taken his retirement pension with him. The Chinese can never be accused of not being enterprising. It now became the painful duty of the pay-roll manager to start balancing the difference between Big Heads and Little Heads and continuing to work off the discrepancy in the kerosene wages. We left him with these apparently insurmountable problems as we headed for Taipei, the capital of Taiwan as we embarked on a never to be forgotten special assignment for THE COMPANY.

Carl and I had divided up the island. Carl was to take the Eastern half and I the Western half after completing part of the Southern area together. We had a list of all the sugar mills that had to be surveyed which had been supplied by the corporation that owned the group. The recommendations were to be prepared in the field and then forwarded to Shanghai to be printed in professional format and bound in folders and distributed to the resident managers by mail.

Arrangements were made to meet at a central point in the North after completing our individual surveys. The initial surveys done in the South and the final ones in the North were to be completed as a team. This served the purpose of both of us becoming familiar with each others method of preparation in the initial surveys. The final ones would allow us to compare our findings and ensure that there were no great discrepancies in our recommendations.

Having completed this program in the comfort of one of the best houses of ill repute in Taipei, we were ready to start our journey; a journey which between us would cover the length and breadth of Taiwan. Immediately after the war, and before the real tourists invaded Taiwan, the most comfortable places to stay and which served the best food were like the rest of the world, to be found among the first class brothels. There was no stigma attached to staying at these places. Many of the families from Shanghai would spend their local two week vacation at these places.

The hot sulfur springs around which the brothel, 'Wun se Go', had been built were magnificent. The service was of a perfection that would have been difficult to surpass anywhere in the world. Of course, it was an accepted fact that you had to live in the same life style as the residents of the country. Taiwan had been under control of the Japanese for over fifty years. Many of the Japanese customs had found their way into the society. Food was served at low slung tables, and at night the visitor slept on a tatami with a wooden block as a pillow. This was the type of accommodation to which Carl and I were exposed during our entire stay in Taiwan.

In the beginning, we were only able to sleep every third night. This third night's sleep came as a result of complete exhaustion. An exhaustion caused by trying to accommodate our Western idea of a comfortable feather pillow to what, in our estimation, was the hardest wood that the furniture designer could find on the island from which to manufacture his wooden pillows. As time passed, we narrowed this ratio to every other night and eventually, on our return to Taipei, we were comfortably sleeping the night through on our wooden pillows.

All of this came with time and experience. We were now faced with boarding the train to proceed to our initial starting point in the South. There were three classes of accommodation available; not surprising as most world travelers are aware. We, naturally, booked first class seats for the entire voyage. We never were able to obtain a refund, when it later developed that certain sections of the train trip did not have what Westerners considered first class accommodations. Although, it was actually only a matter of relativity.

At this time, it was only a short two years since the cessation of hostilities after World War II. This war ravaged country was just beginning to shake itself loose from all the horrors of the many bombings to which it had been subjected. '… in three missions to Formosa with a total of 198 airplanes, the bombers struck the great Okayama airplane assembly plant with 1,200 tons of high explosives; the plant suffered damage, more than 100 planes were destroyed, 50 buildings burned to the ground, three ships in the harbour sunk, and the Einansho and Heito airfields partially demolished.'[15] With the mainland receiving the main focus of rehabilitation, little attention had been paid to what, eventually, was to become Chang Kai-shek's island stronghold.

When our tickets had been purchased, we had been informed that there would be several connections that would have to be made. These connections were due to the fact that the railroad authorities had not been able to completely return the rail system to its original state of excellence, which had been enjoyed under the Japanese administration. The opportunity to use our new found talent from the language school was unique in that very few of the island inhabitants spoke English. There were still quite obviously serious flaws in our command of the every day Chinese needed to travel around the island.

This gap in our fluency in Chinese, and our understanding of the details of our train trip which we had received from the ticket office, was made clear to us after the completion of the first leg of our voyage. We had been pleasantly surprised by the cleanliness and the standard of the coach cars which we boarded, and which we enjoyed for a period of approximately two hours. There was an announcement made, as the train slowly approached the station where we were to make our connection, that there would be less than one and a half hours between train connections inasmuch as we had been slightly delayed in reaching our destination.

This did not give us any cause for alarm. A one and a half hour connection merely meant that we would be faced with a boring wait between trains. Alternatively, we could possibly find something to eat as we hadn't had any food since an early breakfast in Taipei. What did alarm us on our arrival was the way in which the baggage coolies fought over the suitcases for the privilege of carrying them to the next train, which we thought we were going to board at the same station. Surely there wasn't enough money to be earned to cause the almost violent exchange of blows between the coolies as they fought over the entitlement of taking our bags to the next train, only a few yards away from our arrival point at the station, or so we thought.

We lost valuable time during the period it took the baggage coolies to make clear to us that if we didn't hurry we weren't going to be able to make our connection. With an hour and a half between connections, it was not surprising that we had difficulty understanding the need to hasten.

When the logistics of what we were faced with, in so far as making the train connection, finally sank into our minds, we almost cancelled our trip and our engineering surveys on the spot with the absolute intent of returning to Shanghai. The next train connection was five miles down the railroad track.

We barely had the hour and a half to make it. Further more, the only way to travel was on the bombed out railroad bed. The tracks of this section of the rail line had suffered such considerable damage from the Allied bombings that it was apparent that it had been given a very low priority for replacement. It was decided that more efficient use of the resources of the railroad company could be utilized in repairing those sections which were much less devastated by the bombing, than the section between our first stop and the next town. A town five miles away.

And so off we went at a semi-dog trot. It was a marvel to Carl and myself how the baggage coolies were able to not only carry the heavy bags of the well outfitted Westerners, but readily outpaced us as well. These were coolies that were living on a subsistence diet, and yet Carl and I could hardly keep up with them. As we continued on our journey, we were warned of some danger at one stage as we approached a tunnel. Surely there could be no danger of meeting a train head on in the darkened tunnel as, obviously, if there were trains running, we would not be making the train connection by foot.

No. The danger was not from meeting a train head on, but from the possibility of loose rocks and debris falling from the roof of the tunnel. Water had been seeping through the roof of the tunnel for several years since the section had last been bombed by the Allies, and in the process had severely loosened the tiles lining the walls and the roof of the tunnel.

We were warned to keep a wary eye out for any possibility that the vibrations caused by the movement of the many passengers and attendant coolies would cause some oversize part of the structure of the tunnel to be jarred loose. In keeping a watchful eye out for such an eventuality, we often found ourselves knee deep in pools of water that had collected along the rail tracks as the seepage kept getting stronger and stronger as we traversed the tunnel. It was with a tremendous sigh of relief that we glimpsed 'light at the end of the tunnel' without having undergone any serious mishap.

We literally paid the coolies on the run as the train was getting up steam in preparation for leaving as we approached. The coolies threw our baggage into the baggage car, which was the first of the cars that we encountered as we breathlessly entered the station. We were under the impression that we would have our bags moved to the coach cars as we got underway.

It soon became clear that the so called baggage car was ours by the fact of our holding first class tickets. The other cars on the train, that is the third class cars—there were no second class cars—were flat cars with no roofs, no guard rails, and no other means of shelter. And so began the second, or rather the third leg of our voyage if that part covered by foot could be considered the second leg.

This portion of the journey was completed without incident. The train drew to a halt in the town that contained the first sugar mill plant that Carl and I were to survey. There was a reasonable rest house not far from the sugar mill, inasmuch as the large majority of visitors to the town all had business with the mill. The next morning we met the manager and the chief engineer of the mill and embarked on the first phase of our survey. The mill was in quite fair condition in spite of the shortage of parts and lubricants that they had had to endure during the last few years prior to the end of the war, and the subsequent attempt to rehabilitate the plant with no money available after the war ended.

Carl and I were pleased to note as we proceeded with our work that we both employed almost identical methods of analysis for our surveys. We completed our work and prepared to move on to the next one of the mills owned by the corporation which was the buyer of the company's lubricants. We were agreeably surprised to be informed that the next mill was only a short distance away and the journey would be undertaken by road.

Our Chinese was sufficiently good enough not to have misunderstood the word 'road', when we heard it uttered by the manager of the mill. He informed us that our 'road' transport would be ready to depart at six AM in the morning. We wondered why the journey was to commence at such an early hour. We hadn't been able to reconcile the short distance, which we had understood the next mill was from the one we had just surveyed, and the duration of the trip which we had been informed was to be three or four hours.

To 'travel by road' is, undoubtedly, a generic expression used in many languages. In Germany today, it would probably mean traveling over one hundred and twenty-five miles an hour on a perfectly paved auto-bahn. In France, perhaps the same rate of speed, but on an auto-route not so well maintained and with the added possibility of meeting a fellow traveler head-on because he had lingered too long enjoying that last part of his bottle of Bordeaux. In the hilly or high density population areas of Japan you probably couldn't ever reach that lofty speed of one hundred and twenty-five miles per hour. In Taiwan?

In Taiwan, Carl and I learned that not all shock absorbers are the product of the efficient designers of Fisher Body Corporation. The vehicle which greeted our eyes in the morning had been produced by that giant corporation that owned Fisher Body, General Motors. It had been manufactured many years earlier and long before the start of the war. It was a large dump truck with no roof. Only the driver's seat remained in the cab, inasmuch as the other seat had been removed to make storage space available for that part of its cargo that couldn't be exposed to the elements. The passenger area of the truck was in the back, behind the cab.

Carl and I clambered onto what was going to be our means of transportation for the next three or four hours as we took our leave of the site of our first survey. The roadbed from the entrance to the mill was in reasonably fair condition. As we left the mill further and further behind us, the roadbed surface began to deteriorate with alarming suddenness. Bomb craters appeared with startling regularity. We asked one of our fellow passengers as to when we could expect to cease to have to endure the bone jarring, tooth rattling agony of having to travel over a road surface that hadn't obviously had any maintenance since the close of the war. With a big, wide, reassuring, peasant grin he informed us that it would be only a matter of an hour or so when we could expect some relief. In the meantime, he solicitously tried to point out the reason that we were suffering such pain rending results of riding in a vehicle whose shock absorbers had ceased functioning a number of years ago. It was because we were not taking advantage of the God given shock absorbers with which we had been so graciously endowed by our creator.

He pointed downward in the direction of his knees and ankles. At that very moment, we hit an immense bomb crater in the road. We were amazed to see him take the staggering jolt with no indication of discomfort at all while we grimaced in almost agonizing pain. He realized that we still hadn't apparently understood the method of riding in the only kind of transportation available to the residents in this part of the island.

Carl and I had immediately recognized, when we mounted the vehicle, that we were going to complete our several hour journey in a standing position. What we hadn't grasped was the unbelievable jolting that our bodies were going to have to endure. Our fellow passenger continued to try to show us how to survive such a journey by exaggerating the position of his body. He bent his knees almost double. At the same time, he raised his heels from the floor of the truck until he was actually on his tip toes. From this position he alternately rose and stooped in a rhythmic movement. In the midst of this demonstration, we hit another bone jarring depression in the road. He gracefully weathered the jolt by allowing his knees and his ankles to flex themselves to the degree necessary to match the intensity of the vehicle's reaction to the deepness of the bomb crater.

Carl and I both immediately assumed the identical position. Incredibly, we realized that nature had indeed given us built in shock absorbers. Not much more than an hour after this body saving technique had been shown to us, and true to the information given by our fellow passenger, the truck swerved off the road and onto a better maintained roadbed. Better maintained, not by man but by nature.

The balance of our trip was on the river bed. It was obvious to us as we peered over the top of the driver's cab that the river bed had been used countless times by any number of vehicles which had found the it much more 'user-friendly' than the roadbed. The Allies had not thought of bombing it. The only natural obstacles encountered were the many boulders and small rocks exposed by the flowing water. And so we continued on our voyage with our heels elevated from the floor of the truck and knees bent to absorb the frequent and hair raising jolts and swerves of our driver as we traveled down river. By this time, I was having the extreme difficulty of interpreting the meaning of the phrases 'a life of ease and comfort' and 'international oil executive'.

Another survey. Another road trip. Another survey. Another train trip. At one village where we stopped for lunch, Carl and I were appalled by the filth of the eating facilities. We ordered the boiled rice on the assumption that the boiling would have killed all the germs. We, also, purchased the only bottle of beer available, which naturally was quite warm, again on the assumption that there were no germs in a sealed bottle.

We took our purchases out to the street as we couldn't stomach the thought of eating in the over-whelming stench and muck of the restaurant. There we sat on the curb where we shared our repast with each other as the town mongrels and the street urchins looked on in envy.

Time to part company. We reconfirmed the town in which we would meet and the name of the only rest house available in the town. A name which had been given to us by one of the more knowledgeable and traveled mangers of the mill where we had just completed our last survey together. At dinner that night, after my lonely arrival in the town where I was going to be on my own since first arriving in Taiwan, the host from the mill kept on insisting on replenishing my plate with the local delicacies. These delicacies happened to be cold pickled vegetables.

The many chickens that were underfoot in the restaurant were pecking cheerfully away at what ever crumbs fell from the table. They studiously ignored the cold delicacies which I surreptitiously tried to feed them. An action which I hoped would escape the notice of my hosts as I tried to convince the hungry chickens that the pickled vegetables were really delicious.

If only the chickens would consume them. Alas, it was my ill luck to have to finish the majority of them myself. And ill luck it was as I lay on my tatami wide awake at three o'clock in the morning in excruciating agony. My stomach revolted in justified rage at the treatment I had imposed on it by forcing it to accept all those Chinese pickled delicacies, which were the envy of the neighbourhood.

I wondered if I were really going to die of some strange, Oriental illness in this god forsaken, tiny village on the edge of nowhere, on an island, that to the best of my knowledge, had never even appeared in my geography books.

Did I survive five years of a horrifying World War only to meet my Maker and explain to Him in a language that I could barely speak and had absolutely no understanding of the written word, that I was sorry for all my sins of omission and commission? Wave after wave of agonizing spasms racked my body. Should I call out? But to whom and what would I tell them? Mao Tze-tung had interrupted our schooling before we had gotten to that part of the lessons explaining the parts of the body and their attendant frailty.

As I lay there in a tortured stupor, my body took pity on me. I noticed a lessening in the intensity and the frequency of the agonizing spasms. Finally, I was able to take a breath without believing it was going to be my last. I fell into a fitful slumber and was awakened by the crowing of one of the many cocks who had, undoubtedly, spent a peaceful night because he had had the intelligence to spurn my offer of my hosts' delicacies. And so it went. Survey after survey as I worked my way towards the village which was to be Carl's and my meeting place.

At last! I breathed a sigh of relief as the coolie assisted me with my baggage and led me to the room where the other great white master was awaiting my arrival. One look at Carl and I realized that something was terribly wrong. He was sitting on the tatami on several, oversized, huge cushions that apparently the inn keeper had found among the town's relics. He was very pale and had lost a staggering amount of weight.

"What in the name of God happened to you?" I queried him anxiously. "You look like hell! You've lost so much weight that I hardly recognize you." Offense being the best form of defense, he retorted with the comment that I looked like hell myself. While this was true, I knew that I had recovered a great deal from my ordeal of pickled delicacies in comparison to his condition and appearance.

He then went on sheepishly to confess that he grown lax in his eating habits. He hadn't made sure that all the drinking water was boiled. Neither had all the food he had eaten been either subjected to searing flames or had been cooked to the point of being completely tasteless. He, also, had had a sudden desire for some fresh salad. A fatal craving in those days as almost all such vegetation was fertilized with human excrement that was collected from the town's population in 'honey buckets'.

As a result, he had been suffering constant recurring bouts of violent dysentery. The food he ate never had time to linger long enough in his system to provide any nourishment at all. In fact, when viewing his bodily discharges, he came to the conclusion that they hadn't even changed their physical appearance from the time he had ingested them until the time they took their leave through his now, unbearably, painful rectum. In desperation he had appealed to one of his hosts at the mill he was surveying at the time requesting some advice or remedy that would cure him of his affliction. He held up a very small bottle whose label was completely covered in Chinese characters.

"What is that?" I asked him in a somewhat surprised tone of voice, which was caused by the way in which he was gazing balefully at the contents.

"Liquid cement," he replied emphatically. "I haven't gone in seven days since I took the first goddamn dose. Now I don't know what to do."

I burst out laughing in relief that he didn't have some deadly, wasting disease and wasn't going to die in front of my very eyes. I, also, felt some justification for my humour as at least he now had me to help him over the finale days of his ordeal. In my case, he was nowhere to be found when I thought I was going to depart from this vale of tears.

We tried to forget our worries as we compared notes and compiled the data which we had garnered from the many mills over the past number of weeks. The next morning he actually looked and felt better. He said that at one stage during the night he had had the illusion that he was going to have a bowel movement. I assured him that even the thought of such activity was a good sign and that in a short time it would be an actuality, as in point of fact it was.

We had six more mills to survey together and, then, we would be taking the train back to Taipei. Our boss, with the big expense account, had planned to meet us after the completion of our survey and was going to arrive at the end of the following week.

At the close of the long day, I said to Carl that in view of the fact that it was Thursday, we should plan our program so that we could finish after the weekend and be in Taipei in time to meet the boss.

"No." he said. "It is Friday, and we must do the remaining mills in as short a time as possible or we will not be there when the boss arrives." After much arguing regarding which day of the week it was, we called on the innkeeper to verify which of us was correct. Neither. It was Sunday. We both needed a rest and a change of surroundings.

We had to return to civilization and some kind of normality or we just weren't going to make it. We did get back in time to meet the plane, and the boss immediately verified our assessment of our personal condition.

"My God!" he exclaimed in a shocked greeting as he viewed our appearance. "What happened to you two? You both need some rest and recuperation. Immediately after we put these surveys into finale form, I want both of you to fly to Hong Kong for a week's R&R, if you're not already dead before you get there. I'll cable the Hong Kong office that you're coming, and I'll have them put you up at the Peninsular Hotel, and arrange for a car to be at your disposal."

After his kindness in ordering us to Hong Kong to recover from our ordeal of traveling through Taiwan, it was a shame to be the cause of his eventual embarrassment concerning the auditing of his expense account. We did feel very badly about that. Especially since through some oversight on our part, we didn't get the necessary papers signed in time for our exit visas from Hong Kong and had to spend two weeks there at company expense, instead of the original one week, as envisaged by the boss.

There were certain formalities that had to be completed at the mills' head-quarters of the group in Taipei before we could return to Shanghai and consider our survey of the sugar mills in Taiwan complete. We booked passage on a non-stop flight from Hong Kong to Taipei. As we were leaving Hong Kong after our second week of enforced recovery, we were very thankful that we had regained our physical strength and were back to a more normal outlook on the continued prospect of living in the Orient. The plane took off in the usual sweltering heat of that tropical paradise known as Hong Kong. Local flights from Hong Kong to Taipei are not undertaken by the well known, international airline carriers. The plane that started its flight from Hong Kong was, as usual, an old DC-3 that had bucket seats lining both sides of the aircraft.

There is, undoubtedly, some great medical scientist that has the answer to why the Chinese are so prone to air-sickness. Whatever that answer may be, we were well aware of the inclination as the plane rolled down the runway, and the major-ity of the passengers started to exhibit that characteristic. In fact, before the plane had actually left the ground there were a half-dozen or so of the passengers that were giving visible evidence of their inability to retain their breakfast.

The temperature inside the aircraft was well over a sweltering one-hundred degrees Fahrenheit from having been sitting in the sun on the runway prior to takeoff. The sound and the smell of the retching passengers only encouraged the balance of their traveling mates to join them in the orgy of discharging their recent intake of fried rice and beans on to the floor of the aircraft. There were no beautifully laid carpets on these bare boned aircraft that commuted daily around the various cities in that vast country. Consequently, the corrugations in the floor made excellent conduits for the rush of regurgitated food that cascaded towards the tail of the plane as it struggled to gain altitude.

We had scarcely been airborne a short time, when the announcement was made that we were to make an unscheduled landing in Canton. As the plane rolled to a stop, Carl and I hastily exited the DC-3 in order to escape the over-powering fumes of the fetid mess that had accumulated in the rear of the aircraft. As we stood outside watching several mechanics swarm over the plane, we enquired of the pilot what had caused the unscheduled stop in Canton.

"Problems with the starboard engine," he casually explained, "but we should be underway in less than thirty minutes," he reassured us. Sure enough. We were airborne and on our way enduring that overpowering smell of disgorged, half-digested food that had had an opportunity to solidify in the blazing temperature of the Canton airport.

Again, we were hardly airborne when the familiar message of another unscheduled landing was heard over the loudspeaker. This time the pilot volunteered the information that they were having trouble with the port engine. As we impatiently waited on the ground in the soul searing heat of South China, we sarcastically enquired of the pilot in our best Chinese what was meant by a 'nonstop' flight to Taipei. He laconically remarked that we could be assured that the rest of the flight would conform to the time table which had indicated 'non-stop' from Hong Kong to Taipei. We didn't hesitate to show our disbelief, when we asked him on what grounds he was able to make such a definite statement after the last two unscheduled landings. In that wonderfully, fatalistic attitude of the Oriental mind he merely remarked that "the rest of the flight is all over water".

Any unscheduled landing from now on would be our last.

4

Hong Kong—1949

We had hardly been back a matter of months in Hong Kong, when the manager called all of us to his office. We had been avidly reading the newspapers everyday checking on whether or not General Mao Tze-tung had kept his promise to out-general General Chang Kai-shek.

"I've just received a cable from Shanghai," Dave Rowsome announced. "The Shanghai airport has been closed down because of the proximity of the fighting between the Nationalists and the Red Army." This was beginning to sound familiar. "The Managing Director, Phil LeFevre, has decided that all thirty American staff in Shanghai and the out stations in China will be evacuated with their families," he continued. "Since there is no air transport available, they will be coming out on the last company tankers to leave Shanghai," he informed us.

It was plain that Mao Tze-tung had kept his promise. Also, a nice feeling that THE COMPANY would make huge ocean going tankers available to ensure that their prized staff didn't get trapped in the path of the oncoming 'liberators'.

"Inasmuch as hotel rooms are non-existent in Hong Kong, the thirty staff members and their families will have to be accommodated among you all here," he informed us. He then proceeded to detail the size of the families and asked for information on the possible configurations that would be available to house them. The prime object was to keep as many members of the same family together as feasible. While this discussion was in progress, he advised me that there were six bachelors in the group. I was to be in charge of seeing that they were made as comfortable as possible at the bachelors' quarters where I held sway as head of the chummery.

Fortuitously, with four bedrooms and a living room we could have one man share the bedroom with its present occupant by installing a cot in each of the four bedrooms. Pushing all the furniture against the walls would allow two cots to be set up in the living room for the last two of the six. However, bachelors, unlike married staff members, make do with the barest necessities such as sheets, pillow cases, towels and all the other day to day requirements that make up a comfortable living arrangement.

It was essential to call on what would soon be the already strained supplies of the married staff. It was also necessary to double the food supply, inasmuch as the number of occupants of the chummery would have more than doubled. Fortunately, there was no shortage of food in Hong Kong, although periodic shortages of water were a frequent occurrence. It was a customary procedure to fill the bathtub with water when it was in plentiful supply, which then served as a convenient reservoir when the cook needed water for preparation of our daily meals, or we took the usual bucket baths.

One of the evacuee families, Mr. and Mrs. Johnson, was to be quartered with an American Hong Kong staff member, Ed. Ed and his wife were both long time pre-war residents of China. There were, naturally, quite a number of British staff members in the Hong Kong organization. There was considerable speculation at a later date as to whether or not there would have been the deplorable situation that arose had one of the British staff members been assigned the Johnson family, instead of being assigned to an American staff member.

The evacuees were met at the oil terminal at Gin Drinker's Bay when the last company tankers out of Shanghai arrived. They were conveyed to their assigned family quarters, and I picked up the six bachelors. With the crowd milling around and the confusion that existed, there was little chance to meet all of the staff. Many of them were unknown to us, inasmuch as they included the out station staff in addition to the Shanghai staff.

Thus, I was quite unprepared for the abrupt summons from Dave Rowsome the next morning when I arrived at the office. I was even less prepared for the expression on his face. My mind raced in review of all the recent sins I had committed vis-à-vis the office regulations. There were even a few that, while of no official concern to the office, might have merited that look if Dave had ever been made privy to them.

In a voice shaking with rage he declared, "You made the rounds of all the hotels when you first arrived here. I want you to use every contact you have and make hotel arrangements for the Johnsons. I don't care what they cost. Get the bridal suite at the Peninsular Hotel if you have to, but get them the best accommodations that exist in Hong Kong," was his last command in a tone that said someone was going to hang for whatever transgression had caused him to be in such a rage. And a rage it was. He was having difficulty breathing with his face the color of the setting sun over the China Sea.

"But they have been assigned to Ed's family," I blurted out. It was a relief that his fury wasn't directed at me. I completely overlooked the fact that it would have been much safer to beat a hasty retreat and do as I was told. By staying in his office, I might incur his wrath for something which he may have forgotten about the previous week.

"That is correct," he continued in the same deadly tone of voice, "but it appears that Mrs.Johnson is Chinese and Mister Ed has given me twenty-four hours to get them out of his home." The word, 'Mister', rolled off his tongue like venom from a King Rattler's fangs. Woe betide Mister Ed I thought to myself.

I exited quickly from his office. My mind seemed to be saying that this just can't be happening. Here is an American family, evacuees, and a fellow American refuses to put them up because one of them is Chinese? The British always said that their colonialists were more British than the British. Here was an American who had lived in China for so many years that he had acquired the contempt that so many whites have for other members of the human race, because their skin is a different color from theirs. A contempt, so manifest, he would not house a fellow American and his Chinese wife during this chaotic period.

Dave's reaction to the totally uncalled for prejudice of one his staff members was one of the virtues that endeared him to all of us. His decision to spare no cost to try, at least, to partly atone to the Johnsons for the outrageous behavior of Ed was a clue to his character. Dave, eventually, made it so difficult for Ed that he left Caltex and went to work for Gulf.

I put the word out 'on the street'. I was in the market for the best available accommodations, which would be paid for in United States dollars. I visited every one of my old haunts, but to no avail. Word did come back from one of the 'girls' whom I had befriended. She said she would be glad to give up her practice and her home for a few days, and that would literally have cost her money, just to accommodate my friends. Since she was not the only occupant practicing her trade in that particular area, I relayed my profuse thanks to her and filed her offer in the back of my head as a last resort.

It was, indeed, a most generous offer on her part. I had first met her when The Hong Kong Hotel had very kindly extended the duration of my third visit to their premises from three days to two weeks. Her 'station' was just to the left of the entrance to the hotel. Our initial encounter occurred when I was returning home to the hotel alone one evening. She quite naturally assumed that it was in order to approach me. After a few pleasant words and exchange of greetings, she recognized that I was not a potential client and she bid me a very polite 'ming tien'.

On my arrival home at the hotel the following night, she again was customer-less. I stopped to chat with her and to enquire if business was slow, inasmuch as she had been without gainful employment for two consecutive nights. She sensed what was an obvious concern on my part for her well being and took the opportunity to inform me that there were no ships in port from any of the world navies. It was for this reason that her particular trade had not been very remunerative in the past several days. After a few more pleasantries I bid her goodnight and retired to my hotel room.

Over the period of my stay at The Hong Kong Hotel we met frequently. I learned that her name was Rose Petal, and she was supporting her four year old daughter. She was very concerned about her schooling and requested my advice on which of the well run convent schools I would recommend that her daughter should attend. She told me she intended to move to a better area in order to be closer to a more prestigious school.

I relayed this information to Mother over tea one afternoon on The Peak in order to get the benefit of her knowledge of the area in connection with a school for Rose Petal's daughter. Mother, because of her deep inherent kindness, became very indignant. Not because I was talking to Rose Petal, but because Mother felt that I was wasting the girl's time by misleading her into thinking I was a potential client.

"She could be using the time consumed by your chatting with her for much more gainful employment," Mother forcefully informed me. I assured her that Rose Petal was quite aware of my real concern for her well being and that we had established our relationship early in our first encounter. In fact, her request for guidance on a school for her offspring was indicative of our relationship. Mother relaxed somewhat and gave me a few leads on some schools to relay to Rose Petal.

Everyone travels on the Kowloon Ferry between Hong Kong and the Main-land at one time or another. It was, therefore, not a very unexpected encounter one afternoon when I introduced Rose Petal to Mother as we were crossing the harbour.

"What a delightful girl," Mother exclaimed on the ferry pier after disembark-ing and bidding Rose Petal farewell. "You seem to know her so well. Why haven't you invited her to have tea with us one afternoon on The Peak?" It was highly amusing to watch the tell-tale emotions chase each other across Mother's face as the name, Rose Petal, finally penetrated her consciousness.

Although Dave Rowsome had made it quite clear that he was willing to pay for a bridal suite and money was no object, there was a problem with the bridal suites. Because they were so large, the hotels had set up cots in the lounges and had even put extra beds in some of the bigger bedrooms. The bridal suites, as a consequence, were housing ten to twelve people in a suite that ordinarily would have been occupied by two honeymooners. To make one of the bridal suites available would have meant evicting ten or twelve people. Even with my contacts, the hotel managers said it would be next to impossible to find rooms for that many people. At no time was the reason given for the necessity of finding accommodations for the Johnsons on such short notice.

At last, by noon of the following day, there was a glimmer of hope. One of my British colleagues, from one of the trading companies, called with the news that he was going on a ten day trip to the interior of China. He would be pleased to make his home and his servants available to me. He was an old time Hong Kong resident and had many sources of information. One of the sources had told him of my dilemma. So the British came to the rescue.

Strange how some people react diametrically opposite to what one would have expected. Here was an American refusing to have an American family live with them, because the wife was Chinese. When word of their plight becomes known, an old time British resident rushes into the breach as soon as he hears the news.

'Well done, Gunga Din'.

It was as a result of the solution to the problem that made us wonder if, perhaps, the Johnsons could have been accommodated with a British staff member without this deplorable situation arising.

On reflection, such behavior shouldn't have come as a total surprise. It was only a few days after my initial arrival in Hong Kong when word spread like wildfire. An American Army Air Force officer had been refused admittance to the American Club as a guest of one of the members. An officer who bore all kinds of decorations, including the Purple Heart, earned in protecting the lives of those very members of the club who were refusing to admit him.

His sin was quite simple and, conspicuously, not his fault. He was black. This was before the 'sit ins' and the marches and Martin Luther King. Possibly the rules are different today (not that such rules were ever written down). In actuality, there are foul rumours heard today that, and God forbid the fact even be dared mentioned, there are Chinese being admitted to the club. Indubitably, the 'white man's burden' must have become unbearable for such things to have come to pass.

Again, one never seems to learn from history except that, 'you learn nothing from history'. That is not strictly true. Many bad habits that have been perpetuated and have become part of the folk lore of the white man's burden came as a result of learning from history. Buttressed by these two events, the next time such a situation reared its ugly head, I was well prepared.

During my short stay in Shanghai, it was my good fortune to meet one of the great families of Shanghai. The family happened to include a most attractive daughter. When Mao Tze-tung appeared to be going to make life uncomfortable for the wealthy families of Shanghai, they moved their relations and their millions of dollars worth of spinning equipment from their cotton factories in Shanghai to Hong Kong. It was, accordingly, my great luck to renew my acquaintance with Mai Ling shortly after her arrival in Hong Kong.

We celebrated our reunion by dining and dancing at the Hong Kong Hotel. The hotel was one of the grand old ladies of the Island. The food was excellent, the music delightful and my companion captivating. We danced until the small hours of the morning, and I delivered her safe and sound to her family estate on the Peak.

The Hong Kong Hotel was one of the watering places of the old time British residents of the Island. Staid and proper and not given to jazz and the boisterous rock and roll set. It was, thus, no surprise to me to find myself nodding and saying good evening to the wife of one of the British staff members of THE COMPANY. To say that the greeting was not returned in the same manner didn't make any impression on my consciousness, inasmuch as my companion had captured and held all of my attention the entire evening. Truthfully, it now seems strange that I had even noticed that there were other people in the room.

The same did not hold true for the other people, however, as I was soon to learn the next day, when I accidentally came face to face with my nodding acquaintance from the Hong Kong Hotel, the wife of the British staff member.

Her opening words, without so much as a good morning, were, "I say, my deah boy, I saw you dancing with that Chinese ... woman ... last night at the Hong Kong Hotel." The word ... woman ... came out of her mouth like a bad taste. "I must say, you know, it's just not done." Fortunately for my backbone standing behind me were the Johnsons' and the black American Army Air Force officer's experiences.

"Really, my deah," I snapped back imitating her strong English accent on the word, 'deah', "how can that be.... because I've.... done it." I turned sharply on my heel and left her gaping at my disappearing back. Another lesson learned. Perhaps not all the British staff members would have put up the Johnsons during their brief stay in Hong Kong.

There was a time honoured saying in THE COMPANY. 'There are only three problems in this company—company cars, company houses, and company wives—in the reverse order'.

The chummery was located in Kowloon on the mainland. Many of the married staff had to live in Kowloon as well, because Hong Kong was where the taipans lived and was prohibitively expensive as a result. When the company wives, who lived in Kowloon, wished to go shopping in Hong Kong and their husbands had taken their company cars to the office, it was common practice to use the company car assigned to the chummery to pick them up and deliver them to the ferry pier.

One bright and early morning as I left the chummery full of the good spirits of mankind, the company car arrived at the chummery en route to the ferry to pick me up. There were two company wives in the back seat on their way to a shopping spree. In order not to disturb the passengers in the back, I took the seat in the front of the car next to the driver and mumbled good morning to the occupants in the rear. My greeting was scarcely acknowledged as they continued their conversation. Bachelors are an abomination to company wives.

One of the wives, whom I recognized as having just returned from home leave, gazed out the car window at the building from which I had just exited and turned to her companion and asked, "Is that a new company house?" To all intents and purposes I didn't even exist or she could have directed her inquiry to me.

"Oh," replied her comrade, "that is the bachelors' new quarters."

"In a tone so disdainful that even the chauffeur winced, the comment was made loud enough for me to hear."I say, rather posh for bachelors, what?" The British use of English is so precise and exquisite that just a few well chosen expressions, with a deliberate, pointed inflection, sums up an entire situation about which an American might take forever to make his point.

It can be imagined what a bachelor's reaction to that comment would be, or perhaps it can be visualized his wondering whether or not assassination was a viable alternative. Like immediately! In the car! In front of witnesses! No.... 'The wheels of the Gods grind exceedingly slow.' I would bide my time. There was more poetic justice to be paid then pure assassination. That was too clean and quick for the likes of this company wife.

There was no time available that week for selling oil. There were too many details still to be finalized before the furnishing and decorating of the chummery could be considered as complete. That old cliché, 'the exception that proves the rule' manifested itself at this time in the form of a very young and very delightful

British family, Basil and Christine Genders. She not only didn't adhere to that hoary dislike of bachelors by company wives, but she spent considerable time doing hand painted drawings on the walls of the circular staircase leading to the roof garden of the bachelors' quarters.

Basil and Christine had, also, welcomed without question and with open arms, the family assigned to them from among the evacuees. One of the family members assigned to Basil and Christine was Eurasian. If ever there were a person who could have claimed grounds for refusing hospitality to someone of the Oriental race, even if only part Oriental, it would be Christine. At the age of twenty, when life should be the beginnings of all the wonderful things that happen to young people, she went to prison for three years and eight months subsisting on two bowels of rice a day that her Japanese captors rationed to her.

There were any number of details needed to be completed before the bachelors could move into their new quarters and which were very time consuming. These included a roof garden, the standard needs of Stuart crystal ware, Sterling silver ware, linens, and a host of other items. Dave Rowsome had entrusted the entire responsibility to me, inasmuch as I was the longest term resident of the four bachelors that were going to occupy the chummery. Since Hong Kong was tropical in nature, it appeared logical that the furnishings should be in bamboo, plus the fact that it was a staple of that part of China. The Chinese are masters at the art of molding bamboo into the most attractive variety of furniture.

All employees who have worked for huge bureaucracies know that every manager, who has to make decisions as part of his everyday responsibilities, has hidden away in the back of his desk a source of information that tells him exactly what those decisions should be. This source is a reference book. It is known to those who don't have to make decisions and, therefore, aren't privileged to hold one, as 'the big black book'. Officially, it was known as 'The Policy and Accounting Manual'.

The big black book spells out in the minutest detail what you can do and what you can not do, mostly the latter. What rights you have, if any. Who has the authority to sign certain documentation and exactly what the company's policies are in every situation, real and unreal. In some bureaucracies like IBM, the greatest of them all, it is whispered that the big black book even tells you what kind of shirt, tie and suit you can wear (white, navy blue and dark). Some IBM staffers swear that at one time the big black book even told them what they could think.

THE COMPANY, understandably of course, had such a book. In one section devoted entirely to furniture the big black book spelled out graphically exactly what style, size, type and the cost of furniture that could be made available to various levels of management. The bachelors, as to be expected, brought up the rear of the parade.

THE COMPANY operated in many tropical areas. It was pleasing to note that bamboo furniture was an acceptable style. Appropriately, bamboo was the prime selection. While the living quarters and the roof garden were to be completed in bamboo, it was felt that bamboo would not be suitable for the four bedrooms. Light teak was chosen. It was most attractive and even more important it was allowed by the big black book, but only in areas where it was indigenous and, therefore, cheap and consequently fitted into the cost restrictions. It was a marvel of creative financing that even Michael Milken would have envied that allowed teak wood in Hong Kong, where it wasn't indigenous and, consequently, not cheap, to fit into the cost restrictions of the big black book.

Whoever had written the book must have had a mental quirk about desks. The rules stated very unequivocally that desks were not to be part of company furnishings. When such cast iron rules are written down with such force, they only prove to be a challenge to the more enterprising members of THE COMPANY, who rise to such a challenge like hungry fish to bait. As a result of this unbreakable rule, it was necessary to buy eight dressing tables for the bachelors' quarters, two for each of the four bedrooms.

All of the furniture was being made to order. The second four of the dressing tables were designed with a series of three drawers on the left hand side of the table, three drawers on the right hand side of the table and a single drawer in the middle with a green felt covering on the table top. There were fittings for the mirror on the back. Through an oversight, the mirrors were never manufactured and, therefore, never delivered to the chummery. Need it be mentioned that it took many explanations to convince visitors that assuredly, the item was a dressing table and not a desk.

One of the articles on display in the furniture boutique was a most exquisite oil painting of an Hawaiian dancer framed in bamboo, the perfect addition to a bachelor's living room where the frame was a tasteful match for the decor. No matter how the black book was interpreted, misinterpreted, or twisted there was no means by which oil paintings could be purchased with company money. Nor could parts be left off, as with the desks, and call it something else. The closest the bachelors could come to having it be part of the chummery was to buy it with their own money. When the price was made known to me, it came as a rude shock that there were people in the world who had enough money to spend on such items. With the delivery of the last piece of furniture to the chummery, plans were put in hand to have a house warming. The kind of party for which generous bachelors are so well known.

During the arrangements being made for the housewarming, it suddenly occurred to me that while it was impossible to buy the painting, at least, it might be borrowed, just for the occasion of the housewarming. The shop-keeper was loath to part with his valuable property. Finally after much persuasion and promises that all new company arrivals would buy their needs at his establishment, he parted with the Hawaiian dancer. He added the strong warning that if the painting did not arrive back in its original condition, he would bill THE COMPANY directly for the full cost. Under this threat, we took great care to see that no accident befell our Hawaiian lady.

With the picture hung the room was transformed into a luxurious display of wealth and good taste. The transformation only made me lament even more that there was no method of reinterpreting the black book. In reading and re-reading the black book to find some inkling of how to accomplish the impossible task of having the company buy the painting, the instructions to affix brass tags with numbers on them to each piece of company furniture for inventory purposes seemed to be trying to leap off the pages and into my head. For some strange reason, these instructions kept crossing and re-crossing my sub-conscious. What was my sub-conscious trying to tell me? Company tags? Company tags? Company tags?

Everyone knew the pervasive influence of the benign dictatorship for which we all worked. Tags and inventories were a way of life. What was my sub-conscious trying to tell me? A blinding flash! I had not forgotten my 'posh' company wife, but nothing in the way of lawful assassination had my mind found to mete out to her. But here in front of me was poetic justice incarnate. Company tags! That was what my sub-conscious was trying to tell me. Take one of the company tags off one of the chairs just for the evening of the housewarming. Put it on the bottom of the picture in the back with just enough of the tag protruding to announce to all inquisitive company wives, 'here was a piece of furniture for which the company had paid', and the tag declared that it was officially in the inventory.

Done! Ding hao! On with the house warming! If any one of our guests were to examine everything in the room to determine if we had observed the letter of the law in the black book, it would be our 'posh' company wife. Unquestionably, we wouldn't have invited her at all, except that her husband worked closely with one of the members of the chummery and he felt duty bound to do so.

She would be certain to examine the picture in minute detail and discover that bachelors had been allowed to flaunt the cast iron rules of the black book. This would make her life truly miserable, which were just what kind thoughts we all had in mind for her. Understandably, my fellow bachelors had been advised what had transpired in the company car on that infamous morning when that degrading comment had been made.

Dave had enquired in a friendly and fatherly way during the trials and tribulations of getting the chummery furnished, how I was bearing up under the strain of not selling any oil. His question was engendered by the fact that I was devoting my entire time to the personal needs of my three brother bachelors and myself. There was no inkling about how different his attitude was to become after the housewarming.

The day of the housewarming arrived. The servants were in their new uniforms. Their training showed itself in the impeccable way in which the most delicious hors d'oeuvres were served. The beer was ice cold (except for some warm beer which was kept in reserve for the British guests) and one and all made merry. I modestly basked in the many favourable comments from the guests on the tasteful way in which the chummery had been furnished. In particular, on the luxurious impression that everyone underwent when entering the living room and being greeted by our Hawaiian lady on the wall surrounded by bamboo.

Nothing marred the festivities of the evening. Everyone enjoyed themselves by congregating in the usual fashion. All the men in groups talking company business. All the company wives gossiping about the bachelors' wayward life style and the transgressions of the members of the staff who weren't present. Most of the company wives were pregnant. Nothing much else to do in that part of the world surrounded by perfect servants that cater to your every need.

In a moment of what bachelors consider humour, a part of the roof garden had been roped off and labeled with a sign, 'Pregnant Wives Correl'. Although nothing marred the festivities of the evening, Gretchen, one of the pregnant wives, missed her footing on the circular staircase that led from the roof garden and rolled down its entire length. She had had so much to drink that she again gave credence to that time worn statement that 'God looks after the innocent and the drunks'. The baby was born on its due date, sober we understand, and today is a very charming woman. We have often wondered if her mother ever told her of her first encounter with a circular staircase while she was still in her mother's womb.

The morning after—be it a hangover or the rising sun or some aspect of the day like having to go to work, the morning after arrives. So it did after the housewarming. As I entered the office, Mother signaled me with a look that boded no good for my well being.

"The boss wants to see you the moment you arrive," she whispered. She was being motherly as usual. She warned me that he had sent for the inventory and all the receipts of the purchases made for the chummery the instant he had appeared in the office that morning. "If you have anything you want to cover up," she hastened to caution me, "you had better check your files right now before you go in. He's not as mad as he was about the Johnsons' incident, but if you don't have a good explanation for what's bothering him, he might just get that mad," was her finale warning.

I assured her that all was well. If my suspicions were correct and my assessment of his character was well founded on past experience with his nature, she was going to have a most pleasant and rewarding day. A boss that is in a jovial mood is a blessing to even the most experienced executive secretaries.

I knocked and entered his office. "Well, good morning Rembrandt, or perhaps Picasso is the alias you travel under, which is probably more appropriate considering the subject of our conversation," was his morning greeting. "Before you reply under either alias, let me inform you that I have perused in the most detailed fashion your fiscal and inventory files of the purchases made for the bachelors' quarters. There is no evidence, whatsoever, of the purchase of an oil painting. Yet strangely enough three company wives, who were at your house warming last night, telephoned me this morning. They emphatically assured me that the company has made the purchase, apparently the first of its kind in the company's history, of an oil painting. In fact, one of the company wives couldn't wait until my arrival in the office. She telephoned me at home. She," and he mentioned her name—it was my 'posh' company wife, 'Oh revenge, how sweet thou art,' "was almost beside herself that I had granted special dispensation to the bachelors to buy oil paintings and not to the married staff. Would you care to paint me a scenario?" he concluded.

His roar of laughter at the end of my explanation about the company tag, including the reason for the episode, only served to convince me that my assessment of his nature and character was quite correct. I was on very firm ground.

"Well," he laughed, "that is the good news. Now the bad news. What do I tell the three company wives that will be convincing enough to assure them they were mistaken? Or if not mistaken, I have taken the necessary disciplinary action, particularly your traveling companion in the car," was his query.

We pondered this question for a good half hour until he himself came up with the perfect solution. "I'll tell them that thanks to their telephone calls, you were advised that the painting had to be returned. However, the proprietor wouldn't accept it, and THE COMPANY had to retain ownership of it. Without mentioning the painting," he continued, "I'll put a notice in the monthly newsletter that strict attention must be paid to the limitations in the Policy and Accounting Manual. I know all three company wives read the monthly newsletter zealously to see if there is any change in company policy as far as benefits and employee entitlements are concerned. Now the rest is up to you. I'm willing to go along with this story, because of the poetic justice involved."

"You find some way to rent the painting for as long as the bachelors' quarters are in commission. Put the cost of the rental on your expense account under 'entertainment', but get that tag off the painting and don't ever have it show up in any other form in the inventory or I'll have your head," he concluded still smiling. Mother asked me later in the week what magic wand I had waved over the boss to transform him from his initial mood to one of such pleasantness. It appeared that he never raised his voice the rest of the week and occasionally even smiled to himself for no apparent reason.

It was well that our revered manager got some relief from the pressure and the trials and tribulations of trying to cater to an overflow staff of thirty members, plus their wives and children. The office had been transformed from an orderly and efficient work place to a mêlée of bodies and paper and telephone calls, none of which had any connection with selling oil. In the midst of the confusion with cables flying between the New York office and our Hong Kong office (in those far gone days, all communication with the home office was by cable—the direct dial efficiency of today's telecommunications simply didn't exist) an urgent cable arrived. It was an inquiry regarding the potential bi-lingual ability of the conglomeration of staff members hunkered down in Hong Kong awaiting re-assignment.

"MADAGASCAR OFFICE REQUIRES FRENCH SPEAKING EXPATRIATE. PLEASE ADVISE," the cable read.

In times of plenty and in times of famine, one's reactions reflect the then current situation. Dave's relief at getting rid of at least one of the horde of unwanted and unneeded bodies was almost pathetic. It was only one out of thirty, and a bachelor at that, but beggars can't be choosers. The staff member's name, Roger Lanouette, rang out with true Gallic tones. Off to the airport with him with a first class ticket and a bon voyage wish as he winged his way to Madagascar.

Another practice in those days, a practice long forgotten now, was to advise the New York office of all departures and arrivals of all staff members and their families. The expense and time consuming effort of this procedure was brought to the attention of management by one of the Harvard MBA's engaged by THE COMPANY in order to keep abreast of the times. It was rumoured that this particular MBA made his cost saving recommendation by commenting that it really wasn't necessary to send cables about arrivals and departures of staff members in the field to the New York office. The daily newspapers were quite capable of carrying out that function. Only the office at the destination had to be advised of the transfer in order to meet the new arrival. If he didn't arrive, the newspapers would carry the headlines in two inch type, as news of the latest plane crash edged out all other happenings around the world.

The cynical reference about plane crashes made to the rational of the Harvard MBA was undoubtedly caused by the resentment felt by all of us, who only had our names adorned by an undergraduate degree. In addition, our salaries after a number of years in servitude to THE COMPANY still didn't approach the astronomical sums being paid to those new employees. They just happened to be lucky enough to have parents with the 'where-with-all' to allow them to continue in school long enough to gain that coveted and well paying graduate degree of MBA.

The cable was dispatched to the New York office, as well as to Madagascar;

"LANOUETTE DEPARTED FLIGHT PAN AM # 133 LEAVING 1400 NOVEMBER 28TH ARRIVING MADAGASCAR 1600 NOVEMBER 28TH".

No one in their wildest imagination could possibly have envisioned the New York office's reaction to this germane piece of information. Back came the response;

**"WE ONLY WANTED TO KNOW IF HE SPOKE FRENCH.
WE DIDN'T ASK YOU TO SEND HIM THERE".**

Careers have risen and fallen on less momentous misdeeds than sending an employee halfway around the world without specific instructions. Once was enough. The depth of the feeling regarding this gaffe was only brought to my attention when, subsequently, I was to be transferred to Ceylon. In order not to have local management repeat such serious errors, the home office in its wisdom sent out a Vice-President from New York to help create more chaos in an office already overflowing with unneeded and unwanted bodies.

As lunch time approached and Mother and I had decided to have tiffen on the Peak, we were entering the lift for an early departure. At the same time, the manager and the vice-president were taking advantage of an early departure as well and joined us in the lift. As we descended, Mother motioned in my direction and conversationally remarked, "Well, another body on its way. He leaves for Colombo, Ceylon next week."

In tones that can only be described as desperate, fervently hopeful, or 'please don't let it be a repeat of Lanouette', the Vice-President asked, "Does New York know he's going there?"

Inasmuch as he was on site to show all concerned how the operation should be run, he was panic stricken that another body was on its way to foreign parts without the express direction of the New York office which he was representing.

Dave with just a trace of smugness in his voice replied, "Of course they do. This office has the best record of only making the same mistake once." This exchange only highlighted the absurdity of sending out a highly placed executive to assist in an operational problem that was unique to the circumstances. He was suppose to be helping to resolve an almost intractable quandary. He hadn't even been made aware of the fact that another employee was on his way to distant parts, in order to help solve the result of Chang Kai-shek's and Mao Tze-tung's differences of opinion.

The world is full of sad and unusual stories. What makes some more pitiful than others is they could have been so easily avoided with a little forethought on the part of the participants. To read a report of the hi-jacking of an airliner, or even of an ocean cruise liner such as the Achille Lauro in nineteen eighty-five, would not seem so uncommon in today's terror ridden world. To have an unsuccessful attempted act of piracy reported one or two hundred years ago when a sailing vessel triumphantly made home port, was probably not at all unusual either. Or even the frequency with which the British blinked when English pirates attacked French commerce was habitual enough. Of course, the British unofficially blinked as long as the pirates confined their efforts to French vessels and did not have the effrontery to attack English shipping.

During the chaotic period when THE COMPANY was trying to find alternative areas to which to send the evacuees from Shanghai, there occurred a tragic and pathetic event. Such an act probably hadn't happened on the high seas for at least a hundred years or more, and probably hasn't occurred since. It certainly had never occurred in the air.

Macao, a Portuguese colony on the Southeast coast of China, was a haven for every gambler and smuggler in the area. It was, also, a place frequented by the residents of Hong Kong who were in need of a little respite from their hard working lives. By air, it was such a short distance that the aircraft barely was able to gain flying altitude when it would begin to commence its descent.

In all areas of the world where political stability is not commonplace, and the local citizens of the territory do not have unlimited faith in the paper money of their government, gold is the common means of exchange. Neither Hong Kong nor Macao had currency restrictions of any kind. It was just as easy to buy, sell, horde or transport gold as it was to shop at the nearest supermarket.

Two of the staff members of the Hong Kong office, one American with two young teenage children and one British whose wife was pregnant, decided that they and their wives would spend the weekend in Macao. They planned to go by plane. Tragically, it was the same plane that some clandestine organization was using to transport a considerable amount of bullion. Even more tragically, the knowledge of the shipment had become known to three of the very, many, unsavory characters who inhabited that part of the world. When the plane commenced its decent in preparation for landing in Macao, the pilot was advised by one of the trio to alter the destination of the flight and continue on into the interior of China.

There were any number of small airfields quite capable of accommodating the size aircraft used between Macao and Hong Kong. The other two members of the trio, with their semi-automatics at the ready, had stationed themselves in the cabin. One just outside the cockpit and the other at the tail of the plane. This gave them complete command of all the passengers on board the aircraft. It is at times like this when 'discretion most obviously becomes the better part of valor'. The pilot should have merely acquiesced and proceeded to do as he was told, particularly since the command was given at gun point. But.... no! He must play hero. He refused to do as he was ordered, and he continued on his descent path into Macao.

Human life in the East and, especially, in that part of the East, does not hold the value to which Westerners are accustomed. In particular, it certainly did not hold any value to the type of individuals who were at that moment engaged in an act of piracy. As observed earlier, there had probably not been an act of piracy committed on the high seas in one hundred years or more and certainly none in the air since the advent of the airplane. Hi-jacking aside, because it is, in effect, not an act of piracy, the records will undoubtedly show that there had never been an act of piracy in the air until the attempt was made on the flight between Hong

Kong and Macao. There has certainly never been a repeat since this fatal occurrence. With the refusal of the pilot to obey the command to abort his descent and continue on into China, the pirate, as undoubtedly happened countless times on the high seas on many sailing vessels, merely shot his captive dead.

As is often the case with the plans of organized crime, a vital factor had been neglected. The plane was small enough and the voyage short enough not to require a co-pilot during its flight. The pirates had over-looked a crucial part of the possible scenarios to which they might be exposed when engaged in the hazardous act of piracy. None of the trio of brigands could pilot the plane. As fate decreed, there were none of the passengers who were capable of flying the aircraft either. The end result was as inevitable as day following night. The plane crashed into the shallow waters off the coast of Macao with only several survivors. Neither of the company staff members or their wives were among the survivors.

The reason the details of the attempted piracy were so accurately known was that one of the very few survivors was the pirate who had taken his position at the tail of plane when holding the passengers at bay. His survival and that of the other few passengers who were located in the rear of the aircraft emphasized the company's travel recommendations. 'If at all possible when flying on company business, take a position as close to the tail of the aircraft as possible. In the event of a crash, statistics indicate that from this position the chances of survival are more likely than if the passenger is seated near the front exit'.

The forward part of the plane is frequently chosen by those highly paid executives, who feel that they must exit the aircraft immediately on landing if they are to utilize every minute of the company's valuable time in pursuit of the company's objectives. While THE COMPANY may have been solicitous in regard to what position its employees should occupy in the aircraft, nowhere in its terms of employment did it mention the possibility of air piracy. In all fairness, since there had been no history of such an occurrence and there has been no record of a repeat performance, perhaps THE COMPANY can be forgiven for this tragic oversight.

However, neither did THE COMPANY mention in its Employee Relations Manual that while piracy on the high seas was a thing of the past, piracy on the coast of China was a very common occurrence. Fortuitously for those of us who traveled by coastal freighter, the owners of the shipping line were well versed in the hazards of this type of travel.

Passengers would board their ship in Shanghai en route to Hong Kong. They would be taken to their cabin by their cabin steward, who would unpack their belongings while the vessel was getting underway. First time passengers would then emerge with the intent of proceeding to the bow of the vessel to obtain a sweeping view of the mouth of the Yangtze River and the China Sea as they set out on their voyage. That is ... only ... first time passengers would attempt to engage in this harmless undertaking. Old time passengers or 'frequent travelers' as they are called today, would immediately congregate in the bar, where immaculately clad stewards would serve the best Scotch available in the world with just a dash of soda.

As a first time passenger, I was most anxious to view the panorama of the mouth of the Yangtze River, the China sea and have a first hand glimpse of the sun setting over the horizon. I had read about this phenomenon so many times in so many books. It was one of the events that had so whetted my appetite for living in this part of the world. Being an ex-naval type I was well aware of port and starboard and the bow and the stern of the vessel. I had no hesitation in proceeding in the direction that would gain me access to a position at the very prow of the ship.

Vessels on the coast of China resemble their counterparts through out the world. All living accommodations, machinery and the position from which the vessel is commanded are located amidships. There are large open areas forward and aft of this superstructure as it is called, where access to the holds is available, as all coastal vessels are engaged in the transport of freight. When the weather is calm and the sun accommodating, many travelers would be inclined to use this area as a place in which to sun bathe. That is travelers who are traveling on other seas and other coasts than the coast of China.

In times of bad weather, when heavy seas come crashing over the craft and sweep across these open areas, it behooves one not to found there. It is always from these open areas that the Hollywood films depict the 'bad guy', and sometimes the 'good guy', being washed overboard in a thunderous rush of white water.

"May I help you sir?" was the query that greeted me as I rather hesitantly and, frankly a bit uneasily, rattled the barred door at the end of the passageway leading to the forward part of the vessel. The polite questioner was very smartly dressed in civilian trousers and wearing a bush jacket. Not the type of steward's uniform or sailor's garb, that would be expected of a member of the ship's company. What was unsettling was the semi-automatic rifle slung across his shoulder with the barrel pointing downward and his right index finger firmly in place on the trigger.

"Yes, you may if you can," was my response. "I'm anxious to get to the bow of the vessel before we reach the mouth of the river in order that I may see the sun set. Can you indicate the way or open this barred door for me?" I questioned him.

His reply, with no explanation, left me feeling even more uneasy than had the view of the barred doorway. "I'm sorry, sir, but these doors are locked from the start of the voyage until we reach Hong Kong. Only the Captain has a key to them," was his explanation as to why it was not possible for me to proceed any further in the direction of the bow of the vessel. I thanked him and thought to myself, 'I will go topside and see if there is any access to the bow from a ships ladder that might lead down into the hold area'.

I proceeded from deck to deck and took the occasion to glance up and down the passageway as I passed each deck on my way topside. Both forward and aft of each passageway on my journey upwards there was plainly visible a similarly clad individual. Each had slung across his shoulder a twin version of the semi-automatic rifle that I had encountered on my initial confrontation with these cold, business like individuals.

Those familiar with vessels of this type will recall that the superstructure is set back at the highest point. The bridge where the Captain holds sway is set back far enough so that there is no point of access to his command quarters other than to mount the ships ladder from the last deck which passengers and ordinary mortals are allowed to inhabit. I reached this last deck available to passengers, left the sanctity of the passageways and strolled out on to the deck.

To my distinct surprise and adding even more uneasiness to that feeling which had been engendered by my encounter with the semi-automatic rifle on the lower deck, the iron bars which had prevented my gaining access to the forward part of the vessel had apparently been extended in a direct upward path. It was now possible to see that there was no access to either the forward or aft part of the vessel from within the mid-ship section of the superstructure as they were totally barred. At both the port side and the starboard side of the vessel, fore and aft on the open deck, there strolled exact duplicates of the individual and his rifle, who had first queried me as to whether or not he could be of any assistance.

It now, finally, dawned on me that we were caged in. Restricted to the use of only the mid-ship's part of the vessel. As this realization dawned on me, I glanced downward at what under ordinary circumstances would be the open areas where access to the holds was to be had. Surprise would hardly describe my reaction to the view that greeted my eyes. Milling around in indescribable confusion were hundreds of Chinese passengers in both the forward and aft sections of the vessel. Some of them gazed upwards with the baleful eyes of caged jackals. They looked towards the individuals whose semi-automatic rifles always had a tendency to point in either the bow or the stern direction and, invariably, at the hundreds of passengers scurrying around on the forward and aft decks.

I beat a hasty retreat to the bar lounge with all thought of viewing the sunset and the mouth of Yangtze River having departed from my thoughts completely. I was determined, notwithstanding, to unravel this unique situation to the best of my ability. As with all natural things the explanation was simplistic.

Piracy on the China coast was endemic and a natural way of life. The passengers that I had viewed herded together fore and aft of the super-structure were traveling steerage. In among them would be many of dubious character. Piracy would not be an act to which they would have any hesitancy in stooping. It was an enterprise in which they had undoubtedly engaged many times in their careers. Should the occasion arrive or they be given the opportunity to engage in such practice, they would be the first to take advantage of it.

"And what would be the duties of the individuals that I viewed with the semi-automatic rifles slung across their shoulders if such an event should occur?" I continued to inquire of my fellow passenger who was enlightening me as to the status quo of traveling on the China coast in those days.

"Oh, they would machine gun them immediately," was his off hand comment in reply to my question, as he ordered another whiskey from the hovering steward with just a dash of soda.

5

Ceylon—1950

An island paradise. Perpetually green. A race of people, who were instinctively proud and descended from an ancient civilization, that built monuments and dams and irrigation projects that even today are marvels of engineering. Irrigation channels many miles long, but built so hydraulically accurate that depending upon which side of the island was enjoying the monsoon, the water could be run in either direction.

'Ceylon has been known to the Western World ever since 16th century Portuguese traders reaped some of their tidiest profits from the country's gem pits. In Sri Lanka, as it is called today, miners still toil by candlelight. Ceylon, also exported cinnamon, pearls, and elephants and cut and polished treasures, including sapphires and topazes. The Portuguese extracted the island's cinnamon, pearls, ivory, dyes, and gemstones. In 150 years of dominance they left a legacy of Portuguese family names and words and a major port city, Colombo, Ceylon's capital'[16].

Then the Dutch colonized the island followed by the British. In many colonies through out the world, the addition of white blood to the local population produced many strikingly beautiful women. In Ceylon there was, of course, the same biological infusion, but in this race of people, the infusion couldn't improve on the pure blood of the Sinhalese. The women were breathtakingly beautiful with delicate features, indescribable complexions and in their flowing saris they were a symphony of color, grace and radiance.

The commercial interest of THE COMPANY and other international oil companies lay in the fact that the British had introduced the growing of tea into the island. As a outcome, there was a great demand for petroleum products to expedite the cultivation, the drying and the transportation of the resulting tea leaves down to the port of Colombo to be exported around the world. All the world knows Ceylon tea, that is all the world who are fortunate enough to be tea drinkers.

Ceylon was to be home for five years. Unknown to me on my arrival, it was also the country in which I, a perennial bachelor as my New York supervisor told his secretary, would get married. It was known as the 'Pearl of the Orient' and so it was. It was a happy five years in spite of some things which marred its serenity, but those things came later. The initial introduction to this island paradise left nothing to be desired.

There was another American bachelor, Charles Biebusch, on the staff, and it was only natural that the two of us should join resources and set up living quarters together. Charles was the embodiment of what most people believe an accountant should look like; thin, quite spoken, slightly stooped and adorned by steel rimmed glasses and deliberate in every move he made.

What does one do for entertainment on an island that numbers its European population in the hundreds, many of whom lived on the tea plantations, and only visited Colombo when the busy demands of tea growing would allow them to leave the tea bushes to grow by themselves? Happily for me, Charles was addicted to horse racing. This addiction served as an introduction to the wealthy families of Ceylon. He followed the race sheets avidly, even, when he knew that the fixing of the races was so endemic that the race sheets all but gave the odds on who was going to be allowed to win a particular week's trophies.

There was one particularly sad incident, when apparently those in charge of fixing the races inadvertently doubled up on their arrangements. The winner, to be, was doped twice by two different individuals. As a consequence, he jumped the fences, threw his jockey and was in such a state of delirium tremors that the poor animal had to be shot in order to put it out of its misery. It proved to be a bonanza for those who were not privy to the information as to which horse had been selected to come home first in that particular race. The story is told that some of the bookies, and the owners as well, were hard put to find the scratch to take care of the fortunate winners.

There was another connection with horses that, on first examination, might seem strange indeed. This was a dance school. It was owned and operated by a very attractive British woman, Yvonne Bradley. The most unusual thing about this entrepreneur was that she was a polo player. A women polo player in those days, when women were scarcely allowed out of the kitchen where they were supervising the servants, was indeed a rare find. She also had a Sinhalese student named Rohini de Mel who was an avid sports person. Rohini, although a fraction less than five feet tall, was a class tennis player, a scratch golfer and a polo player. Whether I had enrolled in the dance school to enjoy the company of the owner or to improve my dancing was a moot question. In any event it accomplished both.

It also served to introduce me to polo. With my fellow Sinhalese dance student being a polo player and my dance school owner a player also, what course of action was open to me but to take up polo? Having delusions of grandeur, as well, about playing a game that Royalty and the privileged class indulged in was also no small contribution to the decision to take up the sport.

Yvonne, the owner of the dance school, had a mother who was in the dairy business. We bought our milk from her. Often my owner-teacher was busily engaged assisting her mother to either milk the cows or deliver the milk. It was never very obvious in exactly what activity she was engaged. When you are an entrepreneur, you have a myriad of interests. If she were unavailable to give me my weekly lessons, she assigned another member of her staff to take over the onerous duty of trying to convince me that I, indeed, did not have two left feet.

Dancing with this teacher was a dream. She was so poised and so perfect in her execution of the intricate steps of the Latin American dances, which I had elected to study, that even students with two left feet progressed to the point where they actually seriously considered trying for the various medals in that particular dance class. She was an expert. She regularly went to England to compete in the many dance contests held there, particularly in ballroom dancing. All of which added immensely to her professional standing.

Twenty five years later she glided across the dance floor, light as a feather in my arms, with all the admiring glances of the onlookers sitting around the dance floor watching her every graceful movement in one of the better known hotels in suburban Westchester, New York. From force of habit, she absentmindedly corrected me for failure to follow through on the finale beat of the waltz.

Before the advent of the international oil companies, when the pace of tea growing was much more sedate and was more suited to the British way of life, all activity on the plantations was carried out on horse back. At one time, the horse population was so numerous that it supported twenty seven polo clubs through out the island. When smelly gasoline vehicles displaced this charming way of life, so went the polo clubs. There weren't sufficient horses left to allow the clubs to continue to operate. At the time of my arrival, the only club still in existence was the Colombo Polo Club. Since my home base was in Colombo, I could scarcely lament the demise of the other clubs inasmuch, as there were enough gentlemen of the British leisure class in Colombo to allow us to play three times a week.

The ball was 'thrown in' sharply at four-thirty PM on Monday, Wednesday and Friday afternoons. Anyone not there at that time for the line up was most likely to be unable to enjoy the afternoon's four chukkas. The company office, also, closed at four thirty in the afternoon. This presented a problem. It was not possible to leave the office, return home, get suited up and be on the polo field at the same time as the office closed and the ball was thrown in.

I was still a very junior member of THE COMPANY. The boss was rather pedantic and not given to approving the necessities of life such as polo. This required my making arrangements with my secretary whereby I would leave correspondence scattered over my desk as if I had just stepped out the office for a moment. When four-thirty arrived, she would carefully clear off my desk. No one was the wiser that I departed every Monday, Wednesday and Friday afternoon at four PM in order to enjoy some relaxation and continue to endure the rigors of the 'white man's burden'.

A Sinhalese women polo player had, essentially, to come from the wealthy class. The wealthy class and politics were one and the same thing in Ceylon. It was not long before this poor American oil executive was enjoying an afternoon chukka of polo with one of the candidates for Prime Minister and, as well, several members of the cabinet. 'The Prime Minister to be' eventually decided that politics was a stronger calling than the sport of polo. We no longer saw him at our afternoon chukkas. He didn't forget his fellow club members, however, when he became Prime Minister and the Queen and Prince Philip were his guests at his official residence. One of the cabinet members also had aspirations of becoming Prime Minister. This required more time than three afternoons of polo would allow. He requested that I take over his polo ponies and play them in order to keep them in training. It was, unquestionably, a heady experience.

The President of the Colombo Polo Club was the chief tea-taster for one of the larger British tea companies on the island. He was the perfect image of what all Americans think a British colonialist should look and act like. He was tall, in perfect physical condition with a trim black mustache, a head of hair that was just graying at the temples. When he arrived on the field in his immaculate, white riding habit and put on his polo helmet, the onlookers were transported back several hundred years to the days of the British rajh in India. Even his name Brockelhurst, when voiced, had a ring of ancient imperial tones to it. Naturally, fellow members of the club were privileged to call him 'Brock' as he was known to his intimates. That is, if imperialists ever stoop low enough to have intimates among the human race.

He took all newcomers under his wing as a president should. He carefully spelled out, particularly for the rough and crude pioneers from the New World, that polo was a gentleman's game.

"If you inadvertently cause a foul," he impressed upon us, "you must apologize to your opponent." If your polo stick happened to catch your opponent in the mouth, and his teeth and blood were pouring copiously out of the area in which you had struck him, the president emphasized that an apology would immediately pre-empt any argument.

"Polo players never argue on the field," he emphatically stated. And so began a sport that ultimately I was to play in many parts of the world. It was a sport that introduced me to the Queen and to Prince Philip.

The royal couple were on a world tour and Ceylon, which was part of the empire at that time, was one of the stopping off points for the Royal Yacht. What better way to welcome the Royal couple, particularly Prince Philip, than to invite him to captain one of the teams in a polo match set up expressly for his visit. The exhilarating excitement of anticipation that the thought of playing polo with Prince Philip gave the members of the Colombo Polo Club can scarcely be imagined.

Several weeks before the arrival of the Queen and her consort, the annual gymkhana was being held. Major Venn, aide de camp to the Governor-General, Sir Henry Moore, had been asked to be one of the judges at the events. One always keeps his options open as far as connections to the Governor-General are concerned. Unfortunately for the members of the Colombo Polo Club, one of them lost control of his horse during the tent pegging contest. He actually rode the Major down who was acting as a line judge at the time. As the Major was being carried off the field he was heard to mutter under his breath, "I say, worse than a Calvary charge. They must all be mad."

We heard, subsequently, that the Major had argued strongly against letting the Prince join such undisciplined players in a polo match. They say that he became even more adamant when he heard that one of the members of the club, with whom the Prince would be playing, was from the colonies in the New World. That was the last straw. Whether or not there was any truth in that latter statement it was never learned. What we did learn, however, was that there was a strong recommendation that His Royal Highness not be allowed to play during his visit to Colombo.

While polo players may be gentlemen, they are not by nature prone to give up so easily on a project on which they had set their hearts. A project which meant so much to every red-blooded member of the commonwealth. A match that would be recounted time and time again at the club.

'I say, do you recall that backhand shot that took the ball away from Philip in the second chukka?' Oh yes, it must never be said that polo players give up that easily. If the invitation wasn't going to be offered officially through the Governor-General's office, then it would be made unofficially to the Prince himself. But how was that possible? Very easily as the 'old boy school' will tell you.

Prince Philip was known for his love of the sea and the fact that he seized every opportunity he could to be on the bridge when the ship was underway. We all knew it was a foregone conclusion that when entering the port of Colombo, Prince Philip would be on the bridge. What Major Venn didn't know was that one of the members of the Colombo Polo Club, Eric Tucker, was also Chief Pilot for the Port of Colombo. The ideal opportunity to issue the invitation as the Royal Yacht entered the harbor. This is exactly the scenario that developed. Prince Philip expressed his keen pleasure at the invitation. He said he would look forward with great delight to the match. What he didn't know was that there was a host of public officials arrayed against him including, of course, our indomitable Major Venn.

Major Venn's reasons for being opposed to Prince Philip's playing were much more of a personal nature than the other public officials. Their reasons were genuine, official ones. Polo is known as a 'contact sport', just as is American football. Inherent in this terminology is the fact that in contact sports there always exists the strong possibility that the player will suffer some kind of temporary disfigurement, a black eye, a broken arm or a broken leg. Since the British tax payers were underwriting this world tour of showing the flag, the officials recommended that Prince Philip forgo the pleasure of a few chukkas of polo. This would safeguard against the possibility that at his next port of call, he might appear with a black eye or hobble into the ball-room on crutches with a broken leg.

While we were smarting under our disappointment, there appeared in the mail an engraved invitation from the Prime Minister to attend a reception for the Queen and Prince Philip at 'The Temple Trees', the Prime Minister's official residence. While both the momentous events of playing polo with Prince Philip and meeting the Queen at a reception would have been much more to our liking, even one of these portentous happenings would suffice for us to dine out on for many years.

And so the eventful evening approached. Arriving at the magnificent entrance to 'The Temple Trees' in our chauffeur driven car, clad in immaculate evening clothes and ushered into the garden with a flourish was in itself enough to make us believe that we were indeed the 'chosen people'.

To use the words beautiful or gracious when describing Her Majesty, only enhances the words themselves. As she came into the garden, it was immediately transformed into a backdrop for a person of exquisite charm. As all who have read about her or seen her picture in the media, she is, in person, very different from the mechanical reproduction of her likeness on television or in the press. Perhaps, it is because when you are in such close proximity to a royal personage you can physical feel such a presence. In the case of Her Majesty, this is particularly true when the individual is not only born to royalty, but her own nature is symbolic of what the average person believes, or would like to believe, royalty really is. As she and Prince Philip moved about the garden and stopped at various tables to chat with the occupants, all of us could scarcely fail to take our eyes off her. Today, countless years later, that evening lives in my memory as vividly as if it were only yesterday.

Prince Philip and I met a number of years later when he was on another royal visit. This time his visit was to Nyasaland. While we were chatting, I took the opportunity of telling him how disappointed we were that he had been unable to join us to captain one of the polo teams during his visit to Colombo. He, too, expressed his regret, and said he had been very appreciative of the invitation, but unfortunately affairs of state took precedent over his personal wishes. He fondly recalled the visit and we discussed how much we both enjoyed the evening with the Prime Minister.

Where in the employee relations manual of THE COMPANY does it prepare an international oil company executive to be on speaking terms with royalty? Perhaps, the perennial returning thought of assassination might just well fade from my memory forever.

No! Life, like the stock market, tends to disappoint the majority of people most of the time and in its disappointment it is not kind. It, certainly, is not kind to those of us who harbour such insidious thoughts as assassination, even if it is only a fantasy. And it sometimes, perversely, is not kind to those against whom such thoughts are harboured. My colleague Charles, the one who was addicted to the races, perhaps inherited this compulsion because he was an accountant. Accountants by nature find numbers and odds a fascinating avocation. He had a manager who, according to Charles, could be forgiven for being incompetent as not all of us are born to excel. What he couldn't forgive him for was that he was bone lazy, a careless worker and prone to blame his subordinates for any and all problems that arose from his laziness and incompetence.

Charles was forever quoting me odds on how much longer it would be before he would take matters into his own hands. He would, perhaps, resolve that ever recurring question of whether or not assassination was a viable alternative. Since there was no direct official contact between myself and Charles' supervisor, I was inclined to have little sympathy or understanding for his predicament. Very often, after Charles had consumed a number of pink gins at home after a particularly bad day, he would start roaming around the house looking for my hunting rifles with the express purpose of establishing the viability of assassination. I would try to convince him that it was his imagination that made him portray his manager in such a bad light. It was not possible for an individual to be as unprincipled as he painted him.

Suddenly, to my horror, I arrived one morning in the office to find that this very same, incompetent and unscrupulous individual had been transferred to the marketing department. Overnight, he had become my immediate supervisor. It was not long before I began to take my colleague to task for having been so kind, generous and restrained in his assessment of his previous manager who was now mine. Our evening conversations now took on the bizarre twist of my continually harping on how miserable this individual was making my life. Charles, who was totally relaxed and enjoying life under his new, well liked and efficient manager, was now attempting to restrain me physically from searching for my hunting rifles.

He did, however, have a lot more sympathy for my predicament than I had had for his. This was due, understandably, to the fact that he was fully aware of the trials and tribulations that I was undergoing, because he had suffered them himself. At the time he was enduring them, I couldn't believe that the situation could be as adverse as he had painted it. Now I knew. Something had to be done about it. If we both agreed that assassination wasn't a viable alternative, what other option existed for us to rid ourselves of this daily threat to our life's serenity, mine in particular and Charles' since he had to listen to me continually harping on my miserable existence?

Hunting in Ceylon was a very accepted diversion for those who had the time, the money for expensive hunting rifles and the inclination, or if the individual worked for an international oil company, as in my case. Working for an international oil company produced opportunities to indulge in sports that were far beyond the average wage earners imagination and purse if he were a nine to five commuter in his home country. During one of my frequent hunting trips, when deep in the jungles after a day's shooting, I was invited to stay in the village overnight as the guest of the chief witch-doctor to whom I had wisely made the gift of a freshly killed antelope.

There was a full moon. He and his apprentices were taking complete advantage of it by performing their religious rites in the bright, abundant light that the moon cast. He 'rolled the bones' as required by the special ceremonies. One of his junior disciples explained to me that the bones were from the body of a relative of one of the chief-witch doctor's devotee's. It appeared that this individual's relative had died as a result of a spell cast by the witch-doctor of another village.

The rolling of the bones ceremony would effectively act in two ways. It would protect the dead man's relatives from any more incursions into their well being. In addition, if all the signs in the sky were in the correct position and the bones rolled out the appropriate message, they would cast a spell over the witch-doctor who had been responsible for placing the initial curse on the dead man. The guilty witch-doctor would, then, forthwith follow in the path of the deceased.

A blinding flash of insight. Here was the solution to the problem of disposing of the bane of existence of myself and my colleague, our inept and unethical fellow employee and supervisor.

If the bones being rolled by the witch-doctor were those of his client's relative, and the death had actually been caused by the spell cast by his associate witch-doctor, conceivably, it would not be prudent to embark on this method of curing our malaise. Notwithstanding, the opportunity was too providential to cast it aside without further investigation. I explained my dilemma to the apprentice. I emphasized to him that while I might like to see this individual burn in hell, I did not really want the onus on me of being the one that had caused him to proceed there. I really only wanted him to go away, get out of our lives and leave us in peace. The apprentice explained that there were various degrees of the spell that could be cast. Not all spells carried the ultimate punishment. There were countless renditions possible that could be cast by the chief witch-doctor.

On the basis of this understanding, I made an appointment with the chief witch-doctor for the following month when the moon would be at its apex again. He revealed to me that it would be necessary to bring with me an article that the individual, over whom the spell was to be cast, had touched in less than four hours before the rolling of the bones was to take place.

This presented a problem. There were no means by which we could entice the cause of our dilemma to come to the village and have a spell cast over him. In addition the village, even if all went well on the journey, was just about four hours from Colombo. No matter. A solution had been found to our predicament. It was up to us to implement it in spite of any difficulties that we might encounter. I confirmed my appointment with the chief witch-doctor and sped post haste back to Colombo to inform Charles of the wonderful news of our deliverance.

Although he was wildly enthusiastic at the beginning, being an accountant, his conservative nature began to show itself. Hesitation started to set in. "Are you sure that nothing can go wrong?" he inquired. I assured him that all would work out the way we would plan it with the help of the chief witch-doctor. I explained to him the need to have an article that our tormentor had touched in under four hours in the hands of the chief witch-doctor, if the witch-doctor were to roll the bones successfully. And so, we made our plans accordingly.

Charles left the office a few minutes early before four-thirty on the afternoon of the day on which the calendar said there was to be a full moon. The extra few minutes allowed him to obtain the car from the parking area, position it in front of the office and have the engine running, when I appeared with the necessary article which the object of our spell had to touch. The simplicity of obtaining the article had suddenly burst upon us while we were drawing up our plans. Since the ineffectual bane of our existence did nothing but sit in his office, drink tea and sign documents, it was a very simple matter for me to have a document prepared for his signature.

At four-thirty PM sharp, I arrived at his office with an urgent request for a signature in order to post the mail that afternoon. He was always ready to leave at exactly four-thirty. He never put in any overtime and, as usual, his desk was cleared. I approached him with the request for his signature and merely commented that since his desk was clear, he could utilize my pen for the required signatures. This he promptly did without even reading them. Since he never stayed past four-thirty, to read them would necessitate his doing so. The instant he finished signing the documents, I scooped up the pen, was out of his office and on my way to the waiting car. Charles was sitting in the driver's seat with the engine running and the gear shift engaged. With a gut wrenching spurt of speed we were on our way.

With almost a four hour journey in front of us, there was plenty of time to evaluate all the possibilities that could eventuate from this project. We reviewed every step of the proposed plan and exactly how we intended to ensure that the chief witch-doctor fully understood our intentions. As we dashed on our way, we began to ponder if it were really possible that two grown adults from a Western civilization, both practicing Christians and with university degrees, were really headed for an appointment with a witch-doctor in the jungles of Ceylon in order to cast a spell over one of the company's senior employees.

The car was racing south towards Galle. I was clutching the pen in my hand. We had both done nothing for the past month, but look forward with the greatest anticipation to this moment. Yes, we decided. It was possible. Anchors aweigh! We were determined to use whatever means were available to us, including the good offices of the chief witch-doctor, to rid ourselves of this unprincipled and worthless manager.

If God looks after the innocent and the drunks, He must also look after those who have momentarily taken leave of their senses. We sped past Galle, turned inland away from the coast and headed towards our rendezvous with the witch-doctor. Our ride was getting more jarring as we bounced over the many ruts in the jungle trail. Would we be there on time? It seemed that the road had deteriorated considerably since my prior visit and that time was going to run out on us. No! Suddenly, there was the village looming out of the darkness. A darkness, which was alleviated to a considerable degree by the brightness of the full moon. The same full moon which was so critical to the success of our undertaking.

There was little time to spare. The car ground to a sudden halt. We bounded out, hit the ground at a run and headed for the hut of the witch-doctor. Strangely there appeared no sign of life. The perpetual cook fire that was always glowing at the entrance to the hut was out. There was nobody to be seen on the premises. Had we made all these plans, come all this way at a breakneck and reckless speed only to find that our saviour to be was not here? We looked at our watches. Time was indeed running out. Where was he?

Abruptly, the apprentice appeared out of the darkness. He was apologizing profusely for the absence of the chief witch-doctor. It appeared that there had been an urgent call for his services to ward off an evil spell that had been causing a very large number of cattle to die at an adjacent village. All this way for nothing? Were we ever to find a solution to our problem? Were we going to have to make another appointment and undertake that hair rising journey again? What were we to do? Our disappointment was so great that in spite of being pressed to spend the night at the hut of the apprentice, we decided that we would head back towards Colombo and spend the night at Galle on our way. We might find some diversion there to assuage our frustration.

We wended our way back at a more sedate speed and mulled over our various options, all the while expressing our deep discouragement at the absence of the chief witch-doctor. If the truth be known, in the aftermath of our despondency, we were both beginning to feel a slight bit of relief. It had, literally, been a wild escapade. We were beginning to suspect that maybe God in His wisdom was including those of us who had taken leave of their senses among the innocent and the drunks to look after. If we had such feelings of suspicion on the ride back to Colombo, six weeks after our return to Colombo we were positive that God had, truly, intervened.

Initially, within the first two weeks of our return, our unprincipled supervisor was transferred to India and, quite obviously, without the help of our chief witch-doctor. Naturally, we were elated. But even in that feeling of elation, there lurked an uncanny sense of uneasiness in spite of the indisputable fact that the witch-doctor had not 'rolled the bones' on our behalf. What gave us a downright, spine chilling jolt four weeks after his departure was the news that he had died suddenly of what appeared to be an unknown disease, which even the autopsy was unable to pinpoint. That there were two sober and God fearing individuals that spent innumerable hours talking over their part in this bizarre episode needs no telling.

It was a considerable period of time before my mind had the temerity to raise the question of whether or not assassination was a viable alternative.

It was with some sense of alarm that Charles woke up one morning not too long after the most disturbing news of our unprincipled supervisor's demise. He had, apparently, been tossing and turning all night long with a mounting fever. He told me that during his brief waking moments in the night, his mind kept telling him that it simply wasn't possible that somebody had deliberately 'rolled the bones' with him as the chief character in the drama. He decided to remain in bed during the day. I returned from the office that evening to find that his temperature had risen to a fever pitch. I, too, became panic stricken with the thought that there are many people who have access to various witch-doctors throughout the island although with Charles' inherently kind nature it didn't possible that someone could have targeted him.

In pursuit of my dance studies, I had convinced Charles that there was more in life than following the race sheets and that he should enroll at the dance studio. He finally succumbed to my urging and had the opportunity to meet Doreen, my charming and gifted Ceylonese dancing teacher. She was not only professionally proficient, but was a person of deep humanity and kindness. A nature so serene that just being with her gave a person a feeling that indeed there was hope for the human race. Upon viewing Charles lying in a bath of perspiration with not a square inch of the sheet that could be claimed as dry, my thoughts instinctively turned to Doreen. She would know what to do. In her kindness, she would not hesitate to lend a helping hand to two panic stricken individuals in a strange country with one of them, obviously, going to follow the path of our deceased, unprincipled supervisor. I called her immediately. As anticipated, she arrived with just the time spent necessary to get in her car and drive to our home.

What was the cause of the fever or what was the reason that Charles was afflicted so soon after our escapade with the witch-doctor was never determined.

However, thanks to the ministrations of our generous and devoted dance teacher he survived. She kept up a running marathon of changing sheets, sending them out to be washed, replacing them when returned, replacing the pillow cases twice as frequently as the sheets and constantly bathing his forehead with cold water. She unselfishly and unstintingly remained at his bedside until the first sign of a break in his fever a number of days later.

Many patients marry their nurses. Charles was no exception. It was because of his marriage that I was able to have the unique advantage of enjoying that evening dancing at the suburban Westchester hotel many years later. It even made it more enjoyable to have my dancing steps corrected, because it transported me back many years to that Island Paradise and to the days of my dancing lessons.

6

Elephant Kraal—1951

Elephants, in spite of their enormous proportions, are very graceful in their movements. This is particularly true when seen in their natural habitat in the jungle. With the mothers looking after their young and 'Aunty' close by to give a helping hand if called upon, they are truly a symphony of regal motion as they browse their way through the jungle consuming untold tons of vegetation which is necessary to sustain their massive bulk. Four hundred pounds of foliage is not an unusual amount of sustenance for one of these graceful animals to consume in a day.

The youngsters, feeding at their mothers' breasts, are twice blest. Not only is their mother committed to looking after their well being, but there is another cow elephant, that apparently by mutual consent, adopts the offspring. Until the calf is old enough to fend for itself, 'Aunty' as she is known, is a surrogate mother whenever needed. This is especially evident when there is any sense of threat to the herd. It is possible to spot 'Aunty' immediately when the bull leader trumpets a signal of impending danger. All the bulls of the herd immediately form a circle with their backs to the center. As the mother guides the youngster into the center of the circle, Aunty is right by her side to do battle with any intruder that might threaten the life of her adopted charge.

This remarkable scene was witnessed several times as hunting had now become an obsession and was proving to be a distinct challenge to the time spent playing polo in Colombo. The periods spent hunting would not have been possible except for the fact that duties with THE COMPANY entailed making many safaris throughout the island. Innumerable days and weekends were spent in this absorbing sport. Although elephants were certainly never the object of our quest, being in the jungle so frequently gave us the opportunity to observe them regularly. Aunty's devotion to her charge was only excelled by the extraordinary performance showing the commitment of a bull leader in discharging his duty to the herd.

The realism portrayed by the movie industry of events that very few of the viewers will ever see in real life is only authenticated by the actual happenings themselves. Those devotees of the Tarzan movies will well remember the 'round up' of the elephants depicted in the scenes where huge 'kraals' are built in the heart of the jungle. These kraals consist of massive tree trunks anchored rigidly in the ground and bound together with many thongs of sisal. Sisal is as strong as steel, but more flexible and will not snap on sudden impact as I was going to witness in a brief time.

The kraal is constructed in the shape of a huge circle with a single entrance on its perimeter. The entry way consists of a "V" shaped extension of the same massive tree trunks with the mouth of the "V" at the outermost part and pointing in the direction from which the wild elephants will be driven. Every attempt is made not to disturb the vegetation enclosed within the kraal or in the surrounding jungle.

The whole purpose of the manner in which the kraal is constructed is to make sure that there has been no sign of human activity. This might cause the herd, as it is being driven in the direction of the kraal, to veer off on another path. The other prime requisite is that it be strong enough to withstand the charges of the immense bull elephants after they have been driven into the kraal, and they realize that they have become captives. No recent search of history books covering elephant trapping has been made since that unforgettable time to confirm that we were privileged to view, what we believed, was to be the last elephant kraal to be organized throughout the world.

As is usual in jungle societies, news travels exceedingly fast. Although Ceylon had all the advantages of modern communications, it was frequently remarkable how information would first be heard in the stables before either the newspapers or the radio carried the events that had happened or were about to happen. And so it was with the kraal.

Since it is impossible for the majority of polo players to exercise daily all their ponies themselves, it was necessary to engage a 'riding boy'. This individual takes out for a cantor in the morning those ponies that the player hasn't sufficient time to exercise during the day. Of course he is paid, based on the number of ponies in the owner's stable whether he exercises them or not.

The irony of this arrangement is that the owner is paying someone to ride his horses whereas in most Western countries, riders line up to pay for the privilege of horseback riding. But then, if one is a polo player, consorting with royalty, but privately counting every penny spent on shoeing his horses instead of his children, it behooves one not to mention this pecuniary drawback to his fellow polo players.

A very excited riding boy, Ganarus, greeted me early one morning at six AM when I arrived at the stables to exercise the three ponies that I was going to play that afternoon. In his excitement, Ganarus lapsed into his native tongue forgetting his studied effort to always speak English to his 'owner'. His 'owner' only in the respect that he was exercising his owner's ponies.

"My uncle, the mahout in Ratnapura, has communicated to me that there is to be a kraal," he exclaimed breathlessly. "A kraal," he continued in a tone of intense excitement. "A kraal such as we have never seen and will never see again. It will be the last of the roundups. No longer will there be need for these animals to work in the jungle and there will never be another kraal!" And so the electrifying news arrived in the stables a full day before the newspapers heralded the forthcoming momentous event with headlines that, by their size, indicated the extent of the importance of the impending happening.

The other two dance studio, polo players had already cantered off before my arrival. On seeing my car approach, they had galloped back with such extreme enthusiasm that they had even communicated their excitement to their ponies, which were prancing up and down as the riders pulled them up from a full gallop.

"A kraal! A Kraal!" they were shouting. "There is going to be a kraal, and we are going. You must come with us. It is a chance of a lifetime. There will never be another one in the history of mankind."

Their excitement was so electrifying that my response was automatic. "Of course. Of course. When do we leave?" Polo, hunting, and oh yes, the international oil business were very far from being anywhere near the top of the list of my priorities. But then, an international oil executive is not concerned with selling oil. His duties, as enumerated previously, have very little to do with the objective of selling oil.

And so plans were put in hand for this momentous event. Charles was not as enthusiastic as I was until he heard that his 'nurse and dancing teacher' was going. He immediately agreed to accompany us and volunteered his car. This was indeed fortunate for all of us as it was a very comfortable means of transport since it was the only one of its kind on the island. It was a convertible Pontiac, enormous for that part of the world. It drew many stares of disbelief as it manoeuvred and negotiated its way around the narrow and tortuous roads of the Ceylon hills.

After determining the exact days of the start of the kraal and the drive itself, we made our plans accordingly. Even though international oil executives don't have much to do with selling oil, their immediate superiors have a tendency to view with distaste the request to grant special leave to their subordinates. The duration of which is dependant on when the wild elephants decide to allow themselves to be trapped.

The jungle telegraph told us that the drive had commenced and in a matter of days the herd was approaching the kraal. If all went well with the drive, we could leave Colombo very early the next morning. It was an all day excursion of approximately sixteen hours. We would probably arrive well past midnight at the site of the kraal. Indications were that the herd would be inside the kraal before nightfall. We would be able to view the first efforts in the morning when the wild elephants were to be noosed and tethered to the trees.

On that never to be forgotten morning, we packed the car. Tent, cooking utensils, food, bedding, water and extra clothing, all the necessities required to survive at a location far from the civilized amenities one expects when proceeding on a so called vacation. Obviously, the kraal had been built remote from any means of habitation. The organizers weren't in the business of catering to tourists. They were concerned with trapping the maximum number of wild elephants that could be trained and turned into workers for the myriad duties delegated to the huge beasts in this jungle society.

We arrived at the site of the kraal well past mid-night having taken over eighteen hours to negotiate our way from Colombo to the most inner parts of the jungle. In addition, as anticipated, finding a location to pitch our tent without having to clear a place in the jungle at that hour of the night was proving extremely difficult.

Finally, one of our party who had broken away from the group momentarily shouted joyfully. "Over here, over here," we heard from a distance. "Somebody has cleared a whole area here, and they are not using it," was the delightful news. We hastily assembled all our paraphernalia, pitched the tent, which was only a pup tent, by which those little cloth shelters are known, and we crawled into our sleeping bags with a sigh of relief and exhaustion.

To those of us who are completely bi-lingual, it is an established fact that in times of stress or danger or shock, we always lapse into our native tongue. So it was with Rohini, our Singhalese compatriot. As fate would have decreed, she was sleeping in the very midst of the group. Surely not an hour had passed after we had all immediately fallen into a deep and trouble free sleep when we heard a most piercing shriek emanating from the very center of the tent. Almost simultaneously, but preceding the scream by fractions of a second, was heard a harsh rending of the canvass of the tent. Although the buffalo is probably the most dangerous animal in the jungles of Ceylon because he will attack without provocation, the leopard garners more respect from the Ceylonese. This may, possibly, be because they are very seldom seen and even less often tamed.

"Coateia! Coateia!" she screamed. 'Leopard! Leopard!' was the translation known to all who ventured into the jungle whether or not they spoke any of the local language. The tent had collapsed all around us and over our heads. We scrambled madly to free ourselves from the entangling canvass and ropes. Even more mysteriously, there was a large number of branches of a young sapling which, mysteriously, seemed to be moving in several directions at the same time over what was left of the tent. We disentangled ourselves and huddled frighteningly together with our flash lights probing the darkness in all directions.

Our luck in finding a cleared area that no one was utilizing suddenly became very apparent to us. Within arms length, in actuality if we had reached out our hands we could have touched the massive foreleg of a tame elephant that was feeding on the young sapling which he had brought down around our ears. Our good fortune in finding a place to set up our tent without having to clear the area was unmistakable. We had pitched our tent in the midst of the compound of the organizers' tame elephants, the very elephants that were to be used to successfully conclude the trapping of their wild brethren.

Hysterical tones of laughter laced with relief burst forth as we realized that in fact we were not the proposed prey of a man eating leopard or of any other carnivorous beast for that matter. We sheepishly gathered our belongings together and beat a hasty retreat. We were being admonished in the sternest tones possible by the elephants' mahouts who had instantly arrived on the scene at the sound of Rohini's scream of "Coateia! Coateai!" Eventually another site was found. It was researched in great detail for a considerable distance around before pitching our tent a second time. We crawled into our sleeping bags again and fell into a not so sound and not so trouble free sleep for the short balance of the night that remained.

Our sleeping companions, the tame elephants at the initial site at which we had pitched our tent, were to be used in the tethering of the wild elephants which had been driven into the kraal. The tethering of the elephants to the trees was a centuries old method. It was the first step in the transition from their wild habitat to the civilization that was to become their permanent home. After the herd had been driven into the kraal by the beaters with their rattles, drums and other noise making apparatus, two trained elephants with their mahouts and two additional mahouts would enter the kraal.

The two trained elephants, under the guidance of their mahouts, would approach one of the wild captives and manoeuver him firmly in between them. The other two mahouts would then slip off the tame elephants before the confined, wild one got wind of them and quickly 'noose' him by securing strong thongs of sisal to the hind legs of the quarry. The captive would then be forced towards the nearest tree strong enough to withstand the pull of the trapped animal. The mahouts on the ground would secure the sisal very firmly to the tree.

With the trapped animal's hind legs bound firmly together and lashed to the tree, there was very little leverage that these huge beasts could exert in an attempt to free themselves. Any concerted effort put forth in the shape of a lunge with the hope of breaking their bonds only resulted in the animal falling to its knees. Its hind legs could no longer balance it as they were bound so closely together. As the wild elephants continued to be secured to the various trees, all vegetation within immediate range of their trunks was cut down and taken away. In this manner, they were prevented from feeding themselves. In addition, they were given no water to drink. They got weaker and weaker from lack of food and water, and their strength waned and the transition from wild to tame started to take place. They were first given water by their human captors, who always approached them on the tame elephants. This gave the captors a feeling of security in seeing that one of their own kind was part of the experience they were undergoing.

It takes little imagination to grasp what a photographer's paradise all the activity going on in and around the kraal provided for our cameras. Stationed at fixed lengths around the outside of the huge tree trunks that made up the kraal were a series of beaters. They had now assumed the role of attempting to keep the massive bulls from testing the strength of the stockade. Each one of the beaters had a well sharpened spear and a blazing torch. As the trapped animals approached the tree trunks, the beaters would wave the torches and shout at the top of their lungs. If any of the herd were not dismayed by this show of strength and came close enough to resemble a threat to the security of the stockade, their charges would be met by the sharpened spears.

The most advantageous place for dramatic photography was, naturally, on the top of the tree trunks which made up the kraal. Much against the reliable advice of everyone in the party, I was determined to get a close up of the bull leader. He roamed at will from the center of the kraal where he couldn't be seen because of the dense brush, to immediately bordering the kraal tree trunks. It was a never to be forgotten sight to suddenly have him appear out of nowhere and find him in your lens with his trunk swaying back and forth and his huge ears flapping madly as he trumpeted his rage at his captors.

After considerable exertion and with the help of one of the beaters, I gained access to the top of one of the massive tree trunks that made up the perimeter of the kraal. I waited breathlessly for the leader to arrive. There were many sharp admonishments from my colleagues as to the foolishness of risking my neck to obtain pictures that I might never live to see developed.

In the midst of their many caustic comments as to the lack of intelligence with which I had been endowed, the enormous bull appeared right in the direct line of my lens. I immediately pressed the release only to realize that he had instantly turned and was retreating to the inner safety of the jungle inside the center of the kraal. As is often the case with amateur photographers, there was a sudden whir from the camera which told me that, as usual, I had committed the unpardonable sin of not making sure there was sufficient film in the camera to ensure that I could complete the photographic project. A project, which I had undertaken with so much difficulty, and according to my companions, considerable peril.

Reluctantly but with great haste, because in spite of their repeated sound advice not to attempt to take pictures from such an exposed position, I was deter-mined to reload the camera and return to my vantage point. I scrambled down from the top of the tree trunk with much greater ease and alacrity than I had exhibited in mounting it.

As my feet touched the ground, there was suddenly a concerted shouting from all the beaters in the immediate area. A number of others with torches blazing joined the ones immediately adjacent to the tree trunk from which position I had just vacated. I looked up and gazed in between the bound trunks to view, with unbelievable horror, the sight of the massive bull on a direct line of charge for the tree trunk from which I had just descended. Whether it was coincidence, or whether it was because he had spotted me standing there with the camera pointed in his direction, I will never know. In any event, it appeared that he had not turned with the intention of retreating to the safety of the center of the kraal, but rather with the objective of obtaining a better view of his opponents without hav-ing himself exposed.

Elephants have notoriously poor vision and whether or not he actually saw me, of course, will never be known. I am inclined to believe that it was pure coin-cidence. My colleagues were not so generous in their assessment. They, unequiv-ocally, stated that I had provoked the charge by putting myself in a position where he could pinpoint, what he considered to be, one of his universal tormen-tors. All such conjecture was, obviously, academic. The immense leader was on a direct collision course with the tree trunks of the kraal. The shouting had greatly increased in intensity as more and more of the beaters congregated on the site of the object of the charge.

In spite of the waving torches of the many bearers who had joined those beaters who held their sharpened spears at the ready in order to repel the charge, he continued at a breakneck speed for the perimeter of the kraal. Neither the shouting beaters nor the blazing torches deterred him. He continued in a direct line for the tree trunk which I had just vacated. As he struck the ridged trunk bound with the thongs of sisal, the sharpened spears repeatedly thrust in his direction seemed to bother him no more than buzzing mosquitoes.

The massive bulk of the huge leader caused the structure to groan and quiver, but the steely flexibility of the sisal proved its value to the kraal organizers. A few of the thongs had, of necessity, to give way in the face of such an immense weight thrust against them. However, as planned, the remaining ones held securely. On impact, however, the tree trunk which the leader struck head on vibrated in a sickeningly, violent fashion. Any one standing on the top of the tree trunk would have been propelled directly into the kraal as if he had been fired from a sling shot. It hardly needs telling that there were no further attempts to gain the same vantage point for the sake of photography.

If wild animals, such as were at the moment enclosed within the confines of the kraal could realize that with an organized charge, led repeatedly by the huge bulls and concentrated on one objective, they would not have continued to remain captives. There was no means available to withstand the concerted charge of these huge animals. Some, however, were frightened off by the shouting. Some were frightened by the torches. Those, who ignored both the shouting and the torches, were then turned away by the sharpened spears. None of the defenses of the kraal organizers would have proved to be successful, if the bull leader had been able to use his great natural ability to mount a concerted attempt by his charges to breach the wall.

It would be wonderful, if the story were to end by the telling of the incredible way in which the wild animals put into effect an organized plan of escape. But then, if they were capable of such planning, no doubt we would be living on the 'Planet of the Elephants' instead of on the earth as we know it. To see these huge and majestic beasts at the mercy of puny mankind gives rein to those kind of thoughts. Nevertheless, maybe mortals should not become so enamored of the wild creatures of our universe or we might begin to think like them.

Although the bull leader was not capable of organizing a group charge, it was now that he gave the best laid plans of man a serious setback in this particular kraal. As would be expected, the first captives to be noosed were the cow elephants and the smaller bulls. During this activity, a careful eye was kept on the bull leader of the herd who roamed at a frenetic pace around the perimeter of the kraal.

The presence of the tame elephants, as was intended, confused the bull. He was not sure what their proximity meant. However, after a dozen or so of the herd had been secured to the trees, he very quickly realized the reason for the presence of the tame elephants. At that time, it became almost impossible for any pair of tame elephants to enter the kraal without being irrefutably assured that they would be face to face with the bull leader of the herd as he pawed the ground, flapped his huge ears and trumpeted wildly. There was no mistaking his intent as to what was going to happen to the intruders as he made mock charges in the direction from which the tame elephants would have approached. It became almost impossible to get the trained elephants to undertake their dangerous task.

After much consultation on the part of the kraal organizers, it was decided that it would necessary to noose the bull leader if the rest of the herd were to be quickly tethered and a reasonable timetable implemented for completion of the kraal. Four of the largest and strongest tame elephants were selected and entered the kraal with the intent of securing the leader. A number of times the attempt was made to get close to the massive bull but each bid failed.

The bull, as was customary in leaders, was an immense tusker. The tame elephants kept a wary eye on those lethal weapons. Unfortunately to no avail. During one of the attempts to hem him in between a pair of the trained elephants, he gored one of them badly in the underbelly. With the smell of blood now in his nostrils and the tame elephants even more hesitant, if not down right refusing to enter the kraal to face the bull, it was decided that an attempt would made again to return to the task of noosing the balance of the herd. Some success was accomplished, and a few more of the trapped animals ended up with their hind legs lashed firmly to a tree and with nothing to eat or drink.

It was now that the mettle of the bull leader came to the fore, and proved why he was the leader and not one of the lesser members of the herd. When the sun rose the next morning, an incredible sight greeted the eyes of all the onlookers. At every tree to which one of his charges had been tethered with the intent of starving the animal into submission, the bull leader had brought hundreds of pounds of vegetation during the night to each one of the captives. He must have spent every minute of the nightfall collecting the foliage. It was, indeed, a heart warming and awe inspiring sight. Even his adversaries, the kraal organizers, had to give three cheers for his indomitable courage and tenacity.

There now existed a very perplexing situation. There were a large number of people employed in a kraal round up and it all cost money. The bull had already delayed the timetable. His actions indicated that there would be a further substantial slowdown. He, obviously, would continue to feed the captives as well as make it vastly difficult for the mahouts to continue to noose the remainder of the herd.

It was now that a heart wrenching decision was seen to be carried out. The determination was made that there was no alternative but to shoot the leader. Admittedly, the decision was made with the utmost reluctance. The bull would have been a very valuable addition to the kraal owners team of work animals. In addition, the tusks alone were worth a small fortune after the animal had ended its useful working life. The greatest reluctance, however, was the result of the fact that all mahouts have a great love for the huge animals which they train and with whom they work. In many cases they actually live with them. To have to shoot one of the bravest of these great beasts was indeed a heart breaking act. There was no other possible alternative. and so it happened. Right in front of our very eyes. Although the trip, the kraal and everything about it was stirring and never to be forgotten, the loss of the leader put a extreme dampener on our enthusiasm for the event.

7

Paradise disturbed—1951

We returned to Colombo with our hearts saddened at the thought of that majestic bull leader no longer adding to the grandeur of our existence on this puny globe of ours. It was agreed that whenever the opportunity arose, we would try to visit these creatures as they set about their daily work tasks in the jungle under the guidance of their mahouts, or under any circumstances that would remind us of the unforgettable scenes of the kraal.

Little did we realize that shortly after our return to Colombo there would be an announcement that there was to be an elephant race. Charles and I viewed with great skepticism the news that there was such a thing as an elephant race. Our Ceylonese friends assured us that it was an annual event up in the hills of Beruwela.

Fortunately, it was on the weekend which did not compel us to ask leave of our superiors. We were still smarting under their sarcasm regarding our last behest to await the pleasure of the wild elephants in Kerala at the kraal. The car was provisioned again, this time with a generous supply of refreshments, cold beer, snacks and all the necessary ingredients to make our visit to the races a success.

As our Ceylonese friends had faithfully assured us, there was indeed an elephant race. It was more of a village outing than a serious competition between these titans. The Ceylonese nature has an underlying character to it that my colleague had ascertained long before I had. Of course, the fact that he had done so was intuitive I realized afterwards. It appears that they were just as addicted as he was to wagering on the outcome of any contest between four legged animals be they horses or elephants. There were any number of spectators, who were willing to wager astronomical sums on the outcome of a contest comprising animals that certainly had no training, or inclination for that matter, to run a competitive race. However, it was that attitude that added to the spirit of the occasion and apparently there were no sore losers.

In some aspects, it seemed undignified to watch these noble beasts being urged on by their mahouts. The mahouts, actually, were on the ground and not astride the great creatures. In a cloud of dust and amid hilarious shouting from all concerned, the events were run. The mahouts had to keep a wary eye on their rear. Very often the following elephant, who was being egged on to perform even greater exertion for his mahout and his backers, would fail to see the mahout in front of him. Only by the sudden rise in the intensity of the shouting would the potential victim realize he had forgotten to protect his vanguard.

No harm came to anyone. Refreshments, conviviality, the renewing of old friendships and all the reasons that bring people together made a very pleasant afternoon for all told. Another interesting and unique experience came to an end. There can't be many Westerners who have seen, or even believe, that there is such a phenomenon as an elephant race. We found ourselves again in the enviable position of being exposed to a most unusual pastime.

Not so enviable was our return trip to Colombo. In tropical countries rain is a way of life. In this island paradise, monsoons were so intense that sometimes it appeared that the Island had become submerged in the sea. Visibility becomes nil. The heat is stifling. With the inability to distinguish objects within arms length, there is no recourse except to halt all activity until the monsoon shower has passed. Many Westerners with their superior knowledge and study of the climate of countries that experience monsoons very smugly bring with them plastic rain gear to ward off the downpour.

It is always highly amusing to watch them put on their 'plastic sweat suits' the first time that the monsoon threatens. It might be mentioned that it is the first and only time that they don them. In a matter of moments, their bodies are so soaked in perspiration that they might just as well have remained in the pouring rain. During our return to Colombo, we were met by the first showers of the coming monsoon season.

Hydro-planing, skidding or whatever technical term one wishes to employ, the end result is the same. The vehicle does not continue in the direction that the driver intended it to proceed. Unfortunately, this proved to be the case during our return to Colombo. Due to the tortuous roads and many turns, it is impossible to get up to any speed which, actually, is a blessing in disguise. As we turned a hairpin corner on a steep hill, the car hydro-planed across the road. As fate decreed, there was a lorry painfully chugging up the hill in the opposite direction to which we were proceeding. With a resounding crash, mostly caused by the shattering of the plate glass windshield of the lorry, both vehicles came to an instantaneous halt as they had met exactly head on. The lorry, an old and decrepit produce van, was totally demolished. The ancient axles snapped. The sides gave way as the vehicle was so heavily overloaded that the weight of the produce merely took all encumbrances with it as it spilled across the roadway. The grill of the Pontiac was badly smashed. Due to its superior construction, it protected the engine from any harm, and it remained navigable.

Although there were no serious injuries thanks to the slow speed, two of the passengers in the front of the vehicle were thrown into the dashboard, which resulted in some severe bruises and many cuts from the broken glass covering the instruments. I had fallen asleep in the back seat. With the jolting impact following from the head-on collision, I was thrown forward. My legs had been extended under the front seat with my heels resting on the floor. As a consequence, my shin bone acted as a fulcrum as my body was hurled towards the front of the vehicle, which caused the flesh to be crushed against the bone where it met the sharp edge of the front seat.

In spite of the intense pain, there appeared to be very little bleeding. With the vehicle still road worthy, it was decided to continue on to Colombo and stop at the hospital on the way and have the various bruises and cuts attended to. And so ended the elephant races.

We arrived home, tired but grateful that the accident had not resulted in anything more serious than a few cuts and bruises. Early to bed, so that we could arise in the morning and go forth to do battle in the market place and, hopefully, sell some oil to pay for all the enjoyment to which we had been subjected in the recent months. The next morning, I tumbled out of bed after finishing my bed tea which the house boy had brought to my room, got under the shower, and started to soap myself from the top of my head to my ...

'My God! Is that my.... foot?'

Was that dark, mottled, black and blue appendage attached to my ankle ... in fact.... my foot? There was not a square inch of anything resembling ordinary flesh anywhere to be seen on what, apparently, was actually my foot. I started to faint from sheer shock and terror. I realized that I might drown under the shower, if I cravenly gave in to that coward's first port of call when one is frightened out of one's senses. I yelled in unadulterated panic for Charles, who came running in to see what had induced such a tone of terror in my voice.

The look of abject abhorrence on his face when he glanced in the direction that I indicated, as my vocal chords were incapable of carrying any message at the moment, only confirmed my worst fears. His mouth hung open in stupefied wonder, as he gazed at what appeared to be an exhumed piece of flesh that was to undergo an autopsy to determine the cause of death.

"You must go see a doctor immediately." he gasped. "Can you walk on it?"

I had regained some control of my vocal chords at this time. I confirmed that I must be able to walk on it. I had entered the bathroom from the bedroom and hadn't experienced any difficulty until actually viewing the horrible extremity as I had been proceeding with my shower.

"I'll take you to Mr. Chomberly's office. Although I have never used him, I hear that he has been on the Island for many years. You may have contracted some rare tropical disease. If anyone should know about it, he should. They tell me that he spends sometimes as much as two or three months in the jungle all by himself researching all kinds of rare and unusual diseases," he continued. "Get dressed immediately. I'll have the car out front for you so you don't have to walk too far," was his hastily relayed advice.

In the British medical profession the more you specialize, the more important your title becomes. No mere doctor was going to take care of my problem. Only common and lowly general practitioners are called 'doctor'. Once you have a specialist degree, you drop the doctor and revert to Mister. As I entered Mr. Chomberly's office I began to regret immediately Charles' well intentioned advice on how knowledgeable Mr. Chomberly was, and how much time he spent in the jungle alone on his missions of medical research.

Spread out on the top of a tall secretariat in one corner of his waiting room was a series of dolls with the most grotesque expressions on their anything but doll like visages. They were, in fact, the exact images of what you would visualize if you were asked to describe what kind of doll a witch doctor would have; a witch doctor who practiced the art of sticking pins into them in order to control the life span of the victim. Torn between the devil and the deep blue sea, my horrible foot and the possibility that I was about to get my just deserts from a European witch doctor, I started to back out of the room. At that instant, Mr.Chomberly entered. Not only do the British specialists give up the title of doctor, but they give up that soothing and professional appearance which a white coat gives to a terrified patient.

If his age were any indication, Mr. Chomberly had evidently spent many years in the jungles of Ceylon. He appeared close to eighty or even more. Across his rotund stomach protruding from under his waistcoat was draped a gold watch chain from which dangled several odd shaped bones. He resembled nothing more than what would have been expected of the medical profession, when it was at the stage of using leeches and blood letting as the cure-all for any and every disease.

His greeting of, "You have a problem my dear boy?" only confirmed my worst fears that he hadn't opened a medical journal in the last twenty or thirty years.

I replied that 'yes indeed I had a problem' without mentioning that he was one of the major parts of the problem. I removed my shoe and sock and indicated the badly, mottled, black and blue part of my anatomy. It was beginning to resemble less and less of any relationship to being part of a human being.

He gazed at it with his head nodding back and forth like a kindly, old gnome. "Hmm," he murmured once or twice and then ended his examination with a soul shattering pronouncement. "Internal hemorrhaging," was his diagnosis.

"Appuhamy," he shouted loudly.

Immediately, there appeared before my eyes an elderly and severely bent over Ceylonese with a large white, drooping mustache. He had, apparently, been waiting behind the door leading to the clinic in anticipation of his master's voice calling him to give aid and succor to the sick and indisposed. He padded across the room in his bare feet. Bare feet is the common mode of dress for the average Ceylonese in the villages and, to a great extent, even in the cities as well. Certainly, however, not to be expected in the office of an established European doctor who specialized in tropical diseases.

"Appuhamy," he repeated. "Get the razor blade."

I had been paralyzed with fear and terror, when I had first viewed the horrible sight which greeted my eyes in the shower as I had gazed down at my foot. Now, I was totally incapable of making any movement to escape into the world of light and knowledge that lay just outside the door of this ancient and medieval practitioner of the black arts. He was, apparently, going to amputate my foot with the help of Appuhamy and a razor blade. As I sat there completely powerless of making any movement to rescue myself, he dabbed at the cut on my shinbone where the blood had dried around the edges with a piece of cotton dipped in alcohol.

How had I ever let THE COMPANY entice me into coming to this never, never land of witch doctors, medieval practitioners of so called medicine in their eighties, and bare footed nurse's aides with droopy mustaches?

If ever assassination were to be a viable alternative, it would be right now. If only it were possible to get my hands on the throats of the individuals, who had painted such a rosy picture to me of an island paradise known as Ceylon.

"Appuhamy, take care when you shave around that cut. We don't want any more blood draining into the foot than has already done so," he instructed his nurse's aid. Turning to me, he continued with the kind advice that he was having Appuhamy shave around the cut so that when he put sticking plaster over the wound, it wouldn't be painful to remove when the bandage had to be changed.

Why must doctors always use such frightening technical phrases as 'internal hemorrhaging' when diagnosing their patients' ailments? Internal hemorrhaging indeed! Why didn't he just say that with the cut on my shinbone drying up so rapidly, there was no place for the blood to go, which had continued to flow from the wound, except into my foot? And why didn't I remember my elementary first aid, which now came back in a rush, which would have told me that a bruise is nothing more than internal hemorrhaging?

What had greeted me in the shower in the morning after the blood had drained into my foot all during the night, because the wound had dried up and closed off the escape to the outside, was a massive bruise. The relief was so great that the foot was not to be amputated by the bare footed nurse's aide, under the guidance of this ancient and medieval practitioner of the black arts of witch craft, I was able to relax. I questioned him as to the duration of the appearance of the horrible looking appendage which resembled anything but a foot.

"Bathe it in warm water and massage it gently, and in due course it will regain its former appearance," was his well intentioned advice. I never returned to his office again, because there was always the lurking fear that he actually utilized those dolls spread out on the secretariat in his waiting room as part of his medical practice. Indeed, my basic psyche had gotten such a fright that I never had the need of the services of a medical practitioner the entire five years that I remained on the Island.

Charles, when recommending Mr. Chomberly, had commented that he had never used him. This comment was a result of the fact that he was a frequent visitor to several specialist's office to have a leg wound treated. This wound, and it was a wound, was open and drained constantly. The bandage had to be changed frequently, because of the matter draining from the laceration. In his reserved and philosophical way he would comment, if asked how it had happened, that 'one should never sit in a restaurant with your back to the door'. Evidently with your back to the door, you didn't have time enough to turn and exit when the hand grenade was being tossed through the window.

Not to sit in a restaurant with your back to the door was a standing company rule in Saigon, where he had previously been assigned by THE COMPANY. He had broken this cardinal rule one evening. Consequently, the hand grenade went off before he had been able to completely exit from the restaurant. 'Vietnamese who were suspected of sympathy with the French, who held any sort of office in rural or village government, or who even accepted French money were marked for murder. In the cities, especially Saigon, the killings were less discriminatory. There were some selective murders of collaborators, but more often bombs were thrown into a sidewalk café or left to explode in a crowded street'[17].

Charles was not the only American to be unfortunate enough to be caught up in this deadly campaign to intimidate the residents of Saigon as was recorded during the night of March 17, 1950.

'At 7:30 that evening, five American sailors from the US Navy destroyer, the *Anderson*, were leaning across a bar with cognac before them, absorbed with the difficulties of conversing in their faintly remembered high-school French with a graying-blonde French bar woman. At the sidewalk tables outside sat a score or more of French sailors and a few Foreign Legionnaires. Across the square, which was crowded with strollers, was the Continental Hotel where the American admiral and his staff had rooms. The crack of the grenade was sharp and the puff of smoke was small. It fell clear of most of the drinkers, wounding two French sailors and a legionnaire. It killed two passing Vietnamese and injured half a dozen others[18].

Charles had suffered a nasty and disabling wound which had not healed for a number of years. The medical profession, in its endeavors to save as much of the leg as possible, since the wound was just below the knee, kept shaving the bone but without success as the wound failed to close. Where does it say in the company's employee relations manual that an international oil executive must learn that he should never sit in a restaurant with his back to the door?

Never in my wildest imagination did I realize that, in the not too distant future, I would be emphatically emphasizing to my very young children that 'they must never swim at the beach with their backs to the shore'. If they did so, they would not have sufficient time to get out of the water when the guns started firing, and the rebels came down out of the hills.

The 'international oil business', as its title suggests, is 'big business'. Its customers are large and varied, and one particular activity is a prodigious user of petroleum products. There was a huge jungle clearing project being undertaken in preparation for building an earth dam. It was on the other side of the island and, it required untold amounts of fuel and lubricating oil. It was only a short time ago in the oil industry's history, that its research staff had discovered what today is very commonplace and known to every motorist, namely 'detergent lubricating oil'.

We had successfully sold to the manger of this project hundreds of barrels of this detergent oil known as Caltex RPM Delo. It was a top quality product manufactured by the Western Sister of the Two Sisters that owned us. It had quickly established a well earned reputation for the qualities that made it unique at that time.

The big selling point in those days was the same as it is today. The engine oil cleans as it lubricates. The chemical additives in the oil keep the carbon generated by the combustion in suspension. When the oil is drained, all the carbon that has been kept in suspension because of the superior chemical additives, drains out of the engine at the same time. We had, also, sold to the project manager an equal number of barrels of flushing oil. This is an oil, which after you have drained out the dirty lubricating oil, you then flush out all the carbon residue left in the crank case by the use of this expensive, flushing oil.

The project was being run under the auspices of one of the many multinational divisions of the United Nations, or the World Bank, or one of those organizations whose myriad initials in their acronym never tell you from where they originate. In due course, the American manager to whom we had so successfully sold all that detergent lubricating oil and flushing oil was transferred.

He was replaced by a much, more, knowledgeable individual who hailed from South Africa. At the time, I was unaware of his origins. With his arrival, it necessitated my making a visit to the project site to establish contact with him. My Managing Director, Phil Sanders, had gotten bored with life in Colombo. He decided that a trip through the island, and in particular a trip to the damn site, would enliven his rather dull existence. The arrival of the new manager was, ostensibly, the reason for his joining me for the trip.

On our arrival, we were treated with proper fanfare. It is not often that Managing Directors of large international oil companies take the time and trouble to visit projects in the jungle. After being shown over the work area with the new South African manager proudly explaining how he intended to make a number of improvements that would greatly increase the efficiency of the operation, we returned to his office.

My Managing Director proceeded to tell him how lucky he was to have the advantage of using our RPM Delo detergent oil, which had only been on the market a short time in Ceylon. One reason it had only been on the market a short time was that there had been a considerable amount of the old style lubricating oil left in stock, which had to be sold before introducing the superior brand. Phil Sanders went on to extol the virtues of RPM Delo. He explained in great detail the advantage of the cleansing action. Even more importantly how all the carbon that the chemical additives cleaned out of the engines remained in suspension.

"When the oil drains out, all that dirty carbon that is being held in suspension comes with it," he stated very convincingly.

The South African Manager was a very impressive figure, as he towered well over six feet, and was built in proportion to his height. Not the kind of individual that you would enjoy meeting in a dark alley, unless he were on your side. Equally impressive was his knowledge of his machinery, and the way it operated. He was, also, very aware of the advantages of detergent oils. Perhaps, he came from an area that hadn't had a large stock of the outmoded type of lubricating oil which had to be sold before the unique brand was introduced. He probably didn't have to wait either, as we did in our territory, at the far end of a long supply chain until the old stock was exhausted.

He very carefully let my Managing Director repeat a number of times, after artfully suggesting that he would like to be assured, that the oil did, in effect, keep the carbon in suspension and that the crankcase would be clean when it was drained. Phil Sanders was oblivious to the trap into which he was falling, as he continued to emphasize the tremendous advantages of our RPM Delo lubricating oil. Then our knowledgeable South African let the bombshell fall.

"If that is true, and your oil does all you say it does, why did you sell us that flushing oil? Flushing oil is used to flush out the carbon that remains in the crankcase after draining the engine oil. You say there isn't any carbon left when we use your detergent oil. What am I suppose to do with those hundreds of barrels of flushing oil? Either you don't have any faith in your own detergent oil or if you do, you shouldn't have sold us that flushing oil."

The time honored situation, when there is a junior and a senior member of management present and there is a difficult, if not impossible question raised, the senior member always turns to the junior member and says, 'Explain it.' Since it was I that had sold the flushing oil to his much less knowledgeable predecessor, I was now about to get my just deserts for trying to make money for THE COMPANY at the customer's expense.

After much hemming and hawing on my part, the new manager took pity on me. He perceived that I was literally beginning to look inadequate in front of my Managing Director. He also knew that we had no defense for our position and was kind enough not to press the point. He felt assured that there was no alternative for us, but to take back those hundreds and hundreds of barrels of flushing oil at our expense. The cost of taking back all those of barrels of flushing oil was tremendous. They were deep in the jungle on the other side of the island.

During our return to Colombo, Phil Sanders pointed this out very forcefully to me and stated, "I don't care how you accomplish it, but we are not going to take back that oil. The expense would be so high that it would actually influence the balance sheet for the month."

Our situation was even further compromised by the information that we had received from Shell at a recent industry meeting. Industry meetings were generally chaired by Shell, because in British colonies they were invariably the largest marketers by far. It was my first industry meeting. I was in considerable awe of the grandeur of that supremely, British organization. They always seemed to leave you with the impression that they were representing the Foreign Office of Her Majesty's Government, and that the oil business was a smelly adjunct to their purpose in life.

The Chair announced that Shell was dropping their price of all grades of lubricating oil effective at the close of the month. They wished to give industry advance notice in order that they would not be taken unawares when the new prices were published. The Chair wished to assure all present that they had no intention of attempting to increase their share of the market by this action. As a novice, I was astounded at the reason given for this reduction in price. "Our profits are embarrassingly high," the Chair announced. All along I had been under the impression that that was exactly what we were all trying to do—get the highest price possible.

If we ever had to take back those hundreds of barrels of flushing oil from deep in the jungle, we now had a compounding problem; not only the expense of taking it back, but in view of Shell's forthcoming action, we were now going to have to re-sell it at a price less than we were going to have to credit the customer's account.

There, then, began a dialogue with the project manager and myself over a long period of time. A dialogue that, at times, became quite acrimonious. He was very insistent that we take back the oil. I was in the unenviable position of not being able to convince my Managing Director that to take back the oil would be the only way out of a very difficult, if not impossible, predicament.

During a visit to Colombo, the project manager called on me at my office. He emphatically stated that it would be the last time he would raise the question of the flushing oil. If the circumstances were not resolved to his satisfaction, he would unilaterally cancel our contract. I informed him that legally he was in no position to do so. His predecessor had purchased the oil. We were under no obligation to take it back.

In his frustration and realizing that we were contractually correct, he rose from his chair, drew himself up to his full height and stated in very dogmatic tones, "You know what you can do … with your oil!" Having been ground down over a long period of time between his insistence that we take the oil back, and my Managing Director's equal insistence that we don't take it back, I had reached the end of my rope.

I eyed him up and down, with just a slight lingering of my eyes on his very ample posterior, and replied, "I'm sure yours would take more of it."

That we remained friends and he remained a customer was a credit to the give and take of the international oil business. Oh, yes, as a matter of fact Phil Sanders was transferred very shortly after that. His replacement, Ronnie Mann an Englishman, was easy to convince that with the end of the contract in sight there was no hope of renewal as long as we continued to refuse to take back the flushing oil.

I suggested that it wouldn't look too good for him to lose the biggest contract that THE COMPANY had ever enjoyed in Ceylon in a matter of weeks after his arrival. He saw the reasonableness of my position. We agreed we would take back the oil and credit the customer's account. That handy technique of crediting the customer's account, instead of refunding the money, tied him to us until he had utilized all the credit in purchasing other products. This customer was not, basically, a perverse client. He had a legitimate complaint. We had immediately recognized it on our first encounter, when he obviously was so well informed as to the capabilities of detergent oils. We were slow in acknowledging it to him.

There are customers, nevertheless, that are inherently difficult, because that is their nature. All businesses have to endure them. The international oil business is no exception. The only substantial difference lies in the interest at stake. If you lose a customer at the supermarket, it does not represent a major problem. In fact, it is highly unlikely that you will ever learn that you have lost him or her. When you have a customer who purchases millions of dollars worth of oil from your company, you are fully aware of the consequences if you lose him.

In the giant, international oil business there are many customers who purchase well over a hundred million dollars worth of petroleum products a year. If an international oil executive lost an account that was worth one hundred million dollars a year to his company, it is very likely that not only the client would go, but the executive would go with him. He would be making the rounds of the employment agencies trying to inadequately explain to the interviewers why he had left such a well paying job.

In spite of the risks involved in such a situation, there comes a time when the international oil executive throws up his hands in frustration and despair. He decides that no buyer is worth the habitual hassle that these perpetually, complaining customers present. It doesn't matter how far over backwards you lean to gratify them. They will never be satisfied. So it was with one particular customer. It didn't matter what we tried to do to appease his every whim. We broke countless rules in the book to try to accommodate his twisted and warped mind.

One Monday morning when everything about life was particularly bleak, and the afternoon polo match had been called because of rain, one of those habitually, criticizing customers called with his perennial complaints. Admittedly, he didn't purchase products worth one hundred million dollars a year. Nevertheless, his account was very sizable. When my secretary informed me that he was on the telephone, she was holding her hand over the mouth piece to warn me that he was on the loose again. A smile spread over my face. "Don't worry," I told her. "I have the answer to all his problems. He won't ever complain to us again".

I greeted him over the telephone with such real pleasure in my voice that for a moment he was completely nonplused. He was well aware that, when he telephoned me, my voice always seemed to indicate trepidation, hesitancy and repeatedly at contract renewal time, dread. I inquired as to his state of health and his family's, which further unsettled him. Then, I went on to say, "My secretary tells me that you have a problem. Before you tell me what it is, would you please note the following telephone number in your file." Still completely surprised, he wrote down the telephone number as I gave it to him. After writing it down, he queried the import of the number.

I replied, "If you call that number, I'm sure that you will have all your complaints resolved. You will no longer have to worry about the poor service which you have been receiving from us in the past. In fact you will never have to call us again with a problem."

His voice immediately turned sarcastic as he regained his composure and reverted to his usual, obnoxious self. "What number is that?" he demanded. "A new department you've set up just to handle all the problems you create for your customers?" was his caustic rejoinder.

"No," I retorted. "That is the telephone number of the Shell Oil Company. Call them and give your business to them. We don't want it."

My time was up, although it frankly had nothing to do with the obnoxious customer which I had just had the pleasure of turning over to The Shell Company. I was six months over due for leave, after having spent three and a half years out of the United States on my first tour of duty with THE COMPANY. I was getting 'channel fever'.

I said my good-byes and left that marvelous, island paradise known as Ceylon. I trailed my way across Europe and boarded a fantastic trans-Atlantic liner of the Cunard Line in Southampton. The Cunard Line had aptly entitled her, the 'Queen Elizabeth'. A ship that probably has never had an equal in all the world of trans-Atlantic vessels, including its sister ship the "Queen Mary". There were many that tried to rival her, but with no apparent success.

I subsequently traveled on the 'Ile de France', the 'Christo Colombo', the 'Veniezia', the 'Adriatica' and a number of other world class vessels that plied their trade in the North Atlantic crossings and in the Mediterranean. Perhaps, it was because it was my first voyage in unrivaled luxury that made such an impact on my very impressionable mind, but no ship ever took the place of my first love, the 'Queen Elizabeth'.

As fate was to decree at a later date, the last trans-Atlantic voyage undertaken by me and my family was on the self-same 'Queen Elizabeth' from New York to Southampton. After that voyage, the relentless demands of time and family prohibited such a luxury of taking five days to cross the Atlantic. We were soon, ever hence forth, condemned to travel by that most insidious method of travel ever designed by man, the trans-Atlantic jet. There was a very happy medium, however, before the airline industry graduated to jets, when they employed that wonderful compromise between the trans-Atlantic giants of the sea and those exhausting jets. This was the period of the propeller driven 'Stratocruisers'. That was an experience yet to come.

When I finally arrived home, my tyrannical mother greeted me with open arms after an almost four year absence. I explained to her that it wouldn't happen again. I was going to the office of THE COMPANY and tell them in no uncertain words what I thought of their life of 'ease and comfort' and their retirement plan. I was going to quit on the spot. It appeared that for an additional contribution by the employee to the pension plan, evenly matched by THE COMPANY, the Caltex international oil executives could retire at the age of fifty-five. I told her that I was going to make it quite clear to them that I knew now why they were generous enough to allow us to retire at that early age. We bloody well didn't live that long.

Of course, all these brave words were voiced without realizing the main reason that THE COMPANY gave us such long home leaves plus travel time after every tour abroad. A tour of duty in those days was for a period of three years. Each year abroad qualified for two months of home leave. Any delay in your departure from your overseas assignment earned a prorata addition to your vacation. I was six months late in departing from Ceylon which added an additional month to the already six months earned for a normal period.

Moreover, THE COMPANY hadn't yet learned that airplanes were here to stay, and that they had become an accepted means of travel. The home leave program was still carried on the books based on the days of travel by sailing vessel.

The employee was allowed thirty days travel time between his present area of assignment, and the city in which his records showed to be his official domicile in the United States. He was then permitted another thirty days travel from his established residence to his next area of assignment. In my particular case, there would be an elapsed period of almost nine months from the last time I had been in contact with any phase of my employer's business, and the next time that I would begin to attempt to undertake, what most people believe an international oil executive's duties to be, the selling of oil.

At the end of a nine month vacation with nothing to do but spend money, you had not only spent every cent you had saved overseas, but you were also very heavily in debt. You had no other choice but to 'go out again'. It was a routine procedure for staff members returning to the field to be met by one of the company accountants at the pier, as their ship arrived at their destination. They had cabled ahead from the ship telling the office how much they owed on their bar bill. One of the accounting staff would be there to meet them with a company check to pay off the astronomical bar bill, which the employee was totally incapable of doing as he already spent every cent at home that he had saved from his last tour.

My mother had been widowed at a very young age when I was only three years old and my brother was five. She had always been a tyrant. I use to vividly recall how she dragged us crying and screaming to the dentist every six months to have our teeth cleaned and filled (filled if necessary—toothpaste didn't have fluoride in it in those days).

Another one of her iron clad rules was that we must always wear clean underwear. She insisted that if we ever had an automobile accident, it was imperative that our underclothes be in immaculate condition when we arrived at the hospital. My brother and I always complained that it wasn't necessary to be so particular about everything we wore, or for that matter everything we did, since we were only at home and not out in the real world.

Her stern response to that childish observation was that, "Since your home is the most important place you will ever be in during your entire lives, that is the place that you will always treat with the utmost dignity and respect and be on your best behaviour. If you act properly at home, you will never have a lapse of honour or behaviour in your place of work or in the so called real world." Her other absolute insistence was about the necessity of proper table manners. Again we complained that we were only at home and it didn't matter. We nursed many a sore knuckle or finger as we often failed to see the eating utensil that she was using at the moment at the dining table as it descended with a resounding smack on the offending digit that was not behaving in accordance with her laid down rules of polite table manners. I was painfully reminded of her method of chastisement only recently. My thirty-four year old son landed his soup spoon on my offending elbows, which I had absentmindedly rested on the table while eating at the sushi bar at which he and his fiancée were entertaining me in Melbourne, Florida.

Although, I was never fortunate enough to have the direct guidance of my very staid and very English father in my formative years, he did leave a legacy of wisdom for us that my mother reminded me of when I was a young teenager working as a boatman at the Sheepshead Bay Yacht Club in Brooklyn, New York. Part of the duties of the boatman, when you were unlucky enough to have drawn the 8:00 PM to 8:00 AM night shift, was to clean all the toilets and urinals in the boat house. I told my mother that I didn't think that that was the kind of work that a person of my standing should be asked to undertake. Her comments at that time were very surprisingly to surface in my mind many, many years later when I was Regional Director for the Australian and New Zealand Division of Caltex Petroleum Corporation in New York and reporting to a very revered Vice-President of mine, Ray Johnson.

"Always remember what your father said about any job that you will ever be asked to do. 'No job is beneath your dignity so long as it only dirties your hands and not your soul'."

Ray Johnson and his very kind and extremely charming wife, Barbara, were hosting a theater and dinner party for some visiting Australian Government ministers as part of his government relations duties as an international oil executive. Unfortunately, there was a severe emergency problem that suddenly surfaced in Manila in the Philippines, another area that was part of his Vice-Presidential responsibilities.

He had had to advance the theater party to that very day as he informed me on the telephone, because he was leaving the next morning. The six orchestra seats to 'The King and I', which were dated four days hence, had to be exchanged immediately for that evening's performance. I knew that there was no office boy, or even my very efficient secretary, Dorothy, for that matter, who would be able to go to the box office and pound on the counter with sufficient force. Hammer on the counter with enough authority to convince them they had to make six of the best seats in the house available for that night's show. A show which was, at the time, one of the most popular plays on Broadway.

I had asked Nick Nikiferow, my extremely able and conscientious staff assistant, to accompany me after explaining my problem inasmuch as I was selfish enough to want company, if the line at the box office proved to be exceptionally long as I had no doubt it was going to be. Nick had joined me without a moments hesitation. From past experience with his character and his attitude towards his work, I had long ago come to the conclusion that his father must have passed on similar wisdom to him such as mine had to me. On our way out, we stopped at the office of the Philippine Division to confirm exactly what Ray's flight plans were.

The Regional Director wasn't there. He was in Manila trying his utmost to hold the fort until Ray arrived, but the young Deputy confirmed that Ray was leaving the next morning on an early flight. After giving us the details, he enquired where we were going as both Nick and I had our overcoats on and it was early afternoon. When I explained that I was going to the box office to exchange the theater tickets, because of Ray's unexpected departure caused by the problems originating in his area, he looked at me in amazement.

"You, a Regional Director, going to a box office to exchange theater tickets?" he questioned in a wondering tone of voice. "I would never do that," he informed me haughtily. "They don't pay me enough money to do that kind of menial work," he ended off his disdainful opinion of my twisted sense of duty.

Ray's visitors were important to him, and he had asked me to accomplish what was almost the impossible. Certainly, impossible to accomplish through the normal routine office channels with regular staff. I hadn't given it a second thought as I hung up the telephone and reached for my overcoat on the clothes rack. Now that this junior Deputy had made his point, it occurred to me that maybe I should give it serious second thoughts. I suddenly looked down at my hands which were holding the tickets that had to be exchanged. 'Hell, they weren't getting even the slightest bit dirty, much less my soul'. "Let's go Nick!"

I did get my revenge on my mother that Christmas after the many years of her tyranny. My home leave coincided with the holiday season, and we were celebrating Christmas at my beloved aunts' home at 1530 East 14th Street in Brooklyn, New York. I told my Mother that due to the holiday rush and just arriving home from a half a world away I had, very unfortunately, been unable to buy her anything that could be put under the tree.

She said immediately that it didn't matter. It was just enough to have me home after such a long time.

I had been watching the clock very carefully. I had timed my comment about being unable to buy her anything to put under the tree with the arrangements I had made with the next door neighbor, who was a member of the New York City police force. At my request, he had donned his uniform for the evening's occasion and rang the doorbell just as I finished my confession to my mother of my dereliction of Christmas duty.

My mother answered the door as my two aunts were busy preparing dinner. The neighbour in his police uniform informed her, in the sternest tones possible, that there was a car with a New Jersey license plate blocking his driveway. Since he knew that his neighbours' sister lived in New Jersey, he was sure that it belonged to her and would she remove it as quickly as possible.

He added the further comment that he hoped that she hadn't driven it all the way from New Jersey with that huge red Christmas ribbon wound all around it, because the ribbon certainly appeared to be a distinct, traffic hazard. My mother gazed at the sleek, brand new, four door Chrysler sedan all bound up in that huge red ribbon as the beautiful white snow flakes drifted down on the two foot square Christmas card which read, 'Thanks Mother. Merry Christmas' and promptly broke down into tears. I joined her.

My brother's revenge was even sweeter and more poignant than mine. When she became a semi-invalid in the latter years of her life at the time that I was commuting between the Caltex New York office, New Zealand, Australia and Florida on a monthly basis, the doctor ordered her confined to a nursing home. His advice was that that was the only place she could receive round the clock care. My brother refused to obey the doctor's orders. He took care of her for three and a half years on a twenty-four hour basis until she died at the age of eighty-nine, leaving behind her two very humble and repentant sons who clearly remembered what a tyrant she had always been.

I had regularly been a very avid reader of whatever literature on which I could get my hands, including some of the then more current novels. In a number of these novels, I read that the ambitious employee, who was attempting to climb the ladder of success as quickly as possible, was able to skip a large number of the rungs by marrying the boss' daughter. My boss, Bill Beiswinger, was the Chief Lubrication Engineer for the world wide operations of THE COMPANY, and it was to him that all of the field lubrication engineers reported, when returning to New York during our home leave. He was the same boss who had been transferred to New York from Shanghai when the China organization collapsed from the weight of Mao Tze-tung's onslaught on the city.

He also happened to be that same, razor sharp engineer that Carl and I had embarrassed so badly in Shanghai about his expense account after his visit to us in Taiwan. In addition to being a brilliant engineer, he also had a forgiving character and never held a grudge against Carl and myself for our oversight about his expense account. I discovered that his daughter was only two years old, which was really a dead end proposition as I couldn't afford to wait until she was of marrying age. He did have a very beautiful and extremely kind natured baby sitter, however, who also happened to be his secretary.

Connie Walters knew every one of his engineering staff in the field by name as he had told her of all our exploits, both official and unofficial. It wasn't long before I had joined his baby sitting staff and was keeping his extremely, attractive baby sitter company at his home. Connie had started work at a very young age. In fact, she was so young at the time that Texaco engaged her, she had had to obtain working papers before she could report to the Chrysler Building where Texaco was housed. Of course, this allowed Texaco to pay her the absolute minimum wage. During her brief stint at Texaco, she had become very friendly with another one of the secretarial staff.

Shortly afterwards, she was transferred from Texaco to the California Texas Oil Company, Ltd. as Caltex was known at that time. The transfer coincided with her colleague's boss' transfer, who was being transferred for development training as he was one of those employees on the 'fast track'. It, also, appeared that he was important enough to be able to bring his own secretary with him for the period of his transfer. The three of them walked over together from the Chrysler Building to The French Building, 550 Fifth Avenue which was then the main address of THE COMPANY. The Chrysler Building was Texaco's home for many, many years before they moved to Westchester, the beautiful and extremely expensive suburb of New York City.

A move, which coincidentally, was only minutes away from the home of the then present Chairman of Texaco. The cost of this multi-million dollar move eliminated the Chairman's inconvenient commute to the city. The Harvard Business Review astutely pointed out when it reviewed the mass exodus of large corporations from the cities to the suburbs that over seventy-five percent of the locations selected in the suburbs were only fifteen minutes or less from the homes of the then present Chairmen or Chief Executive Officer of the company undertaking the move.

She and her colleague and her colleague's boss, Gus Long, chatted amiably on the pleasant trip across town. Many years later, whenever she felt that some of the visiting dignitaries of Texaco were getting a bit stuffy or simply unbearably overbearing, she would wait for the opportune moment and suddenly interject some comment which always started with the phrase, "When Gus Long and I were out walking one day in New York.... .".

The stuffiness and overbearing disappeared as if by magic. They never did hear what ever was said during the walk or even asked why she was out walking with 'god'. The mere mention of 'Gus Long' and the thought that this charming woman in front of them was on speaking terms on a first name basis with 'god' was enough to bring them to dress parade attention. It would start them on a litany of silent prayers on which they concentrated their entire attention hoping against hope that they hadn't compromised themselves during the prior conversation.

'It was Gus Long who dominated Texaco for two decades. He was a granite-faced salesman from Florida who made his name as a 'no'-man and reinforced the tradition of skinflint management and centralized control which Texaco had established. For many years the board was full of Long's men'[19].

There was a close liaison between the lubrication engineering departments of our two owners and THE COMPANY. Haviland Motor Oil, another household name to the motorist and manufactured by the New York Sister, was the motor oil sold in the company's service stations through out the world. These sales by the New York Sister were balanced by RPM Delo, manufactured by the San Francisco Sister, and it was this commercial detergent oil, RPM Delo plus the flushing oil, which had been sold to the dam manager which had been responsible for so much of my grief in Ceylon. Only the technical aspects of the qualities of these oils were discussed at the many meetings between engineers of THE COMPANY and the engineers of The Two Sisters. *Prices* were never the subject of conversation.

These meetings were almost always over lunch which allowed the cost to be put on Bill's expense account. There were two things that were very noticeable about these lunches. One was that the tab was always picked up by Bill. The other was that all the Texaco engineers appeared to be addicted only to drinks that had Vodka as a base. I queried Bill about these two observations of mine after enjoying a number of these lunches.

He laughed and said that, obviously, I didn't know too much about Texaco's skinflint attitude towards expense accounts. "They would never approve an expense account that covered only company employees," he said. "Of course, with you along as an overseas 'visitor' it makes it easier for me to upgrade to a better restaurant, as well as actually get the expense account signed by THE COMPANY."

The other question I had was, why was it that so many Texaco engineers appeared to drink nothing but Vodka. "Haven't you seen those advertisements that read, 'Vodka—It Leaves You Breathless'," Bill asked.

I said, 'Yes, I had seen them, but since I didn't drink Vodka, but only beer, I assumed that it was the effect of the drink that gave you that so called 'breathless' feeling'.

He laughed again and said, "No. The advertisement refers to the fact that Vodka leaves practically no smell on your breath. Texaco staff would never dare go back to the office smelling as if they may have drunk their lunch instead of eating it. They're always scared to death that someone may notice that they have had a drink at lunch."

He continued by adding that just in the event that the 'Truth in Advertising Law' wasn't being too meticulously observed by the company manufacturing the Vodka which said it left you breathless, or the employee enjoyed some other drink than Vodka, all Texaco employees in New York always had a box of 'Chlorettes' in their possession at all times.

'Former Texaco men lovingly exchange stories about the company's penny-pinching, totting up tiny expenses, or refusing to allow their experts to contribute to industry meetings'[20] (or pick up the restaurant bills on their expense accounts either, apparently). 'In Libya, it was said, when Texaco cabled the revolutionary government announcing a new price involving millions of dollars, they cabled by the cheap night-letter rate'[21].

"Oh, by the way," he continued, "Don't ask for a drink when you go out in San Francisco with the Chevron engineers either. They don't have any problems with their expense accounts since it is an entirely different atmosphere with our Western owner, but they sure do have the same problem with drinking.

If you do make the mistake of asking for a drink at lunch time, they will undoubtedly tell you the story about the time that the then Chairman, Mr. Peterson, was asked if any of his staff ever drank at lunchtime. His reply was that, 'Definitely they do. They drink as much as they want to drink. Anyone who has the afternoon off and isn't coming back to the office can have a drink or as many drinks as he wants at lunch'.

In addition to the approach to expense accounts, the startling difference in the attitudes of the Two Sisters was very noticeable in many other aspects of their relationship with their Step-Sister, Caltex. Chevron had a savings plan for their employees that was the envy of the oil industry. For every dollar contributed by their employees, Chevron would contribute two dollars towards the plan. On the other hand for every dollar contributed by the Texaco employees, Texaco would very grudgingly contribute fifty cents.

Bearing in mind that the Caltex Board had two Texaco Directors on it, as well as two Chevron Directors, this presented a considerable problem as to how the savings plan of Caltex would be administered, as well as many other matters. And many of these other matters were of world importance in the oil arena which, definitely, didn't involve the employees in any respect. The Board voted a dramatic solution to the problem of the administration of the Caltex Savings Plan. For every dollar the Caltex employees contributed, Caltex matched it with a dollar of the company's money. This was really a draconian, King Solomon decision, inasmuch as it was only half as much as the San Francisco Sister gave their employees, but at the same time it was twice as much as the New York Sister gave their employees.

While the feelings of the employees of Caltex towards Texaco did not quite approach that of members of the staff of some of the other five Sisters, it is interesting to note the comments of an Exxon man and a Shell man. 'We all hate Texaco', said the Exxon man. 'If I were dying in a Texaco filling station,' said the Shell man,'I'd ask to be dragged across the road.' The other Sisters were united in their resentment of Texaco, and it is not hard to see why. Texaco has always taken pride in being the meanest of the big companies, the loner in the Western, refusing to contribute anything except for profit (apart from their patronage of opera), while their return on capital has been constantly the highest'[22]. No doubt, their being the meanest and most skin-flint was the basis for their having the highest return on capital, and that meanness and resultant high return on their capital was, undoubtedly, the reason, also, for the oft heard comment in the halls of Caltex. "Work for Chevron, but own Texaco stock."

Whatever problems I had with the attitudes of the Two Sisters that owned us, they were very quickly put in their proper perspective when I protested many years later to Bill Chandler, who at that time was Vice-President of the Trans-Arabian Pipeline Company in Beirut. I was complaining to him about the difference in the approach of the Two Sisters to certain problems that we were encountering in our efforts to solve some very contentious, international problems in the Middle-East.

He quickly put my concerns in their proper position when he wearily replied, "Don't tell me about your problems with your two owners. Please remember that your two owners, plus Esso and Mobil, are my four owners." He continued by saying that he could never understand how some of the highest paid legal staff in the world that were employed by the Four Sisters, Texaco, Chevron, Esso and Mobil could arrive at four entirely different interpretations of some of the tax laws passed by the United States Congress.

As this was my first home leave and having been away for over three and a half years, I spent most of it in my home town, New York. Coincidentally, this also meant that I was readily available to 'baby-sit' the boss' daughter by keeping his secretary company at the boss' home. I explained to her during these frequent baby-sitting sessions that being the wife of an international oil executive was anything but a bed of roses. On the contrary, it was very likely to result in evacuations, curfews, extremely unhealthy conditions in certain tropical countries, substandard schooling for children when they arrived and constant disruptions to their daily lives. A way of living that most American women would never consider constituted a happy marriage environment.

I told her that it wasn't fair for any career executive in the international oil business to ask some unsuspecting American woman to share these hazardous conditions. When I asked her to marry me, she was to be faced with all the calamities that I had so vividly outlined to her. However, she was of such a wonderful character that never once did she ever reproach me for putting her into life threatening conditions that I may have inadvertently overlooked in my description of the life of an international oil executive's wife.

We were married in Colombo, Ceylon, and she continued her career with THE COMPANY, but on an unpaid basis for a final total of thirty-nine years. A running total, that she never failed to remind me of through the years, which was five years longer than my indentured service. When I was eligible for the company's twenty year award, Frank Price the Regional Director for the African Division to which we were assigned at the time, gave it to my wife. He said she deserved it more than I did.

Our honeymoon had ended. They say honeymoons last for a year and we had been back from my home leave just over a year. We were both learning a change in life style. Connie, in particular, was faced with living in an environment as totally different from her previous one as anyone could imagine.

She did without one of her favorite meals, corned beef, for almost an entire year until she learned that the English call it 'salted silver side'. She learned immediately, however, the first day she went shopping in my wedding present to her, a convertible Morris Minor, that she should never leave the top down when she parked it in the sun. She stood on the sidewalk for an hour under the shop's awning, after covering the seat and the arm rests with cloth borrowed from the proprietor, while waiting for the seat and arm rests to cool off.

As lady of the house, she immediately took over the bank account. By the end of the first month she was ready to charge down to Barclays Bank PLC and accuse them of stealing. As she told me, she was able to master the new currency of rupees, but there was no way that she was going to allow Barclays to steal her deposits.

"Every time I put money in the bank they reduce my balance. What are they doing with my money?" she demanded. "And every time I draw a check, they increase my balance. Further more that must be the only bank in the world that prints its statements in red ink," she emphatically ended her complaints to me about Barclays banking system in Ceylon. It took a lot of delicate explaining to convince her that every one in the colonies lived on an overdraft. It was a way of life.

"Just ask anyone at the next cocktail party to which we go," I suggested to her. Unfortunately, she soon got the hang of it.

I had been practicing desperately hard trying to improve my polo handicap and had just concluded a most successful match. At the end of the game, the handicap committee advised me that they would increase my handicap from a 'one' to a 'two'. After the match I returned home, tired, but exhilarated by the news of my new handicap.

There had been two extra chukkas of polo as well. The ponies had performed exceptionally well. The field was in matchless condition. The Secretary of the club had been commended by the President for the outstanding way in which the grounds keeper had maintained the grass. Almost the ideal condition that golfers like to see on their greens. Eight horses thundering over grass coverage has a tendency to produce more divots in one chukka than the average golf course sees in a year.

In addition, the sales results for the month of March had just been put on my desk as I was surreptitiously leaving for my polo game at four o'clock. The next time that additional leave would be required for extra-curricular activities, which might interfere with the selling of oil, I wouldn't be so hesitant in asking my erstwhile superior for the extra time.

It was his habit to take the sales figures home the day they were produced and analyze them in minute detail at his leisure. He would be sure to be very complimentary in the morning. It was no wonder that the ponies had performed so well. Polo ponies can perceive the attitude of their riders and react accordingly. My ponies were able to sense that my spirits were indeed in orbit as the result of the quick glance at the sales figures.

Polo ponies are in far superior condition than the majority of their fellow stable mates. More importantly, they have incomparably greater intelligence. One of the ponies that had been played by me that day, according to the fellow member from whom I had purchased him, literally understood the game. When his rider hit a backhand shot and the pony, who had been trained to follow the ball, didn't see it coursing down the field in front of him, he immediately concluded that his rider had hit a backhand. The pony would turn instantaneously and prepare himself to carry the game into the opponents' territory. For his previous owner, who was a six goal handicap player, this gave the player just that added split second edge in a tightly fought match to keep ahead of his adversaries. For me, it often proved to be a devastating embarrassment.

For a long time I had been hopelessly trying to improve that handicap from one goal to a two. Backhand shots are one of the more difficult shots to perform in polo as probably in most games. When successfully executing this shot, my reactions often lagged that of my pony. He would hear the resounding crack of a well hit ball. When he failed to see it in front of him, as would be the case with a forehand shot, he would immediately turn and reverse direction. My delight at successfully executing a backhand shot made me fractionally slower than my pony in preparing myself for an abrupt about face. As a consequence, numerous times I found myself airborne, proceeding in the original direction in which the ball had been traveling. My pony, riderless and traveling in the opposite direction to my airborne flight, galloped towards the opponents' goal and endeavored to keep them at bay without any assistance from me. By this time, I had rolled down half the length of the polo field at a speed equivalent to a full gallop which was the speed at which I had parted company from my pony.

With 'all right with the world' I should have been forewarned that trouble was brewing. I entered the house on returning from the club. My wife called to me with the information that The Post and Telegraph office had delivered a telegram.

"Looks frightfully official," she commented in her recently acquired English intonation. She handed me the document. Indeed it did. I slit the envelope open with clumsy haste. My instincts had finally begun to come alive. A telegram in those days addressed to an individual invariably was the harbinger of grave news.

DATE: APRIL 1, 1953
TIME: 0800
FROM: THE SECRETARY OF THE NAVY
TO: LIEUTENANT (jg) R.PALMER SMITH, SERIAL NUMBER 311390

SUBJECT: ACTIVE DUTY

REFERENCE: UNITED STATES NAVAL REGULATIONS, CHAPTER III, SEC 'C', PARA 13

YOU ARE DIRECTED TO REPORT FOR ACTIVE DUTY IMMEDIATELY. YOUR REPORTING STATION WILL BE THE 13TH NAVAL DISTRICT, 90 CHURCH STREET, NEW YORK, NEW YORK. THE UNITED STATES EMBASSY IN COLOMBO, CEYLON WILL PROVIDE YOU WITH TRAVEL DOCUMENTS TO NEW YORK. YOU WILL BE ADVISED OF YOUR SHIP'S LOCATION BY YOUR REPORTING STATION. THEY WILL SUPPLY AIR TRANSPORTATION TO YOUR VESSEL. ACKNOWLEDGE RECEIPT OF YOUR ORDERS TO COMNAVSURFLANT BY RETURN THRU THE US NAVAL ATTACHE'S OFFICE IN COLOMBO, CEYLON.

SIGNED: COMNAVSURFLANT

CC: UNITED STATES EMBASSY, COLOMBO, CEYLON
US NAVAL ATTACHE, COLOMBO, CEYLON
PERSONNEL FILE, LT.(jg) R.PALMER SMITH, SERIAL NUMBER 311390

No …! Not again …! Totally unfair! The United States Navy had, already, had five years of my life. There were many younger men who hadn't served a day. They were, undoubtedly, even more qualified than I. Why me? I had only been married a year. They are not suppose to take married men. No, not married men I knew, but married officers, yes. Another reminder of that oft quoted maxim of the United States Navy, 'Rank has its privileges, but rank also has its responsibilities'.

One of my frequent hunting companions was a member of the US Naval Attaché's office at the American Embassy in Colombo, Herb Goulden. We had struck up a deep friendship because of our common obsession with the sport. I didn't even delay until morning. Without even changing from my polo habit, I vaulted into the car and drove at breakneck speed to his home. My mind harboured a forlorn hope that there was some advice that he could give me that might help to avoid a second tour of duty at sea. It is not possible for anyone, even a professional solider (General Patton not withstanding) to say that he enjoys fighting a war. Nevertheless, there were many aspects of service in the US Navy that had been thoroughly enjoyable. In reality, enjoyable to such an extent that close to the end of my service after the war, I had seriously contemplated turning 'regular'. It was not that I now regretted to continue to serve my country. It merely seemed that five years was a fair representative part of my life. There were many who hadn't served at all. It would do their character a tremendous lot of good to undergo the discipline of serving in the exceptionally well run United States Navy.

It was fortunate to find Herb at home. I entered with a despondent and apprehensive look on my face. A large smile materialized on his face when he recognized who his caller was; a smile which was slowly spreading over his countenance. His greeting of, "Oh, you must have received the telegram," didn't seem to be out place. He was aware of the correspondence inasmuch as a copy had been sent to his office by COMNAVSURFLANT, which the telegram had indicated.

What sent sudden loud and clamorous bells sounding off in my head was his smile. A smile, that had by now, turned into a mischievous grin. That monumentally, disturbing telegram hadn't left my vision from the instant that I had set eyes on it. I was still clutching it in my hand, and now as I glanced down at it, my vision and the actual telegram itself melded together. The first line finally registered on my consciousness. The date. *April 1st!*

Practical jokes are not one of my favourite pastimes. Unfortunately for me, my hunting companion was addicted to them. The telegram was a prime example of his addiction. The disturbing contents of the telegram were good enough reason for the date not to have registered on my mind.

In addition, not only was the language authentic, the Thirteenth Naval District headquarters address correct, but even more telling, my serial number was legitimate as well. There are two numbers that never leave an individual's mind. One is his social security number. The other, to those who have served in the military, is their serial number.

"How did you ever learn my serial number?" I queried him in startled amazement. The tenseness and apprehension generated by the practical joke was rapidly fading. It began to dawn on me that I did not have to leave this island paradise to resume that relentlessly boring and dangerous task of hunting down the enemy in cold and unfriendly waters.

"That was very elementary," he answered. "We merely asked Washington for it. We asked them to confirm if you were still in the reserves." The apprehension and tenseness which had been receding suddenly began to resurface again.

"What do you mean by … *we* … asked Washington?" I immediately shot back at him.

In a calculated offhand manner he replied. "The Naval Attaché was interested in establishing if you were still in the reserves," he proceeded to inform me.

"And..... ?"

"You are."

Although I have never professed to be a genius, it didn't require a genius' mentality to abruptly realize that there was more at stake here than a practical joke.

"We want your help," he declared with all signs of humour gone, and the smile wiped off his face.

"Help? What kind of assistance can I give to a Naval Attaché's office? I haven't been on active duty for years. Although up until a few minutes ago, I wouldn't have been so emphatic about that statement," was my immediate and caustic response.

Herb then carefully defined the workings of a Military Attaché's office. "Our operation here isn't large enough to require more than one branch of the military to be represented. Accordingly, we undertake the work of all the branches of the forces. My superior is a Lt.Commander, USN. That is why the office is known as 'The Naval Attaché's Office'," he continued to explain.

'... regular exchange of Ambassadors began in Renaissance Italy. Nations deem it so advantageous, in fact, that international custom grew to include specialized representatives called attachés, who ranked below the ambassador. Armed services acquired direct representation through military and naval attachés abroad'.[23]

"Very interesting," I retorted. "But just what relevancy does that information have in connection with your desire to know if I'm still a member of the reserves?"

"We are aware that your duties for Caltex demand that you range over the entire country. Specifically, your travels are invariably by motorcar," he carried on. "There are hundreds and hundreds of bridges throughout the island. You eventually must cross every one of them on your trips."

"What has that to do with your office?" I asked quite naïvely.

"We want you to take the measurements of every bridge that you cross. Your personnel file, which we also took the opportunity of obtaining, shows that you are a graduate engineer. Consequently, you can give some indication of the type of construction as well. Note the measurements and the information on a special map that will be supplied to you and periodically report back to us with the details."

"It doesn't make sense to me,"—apparently my naïvety had no limitations.

"It may not make sense to you," he informed me. "But to the logistical officers that are responsible for supplying the troop carriers, the tanks, and the supply trucks that may be needed sometime in the future, you can be assured that it will make a lot of sense."

I literally recoiled in astonishment. "You're not thinking of invading Ceylon?" I burst out.

"Don't be stupid! Of course not," he impatiently retorted as his long suffering forbearance with my naïvety began to wear a little thin. "This is a friendly country…. now…, but you never can tell when our Russian friends might decide they need it for strategic reasons. They would simply take it the way they did Hungary, Czechoslovakia and a few others. If they do, we want to be prepared as possible if we have to take it back. That means knowing what the roads and bridges can sustain in the way of heavy duty military traffic."

Thus began a long and tedious compilation of the transportation infrastructure of the island. It was, also, the start of a long and uncomfortable series of lies, half lies and simply plain evasions when my wife would unexpectedly, and in surprise, question me about an unforeseen break in my routine. She had struck up a close relationship with my hunting companion's wife, Leda. When I was away on tour, she would spend considerable time with her to break up the boredom of being on her own for several weeks.

I had just dropped off the results of my latest trip at his house on my way home from my recent travels. Arrangements had been made at the time I agreed to undertake the compilation of the information to deliver it as soon as I returned to Colombo. It was manifest, even to someone with my naïvety, that it would not be possible for me to be seen entering the Naval Attaché's office on a routine basis. As I entered the house, my wife was just replacing the telephone.

In a somewhat annoyed tone, she remarked, "I was just talking to Leda. Why didn't you tell me you were going to stop off at their house? I would have liked to have gone with you. Maybe we could have made arrangements to have dinner with them somewhere on your first night back."

I always took my hunting equipment with me on every trip. She was aware of it, since she always very efficiently helped to pack the car for me. Therefore, it was easy to reply quite casually. "Oh, he wanted to borrow my rifle cleaning set when I got back. I thought it would save time if I just dropped it off on my way home. Save a second trip," I added.

"Well, I wish you would have told me," she declared, as she ended the conversation in a slightly aggrieved tone of voice.

I became much more circumspect in the future when delivering the results of my investigations. There were still times when there seemed no logical reason for me to be at his home so consistently without my wife. On those occasions, I simply lied.

"THE COMPANY is trying to obtain the Embassy's petroleum business," I told her. "With my contacts through Herb, the account had been assigned to me." At this time in our married life, she had been working for THE COMPANY in the marketing department for a much longer period than I had. She was very knowledgeable about the company's business.

"Seems to me that that account is hardly worth all the time you spend talking to him, and talking to him about nothing but hunting, I'm sure," she added a bit caustically. "I'm sure, also, that what ever you talk to him about, there is no reason that I couldn't be there."

All happily married couples know that there is an affinity between husband and wife that recognizes, without any spoken words, something which apparently is not what it seems on the surface and very definitely is marring that affinity. I had been severely warned that under no condition was I to discuss with anyone the arrangements that had been undertaken by me to supply the Naval Attaché's office with the detailed information on the transportation infrastructure of Ceylon. This was the beginning of a number of situations that were to be a major source of strained relations between myself and my wife.

Traveling throughout the island suddenly came to a halt. Perhaps my companion at the Embassy was quite correct. Were the Russians behind the trouble brewing in the labor unions? Were they trying to de-stabilize the government by bringing all commercial activity to halt by declaring a major strike? 'Hartel', was the terminology, borrowed from the Chinese, applied to the disruptive, violent, and sometimes, deadly results of the countrywide strike.

The word in Sinhalese carried a much deeper connotation than does the simple word, 'strike', in English. The storage terminals of all the oil companies had to be put under twenty-four hour guard. There had been at least one oil company road tanker set fire to and blown up when making deliveries in the country. Fortunately for THE COMPANY, it was not one of theirs. If the instigators of the troubles were capable of blowing up a tanker, there was no reason to believe that they weren't perfectly cable of undertaking the same objective with the oil terminals.

Who could be trusted to stand guard at these vital and valuable installations? Vital to the government and valuable to THE COMPANY. Not only valuable to the companies, but of extreme concern to the government. Oil is a political animal. No country can function without it. No government can survive if they lose control, or availability, of its source. Whether that source be the crude producing wells of the oil exporting countries (as the Gulf War so amply demonstrated), or simply the storage terminals where the refined products are stored after being imported.

It is from these terminals that the army and the police are supplied with the necessary means to implement the government's policies and maintain law and order. In Colombo, there was only one group of people that the Caltex Managing Director felt could be trusted. Trusted to be beyond the reach of what was certainly developing into a political threat to the government and not just a matter of wages and union demands. That group was the American expatriates on his staff.

An emergency meeting was called by the Managing Director. At this meeting, all American members of the staff were assigned watch duties at the company's terminal. I drew the mid-night to morning watch on the first duty list. All company tank trucks were to be kept fueled and fully loaded. This was in direct contravention of the company's safety regulations, which stated that no tankers were to be stored at the terminal if they were loaded with gasoline or other petroleum products. Obviously, these safety regulations had be superseded at this time. If the instigators of the disruptive strike were successful in rendering the terminal inoperative, the loaded tank trucks would be driven to another site or to one of the other oil company terminals. In this way, at least there would be an immediate source of fuel available for the police and the army.

There was another safety precaution implemented. All privately owned vehicles were also to be kept fully fueled, and in top mechanical condition. Tires were to be checked and replaced, if there was the slightest indication that they were not reliable. THE COMPANY had its own staff of mechanics at the terminal whose customary daily duties were to maintain the tank truck fleet in road worthy condition.

Under ordinary circumstances, it was strictly prohibited to utilize these mechanics for maintenance duties on privately owned vehicles. These were not normal circumstances. For once in a lifetime, privately owned vehicles were brought up to maximum operating efficiency by company employees in the workshops of THE COMPANY. At least at the time, I thought it would be 'a once in a lifetime'. Little did I realize that it was only the first of several times that I would make sure that my wife's car was always fully fueled, in as perfect operating condition as possible, stocked with provisions, and equipped with the newest and most reliable tires available on the market.

What was an international oil company executive doing walking guard duty at an oil terminal on a small island off the Southern coast of India? Guard duty in the sweltering heat of the tropics, in the glaring light of the security floodlights, fully silhouetted against the terminal buildings and a perfect target for any terrorist that might take it into his mind to decide to render the terminal inoperative? And under what misguided sense of duty did this same international oil executive have that made him request his wife to drive him to his duty station at midnight?

What was that individual doing in the middle of the street waving us down to a standstill?

We had spent innumerable hours fulfilling our duty to THE COMPANY, including my wife, who, uncomplainingly, had driven me to the terminal at the start of my every tour. In the same uncomplaining fashion, she would pick me up in the morning at the completion of my guard duty. During the discussions at the emergency meeting, it had been recognized that the company wives had to remain completely mobile during this extremely disruptive and uncertain period. Consequently, it was necessary that they at all times have a vehicle at their disposal. It was for this reason that the company wives drove their husbands to the terminal. This would allow them to take the vehicle home, and have it at their disposal in the event there was an immediate need to evacuate the area.

"Who is that in the middle of the street?", she inquired as she slowly brought the car to a halt.

We were very conscious of the danger that not all individuals encountered on the streets of Colombo at that hour were necessarily law abiding citizens, particularly after curfew. It might become necessary to suddenly change intentions, and speed off in another direction. Not this time.... .however. The individual was wearing a uniform and had a rifle slung across his shoulder pointing in our direction. Not only pointing in our direction, but as the car came to a standstill the muzzle of the rifle was shoved through the driver's window and into my wife's face. She was doing the driving and had, as usual, again graciously undertaken to drive me to my assigned duty station. The rifle bolt clicked into place.

My wife abhorred rifles and hunting for several reasons. Accordingly, she didn't recognize the significance of the sound. The same gut, wrenching sound that I had heard in another country, on another distant shore and which I was to hear many times more in a totally explicit fashion. Not the sound of a rifle bolt clicking into place, but the sound resulting from the hammer meeting the firing pin, and the bullets erupting from the muzzle. At this time, the soldier's duty was to verify the cause for any citizen to be abroad at this hour.

Identification papers are a must in all countries outside the United States. They are required to be carried on one's person at all times and Ceylon was no exception. We were duly interrogated and passed as acceptable security risks. I, quite understandably, did not mention to my wife the implications of that nerve shattering sound of a rifle bolt being shoved into firing position. What I did voice, however, was that perennial thought which was beginning to surface in my mind more and more often as my service with THE COMPANY lengthened.

IS ASSASSINATION A VIABLE ALTERNATIVE!

Those senior officers of THE COMPANY, who had interviewed me prior to my being engaged by THE COMPANY, had made no mention of standing guard duty. Perhaps, I could get them to walk sentry duty here in the suffocating heat. With a little bit of luck, an assassin's bullet would save me from being guilty of coming to the definite conclusion that assassination was a viable alternative.

One positive aspect of the uprising was that it was impossible to travel anywhere in the island for normal business reasons. The compilation of the information required by the Naval Attaches office had to be postponed indefinitely. All tank truck deliveries were being made in convoy with outriders scouting out the route ahead of the convoy. An outrider who had to delay the convoy, while stopping to take measurements of every bridge that the convoy passed over would have been certain to raise many an eyebrow. Perhaps young international oil executives are immune to a failing of the older generation, common sense.

Where in the employees relations manual, or in our position descriptions, did it say that part of our duties was to ride 'shot-gun' on a convoy of tank trucks carrying highly inflammable and explosive material? God again was on the side of the innocent, the drunks and those who have temporarily taken leave of their senses. Or, if not leave of their senses, they had lost all sense of reality and recognition of the duties for which they had been employed, or more specifically, duties for which they had not been employed.

Phil Sanders, the Managing Director, and his wife had spent their honeymoon and the first years of their married life in a prisoner of war camp. He was unfortunate enough to have just returned from home leave with his new bride. He had been assigned to a fresh post with the company in Subic Bay in the Philippines just prior to when the 'japs' had had the audacity to push MacArthur into the sea. Perhaps for this reason, he did not seem to hesitate to assume that it was the duty of all employees to protect the company's property to the best of their ability. To the best of their ability, even including their lives.

Guard duty and riding shot-gun on the convoys became a way of life. The 'Hartel' continued. There were no more tank trucks lost by any of the oil companies. Whether it was because we were riding shot-gun, or the strikers had decided that they had made their mark with the initial attack, it was difficult to know. There were further isolated cases of violence in the countryside. Eventually the strikers capitulated. We went back to our normal routine way of living. Apparently, to the best of everyone's knowledge the Communists did not seem to have had control of the strikers. At least, that was the information received from the Naval Attaché's office via my hunting companion.

Polo, hunting, and, oh, yes, selling some oil were the outward trimmings of our normal routine way of office life. The constant recording of bridge measurements and type of construction, unfortunately, also returned to a routine way of living for me. There were several major steel bridges on the island. They appeared to be large enough to accommodate any type of vehicle that moved under its own power. Thus there was no need to take the measurements of bridges of that type. Or so I thought. No, it wasn't the measurements that the Naval Attaché's Office wanted. It was the actual drawings of the structures themselves. Into what sense of false security did I lull myself? How was it ever going to be humanly possible to get the actual drawings themselves? And why didn't he want just the measurements? My naïvety knew no bounds, or perhaps at that time 'The Bridge on the River Kwi' hadn't been produced.

Every oil company sells a multitude of products that are petroleum based. At least in those days, the main thrust of the marketing effort was to dispose of the maximum number of products that would allow the crude wells to keep pumping out their enormous quantities. Today, the oil companies sell any item that generates a profit, milk, beer, or anything that attracts the customer onto the premises where the basic products sold are manufactured from a petroleum base.

One of the unique products which THE COMPANY sold commercially was a material called 'Rust Proof Compound'. This compound, when applied to steel structures, prevented them from rusting, as it name implies. The maintenance manager in all governments is an important and key figure in the sale of petroleum products used on the infrastructure through out the country. I might be naïve about the duties of the Naval Attaché's office, but I was very knowledgeable about the oil business. The compound used for the prevention of rust was going to be the open sesame for me in obtaining the plans of the steel bridges.

An appointment was made with the Manager of the maintenance department. He had been a dinner guest at my home a number of times, and we were on a first name basis. He was a conscientious and hardworking civil servant. I told him there was a product in which he was sure to be interested, because of the tremendous savings that it would generate for his department. He very quickly acquiesced to my request to set up a meeting with him and his senior departmental staff.

The virtues of this compound, which prevented the metal structure from rusting and eliminated the need for constant repainting of the bridges, was graphically displayed to him and his staff with a detailed sales presentation. Both he and his staff were impressed enough to ask for estimates on the quantity needed and the attendant cost to implement the program, just as I had anticipated they would.

In my presentation, I had studiously avoided giving any indication of how the quantities required could be calculated. He was queried as to the total surface area of the bridges under his jurisdiction. That information was one statistic that was not part of his reporting requirements. The suggestion was made to him that if he could produce the plans for all the bridge structures, it would be possible to calculate the areas with certain measuring equipment which was available in the company's office.

He readily agreed, but hesitated as to the timing. He informed me that the plans were regularly referred to during the working day. I assured him that my doing the necessary investigation over a weekend presented no problem. He merely had to make the plans available on a Friday evening. The calculations would be made, and the plans returned on Monday morning at the time his office opened. Arrangements were made for me to pick up the plans at his office at the close of business on that Friday evening. The fateful Friday arrived. My nerves were beginning to tell me that they were not cut out for this type of activity.

At a pre-arranged locality, well away from any chance encounter with the naturally curious, the plans were transferred to my hunting companion's car. They were cautiously returned to me late on Sunday night. It wasn't necessary for him to inform me that he and his staff had spent the entire weekend meticulously photo-graphing each and every one of the voluminous bundle of documents with which I had presented him.

"Is there anything wrong with you?" my wife inquired. "Every time the telephone or the doorbell rings you jump as if you were about to be arrested. Is there something you're not telling me? This weekend has been the last straw. For the past few months you have been snapping and snarling at the servants, and me in particular. I think it is about time that you took a vacation, or made a clean breast of what ever it is that is troubling you."

Having delivered the plans into the safekeeping of my hunting companion on the Friday evening, my mind had immediately embarked on a fantasy trip which envisioned all kinds of calamitous happenings. The worst scenario was the thought of the maintenance manager calling at the office over the weekend to ascertain how the measurements were progressing and not finding me, or the plans, there. I then imagined him coming to the house with the request to return the plans immediately. There had been an accident to one of the bridges, and they needed the plans to commence repairs to the damaged area. My wife was quite correct. I needed a vacation.

Strangely enough on a much lighter note, my new Managing Director, Ronnie Mann, was about to suggest the same remedy, but for a different reason. During a review in his office of an advertising program on which THE COMPANY was about to embark, he casually asked me how long I had been in this part of the mystical East.

"Almost four years," was my reply.

"Just what I thought. You need a vacation. Go to a different part of the world," was his prompt rejoinder to the information concerning the duration of my stay in this tropical paradise of Maharajahs, Maharanees, waving palm trees and Kandian Dancers. I smiled and confirmed that while I might like a vacation was there any particular reason that had prompted him to make such a suggestion.

"You sent my young son a card on his birthday last week, didn't you?" Upon receiving confirmation of this politically, adroit measure on my part, he went on to ask how his son's name was spelled.

"*R A J A H,*" I carefully spelled out. "His name is *Rajah,* isn't it?"

"Yes, indeed it is,", he laughingly replied, but in the country from which you come, they spell it, *R O D G E R!*"

He was right! I needed a vacation!

8

'Elephant Walk'—1953

"For Christ's sake, Peter, get her home early tonight!" Lawrence Olivier was tired, irritable and was ready to go to bed after his long and arduous trip halfway around the world from London to Kandy, Ceylon. A trip that had been undertaken at the behest of Paramount Pictures, who were under the mistaken impression that Vivien Leigh's husband had some rein over her nocturnal activities. Paramount Pictures had been unable to control Miss Leigh's penchant for late nights, partying and the consequent tardy arrival on location for 'Elephant Walk'[24] which was being filmed in Ceylon.

Peter Finch, the great Australian Shakespearean actor who had the male lead in 'Elephant Walk' looked imploringly in my direction as if to say, 'Do you think we could get her back to the hotel just once before mid-night this time?' I shrugged in a very obvious degree of resignation. We had never been successful in getting her or Danna Andrews back from their nightly sprees in the numerous towns where the filming had been taking place. Communities where native residents normally told time by the lines on the palm of their hands.

'When it was too dark to see the lines in the palms of their hands, it was time to go to bed. When it was light enough in the morning to see the lines in the palms of their hands, it was time to arise'.

With the arrival of the entourage of Paramount Pictures, these time honored customs vanished. To have Vivien Leigh, Peter Finch, Danna Andrews and a host of other lesser lights dinning at your premises was enough cause to neglect all tribal virtues. Tribal virtues such as going to bed at a realistic hour and arising to continue your honest pursuits in the morning when the sun rose, and you could see the lines in the palms of your hand.

Very, very strangely for a Western, oriented society these were the exact parameters that Paramount Pictures was following in this jungle setting. All scenes that were being shot in Ceylon for this extravaganza, 'Elephant Walk', were being shot outdoors and shooting commenced immediately the sun appeared. We came to realize rather belatedly, that the indoor scenes were going to be shot in the safety and reasonable temperature of a more hospitable climate in Hollywood.

Outdoor scenes, even in that advanced age of movie production, had to be shot during the period between sunrise and sunset. There is no lighting system available that will 'light the world' other than the sun, even for Hollywood. Hence, Paramount worked by the same centuries old system of time keeping that the jungle had employed for eons. Bed at night when the sun bid you adieu, and you couldn't see the lines in the palms of your hands. Arise when you could see the lines in the palms of your hands as the sun rose to greet you.

How these newcomers to a devastatingly, torrid, tropical climate survived under the self-imposed arduous conditions of constant dining and wining after their retirement from the set for the day was beyond our comprehension. We had been living in the tropics for a number of years and found it impossible to keep up with them. The only saving grace for us was that we did not have to be on location every single morning when the sun rose.

I asked Danna Andrews at one time, how it was possible for him to be immaculately dressed in his stage clothes, made up and ready to partake in the shooting schedule organized for that day after having been in bed for only a matter of a few hours. His answer? The most honest and straight forward statement that could ever have been envisaged in reply to that inquiry.

"If you were paid as much as I am for doing nothing, you wouldn't take any risk that might jeopardize that kind of income."

- Not so Vivien! She was invariably late. No amount of make-up could erase the vestiges of the previous night's indulgence. There was nothing that the director could do to convince her that the entire shooting schedule hinged on her prompt arrival on location at sunrise.

In all fairness to Vivien, we later came to realize that she had long ago recognized that 'Elephant Walk'" was not a vehicle designed for her great talents. She was already on location, and there appeared to be nothing that could alter that fact. She simply resigned herself to the alternative of thoroughly enjoying herself. When she went to Hollywood and reviewed the 'rushes', they say that all her light nights and partying resulted in a nervous breakdown and, as a result, she had to be replaced as the lead, female star. We, who had worked with her, smiled to ourselves and nodded knowingly, 'it wasn't the late nights that gave her the nervous breakdown. It was seeing the results of all that filming in Ceylon of a story that was best told to children just before they retire for the night'.

That Elizabeth Taylor, another matchless actress, ever consented to replace Vivien in the role of female lead never failed to amaze us. But then, perhaps, like our good friend Danna Andrews, if you're paid that much money for doing nothing you don't refuse roles that might jeopardize your career.

Kandy was the location for the finale scenes of 'Elephant Walk'. The world famous Kandian dancers were to have a prominent part in the filming. It was the end of a three week paid vacation for us. A vacation that started with the innocent announcement in the 'Help Wanted' columns of the local Colombo newspaper. While the expertise of international oil executives might be a welcome addition to the work force of Ceylon, the resident permits of their spouses specifically excluded them from any remunerative occupation. When Paramount Pictures arrived without Hollywood secretarial assistance, which would have been a prohibitively expensive addition to their already bloated payroll costs, they confidently expected to find local talent to fill that gap.

It doesn't take too much imagination to visualize highly paid, intensely driven Hollywood moguls shouting at the gentle, slow moving and shy Ceylonese girls who replied to the help wanted advertisement announcing the need by Paramount Pictures for secretarial help. It requires even less imagination to venture that that relationship wouldn't last more than twenty-four hours. Paramount went to the Government with the threat that, 'if the Government didn't allow Paramount to hire American women who were resident in Ceylon without working papers, Paramount would depart and take their prodigious spending habits to a more accommodating tropical setting'.

My wife and another company wife, Ruth Thompson who was the wife of the Chief Accountant, were chosen to replace the unfortunate Ceylonese girls. Ceylonese girls who were demure, timid, anxious to please and who had never been exposed to the demands of the work pressure atmosphere of Hollywood. A Hollywood transposed from California to an island paradise in the Indian Ocean. One of my wife's first assignments was to prepare an advertisement listing the additional staff and equipment requirements for the filming of 'Elephant Walk':

A stand-in for Vivien Leigh.
A double for Vivien Leigh who, while not necessarily an expert horsewoman, had to be a capable rider.
A double for Danna Andrews who had to be an expert horseman.
Two horses with all the necessary saddlery.
A small convertible, two door, English car.

All to be available immediately and for a three week period. A further requirement of approximately thirty extras needed for the first days of filming at the airport.

She immediately proved her value to her new employers. "I can save you the cost of the entire advertisement," she announced. "My husband will be Danna Andrews' double. He is a polo player. You couldn't find better horsemen than polo players. Vivien Leigh's double will be the daughter of a tea planter. She will meet us on location when we arrive at the site of the first scenes to be shot. She won 'best in show' with her jumpers last year. My husband will bring two of his horses with him, and you may hire my car which is a convertible, two door, English Morris Minor. The stand-in for Vivien Leigh will be the wife of a pilot who flies for QANTAS and is stationed in Colombo. Caltex will provide all the extras you require at the airport and throughout the island if you have a need for any after we leave Colombo."

It was really no wonder that my wife was actually earning more money than I was when we were first married, as executive secretary to the Chief Lubrication Engineer, Bill Beiswinger, in the New York office of THE COMPANY.

When she arrived home from her first day of employment with this momentous news my heart sank. "The boss will never give me three weeks off to go chasing all over the countryside with Paramount Pictures," I lamented, "much as I would love to do it." That she was worth every penny the New York office paid her was evident in her immediate response.

"Oh, yes he will! I've arranged for him and his wife to be the first two extras that exit from the plane with Peter Finch and Vivien Leigh." Peter Finch, a tea planter, and his new bride Vivien Leigh were the storybook owners of 'Elephant Walk'. 'Elephant Walk', from which the picture took its title, was the name of the most prolific tea plantation on the island so the tale would have you believe.

Its name was derived from the fact that the huge mansion, which was to house the honeymoon couple, had been built many, many years ago by the groom's father across a walk that the elephants had used for centuries to wend their way down to an ancient watering hole. "No three weeks? No chance of his ever meeting Peter Finch and Vivien Leigh," she continued. Perhaps she would have done much better working for the Naval Attaché's office than I ever did. She actually proved that contention at a much later date, when she was faced with a possible, physical search by the Egyptian secret police. She very simply and calmly leaned over to kiss me goodbye at the airport and at the same time returned the documents that she had intended to smuggle out of Egypt back into my safekeeping.

The Morris Minor was loaded with all the paraphernalia required for a three week trip into the interior of the jungles of Ceylon. My wife had graciously offered the vacant seat in the back of her Morris Minor to the candidate for the stand-in for Vivien Leigh, the wife of the QANTAS pilot.

Paramount was responsible for the cost of transport for all members of the cast. Consequently, not only was my wife hiring her car to Paramount, but she was receiving the transportation costs for three of the members of the cast, she, myself and Vivien Leigh's stand-in. THE COMPANY really lost one of its star performers when she made the choice of marrying me. She could have remained with THE COMPANY and gone on to bigger and greater glory in the service of that benign dictatorship.

Those who have seen Vivien Leigh in 'Gone With The Wind', and there can't be many that haven't, will well remember her beauty and, particularly, her breathtakingly, blue eyes. The men assembled on location with her had the greatest difficulty to keep from staring at her. Not so the women, particularly my wife. Vivien asked if she could borrow my wife's car during the luncheon break one afternoon. It appeared she wanted to drive out into the countryside just to be by herself and away from all the activity involved in shooting the film.

The answer from my wife was a resounding, "*NO!*" Unfortunately for me, my wife had failed to inform me of the strong stand she had taken. Subsequently, when my wife wasn't present, Vivien asked me if she could borrow my wife's car. I fell all over myself saying, "*YES!*" I had visions of taking the car back to Colombo and having it 'bronzed', the way one does with their children's baby shoes. I would then be able to gaze at it and visualize those blue eyes and that breathtaking beauty of a truly great actress all the rest of my life.

When my wife learned of my unpardonable sin, she announced that on our return to Colombo the car would be sold and another purchased to take its place. She would never drive a car that had been driven by 'that woman'. I never made the mistake again of being so visibly enamored of another female the rest of my married life.

Lawrence Olivier retired to bed. Vivien, Peter Finch, Danna Andrews, the chief cameraman, myself, my wife and several others assembled in the lobby of The Kandy Hotel in preparation for our nightly foray into the countryside in quest of food and entertainment. Food which we found in great abundance in the form of delicious hot curries. Here again, it was remarkable the way these newcomers to our island paradise were able to consume the hottest curries that the local population were able to concoct for them. How they survived the rigors of the heat of the penetrating chilies, which were lavishly served by the staff, was beyond our grasp.

Mid-night came and passed. Course after course of food was still being served and all washed down with great draughts of cold beer. Peter Finch, with that same imploring look which he had exhibited when Lawrence Olivier demanded he bring Vivien home at a decent hour, gazed in my direction with an unspoken request for help. He seemed to insinuate that since I was doing the driving, I was capable of ordering the assembled personage represented by the main cast of characters for Paramount's picture to cease their pleasurable endeavors and at my command return to the hotel.

It was three AM when the car rolled to a stop in the parking lot of the hotel. Peter Finch glared at me as if the whole affair were my fault. He was, obviously, desperate and dreading the confrontation that would eventuate when he had to face Lawrence Olivier in the morning. Even if no one were aware of the hour at which we had arrived back at the hotel, it would take only a matter of seconds after glancing at Vivien when she arrived on the set to know that Lawrence Olivier's admonishment had not been taken too seriously.

During one very overcast day with the threat of rain which effectively ruled out any possibility of shooting film without the benefit of the sun, Danna Andrews asked if he could borrow one of my horses for a quick canter around the countryside. In this instance, the loan of my horses didn't require the permission of my wife. In addition, Danna was excellent company and a most likeable person. We had established a very friendly relationship and, consequently, my answer was definitely in the affirmative. I did, however, warn him that polo ponies were very high spirited, and he should exercise considerable care when mounting them and riding them.

To my utter astonishment, as he mounted the pony and cantered off, it was obvious immediately that he was an exceptionally, well accomplished rider. I turned to the director and asked in a puzzled tone why Paramount would pay me to do the riding scenes in the jungle when Danna was more than capable of doing so. All through life, one's ego is always vulnerable to being crushed. This was one of them.

"If Danna breaks his neck riding through those jungle scenes, we will have to spend a fortune re-shooting them. If you break yours, we'll just get someone else." I was too deflated to get mad at either the director or anyone else connected with Paramount Pictures. Until now as I pen these words, I never confessed to anyone to whom I repeatedly and proudly showed the riding scenes in my film copy of 'Elephant Walk' that Danna Andrews was as good, if not a better horseman, than I was.

My wife regaled us with the stories of how the director, the producer, the writers and even the cast of characters would argue over the wording of the script. It was, indeed, an eye opener to the layman to learn how Hollywood sometimes operates. This was a story that had been written many years ago. The studio had an exorbitant, costly group of people assembled to shoot the film and they had still not decided on the finale version of what words would come out of the actors and actresses mouths. We, in turn, regaled our fellow compatriots in Colombo with some of the bizarre happenings on location.

Ordinary mortals, who are dependent on directors and producers for their stardom, invariably obey with alacrity the director's slightest whim. Not so with those massive beasts of the jungle, the mighty elephants. Those readers, who have seen 'Elephant Walk', will recall the scene in the story when the wild elephants first decided that they would storm the huge mansion built across the route to their watering-place. To re-enact this scene, the tame elephants were assembled at the top of a hill by their mahouts. At the proper signal from the director, the mahouts started them on their downward journey towards the house.

Halfway down the hill, the director decided that the scene would look more impressive if the charging elephants were moved about a hundred feet to the left of the area from which they had started their descent. We gazed at the director in astonishment as at first he shouted, then he yelled, and finally he screamed in exasperation as it became more and more obvious to him that the elephants had no intention of obeying him. Perhaps, or perhaps not, the mahouts might have been able to accommodate him if they had understood English.

However, since they didn't, his repeated shouts of, "Move one hundred feet to the left! Move one hundred feet to the left!" made no impression on either the elephants or the mahouts. It did impress us with an understanding of what monumental egos Hollywood directors must have, if they really believed that with imperial instructions from one of them, hundreds of tons of elephants would 'present arms' and do a sharp military manoeuver to the left.

The most laughable incident was at the time of the filming of the scene where the elephants finally break down the wall surrounding the house. After demolishing the wall, they enter the house and inadvertently set fire to it by overturning one of the kerosene lamps. Vivien Leigh's double had the unpleasant (that's what doubles are paid for—as I had so recently learned) duty of having to leave the house on the run with the elephants, supposedly, in hot pursuit.

Elephants are terrified of fire. The house began to blaze. Vivien's double frantically ran down the front steps of the mansion as called for in the script. She was just in front of the exiting elephants who were now frantic and terrified in their own right, which emotions were not suppose to be part of the script. The action, as it was intended to be shot (we all knew the sequence inasmuch as my wife had just rewritten it for the third time the night before) would show the elephants pursuing, with a vengeance, the wife of the owner of 'Elephant Walk'. They were going to wreak their vengeance on anyone associated with the barricade, the grand home of the owner of 'Elephant Walk', which had been erected many years ago across their natural route to water.

Unfortunately for the director and the script writers, the elephants were much more fleet footed than human beings and in particular the wife of the QANTAS pilot. Halfway down the walk she glanced over her shoulder and was horrified to discover that the elephants had not only gained on her, but momentarily would be in the act of passing her by. They were completing ignoring the script in their haste to get away from the burning house. She made a wild and desperate leap for some thorn bush which was growing just past one of the massive trees that lined the path to 'Elephant Walk'. From this vantage point, she safely watched the 'herd' thunder past her while she nursed her many bruises and scratches.

With the house burned down, the elephants back under the tender care of their mahouts and the remaining scenes of this grand epic called 'Elephant Walk' to be shot in the comfort of a Hollywood studio, their remained nothing further to be accomplished on location. The grips started packing up those items that were to be returned to Hollywood. The balance was given away to the onlookers as the cost of returning them to the United States far outweighed their value. Vivien immediately started to lay her plans for her return to London.

These plans consisted of cabling all her colleagues, who were available, for a welcome home party in London, making arrangements for a stopover in Paris for a night's theater party and setting up tentative dates for parties in Hollywood, when the rushes were ready to be reviewed. Lawrence Olivier had returned to London in the meantime. He had accomplished nothing more than to prove that there was no one person that was able to control Vivien Leigh's nocturnal activities. All of us, who were resident in Ceylon, also packed up our belongings. We said our sad farewells and wandered home still in a rather dazed condition. It was difficult to conceive that we had been not only onlookers to a giant film maker's endeavours, but were on a first name basis with some of the world's great actresses and actors and had actually been part of the making of a Hollywood extravaganza.

9

Cairo, Egypt—1956

The usual custom in large bureaucracies is that the initial advice you receive regarding your next assignment has very little to do with your finale destination. Before leaving Ceylon we had been informed that our next tour of duty would be Madras, India. An absorbing avocation in Ceylon, India, and almost all British territories and ex-territories is the showing of pedigree dogs. It is an engrossing pastime of the British gentry. My wife had been eminently successful in breeding and showing English Cocker Spaniels in Ceylon. She had garnered quite a few blue ribbons in the process and had even established her own kennel name. When we were told that India was our next destination, she was determined to out-do her record in Ceylon by the infusion into her best show dogs, the top champion blood of the Cocker Spaniel breed obtainable in England.

Just prior to going on home leave from Colombo, she made arrangements with the Tree Tops Kennels in England to reserve for her 'the best of the litter' expected in late December 1955. We would transit England on our way to Madras and pick up the puppy at the kennels. It would be only a matter of a few weeks old and would be able to be carried on board as accompanied baggage. In this way, there would no risk of having it freeze to death in the hold, as has been known to happen on some of our better air carriers.

January 3, 1956 was the departure date for our post in India. At the end of November, our landlady was served with a month's notice. We and our six weeks old new baby would move in with my in-laws for the three days of January. On December twenty-third the telephone rang. It was the New York director, the very same individual that had been my Managing Director in Ceylon, Phil Sanders. On his transfer from Ceylon back to New York, he had been given an expanded area of control. It was to him that we all reported when on home leave from that part of the company's world operations. During the latter part of my tour in Ceylon, I had been transferred from the lubrication engineering department to the marketing department. Consequently, I no longer reported to my old boss, Bill Beiswinger.

The purpose of the call was to issue an invitation to lunch, if I cared to come into New York. I gazed at my wife with a look of amazement spread all over my face and whispered to her, "He has to be out of his mind. Lunch on December twenty-third? I have had lunch with him two and three times a week for the last six months." I had actually said my finale farewells in anticipation of the Christmas holidays and our departure for India. The six months that I had enjoyed having lunch with my New York director at his expense, although I always picked up the tab and put it on my expense account which he subsequently approved, was the result of the company home leave program which hadn't changed as yet.

She was much more knowledgeable about how the New York office operated than I was. She had actually spent quite a few years there, as opposed to my exposure which only amounted to a matter of months when I had been initially engaged.

She whispered back immediately, "Go ahead. He is probably all alone, because he has been elected to hold down the fort while everyone else leaves for a five day weekend. He has probably gotten lonesome, since there is no one to whom he can talk. We have finished all our Christmas shopping and have very little packing to do. So go and enjoy," was her finale send off.

Off to New York to relish the last of the company expense account lunches with my director. On my arrival at the office, my host donned his overcoat and handed me a file of cables about one inch in thickness. His comment as he handed the file to me was, "I hope this doesn't spoil your appetite, but you are not going to India. You are going to Cairo, Egypt. You can read the details at the table at The Glhouster House," as he named the restaurant that he had chosen for us at which to have our pre-Christmas repast. He explained that not only was there a change in posting, but it meant a promotion to Assistant Manager as well. What then could possibly be contained in the file that might cause me not to enjoy a lunch at company expense? He was fully aware of my domestic arrangements, which included moving in with my in-laws for the short period of three days.

The reading of the file soon showed the cause for his comment. Not only weren't we going to India but to Egypt, but we were going to leave for the Middle East in April instead of on January third. Now it was clear why lunch might not be so appetizing. Not three days with my in-laws, but almost four months and with a six weeks old baby who would be a half year old when we departed.

He was quick to see the discomfort on my face when I reached that part of the file that indicated the timing of the transfer. "We will stop in after lunch and see the Vice-President in charge of the area. It is doubtful if anything can be done about the timing at this stage, but we can always ask", he observed in a reassuring voice. After our partially relaxing lunch, we returned to the office and called on the Vice-President.

"Your director had already informed me of your domestic problems before your lunch today. He advised me you were coming into New York for what you thought would be your last lunch," he rather humourously started the conversation. The Vice-President was well known to me. I assumed he felt that he was at liberty to lighten the blow of the delayed departure with just a little bit of humour.

"I can appreciate your situation," he continued on a more serious note. "Why don't you go home and check with your wife. If the arrangements aren't satisfactory, you can depart for India on the third of January as planned." Was he really giving me a choice? I had now been in bondage to THE COMPANY long enough to know that such choices were few and far between and were, in fact, non-existent.

"Well, naturally, if it is in Egypt that you want us, we will go wherever you wish," was my reaction to what appeared to be his kind offer. "However, it would be very considerate of you, if you would just let me know why it is possible for me to have a choice of assignment. There is something that doesn't ring true about this situation," I suspiciously followed through on his offer.

He then went into some detail to explain the unusual circumstances that allowed me to have a choice of assignment. "If you decide to accept the offer of the Egyptian posting, we will have to find a replacement for you to fill the position in Madras. Inasmuch as the Indian organization is so large and has so many qualified staff, this will present no difficulty. If you decide that you do not wish to change your plans and leave on the third of January, we have quite a few months to locate a replacement for you. Normally, we don't have the luxury of three months to find a replacement."

At this point in the explanation he paused. Then he carried on in very deliberate tones, "And what's even more critical for your career is that we will … never … let … you … forget … that we gave you a choice." Did I really have a choice?

There was the well recollected remark by the instructor in the orientation sessions at the time of joining THE COMPANY, when one of the group asked if THE COMPANY ever gave its international oil executives a choice of assignment. "Definitely," was the response. "You always have the choice of going…. .or quitting." The extended stay with my in-laws didn't look too intolerable as an alternative at this stage.

In spite of the delayed departure, everything about the new assignment looked extremely attractive. THE COMPANY was setting up a new Middle East headquarters office. I was to be appointed Assistant Manager. The Manger was going to be an old time colleague of mine, Harry Bernard, whom I had first met in Shanghai. The duties and the varied agenda for the Middle-East headquarters was, in essence, a very appealing prospect. If only I could have read Gamal Abdul Nasser's mind.

Over the years, many people who were not in the international business would inquire as to the difficulties which a wife of an international executive would be faced in order to accommodate his career requirements; the complications and inconvenience of sudden transfers, the finding of qualified schools for children as they arrived, the variety of different languages with which they have to cope and a myriad of other problems associated with leaving one's home country. Very luckily for me, I was well aware of my wife's adaptability to these kinds of problems. With this in mind, I assured my director and Vice-President that the transfer would present no difficulty. If, under the circumstances, my wife had any strong objections, I would telephone them both immediately after arriving home and presenting the options to her. On this note, the meeting was terminated, and I made my departure.

On arrival home my wife greeted me with a knowing smile. "Well, how did it go? Was I correct? He was on duty and bored. Had no one to whom he could talk."

With a slight look of chagrin, I acknowledged the astuteness of her assessment of the status quo in the New York office just prior to the Christmas holidays. I described the lunch at The Glhouster House, a restaurant well known to her, and then questioned her as to whether Dards International Packers had telephoned. Dards was responsible for packing and shipping our personal belongings to India. Part of their service was to telephone with confirmation of the date of dispatch of the consignment in order that we would have an indication of the approximate time of arrival of the shipment at its destination.

Upon receipt of a negative reply from her regarding Dards telephone confirmation, I suggested that it might be feasible for me to call them and check on their progress. After dialing and receiving verification that I was connected to the correct number, I gave them my name and the name of THE COMPANY and asked, "Have you shipped my belongings to Madras, India yet? No? Good! Ship them to Cairo, Egypt instead."

I placed my hand over the mouth piece, turned in the direction in which my wife was sitting and inquired, "Is that alright with you?"

With a casual look upwards from the book she had been reading while I was interrogating Dards, she remarked without a moment's hesitation. "Sure!"

If only all international executives were blessed with spouses of such forbearance and adaptability, the trials and tribulations of many personnel departments would be halved. There would probably be no need for a staff of psychiatrists which many international corporations maintain as part of their interviewing process for prospective employees. Why would anyone want to be an international oil executive was their constant questioning theme? Many an international executive's career has founded on the inability of his wife to acclimate herself to the very different, difficult and varied conditions that exist outside her home country. Although no published statistics exist on the number of new recruits that personnel departments must produce as a result of an employee terminating his employment because of his spouse being unable to cope with the problems faced abroad, it must be a very large volume.

If she too, however, could have had the opportunity of reading Gamal Abdul Nasser's mind her reply would have been just as prompt, but much sharper and the word would have had a vastly different connotation. "Never....!"

We moved in with my in-laws on January first. I must confess it was a most pleasant experience. They doted over the baby. We had built in baby sitters for over three months. This gave us unlimited freedom to renew old acquaintances and see all the long running shows on Broadway. The time in the office was efficiently utilized to bring myself up to date on the proposed operations of THE COMPANY in that part of the world to which we were headed. The problems in the office appeared to be anything but of a normal routine nature which no doubt was why the office was being set up. The problems relating to physically moving and settling in Cairo were abnormal and definitely anything but routine. Fortunately for us we were unaware of what lay in store.

Progress for progress' sake has always been a nemesis of many people. Travel by jet today is boring, exhausting and the resulting jet lag is physically debilitating. Not so in those glorious days of the propeller driven 'Stratocruiser'. The airline industry should never have progressed beyond them to jets just for progress' sake.

Phil Sanders, my New York director, stopped at my desk with my travel documents which he had been about to sign. "I just happened to notice that you have booked only two berths on the plane. What about the baby? Don't you want a berth for her?" This was the same director who had, unfortunately, spent his honeymoon and the first four years of his marriage in a prisoner of war camp. Whether or not this had anything to do with his not having any children was a matter of conjecture. Whatever the reason, his suggestion that a six months old baby occupy a full sized adult's berth in an airplane indicated that he had never been on speaking terms with infants. I thanked him profusely and said that we would manage with two berths. The baby would share mine. I was a very light sleeper. Thus, there would be no problem in assuring that she was well taken care of during the night. My wife was a heavy sleeper and only too pleased to be relieved of the responsibility.

Many jet travelers today do not realize that those over size 747's, with the supposed innovation of a cocktail lounge 'upstairs', learned their lessons from the Stratocruisers. On the Stratocruisers the cocktail lounge was 'downstairs'. It was a glorious way to travel. You arrived at Idlewild Airport where a steward was waiting to guide your baggage through the gate. Having completed your passport and ticketing arrangements, you were then escorted to a luxuriously appointed lounge where you were served drinks and hors 'd'oeuvres, all at the airline's expense. The announcement to board the aircraft was made only minutes before takeoff. You were greeted by charming and smiling stewardesses, who offered you a glass of champagne while they helped to buckle you into your seat. No long boring wait strapped in wondering why you had to be on board so early. With the extinguishing of the 'Fasten Your Seat Belt' sign, you were issued with an immediate invitation to retire to the cocktail lounge 'downstairs' for an aperitif while the staff prepared your repast of caviar and pheasant under glass.

The only problems encountered were the difficult choices that had to be made between the various vintages of the several red and white wines served during the meal. The finale choice of which digestif to choose among the half-dozen offered at the end of the meal was the most difficult. The stewardesses kept a constant eye on the progress of your meal. Offers of refills or additional helpings of pheasant were made instantaneously, just before you downed your last sip of wine or the last forkfull of your meal. With an uncanny sense of timing, they were at your elbow before your first yawn with the announcement that your berth had been made up, and you were at liberty to retire to bed at any time you were so inclined. Off to bed. A good night's sleep of seven or eight hours: A full breakfast, with at least a dozen choices to tickle your appetite, and you were landing at Heathrow fully rested and totally unaware of the knowledge that such a thing as 'jet lag' existed.

The steward notified us as we were disembarking that our limousine would be at the gate to convey us to our hotel. After clearing custom and passport formalities, we proceeded to the gate at which the steward had informed us our transportation would be waiting. As the driver was loading the baggage into the trunk, I conversationally inquired if Caltex had had many visitors during the past week. "Oh!" he replied in a surprised tone of voice, "this vehicle doesn't belong to Caltex. It is part of the airline service. As a matter of fact though, there is a limousine belonging to Caltex. I was talking to the driver. He mentioned that he was waiting for one of the company executives who was on his way to Cairo." I thanked him profusely with a bit of embarrassment and asked him if he would be kind enough to transfer the baggage to the company limousine. Since they had been considerate enough to have made arrangements to meet me, I intended to utilize the company vehicle. He unresistantly and graciously proceeded to unload the vehicle and assisted in putting our belongings in the company car.

The driver of the company transportation requested confirmation as to whether or not The Dorchester Hotel was our destination, which his office had been informed by New York was the hotel at which we had been booked. Upon receiving an affirmative reply, he nodded in the direction of another limousine that was parked alongside. "That is the transportation which The Dorchester Hotel has sent to pick you up and take you into London," he apprised us. "I told them that I was from THE COMPANY and would bring you into the city. He insisted he would stay and ascertain if you might possibly require two vehicles."

My wife looked at me and suggested that perhaps we could put the baby in the company vehicle, she would take The Dorchester Hotel transport, and I could utilize the airline limousine. Then in an even more sarcastic solution to a ridiculous situation she said, "Why don't you just ask them to line up side by side? You can ride on the roof of the middle one and drive the troika into the city as a conquering Roman gladiator in his chariot."

She was very prone to lampoon THE COMPANY when she got annoyed at that benign dictatorship that controlled our lives. In this instance, she was highly amused by the obviously, ridiculous situation that had arisen over the transportation put at our disposal. She was enjoying herself with her comical comments to the solution of two people and an infant having three chauffeur driven limousines at their disposal to convey them into the heart of London. We thanked the driver from the hotel and advised him that we would use the company vehicle. Instinct should have told us that such an ostentatious display of wealth was a harbinger of unpleasant coming events. Events that were to be anything but ostentatious, wealthy or even a normal means of existence.

The first sign that the three limousines was the last of the comfort that we were to see for many a day was the quizzical look which the owners of Tree Tops

Kennels gave us. They glanced at the carrying case for the puppy. We had gone to great pains to purchase the smallest and most elegant one in New York in order to guarantee that our new 'champion to be' would be able to ride in first class style with us. After glancing at the carrying case, their eyes traveled down to the puppy. A puppy no longer, but almost a full grown English Cocker Spaniel. Their glances seemed to indicate that with the use of a shoehorn he might just be gotten into that miniature carrying case, but then he would probably suffocate. He would certainly suffer multiple fractures from forcing his oversize body into a area designed to hold, with breathing space, an animal one fourth his size.

They very kindly arranged to produce a shipping crate made from a tea chest, and said that they would make arrangements to have it at the airport. We gave them the time of departure, the flight number, and the name of the airline on which we were traveling, BOAC.

"Not possible!" was their immediate response. "That airline only takes 'carry-on' animals, and noticeably this one is so big it must go in the hold." We now had the ludicrous situation of a five month old puppy dictating on which airline we would fly.

To cheer us up the owners of the kennels gave us, what they visualized to be very encouraging news. "The shows in India have been immensely successful this year. Several of our strain have received 'best in show'. More blue ribbons have been received so far this year by some of our owners than in all of last year," we were informed by the proud proprietors of Tree Tops Kennels. Their kennels were internationally famous. The owners were very knowledgeable about shows throughout the world where their breed was taking first place in almost all the competitions.

"But we are not going to India," we told them. "We are going to Egypt."

"To Egypt?" was the incredulous reaction. "They don't show them there! They eat them!"

We had informed them of our delayed arrival in Great Britain, but we had not enlightened them as to our change in destination. Be that as it may, we had no alternative but to continue with our plans by making the necessary changes. If only we could have read Gamal Abdul Nasser's mind, we would have left our new champion there, and perhaps, or perhaps not.... continued our journey.

BOAC was cancelled. Air India very kindly agreed, albeit reluctantly, to book the three of us and our champion show dog. There are not many airlines that will take the responsibility of carrying live animals in their holds. The flight to Cairo, while physically comfortable, was a mental anguish for my wife. As a breeder, she had a great affinity for her charges. The thought of that young pup in the dark hold all by himself and possibly freezing to death gave her many a sharp qualm.

A kennel bred dog and, quite obviously not house broken, does not take kindly to hotel rooms. This knowledge was gained the first night of our stay in the Semerimus Hotel in Cairo. He was fastened securely to the radiator, surrounded by newspaper in the event he wished to exercise his rightful prerogatives. We bid him goodnight with many a kindly pat on the head and retired to bed for what we hoped would be a good night's sleep. Piercing does not describe the sound that emanates from a young puppy who feels that he has been wrongly sequestered in a strange room, in a strange country. In a country where the citizens possibly may have fed on some of his ancestors.

Three completely sleepless nights were all that my wife and I could endure. There was a cat kennel that also boarded dogs, if you prevailed upon their kindness sufficiently. That is to say if you were willing to pay three times the normal fees. Our champion was ensconced there. My wife actually made periodic checks morning and afternoon to determine if someone might have conceivably kidnapped her charge and sold him on the black market. A black market that might have intended to send him to the countryside where he would have ended up as the 'piece de resistance' with blue ribbons accorded to the chef instead of to his rightful owner.

There were no shows in Cairo. The champion was sold while we were in our second month at the hotel for a fraction of his cost. A fraction of his cost without consideration of the expense of transporting him, boarding him the extra three months at Tree Tops, because of our delayed arrival and the month's boarding in Cairo.

Yes. There was no doubt in our minds now. They eat them here. They don't show them.

It certainly ate into our meager savings left over from our fling in New York for over six months. I wondered what the reaction would be if the costs were to appear on my expense account under the heading of 'costs encountered due to a change in destination'.

House hunting is always a problem in any country, even in your home country. House hunting in a foreign country just compounds the difficulties many times over. For this reason our stay at the Semerimus Hotel was now well into its second month. One of the apartment buildings that had captured our interest intensely early in our search was on the Island of Zamalak in the middle of The Nile River. It was in the process of being completed. The completion date was too far into the future for us to give it any serious consideration. After nearly two months of unsuccessful searching, the building was now that much closer to completion.

The agents were approached again. Their advice was that it would be possible to move in in a matter of weeks. The apartment we chose was on the eighth floor looking directly over The Nile and facing East. We, or rather I was sorely tempted to rent the roof top, 12th floor duplex. There were two very strong arguments that mitigated against that choice. My wife was adamant that it was too dangerous to have our own private swimming pool on the roof of the second floor of our duplex in our apartment with a six months old baby who was quite capable of innocently crawling over the side and into the pool. In my case, my mind harboured an uneasy feeling. An uneasy feeling that when entertaining my New York directors and offering them a dip in the pool after a delightful, pool side lunch or dinner, served by immaculately clad and trained servants, they might just review the compensation package enjoyed by the expatriate staff, mine in particular.

It was an ideal location with a prestigious address within walking distance of The Zamalak Club, where there were two polo fields and stables for the members' ponies. The club had some unnecessary facilities as well. Facilities which polo players consider unnecessary, such as golf courses, tennis courts and swimming pools. The only exception to what the polo players considered to be unnecessary facilities were several club houses with celebrated restaurant reputations.

The lease was signed for three years with the all important inclusion of the 'diplomatic clause'. This is the clause that says in effect that 'if you are transferred, or have to vacate the premises for reasons other than voluntary, the lease may be cancelled without incurring any penalties'. It behooves every international executive who signs a lease in his own name to be irrefutably assured that the 'diplomatic clause' is part of his contractual arrangements with his landlord. Little did I realize how soon it would be before I notified the owners that I intended to invoke the 'diplomatic clause'.

Instinct should have, again, reared its ugly head. It should have told us that being so fortunate as to find an ideal location, such as a new apartment on the Island of Zamalak with The Nile in your front garden and within walking distance of the club, was too much of a good thing. The building was in the last stages of completion. One of the last stages happened to be the lift. After walking up and down eight flights of stairs for a number of weeks, there were very pointed interrogations made to the builders as to the so called completion date, which they had assured us was only a matter of a few days away when we moved in. We were about to have our first lesson in Arabic culture.

The initial response to our barbed questions regarding the date on which the lift would be operational was a very polite, "Bookera,". One of the appealing advantages of being in the international business is the opportunity of learning about the cultural differences that exist between your society and that of other members of the world community. We gazed at the state of construction of the elevator shaft and bitingly remarked that it didn't seem at all humanly possible that the work could be completed, 'bookera', 'tomorrow'.

As we were to learn, 'bookera', 'tomorrow', was an Egyptian's polite way of informing you that 'it will be finished when it is finished'. We hadn't been exposed long enough to such a non-Westernized time table to realize that the builder was being polite. In the usual impatient manner of Westerners, we insisted on a more definite date. He gazed at us for what appeared to be several minutes as if trying to gauge what was the real cause of our annoyance. In a tone of voice that indicated that he was really taking a profound risk in giving us a specific date, he announced that perhaps the lift would be operational, "Bada bookera," 'the day after tomorrow'.

As the years passed in the Middle East, 'bookera', became an acceptable response to us when we wished to know the duration of any particular activity that was engaging our interest at the time. We came to regret our rudeness in pressing the very polite builder for a definite time regarding the completion date that would eliminate that exhausting eight story walk up and down several times a day. We came to regret it, because we continued to insist that he give us a more Westernized version of a timetable than 'bada bookera'. His answer, "Bookera felmishmish!" It was given in a tone of voice that did not in any way border on his initial polite response. It told us that we had overstepped our bounds. "Bookera felmishmish," 'tomorrow when the apricots bloom', if they ever bloom. Nature would take care of the completion date, and we irritable and ill-bred Westerners would just have to wait.

The Egyptians may not be efficient in the area of building completion dates. They are very efficient when it is a matter of clearing customs. We had been very fortunate to discover when we were furniture shopping in New York, that 'Modern Age' was closing its furniture outlets in Manhattan and shifting the main focus of their sales effort to the burgeoning Florida market. Every piece of furniture in their New York shop was marked down by 50%. We bought out the store with the approval of our New York director whose signature was required on the shipping documents. He wanted his newly appointed staff to properly reflect the prestige of the up-to-date fashionable Middle East headquarters.

Egyptian long fiber cotton is world famous. The Egyptians do not take kindly to the importation of furniture that contains any low grade cotton in its padding. Even more important to their concern for maintaining their world-wide reputation is the possibility that the cotton padding may contain some boll weevil that would pose a threat to their crop. In a very efficient manner, which greatly expedited the passage of furniture through their custom's sheds, they very thoroughly slash each and every piece of furniture that might have the slightest possibility of containing any cotton. Within a matter of forty-eight hours after the arrival of our personal belongings, they were delivered to our apartment. Each piece of furniture suspected of containing cotton was slashed in several places. Where there had been cotton, they had removed it. Where the padding was of a synthetic nature, it was not disturbed. The highly visible slash in the fabric marking the efficient method that the Egyptian customs used to expedite the processing of the importation of personal belongings owned by impatient Westerners remained in place.

A place to live, a nanny to take care of the baby, a cook, a maid to serve and clean the house and a chauffeur to drive the car. Upon completion of these prerequisites, an international oil executive may consider himself as having settled into his new assignment. We had our apartment. My wife faithfully took care of the three house servants and the office provided the chauffeur. I was ready to start performing my office duties.

Office accommodations in Cairo were at a premium. Residential buildings converted to commercial space provided a much higher income to their owners. As a result, the company's Middle East headquarters' office was quartered in a five bedroom apartment of what had once been a luxury residential structure. It overlooked the tree lined American Embassy, which fortunately was just a narrow street across from the office. The entrance to the Embassy was only a matter of several hundred feet from a tree whose branches actually grew over the second floor balcony of the 'living room' of the office. The office boy's first duty on arriving and entering the office in the morning was to open the French windows leading to the balcony. This provided the staff with a relaxing view and a soothing atmosphere under which to work. When the weather became colder, it was not possible to have the windows open. A good part of the view was still available to be admired in spite of this drawback.

How was it possible to ever imagine that it would need two international oil executives to supplement the office boy's duties during the winter months, when it was not possible to have the windows leading to the balcony open? That it took two executives to augment the duties of one office boy is not meant to reflect any criticism of the executives. The reason why it took two was a simple matter of double checking. When the office boy performed his duties, the French windows were visibly open and therefore didn't require checking.

At a certain period during our sojourn in Cairo, which happened to coincide precisely with the initial *requests* made by the United States Naval Attaché, it became imperative to be absolutely secure in the knowledge that the windows were unlocked, the hinges well oiled and the area clear in front of the French windows. A split second's delay in exiting the office through those windows, scrambling down the tree overgrowing the balcony and sprinting pel-mel for the entrance to the American Embassy might just be the cause of not gaining political asylum at the Embassy. We would end up as guests of the Egyptian government instead.

Bill Murdock, the American Operations Manager, and I religiously checked each other every morning. One week he would unlock the windows and I would double check to ascertain if he had completed his duties. The following week I would unlock the windows and he would repeat the security check. This procedure was implemented prior to the evacuation and after our return to Cairo subsequent to the evacuation. It continued without letup until we were both transferred.

Another well, thought-out, innovative arrangement was introduced to me by my English neighbour on the floor directly above our apartment in Zamalak. I was unaware as to whether or not he had any dealings with the British Naval Attaché. He was a senior executive in Imperial Chemical Industries, a British chemical company. He had lived in the Middle East for many years. If oil is a 'political animal', surely as night follows day, chemicals must fit that definition as well. His system may not have been foolproof, but it did seem to indicate that it would provide that split second advantage when the need to depart instantly arose. A split second advantage that is so necessary when your liberty, and perhaps your life, depended on its timing.

The dual arrangements were a mirror image of the procedure to be followed if either one of us heard a knock on his door. When the upstairs neighbour heard the visitors announce themselves by pounding on his door, he would telephone me to alert me to the fact that there were unknown callers waiting to be admitted. There was an allowable elapsed period of a maximum of two minutes. If no repeat call was made by him within the allotted time to appraise me of the nature of his callers, I was out the door and on my way to the airport carrying a forlorn hope with me. A forlorn hope that I could book passage and be out of the country before his visitors finished interrogating him and stopped to knock on my door.

The mirror image was when the initial knock took place on my door on the floor below him. I called him. There was the maximum two minute waiting period. I would confirm, or not confirm as the case may be, the nature of my callers. He then either relaxed and returned to writing up his monthly reports on receipt of my second call or was in his car on the way to the airport carrying the same forlorn hope in his mind that I would have carried in his stead. The possibility that he could book passage and be out of the country before my visitors conceivably went upstairs to pound on his door.

There was no idiotic chivalry such as not departing without your friends. If he did not call back, or conversely if I did not, there was no earthly manner in which either one of us could have been of service to the other. There were already three Britons who had been incarcerated by the Egyptians on charges of spying. One of the three was a member of the press, who was apprehended probably just because he was carrying out his duties of reporting the news.... or perhaps not. For public consumption, I always railed at these onslaughts on an innocent civilian's precious liberty. Privately, I remained sanguine until in another world or at another time I might be privileged to view the evidence of their innocence. My neighbour was determined not to be the fourth Briton to be imprisoned, if there were any manner in which he could avoid doing so. I was just as determined not to be the first American to join the unfortunate trio.

A vital part of big oil's business is to be aware of the magnitude of your competitor's operations; What products they were importing, in what quantity and what percentage of the market such quantities represented. Many statistical studies have been completed that prove there is a time at which a further share of the market will prove to be a 'point of no return'. That is 'no return of any profit'. An excessive percentage of the market held by any one competitor invariably generates a price war.

As these words are being written, Americans have only to get into their cars, drive over to the nearest McDonald's and purchase a hamburger for a fraction of what they cost not many weeks ago. McDonald's lost market share. They are determined to regain it. All companies, in every business imaginable, attempt to keep the most accurate statistics available on their competitor's activities. The Government of Egypt was an intense, highly visible competitor of the established oil companies. As with all competitors, the most accurate information procurable was kept on the government's activities by the staff of the international oil companies. To the multitudinous military individuals and members of the Revolutionary Command Council ensconced in senior positions in Gamal Abdul Nasser's bureaucracy, this was … spying! Definitely not so with the international oil companies. This kind of information was their life's blood.

When the Naval Attaché's office *requested* certain *commercial* information on the Egyptian Government's imports into the oil market, the area between competitive statistics and 'other activities' may have become slightly blurred. Not all counter-espionage departments of less developed countries are either incompetent or stupid.

My wife was occupied having curtains made for the apartment and buying the smaller pieces of furniture that Modern Age had been unable to supply. I was busy meeting the staff of our agents. The service stations of the agents all had the familiar logo of THE COMPANY that could be recognized anywhere in the world. The logo, actually, was an incestuous compromise made by the Two Sisters that owned Caltex. All Americans are well aware of what company owned all those service stations in the United States that had the huge red star with a green 'T' in the middle. It was Texaco, one of the Seven Sisters.

When Americans traveled through the Middle East and Northern Africa and many other areas outside of the United States, they still thought of Texaco when they saw the Caltex service stations. This was because the only difference in the appearance of the station was that the green 'T' in the red star had been replaced with the word 'CALTEX'. Everything else about the service stations was identical to their stateside brethren, including the green stripes around the canopy. Chevron (Standard Oil of California—SOCAL), the Western sister, however, was satisfied that they had consummated the incestuous relationship and were in the public's eye because their name came first in the identification as in *CAL*tex. No one looked at, or even noticed, the legal notice posted in extremely small print over the door of every one of these apparently American owned service stations: 'PROPERTY OF *CFP*', (Compagnie Française des Petroles).

'The French had very effectively been shut out of the most prolific part of the crude producing Middle East by the Seven Sisters. However, it was true that they had been allowed their twenty-four percent share of the Iraq oil back in the nineteen-twenties. The then French President, Poincare, had set up a national oil company called Compagnie Française des Petroles to handle the oil from Iraq. As with BP, the fifty-one percent British Government owned oil company, the French Government gave CFP special protection. But like many upstarts in the oil business it had money and grand designs, but lacked the scale of production of crude oil to put them into effect. The French resentment at the Anglo-American domination of the industry was to smoulder, with periodic explosions, over the following decades'[25].

Caltex, as the step-sister of the Two Sisters, was unique in that they were given, and encouraged as well, to sell as much oil as they could, but money was very hard to come by. The Two Sisters preferred to keep that scarce commodity for their own designs. In spite of the resentment felt by the French over the Anglo-American domination of the oil industry, this unusual combination of the two shortages, money in the case of Caltex and oil in the case of CFP, led to a very strange marriage of convenience. This marriage was known as the 'Joint Agreement'.

The 'Joint Agreement' between CPC and CFP covered not only Egypt but Syria, Lebanon, Jordan, Ethiopia, Eritrea, Djibouti, British and French Somaliland and The Sudan. It effectively obligated the French to provide all the money necessary for the huge distribution networks in these countries, and it compelled CPC to supply all the oil needed to meet the marketing requirements of the French. The 'Joint Agreement', in effect, was a single and complete franchise arrangement with CFP for the sale and distribution of all CPC's products in almost a third of that vast continent of Africa and a major part of the Middle East.

Oil is a strange product to merchandise. It is never seen by the customer who consumes it and is very seldom seen by the people who sell it. It is not like the banking business whose product is always on display at their place of business. On the other hand, banking to the oil business is a highly vital necessity. In addition to meeting the staff of our agents, I was also introduced to the senior staff of Barclays Bank PLC who had been delighted to grant THE COMPANY an over-draft facility of $50,000,000.00 in equivalent Egyptian pounds.

The Manager of Citibank in Cairo, Don Hykies, was determined to supplement Barclays by any means possible. Consequently, my wife and I were frequently his and his wife's guests at many lavish diner parties and other functions. Unfortunately for him, the only business that I was able to successfully steer in his bank's direction was in South Africa when we were both subsequently transferred to Johannesburg. I opened a personal over-draft with Citibank's branch there which was used to purchase my polo ponies.

Not that I didn't once offer to augment Barclays in Egypt with Citibank by offering to establish an additional overdraft of quite a few million dollars. At the time that the offer was made to Citibank, neither Citibank nor any other bank in Egypt for that matter, including our esteemed established bankers, Barclays, were the least bit interested or cooperative.

In countries of the political hue of Egypt and many other socialist societies, the government is often the biggest single oil importer in the market. This necessitated meeting The Minister of Petroleum Affairs and many of his senior staff. He was particularly dark skinned, no doubt descended from one of those desert tribes that differed from their neighbours. He was a jovial and likable extrovert. Not all senior members of Gamal Abdul Nasser's government could be classified as having those attributes. Irrefutably, however, the stories were legion as to his emotional and intense dislike of the Americans. He never once exhibited this characteristic in all the times that we exchanged vehement views in his office. More telling than his personality, unfortunately for our business, were his actions. At no time was I ever able to accomplish the special objectives desired by THE COMPANY, that required his ministerial cooperation.

He never did personally relate to me how he had lost his arm. There were many in Cairo who would not hesitate to inform you of the racial prejudice that caused the tragedy and which was responsible for his deep abhorrence of the Americans. He was traveling in Texas, so the story went, when he incurred a severe infection in his left arm. An infection so grave that it spread throughout his body. By the time he arrived at the hospital he was delirious, incoherent and incapable of telling anyone that he was an Arab. His exceptionally dark complexion excluded him from treatment at that particular hospital. The hospital was for whites only. The resultant delay gave the infection that much more of a chance to take hold. It was not possible to save the arm when he arrived at a facility that catered to blacks. To be an American and have to do business with an individual with such an impassioned dislike for you was inordinately unnerving. It left you with a mental handicap that almost matched his physical one.

THE COMPANY was registered in Alexandria. Under Egyptian law all company monthly board meetings had to be held in the city in which a company was registered; an extremely pleasant periodic duty. A visit to Alexandria to attend the monthly board meeting, lunch at the club and a quick flight back in time to enjoy the night life of that rather, unrestrained city of Cairo, a city whose reputation was well earned.

When the company's New York visitors were entertained, they were always startled by three most unexpected events. The first was when they learned they were going to dine in King Farouk's palace in the heart of Cairo. The second was on arriving at the Abdin Palace when they realized that it was the Egyptian custom to sit on the floor at low slung tables when you dine. The third, and we always relished the looks on their faces, was at the end of the meal when the entertainment commenced. They were astounded to find that the oriental dancers were performing right in front of their very eyes. Not only right in front of their very eyes as they gazed upwards from their vantage position on the floor, but the dancers were performing on the very table on which they had just finished dining. It was a delightful start to our stay in that part of the Middle East, even though the stay was of a very short duration.

Tours of the country side to view at first hand the distribution facilities and the service stations is always a first priority of any new assignment for an international oil executive. THE COMPANY prided itself on the cleanliness and sparkling appearance of its world-wide and far flung chain of service stations. Clean rest rooms was synonymous with the name of THE COMPANY. On my first visit to the countryside, it was horrifying to see the dilapidated state of the buildings and the filth of the rest rooms. Filth is the only word that could truthfully be used. Taking the station owner to task for conditions that were so sub-standard to the company's policy that in any other country they would have been cause for immediate cancellation of the franchise, gave me another lesson in Arab philosophy.

The operator very politely explained that he had, indeed, initially followed the company's instructions. He had brought the premises up to more than acceptable standards. The rest rooms were immaculate. The pump islands sparkled. The service attendants were outfitted in new and shiny uniforms.... .and the customers stayed away in droves. This was not the kind of facility to which they were accustomed, and with which they had grown up.

Whether this was true or not I was never able to ascertain for a fact. A look at his sales figures indicated that he was operating at maximum capacity. Any increase brought about by cleaning up the station, if such action actually resulted in increased sales, (or decreased sales if his story were to be believed), would strain his facilities. The situation was a standoff.

It brought to mind that frequently told tale in THE COMPANY about the new sales representative who refused to submit his expense account on time. When it was submitted, it was so filled with glaring exceptions to the company's established practices as to be totally unacceptable. He was called on the carpet by his immediate supervisor, who informed him that unless he made the necessary effort to correct the timing and the discrepancies, disciplinary action would result. The sales representative cordially invited his supervisor 'to go stick his head in a bucket of water'! The prompt response to this retort was to inform the sales representative that his actions and attitude were going to be reported to the manger immediately. "Tell him to go stick his head in a bucket of water also," was the rejoinder to this threat.

The supervisor diligently reported the situation to his manager, with particular emphasis on the fact that the new employee had had the temerity to suggest that the manager 'stick his head in a bucket of water also'. He then asked for instructions on how to discipline the new employee to the maximum extent possible.

"Before answering your question," the manager replied, "would you please advise me how many gallons of product this particular employee sold in the first month of his employment?"

"Fifty thousand gallons," was the answer.

"And the second month?"

"One hundred thousand gallons."

"And the third month?" the manager continued with his queries. "Two hundred thousand gallons," was the supervisor's response. The manger looked at the supervisor pensively for several moments and then turned away. As he turned, he politely asked the employee's supervisor if he would be kind enough to excuse him for a few minutes. The supervisor asked in some surprise, "Where are you going?"

"To look for a bucket of water."

However much one might abhor facilities that were not up to the standard of cleanliness which THE COMPANY insisted be maintained in its world wide operations, there was no denying that the lofty sales results were impressive. One product, whose sales were enough to warm the cockles of any flint hearted sales manager, were those of kerosene. The sales figures might warm the cockles of a sales manager's heart, but it physically warmed the Egyptian peasants as well. To the Egyptians in the country side, kerosene was a necessity of life. It not only physically warmed them, it cooked their food and lighted their homes. Woe betide any political leader that did not make kerosene available in large quantities and at prices the farmers and peasants could afford to pay. Gamal Abdul Nasser's continued hold on power in his country was a constant reminder of this lesson well learned.

Unfortunately for Nasser's successor, Anwar Sadat, he did not learn this lesson very well. On January 17,1976 his government announced that the prices on about twenty-five essential commodities would rise as the subsidies were reduced. Among these essential commodities, very naturally, was the all important one of kerosene. 'Early on the morning of the eighteenth of January tens of thousands of men and women poured into the streets, people for whom life had long been almost unbearably hard but who knew that now they were going to find it impossible. It was a result of this lesson badly learned that the first of the 'Legitimacy

Cracks' appeared in Sadat's hold over his people'[26]. It was no doubt the first of the 'Legitimacy Cracks' that eventually widened enough to rupture the whole fabric of the Sadat government and culminated on October 6,1981 with his assassination.

The curtains arrived and were hung. Invitations went out for dinner parties and cocktail parties. The servants settled into their well trained routines which the lady of the household always insisted upon. The office established a more formal procedure with the arrival of the new Assistant Manager who was now back from his many familiarization trips to the field. Even the lift became operational (when the apricots bloomed).

My first polo pony had been purchased. One pony, naturally, would never allow a player to take part in any games. Providentially, the club had an excellent system that was specifically designed for newcomers, or for players who might have had the misfortune to have one of their ponies go lame during a chukka. The club owned a number of ponies which were available to newcomers while they were building up their string, or for those players who had the need for an extra pony. This allowed a player the opportunity to join a game immediately upon becoming a member of the club.

The fields were probably the best maintained in the world. The reason for this was very simple. There were two fields. Since the club was on an island in the middle of The Nile there was an unlimited amount of water available. The fields had been boarded by short, retainer walls which had been designed to hold the water after the field had been inundated. After every game, the field on which the game had been played was flooded. This served to level all divots that had been produced by the players' ponies during the game. While the one field was being settled, the next game would be played on the adjacent field, and the Egyptian peasant continued to eke out his life on his meager daily subsistence.

Don, the Manager of Citibank and his wife Clair, were becoming very close friends as they were delightful people to know. Don did not resemble the normal, staid, solid looking banker in a pin-striped double-breasted suit from Brooks' Brothers. On the contrary, he was tall and thin and had a delightful smile which was always present even when he was saying 'no' to a desperate supplicant. His branch office was small in comparison to some of Citibank's operations throughout the world. However, Don had the distinction of being at the top of a list compiled by his New York office to show which branch was making the best return on its assets. Under normal circumstances this might have entailed a prodigious effort and unimaginable skill to reach such a lofty position. Don made no pretense of having himself appear as the individual genius who was responsible for his branch being at the top of the list.

"Any branch that has $7,000,000.00 on deposit for which they do not have to pay the depositor any interest could easily make the top of the list," was his explanation. He merely loaned the $7,000,000.00, for which the bank was paying no charges, to commercial establishments in Cairo at very high rates of interest. Rates of interest, almost bordering on usury, were the prevalent fashion in Egypt at that time. THE COMPANY was well aware of this fact from the charges which appeared monthly on Barclays' statements covering the cost of the $50,000,000.00 overdraft which at a later date went unofficially to $73,000,000.00.

Citibank was, obviously, very pleased to have the use of $7,000,000.00 for which there was no cost involved. The United States Government whose money it was on deposit, and who were receiving no interest, were very much less than pleased. The embassy official in charge of financial affairs informed Don to either commence paying interest, or he would transfer the money to another bank in Cairo.

On hearing this threat, Don merely shrugged and said, "It is not my company's policy to pay interest on government deposits. If the US Government wishes to transfer the funds to another bank, all they have to do is give me the name of the bank and I will arrange the transfer."

When the guns of World War II stopped firing at the close of the war, quite obviously there was a considerable amount of very valuable war material still in those countries in which the war had been waged. Rather than attempt to ship this material back to the United States at great expense, it was sold on the open market. Congress had passed a mini-Marshall plan in that the proceeds from the sale of this war material was to be used in the country in which the material was sold in order to help it recover from the ravages of war. These funds were known as 'Counterpart Funds'. They could only be used for the specific purpose of 'foreign aid' for the country in which the funds had originated. In addition, Public Law 480 which permitted payment in local currency for the many tons of wheat and flour shipped to Egypt (part of which could then be turned back to the local government for development projects) also generated substantial sums of money.

The powerful bank lobby, undoubtedly the same one responsible for the Savings and Loan debacle, had Congress add a clause to the bill that ensured that the proceeds could only be deposited in an American bank. This effectively shut out foreign competitors who couldn't then offer the US Government a better return on its money.

Citibank had loaned out the Government's money to many of their clients. They would have been in a very embarrassing position if the US Government had instructed Citibank to transfer it to another bank. Don was on very safe ground when he suggested that if the Embassy wanted to transfer their money all they had to do was to direct him to which bank it was to be transferred. He was fully aware that it would take 'an act of Congress', to use that old cliché, to have the funds transferred. Strangely enough, in this case, that is exactly what it would have taken, 'an act of Congress' to amend the bill to include foreign banks. There were no other American banks in Egypt except Citibank.

No one in their wildest imagination could have foreseen that the situation would ever arise where there would be only one American bank in a foreign country in which there were Counterpart Funds. The 'tax and tax, spend and spend, elect and elect', check bouncing liberals of our Congress would never bother themselves about the minor matter of the taxpayers not receiving a fair return on their $7,000,000.00. They were too busy voting themselves pay increases and ruining the reputations of the candidates for the Supreme Court. My good friend Don remained at the top of the list of best performing branches of his company for a very long, enviable period.

My wife and I started our Arabic lessons. We had both agreed that whatever country to which THE COMPANY would post us, we would make a determined effort to learn the language. At a later date after attempting Tamil, Singhalese, Egyptian Arabic, French, Lebanese Arabic, Swahili and the thought of Afrikaans she drew the line. "Enough is enough," she said.

Fortunately, the only other language that she would have had to learn after that, if she really wanted to make the effort, was Australian. Luckily there were enough words common to both English and Australian for her to decide not to make the attempt. However, when our second daughter, Gayle, called from her boarding school in Walla Walla, Australia, many, many years later and informed us that 'she had cocked a wog and was crook', my wife began to ponder if maybe she shouldn't make the effort to learn Australian.

We both enjoyed our initial Arabic lessons. It was surprising for me to find that Arabic was much more difficult than Chinese. While the language might be difficult to learn, it was very easy to learn to like the food. To dine on a houseboat moored on The Nile with the massive river flowing by your table was truly an enchanting experience.

The level of telephone service one can expect in various countries in that part of the world depends primarily on which contractor had made the successful bid to install the system and how much of the cost of installation found its way into the pockets of government officials. The charge for ordinary telephone calls was a factor of government decision in Egypt. In most countries, other than the United States, the telephone system is part of the postal system, as it was in Cairo, and is a government monopoly.

There is no doubt that the cost of a telephone call to the New York office made by one of the American staff of the Cairo office was astronomical compared to telephone costs in any other of the world-wide, far flung offices of THE COMPANY. Not only was it astronomical, but it was exceptionally time consuming as well.

Technically, the system in Egypt could not be faulted in those days when judged against national telephone systems in other countries. There were the usual hour after hour delays when attempting to get an overseas connection. In addition, the volume of sound would rise and fall depending on how overloaded the system was, but these were common faults that all international staff of every company in every LDC endured as a matter of routine.

There was, notwithstanding, a very major problem in Egypt. Arabic, French and English were the only three languages permitted to be used on the telephone. The use of codes on the telegraphic system was prohibited. Any attempt to circumvent these rules invariably ended up with a dead telephone connection, or the refusal of the staff at the cable office to accept your dispatches. There was no such thing as a secure line for international oil company executives.

Price was a major factor in any attempt to successfully negotiate a contract with the Egyptian Government, as it is with any customer. They were the biggest importers in the country. However, when negotiating with them, you were faced with having your customer 'reading your mail'. They were also 'listening' to your telephone conversations when you were making recommendations to New York as to what level of price and what terms you felt were necessary to obtain the government's business. 'Internal security was tightened during the summer of 1956. Egyptians were advised to avoid "certain" foreigners, members of the foreign community became accustomed to the whirl of a tape recorder as they telephoned'[27].

As with the attractive visits to Alexandria to attend the board meetings, the airline trips to Beirut, Lebanon to make a telephone call and to post the written material that you had no desire for the Egyptian authorities to be reading, were even more delightful; The St.George Hotel on the water front in Beirut with dinner in the Grill Room, The Elephant Noir Night Club at the end of the day, visits to Baalbeck to view the fabulous Roman ruins up in the hills (if you were astute enough to time your telephone call so that it coincided with a weekend), all at company expense.

It was hardly an unbearable price to have to pay to make a telephone call or to post the mail. Perhaps not for the employee, but while New York never questioned the cost of the telephone calls, there must have been many an eyebrow raised at the towering cost of 'communications' of the Cairo Office. Communication costs that included airline tickets to and from The Lebanon, hotel accommodations for at least two nights and days and all the meals and entertainment necessary to sustain the telephone caller. The actual cost that the telephone company in Beirut charged was insignificant compared to the logistical expenditure of getting into position to make the call.

Visits to the Pyramids, to Alexandria, to Beirut, to the desert at mid-night galloping wildly over the sand dunes, to the Cairo museum, which housed the majority of Ramasee's gold relics from his tomb were, unquestionably, experiences of a lifetime. The assignment was beginning to resemble all the advance billing which THE COMPANY had portended.

10

'A Contradiction of Terms'—1956

"He did.... what?", I sputtered.

"He nationalized *the* canal", Harry forcefully repeated for my benefit on the telephone. "Get over to the office immediately! No! On second thought come over to the house. We can talk better here without any of the office staff overhearing us. I'll call Bill and Hank and have them join us."

I had been preparing for a trip to Suez and hadn't intended to go into the office that morning. Neither had I been listening to the radio, inasmuch as I didn't want to disturb the nanny and the baby at that hour of the morning. Nonetheless, I finished packing my belongings in the car. I was under the mistaken impression that after the meeting I would leave to proceed on my way to Suez, although, slightly later than planned. On arrival at Harry Bernard's apartment, I found the other two American members of the staff already settling down and enjoying their second morning cup of coffee which the houseboy immediately offered to me as I entered.

Harry was pacing restlessly back and forth holding his coffee at arms length as he aired his private views about Gamal Abdul Nasser's decision to nationalize The Suez Canal. Clearly a canal that didn't belong to Egypt. At least the French and the British didn't believe it belonged to Egypt and which they believed Nasser had no legal right to take the action that he did. The first indication that surfaced in regard as to how serious Harry viewed the situation were his instructions to me to cancel my trip to Suez. He then informed Bill and Hank that if they had any plans to leave the city, they too were to postpone them indefinitely.

"I've already talked to the American Ambassador," Harry informed us, "but, naturally, it is too early for him to have had any reaction from Washington. The time zone difference hasn't allowed any meetings to be held yet or any press releases to be made. The French and the British haven't made any statements either other than that they are looking into the situation."

He continued with his instructions on the modus operandi that was to be followed at once. Every attempt should be made not to alarm the wives. However, they should be careful not to make any unnecessary trips to the market and to avoid crowds of any kind. Passports were to be kept physically on their and our persons at all times. All automobiles were to be brought up to top operating condition immediately. Tires checked and replaced where any doubt appeared to exist as to their reliability. My mind suddenly snapped to attention. What was the 'once in a lifetime' situation in Ceylon that I had envisaged not so long when my wife's car was bought up to perfect running condition, the tires replaced, and the car provisioned?

It is a blessing that we are not endowed with the knowledge of what lies in store for us. My wife was pregnant and we were expecting our second child to be born in Cairo. Little did I realize that not only was he not going to be born in Cairo, but he would be six months old before I saw him for the first time. There was no intention to provision the cars at this time. The only requirement was to put them in top mechanical condition.

When our first daughter was born, my wife was rather skeptical about my insistence that she be provided with her own passport, as were our other three children at a later date when they were born, instead of being carried on her passport. To a parent there is no situation on earth that can be envisaged, where they would send off their offspring without the guidance and physical presence of themselves.

The meeting of the children of the holocaust is a heart rending reminder of the fact that there are real life situations when that decision has to be made. We were never faced with any such soul searching determination as to having to put the children on some available transportation which was only sufficient for them with no room for their mother. There came a time, notwithstanding, when my wife agreed that it was comforting to know that they all possessed their own passports. If worse came to worse, there was a possibility that the children could be gotten out of the country in which we were then presently resident even if there were insufficient room for their mother on the same means of transportation.

Experience is a wonderfully, leveling phenomenon as everyone is well aware. My previous Managing Director, Phil Sanders and his wife, having spent their honeymoon and the early years of their marriage in a prisoner of war camp, gave no thought to the fact that he might ask an employee to risk his life for THE COMPANY in pursuit of his duties. This Manager in Cairo had a different philosophy. He had waited in the United States three years before he was able to marry the woman of his choice.

He was returning to his post with THE COMPANY in China after his home leave. He had set sail from San Francisco late on a beautiful, star lit night on a Saturday evening on his way to Shanghai where his intended was living with her mother and father. She was a long time resident of China, the daughter of missionary parents. She had been born in that vast and highly over-populated country. Twenty-four hours after the commencement of the voyage from San Francisco, the vessel, on which Harry Bernard was traveling, made an abrupt about face and sailed back into its port of departure.

He had sailed from San Francisco on Saturday night the 6th of December 1941.

Three long years later, his fiancée was released from internment as part of a negotiated prisoner of war exchange arrangement with the Japanese. She was taken back to the United States where the marriage ceremony was held, albeit, three years late.

He was determined that there would never be a repeat of that experience for her. Nor for any of the other wives or children if there were even the slightest indication that the crisis would erupt into a situation that might cause any of the families to lose their liberty. Not only lose their liberty, but his wife would face the consequences of another prison term and in the case of the other wives and children, an initial incarceration. All indications in his assessment were that the situation was going to explode violently and the women and children were to be sent home immediately.

Bookings were made for air passage for the three company wives, the managers' two children and my daughter. Cairo was a natural transportation hub and stop over point between the West and the Far East. At the best of times to obtain passage out of Cairo on short notice was next to impossible. The earliest bookings that could be obtained were fifteen days hence. Being in the oil business has its responsibilities, but to reverse the old United States Navy maxim, it has its privileges as well. Privileges, that were particularly welcome when part of your business involved the supplying of aviation fuel to the American international air carriers with the resultant close contact with their management. When it became apparent that departure from Cairo was going to be delayed longer than Harry desired, considerable pressure was put on TWA's directors to make additional flights available. TWA, recognizing the public relations value of unexpectedly filling one of their large aircraft completely with evacuees, decided that they would divert a flight from another route. We were the first to be made aware of their decision. The bookings were moved up from a fifteen day delayed departure to only a four day wait.

Twenty-four hours before the families departure, an announcement was made that Gamal Abdul Nasser was going to make a major policy speech at the Town Hall in Cairo. Unfortunately, the speech was to take place in the afternoon prior to the late night departure of TWA's special flight that had been arranged. The Town Hall was located between the airport and the residential areas where all of the company staff lived. All signs suggested that the speech would be a rabble rousing, political harangue against the Western Powers.

Western powers that were now beginning to make ominous sounds that indicated that no 'WOG' was going to trample on the legitimate rights of the world's greatest colonizers. What gave all of us chills, that is all of us who had rubbed shoulders with that vast community of experts and long time colonial residents of the various European empires, was Anthony Eden's statement to Parliament in London. He announced that there was no cause for alarm. He had had considerable experience through out the far flung empire of Great Britain, and in particular the Middle East, where his expertise was unrivaled. He knew precisely how to handle this delicate and distressing situation.

BASH THEM!

That was how any WOG, who had had the insufferable temerity to question the rule of the white man, was handled in the days of the empire builders. As soon as Anthony Eden referred to his experience in this part of the world, experience which was gained under the old empire rulers, we knew with a certainty that that was exactly what he intended to do.

BASH THEM! But when? And how?

There were twenty fours left before departure of the families. Nasser was going to gather a crowd of tens of thousands of excitable listeners. Listeners in whom he was going to instill inflammatory, emotional hate for the Westerners in order to prepare them for any eventuality that the great powers had in store for them. Town Hall was directly in the path of the way to the airport. When the time came to depart, it was highly likely that it would be physically impossible, at best, to transit the area because of the crowds. At worst, the crowds might seize the opportunity to wreak their revenge on the first available Europeans on which they could lay their hands, as the families attempted to pass through the area en route to the airport.

Harry ordered immediate hotel arrangements to be made to accommodate all the families in Heliopolis, a district well past the Town Hall and in close proximity to the airport. The evening before the scheduled departure of TWA's special section for the United States, all the families and their baggage were assembled and a leisurely departure was made for the hotel.

The arrival was timed to enjoy a delightful dinner in the three star restaurant for which the hotel was famous. A good night's sleep, a relaxing day lounging around the swimming pool and the radio turned on to listen to the 'rabble rouser'. With the move to the hotel, some of the tenseness which had been gathering momentum in the men, as well as the women, had begun to evaporate. With the commencement of the speech and the approaching time for departure, the tenseness began to reappear. By the time of arrival at the airport all concerned were on the thin edge of emotional explosiveness.

There were many restrictions under which residents of Egypt, both citizens and non-citizens, were forced to endure. One of these rules was designed to prevent the exodus of foreign currency and precious metals. The rule merely stated that upon entering Egypt, travelers had to declare all currency above a minimum amount that they had in their possession. They, also, had to declare all valuables that they were importing and intended for their own personal use, such as Sterling Silverware, gold jewelry and any similar items that had precious metal as part of their contents. When the luggage was being searched on departure, the original list was compared with the contents the travelers were taking with them. If all the items were shown as being imported by them on their arrival, there was no problem evidenced by the customs officials. Whereas the edict was in effect, it was difficult to find any place where it was published. In addition, in many cases, it had become operative after the entry of the individual concerned.

In Hank's case and after my short experience with some of his office lapses, one of which at a later date was to be a most embarrassing predicament involving millions of dollars, I took the very uncharitable view that he had failed to observe this particular requirement when he initially arrived in Cairo. His wife's reactions when her luggage was about to be searched at the airport merely served to confirm my suspicions. As the search of her luggage continued, she started to become extremely, emotionally disturbed. A disturbance which eventually culminated in an out-right burst of hysterical crying. By now, I was convinced that not only had Hank conveniently ignored the required recording of the valuables and currency he brought into the country, but he undoubtedly was 'exporting' something of considerable value in her suitcases. Her hysterical crying so unnerved the custom officials that they actually ceased searching her baggage.

Her luggage had been the first of the company's wives to be searched. There had never been such an intensive search made at any time of any European's belongings prior to this departure. It was almost midnight. The temperature was hovering around ninety-five degrees Fahrenheit with the proper attendant humidity of one hundred percent. The ten PM departure had already been delayed almost two hours by the custom officials' sudden adherence to their duties. Duties which they had never performed before except very perfunctorily. My wife in her pregnant condition was physically and emotionally exhausted. The perspiration was pouring off her face as if she had been caught in a sudden monsoon shower.

Had Hank anticipated this unexpected change in the custom officers' attitude, he would never have attempted to smuggle out what ever it was he had sequestered in his wife's baggage. For that matter neither would I have asked my wife to pack the current 'mail' in her valises. Mail that couldn't be posted in Egypt and which she was taking with her to New York for delivery to the office.

We had already been made aware of the translation of Nasser's speech. It was highly inflammatory and directed against the European powers. The custom officers were taking their cue from their leader's speech. They were going to make life as difficult as possible for all Europeans. Normally they were extremely polite and deferential. That evening they were rude and arrogant. They deliberately used every tactic in the book to delay the departure of the plane. To the Egyptian if you were 'white' you were European. They didn't differentiate between 'white' Europeans and 'white' Americans.

Under normal circumstances, the visitors bidding farewell to their friends and relatives had been allowed to accompany them to the exiting gate to the airfield. In many instances, where there was considerable baggage to be carried on board, the visitors were allowed to assist the departing passenger right up to the ramp of the aircraft. In the case of pregnant women, this actually included entering the plane and assisting them to get settled into place.

Not so in this atmosphere. We had all been brusquely and physically restrained from accompanying the wives into the custom's area. My wife's baggage was next in line to be searched. In our case, the regulation concerning valuables and currency had never been made known to us. It was of no consequence. There was nothing in the luggage that would arouse the interest of the custom officials.

The custom officials.... no! But definitely something of interest to the two nondescript individuals who, apparently, were merely lounging around the custom counter with a profound and noticeable attitude of studied indifference.

The studied indifference of certain individuals observed by the causal traveler is exactly what registers on the tourist's mind. Indifference. There is never a second glance made in the direction of such individuals by the 'innocent' traveler abroad. To those of us who are constantly on the alert, because we can not safely pass the rigorous search made by such onlookers, 'studied indifference' is exactly what registers on our minds as well. But with entirely different implications, as we view the very distinct, unnatural stance of anyone connected with the secret police of the country in which we are resident.

'They had become very common sights on the streets of Cairo, the CID (Criminal Investigation Department) man in his small black car and the 'gal-abiyaed' lollers with their well-polished shoes'[28]. They were becoming increasingly easy to identify, particularly for those of us who had cause to be extremely concerned about their surveillance.

The extraordinary and unusual, hysterical outburst of crying by a women passenger riveted all eyes in the surrounding area on the unfortunate victim. With the attention of every person focused on the disturbance, my wife immediately took the opportunity to surreptitiously remove all the folders of mail from her baggage. Mail which had been very carefully hidden by layering it between her lingerie. Items that a custom inspector, particularly an Egyptian inspector, would hesitate to disturb if the usual perfunctory search were to be made.

As the examination of the baggage of Hank's wife had been progressing, I never took my eyes off my wife. I was well aware that she had been making every effort to remain calm and at the same time had been attempting to find some method by which the mail could be retrieved and returned to me. She now had the mail thanks to the disturbance created by Hank's wife. Her next move was to return it to me. There would have been no reason not to destroy it if that had been possible. But, understandably, in full view of the customs' officers and the two nondescript individuals, such action would have resulted in their apprehending her immediately.

As I watched her in fascination, the fascination of someone locked onto the hypnotic and deadly fixed stare of a cobra, she placed the folders of mail between her body and the baby in her arms. The baby, soaking with perspiration and exhausted by the unnatural break in her normal routine of retiring to her crib at six-thirty PM for her night's repose, had collapsed into a total sleep of unconsciousness.

While my wife stood there stoically enduring the rough and arrogant search made of her luggage, she kept propping our daughter up in her arms and repeatedly appearing to try to wake her up so that she would be able to acknowledge a farewell from her father. Immediately prior to the completion of the search of her luggage and with the attention of the customs' agents and the two nondescript characters waning, she suddenly moved in my direction with the obvious intent of my kissing her and my daughter a finale farewell. As she leaned across the barrier, she released the pressure on the folders of mail by holding up our daughter for her goodbye wishes. As I kissed my wife, I was able to retrieve the mail from her person and slip it inside my shirt with none of the onlookers any the wiser. As she told me the next time that we were finally able to talk privately, her nerves were in such a state of chaos that it was quite a few hours into the flight before she could allow herself to relax.

TWA had generated tremendously, good customer relations by making the special flight available. They had been able to get all the women and children of the various international enterprises out of Cairo who wanted to depart, rightly or wrongly, before any break occurred in the relationships of the Western Powers and Egypt. These good customer relations evaporated immediately on the following morning twenty-four hours after arrival in Paris. There had been an announcement made, while en route to Paris, that there would be a one day stop over in Paris. The flight was unscheduled and, therefore, had to wait for a New York connection.

The station manager of TWA telephoned my wife at the hotel the morning of departure to advise her that it was not possible to accommodate her and the baby on the connecting flight to New York. It appeared that some members of the Rockefeller family had suddenly decided to return to New York from Paris and her seat had been allocated to one of them. It was possible for her companion, Hank's wife and her French Poodle, to continue on to New York. Her seat and the poodle's had been confirmed as had Harry's wife's and their two children.

Hank had always claimed that the dog belonged to his wife, and he had no responsibility for it inasmuch as it was a very badly behaved animal. It was a Standard size poodle. Those familiar with the breed are aware that Standard is the very largest strain of the poodle family. In fact, it was so large that TWA had had to allocate a seat to it as the special section was not equipped to carry live cargo in the hold. Since our daughter was an infant under the ticketing arrangements of TWA, she was not old enough to qualify for a seat. My wife had to hold her in her arms during the entire flight from Cairo to Paris, while the French Poodle stretched out his full length and enjoyed his sleep the whole journey.

To be told by the TWA station manager that her seat was not available, while that of her companion's and her companion's French Poodle's were, was not the information to convey to a pregnant woman. A pregnant woman holding another infant in her arms who had to all intents and purposes just been evacuated from a potential war zone.

She calmly informed the station manager that it was not her place to tell the member of the Rockefeller family that it was not possible to have the seat available. She intended to proceed to the airport and board the plane to New York. It was plain that one of the members of the Rockefeller family would have to remain behind. The station manager repeated his advice that it was useless for her to go to the airport. She would be unable to board the plane. This man, very obviously, hadn't dealt with pregnant women who have just been evacuated and watched French Poodles sleeping soundly while she held a cranky infant in her arms all the way from Cairo to Paris.

She thanked him graciously, and said she would look forward to seeing him at the airport since she was just in the process of departing from the hotel. As she winged her way over the Atlantic on the way to New York, she was never advised the name of the other passenger on the connecting flight, who was finally informed by TWA that his seat had been allocated to a member of the Rockefeller family.

Similar to the oft paraphrased statement, 'If your so smart, why aren't you rich?', we in THE COMPANY often found ourselves wondering, 'If you're Chairman of the Board, why aren't you so smart?'

After seeing the TWA evacuation plane roll down the runway and take off, all the onlookers breathed a sigh of relief and headed home for some sleep, at least some sleep for what was left of the night. In spite of very little rest, the 'dedicated' American staff of THE COMPANY were at their desks early the next morning. Maybe we should have lingered a little longer in bed. At least that would have delayed having to read the first cable laid on our desks from the New York office:

"IN VIEW OF THE EXTREMELY UNCERTAIN CIRCUMSTANCES NOW FACING YOUR OPERATIONS IN EGYPT IT WILL BE NECESSARY TO CANCEL ALL SALARY INCREASES THAT HAVE NOT BEEN ALREADY IMPLEMENTED. ALL PROMOTIONS WILL BE DELAYED INDEFINITELY AS WELL. signed: CHAIRMAN OF THE BOARD"

This is the wisdom exhibited by what is suppose to be the most exorbitantly paid segment of the commercial world? We were not unique in that we thought we were the only field staff to hold those feelings. Over fifty years ago, the Burmah Oil Company geologists '...in the barren hills of Masjid-Sulaiman ... cursed more freely, as is the custom and privilege of the man in the field when confronted with unintelligible and apparently insane decisions by the general staff at home'[29]

Further to this non-existent wisdom shown by a highly paid CEO, we, who are literally on the 'firing line' of international survival, often similarly cringe in abject horror as to what 'intelligence' is going to be exhibited by the members of the State Department or the military. The very ones who are responsible for the well being of the United States, and particularly in our case, its citizens abroad.

I was out of my chair in an instant and on my way to Harry's office with a copy of the cable in my hand when we collided in the corridor. His reaction had been identical to mine, as was evident by the manner in which he was waving the offending cable in front of him and headed in the direction of my office.

Within minutes after settling down in his office, we had summed up our response to this preposterous situation that our all knowing mentors in New York had placed us. In essence, although we couched our objections in as diplomatic terms as possible, our position was made plain in two very simple and concise scenarios.

There were only two possible options open to THE COMPANY:

THE COMPANY would stay in business in Egypt, or
THE COMPANY would go out of business in Egypt.

Based on these only two possible alternatives for THE COMPANY to follow, what knowledgeable and experienced staff would have to be available to implement either of these choices? Who would ensure that the company's best interests would be looked after in the event that THE COMPANY decided to liquidate its assets and go out of business? And who would promote the interests of THE COMPANY if the decision were made to stay in business in Egypt?

It didn't take very long to draft up our reply to the inane circumstances in which the cable had put us. Every member of the staff had been supplied with a copy by their loyal colleagues in the cable department. At first, it was our intention to reply by letter. After realizing that all of the office staff had been instantly made aware of the contents of the cable, we were quick to realize that a cable would be the best method of damage control response that we could make. Our reply was simple and direct as possible:

A) If you intend to have us go out of business, we desperately need every man and women on the staff to help liquid the assets of THE COMPANY in the most efficient way possible.

B) If you intend to have us stay in business, we desperately need every man and woman on the staff to help us maintain the market position of THE COMPANY in the years to come under what are, obviously, going to be the most trying and difficult circumstances imaginable.

C) If we cancel all salary increases and delay all pending promotions, our staff will immediately start looking for employment with other concerns in Cairo who seem to have a much more optimistic outlook of the future of the Egyptian economy than your office in New York has.

Which ever scenario was going to develop, THE COMPANY would need each and every person on the payroll at this time. By canceling salary increases that had yet to be implemented and promotions that were soon to be conferred on the most valuable and enterprising members of the staff, the Chairman would surely guarantee that we would get the worst of both worlds.

In all of our deliberations about how we would answer this piece of moronic and soul shattering stupidity, we had assumed that the instructions applied to the local Egyptian staff only and not to the American expatriates. At one point in our discussions, I queried Harry as to whether or not the same procedures were going to be applied to him and myself and the other two Americans in the office. Before he could answer my question, I went on to say that he should add a closing paragraph which, in essence, would state, 'If the instructions contained in your cable of today's date are to be applied to the members of the American staff, as well as to the Egyptian staff, we have only one comment to make; Just what the hell do you think you are doing?'

Although he had the exact same basic feelings as myself, he didn't get to be Manager by pointing out how stupid the New York office could be. Consequently, we wrote the cable with the understanding that the instructions applied to the Egyptian staff only.

The consistent practice of the Two Sisters had been to appoint the Chairmen of Caltex from their respective company boards to the board of their Step-Sister on a rotating basis. This particular Chairman, W.M.Pinchard, who had been appointed by the Eastern Sister, was just exhibiting the usual stupidity that very often emanates from these high offices, as well as the dogmatic and arrogant, iron fisted control which he had learned from his mentor, Gus Long. In addition, in typical Texaco fashion, he was just looking at the bottom line and thought he would save a few dollars on a short term basis at the expense of some very loyal employees.

What was very surprising was that this same penny pinching attitude was exhibited by his successor, who was shortly afterwards appointed by the Western

Sister. This Chairman from the Western Sister had had very little, if any, experience abroad. Local wars, evacuations, curfews, malaria, uprisings and a host of other every day occurrences that the American expatriate faced in those days were just something he read about at his leisure at his country club.

Nowhere was his attitude more manifest than when he decided that he would override the terms of compensation that the expatriates received. Terms which the expatriates had been told were the formula for their remuneration when they had been engaged by THE COMPANY.

Caltex had an excellent system for recognizing the differences in living and working conditions for the expatriate Americans and those Americans who commuted daily to the company's office at 350 Madison Avenue, New York. It was the expatriate Americans who toiled in offices in the tropics without air conditioning, lived in war torn territories and in politically unstable areas, exposed to sub-standard levels of medical care and schooling for their children and a host of other conditions that formed the base for their remuneration. The formula was simple. The basic salary of the international executive was the same as that of his fellow employee in the New York office who was handling the same responsibilities.

To compensate the expatriate for all those onerous conditions under which he had to labour, he received in addition to the equivalent salary of his fellow executive in New York, a free company house with all utilities paid, a 20% salary bonus and a company car. All of these extras were tax free. This particular Chairman, with no experience of service abroad in any of those many areas that had the conditions of daily existence with which the average international executive faced, looked at the 'bottom line' only of the expatriate's compensation. He couldn't understand why they were receiving, what he considered, exorbitant compensation for doing the same job that their fellow compatriots did in New York (Caltex Petroleum Corporation), or San Francisco (Chevron) or The Chrysler Building in New York (Texaco).

Although he wasn't particularly bright, he did recognize that to arbitrarily cancel or reduce some of these additional incentives for working in foreign territories would bring the attention of those concerned immediately to the forefront. He devised, instead, an underhanded system which was difficult to detect by the expatriates in the field and which was more the style of Texaco, rather than Chevron.

When the basic salaries of all of the state-side employees were increased to compensate for inflation and for the higher entry salaries of newer employees, he simply issued the edict that when those increases were awarded, none of the

American expatriates in the field were to receive them. Because of my continuous extended service abroad for twenty-two years without an assignment to New York, this action in my particular case amounted to three 5% salary adjustments, or a total of 15%, that was never received.

Some MBA could probably extrapolate to what the loss of these increases amounted when compounded over the years. In addition, not only were they lost and the compounding effect as well, but the loss was on the basic salary that was used for the calculation of retirement pensions and benefits.

If ever the dedication at the beginning of this thirty-four year saga of the international oil business to the individuals responsible for the writing of it were to pin point any one individual, it would be that Chairman from the Western Sister. The one who was responsible for the decision to unilaterally change the terms of employment of the expatriates of the Caltex Petroleum Corporation, mine in particular. To those of us who later became aware of what he done and who were affected by this underhanded method of reducing our remuneration, he became known as 'Willie, The Bastard'. His name had all the qualifying letters to spell out that loving term—William F.Bramsted.

The only redeeming feature that was of even the slightest satisfaction was that at a later date we heard that 'Willie, The Bastard' had been playing so much golf in Japan with our Japanese associates and, consequently, not paying too much attention to the needs of Caltex, that he was 'promoted' upstairs and transferred back to San Francisco to Chevron's headquarters, which was not the normal way that the Two Sisters' Chairmen exited from Caltex.

The customary practice with the rotating Chairman appointments was that the Caltex Chairman retired after serving his tour of duty with Caltex Petroleum Corporation. It is easy to understand the rousing cheers which could be heard 'around the world' in 1970 when a newly appointed chairman, by the name of James Milton Voss, was announced. Jim was *CALTEX*. He had joined THE COMPANY as a Caltex employee and worked his way up to that rarified position without the help of any service with our two owners.

It was now a number of months since the families had left Cairo. The Egyptian army officials were establishing themselves more and more firmly in all aspects of everyone's daily living, particularly those people in the oil business. The Army, under the guise of the Petroleum Ministry, had taken charge of the refinery in Alexandria. All the Europeans had been replaced.

The Egyptian Government was using the refinery tanks as storage for the products that they were systematically importing outside the contract they had with THE COMPANY. Because of our frequent trips to Alexandria, we became aware that the majority of the products being imported and stored at the refinery under Egyptian Government ownership came from the Russians. This was not surprising in that Mr. Dulles had cut the Egyptians off from United States support. The Russians were delighted to take over in this very sensitive area of the Middle East.

The office routine became just that. Routine. There was little that we could do. Everything was on a semi-war footing. Everyday articles became more and more scarce. There was plenty to eat, but some of the more exotic delicacies disappeared. With the families away and the cost of what Americans consider necessities skyrocketing, we were on a permanent expense account basis for our daily living. The expense account, also, covered our nightly forays to the Auberge des Pyramides as well as every other night club in Cairo. I wondered how it would be possible to put the cost of maintaining my polo ponies on the expense account. However, discretion being the better part of valor, I decided against that.

There was one miraculous break in the nerve deadening atmosphere of survival in this city in the land of the ancient Pharaohs. The telephone rang on my birthday, October 16th. The operator announced that there was a call from New York for R.Palmer-Smith. Was he available to take the call was her query?

How wonderful. My wife, with all her day to day duties of caring for our baby daughter on her own with no servants and pregnant as well, had remembered to call me on my birthday. Her tone of voice on the telephone told me immediately that it was much more marvelous news than just greetings on my birthday. We now had two celebrations to observe on the 16th of October. Jim, our son, had been born on my birthday just two hours prior to her call. It was an unbelievable experience to be talking to the mother of your first born son from Cairo, Egypt just two hours after he had been born in the New York Hospital, a half a world away from where you were living.

Jim and I still talk about that call and, even more importantly, why it was six months before I ever saw him. I tried to explain to him that I was a member of the 'war generation'. Those of us who had seen service to our country had given up many years of our lives in the process of defending our nation. At the moment, it appeared that we might just be embarking on another world-wide conflagration. Whatever contribution I had made to the previous war effort, it appeared to me that in the essential service of the oil industry that I would able to make an even greater contribution to my country than I had been able to make when I was in uniform. For this reason I never left my 'assigned duty station' to go and see my son and his mother whether I was in Cairo or Paris or Nairobi or

Ethiopia or Eritrea or Djibouti or British Somaliland or French Somaliland or
The Sudan.

It was surprising to find the US Naval Attaché a spectator at a mid-week polo
match. He had never evidenced the slightest interest in the game before. Surprising at first glance, but then my instincts told me almost simultaneously as I
glimpsed him that it was not just an innocent visit.

For a long period after our initial meeting in his office, we had been very selective whenever we held conversations that we did not want overheard or recorded.
These conversations were almost never held in his office or mine, at home or on
the telephone. They were invariably held at restaurants. But only at restaurants
that had no carpets on the floor and, in addition, the floors were laid in marble.
There was no way that a table in the middle of the room, on a marble floor, could
have been wired. In addition, one of us would always accidentally bump the table
moving it an inch or two off its set position. A surreptitious glance under the
table at the legs would confirm that there was no wire, even though we were sure
that the marble floor provided an almost one-hundred percent guarantee that it
couldn't be bugged.

The match ended and I returned to the sidelines on my pony. The Naval
Attaché had left the stands and was waiting for me with admiring glances directed
at my pony and very complimentary comments about the skill with which I and
my team had exhibited in defeating our opponents. Instantly, I realized that the
polo field presented an even more secure area than a restaurant in which to hold a
discussion. With ponies galloping madly all over the field and often entering the
sidelines, because their opponents had forced the defending team's pony off the
ball with a classic side maneuver, it was an impossibility that the field could have
been wired. Further more, the repeated flooding of the fields after every game to
abolish the divots effectively eliminated any chance that the ground could carry
any electronic devices.

The groom took my polo mallet and assisted me to dismount. He then took
the bridle and commenced walking the pony. After every chukka this was a most
important part of maintaining a polo pony in top condition. They were invariably dripping with sweat. There is no better way to lose a pony than to have it get
a chill and then colic and, then, you find yourself with a reduced string. As the
horse keeper moved away at a brisk pace, the Attaché took my arm in order to
ensure that I didn't walk too rapidly in the direction of the stables and the club
house showers.

His first question, in a lowered and guarded voice, was an inquiry as to whether I had been to Alexandria recently. Upon receiving confirmation that I had just returned a few days ago from a Board meeting there, he asked if there had been any change in the import program of the Ministry of Petroleum affairs. I knew from past questions of this kind that he was looking for confirmation that the Russians were still continuing their supply to the Egyptian Government. I nodded my head without saying anything, and he realized that no change had taken place since my last report to him.

Shortly after my arrival in Cairo, as should be the usual habit of all Americans taking up residence in a foreign country, I had gone to the American Embassy to register myself and my family. Even today, many years later in 1989, as a matter of habit I registered at the Embassy in Paris, although, it was then over forty-two years since I first registered at the Embassy in Beijing.

It was, fortunately, an early lesson learned in Beijing. If you hadn't registered, it might be possible that you wouldn't get an invitation to leave under the auspices of the United States Government, ably assisted by the United States Marines when the occasion arose. Within a matter of days after my registration at the Embassy in Cairo, I received an invitation from the US Naval Attaché to have coffee with him. I was no longer a stranger to the workings of Military Attaché's offices.

Over coffee, I explained to him that I had just arrived. It was doubtful if I could be of much assistance to him, but I was always willing to help if the occasion demanded it. He thanked me and confirmed that he was aware that I was a recent arrival as he had gotten my name from the registry at the Embassy. For some strange reason, he was also aware that I was a Naval Officer in the reserves. This no longer astounded me or caused me any great concern. I was becoming fully cognizant of how information of this type could be obtained or exchanged between like members of the same profession. I wouldn't have been at all surprised if the Naval Attaché in Madras (if they had one there) had called on me the very day I arrived if our destination hadn't been altered.

He acknowledged my recent arrival and said that under ordinary circumstances a new arrival couldn't be of much assistance to the Naval Attaché's office. However, in this instance the request was a very minor one. They simply wanted our statistics on the Egyptian Government's imports for comparison with information they had received from other sources. I said I would be glad to oblige. The information was made available to him at our frequent dinner meetings. Since obtaining this information was an ordinary part of any international oil executive's normal duties on the basis of competitive statistics, there was no additional risk or exposure involved caused by the Attaché's request. The only added risk appeared to be when making the information available to him.

We strolled leisurely towards the club house. Both of us were making a determined effort to stay on the playing part of the field where it would have been physically impossible to have installed any listening devices. After receiving my confirmation on the program of the Egyptian's Government's import program, he broached the real subject of the purpose of his visit to this very secure and impossible to bug area.

"We would very much like to have confirmation of the actual quality of the kerosene imported into the refinery in Alexandria," he stated. "From past experience with other countries over which the Russians have gained influence, it has been our experience that they sell them extremely inferior products at very high prices. In addition, they even have the audacity to make them pay in hard currency," he informed me. "This kind of information can be very helpful on a diplomatic basis, when you are trying to make these LDC's understand that their Russian sponsor, 'Big Brother', isn't really doing them any favours."

"But I have already confirmed to you that the last three tankers were standard lighting kerosene," I said. "Our informant has viewed the documents. There can be no mistake in the quality. He is a very capable individual. I can assure you of this as he was in our employ before the Ministry took over the administration of the refinery. I can vouch for him. Our Operations Manager, Bill Murdock, has absolute faith in him and his ability. If he noticed any lowering of quality in the specifications in the documents, he would have brought it to Bill's attention immediately," I insisted.

I was puzzled as to why he continued to query the validity of the information that I had given to him. "What do your other sources say?" I asked him.

"Same thing," was his reply, "but they don't have access to the actual product as you do. As a consequence, we would like you go to Alexandria and visit the refinery and obtain a sample of the most recent shipment received from Russia," was his earnest request. He left no doubt in my mind that he was serious and determined to have his way in this matter.

Again I futilely reiterated, "But our informant at the refinery has already confirmed that the last three tankers to unload at the refinery carried lighting kerosene. Your office has been supplied with this information on a current basis, cargo by cargo," I emphasized. Everyone in the Middle East, who was in power, knew that one way to keep the populace satisfied and under control was to be sure that there was an abundance of kerosene to heat and light their homes and to cook their food. And of even more importance, at very low prices. THE COM-

PANY had shipped many a cargo of lighting kerosene into Egypt based on this premise. As noted earlier, Gamal Abdul Nasser was a canny and astute ruler and well knew the importance of this product for his peasant populace.

"Be that as it may, we would like you to obtain a sample for us," he continued dogmatically in the same vein. "In addition, to avoid contamination of any kind, we will supply you with the sample container," he ended his very forceful demand. I reluctantly agreed that if he felt that strongly about obtaining a sample, arrangements would be undertaken to satisfy his request.

"Although, personally, I am quite willing to take the risk, I must emphasize that for me to go to the refinery on such an errand is out of the question. As Acting Manager, any visit made by me is complimented by having the Refinery Manager always in attendance. They will arrange a luncheon, as has always been the practice in the past, and it will be impossible for me to be out of their sight at any time. If you have no objection, I will ask my Operations Manager, Bill Murdock, to get the sample. I know from his personnel file that he is a member of the US Army Reserve and is absolutely trustworthy. As Operations Manager, he has much more flexibility than I could conceivably have and will be allowed considerably more freedom on the refinery grounds." He quickly realized the validity of my position and promptly agreed.

"How do you intend getting the sample container into my possession?" was the next logical question. It would not be possible for me to enter the Embassy grounds, visit the Naval Attaché's office and exit with a package. A package that would be the object of every eye of every member of the Egyptian government staff that had been detailed to keep the Embassy under twenty-four hour surveillance.

"When is your next match?" he enquired. On being informed that it was on the following Friday, he was, obviously, pleased that it fell on the Sabbath, and therefore there would be less reason to suspect his visit to view a game at that time.

At the end of the match on Friday, the Attaché was there with his sample container. It was all nicely boxed in cardboard and sealed. It is a common practice for spectators, who visit players on the field, to 'give them a hand' when returning to the club house. A polo player has any number of mallets, at least two helmets, knee caps and assorted gear with which he always welcomes some assistance. As pre-arranged, the Attaché picked up one of my helmets, several of my mallets and while on the way back to the club house deposited the sample box inside the helmet. At the club house we bid each other adieu and went our separate ways.

There had been no hesitation on Bill's part when I requested him to assist me in fulfilling the Attaché's request. However, he too queried the necessity, as it was his contact at the refinery that had been supplying us with the product names, the quantity and the quality of the imports of the Egyptian Government. Arrangements were made with Bill to receive the sample container at a 'neutral' point. I did not want to bring it home with me. Neither did I want to proceed directly from the club to his apartment with a package after visiting with the Attaché and leave without such an obvious article that had been in my possession on my arrival.

There was a British staff member from the Shell Company who was being transferred in a few days. I had promised to have a farewell drink with him. Bill knew him quite well, also, as they were both in the operations side of the business. Bill's apartment actually adjoined our colleague's, and the two buildings were connected by a dual purpose fire escape and servants' stair case.

They were both bachelors and lived on the upper floors of their respective buildings. Rather than descend to the ground floor, exit the adjoining building, enter and take the lift to the upper floor, they had developed the habit of crossing over from one building to the other via the servants' staircase. Therefore, it was no surprise to my host when shortly after my arrival, Bill entered his apartment from the kitchen.

To the casual visitor to a police state, who has no knowledge of how detailed the surveillance of foreigners is, such arrangements as Bill and I were making in order not to appear suspicious in any way would lead such visitor to believe that we had become paranoid. However, long before the international experts on terrorism had begun to garner their exorbitant fees for their advice on how to avoid being under the watchful eye of those who might intend to do them harm, those expatriates that had reason to protect themselves from such surveillance had instinctively established their own methods, just as Bill and I were doing in this instance. Today, everyone is familiar with those experts' advice—never take the same route to the office every day and never at the same time, never fall into habits that are predictable to those watching you, never, etc.

In those days in Cairo, 'surveillance was accomplished by the famous 'city eye' system which Nasser inherited from the previous regime and which has probably existed in Egypt for centuries. It is entirely unobtrusive. A CIA officer, formerly an FBI man, who had undergone the most sophisticated modern training in surveillance once went from one end of Cairo to the other and was prepared to swear that he had not been under surveillance for one moment, only to learn later from the smiling chief of security that every move he had made had been observed, every telephone call monitored, and every contact identified and recorded. The secret is simple: doormen, taxicab drivers, telephone operators, beggars, street vendors, and hordes of other people know that they may be rewarded by a few piasters should they be able to give helpful answers to some security officer coming by to ask questions about a foreigner who just passed. Such persons, who work the blocks around the best hotels and other places where foreigners congregate, have been rewarded so many times in the past that they have developed remarkable powers of observation and memories, together with an ability to spot details which security police most frequently ask about'[30].

During our friendly visit over drinks with our Shell host, Bill mentioned that another bachelor companion of his in the Shell company had also been suddenly transferred and was leaving in a few days. Neither our host or the other Shell staff member had been able to supply the names of their replacements or for that matter where their own next assignments were to be. A really unusual situation for an organization of the efficient reputation that Shell had.

The Shell Company was the operator of the pipeline that was owned by the Egyptian Government. Because of this and other mutual interests, we were anxious to learn the names of their replacements. We, naturally, intended to maintain a close working relationship with them. Knowing the way the Shell Company operated, we were very surprised that two of their key people were being transferred without having their replacements broken in by the experienced men on the spot.

Although 'comparisons are odious', I was soon to learn that Don and Citibank were not the only ones to take advantage of the use of funds for which they did not have to incur any cost. Even more to the point, Don was an amateur when compared to that urbane, worldwide organization of what they would like people to believe is an extension of the Foreign office, The Shell Oil Company. I was, also, very disagreeably surprised to learn that Caltex was one of those who enjoyed part of that same advantage of the use of funds for which there was no cost incurred. Not disagreeable in the fact that THE COMPANY was enjoying it, but disagreeable in the way the knowledge was made known to me.

In all fairness to Shell, their use of $29,000,000.00 of the Egyptian Government's money averaged over a period of several years for which there was no cost involved did not entirely accrue to their benefit, although the majority of it did because they were, as usual in past British dominated countries, the biggest marketers. It represented unpaid bills for the thru put fees for product which had been transported through the Egyptian Government owned pipeline by the industry. The amount was prorated to all the companies that used the pipeline that Shell operated on behalf of the Egyptian Government. Unlike Citibank, however, there was a day of reckoning for the oil companies, who collectively owed the Egyptian Government the overdue throughput fees of $29,000,000.00.

Hank knocked on my door, as he was leaving the office, to advise me that he was on his way to the Shell office for a meeting in connection with the Government owned pipeline. I barely looked up from my desk to acknowledge his comment. His duties frequently required his attending meetings at The Shell Company office for the purpose of product transfer through the pipeline and his informing me of his leaving was just normal, office protocol.

That was the last known communication that I received from Hank on the subject of product transfers through the pipeline, until the Chief Accountant also knocked on my door several days later. It was the Saturday morning after Hank had attended the meeting at Shell.

The Chief Accountant asked me if I had any knowledge of an amount of $6,000,000.00 that was owed to Shell by THE COMPANY. My reply was that I didn't know. My tone of voice left him with the inference that that was a matter for his attention. I had other duties more pressing at the moment. Nonetheless, he continued in a puzzled voice by saying that the Shell Company appeared to be very insistent that the amount was due and payable immediately.

"What's it for?" I impatiently enquired.

"They say it is the accumulated, overdue amounts owed to the Egyptian Government over the past three and a half years for product transfer through the pipeline. They further insist that we are well aware of the charges. It was agreed at the last industry meeting that Shell would make the payment on behalf of industry, and each member of industry would reimburse Shell the very same day.

"Well, get hold of Hank. He went to a meeting this week I seem to remember. He should know about it." The next knock on the door revealed both Hank and the Chief Accountant standing in the doorway. Hank with a very sheepish look on his face and the Chief Accountant with considerable alarm on his.

Hank acknowledged that Shell had advised all the participants at the meeting during the week that apparently there had been a change of management staff at the Egyptian's Government's accounting office. The new manager was a Lt. Colonel from the supply department of the army. He was very much more knowledgeable than the Colonel, a tank commander, who had held the job previously. The Lt. Colonel from the supply department had immediately recognized that Shell had not made payment of the throughput fees on a current basis. In fact, Shell had allegedly avoided paying them for a number of years.

An overdue amount of $29,000,000.00 for which no cost or penalty was incurred. Even if it were spread over a number of recipients and averaged out over a number of years, it made Don's $7,000,000.00 look puny by comparison.

I eyed Hank suspiciously. "What happened?" I demanded. "Do we owe them the money?" He again acknowledged that he had confirmed the volume of the amount of product thru put by Caltex. Although Shell didn't have the exact total amount of money due by each member of industry at the time of the meeting, they were going to make the calculation and advise each member of the industry. He ended his explanation with the comment that it appeared that we owed them the amount of $6,000,000.00, and that he had agreed, along with the rest of industry, to make payment to Shell immediately they advised us of the amount due.

"Why didn't you tell the accounting office?" I demanded again in an accusing tone of voice. He had to confess that he had stopped off for a drink with several of his conferees from the meeting, which had apparently turned into more than one drink, and he had not come back to the office. Consequently, the next morning he had completely forgotten the matter and did not report the overdue amounts to the accounting office. Even more importantly, he failed to inform the Chief Accountant that payment would have to be made immediately after Shell had calculated the finale figure, paid the Egyptian Government on behalf of industry and notified us of our share.

I hated to have THE COMPANY in such an embarrassing position, particularly, where it involved The Shell Company. I turned to the Chief Accountant and said, "It looks like we have no alternative but to make the payment immediately. Go ahead. I'll sign the papers." Now the alarm on the Chief Accountant's face began to register more than it had when he had first entered my office with Hank.

"When Hank gave me the details, I felt sure that you would agree that we had no choice. Because of our overdraft position, I took the liberty of forewarning Barclays that you would be drawing a check in the amount of $6,000,000.00. They said that as much as they would like to accommodate us it just wasn't possible."

My immediate reaction was to reach for the telephone. When the manager in charge of the company's account at Barclays answered the phone, I indigently asked him what was this nonsense that my Chief Accountant had informed me about them not being able to accommodate us for an amount of $6,000,000.00.

"If it means that we will go over our $50,000,000.00 overdraft limit, just draw up the papers for an increase in the limit and I'll have them formalized when Mr. Bernard gets back from New York," I instructed him.

"No, sir," was his answer, "that is not the problem. As a matter of fact, you are already, unofficially, $17,000,000.00 over your $50,000,000.00 limit at this time. Your overdraft stands at $67,000,000.00. The $6,000,000.00 normally wouldn't make any difference, but frankly we just don't have the money at the moment. We simply can't make it available."

All my life, every minute of the thirty-five years of it, if you were to count every minute from the day that I was born, I had laboured under the illusion that banks had all the money in the world. To be told that a bank could run out of money was an even greater, psychological shock than when I learned that there was no Santa Claus and no Tooth Fairy.

As a child, I had only carried those illusions for a short time. I was much more resistant to calamities of that nature as a youngster, and over the years I recovered slowly. But to have carried an illusion for thirty-five years and to learn at this late date in life that a bank could run out of money was soul shattering. It was like hearing that one of the world's vast oceans had run out of water. It was unheard of. It left me with a strange, unnatural, eerie feeling.

In a much more, subdued voice, I again asked if I had understood him correctly: That he couldn't possibly make the money available under any conditions. He very regretfully informed me that he was sorry indeed, but that was the case. I thanked him and hung up the phone.

Now, I thought to myself, 'I can accommodate you my good friend Don Hykies of Citibank. You wanted some of our business? Well, I'm pleased to inform you that you have it'.

"Good morning Don. Have you heard from the family?", I queried him on the telephone. "How are they? Great. By the way, I've got good news for you. There's an opportunity for which you have been looking for a long time. We need a facility in the amount of $6,000,000.00 in equivalent Egyptian pounds. I have no doubt that we'll be able to keep the line on a permanent basis and maybe even increase it in the near future."

Total silence.

I felt compelled to carry on and enlighten him as to why we needed the overdraft. "Apparently, Barclays is in the embarrassing position of having run out of money. How is that possible Don? I never heard of such a situation in my life." His explanation was as much of a blow to me as the initial advice from Barclays that a bank could run out of money.

"I can imagine that they're down to their reserve requirements. In fact, knowing how we all operate here, I'm sure they're well below it. That is why they can't accommodate you. Ordinarily, you wouldn't even be aware of their problems. In order to increase their reserves to cover your needs, they would have to transfer the money from London. No bank represented in Egypt is willing to do that under the circumstances under which we are operating now, particularly, with Egypt's foreign reserves completely frozen by the West. No head office would authorize its local branch to increase its reserves until this canal situation is settled."

The Western Big Three had reacted violently to Nasser's nationalization of the canal and the initial response of Britain, France, and the United States was to apply economic pressure against Egypt by freezing Egyptian assets in their countries.[31] When Nasser drove to Alexandria's Midan Gomhouria to make his "nationalization" speech he referred to the action taken by The Big Three, "..... one hundred million pounds is blocked by the Bank of England? Maalish. The Canal is ours and we will keep it'"[32].

Why was that sinking feeling in the pit of my stomach beginning to manifest itself? Did I know the answer to my next question? "And you Don? You're in the same position?" was my query. The regret in his voice was almost physically transmitted over the telephone as he probably thought of all those extravagant dinners he had put on his expense account for me and my wife in anticipation of being able to justify them at some later date in the future.

"Yes. I'm sorry, but we're in the same position as Barclays. But keep in touch, maybe we can do something when this whole mess is over," he encouragingly ended his depressing sum up of Citibank's dilemma. "By the way," he suddenly added, "Why don't you try the French banks? They operate a little more loosely than the British and the Americans. Maybe they can make the facility available on a short term basis. Good luck." And good luck to you my friendly Citibank manager. If ever that old saying about 'banks are always willing to lend you an umbrella when it isn't raining' had real validity, it certainly appeared to be the case at the moment.

Then began a marathon of calls to Paris after talking to the local branches of the French banks. We even tried Barclay's in London on our own initiative. They were all very polite even when we could get an answer on a Saturday morning. But they all had the same story. It was Saturday. There was no one with authority who could approve such a request. One did say they would try to contact one of their directors and would call back as soon as possible. In the meantime, I had issued instructions to the telephone operator and my secretary that I would not take any calls from Shell until further notice.

While I was sitting there dazed by the events that had made the morning another monument to the 'life of ease and comfort' of an international oil executive's daily routine, the telephone rang. In my desperation, before the echo of the first ring had died away, I mistakenly grabbed the phone in anticipation and hope that it was Paris returning my call.

To this day, I can hear those reserved, but sharp and pointed tones of the Shell manager's voice, "Palmer-Smith, these stalling tactics are entirely unjustified. You will have that money in my office before noon today."

I didn't know what his problems were, but he certainly was making mine impossible to bear. In hopeless resignation, I called Barclays again. I explained to them that I had explored every avenue, but to no avail. I, actually, admitted that I had tried their head office in London on my own initiative. I even confessed that the situation was doubly embarrassing, because we owed the money to Shell, and that I hated THE COMPANY to be in debt to any organization, but even more so to that one in particular.

"Shell? You owe the money to The Shell Company?" was his extremely surprised and almost incredulous response to my information. "Why didn't you say so when you first called?" He continued in what even to my desperate ears sounded like a tone of relief. "It is because Shell drew a check on us for $29,000,000.00 payable to the Egyptian Government this morning that we couldn't accommodate you. Your $6,000,000.00 payment to them is only an off setting transaction. It just entails us doing the paperwork. There is no other requirement involved. By all means, go ahead with your payment. We'll take care of it when it reaches our office. In the meantime that will increase your overdraft to $73,000,000.00. Under the circumstances," he continued politely, "and as suggested by you earlier, perhaps when Mr. Bernard gets back from New York you will be so kind as to formalize your new overdraft limits. I'll have the papers prepared early next week and sent around for the necessary signatures."

So I was wrong again. There is a Santa Claus and a Tooth fairy.

It is not re-inventing the wheel to say that there is no doubt that training and experience are invaluable tools in whatever profession or job in which an individual labours. I was neither trained or experienced in any other profession than my own, plus the military a number of years ago during the war.

Two of the Barclays Bank British assistant managers that were associated with handling the company's account had been transferred also, as well as the two

Shell staff members. No mention of who their replacements were going to be was given by Barclays either. Since THE COMPANY was the client in this case, I didn't press the matter. Let them come looking for me. The fees we paid them warranted my attitude. At least in my opinion, it did.

Had I been trained in the diplomatic field would have I questioned this rather, extremely, unusual coincidence? An unusual coincidence of two very large British corporations that were transferring people and not bringing in their replacements prior to the respective incumbents transfer? Maybe not. Had I been trained in the military would I have questioned it? Apparently not, since I had been trained in the military and didn't question it. Neither did the Naval Attaché, but in all fairness to him, he wasn't in constant contact with the Shell Company or with Barclays as I was.

To this day, I can't remember any French national on our agent's staff being transferred at this time. Of course, there was always the likelihood that it may have been common practice for the French to transfer their employees without the necessity of having their replacements in place prior to the incumbents transfer. Or maybe they just didn't care, and so they transferred anyone with or without a replacement.

Had I been trained in the intelligence service would I have made any connection with this unusual occurrence or come to any conclusions because of it? I think I would have. But, then, if I were in the intelligence service, would I have been in constant contact with the Shell Company or with Barclays or with the company's French agents? Perhaps not. Even so, how was it possible, as we learned later, that the Shell Company reduced its British staff from two hundred and thirty members to twenty seven and I didn't notice; the US Embassy didn't notice; the Naval Attaché's office didn't notice, and what ever other intelligence network the United States Government had in place in Cairo didn't notice either.

The fact that they didn't notice is the only conclusion to which I can come. A conclusion based on the rather bitter and un-diplomatic remarks made by President Eisenhower directed at the British Government and the French Government at a not too distant later date. He, also, included the Israelis for good measure. As was confirmed later, 'it appears that not only President Eisenhower, but Secretary Dulles as well, felt a sense of outrage because Eden and Mollet had not bothered to consult them on a matter as important as military action in the Middle East'[33].

After being honest enough to admit that two companies with whom I was in constant contact reduced their staff by major proportions and I didn't notice, perhaps a presumptive question could be asked.

'Were the respective staffs of the British and the French embassies also reduced' (the Israelis, obviously, didn't have an embassy in Cairo)? If they were reduced, were our diplomats as unobserving as I was and didn't notice? Then again, maybe diplomats having diplomatic immunity can be expected to be treated on a different basis if a war erupts. Therefore, they don't transfer their staff, but that is not a valid assumption as there is documentary evidence to the contrary.

When the Caltex wives and children were sent out of Egypt immediately after the nationalization of the canal, not a single diplomat's wife or any of their dependents were on that plane. This presented a tremendous, logistical problem at a not too much later date for the embassies in Cairo.

Maybe the staff of the British and French Embassies weren't reduced. Maybe they were, and our diplomats didn't notice, just I as I didn't notice the Shell Company's and Barclay's reductions. Or maybe they weren't reduced, because wives and dependents are pawns used by some powers in the world game of diplomacy and war.

'Don't alert the Egyptians by sending diplomats' wives and dependents out of the country. Keep a stiff upper lip. C'est la vie!'

After finishing my drink, I took my leave and wished my Shell colleague and host good luck in his new assignment, where ever it might be. As I entered my car at the front of the building, I could almost hear Bill saying as he took his leave also, "Looks like the boss forgot his package. No problem. I'll just take it home and bring it into the office in the morning." Early the next morning, Bill was on the first flight to Alexandria

In spite of the fact that Saturdays and Sundays were working days in the Muslim world, it was hard for Westerners to divorce themselves of the mentality that Saturday night was a 'night on the town'. In any event with all the families away, Bill and I had developed the habit of making the Auberge des Pyramides a rendezvous for Saturday nights. Consequently, when his late flight was to arrive from Alexandria that evening, the arrangements were for us to meet at the Auberge.

After spending our usual Saturday night at company expense, we would leave. In leaving, the sample would be transferred to my safe keeping as we proceeded homeward. I had arrived early and been dropped off by my chauffeur. I went immediately to our usual table which my secretary had reserved that morning. It had an excellent view of the dance floor and the stage and also of the entrance as the evening revelers joined the regulars.

From my vantage point, I glimpsed Bill immediately as he entered the club. He did not seem to be in his usual sprightly mood. His always, very noticeably, jaunty step was quite conspicuous by its absence. In addition, as he approached the table, I noticed that he looked wan. In fact he was almost ashen.

"Have you been airsick?" I queried him. "I thought you were a better traveler than that. The weather here in Cairo didn't seem to indicate that you would have a rough trip," I finished off.

"It wasn't the atmosphere in the air that did it, but rather on the ground," was his rejoinder. "I don't really feel much like spending the evening here. Perhaps, we can take a rain check. I would prefer to go home," he said.

My chauffeur had taken my car back to the apartment after he dropped me at the Auburge, as the arrangements were that Bill would drive me home. We didn't want any witnesses to the transfer of the sample. As we entered Bill's car, he appeared to come a little bit alive. I realized as I recognized the anger in his voice when he spoke, that it was a surge of adrenalin from his anger that had given some life to him.

"Goddamn it!" were his first words as the car pulled away from the parking area. "That friggin' military screwed me around enough when I was in uniform. I swore when I got my discharge that they would never do it again to me. Well, all I can say is that this is the last time they will ever do it! I'm finished! Reserve or no goddamn Reserve!" Before I could even question him to determine what had brought on this tirade of anger and disgust, he continued in a bitter tone of voice.

"When I was an officer with the grunts, we use to have a good laugh at that expression 'Military Intelligence—A Contradiction in Terms'. Well, I can tell you now, it's no laughing matter. It's a fact." He let out a breath, leaned back in the seat and appeared to have gotten a grip on himself. He continued with the comment that naturally I was the only person with whom he could release some of his pent up anger. Anger that had apparently been bottled up all the way from the refinery in Alexandria to the airport, on the plane and back to Cairo.

"Let's start at the beginning. Did you get it?" I queried him.

"Yes!" was his immediate and vehement response.

"How come you were able to get it if something went wrong?" I asked. "And something must have really gone wrong to have put you in the state you're in right now. Why you were absolutely ashen when I saw you come through the door at the club. What happened?"

"Nothing!"

"Now you've lost me. If nothing went wrong, how come you're here in such a state?"

"That's why I'm here. Because nothing happened. If it had, you would have been the object of a visit by the Egyptian army or the secret police tomorrow morning. Or more likely under the circumstances, the visit would have been this evening."

"Okay. Relax, if you can. Apparently, you were successful, so give me a play by play description of what happened, or as you seem to state so emphatically, what didn't happen. And, also, if you don't mind you seem to have forgotten that there are speed limits. I would much prefer to arrive home in one piece, although, I appreciate that under the circumstances you aren't paying too much attention to your driving." Bill dropped his speed to a more reasonable pace, or at least to a pace that might have given us some chance of emerging alive if we were unfortunate enough to collide with any manner of vehicle on the road.

"Okay. Here it is—blow by blow! I took the lead from the Attaché's reason for wanting the sample. I went to the lab where they know me quite well, obviously, and told them that we wanted a sample for analysis. We were anxious to see if the Russian kerosene was as smokeless as the kerosene that THE COMPANY supplied to Egypt. The lab assistant didn't question the request in any respect. He well remembered the one or two occasions that our product was off specification, because it hadn't taken the peasants long to let us know with their howls of indignation as their homes filled with smoke. He was most cooperative. He even helped to open the package as we approached the tank farm. He pointed out the tank from which he was going to draw the sample with the comment that the tank contained the latest shipment which had arrived only a week ago from Russia.

By the time we reached the tank, he had finally broken the seals on the box which held the sample container. He removed the container and approached the draw off valve in preparation to opening it to obtain the sample. All I can tell you is that no one with a weak heart should be in this business. Certainly no one with a weak heart, or in his right mind for that matter, should undertake anything for this no-brainer government of ours."

"Okay! Okay! I asked for it blow by blow, but get to the point. If nothing happened—whatever put you in the state you're in now?" I interjected.

"You know," he continued as if he hadn't heard a word that I had said, "God looks after the drunks and the innocent. In addition, he looks after those who have taken leave of their senses and volunteer to help out those goddamn morons that run our government. What do you suppose was in that sealed, cardboard box?"

"A container for lab samples, naturally," I promptly replied. "That's what the Naval Attaché said it was going to be. Why? Wasn't it?" I asked with a beginning sense of doom. Although, I had no earthly idea of what Bill's answer was going to be, I had this foreboding that had all the portents of catastrophe.

"It was just as the Attaché said it would be. A container for lab samples."

"You've lost me again. If that was what it was, and you got the sample, and you are here—then what in the world 'didn't happen' that so unnerved you?"

"The lab assistant at the refinery, who was being so helpful, has been a civilian all his life. He is, also, too young to have served in the Egyptian armed forces as yet and definitely too young to have ever been around the military during the last war."

"How do you know that? What makes you so positive?" I shot back at him. "And besides, what difference does it make?"

"Because he didn't recognize the container. You were in the service. You handled samples many times, not only in the service, but as a chemical engineer in civilian life, didn't you?"

"Yes, yes, of course." I replied impatiently. "All the containers are standard, both the civilian ones and the military ones, except that the military ones are very easy to recognize. The only difference.... Oh my God! No! It wasn't! It couldn't have been! You mean to tell me that they asked us to risk a possible jail sentence and maybe even our lives, and they had the stupidity to do that?"

"You're goddamn right! It was painted in standard US Army khaki colour! The only thing they didn't have on it was *USA* or *USAF* in big friggin' letters."

All the military in every country of the world knows the significance of the colour 'khaki'. Certainly the members of the Revolutionary Command Council in Egypt did, who were in charge of the refinery. The recognition and significance of the colour khaki was made very emphatically at one time 'by Anwar Sadat when he was still Vice-President of Egypt before he became President. He turned up at a meeting of the Socialist Union wearing a khaki outfit on one occasion. When he was asked what the significance of wearing khaki was, his answer was that war might break out at any time and it was necessary to be prepared'[34].

"And you want to know something else? That mother lied to us. It's bothered me ever since he told you that the government was concerned about the quality of the kerosene the Russians were supplying. As if he and our striped pants liberals in the State Department gave a good goddamn what junk these rag heads got from those pinkos. I had the whole plane ride back to think about it. There is only one spec he wants confirmed by the lab. The freezing point. If I were doing the analysis, I could write the report before it was even run. The freezing point is going to be minus fifty degrees Fahrenheit," was how he ended his tirade.

"For the third time, you've lost me Bill," I said in a strange voice. "What has the freezing point got to do with kerosene, particularly in Egypt where the temperature seldom, if ever, gets below the boiling point, even in the winter?"

"I thought you told me you were on an aircraft carrier during the war? Oh, but of course, you didn't have jets in those days. You used aviation gasoline, not kerosene jet fuel. And you didn't fly at thirty thousand feet where the temperatures hang around minus twenty or thirty degrees. What he really wants to know is whether or not the Russians are sending in jet fuel for Nasser's air force and, if so, in what quantities. Well, the quantities he knows, and if all of these last cargoes were kerosene jet fuel our friend Abdul is really building up a big reserve. And building up a big reserve for.... what?

And you want to know something else that I really hate to admit? He was right to want the sample. I not only think I can write the report on the specs before they run the analysis, but I'll wager the ten years of my life that I just lost in the last few hours that the documentation on the shipments is false. How's that for little green apples?"

"What in the goddamn hell am I doing in this business anyway?" he suddenly snarled. "I started as a 'roughneck' in the oil fields and that's where I should have stayed. The only security we had to worry about in those days was job security. And let me tell you something," he emphasized. "I felt more secure then, than I do now ... even if I do remember eating my lunch on the way to the oil fields in the morning right after breakfast, because I was never sure whether I would have the job come lunch time," he wistfully said as he finally slowed down having apparently run out of words.

As Bill's analysis finally permeated my consciousness, my mind suddenly took off into uncharted and dangerous waters. We had only been asked to obtain a sample of kerosene from the storage tanks in Alexandria. Storage tanks that held a material about which the United States Government had an inordinate curiosity. But that was all we were asked to do.

No one had asked us, or even wanted us, to do any deductive reasoning. Not only didn't they want us to do any deductive reasoning, but they had taken great pains with their cover up story of poor quality imports from the Russians to ensure that we didn't even begin to think. But with Bill having opened Pandora's box, through no fault of his own, there was no stopping now.

What was Nasser going to do with that massive build up of jet fuel? If it were jet fuel? Bill had left no doubt in my mind that it had to be jet fuel. Every indication pointed in that direction. The unusual number of cargoes, our own statistics on the country's consumption, which on reflection left only the obvious implication that there wasn't a demand big enough among the peasant population for those huge quantities. What wonderful hindsight—why didn't the numbers hit us over the head when we were first told of them by our informant?

Apparently, the numbers had made a very firm impression on the Naval Attaché's mind. Putting the question of the numbers aside—why the sudden interest of the Naval Attaché in a quality check? A farce—the US Government's concern about quality for the poor, labouring peasants in the field. The indisputable fact, actually the undeniable indication of the fact, was that the sample was going to the United States Army or the US Air Force labs and not to some civilian lab for analysis.

"Bill, your reasoning has me convinced that you're absolutely correct. That is jet fuel. The circumstantial evidence is incontrovertible. Okay, let me pick up from there.

Item; The report comes back from the lab—minus 50 degrees Fahrenheit.
Item; The US Government now knows that the Egyptian Government is stock piling jet fuel.
Item; So what???

Are the Egyptians going to attack the United States? Should the US bomb the storage tanks before they attack us? Ridiculous! There isn't a country in the world, except Russia, that even harbours such delusions that they could successfully attack the United States. The information is useless to them—an exercise in futility. Except that US Naval Attachés don't embark on these kind of exercises in futility on their own initiative. Was it possible that those orders came from a source with a lot of authority? The Pentagon? And who asked the Pentagon to get the info? There is only one other organization with that kind of clout. And after the analysis and they have the information? Are they just going to file it? No! There is a lot of talent in those huge departments of the the US government and they were going to exercise it in this instance.

You and I have seen a lot of stupidity in our military careers Bill, although greatly out numbered by all the competence of the intelligent women and men of all of the services, but with all due respect that kind of stupidity isn't necessarily confined to the military. This is not stupidity, other than the inexcusable use of a military sample container. Nor is it an exercise in futility. There are too many people involved. The danger incurred in obtaining the information is too great to be just the brainchild of some idle US Government employee looking for something to occupy his time. If they don't need or can't use the information on a real time basis, who can? What country? What country would take the initiative to bomb those tanks and get away with it? Who would be threatened by the build up of jet fuel in those tanks? Syria? Jordan? Iraq? Lebanon? Our Arab brothers? Never!"

The realization finally struck me with a chilling blow. Would the US Government make that information available to the only country that had a life surviving need for it? A country that, with all its expertise and world renown espionage service, didn't have the opportunity to obtain the vital information needed for their survival that Bill and I had just obtained. And just who was that country? Was it possible that 'The governments of Israel and the United States had agreed to exchange intelligence secrets'[35]?

'Ours is not to question why. Ours is just to do and die.'

Why did Israel take that pre-emptive strike in the Sinai just prior to the French and British attack? Why did they take the opportunity to wipe Nasser's air force off the face of the earth before it ever had a chance to get in the air? Why did the Israelis think that the Egyptian Air Force was a threat to them? What information did they have that might have convinced them that a massive build up of war material was indicative of a possible or, in their paranoid minds, a definite threat to their survival? And if they had that information, who gave it to them? And whoever gave it to them, from where did those people get the information?

'Ours is not to question why. Ours is just to do and die.'

Why was my mind racing like this? Caltex didn't pay me to have these thoughts or to spend my productive time on matters that didn't enhance the company's balance sheet. What in the world was I doing in a car tearing into Cairo having left the Auberge des Pyramides early without spending the evening there? In a car with a colleague who had just returned from Alexandria having visited the Egyptian Government run refinery and had obtained a sample of their Russian imports. And all the while my insides were tying themselves into agonizing knots and my stomach flip flopping like a fish thrown up on the bank of the river just after the angler had cast him there.

A colleague that under no circumstances could have provided an acceptable alibi to the Egyptian Intelligence Service as to why he had just procured a sample of their Russian imports of kerosene jet fuel. A sample in a container that simply screamed that it was the property of the United States Army or its sister service, the United States Air Force.

Where were those senior officers of THE COMPANY that had interviewed me when I had mistakenly believed that I wanted to be an international oil executive in order to live a life of 'ease and comfort'? Why weren't they in this very vehicle careening into that vastly, overpopulated city of Cairo which was on a semi-war footing? If assassination were a viable alternative, and at this very moment I was thoroughly convinced that it was, nobody would ever find their bodies. I knew the desert too well after all those mid-night gallops that I had undertaken over the shifting sand dunes on those moon-lit rides. Right now, I was quite willing to take the risk that their bodies would never be discovered in that massive waste of the Egyptian desert.

11

Cairo—King Saud—Mid 1956

"Did you get it in writing?" I removed the telephone receiver from my ear and gazed at it in astonishment. The telephone had only rung once before it had been picked up. We had been waiting for the call for almost three hours at Harry Bernard's, the Manager's apartment in Cairo. Everyone was getting somewhat impatient, in spite of the fact that there was a high stakes game of putting in progress on the deep napped rug in Harry's living room while his house boy served some of Harry's Chevis Regal and Remmy Martin. I had already lost two hundred dollars to the other three members of the office staff, who had also been waiting for the receipt of what, we believed, was going to be a telephone call of the utmost importance. I, subsequently, put my putting losses on my expense account under 'associated communication expenses'.

When Harry queried the entry, I didn't hesitate to tell him that it was due to the long and frustrating delay on his call from New York with instructions to obtain Colonel Ahad's request in writing; plus the ensuing drama caused by the attempt to fulfill those instructions. Otherwise, I informed him, I would have been out at the Auberge des Pyramides spending the two hundred dollars and putting it on my expense account instead of losing it putting a golf ball on his carpet. At the time of the submission of my expense account, we had put behind us the ordeal of the cause of the telephone call. He withdrew his request for details of the entry and signed the expense account with alacrity.

The other three members of the staff were looking at me with quite some trepidation because of the expression on my face. What could Harry, who was making the call from Caltex Petroleum Corporation's New York office, possibly have said that would have produced the look they saw on my face?

A cable had been received very much earlier in the day from New York. Because of the time difference between Cairo and the New York office, it had obviously been sent by some hard working clerk who had been forced to go to the office in the small hours of Monday morning to alert us beforehand of a very important telephone message which would arrive on the evening of the same day.

"No! I didn't get it in writing. It was a routine ..."

"Get it in writing!"

"That will be very difficult, because..... ."

"Get.... it.... in.... writing!"

Time was running out. The other listener who was tapped into our call was not going to be able to make any sense out of this conversation. We would hear the click of an interrupted connection at any minute if we didn't give him something he could understand. "Is the Chief Accountant there? Let me talk to him. There has been a mix-up on the last billing for the recent shipment of lubricating oil to the agents," was the next innocuous piece of conversation that the Egyptian government heard over their tap. We could almost see the listener relax. He wasn't going to have to concentrate any more on this telephone call. After a few perfunctory comments to the Chief Accountant regarding the invoice of an insignificant shipment, the conversation was terminated. Everyone assembled in the room looked at me for an explanation.

"Harry wants it in writing," I explained.

"Wants ... what ... in writing?" Bill echoed.

"That telephone request from Colonel Ahad to charter that Russian flag vessel in the Gulf."

"Those requests have never been in writing before, and besides that's out of the question," Bill emphatically stated. "I talked to the Colonel this morning. He was very acid about the time it has taken to reply to what, he assumed, was a very routine matter under the terms of our supply contract with his department. Do you mean to tell me that we have been waiting for three hours for a telephone call, and that is all the call was about, 'get it in writing'? As I told you at lunch today, the Colonel said that the vessel had already left the Gulf. At $25,000.00 a day demurrage, he wasn't about to continue to hold the vessel waiting for our response. He considers it a closed matter. However, he certainly implied that we had better not let it happen again or he would have a lot to say about THE COMPANY at contract renewal time."

Five days ago on a Thursday morning, there had been a telephone call from Colonel Ahad of the Petroleum Ministry. He had requested that the Egyptian Government be permitted, under the terms of the company's contract with them, to spot charter a vessel for a cargo of kerosene to be loaded at Ras Tanura in Saudi Arabia.

As is well known, all international oil companies are not only in the business of selling oil, but they are in the huge and massive task of moving that oil around the world in ocean going tankers. Ocean going tankers which approach a half million ton capacity, a half a million ton vessel, almost six times the size of the original Queen Mary; Quite obviously a very remunerative business. The company's customer, the Egyptian Government, was very often able to spot charter a vessel that did not belong to one of the international oil companies. This vessel could be obtained at rates that were much more favourable than those stipulated in the contract with THE COMPANY. In instances of this nature, the contract allowed the customer to charter his own transportation, but only if THE COMPANY were first given the opportunity to provide a vessel at the equivalent rate and terms.

When the telephone had rung in my office early on that fateful Thursday morning of the prior week, and the well known voice of Colonel Ahad greeted me, little did I realize that it was the commencement of an epic drama. A saga that was to involve not only THE COMPANY, but the company's suppliers, Aramco, the State Department, the Saudi Arabian Embassies in Washington and Cairo, Gamal Abdul Nasser's office, the United States Naval Attaché's office in Cairo, the United States Information Service in Cairo, and last but not least since he was person that caused the saga to unfold, the King of Saudi Arabia, King Saud. None of this could possibly have been known to us, as we conferred on the telephone with Gamal Abdul Nasser's representative in the Petroleum Ministry of the Egyptian Government on that crucial Thursday morning.

The Colonel informed me that there was a spot charter available in the Arabian Gulf. Under the terms of the contract with THE COMPANY he would like to exercise the right to charter it. The contract permitted this substitution, if THE COMPANY couldn't supply a similar vessel at the same terms with the approximate availability. He was requested to supply full details of the charter which were meticulously noted down. Admittedly, my eyebrows didn't elevate themselves by even a fraction of an inch, when in replying to my questions regarding the tonnage of the vessel, the day of availability, which was in four days, clean or dirty and the rate, I, from force of habit, asked for the 'flag' of the vessel.

"Russian!"

To this day, I honestly believe that the Colonel had no intention of trying to miss-lead me into believing it was owned by one of the independents or one of the other international oil companies, if I hadn't queried the flag. Panamanian flags, Liberian flags and a host of others gave the international oil companies hospitable flags under which to operate their ocean going tankers at considerably less cost than they would have to incur, if they were operated under the American flag or the British flag or any flag that corresponded to the Western nationality of the oil company concerned.

Greek shippers had become world tycoons by building up massive fleets of independently owned oil tankers. There had been a number of times in the past when the Egyptian Government had been able to obtain a spot charter at most advantageous rates from these independents. At other times, one of the international oil companies itself would have a 'distressed' vessel available. Rather than send it on a lengthy voyage in ballast without any cargo, they would often offer it on the open market at a considerably lower rate than AFRA, which was the standard international rate. THE COMPANY had done this many times in the past with their distressed vessels. To the listener, it was a routine request under the terms of the contract.

The Egyptians had been cozying up to the Russians, again, for some time, much to the consternation of the State Department in general and to John Foster Dulles in particular. However, there was no reason to believe that there was anything more behind the request other than the fact that they had found an opportunity to obtain a vessel at a more reasonable rate than under the contract they had with THE COMPANY.

Harry Bernard was in New York for face to face discussions with the Board of Directors of THE COMPANY. Open telephone lines from Beirut still left a lot to be desired because of the magnitude of the problems that we were encountering in Egypt. These problems required continued verbal advice and consultation which no letters, cables or telephone calls were capable of consummating satisfactorily. His visits to New York were so frequent, he once asked TWA, half in jest, if they issued commuters' tickets. As a result of his frequent absences, I would often find myself in charge of the office as I was at the time of Colonel Ahad's telephone call.

As is well known, the various functions in huge bureaucracies are broken down into their disparate parts. The Cairo office of THE COMPANY did not have the authority to tell Colonel Ahad that he was at liberty to charter the vessel that had been offered to him by the Russian Government (there are no independently owned tankers sailing under the Russian flag). Nor did the Cairo office have the information on the availability of a Caltex vessel that could be substituted for the proposed charter. As a consequence, the request was immediately referred to the shipping department in New York by cable as had consistently been the practice in the past.

Friday is a non-working day in the Muslim world. Non-working for those who profess the Muslim faith and intend to go to the mosque on their Sabbath. For those of us who laboured in Cairo under a different religious atmosphere, Friday was an un-official working day. Un-official in the respect that the office was closed, but New York expected us to be there and available to answer any and all of their queries the entire time the New York office was open.

When Saturday and Sunday appeared on the calendar and the New York directors were playing golf at their favourite country club, the Egyptian economy was humming. The Egyptian Government looked askance at any foreign company that had the audacity to publicly show non-observance of their proclaimed religious work week by closing their offices on a weekend; that they considered themselves above the Islamic faith. As a consequence, Saturdays and Sundays were working days for us in the Muslim world. It made a long week, seven days in a row, week after week.

In addition, because of the time difference between Cairo and New York, telephone calls were often made or received after the Cairo office hours which resulted in many long and sometimes dreary days. It was for this reason of time difference, that we had congregated at Harry's home to receive the call which we had been advised by cable was of the utmost importance.

Colonel Ahad had placed his call on Thursday morning. It was fortunate that he was not available on Friday to be told that there had been no reply from the shipping department of THE COMPANY in New York. To all appearances it was a customary request that should have been answered in the affirmative immediately. Alternatively, we would have been advised the name of a similar sized vessel with identical rates that THE COMPANY would make available to meet the Colonel's needs. Although I had not embraced the Muslim faith, after countless weary weeks of seven days duration, I was well aware of the telephone call that would be forthcoming on Saturday morning when ... we ... all ... returned from our prayers at the mosque on Friday. Therefore, I placed a call to New York from my home on Friday evening when I had arrived from the office and should have been relaxing or going out on the town.

The time difference would allow me to find someone in the office who hadn't left after lunch for a long weekend in the country. They would be able to give me the necessary information to relay to the Colonel on Saturday morning. Perhaps, if not the details, they could give me some inkling of why there had not been an immediate response to my cable. A cable asking authority to allow Colonel Ahad to go ahead with his request, or alternatively give him the details of the vessel that would meet the terms and availability of his proposed charter.

Being familiar, now, with Fridays in the New York office, which entailed all senior personnel leaving for their country homes before the early afternoon traffic rush, the call was made with the hope that a decision had been made, but the information hadn't yet been cabled. Hopefully, on the other hand, if it had been cabled it was delayed somewhere en route. When the connection was finally made, the facts received from the shipping department in New York were that the request had been forwarded to our suppliers, Aramco. Aramco, The Arabian American Oil Company, had an office in New York not too many blocks distant from the Caltex office. That physical proximity was the only thing that appeared to be working in favour of the Colonel's request. Aramco's response to our shipping department had been that the request had been forwarded to Washington, D.C.

"To where?" I literally yelled in exasperation.

It had taken hours from the time I had arrived home from the office until long after dinner trying to get the telephone connection to New York. I intended to inform them that on Saturday morning there was going to be a Colonel from Gamal Abdul Nasser's army who was going to be very irate. He would be about to start his own local war when he arrived at his office and found that he hadn't received a satisfactory reply to his customary request to spot charter a tanker in the Arabian Gulf for loading at Ras Tanura in Saudi Arabia.

The details received from my informant in the company's New York office that the request had been forwarded to Washington D.C. couldn't be relayed to the Colonel. I was so non-plussed by the results of the telephone call that, even, if I did inform the Colonel of the outcome of the telephone call, there was no justification that I could offer in support of the decision to refer the request to Washington. There wasn't much further intelligence that could be elicited from New York as the mere mention of the city of Washington D.C. might automatically have caused an 'interruption' to the telephone circuit.

There then ensued a continuing dialogue between the Colonel's office and the company's office in Cairo during the entire weekend. He just couldn't comprehend that a simple and ordinary request couldn't be handled in a matter of hours. My rather lame excuses that it was a weekend in New York and people with authority were difficult to gain access to at that time didn't seem to impress his military mind very much. The exchange finally culminated in his advice on Monday to Bill, the Operations Manager, that the vessel had sailed from the Gulf and was no longer available for charter.

The reason for referring the request to Washington was eventually made known to us at a much later date. However, at the time, it was extremely frustrating and very disconcerting to be unaware of what had engendered such bizarre instructions as to 'get it in writing'.

It was now necessary for us to accomplish a very difficult and unusual task. As Bill had so emphatically stated, the Colonel had never been asked for his requests in writing before. Furthermore, we were now going to have to open, again, what was a very sore subject to the Colonel. We pondered how it would be possible to convince a government employee, even if he were associated with the military who put everything down on paper, to put in writing a request that hadn't even been fulfilled and was already outdated.

A finale strategy was worked out. We would acknowledge in writing his verbal request by telephone to spot charter a vessel in the Arabian Gulf to load at Ras Tanura. In our letter, we would express our regrets at being unable to meet his needs. We would add that in the future we would definitely not disappoint him again.

At the time we were forming this strategy, we were totally unaware of the fact that it was the 'flag of the vessel' which had caused the unusual request 'get it in writing' to originate. In our letter to the Ministry, we meticulously noted the details which the Colonel had relayed over the telephone during his initial call, the tonnage, the availability, etc. Just as I had routinely asked him for the 'flag of the vessel', just as routinely we included it in the details listed in the letter when the vessel was described. Again, unknown to us, without that particular piece of information concerning the flag being included in the letter, the whole exercise of successfully obtaining his request in writing would have been a fruitless endeavour.

In the strategy meeting at which we worked out the details of how to obtain acknowledgment of his request in writing, one important factor was paramount in our plans. The request for acknowledgment had to appear to be as inconsequential as possible. This meant that the letter couldn't simply be mailed. It would just lie on his desk unanswered, as he was a very busy civil servant and didn't have time to answer letters about events that hadn't happened. On the other hand, if we made an appointment just for the express purpose of bringing the letter requesting his reply, it would draw too much attention to the matter and might even raise his suspicions to the point where he would refuse to acknowledge it.

Several members of the staff gazed at us with some bewilderment as Bill and I rehearsed our tactics. The two of us would approach the door to my office and knock respectfully on it seeking admittance. When an unseen and unheard individual representing the Colonel would bid us welcome from behind the closed door, we would open it and enter. After the usual greetings, and on the assumption we would be invited to take seats in front of his desk, it was our intention to offer our apologies for the disappointment THE COMPANY had caused him by not being able to follow through on the offer he had received for a charter in The Gulf. We would add the assurance that we would do everything in our power to see that the incident was not repeated.

At no time during the conversation was the letter to be mentioned. The letter was actually going to be in Bill's possession. After the normal and polite farewells of, "Bookera, Insh'Allah," we would then commence our exit from his office. In the formal protocol of that part of the world, the senior man always precedes the junior when leaving a meeting. Our tactics called for a reversal of this procedure. We would say our farewells, and Bill would lead the retirement from the Colonel's office. As he opened the door to depart and had proceeded halfway through the doorway, I was to prompt him with, "I say, Bill, you forgot to give that letter to the Colonel."

"What letter?" would be Bill's response.

"You know, the one acknowledging the Colonel's request to charter that vessel in The Gulf."

"Oh yes," Bill would reply as he turned to the Colonel and casually say, "Just to keep this unfortunate incident from repeating itself, would you, simply, be kind enough to acknowledge our letter by confirming your request to charter that vessel. By having a file copy, it will help us to keep from disappointing you again."

The good Colonel could never hear us holding our breaths as I would continue, "Since it is such a short letter and we know how busy you are Colonel, why don't you just have your secretary confirm it now while we wait?"

On that critical day of our actual visit to the Colonel's office, we found it increasingly difficult to hold our breaths, as we were successfully taking leave of the Colonel for the second time from the same meeting. The second exit was in accordance with the established protocol of the senior man first followed by the junior. This time it was the senior man who held the letter. I gripped it as if my entire future career with THE COMPANY depended on it, as it might well have, although I was totally unaware at the time of the magnitude of the importance of the document. It was the letter that the Colonel's secretary had just finished typing acknowledging his request to charter a Russian flag vessel in The Gulf.

There was no advance, cable warning of the second telephone call from Harry who was still in New York. Neither was it necessary to introduce the subject. This time the telephone rang at my home just after I had fallen into a deep and trouble free sleep.

"Did you get it?" was the abrupt greeting.

"Yes!" was my equally brusque answer.

"Thank God! Make fifteen copies. Drop five copies off at the Saudi Arabian Embassy. No explanation necessary. Five copies at Nasser's office. No explanation necessary. Five copies at the American Embassy. The American Ambassador is aware of the situation and will forward the copies to the appropriate division in Washington, D.C ..." Click! Disconnect! It was fortunate to get all of his instructions over the telephone line before the mention of Washington told our Egyptian colleague who was tapped into our call that he should disconnect us.

My trouble free rest deteriorated into another sleepless night. For the average businessman in the West to obtain fifteen copies of a letter simply required him to issue instructions to his secretary to produce them. To those of us labouring under the semi-war conditions that had been brought about by Nasser's nationalization of the Suez Canal, obtaining fifteen copies of anything was a major achievement. When Lloyds of London imposed their prohibitive war insurance premiums on vessels trading in the Middle East after the nationalization of the canal, most unessential shipping traffic came to a stand still. THE COMPANY had long ago been unable to obtain any photo-copy paper.

There was always one positive source, the United States Embassy. They brought in their own supplies when the local market was unable to meet the normal demands of their office requirements. I held an IOU on the United States Naval Attaché, which I now intended to call in. With this solution in mind, I finally fell into a troubled sleep.

Early the next morning, I was in the Naval Attaché's office explaining my problem and requesting that he have a member of his staff produce the fifteen copies for me. He was very cooperative. He immediately called in an United States Navy enlisted man. He instructed him to make fifteen copies of the Petroleum Ministry's letter which, naturally, had the Ministry's logo of a huge red blazing torch boldly embossed on the letter head. I breathed a sigh of relief. The letter was in safe hands. I would have my copies before the day was out.

There were one or two commercial establishments, if they could be found, that still had a few sheets of photo-copy paper and would make copies at exorbitant prices, but they lacked a very essential ingredient. Security. Cost was of no consequence, but security was definitely a necessity when you are making copies of official correspondence received from the Egyptian Government. With the process of making copies entirely in the hands of United States Navy personnel, I was able to relax and arrangements were made to pick up the copies immediately after lunch.

For some strange reason as I left the office on the way to the Naval Attaché's after lunch to pick up the fifteen copies, my mind drifted back to my pre-employment interviews and to those senior officers of THE COMPANY who had conducted them. Not one of those executives had discussed the subject of selling oil. Mainly their questions seemed to be directed at finding the elusive reason of why anyone would want to be an international oil executive. Of course, they very determinedly painted the rosy picture of a substantial income, an opportunity to see the world and enjoy what they said would be an extremely, comfortable way of life. Still, it appeared in retrospect now, that they were continually probing the sub-conscious mind of the candidate. Why would anyone want to be in the international oil business seemed to be their constant hidden inquiry.

All of them had had considerable years of experience in foreign service. I was, now, beginning to understand, from my present vantage point, why there was that air of probing in their attitude towards the desires of the candidate in front of them who wanted to become an international oil executive. An attitude which I hadn't been able to fully explain to myself at the time, but over the years, and particularly now, was becoming most evident.

They had all gone through various phases of the experiences which I was presently undergoing and quite a few of them, as well, had spent a number of years in various prisoner of war camps. In fact, there were so many alumni of those various camps in the office that the past inmates use to have an annual get together dinner party for each camp to celebrate their deliverance and count their many blessings.

Their consciences bothered them in that there was no way that they could convey to a prospective employee what was actually in store for him. Why would anyone want to be an international oil executive? If they made an honest attempt to explain what the prospective employee could possibly face, they would find themselves without any candidates for employment. However, there were still certain people that thrived on the prospect of the unknown. It was the duty of these senior personnel to ferret out from the many individuals they interviewed those that would survive in that kind of environment.

Experience in the foreign field is an indispensable ingredient for all personnel of American firms which do business abroad. It is vitally important both for the ordinary employee and for those very senior personnel, including the Chairman of the Board, as I had learned not too much earlier.

In the meantime, all these thoughts were vague recollections in my mind as I crossed the street from the company's office to the Embassy of the United States, which housed the US Naval Attaché's office. As I entered his office, I thanked the Commander in advance for his kindness in making his Navy staff available to supply me with the fifteen copies, which I had been unable to produce in my own office. However, I left no doubt in his mind that I was calling in the IOU which I held in respect to his past request to me for my cooperation.

The same US Navy enlisted man arrived in prompt response to the Commander's call. Something was drastically wrong. I could feel it in my very bones, and it wasn't just because the enlisted man didn't have the fifteen copies in his hand with the ready explanation that they would be available in another few minutes.

I looked at him in stark amazement as he causally explained that he had temporarily run out of paper and had given the reproduction job to the United States Information Service. I have no fault with the USIS. On the contrary, they do a sterling job in every country in which they are located, no matter how difficult the conditions under which they operate. As the main reason for their existence is to disseminate information to the local population, they do not have any need for a system of security or locked files. Outside of a few very senior American managers, they are always staffed with the nationals of the country in which they are operating. Staff, who in the opinion of this particular representative of Caltex sitting in the US Naval Attaché's office, would immediately recognize the significance of the huge blazing red torch on the letter head of the Petroleum Ministry of the Egyptian Government.

I was still unconsciously smoldering under the possible, catastrophic situation in which the Naval Attaché's office had placed us in obtaining the kerosene sample. I leapt out of my chair, grabbed the enlisted man by the arm and forcibly told him to take me to the USIS and show me the individual to whom he had given my letter to be copied. Without any thought of protocol, or so called respect for my senior officers, I marched the enlisted man passed the Commander and out of the office in the direction of the office of the USIS. As I exited the Naval Attaché's office, I turned and bitterly commented to him that it was the last time that I would ever have anything to do with the United States Government and its representatives.

That familiar icy hand was beginning to clutch my heart again. Would anyone have recognized that flaming red torch on the letter head of the Petroleum Ministry's letter addressed to THE COMPANY? Was the US Naval Attaché's office going to be responsible for me joining the three British nationals as another guest of the Egyptian Government?

My heart took turns beating at an uncontrollable rate, or slowing to an almost imperceptible standstill, as that icy hand continued to appear by its grip to shut off the flow of blood to my limbs. Where were those senior officers of THE COMPANY to whom my mind had just unthinkingly been sympathetic? Why were they not there in front of me so that I could wreak my vengeance on them? Assassination? Too kind for them! A slow, lingering death would be all too generous. If ever assassination were going to be a viable alternative, it would be whenever I could get my hands on their throats.

Why do guilty people always suspect the worst? Probably, because they are guilty. I was quite ready to believe that every member of the Egyptian staff of the USIS had pounced on that letter the moment they recognized the Petroleum Ministry's logo. They would have immediately removed the letter from the reproduction machine and surreptitiously conveyed it to the Egyptian secret police. There was no doubt in my mind at this time that all of the staff of the USIS were informers on the payroll of the Egyptian intelligence service. I was ready to believe any scenario that my tortured mind could imagine except the real life one.

"That's the one," the enlisted man said as he pointed out the individual to whom he had given the letter and had asked him to make the fifteen copies. As he was pointing him out to me, the staff member, apparently a long time employee of the USIS and exposed to American phraseology, looked up and recognized the speaker.

"Hi, there you are," he greeted him. "I was about to call you. Your job just came out of the machine. We gave it the colour treatment as that Petroleum Ministry's logo is really impressive. Here you are," he exclaimed as he ended his friendly greeting by handing the bundle of copies to my companion. My heart surged as it forced the blood back to my limbs, which told me that my body was still free to follow the instructions of its owner and was not under the jurisdiction of a foreign government.

Guilt? Guilt complexes? Wild imagination? Trepidation? Fear? The ordinary every day routine of some honest civil servant doing the job for which he is being paid would be the last scenario that would enter the mind of an individual who was undergoing those emotions. An individual, who had just experienced the traumatic events of the past few days that we had had to endure as a result of Colonel Ahad's telephone call. However, that is, obviously, exactly what had happened. As a lowly staff member on the payroll of the USIS, he had been asked to make fifteen copies of a letter. He did as he had been asked and was even a little bit pleased that he had been able to accommodate his colleague from the Naval Attaché's office so promptly and so professionally by adding colour to the copies. I turned and headed for the exit in company with my companion who continued to hold the fifteen copies in his possession. In the corridor in which there was no other passerby, I quickly shifted the bundle to my care. We came to the exit of the building and I bid him goodbye without so much as a thank you.

One more task to be completed and, then, this ordeal would be behind us, permanently; I sincerely hoped. I walked back to the office, asked my secretary to arrange to have my car and chauffeur ready for departure in a few minutes. I located Bill in his office and instructed him to accompany me while we made the deliveries. I wanted a witness to the finale phase of this seemingly disastrous and unending saga.

◆   ◆   ◆

King Saud's nine year old son had a serious eye problem that required surgery. The King had decided to have the operation performed in the United States, where he was assured that the best surgeons and medical facilities were available.

The Eisenhower Doctrine had just been promulgated and while King Saud was in the United States, he had announced his support of 'The Doctrine[36]. The State Department was delighted with this public recognition of the very important position the United States Government had taken, although '… our diplomats in Arab countries were bitter about the Eisenhower Doctrine (which they had almost unanimously opposed)'[37]. The State Department had taken advantage of the King's presence in the United States to entertain him in 'royal' fashion in Washington and meet with President Eisenhower.

The King's support was considered a notable victory for Western policy at this time[38]. The State Department was determined to cement the relations between the United States Government and that of Saudi Arabia to the very best of their ability by strengthening the personal relations between the heads of the two countries. This was particularly important to them after the meeting of King Saud and Nasser in Cairo. A meeting, which had been attended by King Hussein of Jordan as well as by President Kuwatly of Syria.

The King never traveled very far without the most senior members of the Arabian American Oil Company, the suppliers of THE COMPANY, being in exceptionally close contact with him (if nothing else than to just pay the astronomical bills which the King appeared to have no difficulty in running up). The

New York office of Aramco had taken the opportunity to refer Colonel Ahad's request to charter a Russian flag vessel in The Gulf to their directors in Washington, who were accompanying the King. Whether it was because they didn't want to make the decision themselves or because those with the authority to make such a decision were traveling with the King, obviously, couldn't be ascertained by our office a half a world away.

Do highly paid directors have a special sixth sense that warrants those lofty salaries which they receive? Does their antenna start to emit warning signals when there is something that on the surface appears to be normal and routine, but still just doesn't seem to have the ring of orthodoxy? To Colonel Ahad, and quite frankly to me, his request to charter a vessel in The Gulf was routine. A request that had been made many times before and which had been normally answered in a very prompt manner. Promptly either in the affirmative or with the details of the substitute vessel that would be made available to meet the Egyptian Government's needs. The highly paid directors traveling in the King's party, those executives with the sensitive antenna, referred the Colonel's request to charter a Russian flag vessel to load at Ras Tanura in Saudi Arabia to the King.

"A Russian ship in a port of my country?" queried the King. "Those non-believers,.... .those atheists! Absolutely not! Never! My good friend Nasser should know better than to ask me to entertain any such proposition. Tell him under no condition will I allow a Russian ship to enter a port of my country. On second thought, I will have my Embassy tell him what I think of his proposition. In this way, he will realize the seriousness of my feelings about the Russians and his most unorthodox request."

The Saudi Arabian embassy in Washington immediately informed their counterparts in Cairo to relay the intensity of the King's feelings to Nasser about his request to have a Russian flag vessel load in a port of Saudi Arabia. Back came the response from Nasser's office, relayed through the Saudi Arabian embassy in Cairo to their counterparts in Washington, who in turn informed the King of the contents of Nasser's reply.

"What ... Russian flag vessel?"

The Kings reaction was immediate and true to the mentality and suspicions of those inhabitants of thousands of years in the Middle East, with an ancient history of tribal warfare, deception, treachery and mistrust in that part of the world.

"What are you trying to do?" he exclaimed as he turned menacingly to his hosts in the State Department. "Are you trying to have your people in Cairo break up my relationship with President Nasser?"

The sequence of the ensuing questions was as inevitable as night following day. The senior State Department officials, who were obviously aghast at what appeared to be a direct threat to their diplomatic victory of acceptance of the Eisenhower Doctrine by the King, turned to the directors of the company's suppliers, Aramco.

"My God, what are your people in Cairo doing? You had better have a good explanation for this fiasco!"

The Aramco directors from Washington to Caltex in New York, "Whose the trouble maker you have in Cairo?" they demanded with a vengeance. "Get his personnel file out! We want to know his complete background, and his file had better have all details concerning his political associations, to what periodicals he subscribes and has subscribed and, particularly, his religion and he better not be Jewish, and the file had better be up to date!"

The Manager in New York to his long suffering staff, who had been waiting three hours for his telephone call after having been alerted earlier in the day of an important call that would be made that evening;

"Did you get it in writing?"

◆   ◆   ◆

As we were returning to the office after having completed our deliveries of the fifteen copies to their destinations, I leaned back in my seat in complete exhaustion and rested my head against the car cushion. My aching limbs were stretched out to the extent the chauffeur's seat would permit. They ached not from that delightful result of welcome, physical exercise, but from that energy, sapping cause of mental tenseness. A tenseness that grips the entire body, as your tortured mind tries to come to grips with all the cataclysmic events that had happened, might have happened, or conceivably could still happen in the tumultuous times that it appeared we were now living.

The car twisted and turned through the narrow streets, dodging pushcarts and unwary pedestrians. The perpetually honking horns, an instrument without which no Egyptian driver would be able to successfully navigate his city's cramped thoroughfares, were a caterwauling of distant sound. I turned wistfully to Bill and in a tired and weary voice remarked, "By the way, do you know if we have sold any oil in the past two or three weeks?"

12

Paris—Late 1956

It was bitter cold. The hotel management on Avenue George V in Paris had made a determined effort to keep out as much of the freezing wind as was possible. They had provided large plywood sheets with which the luxurious hotel entrance had been surrounded. Even with these well placed buffers, the icy air seeped over, under and around them and chilled all the hotel residents to the bone. The heating system was turned down to a bare minimum in the early evening. At midnight, it was turned off completely and only turned on again in the early hours before sunrise. The hotel administration in Paris had quite correctly assessed that their clientele would rather do without heat than have to suffer the painful task of bathing or shaving with ice cold water in the morning.

The Suez Canal was blocked with sunken ships. Oil tankers were now in the process of making the long and torturous trip around The Cape instead of the abbreviated voyage to which they had become accustomed over the years when transiting The Canal. Furthermore, Saudi Arabia was not at all inclined to help with extra oil to alleviate the suffering of the French after they had so impolitely attacked Saudi Arabia's client state, Egypt.

The French were not only bitter cold, but they were very bitter about the position that the United States had taken when President Eisenhower was made aware of their plans to attack Egypt in concert with the British and the Israelis. Eisenhower's awareness of their plans to attack apparently didn't surface until the very moment that the bombs rained down on the airports throughout Egypt, 'and the Israeli planes strafed Nasser's air force on the ground in The Sinai before it even had a chance to get in the air with, perhaps, half of Egypt's air force destroyed'[39].

As I sat in that frigid, bone chilling lobby and chatted with some of my fellow travelers, who were French, they would immediately pose the identical question with which I was always faced when the French learned that I was an American.

"Tell us honestly and, above all, objectively; do you really believe that your country should have stopped us when we were about to show that Arab international thief, Nasser, what happens when usurpers take property that doesn't belong to them? Not only property that doesn't belong to them, but a canal that was built by us, the French. Now be objective! Don't take the stand your country did just because you are an American." 'Be objective' was the constant theme of the questioners.

They always retired into dignified silence behind their newspapers when I informed them it was very difficult for me to be objective.

"Why can't you be objective?" they would continue to press their point. "You Americans are always priding yourselves on the independent stand you take as citizens of that great democracy of yours."

My answer? "The only reason that it is so difficult for me to be objective is the fact that you and the British were dropping your bombs on me."

◆   ◆   ◆

It was considerably after midnight when the telephone rang at my apartment in Cairo. I had just returned from the usual foray into the night life of the city. The families had been away for so long now, that it was hard to remember what a typical family existence was like. However, the city had assumed a more normal atmosphere and ships were actually trying to resume their regular schedules. There had been several air raid alarms in the last few days. In fact, there had been a prolonged one that very day, October 29th, but knowing the Egyptians, we assumed that it was just an exercise to keep the population's emotions at fever pitch and directed against their hated, prior, imperial masters. It was no longer so difficult to find the specialties in the market place that we had gone without for so long. In fact, the Citibank Manager's wife, Clair, and their children had arrived back that very morning from Europe.

It appeared that after supporting Don's wife and children in Europe for a number of months on a full expense account, the Citibank management in New York very ungraciously overlooked the fact that their Cairo branch had been at the top of the roll of 'best return on branch assets' list for a long time. They had strongly suggested that Don's wife come off the expense account by returning to Cairo. They informed him by telephone from their New York headquarters that they had every reason to believe that Anthony Eden had the whole situation under control, and there was no longer any need to worry. And so, with this exhibition of the expertise of Citibank's headquarters staff, arrangements had been made for her and the children to return to Cairo.

It was difficult to believe that it could be the American Embassy that was calling at this early hour of the morning. The caller gave his name and announced that he was liaison officer for the Zamalak area. My name was on his list, because I had registered at the Embassy on my arrival. He, also, noted that my wife and baby daughter were also registered and asked confirmation that they were still in Cairo. After having just returned from a rather strenuous evening on the town, I suspected that my caller was the night duty officer who was taking the opportunity to up-date his records. I very sarcastically replied that if he wanted that information, I would be glad to oblige him during normal office hours. He could call me then, and I would supply the details but certainly not at this late hour.

"I have been trying to get you all evening. Tomorrow morning will be too late," he wearily replied. "The convoy is being made up at dawn and will depart at two PM. We must know, before then, how many people will be leaving, and how many vehicles you can make available. We need every spare vehicle that you can supply, as we have many more people than for which we can supply transportation." were his startling words.

"Convoy?" I gulped. "Convoy to where? Why? Whose leaving?"

"The Ambassador has ordered all American Embassy wives and dependents to leave by tomorrow at the latest. Most of the Embassy staff are leaving as well. The Ambassador and a few key personnel are the only ones remaining," he continued with his explanation. "Now, please let me know exactly how many of your staff, and how many wives and dependents are going to be in the convoy tomorrow. Also how many vehicles you can make available."

I informed him that all the company wives and dependents had left several months ago, and there were only three American staff and an American visitor in Cairo presently that were connected with Caltex. Hank had been transferred for reasons that were entirely divorced from the situation in Cairo. Transferred or fired. I never did ascertain as I never saw him again or heard of any area to which he had been assigned. After my very embarrassing situation with the Shell Company caused by his lackadaisical approach to his responsibilities, I didn't even want to know if he were still working for THE COMPANY.

"I will call the manager immediately to confirm with him who will be leaving and get back to you as soon as possible. In the meantime, I would suggest that you count on at least two vehicles being supplied by THE COMPANY. Since they are both American cars, they seat six people. On the assumption that the four company people plus the two drivers occupy six of the twelve seats, that will give you at least six seats that you can allocate to those people that don't have transportation," I advised him.

He paused for a moment while recording the information that I had given him, and then in a tired and almost morose voice added, "Do you have any idea how many American tourists are actually in Cairo at this time?"

I replied with some feeling, "I can't answer that, but I can assure you that you have my full sympathy. That visitor whom I mentioned to you is one of our top legal people from New York. When he arrived without notice, we thought he had come with special verbal instructions for us. But no, he was on his way back from Beirut and thought he would stop over and spend a few days resting in Cairo. I frankly believe that there is no limit to the lack of intelligence exhibited by people far removed from the scene of the crime." I could almost see him nodding his head in complete agreement. I hung up the phone and was on the verge of dialing Harry's home when it rang almost instantaneously with my terminating the call from the embassy officer.

"Whom are you talking to at this hour?," Harry's voice demanded with a note of impatience. "I have been trying to get you for the last five minutes."

"The Embassy," I replied. "And what is this about a convoy? And who is leaving? Have you heard from the Embassy?" I anxiously queried him.

"Yes! I've relayed their instructions to New York. New York has told us all to get out. When I couldn't get you on the phone, I called Bill and have just finished talking to him. I told him you and he will leave with the convoy tomorrow. Take your car and his. I have decided to stay here and will have to keep my car for transportation while your two cars are gone much as I would like to make it available to the convoy."

He continued with a note of hesitancy in his voice, "Although New York gave me the option of leaving with you two, I feel that one of the three of us must stay behind. We have too much at risk here for all three of us to just pull up stakes and leave THE COMPANY to who knows what."

"And where the bloody hell is Henry?" he demanded in what was suddenly quite an aggrieved tone of voice.

Henry Kieran, our visitor, had been at the Auberge with Bill and myself. He was probably just walking into his hotel room at this very moment. I suggested that Harry call Henry. I would phone the Embassy back and confirm that the two company cars were available, and that only three of us would be leaving. This would give the Embassy seven seats to allocate to their wives and dependents or to some tourists.

As I was calling the Embassy, it suddenly occurred to me that the Embassy officer had made no mention of any air transportation being available. When he answered the phone and I had identified myself my first query was, "What about air transportation? Can't some of the dependents get out from the Cairo airport?"

His voice carried all the frustration of a logistical officer who had failed in his initial encounter with the unexpected. "We had bus loads of them at the airport this afternoon. All civilian flights have been cancelled. The Egyptian Air Force has taken over the Cairo airport, and no civilian traffic is to be allowed for the foreseeable future." I advised him of the availability of the two company vehicles and that there were seven seats for allocation to his list of dependents and tourists.

After finishing my call to the embassy, I glanced at the clock. It was just three AM. I leaned back resignedly in my chair and thought to myself, 'not a single Embassy wife or dependent was on that TWA plane. On this chess board of life, the Knights are now going to put on their armour, take over and move into front line positions while they sacrifice their pawns'.

So our State Department didn't want to panic the Egyptians a number of months ago, when they could have gotten all the wives and dependents out while there was still a decent interval of time to leave by normal means of transportation. And what were tourists doing in Egypt at this time? Surely the State Department had declared travel to Egypt to be on the embargoed list. Really? Why did I still have that in-built feeling that our State Department knew what they were doing?

When Bill and I had picked up Henry at the airport, his first comment on greeting us was, "What are you doing with those passports in your shirt pockets? Are you going somewhere?" We explained to him that due to the circumstances that we were living under, it behooved us to be ready to leave at a moments notice. This included the possibility that we might not be able to get back to our homes or to the office before heading for the airport. We told him that it was very decent of him to take the chance of coming to Cairo with verbal information for us considering the risk. We were still very naïve when it came to our faith in the good judgment of some of the people in the corporate headquarters in New York who were responsible for our well being.

"What risk?" he replied. "I've just had some tough negotiations over the Joint Agreement in Beirut, and I need a rest. I thought I would stop over here a few days before getting back to the rat race in New York."

The tourists and the wives and dependents of the embassy were a formidable number of people. There weren't enough airplanes in the Middle East, much less in Cairo alone, to accommodate a number that large, even if the Cairo airport were available for civilian flights. Why didn't the State Department get their dependents out when they could have as we had done? And why did they even allow American tourists to come to Egypt? And why, in any case, were they leaving now? What circumstances had changed that had now finally convinced the Embassy to evacuate their dependents at this time?

I had this awful feeling, of which I was now more and more convinced, were the facts of the case. The diplomats' wives and dependents were pawns in the diplomatic game of showing the flag. If you move them out, you tell the world that you don't have much faith in the government of the country in which they were resident. Or, on the other hand, depending on the nature of the government in question, by moving them out you announce in unmistakable terms that you intend to mount an attack. Diplomats just don't do things like that. They never say 'no' when they mean 'maybe', and they always say 'maybe' when they mean 'yes', and if it is 'yes', that they are going to attack, they leave their wives and dependents on the firing line to lull the objects of their mayhem into a false sense of security that all is well.

Even the Nazis, who were no respecters of human life, particularly women and children, 'sent them on their summer vacations' in June 1941. At least, that was the response Ambassador Schulenburg gave to Molotov on June 22, 1941, when Molotov questioned the German Ambassador as to why the German Embassy women and children had left. Molotov must have known Schulenburg was not telling the truth.... The next day, June 23, 1941, the Nazis and the Soviets were at war'[40].

While my mind was dwelling on these insidious thoughts, the phone rang again. This time it was Henry, our visitor. "I'm not going in any convoy," he immediately informed me without even a greeting and in a tone of voice that said, 'I'm a top executive with THE COMPANY, and I don't intend to travel steerage with the cattle.' "You get me on a plane out of Cairo in the morning! I asked Harry to do it, but he says he must keep his line open in case New York wants to talk to him. He told me to contact you, and you were to get hold of TWA management and get me on the first plane out of Cairo in the morning," were his rather imperious commands.

There was no use giving him the information that I had received from the Embassy officer when I had asked that identical question about the dependents leaving by plane. I told him to relax, and I would get back to him as soon as I had talked to TWA. I immediately phoned the TWA manager. I was positive that there were no Americans in Cairo that were asleep, even at this ungodly hour. I was, also, anxious to confirm the information that I had received from the Embassy about the airport being closed.

"Say that again," I exclaimed as I listened to the TWA manager verify the details that the embassy officer had given to me.

"The chances of a plane for anyone out of Cairo in the morning are absolutely nil. The airport is closed to all civilian traffic, although I don't know why," he explained. "The Egyptian Air Force has taken over control of the tower. All passenger planes have been removed from the runways. I've just returned from the airport. The Egyptian Air Force is flying in some of their planes at this very moment. That's why you heard from the Embassy. They had whole bus loads of their people on the way to the airport this afternoon, but they were turned away at the gate."

Henry was telephoned with the news that it was not possible to book him on a plane out of Cairo and he would just have to travel with the cattle. It gave me a little bit of personal satisfaction to inform a 'top executive' of THE COMPANY that he was going to have to travel with the peasants, because he didn't have the goddamn sense to avoid a potential tinder box like Egypt.

He, and everyone else in the New York office for that matter, was fully aware of the fact that we had sent the families out of Egypt on the first sign that there was going to be any trouble. But if he didn't care and thought he would avail himself of a short holiday in Cairo at company expense, neither did we care.

Bill and I met early in the morning in the office to confirm that there had been no change in plans for a departure at two PM. We had our personal belongings with us. Belongings which had been packed for a number of months. The servants were informed that their salaries would be paid by the office at the usual time, and they would personally be held responsible for the condition of both our apartments on our return.

The Embassy confirmed that our particular convoy was making up just outside the Zamalak Club grounds and would depart at two PM. We reviewed all correspondence and destroyed that portion that we didn't want anyone reading during our absence, although Harry would still be in residence. However, there was no guarantee that he wouldn't have to avail himself of the offer by New York that he was free to depart at anytime he thought the situation became too dangerous.

We hastily consulted with Harry to determine what the modis operandi would be after we reached our destination, what ever that destination was to be. Neither the Embassy or anyone connected with the operation had any idea of exactly what plans were in hand for the finale destination of the evacuees. The only knowledge available was that the convoy would depart from Cairo at two PM. It would proceed to Alexandria where we would be met by the United States Navy and, thankfully as we learned later, by the United States Marines. No further information was available.

There were one hundred and twenty-five vehicles in the convoy. We learned that our convoy was only one of a number and that the others were starting from various points around the city. Every vehicle in our group had every seat occupied. Henry elected to travel in my car which was a Roadmaster Buick and was a lot more comfortable than Bill's Chevrolet. His companions, also, happened to be some very attractive tourists which, undoubtedly, contributed to his decision. Bill and I took the front two seats in his Chevrolet with the driver. An embassy wife and her three young children had been assigned to Bill's vehicle and had taken up their positions in the back of the car.

Convoys that are designed to evacuate unfortunate residents from a troubled area do not run like clockwork. After an agonizing delay of over four hours the convoy got underway and headed for the Half-Way House, a mid-point stop on the desert road to Alexandria. Bill and I were crammed into the two front passenger seats with the driver of what General Motors advertised as a full, three passenger bench seat in their top of the line Chevrolet cars. The Embassy wife and her three young children were spread out over the back seat. The children instinctively sensed that something was seriously wrong and reacted accordingly by being cranky and irritable. There was nothing their mother could do to settle them down. There was no way that they could be blamed for reacting to a chaotic situation that had been brought about by their elders.

Whether or not it was the close proximity of myself to Bill or his being so close to me that transmitted the flu germs will never be known. Whatever the cause, we both suddenly realized that we had the beginnings of a dangerous bout of—who knows—the Asian Flu? Were the Asians about to wreak their revenge on two innocent bystanders in this world drama? Yes, indeed! By the time we reached the Half-Way House at midnight, after traveling for six hours on a voyage that normally took only three, Bill and I were weak with fever, constant cramps and an overwhelming desire to just lie down and rest.

Lying down was out of the question as we were elbow to elbow in the front seat. The peevish infants in the back of the car had fallen into a troubled and uneasy sleep. It was impossible to even think of asking their mother to disturb them. At the Half-Way House, Bill and I made a mad dash for the toilet facilities. The flu was no respecter of the body's normal functions and had signaled that we were about to have a monumental bout of diarrhea.

Unfortunately, we weren't the first vehicle in the one hundred and twenty-five car convoy. We weren't going to make it if we had to wait in the line that had miraculously materialized at the entrance to the rest rooms, as the monstrous convoy ground to a halt for an hour's stop-over. An hour's stop-over which we had been informed by the convoy leader would occur when we were mid-way to Alexandria.

Bill and I weren't the only ones that weren't going to be able to make it if we had to wait in that endless line that had formed just outside the very inadequate toilet facilities of The Half-Way House. Actually, it was not surprising that many of the passengers in the convoy had no other choice as well. We found any privacy almost impossible to come by. The facilities at the Half-Way House were not intended to cater to hundreds and hundreds of visitors at one time. It was a small way station designed to refresh the casual visitor on his trip to or from Alexandria. Many travelers in their high-powered vehicles driven by their well trained chauffeurs didn't even bother to stop on their voyage to or from Cairo. Of course, with the number of children and the need for refilling water containers and all the other myriad needs of families with only one parent, and that generally the mother, a stop at the Half-Way House was mandatory.

At one AM the word came down from our convoy leader that we were about to get underway and all passengers should return to their original vehicles. Naturally, there had been any number of people trying to find out from other members of the convoy what news there was to be had. At this stage there was nothing. Nobody knew any more than their fellow evacuees. We all rejoined our respective vehicles, and the convoy audibly groaned as it got underway. Within an elapsed period of less than five minutes, it ground to halt.

As sick as Bill and I were, and every hour told us that we were going to be sicker, our hearts went out to the mothers of the children and particularly to the very young infants. It was impossible to heat their bottles. Some of the families in the rush of leaving had even failed to bring sufficient supplies, and there was many a heart rending hungry cry that could be heard as we sat in our various cars with the doors open to capture whatever breeze might come our way as hour after hour passed.

It was now two and a half hours later. The convoy had not moved an inch from its stop after the first five minutes of starting away from the Half-Way House. There was no news at all. Just sit and wait. Sit and wait for what? Nobody knew. The desert road to Alexandria is not a well lighted highway. In fact, there was no means of illumination of any description. Small lights could be viewed along the length of the road, as people kept their spirits up with the use of the dome lights in their vehicles and some kept their headlights on to help illuminate the area. Soon, however, the convoy leader ordered the lights extinguished. It was imperative that the batteries of all the vehicles respond immediately if, and when, we got the signal to proceed.

Finally there was news. It was all bad. The Egyptian Army, desert troops were utilizing the highway in the Alexandria area and moving all their equipment to Alexandria. There was no hour given at which the highway would be clear for the convoy to resume its way to the coast. By this time, Bill and I had reached the third stage of the flu. The three stages of the flu have often been compared to that of seasickness. The first stage is when you realize you don't feel very well. The second stage comes on abruptly and devastatingly, and you are afraid you are going to die. The third stage is when you have that awful feeling that you are not going to die.

Within thirty minutes of the news that the supposedly well heralded, crack desert troops of Gamal Abdul Nasser's army were in command of the highway, we suddenly received orders from the convoy leader to get underway. It wasn't until a very much later date that we were made aware of the reason for the sudden willingness of the Egyptian Army to clear the road for us.

When no word of the convoy reached the Commanding Officer of the United States Marine contingent that had been waiting in Alexandria to greet us, he enquired of the American Embassy in Cairo by telephone what was the cause of the delay. When informed that the Egyptian army was the cause of the delay by taking over the right of use of the only highway between Cairo and Alexandria, the Commanding Officer requested that a message be sent to President Nasser's office. To wit:

Sir: You will immediately release the convoy by ordering your troops to give way to them, or alternatively we will come and get them!"

Is it any wonder that those of us who have had the grateful opportunity to have had some relationship with that organization known as The United States Marines often include them in our prayers at night?

We were on the move again, thanks to that dedicated group of men and women to which so many of us owe so much. The next stop was a small hotel, just on the outskirts of Alexandria. Again, a very necessary stop for those of us who had to take care of our personal needs and, even more importantly, for the mothers who had to replenish their water bottles for the children and heat the milk for the infants. The word from the convoy leader was that we would rest until after sun-up. He felt it was safer to enter the city by day. As we all sat around on the floor in the lobby, or on the steps or in the garden commiserating with each other, some enterprising young teenager had gotten his portable radio activated.

He suddenly sat bolt up-right in our midst in the lobby of the small hotel, as we tried in vain to find a comfortable position to extend our legs. An effort hampered by the fact that there were hundreds of people crammed into a space that was meant to cater for the few and far between, with many stretched out lying on the floor of the lobby. The teenager's eyes were as big as saucers. His voice had the stark, hollow tones of someone who had just witnessed the start of the Apocalypse. But this time there only three horsemen.

"Oh, no!" he wailed. "They've attacked Alexandria! BBC says that the second air wave has rendered the airport completely inoperable. Who could have done such a thing?" was his plaintive cry at the end of his announcement.

Henry Kieran, our visitor whose name left no doubt where his ancestry lay, immediately took command of the situation. "Those goddamn Jews! They're never to be trusted! We should cut them off from all support from the United States! That will teach them a lesson for bombing Alexandria."

Bill and I looked at each in our agony wondering which was worse. To try to carry on living, or just hope that the attackers might miss the Alexandria Airport and one of their bombs would land on us and put us out of our misery. As Henry was ending his tirade against the Jews, an advance scout from the Marine forces arrived. He was going to lead us into Alexandria, and he appeared on the scene just in time to hear Henry's words. He turned to address him. "Pardon me sir, but we have had been on full air raid alert for the last forty-eight hours. I can assure you that not one Israeli plane has been sighted."

"Don't tell me that! There isn't anyone else in the world that stupid that would do anything like bombing Egypt!" Henry announced to the Marine Officer.

"I'm very much afraid that there is, sir," replied the Marine Officer politely. "Every plane sighted so far has been either French or English."

There was an almost audible sigh of unbelief from all within hearing of this unthinkable news. The Marine Officer continued with the shocking information that the airport was under constant attack. All members of the convoy were to keep alert for possible shrapnel from the defenders anti-aircraft firing. Up until the present moment, the French and the English had concentrated their bombing on the airport he advised us. The United States Navy had informed the French and British Navies and their Military units that the convoys were on the road and headed for the port. They were to make very effort to see that no chance bomb went astray and hit any one of the convoys.

The Marine Officer then consulted with the convoy leader. Now some of the diplomats heard, probably for the first time in their lives, some of the facts of life. Facts of life associated with staying alive in situations that could have been avoided for their wives and dependents had they moved them out at the first sign of trouble, just as we had with our wives and dependents. The convoy leader relayed the Marine Officer's instructions to us.

The convoy would get underway at the crack of dawn. All vehicles were to stay as close to each other as possible. The port, as is the usual case in all parts of the world, was not the most secure area in which to travel under ordinary circumstances. Certainly not when the enemy bombs were raining down on the airport, and the local citizens were unable to distinguish friend from foe in a convoy.

The information was that thousands of excitable Egyptians had gathered on the road and, in some cases, were trying to evacuate the city themselves. The main road had been kept open with the help of the Marines, and we were to proceed directly to the port as fast as was safely possible.

"Do not leave enough space or go slow enough to allow any of the onlookers to get between you and the vehicle in front of you. Keep bumper to bumper!" were the emphatic and stern orders from the convoy leader as he relayed the Marine Officer's instructions.

"At the first sign of any rocks or stones being thrown, roll down your car windows. This will save you from what could be some very serious injuries. The rocks or stones could give you some bad bruises, but at least there won't be any chance of bleeding to death if you have a cut artery from the broken glass. We have no medical facilities available in the convoy. Any wounds will have wait until we board the Navy vessels. So keep alert," were his finale words. "Let's move it out!" he shouted as he headed for the lead vehicle.

We all re-entered our assigned cars and headed for Alexandria at as fast a pace as could be maintained considering the size of the convoy. Everyone obeyed the convoy leader's instructions and kept bumper to bumper as we went through the city and headed for the docks. Now was the time that, if there were going to be any trouble, it would be in the port area.

The embassy wife, whose husband was apparently one of the key people who had had to stay behind in Cairo, opened her windows in the back as we entered the city in anticipation of avoiding any shattered glass. She instructed the three children to lie on the floor of the car in hope that this would lessen the chances of their being hit by anything thrown by the bystanders. I was pinned between Bill and the driver and suggested to Bill that it might be a good move for him to open our windows also.

"You know it's a strange thing, but I have a special aversion," Bill replied with a very noticeable air of revulsion on his face in answer to my suggestion. "When I was assigned to the Indian organization of THE COMPANY in Calcutta, we had a civil disturbance there. Before taking up the threat of throwing anything at us, the Indians took the opportunity to spit on us. Frankly, I prefer taking the risk of broken glass and the possible cuts and bleeding to the ordeal of having some Egyptian spit on me. So if you have no strong objection, we'll leave the windows rolled up."

We had to assume that it was pure coincidence that the next attack wave came as the convoy slowed to a quick stop at the warehouses of the port. Certainly, the French and the British wouldn't have deliberately started the attack just as we arrived. The air raid sirens screeched in agony almost as if they were protesting the effort of having to be constantly activated as the bombs rained down. Every anti-aircraft gun that the Egyptian military owned appeared to begin firing at the same time. The volume of sound was devastating.

We had just opened the doors of the car, and I had the first child in my arms as I assisted the mother in getting her brood out of the cramped back of the Chevrolet. The sounds of the air raid sirens, the anti-aircraft guns, the whine of the aircraft zeroing in on the airport and the saturation bombing was so deafening that everyone instantly froze in their tracks.

I had seen the effects of friendly shrapnel falling on bystanders during the war on my carrier when we had had anti-aircraft practice, and the Egyptian barrage resembled the same conditions that existed in Japan during the fire-storm of March 10th, 1945, because in addition to the bombs, 'There *was* another rain from the skies. Tokyo was thick with anti-aircraft guns, and tens of thousands of shells poured into the heavens. After they burst, the shrapnel fell back into the city in a lethal hail. It was impossible to estimate how many hundreds who were exposed and in the open died from the effects of the falling, jagged metal debris.'[41]

I immediately instructed Bill to run for the warehouse as I threw the child I was holding into his open arms. Then, I turned to the Embassy wife who was still standing there transfixed by the screech of the falling bombs as she clasped her youngest to her breast in a futile effort to protect the baby. I reached into the back of the car, scooped up the remaining child as I pushed her in the direction of the warehouse with the stern command that she was to get under cover and I would bring the last of the three children.

Once inside the warehouse, we felt a little more secure. While it certainly wouldn't protect us against any stray bombs, it assuredly provided adequate coverage against shrapnel. As suddenly as the attack had started, it came to an end. From the short duration, it appeared that it might just have been the tail end of a sortie and the majority of the bombers must have already returned to their carrier. All activity in the warehouse had come to a standstill at the first sounds of the attack, but now we could see that the Marines were all set up in their usual efficient manner. There was the embarkation officer standing at the ramp for the purpose of directing the flow of evacuees into the small landing craft that were hovering just at the foot of a long flight of steps leading down to the water's edge. As each craft was filled, it headed out towards its mother ship, and the next one that was standing by a few hundred yards away would dash into the space vacated by the previous one and start loading the additional passengers next in line.

The line slowly moved forward as the marine sitting at a table took down the particulars of the passengers, their names, addresses and next of kin. At the time, I was too numb to question the necessity of this kind of 'paper work' when the bombs were falling. But, of course, the bombs weren't falling on us. Yet. And so the line moved very efficiently. To those of us who were waiting to get on the next landing craft and reach the safety of a United States Navy vessel, it seemed agonizingly slow. I had taken the opportunity of getting all the information from the mother regarding the details of what the marines required in the way of statistics. Therefore, I was in the lead holding the oldest child by the hand. The mother was sandwiched in between Bill and myself, still clasping the baby to her breast while Bill held the remaining one in his arms.

The landing craft was full to overflowing. It pulled away from the steps just as we were the very next in line. The very next. However, we would be the first to board the arriving boat that had been hovering in the background awaiting its turn to approach the steps. I stood there and breathed my first sigh of relief since the convoy had left Cairo. Within minutes, the mother, her three children, Bill and I would be headed for the safety of the United States which, at the moment, was in the form of the USS Chilton, an attack transport floating in the port of Alexandria. Once aboard, Bill and I could find some hole into which to crawl and nurse our flu stricken bodies back to health again.

Life is not that kind. Up until that moment, I had harboured no ill feelings towards the British or the French. After all, my father had been English, and at one time he had represented the Foreign Office in some outlandish area where the Foreign Office didn't have an official presence. Possibly as a result, he had never become an American citizen. France and the French were my favourites, and I had for many years been trying to get THE COMPANY to post me to Paris. Why then would they take that moment to mount the next full scale attack?

An attack that made the first one that greeted as we had driven up to the large warehouses lining the water front seem like child's play. Now was the time to believe that while every anti-aircraft gun that the Egyptian Army owned was firing at the attackers, there appeared to be no doubt, as well, that every plane that the French and the British owned in their massive navies were on a direct line of attack for where we were standing waiting to board the landing craft. What landing craft? My mind suddenly snapped to attention, as the one that was next in line for us to board and had been maneuvering towards the steps, abruptly turned and headed out away from the port and on its apparent way to return to its mother ship.

"Where are they going?" I groaned to the Marine Embarkation Officer, who had immediately taken shelter next to me under the roof of the warehouse as the attack started.

"I'm sorry sir," he replied in his most calming and official voice possible, "they have orders to return to the ship immediately an attack begins. We have too many people already safely aboard to risk the whole operation for those that are left. We can not afford to have the ones already aboard jeopardized. Nor can we afford to have our landing craft sunk, if the attack is diverted from the airport to the city and port since that would leave us with no way to continue the evacuation. They have strict instructions to abandon us, if it appears that the British and the French intend to bomb the city and the port," he ended his cold and quite naturally, basic, military explanation.

"And what about you?" I suddenly exclaimed, as it became apparent that the Marines already ashore would be left behind as well.

"We have orders to take charge of the evacuees and find them the best possible shelter. We have provisions that we brought ashore with the first landing craft in case of just such an emergency."

Thank God again for the United States Marines!

Repeatedly that same ironic thought emerged again. Having survived one of the most deadly and devastating wars of recent mankind hunting down German submarines in the North Atlantic for months, I was now going to become a victim of an attack by the very Allies with whom I had fought alongside. A victim of 'friendly fire'. 'Friendly fire' was a heart breaking, emotional hurdle for the families of those servicemen, who died as the result of just such a catastrophe of missdirected firing by their own side, or as in our case if it did occur, of bombing.

The British and the French knew we were there. What were the pilots' orders? How important was the Port of Alexandria to their military objectives? If they did attack the port, and many of us perished as the bombs rained down in the same massive quantities that apparently they were unleashing on the Alexandria airport, it couldn't be called death by 'friendly fire'. 'Friendly fire' is a mistake. It is undertaken, unknowingly, by those mortals whose lives are forever afterwards profoundly affected by it when they have been made aware of their blunder.

Just to maintain some normal aspect of everyday living after my discharge from the military, I had resolutely wiped out of my mind over the years since the end of the last war, the horrible memories of the dead and dying bodies of my shipmates from the torpedoed U.S.S FREDERICK C.DAVIS. The DAVIS was one of the six destroyer escorts charged with protecting the two carriers in the task force, on one of which I was serving, and they were also charged with hunting down enemy submarines at the same time that they were shielding us from those same, deadly, under-sea craft.

When torpedoed by the German U-Boat 546, the DAVIS parted amidships and sank within a few minutes. Some of the survivors were in the water as long as three hours. What was so devastating about the deaths of some of those, who didn't survive, was that their deaths weren't all caused by the Germans torpedoing their craft or by the giant sharks inhabiting that part of the North Atlantic or the icy waters of the same freezing North Atlantic, but by.' ... depth charges from our own vessels ...'[42]. Depth charges released by the orders of the very men with whom I was serving. Men who must have agonized every time they pressed the release triggers that lobbed the deadly depth charges into the water, because they knew that they were going to be responsible for the deaths of their shipmates, who were still alive in the water. They had no choice. The destruction of the submarine took priority.

It was a tormenting sign of the mental anguish that I was undergoing to have my mind suddenly recall a situation, and a question that I had wiped out of my mind for years, but now was directed towards those very allies that I had fought alongside. What were the orders of the French and British pilots? The same as my shipmates, who had released the depth charges?

It just didn't seem fair. And what about the child whose hand I was holding? Surely he had had nothing to do with the chaos that his elders were wreaking on him. As I thought of that child who was grasping my hand in fear and anxiety, I voiced a silent prayer to Harry Bernard. He had had the vision and the determination to see to it that none of the wives or dependents of his staff were going to be exposed to what, apparently, the United States State Department hadn't even taken into consideration. Or again that insidious thought, the Knights in their armor felt that they were at liberty to use the wives and dependents of the Embassy staff as pawns in the world wide chess game of diplomacy. Or as John G. Stoessinger stated so spine chillingly and devastatingly about the 'October War of 1973' in his book, 'Why Nations Go To War', "Kings played chess while pawns bled on the battlefield"[43].

I stood there immobilized with the flu draining every vestige of resistance that my body and mind could even begin to harness. As I waited in an almost trance-like state, the mother in back of me, who had caught only snatches of my conversation with the Marine Embarkation Officer, asked, "What did he say about the boat?"

I'm sure that at some stage in this present life, or the one to come, I will be forgiven for my reply to her. "He said it will be right back."

The bombs rained down on the airport. The anti-aircraft guns futilely fired at the attackers, and we waited. Suddenly, it was over. We could see our landing craft faintly in the distance. It had reversed direction again, but this time it was headed towards us. It reached the landing area, and Bill and I assisted the mother and her three children as they were loaded on board. With a full complement, we took off for our destination, the USS Chilton, an attack transport of the United States Navy.

As in the case of the LST out of Tientsin in China, the vessel had not been designed to cater to women and children and babies and hundreds of evacuees, particularly since, it already had a full compliment of naval and military personnel aboard. We, and a large number of other unattached men, found the most comfortable storage holds that were dry and warm and curled up to await the departure of the vessel. Bill and I, in particular, were anxious only to be left alone in our misery. We settled down on some very large piles of what appeared to be rope of some kind. It later turned out that what we had chosen to hunker down on were the rope ladders, which actually resemble nets more than ladders, that are dropped over the side of an attack transport when it comes in view of the enemy shores. After the attack vessel lowers its landing craft, the commandos and the marines clamber down the vertical heights of the ship's side with the aid of these rope ladders and leap into the waiting boats in anticipation of storming the enemy shores.

As we were all trying to make ourselves comfortable, there was still another bombing attack by the British and the French. What they had left to bomb at this stage was unimaginable. Perhaps, they were just venting their rage on their favourite WOGS. Everyone made a mad dash for the deck to view at first hand what damage the bombing was accomplishing. That is everybody, but Bill and myself. We just lay there and wished all concerned luck, the evacuees with their viewing and the British and the French with their bombing. We just couldn't have cared less.

At that moment, assassination never entered my mind. I was too sick to care whether or not those senior officers of THE COMPANY preceded me to whatever place we were individually, or collectively, appeared destined to go at the moment or at a later predetermined date.

The crew of the ship and the commandos the ship carried were valiant. They quickly gave up their staterooms or their bunks to the mothers with the older children. The stewards' department had emptied the contents of dozens of boxes of provisions and made impromptu, miniature cribs out of the cardboard containers. It was an astonishing sight to look in the sick bay where the infants were housed. You would see row after row of cardboard boxes with occasionally a tiny foot waving in the air as the babies woke up from their deep sleep of exhaustion. They had been on the go almost twenty-four hours with out any resemblance of their normal comfortable surroundings.

We transshipped from the attack transport vessel in Crete to a MTC military transport. As in the China evacuation after changing vessels, we truly believed that we were living in luxury. Everyone had their own bunk. There was enough to eat. The food was always hot, served on time and there were three meals. Bill and I actually recovered during the latter part of the voyage. When we landed at Naples in Italy, we were ready for the news from the office. THE COMPANY had, as usual, done its utmost for us while we were in any danger. They had kept my wife, Henry's wife and Bill's family informed on a minute by minute basis as best they could of the situation of the evacuees. Never once, in the many months that my wife and baby daughter lived in New York City on a full expense account, did they ever suggest, as Citibank had done, that she come off the expense account and return to Egypt. In fact, she never did return to Egypt. Like TWA, which she never flew again, neither did she ever set foot in Egypt again. Nor did she ever intend to do so.

There was a three bedroom suite in the luxurious Hotel Excelsior, the best hotel in Naples, with a view of the harbour waiting for us when we disembarked from the transport. I immediately phoned my wife with the good news that we had arrived safe and sound and gave her the additional information that we had received from New York via the company's office in Rome. Bill was to proceed to Rome and coordinate the supply arrangements to Egypt with Caltex (Italy) SpA, and the other marketing areas associated with the 'Joint Agreement'. I was to proceed to Paris and coordinate the marketing efforts with our partners and agents, Compagnie Française des Petroles—TOTAL.

It was while I was in Paris that I heard the story about how the Managing Director of our agents in Cairo had been prevented from leaving on one of the United States evacuation ships when he reached Alexandria. For some strange reason, the Egyptians took exception to his desires to leave for a more friendly shore. Some cynical individuals suggested that their attitude might have been occasioned by the fact that he was Jewish, traveling on a British passport and the head of a French oil company.

As was befitting a company enjoying the special relationship that CFP had with the French Government, its offices were located in one of the most prestigious arrondisemonts of Paris. Over the months that I spent in Paris and the many trips to the far flung organization that CFP ran in North Africa from its Paris headquarters, I began to realize just how astute our New York directors were in concluding the 'Joint Agreement' with the French. Putting aside the monetary side of the agreement for the moment, how would we have ever staffed the offices of some of the branches in the cities that the French appeared to take as normal standards of every day living? Their headquarters' offices bore no resemblance to their branch offices in Africa.

As soon as I arrived in Paris and had settled into my cold and bone chilling hotel room on Avenue George V, I paid my first visit to CFP's headquarters. I was greeted with great courtesy and considerable welcome. TOTAL was panic stricken by the unexpected events that had taken place after their country's attack on Egypt. They weren't the least bit interested in any 'objective views' from their American partner. They couldn't have cared less about the politics of the matter. C'est la vie! That was over and done with. What about the oil? Were they going to be supplied on a current basis? Did we have enough? Were we going to have to ration them or could they continue on a normal basis?

I had already talked to Bill in Rome, and he had assured me that all the supply problems were under control. I could tell CFP that there appeared to be no foreseeable, serious dislocation of their supplies in the immediate future. Bill and I were only concerned with the operation of the 'Joint Agreement'. As far as Europe was concerned, it emerged that 'the American companies had been brought together with the United States Government in a Middle East Emergency Committee (MEEC) to provide an 'oil lift' for Europe, pooling their resources and diverting oil to Europe'[44]. The Caltex offices in Europe were in charge of European supplies and were not concerned with the 'Joint Agreement', nor we with them.

True, France was experiencing severe shortages. That was to be expected with the Canal closed, and the supply line lengthened by several thousand miles as the tankers made their labourious trip around The Cape instead of through the Canal; Plus the not so indelicate subject of Saudi Arabia being annoyed at the French. However, all of our agent's North African requirements were on the same side of the Canal as was Saudi Arabia, and Bill had informed me that he couldn't see any serious dislocation to their supplies, albeit, there might be some momentary difficulties.

After my initial meetings with CFP, I suggested that the best way for me to familiarize myself with their marketing problems was to visit their field offices. This would have been done on a normal basis from Cairo, if it hadn't been for the messy and unplanned interruption caused by the Suez crisis. They agreed with dispatch and advised their various field offices of my impending visits. Caltex (East Africa) Ltd., headquartered in Nairobi, performed many of the accounting functions on behalf of the 'Joint Agreement' for North Africa, although, they had no other relationship with the operation whatsoever. Consequently, my first stop was in Nairobi to familiarize myself with our arrangements there. My next stop was Addis Ababa.

In looking at the time table for the airline flights, I commented to my Nairobi associates that it seemed strange that all flights leaving Addis departed early in the morning long before sun-up, like as at four and five AM. There is, always, a very simple explanation for any situation that strikes the casual visitor to certain areas as extremely unusual and out of the ordinary. The casual visitor, or certain Caltex Chairmen from the Western Sister for that matter, just don't understand the day to day problems of plain 'existence and survival' in these out of the way parts of the world where so many of his fellow brethren earn their living.

In those days, all flights out of Addis Ababa were in propeller driven aircraft. Addis was located at an altitude of well over nine-thousand feet. A problem that sometimes resulted in various embassies and commercial enterprises having to reassign their staff shortly after their initial arrival, as they couldn't physically survive. Shortness of breath, heart murmurs and a number of other ailments associated with high altitudes would manifest themselves immediately a particularly, susceptible staff member arrived.

So too with the aircraft. Those propeller driven, winged aircraft needed all the 'air-lift' they could get from the air which supported them in flight. When the direct sun hit the city of Addis at the time of sunrise, the air was warmed and, consequently, even more considerably thinned out than even at that altitude. All aeronautical engineers are aware of the loss of support occasioned by thin air.

And so, it was not unusual to see the many air travelers, dragging their whining and complaining infants by hand, arriving in the cold, pre-dawn, departure time of all commercial flights out of Addis Ababa.

The airfield had been constructed with the end of the field at the edge of a cliff. Whether this was a necessary requirement because of the topography or whether it had been designed by an aeronautical engineer, I never did learn. What I did learn, after several takes offs, was that at that altitude and with airlift problems caused by the thin air, even before the sun had had a chance to warm it, some flights, actually, appeared to descend after take off before gaining enough speed and air lift to start their ascent.

It is, indeed, very distressing to the average air traveler, who is accustomed to having his aircraft gain altitude as it leaves the ground to find that, in fact, he immediately starts to lose altitude as the plane leaves the ground and starts off on its journey. This early pre-dawn departure, also, obviated the traffic problem of the normally very congested main street of the capital. The reason that the main street was no traffic problem at that hour was that all the brothels were closed at that time. The main street of the capital of Ethiopia happened to be the location of most of the brothels of that rather, large and busy city.

Massawau, Eritria was the next stop; a tropical port city on the Red Sea. Not the kind of tropics associated with the rain forests of the various jungles around the world with their overwhelming green vegetation, but a dry, deadening landscape with no relief from the searing sun. Heat that left your skin with a dryness that told you that if you were ever assigned to this city, your appearance would change by adding five years to your age for every year that you lived there. Your skin would burn and wrinkle, and your body oils would leave their depository forever. A process very similar to the salt flats, as the sea water evaporated at a visible rate and left behind tons of salt which was the main export of the city.

CFP had been able to lease the old, war time underground storage tanks of the Italian submarine base from the Ethiopian Government, which at that time was the administration center for Eritrea. It was a most unusual feeling to inspect a tank farm, where all the tanks were underground, and the only light available was from dimly lit bulbs in the overhead earth bomb cover of the base. The manager wasn't too specific on how he was fortunate enough to have been able to lease these tanks, when every other oil company, particularly, some of the subsidiaries of the other Five Sisters, wanted to do the same. He did take me several times to the Ethiopian officers club for extremely delicious meals. A club, which had been newly rebuilt on the submarine base. With just a slight rise of his eyebrows, he would look around at the opulent club and appear to indicate, without any spoken words, that there are ways of being the one fortunate enough to rent the only tanks available, if your accounting procedures are creative enough to include building an officers' club as part of the 'construction cost' of 'leased' tanks.

The hotel in Djibouti left me with a perplexing problem. Was it the unbearable heat of another Red Sea port city that left its residents with so little initiative? None of the streets were paved. There was no air-conditioning of any description. The shower at the hotel was in such a state of dilapidation and filth that I immediately proceeded to put on my tennis shoes. I showered with them on my feet rather than risk what was, obviously, a germ infested depository for every imaginable microbe of that part of the world. Or maybe it only confirmed the comment often made about the French. 'They don't care what they do or how they do it, as long they pronounce it correctly'.

The landing wharf was an old, sunken, wartime casualty of the Allies' bombing. It had, fortunately, sunk bottom up when it capsized. This gave a broad landing area for the coastal tramp vessels to which to tie up, and the occasional small oil tanker delivering drummed products that came calling on this out post of civilization. The French manager very kindly took me swimming with his family on the weekend as my visit happened to coincide with that period of the week.

"Be sure you don't scrape yourself on any of the coral on the bottom," he cautioned. "It is extremely poisonous, and you could get very seriously ill, if you're unfortunate enough to get the poison in your blood stream." He had already warned me that it was necessary to wear tennis shoes when going swimming in water that was so shallow that it was difficult to believe that you could stay on the surface and still avoid the poisonous coral on the sea's bottom. I didn't enlighten him of the fact that wearing my tennis shoes had become a habit, when showering in the best hotel that his city had to offer to its visitors.

A quick trip in a four wheel drive vehicle, and I had visited what was known as British Somaliland and just further on French Somaliland. The French had been operating under the 'Joint Agreement' in this part of the world for some time. Their staff appeared to be able to cope with living conditions that would have appalled most Americans, if they had been told that, in anticipation of a life of 'ease and comfort', their assignment as an international oil executive was to be in a port city of the Red Sea.

Rather than go back to Nairobi and then to Khartoum and Port Sudan in The Sudan, I made the mistake of thinking I could utilize my time more efficiently for THE COMPANY by taking a flight directly from Asmahra in Eritria to Khartoum. This mistake visibly materialized the moment I entered the old DC-3 which was now in service in that part of the world. No regularly scheduled airline would avail itself of craft in the condition that this one was. Perhaps it was not so much the condition of the plane that convinced me of my mistake, as it was the cargo and four of the passengers.

Bucket seats lined just one side of the plane. Only one side was utilized, because the cargo occupied the other side. Those Americans, who follow Dan Rather's CBS Evening News on a regular basis, will have learned some time ago that there is a chewable narcotic in that part of the world known as 'KHAT'. CBS made quite a point of this on one of Rather's broadcasts when he had gone to Somalia to cover 'Operation Restore Hope'. To those of us who traveled in that part of the world in those days, we were long ago made aware of the availability of this narcotic. It was grown in Africa and shipped to the Middle East and Saudi Arabia in particular, although the Arabs often brewed it and treated it similarly to the way Westerners treat tea.

What was so disconcerting was not that it was carried as cargo in the DC-3, but that it was carried as cargo in the passenger cabin of the DC-3. As the aircraft bumped its way down the badly maintained runway, clouds of dust would rise from the cargo which was lashed to the floor and to the sides of the plane just across from your outstretched feet. The coughing and sneezing of the human passengers were no where near as loud as the bleating of the four goats that had been tethered to the aircraft sides in the forward part of the passenger cabin. They were bleating their indignation at having to breath air that was so dense with dust that at times it was impossible to see either end of the aircraft.

Whether they were to be sacrificial offerings in Saudi Arabia or just ordinary fare for the table, there was no way that the customary passenger could learn. The sounds, the smells and the haze of dust emanating from the bundles of freshly harvested 'hashish', as we were more inclined to call it in those days, was overpowering. The dust, from either the hashish or the Khat, didn't differentiate between human and animal passengers. It smothered us both.

Christmas in Khartoum, New Years in Port Sudan and the airline flight between them told me I was better off flying with my fellow passengers, the goats and Saudi Arabia's narcotics. To the best of my recollections, the flight between Khartoum and Port Sudan was the only time that the passengers of any aircraft utilized in commercial transportation, myself in particular, took part in the navigation. When the old wartime d'Haviland sixteen seater rolled up the landing strip in preparation for loading, I had had my initial misgivings.

With the French, 'form over substance' is the paramount ruling dictum. With the British, form is an afterthought and in the instance of this particular aircraft, substance seemed to have taken a back seat to the same national leanings.

Remembering the company's advice to sit in the back of the aircraft, as in the event of a crash, the passengers in the back of the aircraft were much more likely to survive such an unscheduled landing, I seated myself in the last of the eight seats on the port side.

The pilot and co-pilot, which I was, incidentally, very pleased to realize the plane carried such a wealth of talent, settled themselves in the cockpit. The aircraft was small enough to allow the co-pilot to lean out of his seat without getting up in order to secure the door leading to the cockpit in anticipation of take off. The latch failed to function.

Whether the aircraft had seen such extensive service on the rough airfields of this part of the world and had caused the plane's frame to become so warped that the catch of the door wouldn't line up with the socket in the frame, it was impossible to determine from the eighth row seat. What was very evident was that the door wouldn't close. With a semi-apologetic look at the passengers, the co-pilot ceased his efforts to latch the door shut. He turned his attention to the task of assisting the Chief Pilot in taking off. In the process, he left the door idly swinging back and forth.

In one respect, this was a fortune indication to me that I should not take the opportunity to relax on this particular flight. From being familiar with the geography of The Sudan, I was well aware that our entire flight was over land with no water to be encountered. However, this knowledge did not allow for the sudden monsoon that engulfed us and stayed with us the entire voyage. By habit, I had committed to memory the time table and the knowledge of the time of our arrival in Port Sudan.

Ten or fifteen minutes after our scheduled time of arrival and we were still airborne, my sixth sense of survival began to make itself felt on a real-time basis. I constantly searched for some indication of our location by peering out the window of the aircraft. We had been flying over a continuous and dense bank of low hung clouds the entire trip having left the monsoon showers below us. While this made for a more comfortable voyage, it didn't give the passengers much scenery to enjoy.

Suddenly, through a quick break in the clouds, I was startled to see that we were flying over a sheet of sparkling blue water as the sun had also seized the opportunity to shine brightly through the break in the clouds. This can't be my mind said to itself. There is no water between Khartoum and Port Sudan. The extended period of the time of the flight and the quick glimpse of the blue water told me that something was seriously amiss. I immediately roused myself and headed for the cockpit. There I found the aircraft on automatic pilot, the Chief

Pilot asleep and the co-pilot absorbed in one of Agatha Christie's mystery thrillers. Quite appropriately, it was 'Ten Little Niggers'.

The co-pilot looked up from his reading with an air of obvious annoyance. I politely asked him if blue water was any part of the scenery to be encountered on our way between Khartoum and Port Sudan. His answer was an off hand 'no' and he went on to enquire why I had asked the question.

I revealed that through a break in the clouds I had glimpsed quite a body of such appealing colour. He suddenly sat bolt upright in his seat, took a quick look at his watch, switched the automatic pilot off and with a rather sickly smile told me that we had over flown Port Sudan. He would wake the pilot and we would be back on course in a matter of minutes. He assured me that there was nothing to worry about, as we still had twenty minutes of flying time left as they carried a reserve of fuel. My mind immediately told me that it would take all of the twenty minutes of fuel to get us back on our regular route and landed safely.

We dropped below the clouds and entered the heavy rain showers. Port Sudan appeared on the horizon as we approached it from the sea side instead of, as originally planned, from the land side. The plane slowly landed and appeared to be taxiing towards what passed for a passenger terminus, although, there was no way to actually determine what lay in the distance.

The windscreen wipers were swishing backwards and forwards at a hectic pace but quite futilely. The airfield had been so poorly maintained, that with the combination of the torrential down pour of the monsoon and the mud and gravel of the surface of the airfield being thrown up on the windscreen by the wheels of the aircraft, there was no way that the pilot could even glimpse the terminus building.

No doubt, he had made the landing quite often and used 'elapsed time' as his measurement of distance, inasmuch as when we rolled to a stop the plane was quite close to its destination. Since the cockpit door was still idly swinging back and forth, because it had never latched shut during the entire flight, all the passengers were uneasy onlookers to the mud bath.

The airport management very efficiently recognized that it would be impossible for us to alight without being ankle deep in mud and water. Their evidence of this recognition was the appearance of, at least, a dozen of the local residents hurriedly arriving at the side of the aircraft with each one holding two of those common, ordinary concrete blocks used for building material. They lined them up at the exit to the aircraft, and as we were disembarking they scurried back for another set. Now with the passengers lined up on the building blocks laid end to end from the aircraft, the local airport crew carried the initial ones to the front of the line and laid them out for us to step on. They continued this process until we were safely ensconced within the shelter of the building. And so ended my one and only effort in assisting an airline crew to navigate their aircraft.

13

Beirut, Lebanon—"Paris of the Middle East"—1957

However traumatic, disruptive and nerve wracking the attack by the French, British and Israelis on Egypt was for those of us who had been caught up in the war and subsequent evacuation, there was one very positive aspect of the whole chaotic mess. New York decided that the Middle East headquarters should be moved from Cairo to Beirut.

We had been well aware from our frequent visits to Beirut to make our telephone calls that it justly deserved its title of 'Paris of the Middle East'. Now we were going to live there, not just visit. We would be able to take full advantage of the myriad attractions that this beautiful and serene country had to offer. Baalbeck with the 'Old Vic' from London performing 'Anthony and Cleopatra' and 'The Merchant of Venice' in the ruins of the Temple of Bacchus on a starlit night. The thought of skiing in 'The Cedars of The Lebanon' in the morning and swimming in the dazzlingly blue, breathtaking Mediterranean Sea in the afternoon of the same day gave us the impression that we were, indeed, going to live in paradise.

When the Lebanese were asked in those days what was the secret of their success in having built such a vibrant economy in the center of the normally, turbulent and chaotic Middle East, their answer was, almost, invariably the same. They would tell the story of the analysis they asked the Swiss to make of their business acumen. The Lebanese Government felt that if there were any group of financiers that could be a source of guidance to them in their continuing efforts to improve an economy that was already the envy of many less fortune countries in that part of the world, it would be the Swiss.

After one month's study, the Swiss wound up their investigation by admitting that they were absolutely baffled. Apparently, they had investigated every aspect of the Lebanese economy, but could find no reasonable explanation for its success. The Swiss did, however, have one very strong recommendation to make to the Lebanese. "What ever it is that you are doing, keep on doing it."

Caltex (Middle East) Ltd. was 'housed' in the same type of accommodation that its counter part in Cairo was 'housed'. The office occupied a four bedroom apartment that had been converted to commercial space. However, Ed Gilbert, the very congenial Manager, had arranged to obtain office accommodations in a new building that was only a few months away from its completion date when we arrived. He actually had helped to design the company office inasmuch as the builders, with typical Lebanese ingenuity, had signed up prospective tenants before breaking ground for the start of the construction.

Ed's newly appointed office had its own private shower and toilet facilities. Even more impressive, from my envious point of view, was the wall to wall, ceiling to floor expanse of window that looked out over the broad tree lined avenue. My office had a wall to wall window also, but as befitting the Assistant Manager the window came to a halt half way down from the ceiling. This left a wall just slightly below eye level when reclining in my expensive, adjustable, desk chair. As in Beijing, when we had first cursed the numbingly, cold weather with a vengeance and then suddenly reversed ourselves to blessing it, I didn't realize how soon it would be before Ed and my positions were to be reversed. Then it would be Ed who would be gazing with envy at my wall.

Inasmuch as Caltex (Middle East) Ltd. already had a manager, it wasn't possible for Harry Bernard to move to Beirut from Cairo. During the visits to Beirut to make our telephone calls, we had had the pleasure of meeting Ed and Anne-Marie Gilbert. Anne-Marie was a Parisian and everyone had heard that when they were first married Anne-Marie could speak no English. As a result, they couldn't communicate. The story was easy to believe, because now she spoke fluent English, and they still couldn't communicate. They were a delightful and most hospitable couple. They lived in a strikingly, modern, private home not too far from the sea front where we were to rent our beach house. It was this proximity to the beach that made it possible for Ed, at a later date, to personally deliver the most devastating news to us while we were at the beach with two of the children.

We had moved from our hotel to Ed and Anne-Marie's beautiful home as our arrival coincided with their over-due departure for their six months home leave. As in Cairo, with Harry's frequent absences, this left me with the responsibility of the office. Living in their magnificent house during their six months home leave, and then finding ourselves after their return ensconced in a garden apartment on the Mediterranean 'Sur la Corniche' gave us the sensation that the 'life of ease and comfort' of an international oil executive and his family had finally resumed its normal course of events as promised by those senior directors in New York.

There was only one apartment on each floor of this stunningly located building. Ours was the smallest, because it was situated on the ground floor and consequently had to allow for the luxurious lobby. But we were more than happy to give up that space in return for the lovely, private garden with its mass of lush vegetation. Our smaller apartment, with its towering high ceilings, consisted of two immense living rooms (one with a huge mirrored marble fireplace), one dining room (with a similar fireplace), four bedrooms, an over-size kitchen that any hotel would have been pleased to have in order to cater to its many clients and three and a half baths. Indicative of the life style of the occupants of such living accommodations, there were quarters in the apartment for four servants with two baths for their convenience.

There was also a large covered balcony which extended the full front of the apartment, leading to the garden and overlooking the incomparable Mediterranean. We had lunch served there every day as we gazed peacefully at the romantic sea where so much history had been made. It, also, provided a base the next year from which to stare in awe and astonishment at the United States Marines as they marched on their way into the center of Beirut on the instructions of President Eisenhower. We had only been informed of their arrival by the American Ambassador just prior to the Marines' landing craft running up on the beach between the airport and the city. Unknown to us at the time was the fact that they had been invited to do so at the invitation of President Chamaoun of The Lebanon who had, also, ungraciously failed to inform his Commanding General, Fuad Shehab, that 'The Marines Were Coming'.

Had we been aware of this rather deliberate oversight on the part of President Chamaoun, we would, certainly, never have seized the opportunity to go out to the airport road to cheer the Marines on as they rolled down that thoroughfare with a massive show of strength.

As a sign of the times and the need for increased productivity, the normal office hours had been lengthened. However, the office hours in the Lebanon in no way resembled those in Cairo, either in the length of their hours or in the days of the week. This was due to the prior, colonial, French influence and the many Christian residents in this Paris of the Middle East. Our work week was from Monday to Friday, as it is in most of the Western world, and not from Saturday to Thursday as it was in the Muslim world.

Moreover, the oil industry had, unfortunately for us, become very much more competitive. 'By the mid-1950s, Beirut had a large Western-oriented commercial community.... .: builders, bankers, shipping companies, suppliers of building and oil-well equipment, field offices of companies selling consumer products and a large number of consulting firms specializing in various aspects of the oil companies' (and other large companies') adjustment to the environment'[45].

In addition, the old colonial attitude was dying a slow but sure death. As a result, we now had to labor from 8:00 AM until 2:00 PM in the afternoon instead of from 8:00 AM until 1:00 PM as we had been accustomed to while in China. This still gave us time, however, to go skiing and swimming. We saw the 'Old Vic' perform Shakespeare's classics in Baalbeck at the Temple of Bacchus, and we worked hard; myself liaising with the agents, and my wife being a perennial hostess in this crossroads of the Middle East.

As Assistant Manager in charge of marketing, I had dual responsibilities. Compagnie Française de Ptrole—TOTAL, our same French partners as in Egypt, were also our agents in Lebanon, as well as Syria and Jordan, in addition to those North African territories that I had visited while based in Paris. Caltex, however, was determined to establish markets for its lubricating oil products in a number of other countries without the aid of CFP. These other countries all had crude oil production of their own. Therefore, lubricating oil was the only product that we could market. Perhaps just as important, the sale of lubricating oil products didn't require any capital investment. Consequently, the French had nothing to offer us. We always had lots of oil and no money and, therefore, we didn't need the French in those countries that didn't require the establishment of a huge marketing infrastructure at great capital cost.

The areas that were not associated with CFP were Libya, Iran, Iraq, Kuwait, Saudi Arabia and Bahrain. 'Chevron had bought the sole crude oil concessions in Bahrain from Gulf Oil. Gulf in turn had bought them from a London syndicate for the princely sum of $50,000.00 but because of Gulf's association and agreement with BP in the Iraq Petroleum Company, Gulf could not 'go it alone' in Bahrain without BP. BP thought they had enough oil and didn't want to add to the already unmanageable glut at the time that Chevron was interested in exploring in Bahrain. In any event, BP was insistent that Bahrain would not yield any oil, since it lacked the 'Oligocene-Miocene' formation found in Iran and Iraq. At a later date Texaco bought fifty percent of the Bahrain Concession from Chevron'[46]. This made Bahrain a captive market for me to visit. The Two Sisters that owned us also 'owned' Bahrain.

When a employee working for an oil company in the domestic market in the United States is given an area for which he is responsible, there is no doubt that he wonders if he will be able to cover his area completely and satisfactorily. In my case, I needed a small world globe to determine exactly where my area started and where it ended. It included Egypt, Ethiopia, Eritrea, The Sudan, Djibouti, British Somaliland, French Somaliland, Lebanon, Jordan, Iran, Iraq, Bahrain and Saudi Arabia. In addition, I was a director of Caltex (Middle East) Ltd. and a director of Caltex (Egypt) SpA and had to attend their respective monthly board meetings, one in Beirut and one in Alexandria, Egypt.

In studying the Joint Agreement with CFP, I could only come to the conclusion that the French were more desperately in need of oil than was the step-sister of the Two Sisters, Caltex, desperately in need of money. 'CFP did not have the same scale or range of production as some of the other Sisters[47].' This conclusion, that CFP was in more desperate need of oil than Caltex was desperately in need of money, was based on the, quite obviously, unbalanced terms of the agreement, which in effect were very simple. The terms merely stated that CFP would supply all the capital investment dictated by the marketing and distribution operations in the various countries covered by the Joint Agreement. Caltex, in return, would sell them all their requirements of fuels at the 'posted prices' and lubricants at the 'wholesale prices'. We would both split the retail profits from the sales in the local markets on a fifty-fifty basis.

This gave Caltex 100% of all the profit from the sale at the 'posted prices' for fuels and 100% of all the wholesale profit from the sale of lubricants at the 'wholesale prices' and 50% of all the retail profit, after expenses, from the sale of both fuels and lubricants in the local market. And all this without a single dollar of investment by Caltex, other than for a few desks and chairs (which we actually rented). It really wasn't too difficult to determine who was the more desperate.

It was this unusual calculation of the local profits 'after expenses' that was to be the single biggest impediment to what would, normally, have been a very congenial arrangement, at least from the point of view of Caltex. When the CFP directors looked at accommodations to house their managers or a company car to reward them, somehow or other for some strange reason, the thought always surfaced that, 'Caltex is paying for half of this expense'. TOTAL's managers, in the areas covered by the Joint Agreement, always drove cars twice as big as ours and lived in homes twice as luxurious (in territories where such homes were available). This seemed to annoy Ed, as it sometimes did Harry in Cairo. Naturally, Caltex could have made the same mental calculation that said CFP was paying for half of the cost of our cars and our homes, and we could have lived in the same style that the CFP managers did. It didn't matter that it would have cost Caltex no more money to 'double up' on such expenditures inasmuch as CFP was paying half the cost. What did matter, though, was that Texaco Directors, when visiting us, would have been horrified that anybody associated with their skinflint management and penny-pinching philosophy could live in such a luxurious style. We would never have survived their initial visit. Even our present accommodations were a source of discomfort to them during their visits.

Many years later, I was highly amused to see a cable sent to Dick Wrigley, the Managing Director of Caltex (Africa) Ltd. in Cape Town, advising him of an impending visit by one of the recently appointed Texaco Directors to the Caltex Board who was on the usual, initial, familiarization field trip. The cable ended with the very strong suggestion that the Dick send his chauffeur on vacation for the duration of the Texaco Director's visit, garage his huge Daimler and rent a Ford, drain his immense swimming pool, cover it and keep as low a profile as possible.

The Texaco Directors' attitudes and philosophy imbued all levels of their management. It was while I was in Johannesburg that two of their Chief Retail Service Station Mangers were on a visit to my area. Their visit happened to coincide with a weekend. I had invited them to my club, the Innada Polo Club, one of the most prestigious clubs in the entire Southern Hemisphere. They were my very special guests for lunch on the Sunday that I was to play the afternoon polo match. A match for which they would occupy the best box seats available in the members' stand on the field.

They were seated at a table on the magnificently, luxuriously, appointed veranda at the Club House for lunch overlooking the polo field with myself and my wife. There were, perhaps, another hundred additional guests of the members seated on the veranda. Spread among the other luncheon guests were many of the players who were to play in the afternoon match and who were garbed as I was in our perfectly fitted, spotless, white polo habits and highly polished boots and spurs.

It was while they were being served the most lavish meal imaginable at our immense, umbrellaed, luncheon table that I couldn't help but notice that they appeared extremely uncomfortable. Their discomfort was particularly noticeable as the immaculately, uniformed stewards served them with champagne, pâté de fois gras, roast quail and all manner of delicacies, which was the normal fare prior to the usual Sunday afternoon match. I enquired if there were something disturbing them. They turned to me with very pained expressions on their faces and in the most solemn tones imaginable, but at the same time with a very kind intent, they replied, "You do realize, we hope, that you are aware that you are living in the past. This way of life is going to come to an end, just as the Roman Empire came to end. We trust that you are well prepared to accept that inevitability."

There was nothing that could be said or done to put them at their ease. The way of life that they saw being lived in front of their very eyes made it impossible for them to relax and to forget the mind-set that Texaco had imposed on their very beings.

It's frequently comforting to be aware that all bureaucracies exhibit comparable characteristics, whether it is the one for which you work or the one for which your colleagues work. That is to say 'the left hand doesn't know what the right hand is doing' or there are other similarities in the same vein. It will, always, be recalled what the professor from The Harvard Business School told us during one of the crash courses THE COMPANY had organized for its highly paid executives. He informed us before starting the lectures that he had been invited by Caltex to make a several day tour of its facilities and operations. This would allow him to familiarize himself with the oil terminology and the varied aspects of the organization before beginning his lectures on how to handle 'business crisis' in the international oil arena. He advised us that after only a very short review, he realized that Caltex Petroleum Corporation resembled nothing more than a dinosaur.

"In what aspect," we proudly queried, "size?"

His reply indicated immediately how astute he was, and why he was a senior professor on The Harvard Business School staff. It would take all of us a number of years to reach the same conclusion that he had reached in a matter of a few days.

"THE COMPANY is like a dinosaur," he replied in answer to our query, "because when a dinosaur dies, three days later its tail twitches. It takes that long to get the message from the brain to the tail that it's dead."

It was heartening to know that it wasn't our dinosaur, but ESSO's, which was the cause of the industry wide strike which we were enduring at the moment in Beirut. The firing of an incompetent chief storekeeper, who had been on the endangered species list for a long time, wouldn't ordinarily result in a strike. It certainly wouldn't result in an industry wide strike even in the Middle East. However, the firing of such an individual immediately after the payroll department had awarded him a generous merit increase led the union to have grounds to believe that there was a personal grudge between the chief storekeeper and his immediate supervisor. Of course, it simply wasn't so. It was just a case of the message 'taking three days' on its journey from the supervisor of the chief storekeeper to the payroll department telling them that the employee was not to get his usual annual increase, as he was on the point of being terminated.

"The American Ambassador wants to see you immediately at the Embassy," my secretary informed me anxiously as I entered the office. "He wouldn't tell me over the telephone what he wanted to talk to you about. I've arranged to have your car downstairs and your chauffeur is waiting for you." Hastily clearing off my desk, I left on the run with instructions to my secretary that she was to telephone my wife to say that I might be late for our dinner party that night. I had no idea of how long the Ambassador would keep me. From the sense of urgency transmitted by my secretary's message, it sounded as if it might involve a very lengthy and time consuming meeting.

As I entered the Embassy, which was only a short drive from the company's office, it wasn't surprising to see several managers from the other oil companies arriving as well. As we settled into our chairs in the Ambassador's office, it soon became obvious that all the American oil company managers were present, but what was surprising was that the British oil company managers were also in attendance. It didn't take too long to be made aware of the Ambassador's concern, the industry wide strike.

But why was the United States Government interested in our problems? As a rule it was the other way around. It was industry that was always making overtures to the Government to assist it in ways that could only be handled by the use of Government influence. Alternatively, the companies would be faced with the prospect of using unorthodox methods. There are many situations in the Middle East that the international companies don't have the normal resources to handle, other than the always ready and absolutely guaranteed remedy—money.

"I have some reasonable understanding of what is behind the cause of all of you having to shut down your operations," the Ambassador announced as he opened the meeting. "Would the company, which appears to be the main culprit in this matter, please make it clear exactly how serious the situation is and how close to successfully resolving it they are," he continued. Those of us who had dealt with our own Government and the Governments of other nationalities in the past were very sensitive to the use of specific words that diplomats use. All of us were quite experienced with representatives of various embassies including our own. That is not to say that we wouldn't go on making mistakes when dealing with them, but at least we didn't make the same mistake more than once. We had learned the difference in the meaning of the various words, nuances and tones of inflection in their voices when statesmen discuss policy and world events or specific actions. Actions, which they wish you to take without them actually asking.

It was only necessary to recall the calming words used by Anthony Eden after Gamal Abdul Nasser had nationalized the Suez canal, those calming words just before the guns started firing and the bombs were being dropped. 'There is no cause for alarm. This is a matter that can be handled on a rational basis to the mutual satisfaction of all concerned.' Parliament had relaxed as they had rightly inferred that the Prime Minister was in the enviable position of having his expertise unrivaled in that part of Great Britain's far flung empire. The Prime Minister would know precisely how to handle that distressing and delicate situation. He certainly did. That was one of the reasons our Middle East headquarters had been forced to move from Cairo to Beirut.

Surely there is hardly anyone that hasn't heard that rather oft repeated story of the difference in Webster's definition, a diplomat's definition and a lady's definition of the words 'yes', 'maybe' and 'no'. When a diplomat says "Yes," he means 'maybe'. When a diplomat says "Maybe," he means 'no'. But if a diplomat says "No," he's no diplomat. When a lady says "No," she means 'maybe'. When she says "Maybe," she means 'yes'. But if she says "Yes," she's no lady.

The word 'culprit' was the key to why we had been urgently called to a meeting in the Ambassador's office. He wasn't about to help us with our problems. He was the one who had a problem, note; "Would *the company* who appears to be the main *culprit* in this.... .". The main 'culprit', ESSO, embarrassedly admitted to the sins of poor communication vis à vis providing a generous merit increase to one of their senior union employees and then firing him before he had even received his first pay check with the increase included in it. They had to confess that the problem was a long way from a successful conclusion.

The Ambassador took the opportunity to thank all the managers for taking the time to come to his office. In particular, he acknowledged the presence of the English managers. He explained that he had cleared his invitation to them with the British Ambassador and the British Naval Attaché in the British Embassy. Inasmuch as what was going to transpire would involve all of the oil industry, he needed their absolute assurance that what he was about to tell them would not be conveyed to anyone below their level.

With that said and done, he then announced that there were serious political matters in the Far East that had world-wide implications. The situation was so volatile as to indicate that there might be military action required. In this connection, the President of the United States had ordered the Marines and part of the American Sixth Fleet from the Mediterranean to proceed to the Far East at flank speed[48].

Bingo!!!

I knew immediately what the Ambassador's problem was. The American oil companies all held 'open ended' (supply without limitation) contracts with the

United States Navy. I had developed the habit of filing information in the back of my mind from routine cocktail and dinner party conversations. Conversations that seemed just routine on the surface, but they gave me the signal to file that particular bit of information in that multi-million brain cell part of our heads called a memory bank and wait for the appropriate time for clarification.

So that's why the American Naval Attaché had causally inquired at a dinner party just the other day whether we were having any difficulty with our heavy fuel supplies. The industry had had serious disruptions not too long ago, which had left us in such short supply that the electricity department had had to consider limiting energy requirements for the city and they had so announced their intentions.

He had been assured by me that at the present moment the industry, as a whole, was full to the brim. He wouldn't have to worry about his electric coffee machine in the office having to be turned off. As soon as he had left the party, or even while the party was in progress as I myself had done many times when conveying urgent information to my superiors which I had gleaned at a cocktail party, he must have reported to his Ambassador that there was no problem in having the fleet fueled at Beirut on its way to the Far East. Of course, he could have picked up the telephone in his office and called me with the request to supply the information, but that would have meant one more link in the chain of communications that might be broken either unintentionally by me or deliberately if his telephone were tapped. Obviously, he had no secure line to members of the commercial world.

He had relayed the information that I had given to him to his Ambassador who in turn had relayed it to Washington and the Defense Department. Now his Ambassador had a real problem. There was no one in the industry that could supply the fleet with even one barrel of fuel oil. We were all paralyzed by the industry wide strike. It was obvious now why the British managers had been invited to the meeting. No stone could be left unturned in order to guarantee that the Sixth Fleet would receive its fuel requirements.

"For the information of all assembled here, and I emphasize 'all assembled here', not a single word of what you hear at this meeting is to leave this room. Outside of the various diplomatic authorities involved and the Department of Defense, no one is aware that the major portion of the United States Sixth Fleet is en route to the Far East. As is our usual policy with Her Majesty's Government, the fleet's movements have been made known to the British Government. It is for this reason that we have made the decision to include the British oil companies in our discussions."

He turned in the direction of the ESSO manager. "I obviously can't instruct you to re-instate that Chief Storekeeper in order to bring the industry strike to a halt. I would suggest to you, however, that you seriously consider that alternative. It is absolutely imperative that the fleet be fueled when it arrives. It is only twelve hours out of port. This will give you time to get back to your office and finalize your negotiations with the union this evening and allow the industry to resume operations in the morning," were his closing comments.

The union was absolutely convinced that their actions were correct. There must have been a clash of personalities between the Chief Storekeeper and his supervisor. Why else would a dinosaur as big as ESSO have capitulated so quickly and re-instated their union member employee instantaneously at his newly enhanced salary after only a relatively short industry strike?

Jordan—1958: Arrogance! Defiance! Shock! Defeat!

"No bloody, WOG government is going to tell me at what price I can sell my products," the Mobil Manager in Beirut informed me on the telephone in an arrogant tone of voice. "Have you seen the newspapers this morning? The Prime Minister of Jordan has announced that, effective with the start of Ramadan, the price of kerosene will be reduced by twenty percent." I, too, had read the announcement with great foreboding. I knew that it was the start of another round of internecine warfare between the so called 'have nots' and the 'obscenely wealthy' oil companies. My fellow manager suggested that all the oil company managers meet in his office that afternoon to plan a strategy that would effectively counter the imposed price reduction by the Prime Minister of Jordan.

The timing could not have been more inappropriate. The start of Ramadan is an emotionally, highly charged, religious period during which the faithful renew their vows to Islam by fasting from sunrise to sunset. As the month's fasting wears on, so does the patience of the 'faithful' as well as the 'unfaithful'. The faithful because of the rigors of fasting, when not even the swallowing of salvia is permitted, and the patience of the unfaithful who have to put up with the emotionally, disturbed functioning of their employees who have embarked on this 'pilgrimage'.

The meeting was chaired by the initial caller who was an ex-Marine Officer from the United States Marines and had been infused with the philosophy that 'offense is the best defense'.

"The first signal that we will send to the Prime Minister is that we do not intend to tolerate his unilaterally reducing the price of any of the products that we sell in Jordan. We will stop all shipments of all products to Jordan until he rescinds his price reduction of kerosene," was his opening announcement to the meeting. "I'm sure that you are all in agreement." A typical Marine offensive. Brook no interference from those that you want to join you in your endeavors.

"As a matter of past experience, I have never been fortunate enough to be on the winning side of an argument that was intended to defy a sovereign government," was my immediate response to his statement. The use of confrontation with sovereign governments had been utilized successfully many times throughout the world by the Seven Sisters. However, not in recent history. Certainly not since several of the countries who were now the declared, official, legal owners of the crude oil beneath the surface of their lands had rightfully laid claim to it through administrative fiat. I was the only one of the assembled managers to have any objections to the gung-ho attitude of our stalwart ex-Marine Officer.

"I think we should ask for a meeting with the Prime Minister," I continued. "We can explain the economics of his decree and the devastating results it will have on our profitability, because kerosene is the single, largest volume product we sell in Jordan. After all, we have operated for many years in Jordan under government price control. As long as we enjoyed satisfactory margins, and in some cases more than satisfactory margins, we have never complained. I think it would be a diplomatic blunder to cut Jordan off from its supply of petroleum products, and particularly kerosene, just at the start of Ramadan. If ever there is a product that is politically charged with dynamite, it is kerosene for the peasants," I hastened to add in support of my position. My protestations were to no avail. The meeting voted to immediately suspend all shipments to Jordan.

My suggestion that we ask for a meeting with the Prime Minister was quickly pre-empted by the Prime Minister himself. When the news reached his office that all the oil companies in Beirut had suspended deliveries, the oil company managers each received a personal invitation from the Prime Minister's office to meet with him in Amman on Sunday morning at 10:00 AM. The telephone rang again almost simultaneously with my receiving the invitation from the Prime Minister's office.

"Told you he would come to his senses when we cut off his supplies," my hardy Marine Officer informed me in a jovial tone of voice. I have the greatest respect for our Marines and would in all probability not be alive today if it were not for their dedication to duty. Be that as it may, as in all walks of life, there are some individuals who have a tendency to make you wonder why they didn't stay in their original line of endeavors, such as continuing service in the United States Marines.

Sunday morning all the oil company mangers resident in Beirut boarded the aircraft headed for Amman, the capital of Jordan; I with a great deal of trepidation. Some of the other managers appeared to be having second thoughts on the strategy that we had adopted to deal with the problem. None too seriously though. The Seven Sisters and their subsidiaries had for many years been 'makers and shakers' of international politics.

One had only to reflect on the enormous power the Seven Sisters wielded in 1951 at the time of Mosadeqh's nationalization of BP's oil complex in Iran at Abadan. A power so great that they were able to deprive Iran of the majority of its government revenue. This was accomplished by denying Iran the ability to export its crude oil. At that time, the Seven Sisters controlled almost 100% of the crude oil tankers in the world required for such export, and even more importantly, the markets to which it was going. By jointly agreeing to refuse to make their crude oil tankers available to Iran or opening the world markets for the export of Iran's crude oil (although the British felt the crude oil belonged to them), they were able to bring down Mosadeqh's regime without firing a shot in anger. A result that the United States Government, with all its might, probably would not have been able to accomplish on a diplomatic basis only.

The oil industry seldom agreed to do anything jointly except, as often alleged, to divide up the crude concession areas, set prices and agree on shares of the market. They were bitter adversaries in the markets where allegedly there were no agreed shares. However, like the Mafia and the Wall Street brokerage and investment bank houses, as James B. Stewart points out in his "Den of Thieves",[49] the oil companies 'circled the wagons' whenever they were threatened as an industry by outsiders.

As the plane landed and taxied up to the terminal building at the Amman airport, several official looking vehicles could be seen awaiting the arrival of the aircraft. There were no passport or custom procedures required. It was obvious to all concerned that we were high-level guests of the Jordanian government. We were whisked through the streets of the capital and taken directly to the office of the Prime Minister where we were greeted personally by the Prime Minister himself. After the usual, but very necessary formal exchange of greetings and drinking of mazbout that precedes every visit of residents of this part of the world, social or business, the Prime Minister steered the conversation towards the subject of the petroleum trade.

He politely enquired if business was satisfactory in our far flung empires throughout the world. A few murmured comments about the unstable conditions in the areas with which we all had to contend were the only answers he received.

He then asked a few questions about the technical aspects of the petroleum industry after apologizing for his lack of knowledge of the very fundamentals on which all modern societies survive, i.e.; the availability and consumption of petroleum products.

"In a refinery," he questioned, "do you actually take in that very rough and dirty raw material called crude oil and put it through a process that results in the clean and much better smelling products known as 'petrol' and 'kerosene'?" he asked. His seemingly, naïve understanding of the petroleum industry was beginning to put all the oil company managers at ease.

My Marine Officer was the first to glance in my direction with a half hidden, knowing smile that seemed to indicate, 'I told you so. He not only doesn't know the first thing about the petroleum business, but he is making every effort to set a friendly atmosphere in order to find a face saving device to backtrack on his badly, ill advised price reduction of kerosene.'

The Prime Minister continued in this vein of questioning. More and more of the assembled managers began to relax and glance in my direction. Their looks appeared to confirm that the Prime Minister's attitude was now evidence of how wrong and timid my approach had been to the confrontation and how right the strategy was that the industry had adopted.

'Bash the bloody WOGS! That's the only language they understand.'

The more technically oriented members of the group now took over the lead in the answer and question period. "Yes, Mr. Prime Minister," one of the very specialized, knowledgeable managers confirmed, "that is exactly how the industry operates. We receive the crude oil at the refinery in Sidon and put it through a process known as reduction. The resultant products made from the crude oil are known as 'refined products', because of the 'refining' process which they undergo," was the profound knowledge purveyed to this innocent savage of the Middle East.

"From where does the crude oil that you refine originate?" was the Prime Minister's next question. Even our intrepid Marine Officer knew the answer to this question, and he didn't hesitate to make his knowledge known. "It all comes from Saudi Arabia," he exclaimed as he forcefully interjected his answer into the scientifically trained, expert managers group that had been fielding the Prime Minister's apparently naïve questions of the petroleum industry. "And how does it get to Sidon," was his next guileless question. Obviously, he was at a complete loss as to understanding the profound complications of the highly, technical logistics of the international oil business.

Our ex-Marine officer lived in the same beautiful building complex facing the Mediterranean in Beirut in which Bill Chandler, the Vice-President of The Trans-Arabian Pipeline Company lived. Therefore, he was very well informed on that aspect of the logistics of the oil industry as, in point of fact, all of the company managers were. He, again, took command of the conversation and continued to enlighten this poor, backward, out-negotiated and cowered inhabitant of the desert.

"It comes through TAPLINE, the biggest crude oil pipeline in the world. TAPLINE is short for Trans-Arabian Pipeline Company," our Marine explained. "The start of the pipeline is in the Daharan/Ras Tanura area in Saudi Arabia, and it terminates in Sidon. Of course, only a very minute portion of the crude oil is off loaded at Sidon for the refinery. Millions of barrels of the crude oil are loaded directly from the pipeline into VLT's (Very Large Tankers) or holding tanks waiting for delivery into tankers and then shipped to Europe and other parts of the world. Without TAPLINE, Europe would find itself in a very dangerous position cut off from one of its major sources of crude supply," he continued to amplify very knowledgeably as he closed in for the kill on this benighted tribesman.

The Prime Minister appeared to indicate that the question and answer period was over and that we would now get down to the basic problem which was the cause of all of the assembled mangers being in Amman. "I can appreciate your concern, gentlemen, in connection with my recent price decree," he announced. "Nevertheless, I would like you to understand the economic and political problems with which I am faced at the present time. Our economy is in a very bad condition. We have some insurmountable, fiscal problems which are, certainly, not of our own making and which, of course, played a large part in my recent decision to reduce the price of kerosene. And these fiscal problems would have easily escalated into political problems without my reducing the price of kerosene to the peasants. However, one more question before we get onto the subject of my country's problems," he continued. "This TAPLINE of yours, is that the very same pipeline that crosses my country from Saudi Arabia on the way to Sidon in The Lebanon?" was his question.

"Yes! And we pay you very handsomely for the privilege," our gung-ho Marine officer replied knowingly.

Every head in the room suddenly twitched fractionally.

It was as though a hand of ice had abruptly gripped my heart. I, now, realized where the Prime Minister's apparently ingenuous questions were leading. Our savage from the desert held a royal flush over our four aces. What in the name of God was I going to tell our New York office when Europe ran out of crude oil? Tell them that I disagreed with all the other managers, but didn't have the guts to refuse to join them in their WOG bashing or simply tell them that I hadn't stuck to my guns? Possibly, I should tell them the truth; admit to the fact that the thought that the Prime Minister and a few of his renegade, camel riding citizens (as he would call them when they shot up the pipeline—'a pipeline that was an ideal target for guerrillas'[50]) actually controlled Europe's fate had never occurred to me. Nor, quite obviously, had it occurred to the other managers assembled in this dessert Kingdom on a startlingly, clear, bright, Sunday morning. His next question was a rhetorical one.

"Do you mean to tell *me* that *you* are refusing to send *me* 'refined products', as you call them, that are made from the crude oil that must first come through *my* country before *you* can refuse to send it back to *me*?"

Frantic capitulation would hardly describe the chaos that ensued after the Prime Minister's question. None of the assembled American or British managers had conferred with their head offices in London or New York on the drastic decision to cut off Jordan from its source of petroleum products. It goes without saying that had we been astute enough to do so, someone would have pointed out the logistics of the situation, just as the Prime Minister was doing now. In fact, no one had even consulted with the Vice-President of Tapline who lived in our very own community. He would have been the first to recommend caution when dealing with a sovereign government through whose country his multi-million dollar pipeline transited.

The plane ride back to Beirut was a glum and subdued flight. No one even discussed the magnitude of the wrath that would have descended on all of our heads if we had had to advise our New York and London offices that because of certain actions we had taken to protect an infinitesimal portion of our various companies' world-wide profits, we had jeopardized the supply of crude oil to all of Europe. Our ex-Marine was the most crestfallen. Nobody took him to task for the unenviable position that we had found ourselves in the Prime Minister's office. Human nature being what it is, however, one could almost read into the glances cast in his direction that the predominate thought was that 'if it hadn't been for the Marines, we wouldn't be in this fix'.

Beirut was to be our home for two years. There were highs and lows as were to be expected of any new assignment. The highlight of our stay there was the birth of our second daughter whom we nick-named 'Habibty'. We were studying Arabic and learned that this was a term of endearment. It seemed to fit her exactly.

The worst low was when we left her at home one Sunday afternoon. She had fallen asleep just prior to our leaving for the beach and we didn't want to disturb her nap. The burst of gunfire heard at our beach house hadn't disturbed us too much as such an occurrence was not that infrequent. We had repeatedly taken every occasion to warn the two older children that when they were playing in the sand they must always keep in between the beach houses and not play on the walks. Using the houses as a shelter prevented any chance that a high powered rifle that might have sent a spent bullet in our direction would hit them.

They were, also, repeatedly instructed never to play in the water with their backs to the shore. They must always keep an eye open for any signal from us that they must immediately exit from the water and run to the beach house. We told them that when they were swimming they must, as frequently as possible, glance up into the hills and note if there appeared to be any unusual activity which might indicate that the rebels were mounting an offense that could possible lead them into the city. Of course, with children that young we made every attempt to make a game of it. They never really understood the seriousness of the situation, nor did we really want them to understand other than that they must always look to us and the hills for an indication of what 'play acting part' they were to assume.

The engineer from the refinery had made a study of the hallway and the children's bedrooms and their windows in our apartment. He was able to calculate the three exact locations for their two beds and the crib in the central hallway that avoided, absolutely, any exposure to any stray spent bullet that might come through the shutters in the evening after they had been put to bed. I can still close my eyes today and see the three rectangles marked out on the floor in the hallway on which they were placed every night for months during the fighting.

It was shortly after the burst of gunfire that Ed Gilbert ran down from his home just above the beach house area. He delivered the devastating news that the rebels were in the very process of successfully broaching the main road between the beach and close to the city. That meant that we were on the verge of being cut off from our daughter. We were frantic with fear and anxiety. I insisted that my wife was to remain at Ed's home with the two children while I raced into the city to be sure the baby was safe. She wouldn't hear a word of it. She declared that there was no way that she would remain separated from our new baby while the fighting was going on in such close proximity to our home.

There can't be too many terrified American mothers and fathers who have run a gauntlet in an automobile between the loyalists and the rebels, with the mother and two young children lying on the floor in the rear of the car and the mother's body over the children for protection. The other lows we were fortunate enough not to have had any forewarning about their arrival either.

We surely didn't know about the insidious, underhanded method by which the appointed chairman of Caltex from the Western Sister was slowly but surely decreasing our remuneration by his instructions to withhold the special inflationary, compensating 5% increases from the expatriate staff while awarding it to the domestic staff only. Perhaps he felt that running gauntlets between warring factions didn't qualify for monetary compensation. We should just be thankful that *THE COMPANY* kept us on its payroll, albeit, at a lower equivalent salary than our fellow employees in New York.

The fighting between the loyalists and the so called rebels had been going on for some time. '…. beginning in late 1957, Egyptian subversive activities in Lebanon began in earnest. It became clear to observers in Beirut—or, for that matter, to audiences of Cairo's 'Voice of the Arabs' broadcasts—that Nasser was ready to go to any lengths to bring down Chamaoun'[51]. There did not seem to be any real defined political reason that the Westerners could discern that could account for the warring factions. There were fairly well grounded rumors that the difference was really between the Muslims and the Christians. This rumor was, undoubtedly, based on the fact that the charismatic rebel leader, Jamblatt, was a Muslim. He certainly couldn't claim to have the allegiance of all the Muslims in the country, just as the government couldn't claim to have the allegiance of all the Christians in the country.

One of the reasons for Lebanon's historical stability, in an area whose chief claim to fame was its instability, was that both religions were given equal representation in all parts of the government. This included the army that was a mixture of Muslims and Christians commanded by a Muslim General, and a Prime Minister who was a Christian. However, there was a growing preponderance of Muslims. The preponderance of Muslims was only a reflection of the evolving statistical realities. The Muslims were breeding at a much quicker rate than were the Christians. If the truth were known, this may undoubtedly have been one of the causes for the confrontation. No longer could the populace be represented on a fifty-fifty basis. The Muslims wanted a greater part of the power sharing based on their numbers.

What the Westerners did know, without any doubt whatsoever, was that whatever was causing the confrontation, it was making life miserable for them in Beirut. 'The spark which ignited the blow-up had finally come on 8 May 1958, when unknown persons shot and killed one Nesib Metni, a pro-Nasser journalist whom Chamaoun's enemies believed to be so irritatingly anti-Chamaoun that Chamaoun's guilt for the murder could, in accordance with the Lebanese sense of justice, be assumed. In the preceding few weeks some twenty-odd lives had been lost in incidents of violence at various places in the Lebanon, but this particular murder fitted perfectly the specifications of drama and timing which the anti-Chamaounists' outburst required. Within two or three days, Lebanon was in a state of civil war—a stalemate civil war, but nevertheless one which paralyzed the country.'[52] A sunset to sunrise curfew had been declared. The curfew, when announced, was scheduled to last a matter of days until the situation was brought under control by the Government.

At the end of six months of curfew; when after my wife and I had carefully placed the two children's beds and the baby's crib night after night for months in their designated areas in the central hallway; when after a number of spent bullets had been found on the ground outside the windows of the children's rooms; when after the Marines had landed at the invitation of President Chamaoun with the cooperation of President Eisenhower; and when the families had been evacuated, we knew that the wounds of this confrontation would never heal. It only needs a glance at the TV news today to know that the seeds of destruction sown in that initial clash have come to fruition.

The building next to ours was owned by the same delightful family that owned the one in which we lived. We had gotten to know them because the lease negotiations were handled by the family personally. While this might seem strange for what was obviously a very wealthy family not to designate such details to their business office, there were two reasons for this unusual situation. One was that since in our six story building there was only one apartment on each floor there obviously weren't very many tenants and, consequently, there was not too much call on the family's time. The other building was constructed in a similar manner. The owners occupied the top floor, and the next floor below them was a replica of the owner's in that it was the only apartment on the floor as well. The other floors had just two apartments on each floor which again required very little time from the family.

The second reason for the family being directly involved in the leasing arrangements was that the daughter of the family was learning the business. What better way to learn the business then to be involved in managing their real estate properties? For legal and tax reasons the properties were registered in the daughter's name which, in effect, made her our landlady.

The apartment below the owners was occupied by Bill and Clair Chandler and their wonderful family. Bill was Vice-President of Trans-Arabian Pipeline Company at that time. How was it possible that the oil industry didn't consult with him before we cut Jordan, through which his pipeline ran, off from its petroleum supplies?

Bill and Clair were matchless bridge players. They very kindly and pain stakingly indoctrinated my wife and myself into that most fascinating game. There was one condition that contributed to our having the unusual opportunity of progressing in the art of this game so rapidly. The curfew! You could not leave your home from sunset to sunrise so that there were only two alternatives every night for months. Bridge and poker. Inasmuch as there weren't sufficient players in the two building because the few apartments mitigated against large numbers of residents, invitations were extended on a nightly basis to other members of the community.

There was a constant liaison established between all members of the two buildings. Any guests from other parts of city that arrived to play bridge or poker for the evening necessitated that they and their children (no one left their children at home if they were going to be away for the evening) be accommodated until morning. The children and the adults were all distributed throughout the two buildings. It was a way to survive a stifling way of life of month after month of remaining at your home from sunset to sunrise and hearing the gunfire in the distance. The bomb explosions were much closer since the rebels use to infiltrate the city and place their bombs in abandoned doorways or under parked vehicles during the day.

My wife became an excellent bridge player and actually, eventually, taught the game at a later date. She became so expert at it that she was invited many years later by the Minister of Finance of Tanganyika to be his doubles' partner in the Dar-es-salaam Club in the men's card room, an unheard of accomplishment for a woman. No women had ever set foot in the men's section of that club, much less played bridge there. It was truly a measure of her expertise.

Two of our overnight guests had reciprocated our frequent card playing invitations by inviting us to their home for dinner one evening. We arrived at their apartment and put the children to bed along with the other guests' offspring and sat down to a most enjoyable meal. Don Speilman, our host, was the Assistant Manager for Mobil. He and Nancy, his lovely wife, had two young boys that were very, well behaved children, but like all youngsters, they were charged with energy.

Don had just returned from a quick business trip to New York and had brought back the first recording of a new musical which we had all read so much about, 'My Fair Lady'. He had placed his record player behind the couch that occupied the area just in front of his living room window. This would obviate any chance encounter with it by his two young exuberant children while they were confined to the house week after week and month after month because of the curfew.

After dinner, Don, with an almost reverent air because he had been privileged to have heard the score a number of times during his visit to New York, placed the record on the turn table. We all sat around on the floor and the couch while the most enchanting music that we had heard in many years flowed through the room. We forgot our trials and tribulations of living in Beirut because of the delightful fantasy that the music allowed our senses to explore. Very startlingly, just as the hero was 'walking down the street where she lived', the area just outside Don's apartment came to life with a nerve shattering explosion as an unusually large bomb went off.

We had become quite accustomed to hearing these devices being detonated. Frankly, not in as close proximity as this one appeared to be. That it was more massive than the usual harassment that the rebels were wreaking on the residents of the city was very evident by the way the solid building that was housing us reverberated to the force of the explosion. And why the rebels had chosen that place and time, so different from their usual day time practices, was impossible to fathom. We all sat there in stunned silence for a few seconds.

It may have been that the builders had been delinquent in their duty when attaching the venetian blinds to their fittings on the large window just over the record player. Or whether the reverberations were of such sufficient strength to negate even secure fittings couldn't be ascertained. What was extremely obvious was that the over large, venetian blind parted from its holdings and came crashing down squarely across the record player and the score of 'My Fair Lady'.

I guess it was more a nervous reaction than any real sense of amusement. But the look on Don's face, as he viewed the wreckage of his player scattered all over the floor and the record which he had carried all the way from New York with such tender care and had so carefully placed out of his young children's reach, caused all in the room to burst out into nervous, hysterical laughter.

Don just gazed at us with a forlorn and hurt look on his face. You could almost see the emotions struggling within him as he couldn't seem to make up his mind whether to get mad at us or join us in our jittery laughter. He chose the former course, but with a delightful sense of the quixotic. He turned to us as our laughter subsided and quietly and politely asked how many of us had parked our company cars in the front of the building.

Now the tables were turned with a vengeance. None of us had given any thought to the fact that the explosive must have been placed out of sight under one of his guests' cars, with the timer ticking so that no one could see the bomb before the timer signaled that it was to violently explode. We all made an immediate, mad dash for the doorway and the stairs. We completely ignored the much more convenient but slower elevator as we all harboured the awful feeling that somebody's company car had just joined the casualty list. What explanation would we have when we put the cost of a new vehicle under the column for *'REPAIRS'* on our expense account and had to admit to the fact that we had been careless with the company property by parking it in a not too secure place?

The days were still fully occupied with attempting to perform our office duties as best as possible under the circumstances, but with the realization that it was certainly not at a peak rate of efficiency. The constant news of car bombs in the main part of the city and the resultant casualty lists, hearing the distant gunfire particularly at night, took on an almost normal way of life. Most of the explosions took place during the day, when the rebels could be sure that they would wreak the most devastation on the populace who were abroad at that hour having to perform the necessary duties of buying food or keeping their offices open. The gunfire was confined mostly to the night, when the rebels could infiltrate the city or the loyalists' front lines and unleash havoc on them.

There was one frightening and terrifying exception to the location of these scenarios, when to our horror there erupted during the morning a deafening and sustained sound of machine gun fire immediately in front of the office building. The company office was on the second floor which allowed us to hear clearly the sound of shattering glass as the machine guns swept the store fronts in the area. Everyone in the office acted with the identical sense of self-preservation. We all, immediately, flung ourselves on the floor close to the front wall of our offices as we could possibly get. There was one notable exception to this action on our part. Ed Gilbert! He didn't have a wall.

He would be an open target, if the machine guns were turned in his direction from the ground floor to the second floor. He headed for his doorway which was at right angles to the front of the building and consequently at right angles to that vast expanse of his wall to wall, ceiling to floor window. The rapid rate of machine gun fire was so intense that he just stood there transfixed. He hesitated to expose himself by sinking to his knees and crawling over in my direction to join me where I lay prone and hugging the wall of my office at the same time. So there he stood with a terror stricken look on his face, his stomach sucked in in order to provide the smallest target possible. I gazed at him without any words of comfort that I could think of to ease his frightening quandary. I did voice a silent prayer to myself asking for forgiveness, though, for being so envious of his luxurious office with its huge window as I remembered my biblical teachings and the Ten Commandments one of which said 'thou shalt not covet thy neighbor's property'.

After a prolonged lull in the firing, Ed, eventually, dropped to his knees and crawled over to join me in a sitting position which I had finally assumed during the extended pause in the firing. The sitting position still left us with complete coverage as the wall was of sufficient height to shield us. By this time, there had been considerable shouting between the different offices from all the staff members. All of us wondering what our next step should be. Eventually, we realized that the incident must been confined to only one objective, whatever that might have been, and the perpetrators of the frightening intrusion into our lives had left the scene of the crime. We slowly regained our courage and gingerly unwound ourselves from our protective stances and stood erect, but ready on an instant's notice to fling ourselves to the floor again.

We waited sometime before going downstairs to investigate the damage. There was nothing that could be determined from the wreckage. There were no bodies. No reason for the assault could be found either. We finished off the morning and left, albeit, slightly earlier than usual.

In talking to New York on the telephone, Ed had taken the opportunity of telling them of the rather unfortunate experience we had undergone with the unexpected machine gun barrage immediately in front of our office. In times of stress and danger, the best in men and corporations, particularly THE COMPANY, comes to the forefront. New York insisted that the wives and children leave the area. Immediate plans were put in hand for Anne-Marie, my wife and the three children to leave Beirut. The Sales Manager was a bachelor. The Chief Accountant, who was English from the company's East African staff, was married to a Lebanese and she elected to stay. So the evacuees consisted only of my family and Ed's wife, Anne-Marie. Since she made frequent trips to Paris, which was her home before she met Ed and was married, she was packed and ready to go immediately. She took off the next day for Paris with a heartfelt farewell as she was delighted to get back to a more civilized way of life than she had been enduring for many months.

Packing for three children and getting all their necessary paraphernalia that goes with traveling with children of that age was going to take several days. Frankly, we were naturally quite moved by New York's concern, but having lived under the trying circumstances that we had had to live under for the past months, it didn't seem all that urgent to leave 'the next day' as had Anne-Marie, who had wanted to in any event. And besides, we had several poker and bridge parties scheduled that we would have had to cancel leaving the players with no partners and no place to stay without us.

As is usual in 'the best laid plans..... .' fate intervened again as it always has a habit of so doing. The fighting became so intense and, again as probably in all military campaigns, the fighting moved to the airport which was the object of the rebels drive. It closed down forty-eight hours after New York had insisted that the wives and children leave and just one day after Anne-Marie had departed.

Now there was great consternation even among the hard bitten and long term expatriate residents of Beirut, who had stoically been enduring all the nerve wracking atmosphere of living in a 'war zone' for months. New York was immediately informed of the sudden and abrupt deterrent to the plans to evacuate the wives and children. Again, Caltex's inherent concern for its employees and their families came to the forefront. They instantly cabled the detailed information that there was a Caltex tanker, which was under long term charter from one of the privately owned shipping companies, just two days off the coast of the Lebanon. The vessel would be diverted to Sidon to pick up the evacuees. The owner's stateroom would be made available for my wife and the children, and there were several additional cabins available for any of the wives and children of the other oil companies that might wish to take advantage of the offer by THE COMPANY. Fortunately, it was a long term charter from one of the privately owned shipping companies and not one of the company owned tankers. Tankers built for and owned by the Two Sisters didn't, in any way, have owner's staterooms and spare cabins.

Byron Brown, the Manager of the jointly owned Caltex and Mobil refinery in Sidon hadn't been to Beirut in a number of weeks. He normally made it a practice to visit our offices at least weekly for routine discussions. When we talked to him on the telephone, he said that based on just plain random statistics, he didn't want to be on the road between Sidon and Beirut when there was a constant danger of being caught up in the cross fire between the rebels and the loyalists. The government troops had made Sidon one of their strongholds, because of the necessity of keeping the refinery on stream as well as to ensure that the crude oil coming from Saudi Arabia would be sure to find an outlet to Europe and continue to earn the transit fees generated by the movement of the crude through Lebanon.

The cable from New York giving the details of the tanker that was to be used for the evacuation had been copied to Byron Brown. He telephoned our office at once. He advised us that in view of the anticipated evacuation from Beirut of the wives and children, we should maintain almost constant twenty-four hour liaison with his office. This was due to the fact that the fighting had intensified considerably around the refinery and the main road leading to the refinery from Beirut. Just as important was the information that there was considerable danger that any vehicles traveling between Sidon and Beirut, a matter of some miles, would almost definitely encounter difficulty on the way and be exposed to some possible gunfire from the rebels in the hills.

On hearing this information my wife, particularly after her hair rising experience of running the gauntlet between the beach house and Beirut, flatly refused to go. She said she felt safer at the moment staying at home in our well built luxury apartment with its tremendously stout walls than trying to dodge bullets sheltered only by the tin sides of what the American car industry was building in those days. I confessed that I had to agree with her. We telephoned the Mobil Manager, whose wife had made her decision to accept Caltex's invitation to leave on the tanker and offered the owner's stateroom to his wife.

In retrospect, it was one of the decisions that turned out to be the correct one. The wife of the Mobil manager, who had been delighted to be advised that the Caltex tanker was available to evacuate her was even more delighted, if that were possible, when she heard that she could occupy the owner's stateroom. When we talked to her after her return to Beirut, she told my wife that, while she enjoyed the voyage, it would have been impossible for my wife with the three children to have 'survived' the trip. Obviously, the tanker didn't cater for mothers of small children. Just as obviously, it didn't cater for children and, especially, small children. There were no guard rails that would have prevented them crawling over the side of the vessel into the sea. There were no play rooms or any kind of area that could be designated as a playroom. The voyage took seventeen days, and the first port of call was Halifax in New Foundland.

None of this detracted from the sincere feelings of thankfulness that we felt towards THE COMPANY. It was not their fault that their efforts didn't result in the successful evacuation of my wife and three children. It didn't matter. We were truly grateful that we worked for a company that never hesitated to make every facility at their command available for their employees when a life threatening situation arose.

Conditions worsened from day to day. The bombings downtown became more frequent and more intense. The fighting in the hills escalated and there were daily clashes between the loyalists and the rebels. Naturally, we now began to wonder if we had made the correct decision of having my wife and the three children remain in Beirut. Just as this doubt was beginning to weigh exceptionally heavy on my mind there was an urgent call from Ed Gilbert to my home at 5:30 AM in the morning. He informed me that the American Ambassador, Mr.McClintock, had called a crucial meeting of all American company managers and senior personnel in his office at 6:00 AM for an extremely, momentous briefing. Ed said that he would pick me up at my apartment as my home was on the way from his house. Now I was sure that we had made a grievous mistake in not evacuating my wife and children when we had the chance, particularly after my scathing comments to myself about the absence of the knowledge of the 'facts of life' exhibited by the State Department Staff in Egypt.

On arrival at the Embassy, we recognized the managers of the other American oil companies as well as a large number of Americans with whom we were acquainted. His Excellency, Ambassador McClintock looked exceptionally well and relaxed. His announcement soon told us why he had finally reached such a more normal outlook on the situation.

"The Marines Are Coming!"

He delightedly informed us that at the invitation of President Chamaoun of the Lebanon, President Eisenhower, under the terms of the 'Eisenhower Doctrine', had dispatched part of the Sixth Fleet and an amphibious force of Marines to bolster, what was now, a seriously besieged Lebanese Government. The amphibious forces were at that moment only an hour or two away from their designated landing area, which was the beach section between the airport and the city.

The choice of this location would provide a cover for the airport operations and allow the landing forces to enter the city by the most straight forward route. Any attempt at a direct landing in the port of the city would present severe physical obstacles. There was no place that the landing craft could run up on the beach in the port, inasmuch as there was no beach, and disgorge their cargo of light tanks, troop carriers and all the assorted mobile equipment necessary to support a venture of this kind. I didn't have the temerity to ask him if the logistical officers had records of the bridges or the weight carrying capacity of the roads that the marines were going to traverse on their way into the city.

There were no admonishments about keeping the information secret, just as there had never been about the prior briefings which we had been given on the information available to the American Embassy and relayed to us by the Ambassador. As a consequence, on my arrival home and after informing my wife of the wonderful news that 'The Marines Are Coming', I immediately telephoned the group leader of the families of a number of White Russians living in Beirut. These families had taken sanctuary in the Lebanon from the world wide harassment to which they were subjected, because they had chosen to leave their home country when the character of the Marxist-Leninism peoples' revolution was finally exposed in its brutally, true colours. Which now, as the whole world has finally realized, was 'the subjugation of the Russian population for the sole benefit of the ruling revolutionaries'.

I had first met a number of these White Russians when in Shanghai. They were a delightful addition to the expatriate community there. We spent many hours together over bottles of vodka, while we exchanged views on the depraved character of the leaders of the USSR and their political philosophy. I had developed a very firm relationship with several of that community and after my departure from China I had kept in correspondence with them.

At this stage in my awareness of the real world, it was no surprise to me that there was a constant world wide liaison among these refugees from their beloved Rodina. No matter what part of the globe they had chosen to live or had been accepted, since in many cases they didn't always have the choice of the country in which they would be allowed to reside and attempt to carry out what they hoped would be normal existence, there was a communications apparatus in existence. This communication system kept them informed of any possible danger to their physical well being.

Their concern was always that in the event of any local uprising in the country in which they might be resident at the time, the persistent question invariably was, 'Are the Soviets behind this disturbance? If so, and they are going to be successful, we had better make preparations to move on to another country that will accept us. Because the first ones on whom the Soviets will turn their vengeance will be those of us who left their initial, lawless control of the populace in our beloved homeland'.

Consequently, shortly after the fighting started, I had received a very, deferential caller to my office who told me that he represented the White Russians in the Lebanon. He had been given my name by the Central Committee that kept track of those individuals that were known to be adamantly opposed to the political philosophy of the ruling class of the USSR. At all times after our initial contact, I kept him informed of any information which I had obtained from the American Embassy on the status of the fighting between the loyalists and the rebels.

I assured him that all of my contacts had categorically denied that the Russians were in anyway involved in this unpleasant situation. He politely informed me that his sources in Syria gave his committee reason to believe that that was not the case. I was so sure that he had been misinformed that I never relayed the details of the information that he had given to me to the American Ambassador. On reflection now, it is very obvious that that is exactly what I should have done. Undoubtedly '.... he may have been advised by his Syrian Russian contacts that the Russian military had been mobilized.... . It is true that Khrushchev ordered everything brought to combat readiness, but actually he did not intend to send his troops into Lebanon'[53].

One has only to look at the involvement of the Syrians, in the present Lebanese convulsion, to realize that there are very often unseen forces at work behind the chaos being created by what appears to be only a domestic difference of opinion; Even though that difference of opinion may well result in outright mayhem without any help from outsiders. Although, I was unaware of any official knowledge that the US Government had of outside interference in the affairs of the Lebanon, inasmuch as the Ambassador had never mentioned any such details in his briefings, there was quite sufficient evidence to be gleaned in the streets that such interference was on a massive scale.

It appeared that the concern of the White Russians was centered around the fact that '... the Egyptians gave Kamal Jumblatt the material aid he desperately needed. Their strategy was built around massive support to the 'Beirut Four' who, they believed could eventually call out 'the street' (the city mob) and gain control of the key area, Beirut itself. The Egyptian GIA chief assigned to Beirut was an intelligence officer who would do credit to any intelligence service, and his 'staff' team were all high quality officers. His 'field' team were Syrian desperadoes, sent over the mountains by the Syrian intelligence chief, Abdelhamid Serraj, who provided an ideal link between the Egyptian professionals and the Lebanese 'street'. It was a formidable capability which confronted Chamaoun and his western supporters by June 1958, one month after the civil war started. The 'Beirut Four': Sa'eb Salaam, Abdallah Yafi, Adnan Hakim, and Abdallah Mashnuq depended entirely on aid from the Egyptians, not only in weapons but in funds with which to buy support.'[54] It was not so much the direct aid from Egypt to the rebels, but Egypt's indirect links to Russia that so unnerved the White Russians.

Ed, also, immediately telephoned the Chief Accountant after the meeting to give him the news and let his wife know that more secure times were coming for her and countrymen. At this point, Ed suggested that it might be a once in a life-time chance to go down to the shore and watch the United States Navy and The Marines arrive. The Sales Manager had been transferred for reasons that were not connected with the insurrection. I was delighted with the invitation. I had been wondering how to make the identical suggestion to Ed, but since he was the one that made out my performance report for my salary increases, I didn't want to give him any indication that my judgment left anything to be desired. Since I had nothing to do with his fitness report, it didn't bother him to make such a sugges-tion.

We took off in the direction of the shoreline which lay on the way to the air-port. As we rounded a broad curve just over the bluffs that led to the wide beaches bordering the airport road, there was a sight that must have warmed the hearts many times of countless hundreds of thousands of besieged people around the world who were looking for deliverance.

The United States Navy ships were just in view as they loomed majestically over the horizon. We both heaved a deep and fervent sigh of relief as we took our first breath of total relaxation in many a day or week or month for that matter. We parked on the edge of the bluff and watched them as they approached the distant shore. When it appeared that they had put their landing craft in the water and the Marines were ashore, we continued on our way to the airport road to cheer them on.

As we approached the junction of the main road leading into the city and the shore drive which we were on, we were surprised by the rapidity with which the Marines had, apparently, not only landed, but were already on their way into the city. What was even more surprising, and what we thought was very comforting, was that the Lebanese Army Tank Command had also come out to greet the arriving Marines.

Everyone has remarkable coincidences in their lives and the writer experienced just such a happening at this time, although strangely enough this extraordinary coincidence surfaced many, many years later. At the time this coincidence sur-faced, it actually produced an almost eerie feeling, even at that very late date and even caused the hairs to rise on the back of my neck. It was a coincidence that provided an instantaneous and total recall of the incident of meeting the United States Marines and the Lebanese Army Tank Command at the airport road junc-tion with its later attendant, spine chilling confrontation. Strangely enough, the coincidence wasn't a real life experience, but one that I was reading about in an episode in Tom Clancy's well known novel "Red Storm Rising"[55].

Those, who have read Tom Clancy's fascinating novel, will recall that a group of elite Soviet Spetznaz forces left their safe house in Aachen in the Federal Republic of Germany to attack and destroy the NATO communications head-quarters in Lammersdorf as a prelude to the start of World War III. On the way to the NATO base, they encountered a military convoy of NATO tanks on low-hauler trailers. The Russian Major, who was in charge of the attack and destroy unit, immediately noticed that, strangely, the tanks were loaded backwards with their guns facing aft. Obviously, a most unusual change from their normal proce-dure of loading the tanks with the guns facing forward. He was totally unaware, of course, that the purpose of his mission had been uncovered, and the tank guns were being deliberately trained on him and his unit. They had been loaded in that most, unusual position with this exact purpose in mind.

Years before Clancy's Russian Major in the novel made his observation, I had made the identical observation. In my case, it was a real life situation. Not only a real life situation, but life threatening as well. We, as onlookers to this drama at the time, like Clancy's character at the time his mental observation was made, were totally unaware of the implications.

I turned to Ed and commented, "Strange isn't it? But have you noticed that the tank guns of the Lebanese are pointing up the road *at* the Marines and *not* *towards* the city, as if they were going to oppose the Marines instead of being the advance units?"

In fact, from the vantage point that we had assumed slightly off the junction of the road, we had only to look to the right and we were greeted with the awe inspiring view of a massive armada of United States Marines and all the might of their back-up, logistical support. A look to the left showed a smaller armada, but not that much less awe inspiring as to make one believe that they could be ignored. The Lebanese Army Tank Command had always had a most well grounded reputation for fitness and trained expertise in the art of tank warfare.

There were a number of what appeared to be very senior members of the mili-tary from the Lebanese gathered at the junction, as well as one imposing figure that left no doubt that he was the ultimate, military, command figure of the whole country. There were several Americans in the way of foot soldiers in the group, plus what was also very obvious, the Commanding Officer of the Marine Assault group. They were all conferring on the modis operandi of joining in a concerted march on the city—or so we assumed. We happily unzipped our cam-era cases and proceeded to take as many pictures as we could from our vantage point in the trees lining the two roadways.

After a period of some time, which in all likelihood was no more than five or ten minutes at the most, and during all of this elapsed time there was not a single sign of any movement from either of the two forces facing each other, there suddenly sounded the screech of sirens. In between the two opposing forces there appeared at breakneck speed three vehicles. They came to a stop with a neck snapping lurch as the first police car came to an abrupt halt, followed by the American Ambassador's limousine and the second police car with its lights flashing and its siren just slowing to a dim wail.

Before the Ambassador's car had even come to a full stop, the door was flung open. The Ambassador and his ubiquitous French Poodle exited on the run for the group of American and Lebanese officers that were still apparently trying to decide which was the best route or best method to secure the city. We happily continued to provide unforgettable entries to our photo albums by snapping every possible sequence that was going on before our very eyes, including the antics of the Ambassador's French Poodle.

When I was having lunch with Ambassador, The Honorable Ridgeway B.Knight, many years later in Paris in 1991, I mentioned to him that I thought it a bit incongruous that the American Ambassador would bring his French Poodle with him at a time like that. Ambassador Knight replied that Ambassador MeClintock had become well known for this eccentricity, and that as long as he only took the poodle to certain occasions, it very definitely enhanced his recall image. He did continue by saying, however, that he had brought the French Poodle to a certain diplomatic function which raised quite a few eyebrows and Ambassador's Knight's as well.

Outside of the official representatives to the gathering, which were the Lebanese Army Tank Command and the Lebanese Army Commanding General, The United States Marines landing force and its Commanding Officer, The American Ambassador and his police escort, Ed and I were the only other two individuals present at this momentous meeting in...

'NO MAN'S LAND'

The Soviet Spetznaz Major, in his van on his way to destroy the NATO communications headquarters in Clancy's novel, was unaware of why the tank guns were pointing in the wrong direction, but he was soon to find out that they were trained on him. We, too, were to find out why the Lebanese tank guns were pointing at our Marines, but not so soon as the Soviet Major was to discover his mistake.

After the arrival of Ambassador McClintock, there ensued about fifteen minutes of conference, with what appeared to be some very determined argumentative statements emanating from the Lebanese Commanding General Fuad Shehab. There were only polite acknowledgments from the Marine Commanding Officer. The arguments from the Lebanese side appeared to be expertly fielded by the Ambassador in the middle of the confrontation. Finally, General Shehab slowly walked away and entered the command tank with the large antenna indicating that it was the communications center for the group. Within minutes of his entering the tank and, apparently, having been in radio communication with his other tank commanders, the Lebanese tanks all wheeled clumsily in a hundred and eighty degree turn and led the way into the city.

It wasn't until a considerable period later that we learned that President Chamaoun had been so ungracious as to fail to inform his Muslim Commanding General, Fuad Shehab, that he had asked President Eisenhower for assistance and as a consequence "The Marines Were Coming". 'The General, who had refused to support Chamaoun's position beyond keeping the combatants apart'[56], took it upon himself as soon as the news flooded all of Beirut regarding the arrival of the Americans, that he would stop them from entering the city. As a result of the General's decision we had been taking our pictures in....

'NO MAN'S LAND'.

What apparently convinced General Shehab to alter his plans was the statement made by the Commanding Officer of the Marines. We were told by a very highly placed individual, who was present at the meeting in 'No Man's Land', that the Marine Commanding Officer stated to his opposite number, "General, I have been ordered by my Commander-in-Chief, President Eisenhower, to secure the City of Beirut. As a General, you are fully aware of the implications of such an order from your Commander-in-Chief. You have exactly five minutes to decide whether or not to join us in this operation, at which time we will proceed down this road with or without your assistance." It is obvious why the General changed his intentions.

By this time, we had noticed that several of the Marine amtracks had pulled off the road and started to discharge their 'cargo' which consisted of a large number of battle clad and equipped grim faced Marines. They immediately started to shoulder their packs and line up in formation. We thought it the better part of discretion to beat a hasty retreat at this time and return to our homes and maybe, even eventually, go to the office and perhaps sell some oil.

Without much to do in the office and with the momentous events of the day only hours behind us, Ed decided that it would be better for all the staff to call it a day. So we turned off the lights, turned down the air conditioning for what had been the beginning of an unbearably, scorching and muggy day and we all headed for our respective homes. On arrival at the entrance to the driveway of the apartment, I was utterly astonished to see what appeared to be about one hundred hot and sweaty Marines camped on the doorstep in front of our garden and in the street and spread out in a defensive manner near the walk along the sea.

I immediately stopped the car. It occurred to me that there was no way that the Marines could distinguish between friend and foe at this stage. I did not want to the victim of 'friendly fire', no matter how well intentioned it might be. I exited the car as quickly as I could and watched the Marine Captain approach me cautiously with his machine gun held at the ready. I was dressed for the air conditioned office, which I had just left, so that with a shirt and tie and coat and no objects in my hand, the Captain could get a good look at what or what might not be a threat to him and his men. Without lowering his gun, which was still pointing in my direction, he enquired if he could be of any assistance.

I immediately answered and said, "I live here," in a quite nervous manner. The sight of all those heavily armed Marines, while they might be on my side, that amount of fire power was enough to make anyone nervous. I blurted out, "What are you doing here?" He visibly relaxed somewhat when he recognized my American accent. "What's your name?" he instantly questioned me without apparently intending to give me time to think.

"Palmer-Smith," I replied hurriedly.

"Oh," he continued, "I've checked with the residents in the building, and your wife said she expected you home shortly. You're free to go and please don't worry about anything. We are here to see that the area is as secure as we can possibly make it. You can understand that we must be very cautious when anyone approaches our position, particularly, in view of all the information we were given in our briefings about car bombs. I'm sorry if I appeared to be unfriendly," were his closing remarks. I assured him that I understood completely and could only extend our deepest gratitude and sincerest thanks to him for his presence.

I greeted my wife with the tale of my encounter with the Marine Captain. She, in turn, told me that she had seen them coming up the Corniche doing double time in the oppressive heat of the early morning. As soon as they had arrived, they had apparently decided to make their first rest period right in front of our garden. The Marine Captain had ordered several of his scouts to check out the residents of the building and to obtain their names if any further contact or verification were needed.

She said that they looked as if they were all going to melt like candy soldiers from the heat, because they were perspiring so heavily. She informed me that while waiting for me, she had prepared a massive amount of ice tea. She had, also, alerted all the other residents in the building to her need for ice cubes and a continual source of additional tea, as she intended to make the Marines as comfortable as possible. In addition, the larders of all the apartments in both buildings were stocked with many kinds of dry biscuits and cookies, which had been part of the instructions from the Embassy as a safety precaution early in the fighting.

The original instructions from the Embassy had been to stock up on as much frozen food as possible. As the period of fighting had lengthened from the original one or two weeks that the Lebanese Government had first announced, the American Embassy under the excellent guidance of Ambassador McClintock, had set up regular meetings to brief the American residents on the status quo of the 'insurrection'. At the next periodic meeting shortly after the instructions to stock up on frozen food had been issued, I pointed out that we had stocked up in the same manner in Beijing. Although, we had lost our electricity supply a number of times and for several days in a row, our problem in Beijing was, in fact, directly opposite to our problem in Beirut. It was so cold in Beijing that everything had a tendency to freeze solid immediately, if there were no heat available. The same, however, was not true of Beirut. If the rebels were successful in cutting the power to the city even for a short time, we were all soon to have an immense amount of rancid meat and other spoiled food on our hands. The instructions were immediately changed to canned food and dry groceries.

My wife had also put out an urgent call for the stores of such edibles as the cookies and biscuits to accompany the tea. They were to be delivered to our apartment with an additional request for volunteers. It was going to need many hands to help serve what looked like a company of over one hundred men. All the residents responded with alacrity. We were now ready for our surprise offering of ice tea and cookies for our fighting men who were still enduring the sweltering heat of the blazing sun of Beirut encamped in front of our garden.

I exited the building and approached the Marine Captain who greeted me with a very definite, friendly smile compared to his initial response on my first arrival. I informed him that we had made ice tea and there were excellent cookies to go with the offering. My wife and I, and the other residents of the building would very much like to have him enjoy a cooling break from his hot and arduous guard duties in front of our buildings. He thanked me profusely, and said that as much as he would like to take advantage of my kind offer, there was no way that he would leave his men to enjoy the comfort of ice tea and a snack in a cool apartment while they were still subjected to the onslaught of the overpowering heat of the city.

"Oh, no!" I hastened to inform him, "the invitation is for you *and* your men." He was momentarily stunned.

"You mean that you have enough supplies and are willing to serve over a hundred of us and have them enter your beautiful apartment in their hot, sweaty and dusty condition?" he queried me.

"Absolutely!" I replied with very intense feelings. "That is the very least of our problems."

The look of gratitude on the faces of the Captain's men as they trooped through our apartment and helped themselves to the generous portions of ice tea and cookies was a sight that will always be remembered. They, too, were astonished that there was sufficient refreshments for all of them. A cooling break in our apartment from the hot sun was also just as welcome as the refreshments. Shortly after the last of the Marines had finished their tea and consumed a plentiful helping of cookies, the Captain paid me the courtesy of telling me that they had received orders to move on further into town. Their new post was at the junction of two of the main streets in the port area. We waved a fond farewell to them from the balcony as they bunched up into marching formation with scouts on all four exposed corners of their column.

In the following days the sun continued to beat down unmercifully on all the residents of the city and, in particular, the Marines who were bivouacked in the streets in the dock areas. My wife greeted me with the announcement on my return from the office one day that she had just decided that since the Marines couldn't come to us, we would go to them.

"What do you mean by that?" I asked in a puzzled manner.

"We will make all the ice tea here and bring it and the cookies to what ever location at which they are. You did say that the Captain had told you where they were going didn't you?" she asked.

I confirmed that I did know the location. We immediately contacted the other residents of the buildings and told them our plans and they generously provided all the ice and tea and cookies that we could load in the car. We headed for the dock area. The surprise and welcome on the faces of the Captain and his men was a sight to behold. We told them of our plan and they fell into 'tea and cookie' formation, and we started serving each one of them from the back of the open trunk of the car with the encouragement that they were to take as much as they wanted, as we had ample supplies in reserve which we would go and get when these were exhausted.

It was a heart warming experience to see the gratitude on their faces for a simple gesture such as we had made in making a little bit of ice tea available and some cookies. I guess it was more the thought than the actual refreshments themselves that evoked the looks on their faces. It must have been a lonely experience for most of these very, young men so many miles from home in what was obviously a very, unfriendly country or they wouldn't have been asked to take part in the sad and tragic undertaking.

My wife was the first to notice a tightly knit group of Marines standing shoulder to shoulder in a semi-circle around the back of our vehicle. They had approached as close as they could possibly get without interfering with the traffic of the Marines that had lined up to receive their ration of tea and cookies. She asked the Captain what was the significance of this shoulder to shoulder display, as it appeared that these particular members of the company weren't getting in line for their servings.

"We've had several stray, spent bullets come down this section of the road from just outside the dock area at about this time," he explained. "There really isn't much danger from them, but I've instructed the men to act as a shield to provide you with protection in the event that while you're here we receive another unwelcome, spent bullet which might hit you or your husband."

To say that my wife was aghast by this reply would be an understatement of epic proportions. She instantly replied, "Captain, there is no way that I'm going to stand here for the simple purpose of serving you and your men ice tea and cookies while you use these very same men as a human shield to protect us. Much as I would love to see your men made more comfortable with our refreshments, I am sorry to say that we are departing immediately." With these words she slammed the cover of the trunk of the car and told me that we were leaving instantly. And so ended our attempt to show the United States Marines how much we appreciated their presence at this most difficult time of our stay in the "Paris of the Middle East".

As time wore on and there seemed no solution in view to this stand-off between the loyalists and the rebels, everyone's nerves became more and more on edge, particularly, those of the Marines who were in the front line positions. Rumour had it that the Marine Commanding officer had told General Shehab that as far as he was concerned about the rebels, "Either they pick a fight with us, or we pick a fight with them or we go home."

The Marines needed some break in the long and boring, monotonous need to keep the two groups of antagonists apart while the diplomatic maneuvering was in process. I told my wife that since there was no possibility of an official USO being set up in the area, I was about to form an unofficial one.

We had been privileged to see some of the most exquisite, Oriental dancing by the well recognized professionals of the area during our stay in Beirut before the confrontation had erupted. 'Oriental Dancing', which very unfortunately, had been entitled as 'belly dancing' by numerous Western observers.

On the contrary, it was a superb art form that the stars of the profession had started their training at the early age of childhood. Nadia Gamal was, without a doubt, at the top of the list of these professionals. She had been in training from the age of seven and after many years had reached the pinnacle of adoration by the entire Arab world as the best of the classics.

I immediately contacted a Marine officer, a Lt.Colonel, who was in charge of the forces' non-military activities and outlined my program to him. He was delighted with my suggestion, and he put the performance on the priority list. Life size, picture posters of Nadia Gamal were distributed through out the land based forces and the floating forces which were anchored in the harbour. Because of the necessity to maintain duty rosters, inasmuch as we were in a war zone, it was necessary to schedule three shows. I arranged to hire the hall and engaged Nadia Gamal. She happened to be a loyalist and was most cooperative. Normally, a professional of her standing would never have consented to perform during the sweltering heat of the mid-afternoon and under the obviously, make-shift arrangements that we would have to undergo in order to ensure that all of the military who were in the dock area would be able to view the performance.

The initial, ominous sound of difficulties arose when I answered my telephone early in the morning of the first engagement, even before I had had time to finish my breakfast. It was my Lt.Colonel in charge of troop activities.

"I've got what might be bad news for you," he opened the conversation. "The three Chaplains, Protestant, Catholic and Jewish attached to the fleet have requested, and let me assure you," he continued, "requested means executive order, that they be given ring-side seats at your first performance. There have been a number of rumours floating around that a local American expatriate has organized a 'sex party' for the troops. They are determined to see what it is that you are going to show to their 'flock'." After reluctantly confirming that his three guests would have the best seats available in the house, my mind took off on its usual, mind-boggling, hell-bent, fantasy trip starting with:

'When the hell will I ever learn to mind my own goddamn business?'

The Marines were big boys and able to take care of themselves. They didn't need me to meddle in their affairs and create headlines that everyone in the New York office would read when the three Chaplains got through reviewing the sex show that I had organized for their flock. It doesn't matter to Westerners, and without singling out the Chaplains in particular, how well accepted to the indigenous population the mores of certain cultures in the world are to the areas in which they exist. An 'Oriental Dancer', to whom the stigma of 'belly dancer' had been affixed, was going to raise the Chaplains' eyebrows to such an extent that the New York Times' headlines would look tame compared to the treatment that I would get from the Board of Directors of Caltex Petroleum Corporation. I could just imagine their reaction when the Marines' families organized a boycott of the Texaco and Chevron service stations as a result of the screaming headlines which I, quite rightly, envisaged would read:

AMERICAN OIL MANAGER CORRUPTS OUR FIGHTING BOYS' MORALS

An American, R.Palmer-Smith, assistant manager of the subsidiary owned by Texaco and Chevron has been alleged to have organized a 'sex' show for our fighting boys who were sent out by President Eisenhower to protect the lives and property of Americans in the Middle East war zone. Three Sixth Fleet Chaplains have vehemently protested to their commanding officers about the show. An official complaint will be lodged with the two well known international oil companies headquartered in New York and San Francisco, who it is further alleged, also, were well aware of these activities. It appears that Caltex, as the Texaco and Chevron subsidiary is called, was entirely responsible for the event and paid all the costs of promoting what is alleged to be the most....!

Every executive in the international oil business is paranoid about the media. One of the strict instructions we received before we left for our first overseas' assignment was, *'DO NOT TALK TO THE PRESS.* If you ever receive any enquiries from the press, refer them to the Public Relations spokesman for your area,' was the further admonishment we received. I had just had a prime example of their rabble, rousing journalism shortly after my wife and the children had been evacuated by air. Thanks to the arrival of the Marines, the airlines had resumed their regular schedules within a short period and my family had been able to take advantage of this return to normality. New York had continued their insistence that she be evacuated with the children. Ed had, also, left to consult with our partners, CFP, in of all places, Paris.

It was a correspondent for Time Magazine who reported that 'due to the bombings by the rebels the water supply to Beirut has been ruptured. Severe water rationing has been imposed'. He further reported that, 'food was in such short supply that two American wives were seen to be fighting over the last loaf of bread available in the only supermarket open in the city'.

Had my wife still been in Beirut reading this absurd report, she would have been highly amused. Unfortunately, as soon as you are away from the 'scene of the crime' your imagination tends to get the better of you. She read this report in the breathtakingly, beautiful city of Lago Majori, Italy, where the Caltex office in Rome had taken her and the children after they arrived in Rome. As a result of her being away from the activities being reported and forgetting for the moment that the article only emphasized to the knowing the need by journalists to sell their periodicals, I received an urgent cable. The cable referred to the report about the water shortage, the lack of food and requested confirmation that I was well and to please reassure her that her concerns were, hopefully, unwarranted. I replied in the best manner guaranteed to end her worries.

> **SALES OF UNDERARM DEODORANT HAVE INCREASED TRE-MENDOUSLY. HAVE NEVER LIKED THAT IMPORTED AMERI-CAN BREAD ANYWAY SO AM STICKING TO KHEBEZ WHICH IS PUTTING ON WEIGHT BECAUSE I EAT SO MUCH OF IT. LOTS OF LOVE TO YOU AND THE CHILDREN AND STOP, REPEAT, STOP WORRYING UNTIL YOU HEAR FROM ME TO THE CON-TRARY.**

As far as the Time Magazine's reporting was concerned it was a classic case of 'sins of … omission'. It was, factually, true that the 'fight' over the last loaf of bread available took place in the *'only supermarket which was open'*. The reason it was true is that there was only one American style supermarket in Beirut. It was always open and never closed during the hostilities. Nonetheless, since there was only one, it was the *'only supermarket which was open'*. All the other food stores, of which there were hundreds and hundreds in Beirut, were also open and well stocked with food, but they weren't 'supermarkets'.

We had received an eye witness report to the so called 'fight over the last loaf of bread'. In reality, it was the typical argument over which one of the shoppers had first reached for the last loaf of what appeared to be diet bread—dieters are notoriously aggressive when they are hungry—left on the shelf. The news article again failed to point out that it was the 'last loaf of diet bread left'. There were plenty of other kinds and brands of bread heavily loaded with calories, but this wasn't mentioned in the news item. After all, shoppers' arguments in supermarkets are hardly the grist of the mills that sells news periodicals unless they happen to be in a war zone in *THE ONLY SUPERMARKET OPEN AS TWO AMERICAN WOMEN FIGHT OVER THE LAST LOAF OF BREAD.*

There had been a slight period of water rationing. This was, also factually true because the filters on one of the main supply sources to the city had become clogged, and the city had to shut it down while they cleaned it. Due to the constant car bombings and bomb scares throughout the city, the general maintenance of the city's water supply had been neglected. Here again, the cause of the shortage was the conflict itself. But in no way imaginable was the rationing severe or due to a direct bomb hit on the reservoirs or the water lines of the supply system to Beirut.

Consequently, being in the oil business I was, naturally, paranoid about the press. This recent example of their lack of journalistic honesty only made me more so. If anyone has any doubt about the lengths the media will go to appeal to the public, they will only have to refer to NBC's apology to General Motors for their staged event of the gas tank explosion of GM's pick up truck which they themselves had deliberately booby-trapped.

Further more, I could envisage just how gleefully they would latch on to anything that could be used against their favourite whipping boys, the obscenely, wealthy, international oil companies. The ones who were responsible for a 'sex orgy' organized by a subsidiary of two of the Seven Sisters, Texaco and Chevron. The paranoia of the oil industry about the news media was highlighted in 1973 when.... 'Mobil, always the compulsive advertiser, finally seemed to give up trying to establish their credibility at the time of the Arab embargo when the oil companies were announcing record profits. They put a sad advertisement in the New York Times headed 'Musings of an Oil Person'. 'Wonder if oil company advertising isn't risking indecent exposure these days,' it began, and complained that in thirty seconds the TV news 'can suggest enough wrong doing that a year of full-page explanations by us won't set straight.'[57]

In any case, I had three children and a wife to feed and it looked like I had put that main obligation in jeopardy by my efforts to bolster the moral of our fighting Marines. It was too late to back out of the arrangements, which in any case I would never have done just to assuage the fear that the press would give the Two Sisters that owned us a hard time. In addition, I owed too much to my fellow citizens, who wore the uniform of the United States Marines, to ever have cravenly given in to a selfish need for self-preservation. Although, frankly, I spent a very sleepless night after the first performance.

The three Chaplains marched into the show hall almost as if they were in military formation on parade. Without even a glance in my direction, they settled themselves down in ramrod like stances in the three front row seats which had been reserved for them. Nadia Gamal put on what was, probably, one of her most superb performances. This only meant that my three viewers in the 'box seats' were exposed, not only exposed but within touching distance, to her most professional rendition of 'Oriental Dancing'.

It is not 'belly dancing' my mind kept trying by extra sensory perception to impose on their watchful glances as she glided across the floor. At the close of the show amid a standing ovation from the on-looking Marines, my three religious critics exited the hall in the same military like formation. Again, without even a glance in my direction.

Early the next morning at six AM my telephone rang. It was my Lt.Colonel with the news of the results of the Chaplains' reactions to the show.

He opened his heart wrenching comments with the exclamation, "You're not going to believe this! The Chief Chaplin wrote in large letters right across one of your full length publicity posters of Nadia Gamal that we plastered all over the fleet his reaction to the performance."

I thought to myself, 'so ends what was really a very interesting career in the international oil business'. I was too crushed to even ask the Colonel what the Chief Chaplin had written.

"Don't you want to know what he said?" the Colonel asked anyway.

"Yes, you might as well tell me," I replied in a resigned tone of voice. At this point, the Colonel chuckled and took pity on me, although he, too, had had a sleepless night as he confessed later in the conversation. While he could claim innocence in some ways as to what the show was going to be, he had been very instrumental in organizing the performances and arranging the roster schedules in order that every service man that wanted to would be able to take advantage of the performances.

"The Chief Chaplin wrote in very large letters across the front of one of the posters, 'WHOEVER DOESN'T SEE THIS SHOW, SHOULD SEE HIS PSYCHIATRIST. Signed: CHIEF CHAPLIN'".

By this time I too, like the Marines, was looking to 'pick a fight or go home'. Home to me was wherever my wife and children were and at that moment that was in Rome. The Italians, in their imitable way, with their gracious hospitality had kept the Hotel Excelsior in Laga Majori open a week longer than the usual, seasonal duration. Laga Majori was an exclusive resort town on the lake that catered to the many wealthy Italian entrepreneurs. At the close of the season, my wife and children were the only residents left in the hotel. It was a magnificently, large, luxurious building with over four hundred rooms and suites.

My wife, the three children and the nanny whom she had taken with her, occupied two of the adjoining suites on the second floor overlooking the lake. She had been in residence for well over two months when the season ended. The entire staff had gotten to know them and had unofficially adopted the whole family. They had even taken to reading the daily Italian newspapers intensely to determine the progress of the fighting in Lebanon so they could keep her informed of the progress of the Loyalists. However, with a hotel consisting of four hundred rooms and the necessary staff to keep it open, even the wonderfully, hospitable Italians had to finally, reluctantly inform my wife that it was necessary for them to close the hotel until the next season, and she would have to leave. She promptly cabled me with the information that the only place she could think of going was back to Rome.

Ed had returned from Paris, and I told him that with all the fighting in the hills, I had really been unable to perform my marketing duties adequately by visiting the many service stations through out the country. I suggested to him that now would be a good time to visit another one of the territories under our jurisdiction and utilize my time more efficiently for THE COMPANY. I suggested that Libya would be a good place to start. I, also, informed him that I was sure that he would have no objection if I detoured on my back to Beirut by going through Rome. Since he had had the advantage of visiting Paris, I knew that he could hardly object to my suggestion. He had readily agreed, and I gave my passport to the Administration Manager on the morning of my departure and requested him to obtain the necessary visa.

Visas to Libya were normally obtained by merely submitting your passport to the official at the Libyan Embassy who would stamp it and return it to you in a matter of minutes. There was never any delay as there were very few people in the Lebanon who had any interest or business in Libya. Even so, I was very surprised when the Administration Manager appeared back in my office in what was considerably less time than required to drive to the Libyan Embassy. Even more surprisingly, he was in what appeared to be an absolute state of terror. His eyes were darting frantically in all directions with his pupils dilated and rolling backwards in his head. His breath came in deep gulps, and he was shaking like a young sapling in an hurricane force wind.

"What happened to you?" I demanded in a rough voice. He was one of my least, favourite employees as he was born lazy. I had, also, long suspected that many of the hotels and other service agencies, that we used quite frequently for our many visitors in this very popular cross-roads of the Middle East, were lining his pockets in order to guarantee that they would be first on his list of calling priorities.

While he was trying to bring his emotions under control, he gasped out that he had stopped for a traffic light only a few blocks from the office. While parked next to another car which was waiting for the same traffic light to change, a small van from the street on his left pulled up in front of the other car and came to an abrupt stop. The passenger in the front seat of the van then calmly rolled down the window, leaned out and proceeded to machine gun the driver and the passenger of the other vehicle. With the driver's and the passenger's blood spattered bodies slumped over among the shattered glass from the windscreen, our terrified Administration Manager wheeled in a sharp 'U' turn and came scuttling back to the office. He wasn't prepared to continue to complete the duties with which he had been entrusted which were to obtain a visa to Libya for me.

I was not the least sympathetic about his predicament and was even more annoyed at myself as I had left the obtaining of the visa until the very morning of the day of my departure. I knew that it was useless to insist that he return to the area where the shooting had taken place. By this time what little courage he had had evaporated completely, and he was collapsed in one of the chairs in my office.

"Give me that passport, you bloody coward," I snarled at him. I'll go get the visa myself." I grabbed the passport out of his shaking hands, yelled a quick farewell to Ed with the suggestion that he interrogate the Administration Manger to elicit any further details that might be forthcoming as to the possible identity of the victims. I made a running exit from the office. My car and chauffeur with my packed bags were waiting for me downstairs. I flung open the door before the chauffeur had even had a chance to exit from the front seat to open it for me and instructed him to proceed to the Libyan Embassy without regard for speed limits or traffic lights.

From the imploring look on his face that I was able to see in the rear view mirror, I realized that he was fully aware of what had transpired with Administration Manager's abortive attempt to reach the Libyan Embassy to obtain my visa. He had been waiting in front of the office when the Administration Manager had returned and had received a half-garbled tale of the events. He was a very conscientious and loyal employee of THE COMPANY and been in service for many years. He had never once failed to report for duty during the entire time the city had been under siege. He would never refuse a direct order given by one of the company executives, but there was no doubt that at this moment he fervently wished that such an order would be rescinded.

Perhaps it was my sympathy for his predicament or perhaps a slightly guilty feeling about the way I had treated the Administration Manager or, in reality, it was probably the return of plain common sense that made me alter my instructions to him. "I've changed my mind," I informed him after we had proceeded only a few blocks in the direction of the Libyan Embassy. "Go directly to the airport. My plane is leaving in a short time. You can drop me off there and then go home. It won't be necessary to return to the office."

Since the evacuation of the wives and children, Ed's chauffeur and mine had been allowed to take the company cars home with them when we no longer needed them. This arrangement ensured that they would be at our homes on time in the morning. Frequently with the previous day's bombings or nighttime shooting, it was often difficult for the residents of the city to reach their appointed place of employment with any regularity.

As the old DC-3 took off and winged its way towards Libya, there was no doubt in my mind that the Libyan immigration officers would understand why it hadn't been possible for me to obtain the customary visa. Based on my explanation of the life, threatening hazards of moving about the city of Beirut, they would promptly issue me a visa at the airport.

The plane touched down at the Tripoli airport in a shimmering haze of suffocating heat. The DC-3 was totally ignorant of such a facility known as air conditioning; neither did airports in those days, at least certainly not Third World airports. Nor did they have that convenience whereby they hook you up to a portable air conditioning unit that keeps the passengers cool and comfortable while they are disembarking. Momentarily, my mind sent an unvoiced message of sympathy to the next passengers who would have to endure the heat of this man made oven, shaped like a cigar and constructed of aluminum. Sympathy should have no place in the character of an international oil executive, either knowingly or unknowingly.

As I tended my passport, I started to explain why it hadn't been possible to obtain the necessary, official adornment to my travel documents.

"Because of the shooting in the area of...."

"Where is your visa?" was the query that interrupted my explanation.

"I couldn't get one because....!"

"I asked you, where is your visa?" the Libyan immigration officer repeated again with what was now the beginning of a serious note of irritation.

"I don't have one because...."

"You don't have one?" he repeated in an incredulous tone of voice.

"No. As I started to explain I was ..."

"Are you sure you don't have one?" he queried in what now was a change from a deep note of irritation in his voice to one of ominous overtones.

"Yes. I am sure. I couldn't get near the Libyan Embassy due to...." Without even any further attempt to let me complete my explanation he turned to one of the many, heavily armed sentries standing around the area and snapped his fingers in an imperious manner. I had watched his face change expression from bored hostility to one of antagonism and finally to what was, almost, sadistic delight. I realized, immediately, that I had forgotten what a short time had elapsed since these denizens of the desert had been freed of the yoke of white imperialism and they were now able to vent their spleen on a representative of their previously hated white masters.

He spat out his orders to the armed sentry whose sleepy expression had altered to one of grim determination as the knowledge sank in that he had a dangerous intruder on his hands. I couldn't understand what character assassination the immigration officer had wreaked on my innocently believing that a simple explanation of how dangerous it was to try and get a visa in Beirut was the reason I didn't have one.

However, there was not any doubt from the Arabic that I could understand, that the sentry had been instructed to take me back to the plane at gunpoint. Not only at gunpoint, but as part of showing their importance, the Libyan sentries had affixed their bayonets to their old World War vintage rifles. With the tip of the bayonet only inches from my scantily clad back, I moved with dispatch in the direction of the plane. As I passed the fenced area where the visitors were gathered to await the passengers, the look on the face of the Caltex employee who had been sent out to pick me up from the airport would, under different circumstances, have sent me into gales of laughter.

"What happened?" he gasped out. "Where are you going?"

I momentarily slowed to a less rapid pace, although, the thought of that bayonet only inches from my unprotected back kept me moving with a very determined effort.

"I couldn't get a visa in Beirut, because of the fighting. I thought that they would issue me one at the airport here, but apparently not. So I'm on my way back to Beirut in the same, bloody plane that I came on," I hastily explained. By this time, we had reached the end of the fenced area, and he could no longer keep pace with me. I waved a hesitant farewell to him and headed in the direction of the parked DC-3 on the sweltering tarmac. Any thought of entering the plane and occupying one of the comfortable seats while awaiting take off left my thoughts immediately, as the overpowering heat made it almost impossible to even draw a breath within the cabin. I disconsolately sat on the small steps leading up to the plane that had been wheeled out from the terminal building for the convenience of the disembarking passengers.

My mind took off on one its most determined, fantasy trips to resolve just how I could accomplish the act of assassination. Whether or not it was a viable alternative was immaterial. I could have wrung the necks, with the most exquisite pleasure, of each and everyone of those senior officers of the company who had convinced me that the life of an international oil executive was one of comfort and ease. As the perspiration poured off my brow and into my eyes in constant rivulets, I made a solemn vow to myself that I would assassinate each and every one of them by shooting them, if only I could wrest that rifle from the ever watchful sentry.

The scorching heat being reflected from the shimmering airstrip was beginning to make me feel giddy. I glanced at the sentry and saw what I believed to be, now, two sentries. I felt that I was going to either be seriously ill or faint from heat exhaustion, particularly, since my vision had been become so blurred as to make me believe that there were now two armed sentries delegated to ensure that I re-boarded the plane and left their desert homeland. Suddenly, the second individual assumed a real life stance and spoke to me.

"You will please come with me," he announced in a most respectful tone of voice. I, now, realized that he was not a hazy twin of my guard sentry, but a well dressed official from what was, undoubtedly, the Office of Immigration. He escorted me to the visitors gate, where my Caltex employee was waiting anxiously, and left me in his care with instructions to report to the central immigration office at the opening of the day's business in the morning at which time I would be issued a visa.

As is true through out the world, where ever the Seven Sisters or their subsidiaries operate, powerful relationships are maintained with the governments of the countries in which they are guests. A quick telephone call from the Caltex employee at the airport to the Caltex office in town outlining my problem resulted in immediate contact with the immigration department of the Libyan Government. The senior official at the airport of that department was the individual who came out to the plane to 'welcome' me to Tripoli.

The Caltex employee escorted me to my hotel where after shedding my clothes which were now stuck to my body like determined leeches because of the perspiration, I had a quick shower and went to bed. I told him that I was too exhausted to go to the office, but if he would have a car sent around in the morning I would go directly to the central immigration office as instructed by the senior official at the airport. The next morning, I was courteously greeted by the officials of the immigration department, my passport was stamped with the necessary visa and I was free to go to the company office. I quickly finished my business in Tripoli because, in reality, it was only a way station on my journey to Rome to join my family. Arrival in Rome for a joyous reunion with my wife and family and a week that passed all too quickly. It was only a short period after my visit to Rome that diplomatic negotiations successfully resulted in ending hostilities in the Lebanon with the subsequent withdrawal of the Marines and we resumed our idyllic way of life in the "Paris of the Middle East".

14

Nairobi, Kenya—1959

As the wheels of the aircraft touched down at the Nairobi airport in Kenya, my wife and I gazed at each other with a wondering air. Were we really going to live in the dark continent for ten months? What strange experiences would we have, and what exotic things would we see during this temporary tour of duty that THE COMPANY had asked us to undertake?

The first indication, that our continued existence wasn't going to be based on the cocoon like atmosphere of city living in which we had both been reared in the Boroughs of Brooklyn and Queens of New York City, were the many road signs dotting the landscape on our way into the city. Lynn, our five year old was reading each sign avidly to her four year old brother and her two year old sister. They were growing more and more excited with each notice that we passed. My wife and I looked at each other with the same questioning air that we had exhibited as the plane touched down on the runway. A small part of our speculation about what strange and exotic experiences we might undergo in this city, a city that had undoubtedly been a retreat from the overwhelmingly, oppressive heat of the African coast for the depraved Arab slave traders for hundreds of years, appeared to have been answered by a simple road sign.

IN THE EVENT OF ENGINE FAILURE OR NECESSITY TO CHANGE TYRES DO NOT LEAVE YOUR VEHICLE. WAIT FOR ASSISTANCE. LIONS FREQUENTLY CROSS THIS THOROUGHFARE.

All the international oil companies were on their usual cycles of lean and fat years. Profits had been high and not too much attention had been paid in the last decade to the ballooning staff. We were now headed for a lean year. A reduction in staff and a reorganization was in the making. My Vice-President had told me that if I could accomplish the reorganization in ten months he would be extremely happy, but if I needed a year I was not to hesitate to take it as he would still be satisfied. He wanted me back in New York not later than a year. There was a special New York assignment outlined for me.

The main purpose of my appointment was not made known to the local staff. It would be they who would have to bear the brunt of my recommendations. My title was 'Assistant to the Marketing Director', who was Harry Bernard. The very same colleague whom I had first met in Shanghai, worked for in Cairo and, unknown to either one of us at the time, would relieve me in Salisbury when I was transferred from Salisbury, Rhodesia to Johannesburg, South Africa.

Why the directors of any big organization delude themselves continuously into believing that they can cloak the purpose of appointments they make from the employees of their companies will always remain a mystery. If they can't keep it from outsiders, there is no possible way that it can be kept from the staff. At one of the many cocktail parties hosted by THE COMPANY for the prominent businessmen of Nairobi which my wife and I attended a few days after our arrival, I was introduced by my Managing Director to Marilyn Hatos, the wife of one the clients of THE COMPANY. She was dressed in the latest fashion imported from Paris and had the air of a worldwide traveler that seemed to announce that there was little that she did not know about the trials and tribulations encountered on the various journeys undertaken for international companies. She was the wife of Jim Hatos, manager of the Caterpillar Tractor Company office in Nairobi.

Although I have committed many faux pas during my career in the international oil business, one mistake that I have never made is to discount the intelligence of the women who make up the team of two. A team of two that is always required by the employers in global companies, while they only pay one member of the team. On being given my name and told by my Managing Director that I was in Nairobi on a ten month temporary assignment as Assistant to the Marketing Director, her reply was as sharp and as pointed as anything you might hear in a court room exchange between the prosecutor and the defendant's attorney.

"Oh, you're one of those head-hunters, aren't you?" was her instant comment.

One of the things I did learn at the cocktail party was that 'pole fishing' was endemic throughout the city and, particularly, in the sparsely settled suburbs. The suburbs were where the majority of higher paid expatriates lived and, naturally, as it turned out, where we were to live also. 'Pole fishing' was the expression used to describe the efficient way in which the unemployed members of the local population earned their living. All windows of all homes, particularly in the suburbs, were barred. There was no air conditioning in those days, although at Nairobi's altitude this was not always an extremely serious drawback. During some particular mid-summers, however, it could prove to be a significant drawback as my children were wont to remind me constantly as they languished in the back of the parked station wagon outside the house where the cocktail party was being held. In any case, although the windows were barred, the shutters were seldom, if ever, closed.

This gave free rein to those enterprising members of the indigenous population to develop the technique of using very light, fly fishing rods to efficiently remove any articles of value that were left strewn around the bedrooms after the owners had retired. The men, in particular, were in the habit of leaving their wallets in the back pocket of their trousers after disrobing. On awakening in the morning, they were sometimes pleasantly surprised to see that their trousers had been left behind after the intruder had expertly 'pole fished' the wallet out of the back pocket. Pleased to see that their trousers had been left behind, although disappointed on the other hand to see that the 'pole fisher' had taken the pocket book of the lady of the house for good measure.

There had recently been a number of serious violent incidents in and around the city and a disproportionate number in the countryside, as well as in the suburbs. There appeared to be sufficient evidence to suggest, although never proved, that these incidents were an aftermath of the Mau Mau terrorism that had recently murdered so many thousands and thousands of black residents in this wild and beautiful country.

'Terrorism is a specific branch of modern warfare. It has been called the weapon of the weak because it is most often used by those attempting to size power from an established government and it goes hand-in-hand with propaganda in an attempt to win the uncommitted populace. The technique in every country is quite similar. A raid is made on a small village in the night. The mayor, the schoolteacher, or someone who has helped the government is singled out. His hut is burned, his family killed, and he himself is hauled away or murdered on the spot. Later his body is discovered with the message of the terrorists pinned to it: "Traitor." Although the instrument of terror may be used directly against the enemy in a more conventional and selective way, this calculated, almost surgical terrorism which operates against the people among whom the terrorists live is far more deadly. The Greek terrorists, for example in Cyprus, murdered three Greeks for every two non-Greeks. In Malaya, the Chinese guerrillas likewise turned their terror on their own people, killing more than twice as many Chinese as other nationalities. And in Kenya, the Mau Mau slaughtered seven hundred Africans as against twenty-one Europeans in the first year of their anti-British uprising[58].'

Although the Mau Mau terrorism was over, the grisly murders and organized mayhem that had been employed by them had left the Europeans on the verge of paranoia. The rules were standard in that you never left your children at home alone. When going to a dinner party or cocktail party, it was startling for a newcomer to see dozens of station wagons, which were the usual mode of transportation in that part of the world, scattered around the yard of your host and hostess. The majority of these station wagons had children of every age and description sleeping in the back. In addition, there was a very noticeably, armed individual charged with sentry duty diligently patrolling the lawn area where the vehicles were parked and the children quartered.

If my grown children were to be asked today what it is that they remember most about the ten month assignment in Nairobi, Lynn, the eldest, would be the quickest to reply. She would instantly point out that she couldn't really decide which was the worse thing about the frequent cocktail and dinner parties that her mother and father had to attend. The first choice was probably having to be placed between her younger bother and sister in the back of the station wagon to keep the antagonists apart, as there was a perpetual state of war existing between the two of them.

The second choice was having to fight off the overwhelming numbers of mosquitoes that were endemic to the area and all of this in the oftentimes stifling, oppressive heat of the early evening of the summer. Jimmy was really too young to have any definite memories. He vaguely recalls that he never felt secure, when we said goodnight to him, locked his door and made our way down the veranda to our bedroom quarters after carefully bolting in the boxer dog that I had so knowingly purchased two weeks after our arrival in this really, amazing city of Nairobi. Gayle, our Lebanese, would just smile at you with an enigmatic grin, as you could almost visualize what diabolical schemes she was hatching in her two year old mind at that time.

I had always wanted a boxer dog. I relished that look on their faces with their pushed in soft noses. Although my wife's first love was English Cocker Spaniels, she was easy to convince that since she wasn't going to be a breeder in this part of the world inasmuch as it was only a ten month assignment, it didn't really matter what kind of dog we purchased. The telling point I had made in my original argument clinched the deal for me. I was convinced that I had a method of beating the constant 'pole fishing' that we had heard about at the original cocktail party which we had attended and later from my colleagues in the office. The boxer would serve both purposes. He would satisfy my longing for owning one of his breed, and he would earn his board and lodging by patrolling the outer premises of our home, wherever we might settle.

Luck was really on our side. There was a very large house which had previously been occupied by the French Chargé d'Affaires. With the coming independence of Kenya, the astute French with an eye to such a possibility, were planning to up grade their representation to an Embassy, and their Chargé d'Affaires had moved into more prestigious accommodations. The house that he had vacated was most unusual. In fact, it was very well known because of its uniqueness. It was well known, not only because of the constant entertaining that the French occupant had been undertaking during his stay there, but because it was owned by a long time resident family of a white hunter. The white hunter had originally used it as his headquarters when he was in Nairobi and not out hunting the denizens of the jungle.

Since a white hunter's stock in trade consists of a number of four wheel drive vehicles, he had built garages in a row adjoining the house. At the back at a ninety degree angle to the house and the garages, he had constructed a large open work shop for the purpose of maintaining his vehicles on their return from a safari. All this was situated on six acres, which boarded on a river located in the lower section of the lush vegetation. Only two of the six acres were maintained. The other four were left to the rain forest. It would have taken an army of gardeners to keep any semblance of order in this part of Africa.

Everything grew with a vengeance. It appeared as if the vegetation was determined to force out any alien member of the earth's planet that had had the audacity to believe that he could take up a normal residence by intruding on nature's plans. A resident that was in direct defiance of such nature's plans to cover the jungle floor with flora and fauna. The river was out of bounds to the children, which raised howls of protest when we informed them of this restriction.

It is difficult to explain to a five year old, a four year old and a two year old the deadly results of wading in the brackish waters of a river that harbours the snail which transmits that liver attacking, deadly and debilitating disease which robs millions of Africans of the initiative to progress beyond a daily need to survive. *Bilharzias!*

The white hunter had long since passed away, and there were no longer any white hunters left in the family. As a consequence, the remaining family members, who had inherited the estate, had enclosed the garages and turned them into bedrooms and had added two bathrooms, but had left the work shop open as an entertainment area in the back yard. There were five of these bedrooms, in addition to the two that made up the original living quarters. The original arrangements consisted of a master suite with self-contained bath room facilities and another bedroom with separate bathroom facilities. In addition, there was an immense lounge with a huge and most hospitable fireplace, a dining room and a kitchen as well as all manner of storage facilities, servants' quarters, a gun room and many other such essentials.

Whether the white hunter had designed the original part of the house or it had just 'growed like topsy' couldn't be ascertained. What was known and extremely disconcerting about the whole arrangement of the rooms was that not one them was interconnected. At any time that you wanted to go from one room to another, you had to use the tremendously wide, covered veranda which surrounded the house on the side facing the river in the back. Even the house boy, when serving dinner in the dining room, had to cross the veranda from the kitchen in order to enter the dining room with the hot food. Although we had had some hesitation initially in signing the lease, the boxer dog had convinced me that the openness of the house would present no problem, because of his conscientious attention to his guard duties.

News travels fast in jungle societies, even if the entire jungle society is composed of white colonialists living in a comfortable city perched atop the incomparable, beautiful, mountainous hillsides of East Africa. "I say, old boy, hear you've taken the Safari House on Muthega Road in Muthega," was how I was greeted when being introduced to a fellow guest at the fourth cocktail party that we were attending in the almost less than two weeks since our arrival. He was dressed in a bush jacket and was nursing a meerschaum pipe and appeared as if he had just returned from the jungle, although his clothes were immaculately pressed and his boots shone as if they had a double coat of shellac. "Doubly barred that place, you know. Good digs. You'll like it, even if you will be occasionally fish poled," my companion quite cordially informed me. With just a slight trace of smugness, I took the liberty of informing him that I had eliminated that possibility as that very day I had purchased an impressive sized boxer to forestall any such activity as had been plaguing the residents of Nairobi in the suburban areas.

"Oh," was his response as his eyebrows raised themselves quizzically. He slowly removed the pipe from his mouth as he gazed at me with the air of a schoolmaster confronted with an errant student who had just joined the boarding school. "Perhaps, I should introduce you to your next door neighbour over there on the other side of the room. The leopards just got his dog the other night, because he got home very late from a party, and he had failed to lock him up before he left for dinner. Do you know that leopards love dog meat?" he continued in a quite cheerful voice. "You are aware, aren't you, that there is no building beyond your property? The river in your back yard is the end of the city. You can hear the leopards bark every night. It is a fascinating sound," he went on with his blithe, devastating description of the area in which we were just about to call home.

We had named him Beau for Beau Geste, and he just couldn't understand why he was sequestered in the lounge of the house, when he could have had the full run of the six acres and been performing his nightly duties for which he had been purchased.

The children, also, couldn't understand why they were securely locked in their rooms every night. Being wheeled into the main hallway night after night in Beirut to avoid being hit by stray bullets was not even a vague recollection in their minds now. At the time they were living in Beirut, they didn't know the reason or, possibly, they just assumed that that was the way everyone lived. They couldn't connect that necessity with the present precautions of being securely locked in their rooms when they had been put to bed. If we had used the expression 'Mau Mau' in explanation, they might possibly have come to the conclusion that we had descended to the depths of talking baby talk to them, a device that my wife and I steadfastly refused to utilize over the formative years of our children.

We had engaged an English nanny, who was delighted to join our employ when she heard that she was to have her own huge bedroom and another bedroom to serve as her sitting room with a bathroom all her own just down the hall. We did experience a little difficulty with her, when she realized what we meant by 'just down the hall'. This entailed her leaving the safety of her bedroom and going down the veranda with its open guard rails and at the same time listening to the continuous sounds of leopards prowling the jungle just across the river, before she could enjoy the privilege of relieving herself.

We hadn't taken the sign at the Nairobi Hotel, which was situated at the edge of an eighteen hole golf course, too seriously when we had first glimpsed it while attending a company luncheon on the Saturday. We assumed it was just a bit of nostalgia left over from the early settlers' days. Now after having heard how our neighbour had fared with his guard dog and recalling the rather prominent signs on the route into the city from the airport regarding the necessity to '*STAY IN YOUR VEHICLE*', we weren't so sure that the sign was only nostalgia and not currently in effect as it proclaimed in large bold letters:

BEWARE OF LIONS
AT THE 16TH HOLE

During our stay in Nairobi, we took the opportunity of obtaining season passes for the Nairobi Game Park, as the children were thrilled with the thought of going to a 'zoo' that had no cages. They became experts on spotting the animals in the bush. They never really became bored with the constant visits. There was one time, however, when the tourists in the rear of the viewing park vehicle became very agitated at spotting an animal in the bush, but they had trouble identifying it. On hearing their excited tones, Jimmy squirmed his way to the rear of the vehicle from his always permanent vantage post of hanging over the top of the driver's cab. As he reached the rear of the vehicle, he spotted the cause of all the excitement immediately. In a quite bored and superior four year old manner, he turned to the tourists and proclaimed, "Oh, it's only a lion." With which he retired to his reserved spot in the front of the vehicle looking for that much more difficult game to spot, the jaguar.

The entrenched, local East Africans in the office could see no reason for my assignment. If there were any reorganization to be done, they were perfectly cable of doing it themselves. They had a tendency to forget that if they had done it themselves, there wouldn't have been any need for my presence in Nairobi. The East African company at that time consisted of a Head Office with three branches. The other two branches, in addition to the Kenya one, were Tanganyika and Uganda. They were all staffed identically. One manager, one sales manager, one operations manager, one accountant and the same corresponding number of members in each department in the three branches.

What took a monumental effort was to convince the head office in Nairobi, who were overseeing the three branches, of the fact that even if the sales in the three branches were of equal volume, which they weren't, there was a slight ratio of difference in time factors that should be taken into consideration when staffing any organization.

The Uganda Branch Manager could leave his home very early in the morning by car and visit the furthest sales point in his area and be home for a very late dinner the same night. The Tanganyika manager could leave his home very early in the morning and be about two thirds of the way to his furthest sales point and he would arrive in time for a late lunch. A late lunch that is, if all went well with the flight. The reason that he disembarked only two thirds of the way from his furthest sales point was that the planes didn't fly any further. From there he had to travel by car for another day. Since the next return flight back to Dar-es-salaam was three days after his arrival, he had to make plans well in advance of what he was going to review with his field staff as there was no spur of the moment trips that could be undertaken by the Tanganyika Manager.

While in the Dar-es-salaam office in Tanganyika during one of my trips from Nairobi, I noticed that the sales manager was checking out the tide tables during office hours. I rather pointedly queried the manager as to the necessity for the sales manager to know the highs and the lows of the tides affecting the Tanganyika shores, and how it affected the sales results of the area or was he just planning a fishing trip? "Oh no, he's not really checking the tides themselves," the manager informed me. "He's actually checking the flight times of the air service to the south," he ended his explanation to me rather off-handedly.

I debated with myself as to whether or not I should show my ignorance by following up on his explanation. Since I was on a learning trip, I decided that I would ask the obvious. "What do the tide tables and the flight times of the air service have to do with each other?"

He looked up in surprise. "I'm sorry," he said in a quick attempt to apologize for his off-handedness in response to my previous question. "We keep forgetting that not everyone from Nairobi knows how we have to operate in Tanganyika. There is no airfield down there. The service is a single engine aircraft owned by an ex-British Air Force Officer. He goes down twice a week when the tide is at its lowest. He doesn't have the money to print a time table, but since he has to land on the beach he can only go when the tide is at its lowest. It's easy to check out his departures by merely looking at the tide tables and finding the day and time the tide is at its lowest for the week." Then, and at a later date when I actually took that flight, I wondered why THE COMPANY hadn't indoctrinated us at the orientation classes on the use of tide tables, and how they related to the flight schedules used by a so called international oil executive.

The Kenya Manager was only a floor away from the head office and his immediate supervisor and the Board of Directors. The greatest majority of his communications were verbal. His letter writing and telephone calls were at an absolute minimum which meant the time demands on him were extremely less onerous than the other two branches, when he had problems necessitating consultation with the Directors. And yet, the three branches were staffed on an identical basis.

In addition to the planned staff reduction, Harry Bernard was determined to divorce the two sales activities of retail (service stations) and wholesale (customer direct purchase) from each other. He was convinced that any salesman charged with the responsibility of sales to the service stations and sales to a customer who actually consumed the product at his place of business, would be faced with a conflict of interest. The salesman would always relegate the service stations to second place, when a 'real live customer' made demands on his time. The customer could always leave THE COMPANY. The agent in the service station was generally tied contractually for decades. In many cases, the service station was owned by THE COMPANY. The separation of these two activities was another one of the almost insurmountable tasks, which were part of my terms of reference.

When advertising to the public by The Seven Sisters or their subsidiaries, the emphasis was always on 'service' as in *SERVICE STATIONS*. These very same dispensers of petroleum products to the motorist, 'service stations', were known as 'outlets' in the offices of the international oil companies. The companies realized that the more profit they made from their business 'upstream', producing crude oil and the less profit they made 'downstream', selling oil to the consumers, the less tax they would pay locally[59].

Since I was attached to the marketing department by virtue of reporting directly to the Marketing Director, I was a natural for the field staff to solicit my advice on what was a 'going' acceptable payout rate for an 'outlet'. I had no hesitation in supplying the figure. It was a great savings in time for the field not to have to keep re-submitting the same proposals to the Head Office to build 'outlets', after having been initially turned down, because the current payout rate had been altered. This is what would frequently happened when the proposals were submitted in completed form directly from the field without the field realizing that there had been a change in the economics of the payout.

The proposals would be reviewed at Board level in Nairobi. Since the field always had to rely on the last number used for the economics of constructing an 'outlet', they would naturally tailor their submissions based on that number. Unknown to them, there would have been a change in the producers' relationships with The Seven Sisters. This always altered the internal accounting of the companies[60]. At the time that I was making the information available to the field staff, the payout was in the general neighborhood of between twenty-seven and thirty years. Can any businessman in any other business requiring the investment of hundreds of thousands of dollars ever consider making an investment in which he would have to wait thirty years before he received a return on his money?

Always being willing to gamble when the odds were infinitely on my side, I had been very voluble in my invitations about going on safari to one and all in Beirut after being told of my pending transfer to Nairobi. For anyone who would want to come to Nairobi, I would make all the arrangements. I would hire the white hunter, and we would go big game hunting. Take off into the jungles of Africa and track down those powerful and vicious killers that prowl the deep jungle at night.

We would experience one of those unforgettable flights of fancy that Hollywood had depicted so vividly as their millionaire characters were blanketed by hordes of jungle wise trackers, stewards, drivers, skinners, mechanics, 'house boys' and a radio operator. The radio operator was for those captains of industry that couldn't afford to be out of touch with their financial empires even while enjoying a safari in the dark continent. And last but not least, that all knowing, bronzed, quite, serene and stone faced bulwark of courage and comfort, the white hunter, the most outlandishly, expensive member of the safari.

The odds were overwhelmingly in my favour. Nobody that I knew would be able to take advantage of that invitation. If they had the time, they were too junior and didn't have the money, as in my case. If they were very senior and had the money, they obviously didn't have the time. You would never have been able to obtain the lofty, elevated position which so many of the American residents in Beirut were occupying, as Beirut was a 'head office' paradise, and still have the time to enjoy yourself.

Furthermore, and most importantly, I was going to be in Nairobi for only ten months. The kind of time required for preparation for safaris with white hunters is a lifetime of wishing and planning, certainly at the very least, a number of years. Knowing I was only going to be in Nairobi for ten months, there wasn't a single soul to whom I grandly offered the invitation to come visit that could possibly take advantage of it. Even if they had the money and the time, it just simply wasn't possible for them to get organized and make it to Nairobi. I knew how to play the odds and be a superstar at no cost to myself.

On arrival home from the office after one of the very few more constructive days of constant battling with the head office staff, my wife greeted me with, what she thought was the most thrilling news. "Bill and Clair Chandler are coming to Nairobi," she exclaimed excitedly in a delighted tone of voice as she waved their letter in front of me. "Bill is going on safari with you, and Clair and I are going to spend the three weeks playing bridge and reminiscing about all the wonderful times we had in Beirut. I'm really ecstatic. Isn't it wonderful?" When would I ever learn to keep my mouth shut?

We had hardly been in Nairobi a few months, which had already consumed a fair portion of the ten month allowance that my New York Vice-President had said he would be delighted to support to implement the goal of my assignment. Now, I was going to ask for three weeks off to go hunting? In spite of a lot of evidence to the contrary, I was a very quick learner. That is, a very quick learner in the art of survival that is so necessary when you work for a big corporation. I couldn't lose face with Bill Chandler, one of the sincerest friends that I had made while in Beirut. I, certainly, couldn't disappoint my wife by telling her that one of the very closest friends that she had made over the years, Clair Chandler, wouldn't be able to visit us, just because I couldn't get three weeks off.

The question of not having the thousands and thousands of dollars to pay for this wild extravaganza was a minor detail. I hesitantly mentioned the money first and got the usual reply. "You never have any money. What difference does that make?"

But the three weeks? Getting the three weeks off was my first foray, of several, into the countervailing power plays in connection with the names of the Two Sisters that owned us. I still wasn't senior enough to be present when THE COMPANY was entertaining the directors of our owners, so it wasn't until some time later that I was able to use the name of Gus Long[61] with exquisite relish.

I told Harry Bernard about my dilemma with my very close friend, Bill and his wife Clair, expecting to be given the dates for their three week vacation. How excited they were about coming to Africa. It would be the first visit that they would have ever made to this part of the world. I was devastated about the thought of how deep their disappointment was going to be, when I told them I couldn't take three weeks off at this critical time of my assignment.

Harry agreed with me almost vehemently. "Definitely! You are absolutely right! There is no way that you can take three weeks off at this time of the implementation of our program. And besides," he suddenly ended rather sharply, "you just got here."

Then in a softer and more conciliatory tone of voice he said, "I'm really sorry. I can imagine how you must feel about disappointing your friends and naturally how disappointed they will be when they hear that you can't make it. But as you know, that's the way it is in the oil business; Business is business."

I said I had written to Bill that very day giving him the news of my inability of being able to arrange the safari for him and to accompany him, but I hadn't mailed it yet. I was so disappointed for him that it was difficult to actually post the bad news. I told Harry that I knew Bill wouldn't want to go hunting alone, as we had talked about the possibility of the trip in Beirut a number of times over the constant bridge foursome that we had with him and his wife.

I mentioned to Harry how in Bill's letter he said that he had told his Board how enthusiastic he was about his forthcoming, big game hunting trip with me. "In any event," I continued, "I know that his Board has to always be aware of what part of the world he is in. He never stirs out of Beirut without their being fully informed of his whereabouts." He was the kind of wealthy client to whom the white hunters catered with their radio operators. I finished off with the comment that I felt uneasy. I hoped it wouldn't cause THE COMPANY any embarrassment, when Bill told his Board he couldn't make the trip, because I couldn't be spared for three weeks. "Even more importantly," I continued, "I hope that you, Harry, aren't embarrassed by my bad judgment in extending an invitation like that to Bill."

Harry immediately dropped the papers he had gone back to looking at under the impression that he believed we had finished our conversation. "What do you mean by that?," he queried quickly in a wary fashion, instantly on his guard. "What has your friend's disappointment got to do with me?"

I looked surprised and said, "Well, with the same set of directors from Chevron and Texaco that sit on our Board, as well as on Bill's Board, they may say something in New York about Caltex (East Africa) Ltd. being so unaccommodating as to spoil Bill's hunting trip. Since you're the boss, I really feel badly about it, inasmuch as it is my fault. Although, I know Bill, and Bill Chandler would be the first to insist that it go no further than his own Board."

Harry instantly sat bolt upright on the edge of his chair. "Bill Chandler? You mean the President of Trans-Arabian Pipeline Company? You never told me that it was Bill Chandler that was coming. Why didn't you say so?"

I looked at Harry innocently and quickly answered, "But I told you his name several times."

"Yes, you said 'Bill', but you never said 'Chandler', and you certainly never indicated in any way that your friend was President of TAPLINE." I sheepishly apologized and said I was sorry. "You said you hadn't mailed that letter yet, didn't you?" Harry abruptly asked. I confirmed that the letter was still on my desk. "Well, I don't think you should mail it. Let me know what arrangements you will have to make to cover your desk while you're away. We certainly can't have Caltex (East Africa) getting that kind of attention from the Board in New York."

'Or you Harry,' I thought to myself, but not ungenerously so. I had my three weeks. 'Business is business', unless it just happens to be a possible threat to your career, and certainly Harry didn't get to be the Marketing Director of Caltex (East Africa) Ltd. by offending the Directors of our two owners.

It was everything imaginable. A huge truck for the supplies and what ever trophies we would bag. There was a Land Rover, a staff of nine including the cook and stewards, but not counting the white hunter in his bush jacket and wide brimmed hat with the required leopard skin hat band around it and quietly and confidently puffing on his pipe. It really was a dream. I didn't care that the cash advances on my credit cards would take more years to pay off than my children were old.

The startling contrasts were one of the many striking parts about the whole safari. We would shoot until nightfall, which meant we were sometimes an hour or more from our base camp at sunset. The headlights of the Land Rover could be seen with quite sufficient time for the stewards to have the necessary hot water boiling over the fire. As we entered camp, the first steward would be perched on a high branch waiting to pour the water into a perforated shower head, so that we could wash the grime and sweat of a hard day's trek in the jungle from our weary bodies. I always showered by habit, but every night as you arrived back from your day's hunt, you were quite politely and deferentially asked your preference as to showering or bathing.

One night I couldn't resist changing my routine. I said that I would have a bath instead of a shower. It was a heady experience to leave your tent after undressing, enter the shelter housing the bath and then lie there in the tub in the extremely hot water. And all the while you were contemplating the fact that you were hundreds of miles from civilization. But soaking in a hot tub of water, which was frequently replenished by a solicitous black servant in immaculate white dress, who would continue to maintain the temperature of your bath as long as you wished to lounge in it.

The next thing that always made my eyes widen in wonder was when dinner was announced. The dinning room tent had a red carpet spread over the entire area covered by the tarpaulin. The large, oversize dining table was set up in the exact center of the tent with wine glasses, silver ware, and some of the finest china available for the type of service it was expected to have to endure. The stewards were in spotless white uniforms with a red sash, white gloves, and wearing the usual red fezzes on their heads. And all the while the jungle sounds were muted in the background. The huge radio had been set up near the dinning room table, and the radio operator was standing by in the event the 'great white bwanas' wished to establish contact with the organizations that had made this all possible by maintaining us on their payrolls. It was all a exhilarating experience indeed.

We waved goodbye to Bill and Clair and returned to a more normal life style of having to go to the office on a daily basis and my wife restricted to her new bridge companions. Her bridge partners had been delighted to have the opportunity of playing bridge with a player of the caliber of Clair Chandler and to have the opportunity of exchanging views with a person who was very knowledgeable about a distant part of the world so foreign to theirs.

During our last home leave after Beirut and before proceeding to Nairobi, New York had explained why the assignment in Nairobi was for a period of only ten months. They had planned our return for a New York office assignment at the completion of my duties in East Africa. My very shrewd wife remarked to me that if we were returning in ten months for a New York assignment, we would have to find a place to live as soon as we arrived back in New York.

If we couldn't find a place quickly and were living in a hotel for any length of time with three children, we would purchase the first tin shack with a roof on it just to get out of the hotel. Her brilliant idea was that since we still had several months of our six months leave left over, we should take the time to look leisurely for a place to buy. Then, on our return, we wouldn't be pressured into buying something that we didn't want just to get out of the hotel. And so we bought our first home. It was in Hartsdale, Westchester, New York. The same Westchester 'home to be' of one of the Big Sisters that owned us.

She was most unhappy, when at a later date I suggested that we should sell the house and invest the money in a much better paying proposition than we were getting by renting our home. "But surely we are going to live in it some day," she said wistfully.

"That may well be, but as a businessman I play the odds. Owning a home in which you have never lived, and haven't lived in for ten years, is not my idea of good odds." To borrow a metaphor based on the dark continent in which we had now been living for ten years instead of ten months, 'the leopard hadn't changed his spots'.

That monumental, bureaucratic, benign dictatorship for which we both laboured had done what it had always done. Having told us we were going to be in Africa for ten months, they had slowly, but surely, changed the period of months to years. The ten month assignment in Africa had now lengthened to ten years with no end in sight. My wife and I were discussing the selling of our home while we were in Johannesburg, South Africa. At that time we had been there for over two years having progressed through Manager of Caltex (Tanganyika) Ltd., General Manager of Caltex (Rhodesia) Ltd. and Manager of the Johannesburg branch of Caltex (Africa) Ltd; The Johannesburg branch which did fifty percent of all the business done by Caltex in South Africa.

However, when I had finished the Nairobi assignment we didn't know all that and were looking forward to returning to New York and living in a beautiful home on one and a half acres in the incomparable, rolling, green hills of Westchester county. As we were packing to leave Nairobi, I was offered the assignment to one of the branches in East Africa as Manager. They simply told me that since I seemed to be able to quite easily make all kinds of recommendations from the comfort of the Head Office, perhaps I should go to one of the branches and see how life was really lived. And to which branch was the most generous offer made? The one with the longest communication lines to the Head Office, the one with the largest territory, the one with agonizing transportation problems, the one that was on its way to independence, the one that was always at the tail end of anything good that happened in the East African organization. Tanganyika!

I loved it!

15

Dar-es-salaam, Tanganyika—1960

INTERNATIONAL HERALD TRIBUNE, WEDNESDAY,

NOVEMBER 27,1991

Milan, Italy—With the breakup of the Soviet Union concern has been expressed by ENI (Ente Nazionale Idrocarburi) the Italian state owned oil company, that their supply of gas to the Italian market could be in jeopardy. Out of the 47.6 billion cubic meters supplied to the market, 13.9 billion came from the Union of Soviet Socialist Republics. This represented 29.2% of the market.

"You didn't mail it! You couldn't have mailed it! You know that correspondence is never mailed! It is always sealed and hand delivered! How could you possibly have mailed it?" By this time my voice had raised itself to the pitch of an agonizing wail. As my secretary broke out into a flood of tears, I ended my tirade with the hopeless exclamation of, "Oh my God, what are we going to do now?

There had been a special lock installed on the bottom drawer of my desk in the office. All information on the progress of the bids by the international oil companies to the Government of Tanganyika for the privilege of building a refinery in Dar-es-salaam was kept under secure lock and key. All exchange of information between the Governor-General of Tanganyika and the oil industry concerning the proposed refinery was also kept in that self-same, securely locked drawer. The drawer contained all the official correspondence between the company's office and the Governor-General's office. The originals in the drawer, which had been hand received in the company office from Government House, bore the seal of Government House with the impressive red ribbon binding that told any onlooker that this was official correspondence of Her Majesty's Government. All of the originals from THE COMPANY had been similarly sealed with the company's appropriate wax impression and red ribbon binding and hand delivered to Government House.

In all instances, the Governor's aide de camp himself had delivered the documents to the company's office. When delivering the company correspondence to Government House, the only recipient to whom the mail would be delivered was the same ADC. If he were not there to receive it, the company Sales Manager would express his regrets and return to the office with the correspondence still in his safe keeping. The Sales Manager was the only other person in the office, besides my secretary who was typing the correspondence, who was privy to the arrangements that had been entered into between Government House and Caltex (Tanganyika) Ltd.

Many times when being driven home with my mind racing in review of the day's events and having covered half the distance between the office and the house, the chauffeur would be instructed to reverse direction and return to the office. He must have surely wondered what had prompted me to repeat this procedure frequently over the past few months. I knew in my heart that I had locked the drawer. The key was in my possession. In fact, I was staring at the key this very instant. But had I locked it? Was I sure? There was only one way to satisfy myself.

What went on in the chauffeur's mind was a matter of some conjecture as he watched me re-enter the building from which I had just departed only a short time ago, return in a matter of minutes with nothing in my hand and no sign of having accomplished anything constructive. Naturally, he could not have possibly known the number of times that I tugged at that locked drawer to ease the qualms in my heart that told me that perhaps I hadn't actually locked it.

I hadn't been sleeping too well recently and to spend the night wondering whether or not the desk drawer was locked would only further irritate my wife. She had very forcibly pointed out that I was again in the habit of rising and pacing the floor at all hours of the night. I appeared to be re-entering that self-same state of mind that I had forced her to endure during a certain period of our stay in Ceylon. It was beginning to be almost impossible to get a decent night's sleep. My mind was continuously trying to grapple with the needs of having Caltex successful in its bid for the refinery. And even more distressful was the constant need to get some peace of mind over the clandestine procedure that had developed between Government House and the company's office regarding the exchange of information between the Governor-General and the oil industry.

After having been granted the royal favour of independence by their previous imperial masters, and in keeping with their recently acquired world status, newly independent countries formed their own airlines. After losing countless millions of dollars in these fruitless endeavours, they turned their attention to other prestigious, money losing propositions, which included building their own refineries. In the case of Tanganyika, however, it only had 'internal self-government' and was not yet fully independent. It certainly didn't have the money to start its own airline, even after independence. Boeing and the other aircraft manufacturers weren't in the habit of selling their multi-million dollar aircraft to customers such as newly independent black countries, who couldn't conceivably meet their obligations.

Tanganyika did have some legitimate reason to consider building its own refinery. This was, particularly, true when one of the members of the international oil industry was willing to finance such an endeavour. In those happy days, the international oil companies still controlled the majority of crude oil produced around the world. The sale of this crude oil was the main 'cash cow' that greatly enhanced their balance sheets. It also made their stock acceptable for purchase to Wall Street and to the huge employee funded pension plans that purchased the millions of shares of the publicly traded oil companies.

The international oil companies didn't agree to finance these refineries in God forsaken outposts of the Third World for altruistic reasons. In point of fact, they would have much preferred to continue to sell the refined products made in their own refineries located in the producer countries to these Third World customers. This would not only give them the profit on the crude oil, which they supplied to their own refineries, but also give them a substantial profit on the clean products such as gasoline, kerosene, aviation fuel and diesel oil produced from that profitable crude oil and sold to such 'less developed countries'. However, once these newly independent governments had embarked on the grandiose plans of elbowing their way into the world ranks of their previous masters by attempting to emulate them by owning airlines and massive refineries, it behooved the internationals to take their intentions seriously.

There was no heavy industry in these LDC's. Clean products enjoyed a much more substantial profit than did heavy fuel oil, which was in demand in huge volumes in the industrialized world. In practice, heavy fuel was very often sold to those industrialized countries at a loss. The sale of these large quantities at a loss was a necessary evil, if the company owned refineries were to make room in their storage facilities. Without disposing of this heavy fuel, it would not be possible to keep pouring out the profitable gasoline, kerosene, aviation fuel and diesel oil products. The LDC's, in this respect, were supporting the heavy industry of the developed countries through the profit generated by the sale of clean products to them. This fact, certainly, never gave pause to either the oil companies, Wall Street or to the employee funded pension plans that enjoyed a very satisfactory return on the ownership of the shares of these oil companies.

The building and the financing of a refinery, by one of the international oil companies in countries whose total petroleum consumption was only large enough to support one such refinery, was actually a marketing strategy. A strategy that was designed to ensure that the oil company, which was the successful bidder for the project would, in effect, have a captive customer. Until the refinery was paid for in full, part of the terms of the contract would be the exclusive supply rights of the profitable crude oil to the refinery by the company which had built and financed the project for these LCD's. In many cases, based on the financial resources of the countries in question, this might well prove to be eternity.

Of course, the taxpayers of the West might, unknowingly, kick in some of their hard earned tax money to bail out these LDC's when they got in over their heads with their vaunted airlines, refineries and other national follies. The West, with the able help of the World Bank through loans and transfers, would pay off the remaining balance owed on the national airline or accelerate the redemption of the outstanding amount owed to the international oil company, which had financed the refinery. All of which was accomplished by transfers or loans or some sort of esoteric financial deal that never seemed to identify the real purpose of the transaction. The average onlooker to the activities of the World Bank would never be able to perceive that these loans and transfers from the West were, in fact, going to be used to offset the disastrous programs of the Third World[62].

It was even impossible to see that many millions of dollars of these payments from the taxpayers of the West would end up in the Swiss Bank accounts of some of the most ruthless dictators the civilized world has ever known. The World Bank repeatedly seemed to be in the habit of doing this. They would thus, inadvertently and unknowingly (?), frustrate the marketing endeavors of the very companies whose stock the taxpayers owned and were providing the taxes from the handsome dividends that were funding the World Bank.

With the payment of the last installment on the refinery, either with the help of the World Bank or, even in some unusual cases, by their own efforts, the LDC in question was now free to shop around the international oil market. They were now in a position to obtain the most advantageous crude oil supply agreement which they were capable of negotiating. Many a shocked eyebrow was raised by them, when they first ventured out into the intrepid waters of the international crude oil market and discovered what price they had been paying for that crude oil to their 'captors' who had financed their refinery.

However, price was not to be the subject of the meeting of the oil industry managers which had been called by the Governor-General of Tanganyika in Government House in Dar-es-salaam. Until he opened the meeting with the extremely disturbing and momentous news that Ente Nazionale Idrocarburi (ENI) had entered the bidding for the contract called for by the Tanganyika Government to build a refinery in Dar-es-salaam, the oil company managers in Dar-es-salaam were entirely unaware of this new entrant.

Even in the 'obscenely wealthy' oil industry, there are 'haves' and 'have-nots'. Unknown to many of the general public, some of the biggest international oil companies in the world are in the position of being 'net buyers' of crude oil. In explanation to the layman, this means that their sales to the market of refined products, i.e.: gasoline, kerosene, aviation fuel and diesel oil far exceeded their own, available crude oil supply needed to feed their numerous refineries. Consequently, they have to purchase the shortfall of crude oil on the open market at a very much less advantageous price than they would enjoy when supplying the crude oil, whose ownership was theirs and on which they enjoyed huge profits.

If anyone wondered years ago why Standard Oil of California bought the Gulf Oil Company, it was for this very simple reason. Chevron (SOCAL) was, or very soon could possibly become, a 'net buyer' of crude oil. Most unsettling for them at the time was that one of their main sources of supply, Aramco, was in Saudi Arabia, not the most stable part of the world in so far as the international oil business is concerned. It was where Sheikh Yamani was making life very difficult for four of the Seven Sisters, Texaco, Chevron, Mobil and Esso, of which Chevron was probably the most concerned. On the other hand, the Gulf Oil Company had always been a 'net seller' of crude oil. It had huge reserves in Kuwait, even though it had lost its half-monopoly of Kuwait oil with BP. Although Kuwait was still in very close proximity to Saudi Arabia in that rather unstable part of the world, Kuwait didn't have Yamani. Gulf's reserves were much greater than its refined oil market requirements. At the time those reserves appeared to be inexhaustible. What better way for Chevron to assure itself of a guaranteed supply of raw material than to purchase the company that owned such raw material called crude oil?

There was, undoubtedly, another important reason. The combination of lower oil prices and rising costs of exploration within the United States at the time that Chevron purchased Gulf had made all the oil majors more vulnerable to raids from outsiders. Raiders who believed that the internationals' oil reserves were very much more valuable than their share-prices suggested. It was T. Boone Pickens, one of the new corporate raiders, who perceived that it was cheaper, as he put it, 'to buy oil on Wall Street than to go out and look for it yourself'[63]. Chevron took his words at face value. They promptly entered a bidding war against him. It was T. Boone Pickens, who had targeted Gulf as one of The Seven Sisters whose share-price was so low that it was cheaper to buy Gulf with its huge reserves than to explore for new oil.

This was the first question raised by all the assembled oil managers in the Governor-General's office in Government House. 'ENI is a net buyer of crude oil,' or as The Seven Sisters derisively referred to Mattei, the head of ENI, he was 'an oilman without oil'[64]. 'Why would he enter into an expensive bidding for a refinery for which he would have to purchase the feed stock on the open market?' was the general query.

By a bizarre set of circumstances there was a lowly, American, newly appointed manager who was much later to become privy to certain rumours then in existence which indicated that perhaps Mattei was not 'an oilman without oil'. These rumours seemed to point to the fact that Mattei was in the very process of assuring himself of his own source of crude oil

'We, collectively, never considered that ENI would be a potential bidder for this contract,' was the consensus of the managers. "Are you positive of your information?" was the question put to the Governor-General by one of the mangers present.

This is not the doubting attitude that ordinary citizens, even international oil executives, should take towards the ruler of one of the colonies of the British Empire, especially the bearer of the Order of the Knight of the Garter, Sir Richard. "You understood me," was the response from His Excellency. "I didn't call you all together to have you question my source of information," he disdainfully announced. "I merely wish to inform you that Her Majesty's Government has serious reservations as to the advisability of ENI being the successful bidder for this refinery," he continued. "These reservations are the result of Italy recently concluding a major supply contract with the Union of Soviet Socialist Republics for a substantial portion of her gas energy requirements. Her Majesty's government has made its views known to the Italian Government through NATO. Her Majesty's Government has emphasized to Italy the strategic necessity of not placing herself in the position of having a disproportionate part of her energy supply at the discretion of the Union of Soviet Socialist Republics."

"Unfortunately, these representations have been to no avail. It has now become necessary to ensure that Tanganyika does not become the victim of an energy shortfall in the future. A shortfall caused by default of a government that does not recognize the absurdity of placing itself at risk to the USSR if the 'cold war' erupts into a 'hot war'."

By no conceivable stretch of the imagination could anyone in that room, at that time, have been able to visualize that thirty-one years later it would not be the eruption of a 'cold war' into a 'hot war' that might be the reason to put Tanganyika's energy supply in jeopardy. It would be the total, economic collapse of that monolithic empire of the Union of Soviet Socialist Republics, and the consequent threat to Italy's gas supply as detailed in the edition of the Herald Tribune of Wednesday, November 27, 1991[65].

To a lowly, American oil company executive just recently appointed to his first managerial position, and to what he thought was a wonderful opportunity to prove himself a marketing strategist, this was all getting to be beyond his depth. At no time during my pre-employment interviews had those senior officers of the company, who were conducting the interviews, even vaguely intimated that I would be sitting in open-mouthed wonder in a Governor-General's office of the British Empire. Sitting there trying to absorb the knowledge that I was now about to get involved in the machinations of one of the great powers of the world. And to compound the dilemma, I was going to be privy, in the distant future, to the knowledge that 'an oilman without oil' had allegedly embarked on what, unknown at the time to everyone in the Governor-Generals' office, was a deadly, perilous path to rectify that epitaph of 'an oilman without oil'.

In one respect, all the oil company managers who were tucked away in this obscure port of Dar-es-salaam on the East coast of Africa could not possibly have known of the internal power struggles going on within ENI at that time. Enrico Mattei, the Chairman of the Board of Ente Nazionale Idrocarburi, the same one who had popularized the expression, 'The Seven Sisters', was engaged in an ego trip. He had convinced himself that he was capable of meeting The Seven Sisters head on. He had vowed that he would show them that ENI, a recent entry to this prestigious arena of economic world conquest, was a force with which to be reckoned. He would build refineries all around the world to gain representation for ENI. Even more importantly, this would gain him personal recognition, which would greatly enhance his reputation and satisfy his oversize ego.

It did not matter how little known or obscure the piece of real estate in question on which he intended ENI to build these refineries might appear to those of the internationals who had been engaged in a power struggle for decades in this type of endeavour. Enrico Mattei was Chairman of the Board of a state owned company and didn't have to show a profit.

His power struggles arose because he was attempting to wrest money from other powerful government figures, who were just as determined as he was to enhance their reputations at the Italian taxpayers expense. As it turned out afterwards, he was in the process of being severely censured by the Italian Government. Not because of what he was attempting to do, but because of his failure to achieve it. At the same time, mismanagement, alleged misappropriation of funds by many of his subordinates and several other failures of a like kind were building up in his industrial empire. He would have been faced with these plaguing problems in the very near future except that he, also, had the additional misfortune of being killed in an air crash in 1962. As the recent elections in Italy have confirmed, nothing has changed as long as you are successful in accomplishing what ever power struggle or objective you are trying to achieve for yourself and those of your supporters, be it the Mafia or otherwise.

Nor could the other, allegedly activities of Enrico Mattei in his quest for his own source of crude oil be known to the Governor-General at that time. Or for that matter could it be known to all the other oil company managers gathered there, particularly, to a single American who was simply over awed with the turn of events.

Prior to the departure on an assignment of a newly appointed manager, a short period is spent at Caltex's head office at 350 Madison Avenue in New York to brief the new appointee. During this period, he is often wined and dined by all the senior members of the board in order to inflate *his* ego so he can handle what are surely going to be almost insurmountable problems in the field.

And ego was the subject of considerable discussion at this time as two of the Seven Sisters at 350 Madison Avenue continued to laugh derisively at the Don Quixote of the oil industry as 'an oil man without oil' was driven to desperate lengths by his own monumental ego and the contemptuous laughter of the Seven Sisters. Apparently, not so the French. They were furious at the lengths to which the Seven Sisters had driven Enrico Mattei to fulfill his determination to meet the Seven Sisters head on.

As with the Kennedy assassination, conspiracy theories abound whenever there is an assassination. In the case of the assassination of Mattei, oops, sorry, the accidental death of Mattei, the conspiracy theories were almost as numerous as with the assassination of Kennedy. The most prevalent one said that since the Seven Sisters had barricaded the French, as well as Mattei, from the prolific oil fields of the Middle East, there was still one area which, at that time, was not favourably viewed by any of the majors because of the insurrection of the Algerians. The Algerians needed arms and they badly needed a middle man with tremendous influence to get them. What better entrée to Algerian oil could one be assured of if that person became their purveyor of arms? Italy's State owned munitions industry was a most ready and willing supplier. Furthermore, there was a middleman who knew the munitions industries' CEO's on a personal basis that guaranteed him immediate priority to their output. Desperation being the mother of invention, the conspiracy theory stated that the French firmly believed that Mattei had embarked on just such an endeavour. They were murderously enraged at him because of this belief. A considerable time later they were, in their opinion, able to confirm their alleged suspicions of his actions. Actions which, they believed, continued to deny them success in bringing the Algerian insurrection under control.

Perhaps if Mattei had been a Godfather in the Mafia, which nobody believed he ever was or could have been, he would have had the experience and the background to learn to watch his back more assiduously than he did. No Godfather in the Mafia would *ever* fly in a plane that was being maintained by a company owned by another family into whose territory he was encroaching. The company that was maintaining Mattei's plane was, allegedly, because of inter-locking relationships, of French origin.

None of this could possibly have been known to anyone assembled in the Governor-General's office. With all due respect, it could not possibly have been known to the Governor-General either or to the British Government whom he was representing. However, what was known to the Governor-General, because he had been so informed by the Foreign Office, was that the Italian Government had recently finalized an agreement with the Union of Soviet Socialist Republics for a very large portion of their supply of gas energy. This gas was to be delivered through a pipeline that was to be built directly from Russia's gas fields to Italy with, of course, the steel pipeline to be manufactured in Italy.

"For the information of all assembled here, I wish to inform you that the recent supply agreement concluded between Italy and the USSR covers almost 30% of their gas consumption. This, in Her Majesty's Government's opinion, is an intolerable percentage of their energy requirements which might be needed in the event of war," the Governor-General ended his opening remarks.

"Bitter experience in the past reminds us that when a cold war becomes a shooting war, the first casualties of energy shortfalls are the outposts of commercial empires, not the outposts of territorial empires. In this case, if Italy is short of energy, because the USSR has closed the valve on their gas supply simultaneously with the dropping of the first bombs, the initial victims of the shortfall are going to be the far parts of their commercial empire. One of these will be Tanganyika, if ENI is successful in being awarded the contract to build this refinery. It will not be Italy herself, or parts of their territorial empire that will be the victims of the Soviet's action of closing the valve on the gas line. Italy will simply stop supplying the commercial outposts and keep the residual energy for itself and its territories," was the diplomatic wisdom imported to the assembled oil managers by Sir Richard.

The next announcement by the Governor-General made a deep impression on the listeners. "The reason you are all present here this morning is to make you aware that Her Majesty's Government is not the least bit concerned or interested in which one of the international companies that are represented at this juncture are the successful bidders for the refinery project under consideration by the Government of Tanganyika. What does concern Her Majesty's Government, however, is that Ente Nazionale Idrocarburi is not awarded the contract. For them to be the suppliers of crude oil to Tanganyika, when they have thirty percent of their gas energy requirements at risk with the USSR, is unacceptable to Her Majesty's Government. In the event of war with Russia, we would find ourselves without a reliable supplier of energy to this project and that is totally and strategically unacceptable."

The statement of the Governor-General made a profound impact on me. In particular, that part about Her Majesty's Government not being the least bit concerned or interested in which international oil company in the room was to be the successful bidder for the refinery. Nonetheless, in spite of what Sir Richard had said, I found myself with a deeply, perplexing problem. Her Majesty's Government was 'talking to itself'. With a fifty-one percent ownership of BP by Her Majesty's Government, BP *was* Her Majesty's Government. Even more disturbing to me, there was still another very, incestuous relationship with one of the other Seven Sisters represented at the meeting.

Very shortly after I had arrived in Dar-es-salaam and had not had the time to fully settle in, establish myself and meet all the other members of industry, I had had to take the opportunity of calling the Shell company. The call was about a matter that did not concern the oil business, but was a case of raising money for a private school project. After successfully concluding my talk with the Shell manager, I requested my secretary to call the BP manager. I hoped to have the same successful outcome in the way of a large donation from that other giant British oil company as I had had with Shell.

When the call to BP was answered, the name given by the person answering the call and the voice were identical to the one with whom I just concluded my previous call when talking to Shell. I apologized for calling a second time and said that my secretary must have misunderstood me as I was calling the manager of BP. It was the first time in my relationship with the other international oil company managers that I found myself totally speechless. "No," was the response, "she didn't make a mistake. This is the Manager of BP."

Two different British oil companies? Two different gasolines to sell? Two different advertising campaigns? Two different trade marks? Two different storage facilities? Two different telephone numbers? One manager!

What kind of an impenetrable, Chinese wall was this individual going to build in his mind? Not only would Her Majesty's Government, as represented by BP, have access to all the information which Caltex and the other members of the oil industry would supply to the Governor-General, but in his dual capacity the Shell manager would also be privy to it.

The Governor-General continued to address the gathering. "This office will keep the industry, as represented by your presence here this morning, of the progress of the ENI bid. You, in turn, will keep me advised of any information that you obtain through your various sources as to what action it would be advisable for this office to take to ensure that ENI does not successfully conclude a supply agreement with this future member of the Commonwealth."

So that is how empires are made and ruled. For the average onlooker to the pomp and ceremony of the diplomatic world, it seemed that they did nothing but entertain various, visiting dignitaries and go to garden parties. To be exposed to the inner workings of the international world of countervailing powers was, indeed, a sobering experience. Thus began an ongoing exchange of information between the oil industry, excluding ENI, and Government House concerning the progress of the negotiations with the Government of Tanganyika on the proposed refinery project.

It is remarkable in one respect that in 1960 the supply agreement between Italy and the USSR covered approximately 30% of Italy's gas requirements. Thirty-one years later, the agreement still covered just under 30% of those requirements as noted in the International Herald Tribune's article. This percentage remained the same over thirty-one years in spite of the fact that Italy's need for gas must have increased tremendously over that thirty-one year period. Perhaps 30% was a maximum figure that Italy felt could be a livable risk in the event of war. From this late vantage point, it now appears that the only difference between Her Majesty's Government's opinion and that of the Italian Government's opinion in the event of war, was a matter of percentages.

Many of the British civil servants putting in their time in the outposts of their government's shrinking empire could see the hand writing on the wall. With the collapse of their country's world wide influence, it was becoming very obvious that their ranks were going to be considerably thinned out and, probably, in many cases decimated. Should they opt for citizenship in the newly independent countries on the theory that their expertise was badly needed, and they could finish their careers being assured of ongoing employment? Or should they remain on the payroll of the shrinking empire and face possible early retirement or even outright termination?

If they opted for service in the newly independent countries, they were faced with another dilemma. How honest could they remain in these newly independent governments if that were the option they selected? There was already considerable worldwide evidence of massive corruption in the government ranks of the new born, national services of the independent, Third World, black, civil servants.

It is, naturally, impossible for any person to know what moves another person to take the actions that are only publicly visible to the onlooker. Do such actions indicate that one is a sincere, hardworking and honest civil servant? Or is the individual taking advantage of a once in a lifetime situation to enhance his personal well being at the expense of the newly independent black governments? This was the predicament that I faced with my nemesis in the Ministry of Commerce of the Tanganyika Government. From a member of the white, ruling class of the royal imperialists, he outwardly appeared to become a fawning and ingratiating lackey of his previous subjects. His name was Colin Wood and his title still identified him as Permanent Under Secretary to the Minister of Commerce. It was his Ministry that was the life blood of the oil industry. They literally controlled the industry's existence. Under the British colonial rulers, you could expect, and you would get, the utmost in fair and equitable treatment. With the gradual shift to independence, the words 'fair and equitable' took on an entirely different connotation.

When the United States Congress in its eternal wisdom legislated the eleventh commandment, "Thou Shalt Not Bribe", they took away the only useful tool the international community of Americans had at their disposal to combat their commercial adversaries of other nationalities. There was no doubt in my mind that Colin Wood was 'on the payroll' of ...????? ENI? Perhaps. 'On the payroll' of ...????? my British colleagues? Perhaps. The British oil companies were determined to see that the Americans didn't gain yet another economic foothold in their commercial empire by being awarded the contract to build the refinery in

Dar-es-salaam. Or was he just doing his honest daily duty and earning his monthly pittance from his newly adopted country of which he had decided to become a national ...???? Perhaps. Or did he have his fingers in the drawer of some unseen and unknown till.... .? Perhaps.

It was impossible to pin him down to anything specific. Any request for information was met with an avalanche of inconsequential details of analyses that been undertaken by those self-same, self-defeating organizations that had brought ruin to many a newly emerging independent country, the World Bank and the International Monetary Fund. He would continually postpone or outright cancel appointments. Appointments that in the opinion of myself, the representative of Caltex, were critical to the future economic well being of the country of which he was soon to be become a national. A country that, in the not so distant future, was soon to be both politically and commercially independent of its previous imperial masters.

It was the abrupt and unofficial cancellation of a very important appointment with the infamous Colin Wood that finally convinced me that I should commit myself to writing and inform the Governor-General about my misgivings concerning Mr. Wood, and where his loyalties lay. This was of particular concern to me, because the Governor-General had been in the habit of quoting him repeatedly on various occasions, which gave tremendous weight to whatever pronouncements our esteemed Mr. Wood had made.

I felt it my duty to warn the Governor-General that his source of information was of 'dubious value' to put it in diplomatic terms. In fact, in my humble opinion, it was downright dangerous. In reporting the activities of the progress of the bids for the refinery to my fellow directors in Nairobi, I had repeatedly stressed that Mr. Wood was a serious obstacle to our success in concluding an agreement with the Tanganyika Government. At one of the numerous Board meetings in Nairobi, which I had to attend, I informed them that Mr. Wood had decided to become a Tanganyika citizen. He would soon join the ranks of the newly formed, black civil servants. He would thus further be allying himself very strongly with them and making our situation even more difficult. One of the directors at the board room table in Nairobi, Bill Temple, succinctly pin-pointed my problem. "The main situation that you don't appear to have recognized," he remarked to me sardonically, "is that you have a Wood in the nigger-pile".

As was my habit when keeping appointments with government officials, particularly government officials of tropical colonial empires around the world, I was on my way to the building that housed the Ministry of Commerce a good fifteen minutes earlier than the time for which my appointment called. As I was reflecting on what the outcome of this meeting would be, the car entered the grounds of the government complex. The chauffeur had driven me there so often he could have found the entrance to the building even if he were blind-folded. Therefore, he was astonished and at a loss to understand my shouted command, "Turn to the right! Turn to the right!"

The car had entered the long driveway and had only traversed half its length to the Ministry of Commerce's building. There was no other driveway to the right or anyway that he could turn to the right except to straddle the road and actually obstruct the path of an oncoming vehicle. I lurched forward, wrested the wheel from his hands and turned it sharply to the right. At the same time I shouted a further command of, "Brakes! Brakes!" A command which was entirely unnecessary as he immediately could see that the only alternative to applying the brakes was to run into the trees lining the driveway. The car halted with a neck snapping pitch. The other vehicle, which was headed for the exit of the driveway to the government buildings, came to an abrupt stop just inches away from ours.

Sitting behind the wheel of the other car was the object of my appointment. The man who had finally promised to provide me with important information. Information, which I fervently believed would fully substantiate the recommendations I had recently made to my directors concerning the terms of the offer to build the refinery. A bid which, I felt, would award us the contract. I had suddenly seen him as his car approached us on the long driveway from the Ministry. It was as I instantly recognized him that I had simultaneously ordered the driver to turn to the right with the intention of blocking his way. I was not going to bear the ignominy of being told again by his secretary that he had been unable to keep his appointment with me.

I leapt out of the car and almost physically accosted him by pulling open the door of his vehicle. "Where are you going?" I demanded. "We have an appointment in less than fifteen minutes," I almost shouted at him.

To my utmost amazement, he sincerely apologized with the comment, "I was going to call your office, but I didn't have time," he said in a dazed voice. He appeared to be in a state of shock. A condition that could certainly not have been brought about by the desperate and precipitous method I had employed to stop his car.

"I must go now," he said. To my further amazement, he exited his vehicle without another word and hastened down the driveway on foot as if there were not even sufficient time to disengage the vehicles and proceed by car. In the process, he left me speechless. Something very serious, indeed, must have transpired in the Ministry to have put him in such a dazed state. Since the car was a government owned vehicle, his leaving it in the driveway was of no great loss to him personally. This bizarre episode was never explained by him nor did we ever learn of any circumstances that could have induced him to act in this manner inasmuch as he was never seen again.

If ever there was reason to inform the Governor-General of my suspicions concerning Mr. Wood, this event was the finale straw. I returned immediately to the office and committed all my doubts and frustrations to paper with the express warning to the Governor-General that here, in my opinion was a man that was not to be trusted; that he could no longer be considered a loyal servant of Her Majesty's Government. Allegedly, it was doubtful if he could be considered a loyal subject of any government other than the one he ruled himself, his own self-interest. In my indignation at what I thought were slights and insults that I had received at the hands of this individual over the past months, I was less than cautious in the statements and fears that I recorded. I was so incensed by his recent behaviour that I affixed the customary wax seal myself to the finished document with the express intention of delivering it to Government House personally.

After a few moments of sober thought, I realized that my presence at Government House would require the attention of more senior personnel than would be necessary if the Sales Manager made the customary delivery. I informed the secretary that we would wait an hour before delivering the correspondence. I knew that the Sales Manager was returning to the office at that time.

Also within the hour, the daily post was to be delivered and the mail to the post office picked up for dispatch. 'The best laid plans of mice and men ...' It was the postman who arrived first within the hour, not the Sales Manager. The letter to Government House, somehow or other, got caught up in the massive volume of mail which was the daily reason for our existence. It was carted off to the post office as ignominiously as any other piece of correspondence in spite of the fact that it bore the usual red ribbon binding, the official wax seal of THE COMPANY and no postage was affixed to it. But of course, at that moment I was unaware of that.

As soon as the Sales Manager arrived, I recounted what had happened concerning my abortive appointment with the Permanent Under Secretary to the Minister of Commerce. I told him that there was no doubt in my mind that the Governor-General had to be warned that there was a potential threat to his plans to prevent ENI from becoming the successful bidder for the refinery, and that, allegedly, Mr. Wood embodied this threat. I informed him that I had committed my suspicions in writing, and that it was imperative that the correspondence be delivered immediately. I instructed him to obtain the letter from the secretary, take my car and chauffeur and leave immediately for Government House. He turned instantly and headed in the direction of the secretary's office. In a matter of minutes he was back in front of me with a shocked and a bewildered look of desperation on his face. In a hesitant and apologetic tone of voice he advised me that the letter had been picked up by the postman. "Your secretary mailed it," he explained.

"She didn't mail it! She couldn't have mailed it! She knows that correspondence is never mailed! It is always sealed and hand delivered! How could she possibly have mailed it?" I gasped. By this time the secretary was in my office. I directed my same enquiries to her in nothing resembling the hesitant and apologetic tone of voice which the Sales Manager had employed when informing me of her mistake and her tears became a rushing torrent streaming down her face. In examining the obvious implications of why the letter was not still in her possession, there was no doubt that it had mistakenly been mixed in with the mass of daily mail and bundled together with the other correspondence and been hauled off to the Central Post Office. I repeated my anguished wail, "My God, what are we going to do now?".

I abruptly apologized to my secretary for my outburst and told her she could be excused. There was no helpful input that she could give us now in her state of mind. We needed cooler heads. "Get hold of George," I ordered the Sales Manager.

"But he isn't aware of what has been going on," the Sales manger responded immediately.

"I know that, but the only reason that he isn't aware of it has been based on the 'need not to know'," I replied.

George Mammarat was the Manager of Operations of Caltex Tanganyika. This meant that he was responsible for all of the company's day to day activities. His was the department that made all the truck deliveries and was responsible for the storage of all product. It was his staff that kept the physical property of the company in a safe and orderly manner. He was the individual that was in charge of all the black labour that produced the immaculate looking tanks and pipelines that handled the petroleum products as they came ashore from the huge ocean going tankers owned by THE COMPANY.

He was far removed from the activities involving the bid for the refinery and, particularly, from the clandestine strategy of the exchange of information between the Governor-General's office and the office of THE COMPANY. It was decided very early in the negotiations that the fewer people who were aware of these activities, the less likelihood there would be of an accidental leak. Based on that old and familiar basis, 'the need not to know', George had never been told of the relationship between the Caltex office and that of the office of the Governor-General. Not that George wasn't to be trusted. I would have trusted him with my life, if it had ever become necessary. My trust in him arose during one of the strikes that we had undergone as Tanganyika was approaching its independence.

There had been some horrifying stories of what had happened in some of the newly, emerging, independent countries of Africa as the black citizens of those countries had gained control of their own destiny. Not only their own destiny, but the destiny of the white, imperial masters who had ruled them with an iron and brutal hand for so many years. Uprisings, mass killings and even torture had gained ascendancy in the headlines of the news media of the West.

There was no evidence, whatsoever, that Tanganyika would follow this pattern. However, it behooved every one in residence in a black country, that was soon to become master of its own fate, to take every precaution that ordinary mortals should take to preserve their lives and property should their assessment of the situation be erroneous. In this respect, George had been charged with seeing that all the vehicles of the company were in top operating condition. This, again, included those privately owned vehicles of the expatriates. My wife's car was thoroughly overhauled. The tires were replaced with the best and sturdiest ones available in the market. Extra oil and water storage were provided in the trunk of the car.

At this time, my mind no longer suddenly snapped to attention as I recalled the 'once in the lifetime' experience that we had undergone in Colombo, Ceylon when I had first embarked on these security measures for my wife. It, now, seemed that this was the modus operandi of the American expatriate in foreign service with an international oil company. Perhaps, also, there was the added factor that it was, now, I that was issuing the instructions that all company wives' cars be in perfect operating condition, fully fueled at all times and ready to depart on a moments notice for the countryside. A countryside, where the very much less sophisticated members of the citizenry would, in all probability, welcome us with open arms and protect us from their rabble-rousing, city cousins, or so we fervently hoped.

George Mammarat was a Frenchman, who had the reputation of being a hard driving taskmaster. He and his staff kept the company's property and equipment in perfect condition. In addition to having the reputation of being a hard driving taskmaster, he also had the enviable qualities of being absolutely fair and honest in his dealings with his black staff. The majority of the French, in their imitable way during their colonial days, had always treated the majority of their black subjects almost as equals. Colour to the French was not a problem. In fact, in some of their colonies the non-white citizens were, in effect, Nationals of Metropolitan France and enjoyed all the advantages of being citizens of that great country.

Prior to the wave of newly, emerging, independent countries being granted their independence, strikes were almost either unknown or were treated as face saving devices for negotiations between 'The King' and 'his subjects'. Now there was a different atmosphere.

There had been countless thousands of blacks that had been murdered in Kenya during the Mau Mau uprisings there. In other parts of the world, 'The cost in lives to Malaya for those who had fought for it, had been heavy. The Security Forces had lost 1865 killed, 2560 wounded; 2473 civilians had been murdered, 1385 wounded and 810 were missing'[66]. Very few whites had suffered a similar fate during the Mau Mau. However, there had been enough of them killed to give pause to all white members of the human race that were resident in Africa at the time.

This was a period when more and more of the black race were gaining control of their destiny and the destiny of those whites, who had remained in the old colonial empires. Although only a small number of whites had died in the Mau Mau uprisings in Kenya, almost all of them had been killed by valued and trusted servants, who had been in their employ for many years. Black servants who had, in the opinion of their white masters, been treated on a more than fair and equitable basis

George and I sat in my office and gazed out the window as the strikers began to congregate under a shady tree on the front lawn of the company building. The meeting had been set for the close of the working day. I wanted as few members of the staff involved as possible in the event the negotiations turned physically nasty. We had decided during the day the limits of the concessions that we were prepared to grant them. Generous in our terms, but perhaps not to be regarded so generously in their eyes. What would be their reactions? Would they get carried away by their emotions? Would they turn on their supervisor who had so fairly and honestly treated them over the years? Who could tell in these emotionally charged times? None of the whites in Kenya, who had held such convictions that their loyal and trusted servants would never turn on them during the Mau Mau uprisings, were alive to tell us.

George had insisted that he, alone, should remain on the company premises during the negotiations. This would limit 'damage' to only a single member of the staff if, in fact, the strikers took matters into their own hands, got emotionally carried away and physically decided to wreak their frustrations on an individual.

When George had insisted that I not expose myself to physical harm by remaining in the office during the negotiations but should go home, he had added a heart warming admonishment. "Look, you have three young children and a wife that are going to need you over the coming years. I haven't any children. My wife is perfectly capable of supporting herself if anything happens to me. And besides, if things go wrong, it will be my fault, and you shouldn't have to suffer for my mistakes," he concluded. All of his warnings in such a vein only reinforced my contention that, as Manager of Caltex Tanganyika, I would never ask a member of my staff to expose himself to a danger that I was not equally prepared to share with him. There was nothing that he could say that could dissuade me, and so I sat there with bated breath as he left my office to meet with the strikers.

We had not left everything to chance. The police had been alerted to possible trouble brewing at the company installation. We had not physically wanted them to be in evidence, as this might only inflame the strikers' emotions. The telephone number of the police station was written in large numbers right at the base of the telephone, as well as being indelibly imprinted on my mind. George and I had made sure that the large window of my office was unlocked and ready to be opened at a minutes notice, if he had to beat a hasty retreat. He securely bolted the door to the office as he exited. The assumption was, if things turned nasty, that the strikers would head for the door. They would not think of the window, even though they were sure to have seen him tumble pel-Mel over the sill, if it became necessary for him to seek sanctuary prior to the, hopefully, timely arrival of the police.

I watched him as he walked across the lawn to meet with the strikers. I reflected sadly on how ironic it would be if he were to suffer bodily harm or, even, conceivably be killed in this obscure outpost of a fading colonial empire after having successfully survived the war years.

He and I had been on opposite sides during the last war. In my case, I had only spent a number of months relentlessly hunting down the enemy in the cold and dangerous waters of the far North Atlantic. Waters that were infested with killers of two different stripes. Not only the German submarines that were committed to cutting the life line to England, but to our astonishment and horror at that latitude, by huge sharks. It was a shocking and sobering experience, which we sadly learned when we took aboard the few survivors of a successful attack on one of our escort vessels by the undersea boats. Survivors, whose bodies had been horribly mangled by the massive jaws of those other predators of the deep.

Although George and I were on opposite sides during the war, inasmuch as he was working for the Japanese, I came to know that he had made a much greater contribution to the Allies' war effort than I could ever have dreamed of making. He had been employed by a French engineering firm in Shanghai when the Japanese finally took that great city under their protection. 'Under their protection', as stressed in the Konoye statement, 'Japan's purpose in the present conflict is not a petty territorial acquisition It is rather to safeguard China's independence, and, respecting her sovereignty, to establish a New Order in East Asia.'[67]

The Japanese had done their intelligence work to an excellent degree during their initial occupation and before their attack on Pearl Harbor. They were aware of all the expertise of the expatriate employees, who were unfortunate enough not to have been able to evacuate the city when their new found hosts decided to take on the United States and the Allies at a later date.

George's firm in Shanghai was engaged in the reclaiming of used engine oil. As is well known, one of the reasons for Japan's embarking on their conquest of the Asian continent was the need for oil. During the war years, they were woefully short of this essential material needed to conduct a successful war effort. In Shanghai, the Japanese had made sure that George continued his efforts in the same direction that he had followed for his previous employers, which was the process of reclaiming used engine oil, but of course, now, under a changed proprietorship.

George was one of the many unsung heroes of the war. He risked not only his life, but exposed himself to what would, undoubtedly, be a horrible and lingering death had he been discovered doing his duty for his country. He continued to perform his daily chores meticulously for his new found employers, the Japanese, just as thoroughly as he had done for his former French employers. He went even a step further for his new employers, than he had done for his former ones. To each drum of finished, reclaimed oil that rolled out of the factory that he had been put in charge of by his captors, he added a barely, traceable amount of sulfuric acid.

Certainly to an engineer and even to the layman, it does not take too much imagination to understand the results that the addition of sulfuric acid would have on the operating war machinery of the Japanese. Many a tank or similar vehicle must have been returned for extensive engine repairs to the machine shop as the acid took its inevitable toll on the working parts of such modern and necessary war equipment. Equipment that then took many man hours and scarce material to return to operating condition.

There was no way that his captors could trace the failure of part of their war effort to George, other than the possibility of apprehending him in the act of physically adding the acid to the newly reclaimed oil. A possibility that was, naturally, always in George's mind. And as he confessed to me, it gave him countless numbers of tortured, sleepless nights. Sleepless nights, similar to my confession to him, that I had tossed and turned eternally in my bunk on that United States Navy aircraft carrier, that could be at any moment a target for a German torpedo, and I would find myself in the icy, cold waters of the North Atlantic, inhabited as they were by those huge sharks.

When taking over a new assignment for THE COMPANY, it was my established habit to review the employment records of all the senior employees who were to report to me. It was very noticeable in George's records that there was no war service listed. In fact, there was an embarrassing lack of detail covering the very late thirties and the forties. On my initial brief acquaintance with George, he did not strike me a an individual that would shirk his duty to his country. As we established a close personal and working relationship and exchanged information on the nerve wracking fears we had each undergone during the war years, his story had eventually evolved in its entirety.

This was the man that I wanted to join us now to help with his cool headed advice. Advice on how to handle a situation that might end up in the headlines of the news media around the world, if we did not successfully solve the dilemma of, possibly, having our letter to the Governor-General in the hands of the Tanganyika Government.

As was his habit, George appeared instantly at my request. The Sales Manger and I briefed him as completely as we could in a short period of time. He accepted without question the fact that he hadn't been made aware of the relationship between the company office and the Governor-General's office. The question put to him was, "What are we going to do about the potentially explosive contents of the letter to Government House that the secretary has mistakenly mailed?" A letter, we informed him, that was sure to draw detailed examination by the postal authorities, adorned as it was with wax seals and red ribbon binding and addressed to Government House.

"When was the letter picked up?" was his first question to us in reply to our problem.

"Less than an hour ago," was our response.

"Then it is still in the post office," was his assessment. "There are no mail deliveries at this time of day because of the heat. I propose that the three of us go right now to the Central Post Office. We will demand that we be allowed to search for a letter that was mistakenly mailed before it had been signed by the Manager. This is a situation that employees of the government will understand instantly," was his quick grasp of the situation. "In addition, since we are white, no lowly employee of the post office will ever question our authority."

George had spent many years of service in colonial empires and was fully aware of the mentality of the citizens of those colonies ruled by white masters. This was one of the major reasons that I wanted him to be part of our problem solving team. On the basis of his advice, we scrambled into my car immediately and proceeded to the post office. On arrival, we approached the building from the rear entrance. There we were greeted with quite and obedient diffidence by the staff. The heat of the scorching afternoon day had not yet been dissipated by the evening, cooling breeze so that few members of the staff were in evidence. Those that were still performing their duties in a slightly perfunctory manner gazed at us in wonder as if to say, 'What are these Europeans doing abroad in the middle of the hot, late, afternoon sun?'

George immediately took charge of the situation as we arrived. In a voice of quite authority, he informed the staff that there was a letter that had been mistakenly mailed before it had been signed by anyone in command. The letter had to be returned to the company's office for signature. After having been duly signed, it would be brought back to them for dispatch to its destination. They accepted his story without question. The three of us then methodically, and literally, tore the mail bins apart. After several hours of fruitless searching, we had to come to the sad realization that the letter was not to be found on the premises.

Where was it?

We beat a hasty retreat, returned to the office and settled down to hold a council of war to determine our next move. We were served tea by the secretary, who by this time was hardly capable of performing even that duty. She knew by the look on our faces as we returned that we had been unable to locate the letter.

George again took the lead. His first point was that the letter had, obviously, been taken out of the normal routine service. The next regular delivery wasn't until the oppressive heat of the late afternoon had worn off, and the postmen on their bicycles wending their way around the environs of the city could endure the smothering humidity of the tropical climate of Dar-es-salaam. Therefore, it was in the hands of some government official. Someone on the staff who had recognized the import of the wax seal, the red ribbon binding and the Government

House address. "It looks as if we have to throw in the towel on this one," he concluded his observations, "and wait until they take action."

As had been anticipated by me, George had served us well in the area of expertise in which he excelled to such a sterling degree throughout his lifetime of service to his country and to Caltex: action. It was my turn, now, to bring to bear all the experience I had gained while serving out my time in the internecine battles of the board room; the dealings with diplomats whose spoken words had a different meaning than Webster's and with the other myriad nationalities around the world, nationalities of many hues and colours. They were the ones, who had given me a vast background of proficiency that told me all sequences that might appear logical on the surface to follow each other will not, necessarily, follow each other in practice.

"There can be no other valid assumption made than the one George has made," was the statement with which I started my analysis. "Someone in authority has the letter. Someone, not only in authority, but someone who is going to take it to the highest official in the Government for the decision on how to handle the situation and that means the Prime Minister," I continued. "Let us recognize that they would hate to pass up the chance of embarrassing their previous royal masters if given the opportunity," I concluded.

"They do have a problem in one respect, however. The date for the celebrations for finale granting of total independence has been set. The guest list has been made up, and the invitations are on the verge of being issued. Someone from the Royal family is sure to be a representative of Her Majesty's Government when they haul down the Union Jack for the last time," were my additional observations.

Independence was being granted to most of the Empire's colonies in two steps. Tanganyika at the moment enjoyed 'internal self-government', which meant it was entirely responsible for its internal affairs. Diplomatic representation and defense were still the prerogative of Her Majesty's Government, and that is why the Governor-General still remained in residence and wielded such a visible sign of power. "For the Tanganyika Government to successfully embarrass Her Majesty's Government," I continued, "they will have to, indirectly, announce that they are opening the Governor-General's mail."

"How so?" was the query from the Sales Manager.

"Our letter to the Governor-General was sealed and addressed to Government House," I countered. "How else could the Tanganyika Government been aware of its contents, if they hadn't been monitoring Government House mail and opening the Governor-General's correspondence?" I asked.

"What does that mean?" George was quick to ask.

"In my humble opinion they will not feel that they can make such a public disclosure, as much as they might like to, in order to embarrass Her Majesty's Government," I quietly declared. "In addition, everything in that letter is already known to them except for the fact that the Governor-General is actively trying to prevent ENI from becoming the successful bidders for the refinery project. If the situation about Colin Wood isn't already known to them, they can take appropriate action without ever having to acknowledge that the information was obtained from a letter belonging to Her Majesty's Government and addressed to the Governor-General."

I ended my assessment with the statement, "I don't believe they will take any action at all, because of the circumstances of the approaching independence celebrations, particularly with a member of the Royal family going to be present."

"Great," was the response of the Sales Manager in a slightly doubting tone of voice, "and where does that leave us?"

"What can we do then?" was George's query embodying the instinctive need to take action.

"We do nothing about the first letter," I said.

"What do you mean by 'the first letter'?" George asked incredulously. "You mean we have lost two of them?"

"No. Certainly not," was my rather testy reply. "We are going to write the second letter now. It will be an exact duplicate of the first. The Governor-General will receive the information I want him to have. He will never know about our losing the first one, if my assessment of the Tanganyika Government's decision to take no action is correct." With this conclusion, I ended my analysis of our quandary and asked for any objections. With none forthcoming, the secretary was instructed to reproduce the first letter in its entirety. The Sales Manger stood by waiting to deliver it the moment it was finished. I drew my first real breath of relief since the announcement that the original letter had been mailed by mistake.

The deadline for the submission of bids to the Tanganyika Government for the privilege of building a refinery in Dar-es-salaam came and passed. Everyone in the industry was aware that all the subsidiaries of The Seven Sisters represented in Tanganyika had duly submitted their offers. No one was able to ascertain if ENI had, also, submitted their tender, but speculation ran high that they had done so. A few days after the closing of the deadline for the submission of bids a meeting was called by the Governor-General at Government House. I informed George and the Sales Manager that it appeared that we were likely to learn from this meeting about the status of the ENI bid.

Although I had breathed a sigh of relief at the finale decision to send a duplicate copy of the 'mailed' letter to the Governor—General, I still seemed to be living on pins and needles as far as my daily existence was concerned. My wife,
again, repeated her admonishments as to the state of mind that I seemed to have,
again, begun to endure, and that I was being extremely difficult with the servants
and had no patience with the children.

Unfortunately, there was no news of any import at the meeting in Government House other than, merely, confirmation that, as we had all suspected, ENI
had submitted an offer. The meeting appeared to be a wrap-up of all that had
transpired during the bidding process. At one point during the proceedings, the
Government-General signaled me to approach his desk. He said that he wanted
me to see some comparison of the figures I had sent to him and some of the other
information he had received from his own sources. He slid a number of documents halfway across his desk in my direction and asked if I thought the comparison was interesting.

On the top of the pile was the duplicate letter that I had sent after our frenzied
search of the post office. Actually, it was not possible to determine whether it was
the duplicate or the original. I had no other option than to assume that it was the
duplicate. Halfway through the mass of documents that he had slid across the
desk partially in my direction, there was another letter. Only just enough of this
letter protruded to provide the onlooker, who had written the letter, with sufficient detail in order that the letter could be identified. It was as though an old
and familiar icy hand had gripped my heart. It was the lost letter. I steadied
myself against his desk and gazed into his eyes. As stern as they were, there was a
slight twinkle in them. The message was clear.

'You blundered. Fortunately, no damage has been done. I am fully aware of
your rationale for the tactics that you employed. Your original letter had arrived
in my office, via the post, only a matter of hours before your second one was
hand delivered in the usual manner. Your grounds for sending the duplicate were
obvious the moment the second letter arrived in my office. I did not inform you
immediately of your error, as with some delay in making you aware of the safe situation, it might provide some incentive for you to exercise more caution when
corresponding with this office.'

Not a word was said. I could read that detailed message in his eyes with precise
accuracy. I nodded in the direction of the documents on his desk and said that I
thought the comparison was indeed very pointed. I would bear it mind when
doing any additional tabulations for my own research. I sat down with an inaudi-
ble sigh of relief. The icy hand that had appeared to be clutching my heart

seemed to release itself during all this exchange of inconsequential, verbal comments and the real, critical exchange of information through the power of body language. The rest of the meeting was a blur. At the conclusion, I confirmed that I had received The Governor-General's implied message by imperceptibly nodding my head again in the direction of the documents on his desk.

While being driven back to the office, I could not concentrate enough to find the reason for the original letter to be reposing on the Governor General's desk. Immediately on arrival at the office, I sent for George and the Sales Manager. I related to them in exact detail what had transpired at the meeting. In telling them of my breath taking reaction at seeing both letters on the desk, my mind finally came out of its stupor and applied itself to discovering how such a situation had arisen as to having both letters delivered to Government House.

As I finished my recital, it suddenly dawned on me that all of our assessments as to the reactions of the post office staff on recognizing that they were in possession of correspondence addressed to a representative of Her Majesty's Government were absolutely correct. We knew that they would recognize the import of the wax seal on the red ribbon binding and give it their utmost attention. They would make sure that a high official of the Post Office was involved. Obviously, a high official of the Post office had been the ultimate recipient of the letter and not the Prime Minister.

It was our collective 'guilt complex' that did us in, as always. We were putting ourselves in their position. We were reacting in the way a guilty person would react, if he ever came into possession of correspondence that he knew should never have been in the ordinary channels of everyday, delivery methods of the post office. Not so the dedicated staff of the post office. Here was a piece of mail that was addressed to the ruling, white master of their destiny, who had held sway over them for many years. Even though there was no regular post scheduled for that hour of the day, it did not matter. Even though there was no postage affixed to the correspondence, it did not matter. Even though it was unbearably hot and humid, as it always was at that time of the day in Dar-es-salaam, it did not matter. The high official of the Post office had the authority to have this visibly, important letter delivered immediately, and he did just that.

We all agreed that that was the only possible solution that could account for the bizarre situation that had eventuated from the mistake made by the secretary.

In the opinion of the international oil community, several weeks later, there was another monumental mistake made at the same time as we had committed our lost letter mistake. A monumental error made by the Government of Tanganyika through its Ministry of Commerce due to the Ministry awarding the contract to build the refinery in Dar-es-salaam to ENI. The Ministry of Commerce of the Government of Tanganyika had badly bungled the decision in regard to whom the contract to build the refinery should be given.

The government officials now in power, many years later, at the Ministry of Commerce in Dar-es-salaam, languidly gazing out their windows and thinking about their refinery, which had been built and fifty-percent financed by Ente Nazionale Idrocarburi, wouldn't agree with the opinion held by the international oil community those many years ago. As they were sitting in their offices on Wednesday the 27th of November 1991 reading the article in the International Herald Tribune, they would certainly never concur with the assessment made by the oil industry in 1960 that to award the contract to ENI was a monumental error. There is nothing in evidence that would lead them, today, to imagine that their predecessors had made even a slight mistake in judgment, much less a monumental one.

There is no 'cold war'. There is no 'hot war'. There is no gas energy shortage. There is no crude oil shortage. The world is awash in a flood of crude oil being produced by OPEC. In fact, there is no Union of Soviet Socialist Republics.

16

Salisbury, Rhodesia—1963

It was puzzling how to describe the feelings that an expatriate had on arriving in Rhodesia. After only a very short period of residence in that wonderfully, hospitable country, a very apt description would suddenly spring to mind. Rhodesia was like one vast country club. The moment you arrived at the airport, presented your passport for validation, you became a member of that country club. No matter where you went in Rhodesia, be it to a large city such as Salisbury or Bulawayo or some small way station in the jungle, you were accorded all the welcome and courtesy that you would receive when you entered the grounds of a country club to which you had become a duly elected member.

The company house in Salisbury at 7 Duthie Lane had been beautifully redesigned and refurnished by its present occupants, Bill Marshall-Smith and his stunning wife. Bill was one of the English speakers of South Africa. His jovial countenance, well kept wardrobe and piercing blue eyes immediately gave you the impression that he would be in full command of any situation, adverse or otherwise, that might arise. The huge swimming pool at the house was a delight to behold in the immense front garden. All the servants were long time members on the company payroll. They had become quite accustomed to adapting themselves to the idiosyncrasies of succeeding managers.

It was a quick and effortless hand over from the incumbent manager. Bill was a very competent individual, which he later proved by becoming Chairman and Managing Director of the South African company. Everything in the office was in proper order. It was a pleasure to be part of such a completely experienced, fully qualified and staffed organization. In his hand over memoranda, there was mention of two other companies to which he advised me that I would be appointed a director. One was to the Board of Central African Refineries Ltd ... CAPREF was owned seventeen and a half percent by Caltex with Shell and Mobil having the same percentage holdings. Aminoil, Total and the Kuwait National Oil Corporation held the balance of the shares. All the internationals had learned a bitter lesson from Tanganyika when we attempted to grab our competitors shares and hog the whole operation only to end up with zero per cent while the 'oil man with no oil', Matti of ENI, got the entire crude oil supply rights by building the refinery. Seventeen and a half per cent was a lot better than no percent.

In the case of being appointed a director to the board of the industry owned refinery, CAPREF, at Umtali, I was very familiar with how those directorships were awarded and conducted where there was a share holding by either one of the Two Sisters that owned us or by THE COMPANY itself. In the case of the second company, since it was not one of the many subsidiaries of Caltex or of the Two Sisters as was the refinery, I naturally enquired if there would be any problem anticipated from the Board of Directors of that company regarding my nomination.

"No problem," was Bill's immediate response. "In any case, even if there were, there are only seven members on the Board. Four of them are right here in your office, one of which is myself. The fifth one is the company's attorney. If you think the company's attorney is going to jeopardize the biggest part of his income by objecting to your appointment, you don't know too much about the legal profession," was his airy dismissal of my apparently naïve question. He did continue, however, by saying that he thought it would be a very interesting operation in which to be involved.

It was a river transport company operating on the Zambezi River. An operation that was quite far removed from the humdrum, daily existence of managing one of the subsidiaries of the step-sister of two of the Seven Sisters. He said it wouldn't be necessary to divert much time from running the company office to the river company operation. The river transport company was managed by the Chairman of the Board, Mr. E. Gilbert Ford, who was Chief Executive Officer as well as Chairman. In turn, the CEO was assisted by Mr. St. Clair-Burke, the only other director, other than the Chairman and the Caltex attorney, who was not an executive of Caltex. In point of fact at that time, these two non-Caltex directors were the ninety-percent actual owners of the company.

In the not too distant future, it was not very difficult to recall those unintentionally, misleading comments Bill Marshall-Smith had made about how much of my time would be spent on the river transport company. Literally, everything he had said about my relationship with the river transport company was the exact opposite of what he had told me. I was spending so much time on the river transport company affairs that I was unable to devote any time to running the company's office. One of my fellow directors of the river company, who was on my staff in the company's office, Stan Hodgkinson the Administration Officer, made a very telling comment one day as we were leaving the board room immediately after a most acrimonious board meeting. A board meeting which had been prompted by the lead story in the Daily News of Salisbury. He advised me that if he had known what was in store for him when he had been nominated as a director of the Zambezi River Transport Company Ltd., he would have elected early retirement from Caltex.

Although, at no time was the name of this river company mentioned by the United Nations Committee on South West Africa, nor by the United States Embassy or by President Kaunda of Zambia at a press conference on 3 June 1965, the Salisbury Daily News of 1 August 1963 didn't hesitate to name it. Further more, the Daily News was most emphatic about who was running the company when its headlines screamed in one and a half inch print:

"OIL CHIEFS TO FACE LAWSUIT"

'Top executives in 'delinquency' case'

Daily News Reporter Salisbury, Thursday

The chairman and four top executives of Caltex (Africa) Ltd. are being sued for alleged delinquency. The company itself is also being sued for its alleged failure to provide more than £60,000 for equipment to enable a transport company to complete a contract with Northern Rhodesia's former Minister of Natural Resources, Mr.Geoffrey Beckett. The executives are the chairman, Mr. R. D. Wrigley Jnr; the federal manager, Mr. R. Palmer-Smith; the chief accountant, Mr.F.E.Price; the operations manager, Mr.J.S.Cudlip; and the administration officer, Mr.S.Hodgkinson. The chairman of Zambezi River Transport Ltd., Mr.E.Gilbert Ford, has sent a letter to Caltex on behalf of 90 per cent of ZRT's dividend-paying shareholders informing the oil company that it is to be prosecuted in respect of its alleged failure to provide the money.

Nominees

The oil company has five nominees on the ZRT's seven-man board—four of the nominees are Caltex executives—and it is alleged they did not tell a board meeting that a monthly installment owed by ZRT had not been forwarded to Caltex. One of the nominees, Mr.Russell Cook, the Caltex attorney, has asked the ZRT's shareholders to accept his resignation from the board at the next meeting.

At least it was nice to know that the press considered me a 'top executive'. There was no way for them to know what little authority the 'big black book' delegated to its so-called 'top executives'.

In referring to me as the Federal Manager, the Daily News was relating to what was, then, the Federal Union of Rhodesia, Northern Rhodesia and Nyasaland. The company to which the article referred, Caltex (Africa) Ltd., was the legal entity of which the Salisbury office was a part. The dissolution of the Federal Union of Rhodesia, Northern Rhodesia and Nyasaland and the approaching independence of these black countries was very close on the horizon. It would not be possible for a company headquartered in Cape Town, South Africa and, consequently, a part of that deeply hated system of apartheid to continue to exercise control over any commercial enterprise in a country with a black majority as its governing body.

Although, I had not been told of the reasons for my transfer from Dar-es-salaam, Tanganyika to Salisbury, Rhodesia, I had suspected that it was because of my experience with the formation of the independent Caltex companies in the East African subsidiary of Caltex Petroleum Corporation. A short time ago, even the East African organization had been part of the South African company.

A continuing number of former colonies of the imperialists were approaching their independence. It finally dawned on the various companies doing business in The Third World, particularly the international oil companies and the subsidiaries of the Seven Sisters, that to have a company that was incorporated in such an independent country was the best public relations possible. Certainly, in the situation in this part of The Third World, it was an anathema to the black politicians to have a company under their legal jurisdiction that was part of that loathed and vicious system of apartheid in South Africa.

Having successfully negotiated the shoals of the piranha filled waters surrounding the formation of the separate East African Caltex companies, I was a logical candidate to take on the same sensitive duties in the next part of black Africa that was going to undergo a monumental change. The monumental change from the old colonial days to the 'enlightened age'. Shortly after my arrival in Salisbury, the then Prime Minister of the Federal Union, Sir Roy Welensky, announced that;

"This Union will be dissolved over my dead body."

As with so many of the promises of our erstwhile politicians, *'Read My Lips'*, he did not take his own life to fulfill this promise, when very shortly after his announcement the Union was dissolved. Nor for that matter, did anyone shoot him to assist him to keep his political commitments.

The paperwork involved in divorcing the Caltex activities of the Federal Union from the South African Caltex company, and the formation of the three separate companies that were to take its place was monumental. In addition, the construction of the industry owned refinery in Umtali was approaching completion, and its on stream inauguration date was approaching rapidly. This directorship was one of the very few directorships in the oil industry that could honestly, almost, be called a 'working directorship'. As a result, the duties involved and the complicated agreements and cross-agreements involving all the oil company owners were massive.

Not only were there the normal refinery board meetings, but these monthly meetings took place in Umtali. This necessitated the regular booking of chartered aircraft. A commodity sometimes very difficult to obtain in that part of the dark continent. There were times when a privately owned aircraft could be borrowed as was often done by me from Tiny Roland of the 'London and Rhodesian Mining Company' (Lonrho). In addition, there were, on a never ending basis, the overwhelming duties of the Zambezi River Transport Company. A company about which I kept remembering that Marshall-Smith had assured me it would not be necessary on which to spend much of my time. It was all of these demands that had moved my very patient and long suffering wife to make that heart felt comment in exasperation one evening on my late return from the office. "I know now what you mean by 'The Caltex Family'. You're goddamn well married to it!"

As she often told me over the years to come, it was bad enough having to sit home alone in the evening in Salisbury knowing that, eventually at some time, I would arrive back from the office. What was devastating to her were the frequent absences that she had to endure as a result of the necessity of my having to run the Zambezi River Transport Company. These demands constantly required my presence in Katima Mulilo in the Caprivi Strip of South West Africa. An area that was soon to become an even more intense focus of the United Nations.

After having suffered the often, nerve shattering effects of the aftermath of the Mau Mau in Nairobi, we had been made aware of the very possible danger of a part of that activity having been 'exported' to Rhodesia. The large majority of violent incidents that had occurred involving the white population in Rhodesia by the so called 'marauding blacks' were, actually, invariably laid to the door of ordinary everyday thieves and criminals. They had seized the opportunity of using the aspirations of independence to cloak their basic aims, which were simply to plunder the wealthy white residents of their country. Whatever the reason, the end result was the same. The whites had to be prepared to protect themselves.

I had been advised on a very confidential basis, shortly after my arrival in Salisbury, that self-protection against such intruders required that my household be armed. It is with great sympathy and understanding that I view the television news from my vantage point here in Paris today. I can truly understand the basic instinct that tells American citizens that it is up to the individual, as a last resort, but as a last resort only, to be the protectors of their home and family.

In the United States, unfortunately, this means that our life time, career Republicans haven't the guts to take on the National Rifle Association and attempt to limit the availability of firepower to the lawless. They are afraid that such a challenge might just lose them enough money and votes to end their permanent careers in the congress. Consequently, the last resort means buying a gun to protect yourself and your family.

Not so in Rhodesia. Here it was the government that was at war with the criminal intruders. They wanted their voters armed. The only votes that could be lost were if their constituents were killed. This meant being armed with the necessary firepower to stop any interloper that was bent on entering your 'home and castle'.

It was a simple matter to make the purchase of the necessary firearms. The reliability of the revolver, the ease and rapidity with which it could be fired were the parameters determining the brand to buy. My Rhodesian colleagues actually procured the firearms for me and indoctrinated myself and my wife in its use. The gun, unloaded, was always kept in a locked safe in the house whenever the children were awake and around the premises. When I was in Salisbury and expected to return home, it was also kept under lock and key, unloaded.

During my frequent absences when flying up to the Caprivi Strip in South West Africa, the gun was removed in the evening from its secure location, loaded, the hammer cocked and then placed at my wife's side in the lounge. It was hidden under a pillow. There it would not be in full view of anyone that happened to be surreptitiously looking through the window. Hiding it under the pillow would, naturally, prevent the onlooker from being able to take advantage of the knowledge of the gun's presence and avoid his circumventing the purpose of its being there.

My wife was hesitant about even the thought of having a gun in the house, much less using it. After the stories of what had happened in Kenya during the Mau Mau, and the way we had lived there under the post Mau Mau effects of locked doors, guard dogs and armed sentries, she reluctantly agreed that for the sake of the children she would concede the necessity of having some way to defend them if an intruder, terrorist or just plain criminal, broke into the house.

She did maintain that she would find it impossible to kill an intruder outright without first warning him that she possessed the capability of doing just that. She insisted that the first bullet in the gun be a blank. If the firing of the blank did not deter the interloper, she felt that she was then within her rights to continue to pull the trigger and end his forcible entry into the building that was housing and sheltering her children. When we left Salisbury and put away the gun forever, it was very noticeable how corroded the handle of the hammer had become. The corrosion was caused by the acids in the perspiration on her hands. A result of constantly cocking the gun just before placing it under the pillow and, then, uncocking it when she returned it to its safe keeping place in the morning before the children arose. We both were extremely grateful that she never did have to make use of this constant reminder of the perilous times and places in which THE COMPANY asked us to live and work.

I knew that any terrorist coming through the window of the small, separate lounge, where she spent her evenings when I wasn't in Salisbury, would neither be deterred by the firing of the blank nor would she have the time to pull the trigger the second time. I never did tell her that the first shell in the barrel was a live bullet. She will never know how I deceived her. She died in nineteen ninety one in August in Punta Gorda, Florida, the month of her sixty-first birthday.

None of the legalities of the formation of the three separate companies was meant in anyway to actually change the 'chain of command' between Salisbury and Cape Town or for that matter between Salisbury, Northern Rhodesia and Nyasaland. I was appointed General Manager and a director of the new company in Salisbury. I was, also, appointed a director of each of the two companies to the North of us. As a director, it was, naturally, necessary to perform my board room responsibilities by visiting those areas that were included in my board duties.

I never gave orders to any of the local staff during these visits. Directors never issue orders. They are not in the 'line of command'. There were service agreements among the three companies. These allowed us to pay the staff, provide product from the storage tanks in Salisbury, take care of the many staff responsibilities such as pensions and health plans and a multitude of other activities identical to what we were performing when we were reporting to Cape Town.

Caltex Petroleum Corporation had had quite considerable experience with this type of paper work in the past. Many years ago it was recognized that the concept of a world wide organization being run from New York was a very sensitive issue to the national aspirations of many of the countries in which THE COMPANY operated. In those days it was not so much a 'matter of colour' as it was here in Africa. The Europeans, particularly the French, had never looked kindly on having some upstart from the New World, who just happened to be resident in their country, receive his orders from overseas. The Arabs, also, were beginning to become restive and assert themselves, spear headed by the powerful Sheik Zaki Yamani, the Oil Minister of Saudi Arabia. In addition, the international companies were beginning to discover that some of their local employees actually had considerable ability and were very much less expensive than expatriate Americans. It was as a result of these previous experiences that our owners, the Two Sisters, were beginning to get the message that perhaps they could pre-empt similar feelings in many of the territories in Africa and Asia, where they operated, by making those local companies totally independent and increasing the responsibilities of the local staff.

The legal department in New York had previously, therefore, set up separate organizations worldwide on the identical concept that we were undertaking in Africa, but on a much larger scale. We were now breaking those larger companies down into their more disparate, distinct, local parts as the world's empires came tumbling down. In the case of Caltex Petroleum Corporation, there was always one or more directors of these many companies throughout the world who were resident in the New York office.

The legal department of Caltex Petroleum Corporation was well aware of the ingrained habits of autocratic managers in the international oil business, who had learned their habits from the Seven Sisters. They knew that lifelong habits were going to be hard to break. Of necessity, they insisted immediately after these separate corporations were set up throughout the world, that all correspondence emanating from the New York office had to be cleared through the legal department before being mailed. This would avoid the unpardonable sin of a director giving a direct order to one of the 'independent' companies in some far corner of the world.

Many a letter in New York was returned to its originator without having been mailed. It had been 'red lined' by the legal department pointing out that the writer was no longer managing the company to which he was writing. He was merely a director. He could not issue orders to such a company or he would be deemed to be in the 'chain of command'. An indication of such 'line of command' order would suffice to show that the far flung empire of THE COMPANY was being run from New York. This could possibly hurt the 'feelings' of the rulers of those countries who were meant to be under the impression that the companies incorporated within their boundaries were totally independent.

There was, in reality, an even more important reason for the Two Sisters to have ever agreed to such a concept in the first place. They, actually, couldn't have cared less about the feelings of the local indigenous population in the far flung empire that they had ruled with an iron hand for so many years. What concerned them was the fact that such direct control would be sufficient to draw the attention of the taxing authorities in the United States to the possibility that there was much to be extracted from a company, whose worldwide profits actually were the responsibility and the result of 'managing' from New York. I came to suspect, at a much later date, that in the beginning it might have been this exposure to the scrutiny of the Internal Revenue Service that gave much, more pause to the members of the New York Board than did the possibility of stepping on the sensitive toes of some potentate living on another continent.

The new system of 'directorship' versus 'management' was very frustrating for both the 'directors' in New York and the 'directors' of the many newly formed companies in the field. They had now, to all intents and purposes, changed places, at least on paper. Frustrating for the 'directors' in New York, because all their life long careers with THE COMPANY had consisted of giving orders to their subordinates in the field. On the other hand, it was also very discouraging for the recently appointed directors in the field of the newly formed companies who were desperately seeking guidance from New York. It was dispiriting, because they had to wait sometimes weeks for a reply to their letters from their erstwhile mentors in New York. The international oil companies' profits float on vast, hidden reservoirs of crude oil. Their visibly, luxuriously and expensively appointed offices, in their various worldwide headquarters, float on an ocean of paper, and it was all dammed up in the overworked legal department of THE COMPANY on the thirteenth floor of 350 Madison Avenue in New York.

I was on my way to the field at the height of this chaotic changeover from 'management' to 'directorship' and was being indoctrinated by my Vice-President into the seriousness of the concept. He emphasized that I would not be receiving any orders from his office in the future. My New York Director would be merely making suggestions. I was free to follow them or not to follow them as I saw fit. I was still naïve enough to ask a very pertinent question. "Suppose that I do not act on the advice or suggestions of my New York Director? After all, I, too, will be a Director, as well as Manager, of the field company. Being in the field and on the spot, it may just be that my assessment of the action to be taken will be more appropriate than his. If I do take such action, what happens then?"

"We will pick up the telephone and fire you!"

So much for the lofty experience of being made a director.

In spite of all the trauma associated with the Zambezi River Transport Company Ltd., there was, no doubt, that being a director of that organization meant, as in the case of the industry owned refinery in Umtali, that you were a working director. The only time that you could not exercise your director's responsibilities was in the case of the capital investment budget when you needed unbudgeted funds. Just as the Two Sisters hoarded their money from their step-sister, so Cape Town kept a tight hold on the purse strings when it came to the cost of capital improvements of the Zambezi River Transport Company Ltd. In fact, this was the situation that had prompted the letter to be written by the Chairman of ZRT to Caltex (Africa) Ltd. informing them that they were to be prosecuted in respect of their alleged failure to provide the money to fulfill ZRT's contracts.

Bill Marshall-Smith had made his efficient hand-over complete in that he had ensured that I met all the important government and civilian leaders in Salisbury. It goes without saying that these included some of our very best customers. It was scarcely a matter of weeks after Bill's departure, when I received an extremely pressing telephone call from one of the most important of these clients, Harry Wuflson. He requested an urgent meeting at my earliest convenience. There was no doubt from his tone of voice in regard as to how compelling he felt that the subject was going to be.

I made myself available immediately. Harry arrived in my office with a deep, worried frown on his face. He had risen from a European, pushcart trader who had transposed his business from his home country in the Baltic countries to the jungle, bush trade of Africa. He made no bones about his origin and his early struggles. He was often to regale us with stories of how, at times, he found it necessary to sleep under that self-same pushcart in the pouring rain, when he couldn't afford a hotel at the site of one of the many fairs where he hawked his wares. He had, by now, reached the exalted status of a millionaire. The wonderful thing about Harry was that with all his new found wealth, he was just as kind, generous and willing to help those in trouble as he was when he was physically pushing his cart around the markets of Central Africa.

He informed me that he had just returned from London, where he had been negotiating with a client on behalf of himself and his partner, Northern Rhodesia's former Minister of Natural Resources, Geoffrey Beckett. He had been attempting to obtain a long term extension of the contract for the company that he and his partner owned, Barotseland Sawmills Ltd., with the parquet floor manufacturers to whom he was selling teak wood from Barotseland. This was the very teak wood that the Zambezi River Transport Company Ltd. was hauling down by road to Katima Mulilo and, then, by river from that inaccessible part of the world, The Kingdom of Barotseland. A Kingdom whose name had probably never passed the lips of any European or American school child in their entire life span of geography lessons. Probably not in African classrooms either, except for the Barotses themselves, if they had schools.

The teak, which grew in Barotseland and the Senanga area, was loaded into huge semi-trailers after being logged and milled. It was then hauled to Katima Mulilo by road. Katima Mulilo just happened to be in the Caprivi Strip, which just happened to be part of South West Africa. It was the Caprivi Strip and South Africa's control of that Strip that was of so much concern to the United Nations Committee on South West Africa.

'From the strategic point of view, the Caprivi Strip is the most interesting part of South West. As can be seen from the following extract from the Odendaal Report (page 49), it has had a curious administrative history. Ever since 1890, when it was secured for German South West Africa by the German Chancellor, Caprivi, under an Anglo-German Agreement, it has been an integral part of South West. But it had a chequered history after 1914.This area, the Eastern Caprivi, which was occupied by Rhodesian troops in 1914, was administered from Bechuanaland for a time and that arrangement was confirmed by Proclamation No.19/1922, dated the 21st December 1921, by the Governor-General of the South African Government by which authority for the area was granted to the British High Commissioner for South Africa in the capacity of Administrator.

By Proclamation No.23/1922 by the High Commissioner provision was made for the administration of the Eastern Caprivi as though this was part of Bechuanaland and for the enforcement of the laws of this Protectorate in the area. Proclamation No.196 of 1929, dated the 4th of August 1929, by the Governor-General of South Africa, however, repealed Proclamation No.12/1922 and placed the Eastern Caprivi under the South West Administration until 1939 when the 'Eastern Caprivi Zipfel Administration Proclamation', 1939 (No.147/1939), vested control and administration in the Minister of Native Affairs of South Africa. Legislative powers in respect of the area were, however, reserved to the Governor-General and reaffirmed by the South West Africa Amendment Act 1951.(Act No.55 of 1951), subject to the final authority of the Parliament of South Africa.'[68]

The only reason that Katima Mulilo was part of ZRT's operation was due to the fact that it was the last part of the banks of the Zambezi, when heading North, where it was possible to find an hospitable landing area. It was, also, the last part of the Zambezi that was navigable insofar as the craft of ZRT were concerned. It lay just below the totally unnavigable rapids from just a short distance upstream.

At Katima Mulilo, the heavily loaded trailers from Barotseland were piggy-backed onto river barges which were capable of carrying six of the immense trailers. From here the barges were 'pushed' down river by pusher tugs to Livingstone, which was one of the largest commercial cities in Northern Rhodesia. This was the manner in which ZRT eventually evolved, but when I first glimpsed the operation it was literally light years away from resembling such a method of operation.

Harry's customer, the parquet floor manufacturer in London, wanted to be assured that if they committed themselves to a long term contract and dropped their current teak wood suppliers that their source of teak wood would be secure. And that such supply could not be put in jeopardy in that distant and unknown part of the dark continent from which their new stock of hardwood was to come.

Harry promptly took out his agreement with the Zambezi River Transport Company and showed them that he, indeed, had a long term contract with the river company for the haulage of their hardwood. He took the opportunity to explain to them that they need not have any doubts as to the viability of the river transport company, even though it had recently changed hands and was now privately operated and no longer owned by the Northern Rhodesian Government. The reason that they need have no doubts about the viability of the river transport company was due to the fact that he had an even more iron-clad warranty that the teak wood would be delivered. A delivery that would be made no matter what dire straits into which the river company might fall, although at that time no such catastrophe was even considered to be in the realm of possibility. The iron-clad warranty was in the form of an 'operating guarantee' that had been signed by Caltex (Africa) Ltd.

"Caltex who?" queried the manufacturers.

"Caltex, you know, the ones who are fifty-percent owned by the same company that owns Regent Oil Company, Texaco," was Harry's quick and adroit response. Harry didn't get to be a millionaire without realizing the importance of dropping the right names at the right time. Regent Oil was one of the better known oil companies operating in the British Isles and had recently been 'gobbled up' by Texaco with all its attendant unpleasant publicity. The name of one of the Seven Sisters, Texaco, was a household word in Britain, as well as the United States, and any where else in the rest of the world, for that matter, where the economy ran on oil.

"How in the world did you ever get Caltex to sign an operating guarantee of that nature?" he was asked. "There are not many companies that would ever sign such a document. Not even the huge international oil companies with all their financial resources," they commented. "Although in this instance, it appears as if they did," they said in an almost, awe struck tone of voice.

"In return for their guarantee, I offered them all of the petroleum business originating in the teak wood operation. In addition, I promised them, also, I would switch the rest of my oil business to them as my present supply contracts run out," Harry finished off explaining how he had successfully obtained the operating guarantee from Caltex (Africa) Ltd.

"Sounds excellent," his clients told him. They were reaching for their pens to sign the exclusive extension to their contract with him, while they finished perusing the river transport agreement with the 'operating guarantee' included in it, in what was almost very bold print. As they were lifting their pens to sign Harry's contract, they came to the end of the ZRT contract. Suddenly they hesitated.

"What's the problem?" Harry anxiously queried. "Is there something wrong with the guarantee?"

"No," was the reply, "the wording is perfectly, legally correct, but where is that part about you giving them your petroleum business?" Harry was asked.

"Oh, we didn't include those arrangements in the contract. I was anxious not to make public that I was going to shift all my business to another supplier," Harry informed them as he leaned back in his chair with the relaxed thought that he had quickly settled their concerns.

The directors of the parquet floor manufacturing company looked at Harry for a moment. Then, they very sympathetically asked, "Where did you have this contract drawn up? Not here in London. We know that," they stated emphatically.

Harry was again on the edge of his chair in an instant as his short moment of relaxation was quickly brought to an end. In what was, now, an extremely alarmed voice he replied, "No. It was drawn up by my attorney in Southern Rhodesia. Why?"

"That explains it," they informed him with a note of resignation in their voices, which Harry panic-strickenly noted. He also noted that they had not only laid down the documents covering the river transport contract, but they had also laid down their pens as well without signing his proposed, extended, exclusive contract.

"What difference does it make where it was drawn up?" he demanded. He was now thoroughly alarmed that what he thought to be an iron-clad guarantee was beginning to quickly unravel around the edges.

"Under English law," they explained, "every contract must have a quid pro quo from each party. In this contract there is only the guarantee by Caltex (Africa) Ltd. that they will ensure that the company continues to operate in the event of a failure by the present owners. There is nothing in the contract that indicates what Caltex gets in return for this guarantee. Southern Rhodesia, in spite of its very obvious English character, is very close to South Africa. As a consequence, it has routinely operated under the terms of Dutch Law. Under Dutch law there is no requirement for a quid pro quo in a contract. If the contract were going to be enforced in Southern Rhodesia, there would be no problem. However, the Zambezi River Transport Company Ltd., as you have told us, operates in Northern Rhodesia which is governed by English law. The contract needs a quid pro quo to be enforceable there. We're very sorry to tell you that you don't have an enforceable contract. Under the circumstances, we regret that we cannot commit ourselves to an exclusive long term supply contract with you until you resolve this problem."

None of the Texaco lawyers or directors, one of whom was John McKinley who was destined to become Chairman of Texaco in 1980, was aware at that time of this type of fiasco. A debacle of how a contract drawn up in another country, a country with a different mind-set, could be unenforceable in the country in which it was intended to be the basis of operation and not in the country in which it had been drawn. It was unfortunate for Texaco that they were unaware of our problems with the Zambezi River Transport Company Ltd. Perhaps John McKinley, that rude and 'autocratic Chairman of Texaco who would perpetuate the self-contained rule of his many predecessors'[69], would have been able to warn 'Texaco's lawyer, Richard Miller, not to let the case of 'Pennzoil versus Texaco' be heard in the courts of Texas'[70]. But rather to ensure that it be heard in the courts of the State of New York. The state in which Texaco operated, and which would have the same mind-set as Texaco's. This would have, undoubtedly, avoided Texaco being forced into bankruptcy at a later date.

It was no wonder that Harry Wulfson was visibly exhibiting his extreme concern right in front of me in my office. He had invested a considerable amount of money in the project of logging teak wood in Barotseland. In addition to the contract with the parquet hardwood manufactures, Barotseland Sawmills Ltd. had firm, long term commitments to supply the Rhodesia Railways with teak railway sleepers. It would be a most sensitive, public relations problem, as well as incurring severe monetary penalties, if they failed to fulfill their contract.

I was unaware at the time that one of Harry's real concerns was not actually for himself, but for Geoff Beckett, his partner. Only a person of Harry's character could exhibit more concern for a fellow human being's travails than for his own without actually saying so. Admittedly, as a millionaire, some of his unconcern for his own predicament was due to the fact that this was only one of his many investments. Certainly not one that was going to bankrupt him. When you're a millionaire, you win some, you lose some. The reason that Harry's concern was for his partner was the fact that Beckett had put his entire life's savings into this project. It looked like it was now in the process of unraveling. Harry's long time friend and business partner was about to stand the risk of losing everything he owned. Harry was sincerely distraught over that painful prospect.

I was quick to inform Harry that I would do everything possible. Under the circumstances, since I was not the signatory to the contract, but rather Dick Wrigley, my Managing Director in Cape Town was, I would have to refer the matter to him. Fortunately for all concerned, Dick was departing from Cape Town on his way to Salisbury the very next morning. I telephoned him immediately and advised him how anxious Harry was to meet with him about the terms of the river transport company's contract. I started to describe the problem to him, but he said that wouldn't be necessary. The situation could be explained in the morning as he confirmed that he would meet with Harry on his arrival in the office from the airport.

Harry was in my office bright and early the next morning when I arrived back from the airport after picking up Dick. He was attempting to enjoy a cup of coffee while waiting for us, but it was very evident that he was finding it difficult to relax. Although, he had met Dick several times when discussing the terms of the contract, they had not really established a friendly and informal relationship. Harry was unable to fathom what Dick's reaction would be when he discovered that the contract that he had signed was not legally enforceable.

Harry's particular concern was centered on the fact that there was now, no doubt, that there were several ominous clouds looming on the horizon over the operation of the river transport company. One of which was the pending threatened prosecution of Caltex (Africa) Ltd., the company of which Dick Wrigley was the Chairman and Managing Director in Cape Town. Dick was a highly visible, prestigious and well known individual in the most, lofty social circles of Cape Town. A town, which though very large, was in many respects very provincial. The Salisbury Daily News had a substantial circulation there as there were many Rhodesians that had chosen to make their home in that breathtakingly, beautiful city. To be accused of 'delinquency' was not something to be taken lightly in the social circles of Cape Town. It, almost, bordered on have an extra-marital affair. Not that there weren't many of those in Cape Town, but not visibly so in Dick's prominent social circles.

After settling ourselves comfortably in the beautiful, large, overstuffed leather chairs which were the part of every manager's office in the colonies, Harry immediately broached the subject of his request for the meeting with Dick. "Due to a certain technicality in the wording of the ZRT contract when it was drawn up, the company's 'operating guarantee' is not valid," was Harry's opening comment. "This, in essence, means that we don't have an agreement. The contract is unenforceable in Northern Rhodesia. I can not get a long term extension to my supply contract with my clients in London, because they naturally want to be assured that their supplies of hardwood will not be jeopardy if the present owners of ZRT are unable to fulfill their commitments. This is seriously endangering our investments in Barotseland."

I had heard of Wrigley's reputation over a number of years, particularly, during my three year stay in East Africa. His first words to Harry left no doubt in my mind how well earned that reputation was. It was, also, the beginning of a relationship with him that convinced me that if ever there were a man with whom I would be quite willing to serve the rest of my life through hell and high water, it was Dick Wrigley.

"I don't understand your problem Harry. You and I have an agreement. If the contract is invalid, why didn't you have it re-written before my arrival, and I could have signed the revised contract this morning? I'll be here for several days so you still have time to get it changed, and the technicality corrected. I can resign it before I leave. Now tell me, how was your trip to London," he continued, "and did you bring Trudy and the children with you?"

Harry was never to forget that moment. He often seized the opportunity during the years I served in Rhodesia to reminisce about his feelings on hearing Wrigley's words. He would never, in the future, take any action that might embarrass Wrigley in connection with ZRT, even if it meant opposing his partner, Geoff Beckett. It had, obviously, made a profound impression on him, much as it had made on me. I voiced a silent resolution to myself, at the time, that I would make every effort to follow Wrigley's example if ever the occasion arose. Little did I realize that the time would come when Caltex Petroleum Corporation would cancel, on an imaginary technicality, a hundred million dollar annual contract with the Aluminum Company of America, ALCOA. A contract which I had negotiated. At that time, as I had related to the ALCOA representative, I stormed into the office of Karl Kerth, the company lawyer who had done the legal preparation of the contract, and had been the one who handled the cancellation based on the so called technicality. "Where is the morals department in this goddamn company?" I demanded.

"You're in the legal division," he politely replied. "The morals department is down the hall in the Chairman's office."

The Northern Rhodesian Government had been trying for many years to make the Zambezi River Transport Company profitable, but with no success. During those many years, they had searched diligently for a buyer that would take the river transport company private and, hopefully, make it a profitable operation in that manner. Their search finally bore fruit, when two of the many entrepreneurs seeking their fortune in the undeveloped, dark continent made a bid for the company. These two gentlemen, E.Gilbert Ford and St.Clair-Burke, backed up their offer with the 'operating guarantee' of Caltex (Africa) Ltd. Obviously, the Northern Rhodesian Government had to have some reasonable assurance that the river transport company would continue to operate after going private. The Government had many of its citizens, as well as the Kingdom of Barotseland, dependent on ZRT for foodstuffs and other necessities of life.

The Zambezi River Transport Company had been a consistent money loser over the years and a constant drain on the Northern Rhodesian Government's treasury. The Minister of Transportation was desperate to find a solution that would off-load this albatross from around his neck. His desperation did have its limitations, nonetheless, if one is to believe the story that circulated shortly after the bid was made by Ford and St.Clair-Burke to take the company private.

Apparently, when describing the terms of the bid, the Minister's aide had emphasized the importance of the operating guarantee provided by Caltex (Africa) Ltd. Like all politicians, the Minister was only half listening to his aide. When the aide reached the part of the offer where the sum of money involved was identified as £100,000.00, the Minister's mind only grasped the name of Caltex and the amount of money. He linked them to his hopelessness in attempting to dispose of his Government's responsibility of operating ZRT. "There is no way on earth that I'm going to pay a wealthy American oil company £100,000.00 to take ZRT off our hands. I don't care how desperate we are, nor how well they will operate it. I just won't do it." he told his aide sharply.

"No, no, Mr. Minister, we are not going to pay them," the aide emphasized. "They are going to pay us."

The Minister looked at his aide in amazement. "They are going to pay us?" he repeated in a strange and wondering voice. "Where are the papers?" he suddenly snapped as he came out of his trance. "Bring them in immediately so that I can sign them before they change their minds." The story summed up, in essence, the sorry state of the river transport company's condition.

Caltex had gone to great pains to train its new employees when I first joined its ranks. Training in service stations, terminals, bulk depots, warehousing and a host of other activities and most importantly in my case, although I didn't realize it at the time, its shipping and transportation systems. However, there was one serious omission in this program. At no stage during the training did they mention hippopotamuses, when they reviewed the problems that might affect their transportation departments.

"You wait how long before you investigate?" I enquired incredulously on my first inspection trip to ZRT in the Caprivi Strip.

"Three days," the local manager who had accompanied me from Livingstone replied. "If the barge is three days late, we send an outboard motor boat down river to look for it. Invariably we will find it 'beached' on the bank. It will have hit a hippo during the night, when the visibility is so poor the pilot can't see the hazards in the river. A partially submerged hippo is such a heavy obstacle that the holding chains on the tug and the barge snap on making contact with the immersed animal. The crew simply run the tug and the barge up on the river bank and wait for us. We repair the damage on the spot as from experience we are sure of the cause of the delay and always have the mechanics and the necessary material on hand." Was I really in the international oil business or was I in fantasy land or perhaps Alice in Wonderland?

At a not too much later date when THE COMPANY had taken over ZRT, and I was CEO and directly responsible for its operation, I was horrified to learn that part of the road and river transportation system was a passenger service. This service included a river passenger barge for that part of the Zambezi that was navigable, and a road bus service after the river service ended. A short time after the take-over, I laid down hard and fast rules about how the passenger service would function. It would be operated on the same world wide standards that all the rest of Caltex followed in so far as its petroleum operations were concerned; that is to say clean, efficient, orderly and *on time*. Part of those hard and fast rules about cleanliness, which naturally would only apply in that part of the world, were that the passengers were not to light any cook-fires within the company's passenger compound.

I was incensed to see that my instructions had not been followed, when on one of my frequent inspection trips I clearly saw several cook-fires set at the base of one of the trees in the passenger compound. I glared at the manager. "What did I tell you about cook-fires?" I accusingly demanded. "I've told you that you are not to allow the passengers to set cook-fires in the compound. Do you have trouble understanding me?" I ominously enquired. "How long have you been allowing this breach of my instructions?" I ended my tirade.

"Two weeks," the manager replied weakly.

"How could you do that?" I demanded indignantly.

"Well, sir, the passengers have been waiting two weeks for the bus and had no other place to stay. I reluctantly agreed that they could stay in the compound until the bus arrived."

Was I really in the international oil business?

On one of my initial trips, I was astounded to see the drivers of the trucks climbing through the cab windows. "Why do they enter the cabs through the windows?" I enquired. "Is there something wrong with the doors?"

The then local manger off-handedly remarked, "Oh, the doors have been welded shut for a number of years. We never had enough money to buy replacement parts when the hinges broke, so we just welded them shut before the doors fell off."

"And the road? Why does it wander all over the place? Isn't it possible to build a road in a straight line?" was another of my naïve enquiries in this heart of the dark continent.

"We didn't build the road. The trucks made it. They just take off in a Northerly direction, and the road just follows the path of least resistance by avoiding the trees," he explained. By now I was well used to a continuous series of shocks in connection with my recently inherited duties involving the Zambezi River Transport Company. Consequently, when I asked why we had forty labourers on the payroll, and I couldn't see anything about the operation that could possibly involve forty labourers, the answer was one that could again only originate in the heart of the dark continent.

"The reason you don't see them," was the explanation," is because they are out in the jungle paving the road. They come back to base about once a month."

I looked around me with a puzzled air. "I don't see any hard surface road that has been paved," my Western oriented mind reacted to his description of the labourers' duties.

"Oh, no, they don't actually 'pave' the road. The only way that we can keep any kind of surface on the roads in this part of the country, particularly during the monsoon season, is with a special grass. It grows to about a three foot height and is very fibrous. The labourers are all out in the jungle along the road. They are constantly cutting the grass and laying the cuttings in the ruts made by the vehicles. It keeps the tires from sinking into the mud. You could never afford to actually 'pave' a road in this country. With the first onslaught of the rainy season, it would disappear into the ground," was his finale explanation of why I couldn't see forty labourers.

What I did see, though, was what I thought was a village of about five or six hundred people. "What's the name of this village?" I questioned. "And why is it so close to our operations? It is so close that it actually appears to be on our property."

"That's not a village, sir. That's the employees' compound," the manager informed me. By now he realized that he shouldn't wait for my seemingly, endless questions that only announced how little I knew about an operation of which I had so recently become the manger. In order to avoid any more embarrassment on my part, he continued with his explanation. "It is an established, tribal custom in these parts that when you engage anyone they are entitled to bring their immediate family with them. Of course, we find it almost impossible to ascertain if every one in the individual's household is his immediate family. We settle for an allowance of five or six per employee which means that there are quite a few hundreds in the compound."

"But there is no sanitation of any kind or even running water for that matter. That must present a considerable health risk," I immediately commented. The lack of these facilities was not only very evident visibly, but we were standing downwind of the compound as well.

"Yes, it does," he remarked very offhandedly, forgetting again with whom he was dealing for the moment. "There are several deaths a month, ranging from infants to the elderly," he finished off his apparently, tiring explanation to this strange creature from another planet who had just become his supervisor.

'Well,' thought I to myself, 'something will be done about that immediately. No operation that is associated with the name of Caltex is going to have this kind of shocking situation.'

Little did I realize the subterfuge to which I was going to have to resort to implement my plans to have running water, showers, drainage ditches around the compound and above all, sanitation facilities.

One of the monthly statements submitted to Cape Town was the all important revenue report. It had been negative the entire time that Ford and St.Clair-Burke had been running the operation. The red ink was flowing even more massively now with the huge injection of capital that had been undertaken by THE COMPANY, when we had taken over the operation in the bankruptcy proceedings.

When the request for unbudgeted, additional, capital funds was submitted by me to the operations manager in Cape Town for the planned water and sanitation facilities, the answer came back with an adamant refusal. I telephoned immediately and explained the horrifying conditions under which employees of a subsidiary of Caltex and their families were living. But to no avail. "When you can show us some indication of a turnaround in the income figures, we might consider your request then. For the moment, the answer is definitely no," was the attitude.

The next morning, I instructed the Chief Accountant, F.E.Price, who was one of the Caltex nominees on ZRT's Board, to add three additional columns to the details of the monthly activity report. This was another one of ZRT's periodic statements in addition to the revenue report. It covered the various types and amount of cargo, the number of employees on the payroll, serviceable vehicles and all the many other details so beloved by people that sit behind desks and don't have to cope with the real world. "What are the three columns?" Price asked.

"ELDERLY, ADULTS and INFANTS are the three sub-titles," he was informed.

"And the main caption?" he questioned.

"*DEATHS,*" was the startling response he received. He gazed at me with his mouth drooping open and resembling nothing more than a gold fish attempting to ingest the maximum amount of food that had just been added to the fish tank by its owner.

The first, newly, revised report, which had read 'one elderly and two infants' under the added caption of DEATHS, had hardly landed on the Operations Manager's desk in Cape Town when my telephone rang. In an outraged voice, which scarcely needed an electronic link from Cape Town to Salisbury to be heard, he shouted, "What the bloody hell is this you've sent me? Is this your idea of how to get money for your goddamn, stupid, pet projects?" he demanded.

"Exactly," I replied. "And you will continue to get them until you authorize my capital expenditure request," I finished off.

"You wouldn't do that," he snapped.

"Try me," I snapped back.

He calmed down instantly as he realized suddenly how determined I was. "How much do you need initially?" he asked in a quite and subdued voice.

"Sixty-five thousand dollars should get us off to a good start," I replied.

"Go ahead immediately. I'll mail you the authorization this afternoon. However, let me know in advance if you need additional amounts to complete the projects," he ended the conversation. "Oh, one more thing. Please delete the additions to your monthly report on all future submissions and send us another original for your current report without the information on the subject we have just been discussing."

The bankruptcy proceedings had been bitter and acrimonious. It was a fact that the, then, current payment owed by ZRT to Caltex (Africa) Ltd. for fuel had not been paid, nor had the monthly payment of the funds advanced to Ford and St.Clair-Burke by Caltex for the down payment to the Northern Rhodesian Government been made either. But at the time of the Board meeting referred to in the Daily News article, the three Caltex directors attending the meeting were unaware of these facts. The Chief Accountant, Mr. F.E.Price the fourth Caltex director who kept these records, had not attended that meeting.

The non-payment of these two amounts technically allowed Caltex to force the Zambezi River Transport Company into bankruptcy. This was, particularly, true since the cash flow from the operation was insufficient for ZRT to meet its monthly fuel bills, which now amounted to almost $200,000 in four month, over due payments. From my frequent trips to the Caprivi Strip, I now realized that Ford and St.Clair-Burke had parlayed a con man's idea, in which they had not put a penny of their own money, into an organization which was going to be worth close to a million dollars, when it finally was put into proper operating condition. And they would be the ninety per cent owners.

It, also, appeared that they had certainly been less than honest when describing the existing operating capabilities of ZRT to Caltex, when they made their request to obtain the infamous operating guarantee. Even the engines on the river tugs, which were 'hauler' tugs at that time rather than 'pusher' tugs, had been allowed to deteriorate into such a state of disrepair that they merely sat on their engine beds and acted as ballast. These derelict engines had been replaced by a bank of outboard motors which were fastened to racks welded onto the sides of the tugs. When carrying bicycles, bakery goods, fresh vegetables, earthen cookpots, cloth, grain, kerosene and the multitude of everyday products that find their way into the villages of Africa, it may have not been so serious a dereliction of duty on their part. With firm commitments to the British Government through a contract with The Rhodesian Railways for railway sleepers and a commitment to ferry thousands of tons of hardwood for a manufacturer in England, you had better be more forth coming and on firmer ground than our two, erstwhile, fly-by-nights were. And all of this was backed up by an 'operating guarantee' from an international oil company,

There was not a single piece of equipment, a single barge, a single tug, a single truck or any kind of engine power that was physically capable or economically able to carry the mass of hardwood for the parquet floor manufacturer and the sleepers for the Rhodesia Railways. This was an operation that had to be re-designed from the ground up. And re-designed by whom? Some naïve, recently, appointed, American Manager, who had been told that he wouldn't have to spend much time on the river transport company operation.

The first step was the easiest and the cleanest. I fired the present local manger, who was based in Livingstone. He didn't think it was necessary that he move himself and his office to Katima Mulilo. The next appointment was a member of the transportation department from the Salisbury office. By a herculean effort a military type operation was mounted, and we built what was, in effect, a very comfortable home for him, his wife and two very young children. This was only possible, because the house was of pre-constructed material from Salisbury. The home, also, included a guest room as well as an office. The guest room and office were necessary adjuncts to the house, inasmuch as there was no place to stay and no office to conduct our business, when we visited the operation from Salisbury.

It is a very difficult and an emotionally, draining experience when you have to fire an employee in whose house you are a guest. It was not long before I realized that I had made a serious mistake in the selection of the new manager. I arrived in the Caprivi Strip one week after the first tractor of the new semi-trailers had been delivered to the site. I had listened to the recently appointed manager's complaints on the telephone that he could not get the tractor to obtain any traction on that special soil which formed the banks of the Zambezi. This was the same soil that extended some distance inland and exhibited the same characteristics in that inland area. Characteristics, which were noted by The Sunday Times of London in a news article dated 19 December 1965[71]. On my arrival in Katimo Mulilo, I stood there aghast at the view that greeted my eyes.

The brand new $45,000.00 tractor was in the mud up to its axles. It was, obviously, impossible that the vehicle was going to move under its own power. The newly appointed manager, who had been telling me on the telephone how difficult it was to obtain traction for these huge vehicles, had attempted to solve the problem by placing over a ton of concrete blocks just behind the cab of the vehicle. He envisaged that this additional weight would provide traction for the wheels of the tractor when it was hauling the tons of hardwood in the trailers behind it. And, particularly, when backing into position at the landing area of the barges when the tractor was going to hook up to the trailers. An area that was in a permanent state of mud from the waters of the Zambezi. He, obviously, intended to haul the tons of concrete between Katima Mulilo and the teak wood forests and back to Katima Mulilo on every trip the vehicles made.

I telephoned Salisbury immediately and told them to charter a plane and fly one of the draftsmen up from Salisbury as there was an urgent design job to be undertaken in Katima Mulilo. That evening, I reluctantly informed the newly appointed manager that his talents were being wasted here in the jungle, and he should plan on being back in Salisbury at his earliest convenience where he could make the rounds of the employment agencies.

On viewing the loading area with the bogged down vehicle, I realized at once that the only way to efficiently load the full trailers that were to be piggy-backed to Livingstone and off-load the empty trailers from the barge was by use of a loading ramp. The ramp would have to be raised and lowered with the rise and fall of the Zambezi and, also, with the change in the level of the barges as they took on the tremendous weight of the loaded trailers. The ramp, in addition, had to be run down to the water's edge on tracks as it was necessary to cater for a considerable distance of totally, un-roadworthy, river mud. A distance that changed dramatically with the arrival of every rainy season. A transformation which occurred as well with the occasional downpour, which constantly moved the banks of the Zambezi as they receded and then suddenly reversed themselves depending on the extent of the volume of the rain.

The draftsman arrived and drew up his plans for the loading ramp, the tracks and the huge oversized hydraulic jacks. He departed by return charter for Salisbury having made arrangements by telephone for a steel manufacturer to start the job immediately on his return. Another frequent stop, the steel manufacturer's, on my way to and from the office in Salisbury. The steel manufacturer was quite willing to give us every service imaginable on a minute's notice. He was busy building the pusher tugs that were to replace the existing river equipment with the outboard motors attached, and we continued to pour money, blood and tears into the operation on a daily basis.

It wasn't that the two non-Caltex directors didn't trust their fellow directors on the Board of ZRT. However, at every recent Board meeting they had developed the habit of bringing their own tape recorder to supplement the Secretary's notes who was taking the minutes of the meeting. She was, as a matter of convenience and cost savings, also, my personal secretary from the company office. Stan Hodgkinson, the Administration Manager, showed up at one Board meeting with his own psychological, warfare equipment. He had brought a company tape recorder, as well, which matched the one of the Chairman's.

At this particular meeting during the discussions, the Chairman's tape recorder, which always occupied a central place on the Board Room table, failed to function. The Chairman signaled to the Secretary to suspend taking the minutes of the meeting while his equipment was to be inspected. Stan, then, volunteered to examine the tape recorder to determine the cause of its malfunctioning. During his examination, he, inadvertently, pressed the erase button and before this error could be rectified over fifty percent of the meeting's proceedings had been erased. Whether he did it deliberately or accidentally, he never did tell me.

This, apparently, so incensed St.Clair-Burke that at a later stage in the meeting, when we tabled the resolution to wind-up the Zambezi River Transport Company, he was so furious that his language in response to the wind-up resolution resembled something that might be heard in a bar room brawl. Certainly not what generally transpires in the hushed atmosphere of a Board Room of one of the subsidiaries of the Seven Sisters.

I turned to address the Chair. In deliberately, measured tones without raising my voice, but with icy overtones, I announced, "Mr. Chairman, if Mr.St.Clair-Burke uses language of that kind once more in front of the Secretary at this Board meeting, I will move, at the close of the meeting under the caption of 'Any Other Business', to have him voted off the Board. I need not remind you that the Articles of the Zambezi River Transport Company allow a director to be removed from the Board, if at least five directors are in attendance, as there are today, and the majority present vote 'Aye'."

I thought for a moment that St.Clair-Burke was going to rise out of his chair to reach for my throat as he was sitting on the Chairman's right hand side, and I was facing him directly sitting on the Chairman's left. It was after the close of this meeting that Stan had made his telling comment about taking early retirement if he had known what was in store for him, when he accepted the appointment of Director to the Board of the Zambezi River Transport Company Ltd.

None of this legal maneuvering was accomplishing anything constructive in the way of moving Harry Wulfson's hardwood from Barotseland. By this time, considerable attention was being paid to the court hearings by the press. The Daily News reporter in Lusaka in Northern Rhodesia had been able to get many more details of the pending injunction against Caltex (Africa) Ltd. than had his fellow reporter in Salisbury. He, undoubtedly, must have had access to some member, possibly two in particular, of the Board of Directors of the Zambezi River Transport Company. Only the Directors knew of the special resolution, which we intended to pass at the next meeting of the Board, which would be the finale step in placing ZRT in bankruptcy and removing Ford and St.Clair-Burke from the Board and from ownership of ZRT. The continual, public relations warfare being waged by Ford and St.Clair-Burke in connection with the winding-up of the operation was beginning to take its toll on all members of the Salisbury office. The story, by-lined from Lusaka, indicated that information was being made available to the press, as if from a leaking sieve:

PETROL COMPANY IN BIG NR LAWSUIT

Daily News Reporter

Lusaka, Wednesday

A £100,000 Northern Rhodesia transport company sought a second injunction against Caltex (Africa) Ltd. in the High Court here today to prevent Caltex nominees on the transport company's board of directors from passing a special resolution to wind-up the company Today's application follows an injunction against Caltex granted earlier this month to prevent the oil company from disposing of assets belonging to Zambezi River Transport Service Ltd. The transport company told the Court it would petition Governor, Sir Evelyn Hone, to appoint an inspector to investigate the management and affairs of ZRT.

RAILWAY SLEEPERS

Caltex have already been sued for £63,000 as part of an alleged agreement to provide ZRT with additional finance for more equipment to complete a £1,300,000 transport contract with millionaire Mr. Harry Wulfson and Northern Rhodesia's former Minister of Natural Resources Mr.Geoffrey Beckett. The two men formed a company, Barotseland Sawmills Ltd. to cut 10,000,000 cubic feet of hardwood and supply 750,000 teak railway sleepers to Rhodesia Railways during the next five years. Under this contract ZRT were to ferry hundreds of tons of hardwood and sleepers from the Senanga area to Livingstone.

Any legal proceedings against THE COMPANY had to be reported to Caltex Petroleum Corporation in New York. This requirement was only a vague recollection in the back of my mind as New York was not my reporting center and, therefore, what ever reports were being forwarded to New York by Cape Town were not copied to me. Naturally, I had kept Cape Town informed of the injunctions which had been obtained by ZRT against Caltex (Africa) Ltd. At the time, all concerned would much have preferred that such a reporting requirement to New York wasn't in existence.

Evidently, someone in the New York office was reading the field reports for a change and had sent them to the Chairman of Caltex Petroleum Corporation. The telephone rang very late one night just as I was returning home from the office. It was Cape Town. "We've just had a telephone call from New York. They want you there on the first flight available out of Salisbury for a Board Meeting of CPC," was the brusque message relayed to me by Pat Stanley, the Acting Managing Director.

Dick Wrigley was in California on home leave, and his last words to me on the telephone before he left were, "Do whatever you think is necessary to meet our obligations to Harry."

My response to Pat carried the full weight of the agonizing trials and tribulations that everyone in the Salisbury office connected with ZRT had been undergoing. "That's impossible Pat. The latest shipment of tractors is arriving this week, and the second pusher tug is going to be commissioned on Monday. I just have to be there. In addition, I have just returned from an 'audience' with the King of Barotseland. I won't bore you with the details of his feelings on the possibility that ZRT may have to shut down for a while and leave his people stranded without a link to the outside world for their essential supplies. It is his subjects that provide the backbone of the labour force for ZRT. One word from His Majesty and they will 'down tools' and, then, we are really up for it."

I continued with the reasons that I felt it was not possible for me to attend a Board meeting of Caltex Petroleum Corporation in New York at this time. "The only way I escaped unscathed from the audience with the King was to agree to accede to his suggestion to take a hunting party out to one of his villages where the lions have been terrorizing the villagers and killing their cattle. In addition, there have been a number of elephants that have been destroying their crops. Since he has absolute control over all aspects of his Kingdom, he has authorized me to take what ever action is necessary to bring both these situations under control. So early next weekend I'm leaving for the Caprivi Strip and after the arrival of the tractors and the commissioning of the tug, I'm going hunting on behalf of the King."

Pat was one of the Cape Town directors that was respected by all members of his department, as well as by everyone else who had any dealings with him in THE COMPANY. He was the Fiscal Director and was quite a reserved individual, as most accountants are by nature. His reply was, typically, in character with the way he ran his department.

"Well, you don't have to go, if you don't want to. You can take care of the details with ZRT next week, and after that you can go hunting. I would suggest to you, however, that if I relay your concerns and anxieties to the Chairman in New York about your feelings for your responsibilities to ZRT, he will, undoubtedly, advise you that your next hunting trip will be when you are hunting for a new job," was the way he succinctly summed up my rather short-sighted view of whether or not I should go to New York at the request of the Chairman to attend a Board Meeting. To soften the blow somewhat, he followed up with the information that he had talked to Dick Wrigley in California. Dick was going to have to interrupt his vacation and go to New York to attend the Board Meeting as well as myself. If I felt that it was an unwarranted imposition on me to have to attend the Board Meeting, he said that I should have heard Dick's reactions about the need to interrupt his vacation with his daughter and grandson. With this news in hand, I told Pat I would be on the first available flight out of Salisbury.

When I arrived at the Dorset Hotel on Fifty-fourth Street in New York and enquired about my reservation, the hotel clerk informed me that a Mr. Wrigley, who had arrived that afternoon, had engaged a two bedroom suite, and I was to join him as soon as I checked into the hotel. This was the same hotel at which Caltex Petroleum Corporation maintained a company suite for the Chairman. The Chairman's suite had not only two bedrooms, but it had large kitchen facilities, a very impressive bar, and an oversize lounge for entertaining important clients of THE COMPANY and guests of the Chairman.

Fortunately for Dick and myself, the Chairman was not occupying his suite that evening as Dick and I had a lot of ground to cover before our meeting with the Board in the morning. After reviewing all the details of what had transpired with the court proceedings, and how far we had progressed with getting the operation in a state of readiness to provide Harry and his partner with the necessary transportation facilities, I took the opportunity of telling Dick about my aborted hunting trip.

I had, instinctively, realized the importance of having the King of Barotseland on our side in the coming unpleasant dissolution of the, then, existing Zambezi River Transport Company. I called on my past understanding of the importance of public relations, and the necessary burden such activities bore for the international oil executive. I knew that it was imperative that the King of Barotseland be made aware of the possible interruption of the river company's service caused by the impending bankruptcy proceedings, which THE COMPANY was engaging

in vis-à-vis Messrs. Ford and St.Clair-Burke. I arranged for one of the senior Barotses on our staff to relay a message to the King's palace that a director, as well as
the manager of ZRT, was anxious to have an audience with His Majesty. In due
course, the employee conveyed the information that the King would meet with us
on the Tuesday of the following week.

Off to the airport again after saying goodbye to my long suffering wife as I
boarded the charter aircraft that was to take me to Katima Mulilo. Actually, the
landing area was not in Katima Mulilo in the Caprivi Strip, but was in Zambia.
There were no airport facilities in the Caprivi Strip at that time, although,
unknown to us there were soon going to be massive facilities of that kind. After
landing, it was only necessary to take the local ferry across the Zambezi, and you
were immediately in Katima Mulilo in South West Africa.

It is not necessary to describe the mode of operation of the local ferry. All
movie goers have seen the hand hauled log rafts referred to as ferries that dot the
shores of the many rivers of the dark continent. These are simply a number of
logs which have been bound together and covered with rough hewn lumber. The
rough hewn lumber serves as a surface for the passengers who are in transit, and
for the many bullock carts that make their way from shore to shore carrying the
multitude of goods that pass for freight in that part of the world. There is a heavy
rope which has been lashed to sturdy posts on each shore of the river. This rope is
passed through secure loops on the handrails of the ferry. With a rhythmic chant
the 'ferry crew' haul the craft from one shore to the other hand over hand.

The plane landed and bounced and rolled towards the end of the runway
strip. There was a sickening lurch as one of the wheels fell into a particularly large
pot hole. The pothole was so deep that the pilot was unable to get the plane moving again. When the bare footed local 'airport manager' came running up to
enquire what had happened, the pilot told him in a voice that left no room for
doubt that the pilot had reached the end of his rope. "I've told you for the last
time, if you do not have these pot holes filled in before my next trip, I will notify
the aviation authorities in Lusaka that the field is not serviceable. You will never
be paid again if nobody uses this strip," he emphasized his stand in his closing
words.

The pilot apologetically turned to me and said, "I'm sorry to have to ask you,
again, to help move the aircraft. I promised you on the last trip that you wouldn't
have to assist anymore." With these words, I exited the plane, placed myself at the
tip of one wing, as I had done on our previous landing, and the airport manager
placed himself at the other wing tip. At the signal from the pilot, we pushed with
all our strength as he revved up the motors, and the plane careened out of the

pothole and on to smoother ground. He, then, taxied down the field to the one room mud hut that served as the administration office of this god forsaken place in the jungles of the emerging continent.

As we were pulled by hand across the Zambezi on a wooden ferry of timeless linage that resembled the countless numbers of its predecessors over the past hundreds and hundreds of years, we could see the hippos down stream with the crocodiles warily swimming past the huge beasts. Crocodiles will take the opportunity to feast on very, young hippos, but they make every effort to avoid the immense adults as it is a losing battle if they challenge the youngsters' parents. I gazed at the fascinating scene. My mind traveled back to the orientation sessions that THE COMPANY had gone to such great pains to provide in order that their new employees were made aware of all the different situations that they may encounter when they became part of that great brotherhood of international oil executives. For some strange reason, I could not recall one instance of the instructor ever mentioning being hand hauled by ferry across a river in the heart of Africa, while the hippos and the crocodiles made a mockery of the white man's claim that he had civilized the world.

I will, certainly, be the first to confess, however, that as night was falling and we sat on the veranda of the company house on the banks of the Zambezi in total silence, there was absolutely nothing in the world that resembled the feelings that engulfed you as the sun set, the white man's activities came to a close and the jungle came to life. The night hunters were just rousing themselves. They had no need to be deathly still as they would soon become, when they began to stalk their prey. You could hear the lions roar, the leopards bark, man's ancestors chattering wildly in the trees as they warned their fellow primates that the flesh eaters were abroad in their constant quest to forage for themselves and their cubs, and the hippos lumbered out of the water to graze on the banks of the mighty and forbidding Zambezi.

As The United Nations Committee on South West Africa had reported, the Caprivi Strip is, almost, inaccessible from the rest of South West on account of the swamp. 'A long canoe journey up the River Mashi is possible, except during the rainy season when this route too is impassable'[72]. The Palace of the King of Barotseland reflected these realities of life also. He and His Court, as well as all his subjects in that part of his Kingdom, vacated the area just prior to the rainy season. There were huge, oversize, royal canoes that carried His Majesty's entourage down the river to higher ground where he would base his administrative headquarters, until the River Mashi had receded after the rains had ceased. As a result of this annual, necessary pilgrimage of having to leave his palace to the ravages of nature, the palace did not resemble in any way the palace of the King of Siam. With full apologies, it must be also noted that the Thais had a civilization that bore no relationship to this part of black Africa. Amazingly enough, however, many of the established customs followed in the court of the King of Barotseland's palace exactly resembled those of the King of Siam.

At the gate of the Palace, we were respectfully requested by the palace guide to remove our shoes. He, then, led us down a vast hallway to where we were to have our audience with the King in his throne room. We had noticed immediately that everything about the building suggested that it had been constructed with the urgent thought in mind that it would be necessary at one time or another to be prepared to resist the onslaught of the flowing waters of the Mashi. All living areas were built with an allowable distance of several feet above ground level. This would not deter the flood waters from entering the rooms of the palace, but it would assist in preventing the force of the flowing waters from sweeping away the structure. Consequently, when the waters receded and the King returned to take up residence again, the building would still be standing.

As we approached the throne room, the palace guide sank to his knees, bent over at the waist with his eyes riveted on the ground, opened the door to the throne room and announced that the 'foreign devils' had arrived for their audience with His Majesty, The King of Barotseland. As we entered the throne room, we were amazed and rendered absolutely speechless to see four forms kneeling in abject obeisance to the King in the same position that the palace guide had assumed on approaching the entrance to the throne room. They were on their knees, bent horizontally from the waist with their eyes fixed on the ground in front of them. There were six chairs arranged around the throne. Two of them were directly in front of His Majesty. The other four were off to the left and out of line of his eyesight. He gazed at the two infidels that had had the audacity to request an audience with him. There was only one comparison that could be made and that was with that world famous movie made by Hollywood, 'The King and I'.

Of course, this was black Africa with no history of the civilization that had made Siam one of the wonders of the Eastern World. But that did not detract from the awe that seemed to emanate from all members of the King's household at the thought that they had been chosen to be of service to His Majesty. As 'foreign devils', we were relieved of the necessity to assume the subservient position of the King's subjects. The two chairs in front of the throne were for us. We bowed and acknowledged our presence by greeting the King in English. There, then, began an exchange between two groups of people that could have not been further removed from each other's daily way of life than if we had lived on different planets.

His Majesty indicated with a nod of his head that we were to assume a sitting position in the two chairs that had been provided for us. Apparently, with the presence of two members of the Western World, His Majesty's four advisors were also allowed what was evidently an extremely, gracious, royal favor in that the other four chairs had been provided for their comfort. As we seated ourselves, the four members of the King's governing body took their places on the other four chairs. Not once, however, did they raise their eyes from the ground where they had been riveted, and where they would stay fixed throughout the entire audience. Although a special dispensation had been granted to them by allowing them to sit in the presence of the King, it was not extended to being able to gaze upon His Royal Personage.

The King was clothed in long flowing white robes with a leopard skin slung over one shoulder. Three of his advisors were also attired in the same manner with the exception, of course, of the all important indication of royalty in that they had no leopard skin adorning their persons. The other member of the group was, amazingly, attired in Western dress. In fact, his clothing matched ours exactly in complete replica of coat, tie, shirt, trousers and, even, a vest which made him better dressed than we were, since in the sweltering heat of Central Africa we did not include vests in our wardrobe. Naturally, everyone was barefoot except the King, who wore those immense, oversize, sandals so frequently seen as a part of that mode of dress in Africa.

The King greeted us in the Barotse language. We were immediately made aware of the reason for the Western dressed member of the audience. He was the interpreter. Even more quickly did we learn, that he was not only the interpreter, but the senior advisor of the King's cabinet. His Oxford English, also, left no doubt where the colonial British had allowed him to be educated in their endeavour to provide a qualified local, civil service for their far flung empire. Although Northern Rhodesia, with its coming independence, was eying the Kingdom of Barotseland, it was still a British Protectorate.

After the exchange of greetings, we were asked if we would care to partake of some refreshment in the shape of what turned out to be British afternoon tea and local delicacies baked in the King's kitchen. On expressing our extreme pleasure for the kindness of His Majesty's offer, there then appeared before our very eyes a team that would have made Gold Medallists in the Olympics. That is, if there had been a category in the Olympics devoted to performing the duties of household servants. The contest would have consisted of the team bringing in on large, oversize trays all the ingredients of afternoon tea and serving it to each individual; without once taking their eyes off the floor; without once rising from a kneeling position, bent over horizontally at the waist and entering and leaving the room without once turning their backs on His Majesty. We had, initially, noted that even the King's senior advisors, when they had assumed their sitting positions in their chairs, that they had studiously avoided turning their backs on their sovereign.

As the tea was being served, the normal opening social remarks were made. It was at this time that we learned of the marauding lions and the loss of crops due to the elephants trampling them underfoot. The interpreter explained that if any elephants were shot in the Kingdom, His Majesty was entitled to one of the tusks as tribute. It suddenly dawned on me that it was below His Majesty's dignity to ask for assistance from the 'foreign devils', but he was indirectly giving us an opportunity to offer to dispose of the raiding lions and the destructive elephants. I immediately seized the opportunity of offering our services. I realized that any problems we were going to have over the future of ZRT and the possible cessation of services would be greatly alleviated if we were able to solve the problems of the King's villagers. He graciously accepted our kind offer, and we launched into the purpose of our visit.

We had rehearsed very carefully what the main theme of our presentation to the King was gong to be. That we were fully aware of the absolute necessity of having the Zambezi River Transport Company continue to provide the essential services required by His Majesty's Kingdom. As we would explain, there might be some temporary interruptions to the service as THE COMPANY was determined to modernize the service to bring it up to the standards that should be expected by the inhabitants of such an important area. We stressed that any minor interruption to the service, that might be caused by the company's resolve to ensure that His Majesty's Kingdom was the beneficiary of all the technical improvements of the twentieth century that could be made, would be a small price to have to pay.

His Majesty always addressed us directly, even though it was in his own language. We would hear the translation of his words from his left immediately, or after a slight pause as the interpreter sometimes consulted with his fellow advisors before answering. After our masterful presentation, based on all the government relations experience I had gained in my international career, and which had absolutely nothing to do with the problems that would probably eventuate in the way of interrupted service to the King's people, His Majesty looked at us. He paused for a moment. He, then, asked what appeared to a short and direct question. This time there was no hesitation from the interpreter, as he translated the King's words directly as he heard them. "His Majesty wishes to know who it is that you are trying to force off the Board of Directors and for what reasons."

So much for government relations speeches. And for that awfully prejudiced state of mind that tells the majority of Westerners, who attempt to deal with so called backward tribes in the heart of the dark continent, that these savages would never understand the complications of the Western World's way of doing business. The intricacies involving bankruptcy proceedings, overdue fuel accounts and fly-by-night entrepreneurs that are looking to make a quick buck or in this case a fast million dollars. And so we launched into the whole sordid tale of what was going to happen in the very near future, including the real possibility that the service to His Majesty's Kingdom would be interrupted. We did take the opportunity to assure him the interruption would be as brief as we could possibly make it, and we sincerely believed that if it did occur, it would be of very short duration.

The King rose. The four advisors slid abruptly off their chairs to a kneeling position with their eyes on the floor. His Majesty thanked us for our efforts and signaled the end of the audience. Although, we didn't actually back out of the room, it was remarkable how we both, instinctively, made a determined effort to appear as if we weren't actually turning our backs. The door to the throne room was not in a direct line with the King, and this materially helped us to give his Majesty the impression that we were not turning our backs on him. We retrieved our shoes at the palace gate and wended our way back to the base of ZRT's operation wondering in bewilderment if we were really living in the Twentieth Century. I, also, wondered at a later date, if I should write to New York and suggest that their orientation classes include the compulsory attendance at a showing of the 'King and I'.

There were two extremely, good friends of mine in THE COMPANY who appreciated the ritual we had undergone when we first arrived at the Palace gate and had had to remove our shoes. Brian Harris and Peggy, his very attractive and hospitable wife, who are now living in Valloris on the Riviera in France, still reminisce during our visits together when they come to Paris or I visit them, about the time when they were house hunting in Scarsdale in Westchester, New York. The same Westchester that became the home of the one of the Seven Sisters that owned us, Texaco. Brian had been assigned to CPC at 350 Madison Avenue, New York for a tour of duty. New York badly needed his refinery experience which he had gained throughout the far flung 'empire' of THE COMPANY. Part of his expertise had been gained from a stint of duty in Japan.

The real estate agent after listening to Brian and Peggy's description of the type of accommodations that they would like to rent replied, "I have the perfect house for you. It is in immaculate condition and fully furnished with the most exquisite oriental furniture I have ever seen. It is owned by a Japanese family. The husband has been transferred back to Tokyo for a period of two years. He is obviously climbing the corporate ladder and has to be exposed to his head office culture. Unfortunately, the wife, who was left behind to lease the house, has not found a single prospective tenant that I've brought around to be satisfactory. I've actually given up taking people there as I'm much too busy to pursue dead end prospects. However, since it is exactly what you want, and if you have the time and would care to have a look, here is the address. Call me after you've talked to the wife and let me know why you think she won't rent the place to you."

Brian and Peggy duly arrived at the address given to them by the real estate agent, knocked at the door and bowed to the owner as she answered their knock. They explained the purpose of their visit and asked if they could view the premises. The lady of the house graciously acknowledged their request and invited them to enter. As she ended her invitation with a gesture of her hand signaling them to cross the threshold, Brian and Peggy automatically reached down, removed their shoes, placed them neatly together at the door sill and entered the house in their bare, stockinged feet. After being served a lovely afternoon tea, they telephoned the agent and asked him to bring the lease papers to the house. The real estate agent couldn't believe that the owner had agreed to lease the house, and even more to the agents astonishment, at a substantially lesser sum than had originally been asked. "One word of caution, though," Brian told the agent, "When you bring the lease papers over and enter the house, be sure to remove your shoes at the front door."

After finishing my story to Dick over dinner about losing the opportunity of going hunting, I sheepishly admitted, on reflection, that I should have responded more responsibly to the Chairman's instructions to attend the Board Meeting in New York.

"Well, I don't how you feel," was his response. "I can only assure you that I don't feel as if I've been on vacation at all. When this meeting is over I'm going to start my vacation from the beginning again. None of the days that have elapsed up this to point are going to be counted by me as applying towards my home leave," was his finale determined, but dispirited comment.

Dick, nonchalantly, and I, nervously, took our respective places at the Board Room table. He, close to the Chairman, while I was at the foot of the table as befitted my rank, surrounded as I was by Directors, Vice-Presidents, the Chief Accountant, the Comptroller, Regional Directors and a host of lesser lights. The Chairman was reasonably pleasant as he opened the meeting. He announced that his invitation to Dick and myself was because of the many conflicting stories he had been hearing about an operation in Zambia in which Caltex (Africa) Ltd. had become involved. He requested that, between Dick and myself, he would like to have all members of the Board and the others present at the meeting, as well as himself, fully briefed on exactly what was transpiring and the present status of the situation.

As back in the 'bad old days' in Ceylon, Dick, the senior, looked at me, the junior, and although nicely phrased he said, "You explain it." Actually, between the two us, we did a very credible job. We detailed how much business we were going to obtain. How the operation was shaping up into an extremely efficient organization, and that, although, we had been somewhat discouraged in the beginning, we were sure we had a grip on the whole setup now. Being Dick Wrigley, he took every opportunity during his part of the explanations to heap praise on my efforts and to emphasize how that it was only because of my guiding hand on the controls that we had progressed as far as we had today.

Dick continued with the explanation by admitting that it was unfortunate that Caltex (Africa) Ltd. had been so unlucky as to have had the adverse publicity of being sued with the attendant, distasteful, media exposure. Nonetheless, all of that had been put behind us. The two individuals, who were responsible for the unpleasantness, were no longer associated with ZRT. Public exposure in the press was at an end. The Chairman could be assured that there would be no more yellow journalism commentary in the future.

Money, so it appears, is the reason why you have Boards of Directors, Chief Accountants, Comptrollers and the like. I, suddenly, found myself being addressed by the Chief Accountant. "Your comments about the progress you have made on bringing the operation up to a proper standard are most interesting and encouraging," were his opening comments. "But tell me, how much progress have you made in reducing the outstanding fuel account, which is now in the amount of $380,000.00, and have you shortened the period of indebtedness?" was the bombshell that landed on the board room table right in front of where I was sitting.

In all bureaucracies that ostensibly operate for a profit, there are certain limits on the period of time and the amount of money owed that require the delinquent accounts to be brought to higher and higher authorities, as the quantity of money and the time it is outstanding increase. I knew, of course, that Cape Town had been reporting the huge fuel account that been outstanding under Ford and St.Clair-Burke's tutorship of ZRT to New York. With ZRT as a customer, it far exceeded any thing that we could keep under wraps and survive an audit. What stunned me was the nature of the question. How could such a question be asked? We had just forced the Zambezi River Transport Company into bankruptcy. We now owned the company and literally owed the money to ourselves.

I knew the Chief Accountant, Bill Carroll, quite well. He was not one to cause trouble just for the sake of embarrassing a fellow employee, no matter how junior. He, also, had a reputation for running a very tight organization. If all this were true, why had he asked the question?

The Chairman picked it up immediately. "What are the chances of your recovering the money?" he demanded, as he took control of the questioning in an imperious manner.

On hearing the Chairman's question, both Dick and I looked at each other in horror as we both instantly reached the same conclusion. No one. That is neither the Vice-President, or the Regional Director in New York had reported to the Chairman and the Board that we couldn't recover the out standings. We owed the money to ourselves. We were committed through the 'operating guarantee' to provide the capital, staff, expertise and everything else that was required to have the Zambezi River Transport Company Ltd. meet its obligations to the Barotseland Sawmills Ltd. to carry their teak wood for a period of at least five years. No wonder some of the previous questions asked made us wonder on what the rational for the question was founded. Now we knew. No one had had the guts to tell the most, unpleasant truth to the Chairman and the Board about the operating guarantee. I guess I was somewhat punch-drunk by then, because I answered in the shortest and most emphatic way I could.

"Nil," I replied.

All the friendly atmosphere disappeared as if by the wave of the good fairy's wand, or in this case, the bad fairy's wand. Dick and I just slumped in our chairs and gazed at each other. There had been several questions concerning how much we had advanced to ZRT, how secure the collateral was, had we ever considered putting them on a 'cash only' basis and several others of a like nature. We had both been at a loss as how to follow up on this avenue of questioning. We hadn't been able to comprehend how these senior members attending this meeting, with the knowledge which we believed that they had of the whole operation, could ask such questions. This was the void in our understanding; the fact that we were under the impression that they were fully conversant with all aspects of the fiasco known as ZRT.

Now we were faced with a monumentally, impossible obstacle to over come. How were we going to impart the information to all present that the reason we couldn't recover the money and had to keep on poring additional sums into ZRT was because of the infamous 'operating guarantee'. Such a disclosure would have to be over the heads of two very senior members present. It was their responsibility to convey that information to the Chairman and to the Board. As we were contemplating how to handle this distasteful and delicate subject, the second bombshell fell. This time right in Dick's lap.

"Well, Mister Wrigley (and the emphasis on 'Mister' had an ugly, familiar sound) under those circumstances, if what Palmer-Smith tells us is a correct assessment of the situation, you had better cut your losses and get out. Write off the $380,000.00, and that will be the end to this unpleasant affair."

Dick's and my eyes met each other's in an imploring manner. Dick had told me only last night that the authority to sign the 'operating guarantee' had required the counter signature of his Vice-President and the Regional Director in New York. He, alone, didn't have the authority to commit THE COMPANY to such an exposure. So there were two other individuals, besides Dick and myself, at the table who knew that we 'couldn't cut our losses and get out'.

Suddenly and blindingly, the absolute knowledge finally sank in. The fact that there were only, only two others who knew, besides Dick and myself—Dick's Regional Director and his Vice-President—about the infamous 'operating guarantee' and the deplorable condition of the Zambezi River Transport Company. The Chairman didn't know. The Comptroller didn't know. The Chief Accountant didn't know and none of the other Vice-Presidents and Board members around the Board Table knew, with the exception of the special four of us. No one had told the Chairman and the Board that we 'couldn't get out'. The 'operating guarantee' committed us to continue to run the river company and absorb the losses on the fuel bills and to keep pouring hundreds and hundreds of thousands of dollars into the operation which, in the finale analysis, would turn out to cost us well over a million dollars.

As Dick and I gazed at each other and tried to reach a consensus on how to handle this totally unexpected and delicate situation, the scene before us resembled nothing more than rats deserting a sinking ship. Everyone was talking at once. No one directed any questions at Dick or to me. Dick's Vice-President and his Regional Director were retreating from the field of battle like lemmings disappearing into the sea, as their fugitive glances around the board room table were met with stony, uncompromising looks from their colleagues. They were making a totally, useless effort to cover their flanks, or their (expletive deleted—as we were to learn from even more ethereal surroundings in the future) and like the lemmings, it only contributed to their ultimate demise.

After the passage of what seemed like eons of time, but was actually only a matter of minutes, the Chairman spoke. "I find this matter totally incomprehensible. The meeting is adjourned. We will reconvene after lunch at two PM, and there had better be a somewhat more rational explanation at that time than the superficial details I've heard this morning." He rose from his chair and left the room with Dick's Vice-President and Regional Director nipping at his heels like two woe-be-gone, bedraggled, young puppy dogs.

As I lay back, physically and mentally drained, in the oversize, first class swivel chair in the upstairs, cocktail lounge of the Boeing 747 and winged my way back to Salisbury and the dark continent, I could only come to a very simple conclusion. The meeting in the throne room of His Majesty, The King of Barotseland, had a lot more to say for itself about how 'civilized' members of governing bodies conduct themselves during extremely unpleasant and sensitive debates, than did the comic opera which had just been played out in New York in the Board Room of Caltex Petroleum Corporation and of which I had been a player.

Apparently the two culprits, the Vice-President and the Regional Director, had caught up with the Chairman as he left the Board Room. They must have 'confessed' to their 'oversight' of not informing him of the actual commitment of THE COMPANY having agreed to guarantee the operation of the Zambezi River Transport Company. No doubt they attempted to soften the blow by taking him to his favorite restaurant, one that is undoubtedly among the best, if not the best restaurant in New York City, Le Cygne. They must have fully briefed him over lunch, because when Dick and I arrived back in the Board Room at two in the afternoon, as we had been instructed, there was a message for us that the meeting had been cancelled. Dick was free to resume (or start in his opinion) his vacation, and I was free to return to Salisbury and the onerous duties of 'guaranteeing' that the Zambezi River Transport Company would continue to operate (and maybe even go hunting).

The new tractors continued to arrive along with the trailers. The loading ramp was a resounding success. After sinking a number of barges at the ramp, the shore crew learned to load the trailers on the barges in an alternate pattern in order to keep the barge level. The new manager was a perfect find. It appeared as if this monumental disaster which I had inherited was going to become an efficient, operating entity. It was now possible to pick up the periodic reports without that awful sinking sensation in one's stomach that announced there was another calamity in the making. The revenue report, while still oozing massive volumes of red ink, actually indicated that our actions were beginning to stem the flow. At the end of one reporting period, and long before any such forecasted results had been anticipated to occur, I found it difficult to believe my eyes. The operation had showed a profit for the month. Slight, it was true, but a profit.

Having my cynicism honed to a fine degree by my association with the Zambezi River Transport Company, I couldn't resist picking up the phone and asking the manager how the accounting error had occurred. "What accounting error?" was his response.

"You actually are running, if I may be pardoned for my pun, in the black. There must be a mistake," was my skeptical comment in answer to his question. "If you really are in the black, it must be a miracle. Please describe how miracles happen. I'm not generally on speaking terms with items of that nature. Certainly not in connection with ZRT." One thing about this exchange between the manager and myself was the fact that we could now discuss the operation with some slight degree of normality and even some humour. Certainly, on a more rational basis than in past when every thing about the operation was cataclysmic.

His explanation was, as was everything about ZRT, anything but normal. "For the last four weeks, we have carried nothing upstream except heavy construction equipment. Caterpillar tractors, bulldozers, fork lifts, trench diggers, paving mixers and all kinds of building equipment and material, particularly tons of cinder block. Since there was obviously no published price list for that kind of equipment, as it was never carried before and never envisaged that it would be carried, I set my own prices. I estimated what I thought the equipment would have cost and charged fifteen percent of that figure."

"The shippers never queried the rates and paid all invoices in advance of delivery. I have warehoused all the other usual freight and have been running the barges on a round the clock basis carrying only their cargo. I have collected tens of thousands of pounds, and I intend to collect every pound available before this miracle comes to end. In fact, I collect more for one trip with a piece of their heavy equipment than I do for several months for all the other items we carry," he commented as he finished his explanation and further proved what an excellent selection his appointment as manager had been. Little did I know as we continued the discussion that I would be the one to bring his new found 'miracle' to an end."

"Who in the world is sending that kind of material and equipment to the Caprivi Strip and what are they doing with it?" I instantly queried with very obvious misgivings. Miracle or no, something was not what it appeared to be on the surface.

"Starting with who the shippers are," the manager continued, "all documents show the owners to be the 'Rhodesian Construction Company' with a post office box as an address in Salisbury. What they are doing with it? I frankly just don't know. One of the very first items of equipment that we shipped up was a flat-bed, loading truck. This truck is waiting in Katima Mulilo every time one of the barges arrives with another piece of equipment. As soon as we off-load the Caterpillar tractor or what ever equipment it is, the flat-bed truck picks it up and takes off down the road with it. How they maneuver on those roads is beyond me," he finished his explanation. "Since we started this exercise, I've been too busy to even have time to think."

"Well, let me tell you something right now. Although, I haven't had much time to devote to the marketing activities here in Salisbury because of this bloody fiasco of ZRT, I can tell you that I know every construction company in Salisbury that has enough capital to own a Caterpillar tractor, much less all that other equipment you've enumerated. And there is no 'Rhodesian Construction Company'. I can assure you of that," I emphatically informed him. "I want you to follow up and let me know as soon as you can for what the equipment is being used and where. In the meantime, I'll book a charter and be up there a week from today."

Within twenty-four hours the manager was back on the telephone. "I've talked to the driver of the flat-bed truck and asked him what he was doing with all that equipment. Incidentally, I was surprised to realize that he is a South African and not a Rhodesian. I assumed he would be Rhodesian, because the equipment is being shipped by the 'Rhodesian Construction Company', although, I should have remembered. He, and quite a large number of South Africans, came up on our passenger barge about two months ago. I remember, now, asking them at the time why they were coming to Katima Mulilo. I was very surprised at seeing so many South Africans suddenly appear in this god forsaken part of the world. At the time, they said they were 'on a bus man's' holiday and were going to do a little shooting and just look around. After our audience with the King, I warned them to be sure not to do any shooting in Barotseland before getting an authorization from the Palace. Further more, if they shot any elephant, they had better make certain they paid the tribute of a tusk an animal to His Majesty."

"You know, come to think of it, now that your questions have forced me to remember, I never noticed any shooting equipment in their baggage at all. And what did they mean by 'on a bus man's' holiday?" he continued in a puzzled voice. "What kind of operation would they be looking at in The Caprivi Strip to be 'on a bus man's' holiday' There is nothing in the area but a small village I believe, although I've never even been as far as the village and don't even know its name. I'm really confused, particularly now that you've asked all these questions. The driver said that he wasn't sure for what the equipment was being used. He suspected that they were going to clear an area for some experimental farming or something of that nature," the manager finished off in a baffled voice.

One week after our initial telephone conversation I was in Katima Mulilo. I was pleased to note as we landed that the 'airport manager' had taken the pilot seriously and had filled in all the pot holes. The ZRT manager listed all the additional equipment that had been ferried up from Livingstone in the week that had elapsed. It was remarkable in that there appeared no end to the flow of heavy equipment destined for Katima Mulilo, or rather for that not too distant and obscure native village inland from the Zambezi. In total, it represented hundreds and hundreds of thousands of pounds worth. I suggested to the manager that we make a quick trip to the scene where all this heavy equipment that he had collected so much money for transporting was being used.

Experimental farming ...??????

I had spent many a dreary day on the numerous islands of the South Pacific, when the aircraft carrier of the United States Navy on which I was serving dropped anchor in the ports of Guam, Guadalcanal, Einiwetok and a host of others during the days of World War II. It didn't need an experienced, naval aircraft carrier officer to recognize 'experimental farming' when he saw it.

I was speechless. I could have been on any one of those numerous islands in the Pacific in the early days just after we had wrested control of them from the Japanese and were hastily building our advance military airfields. I gazed in amazement at the frantic activity being undertaken by the operators of the massive amount of heavy equipment which the Zambezi River Transport Company had ferried up from Livingstone. Equipment which hadn't originated in Rhodesia but rather in South Africa, as I quickly learned by surreptitiously looking at the markings in the cabs. All being operated by South Africans, I was very quickly to learn also. The outer perimeters of the huge airfield had already been delineated by clearing a narrow strip. The bull dozers and Caterpillar tractors were now clearing all the jungle away and working their way towards the center of the delineated area of what was going to, obviously, be a massive military airfield.

Being an ex Naval Officer from an aircraft carrier and having already spent a number of years in the petroleum business, it became a very simple matter to spot what was going to be the tank farm. It was easy to see that the storage facilities were going to be of a magnitude that only a military operation would require. In addition, although the storage facilities were in an early stage of preparation, it was evident that the tanks were going to be protected by very heavy embankments, as well as being placed very strategically some distance from the airfield and well hidden in the jungle. Judging from the amount of cinder block and building material that we had transported, the tanks were, also no doubt, going to be additionally protected against what might prove to be enemy aircraft fire or bombs.

The U.N. Committee on South West Africa commented as follows:

".... the Committee notes that the Prime Minister of the Union (South Africa) stated in Parliament on 1 June 1951 that the reason for placing the Eastern Caprivi Zipfel under direct Union administration was the inaccessibility of the region to South West Africa. The Committee, realizing that the Eastern Caprivi Zipfel can be reached from the administrative centres of the Union only through non-Union territories, is not convinced that the direct administration of the region by the Union has, in fact, made it more accessible to the centres of administration."

As any map will show, and as the United Nations Committee on South West had commented, '.... the Eastern Caprivi Zipfel can be reached from the administrative centres of the Union only through *non-Union* territories.... '[73]

It was now easy to see why the documentation was shown as the 'Rhodesian Construction Company'. The equipment had to pass through Rhodesia, a *non-union* (Union—The Union of South Africa as it was then called) country. Otherwise, it couldn't be loaded on the Zambezi River Transport Company's barges, as Zambia would never allow anything to be received from South Africa. Only after 'acquiring' a Rhodesian 'nationality' could it transit Zambia and be off-loaded at Katima Mulilo in the Caprivi Strip, part of South West Africa and under the direct control of the South African Government through the Mandate.

ZRT's loading port on the Zambezi River for all material destined for South West Africa and Barotseland was in Livingstone, Zambia. Any equipment being shipped from South Africa would never be allowed to transit Zambia no matter what type of equipment it might well be. Certainly not the type which ZRT had been carrying for some time now and in massive quantities.

Our young and conscientious new manager of ZRT had no military experience. He had really no idea of the implications of the scene, which had greeted our eyes as we pulled up to a stop at the edge of all the activity being undertaken by the energetic and determined men who were operating the equipment. "Seems like an awfully big and expensive operation for an experimental farm," was his only comment. "But as long as they continue to ship their equipment on ZRT, I really don't care how they spend their money," he observed as we pulled away from the site in our Land Rover. We returned to Katima Mulilo. I was now satisfied that I was fully informed as to the extent and purpose of the activities being undertaken.

As with everything in connection with ZRT, fate was unkind. It decreed that the Commercial Attaché from the American Embassy in Salisbury (or was it the Charge d'affaires's office—things were changing so rapidly in that part of Africa that it was difficult to keep track) was stopping by for his monthly update with me on the state of economy from the oil industry's point of view.

Possibly, if I had had more time to consider, I may not have relayed the information to him that I did. On the other hand, in spite of my intense feelings that I would never have anything more to do with representatives of the United States Government, I still had that ingrained sense of compulsion that told me no matter how stupid or how incompetent the government staff might be, it was still my country. In addition, stupidity and incompetency weren't limited to service in the United States Government, as I could observe on a regular basis in the conduct of the Two Sisters that owned us and the Chairman from the Western sister in particular.

I had scarcely finished dinner when the door bell rang. The house boy announced my caller from the Embassy. I was still so mesmerized by what I had seen that I automatically and vividly described the whole panorama to him. I knew, instinctively, that it was the kind of information that could be of value to my Government, although, how I didn't know. The only reason that I now philosophically debate whether or not I would have relayed the information to him, if I had had time to reflect, is the reality of hindsight; hindsight because of what happened to ZRT. What happened to ZRT as a result of my informing the United States Government in no uncertain terms, based on indisputable military and commercial experience, that the South African Government was building a massive military air base in the Caprivi Strip just a matter of miles from Katima Mulilo. Katima Mulilo, the very village where ZRT's operations were based, and where we were off-loading the massive quantities of heavy equipment that the South African Government was going to use to build that military air base.

I did not know the name of the area or the village where the base was being built. Inasmuch as it was only a matter of about an half-hour's drive from Katima

Mulilo, I told the Commercial Attaché that the name didn't really matter. The inability to confirm the name of the area was the circumstantial evidence on which I based my accusation at a later date, when I accused the Commercial Attaché of informing President Kaunda and the Government of Zambia about the military base being built adjacent to its borders.

The first apparent result of relaying this information to the United States Government about the construction of the base was a despondent call from the manager of ZRT. "Do you know what happened?" were his first dejected words on the telephone.

"Why, what do you mean and about what?" I replied in a mystified voice. He then proceeded to describe what had occurred several days prior, and the devastating effect it was going to have on his revenue statements. It appeared that while loading a large piece of earth moving equipment, several Zambian police officers, some custom officials and a large number of non-uniformed government individuals arrived at ZRT's office in Livingstone. They had directed the loading supervisor to cease loading the equipment. After he had the half-loaded equipment removed from the barge, they then issued instructions to him that he was to undertake no more further freight movements on behalf of the 'Rhodesian Construction Company.' To ensure that their orders were adhered to, they posted several, uniformed guards at the gate to the loading area of ZRT. They remained in situ on a twenty-four hour basis.

My suspicions were immediately aroused. I requested that the Commercial Attaché visit me in my office at his earliest convenience. In spite of all my previous dealings and naïvety in relation to the members of the staff of the United States Government, I still expected to get an honest answer from them when I asked a direct question. But then, perhaps being naïve is a perpetual state of fantasy for some people, particularly people like myself. As soon as he arrived, I confronted him directly with a specific question. "Did your office report the information that I gave to you last week about the military air base being built in the Caprivi Strip to the Zambian Government?" I indignantly demanded.

He quite calmly and deliberately replied that it had only been reported by him to the Ambassador. Certainly, the Ambassador hadn't relayed the information to any foreign Government, in particular, to the Zambian Government.

He continued by saying that he would investigate the situation in the Embassy and get back to me as soon as he possibly could. In due course, his reply to me was an emphatic, "No. The information has not been relayed to any one." How naive could I continue to remain and stay in the real world that I was ostensibly inhabiting? I knew then, instinctively again for a certainty, that he was a god-damm, bloody liar. Circumstantial evidence confirmed my instincts later.

When I had given the United States Government the information, what did I expect in my subconscious that they would do with it? File it under 'C' for Construction, or possibly under 'C' for Caprivi Strip? How about under 'S' for Strip, Caprivi? And last, but not least, as the reality sank in, I realized it was put in an active file under 'Z' for Zambia.

I must have known in my heart of hearts that they were going to use the information for what ever advantage would accrue to the United States. I guess it was the loss of the revenue to ZRT after all the heartaches and effort that we had invested in bringing that nightmare out into the light of the day that made me revert to my original naivety. Naivety that had first surfaced in my inexperienced questions to the aide in the Naval Attaché's office in Colombo, Ceylon.

'After an early denial that the base was being built at all, the South African Government described it as an emergency landing strip for South African Airways' jets on the long round-Africa haul caused by the refusal of the black nations to allow Dr.Verwoerd's planes airspace'[74]. However, Nicholas Tomalin of 'The Sunday Times' spent five hours in Katima in December 1965 and succeeded in sending back the following report:

> **'It was enough to discover that, despite the South African denials, the base is a big military operation. The 16-mile road from Katima to Mpacha is the smoothest and widest in Caprivi. Sixty White South Africans from the Transvaal are working at top speed to complete the base urgently. 'The airstrip is 3/4 of a mile long and 50 feet wide. The main reason why it is not already completed is that there is a major difficulty in bonding the loose Caprivi soil into a firm surface.' (The Sunday Times,19 December 1965.)'** [75]

Obviously, ZRT wasn't the only activity having trouble with the soil. Tomalin's report must have had a typographical error in it as the airstrip was many times wider than 50 feet. We were a bit cynical when we read the comment on his report about how he 'spent five hours in Katima … and succeeded' in sending back the information. We must have taken him up there on one of the passenger barges. He, obviously, couldn't stay more than five hours as there was no place to stay. He could have saved himself the trouble, if he taken the opportunity to have asked those of us who were spilling our blood and guts on a daily basis on that very soil that was such a problem, what was going on in the area.

At the time of his report, the United States Government had long been aware that a military air base was being built in the Caprivi, inasmuch as I had told them about it. The Zambian Government knew, since the United States Government had relayed the information to them. The South African Government knew, because they were building the base. I guess by that time we were feeling a little bit like 'unsung heroes'.

My analysis of exactly what had happened was supported by my conclusions based on circumstantial evidence. This evidence surfaced at a much later date from the records of a press conference which had been held by President Kaunda of Zambia and referred to in the report of the U.N.Committee on South West Africa. By this time the U.N.Committee had identified the location of the air base as being at Mpacha.

The U.N.report was concerned with the strategic significance of the Caprivi Strip i.e.:

".... Bordering as it does on Angola, Zambia, Bechuanaland and Southern Rhodesia, it is, of course, of strategic significance. It is here that a new air base is being constructed at Mpacha, some 16 miles from Katima Mulilo. The construction of this base was first noted by President Kaunda of Zambia at a press conference on 3 June 1965:[76]

'... On the international situation I wish to state how greatly disturbed we are here in Zambia that the South African Government has chosen to build an £8,000,000 air base at somewhere in the Caprivi Strip. This is an obvious threat to Zambia and I want to state quite clearly that we do not intend to be intimidated into silence by any such activities. An air base such as the South African Government is building in the Caprivi Strip is, as I say, a direct threat to Zambia's integrity. We intend following this up in some other way which I am not prepared to say anything about at this moment. I know that they have moved to this site very heavy machinery worth £2,000,000 which they are using for constructing this air base; obviously the fact that they can move to this site machinery worth £2,000,000 is an indication that they intend to get on with the job very quickly. My Government is watching the situation very carefully and if anything develops further naturally we will let you know.'[77]

First sentence of President Kaunda's comments at his press conference, "... air base at *somewhere* in the Caprivi Strip." Of course, 'at *somewhere* in the Caprivi Strip'. I didn't know the name of the village where we had gone to view the activity of the base construction. When the United States Government relayed the information that I had given them to the Zambian Government, they could not tell them the name of the village or the area because, as I had told the Commercial Attaché, 'I didn't know. It didn't really matter. It was only a short distance from Katima Mulilo.'

How did President Kaunda know that the machinery was worth £2,000,000? Was it, possibly, because when I told the Commercial Attaché about the vast amount of equipment being moved by us, I merely extrapolated the freight revenue we had received, based on ZRT's manager's fifteen percent freight rate based on the value of the equipment, and told the Commercial Attaché that, in my opinion, the South Africans must have moved £2,000,000 worth of heavy equipment into the area.

As it transpired in the years to come, this was the last time that I, ever, voluntarily became involved in any activities that related to the political aims or security of my government. Not by choice, I must 'naively' admit, but from lack of opportunity. The next time that I became embroiled with the United States Government, in the person of the Treasury Department, I was an antagonist and adversary and carefully refrained from volunteering any information.

It wasn't the end of the saga of the blood, sweat and tears of the Zambezi River Transport Company. Several years later, when I was attending a cocktail party in Johannesburg after being transferred to South Africa, I was introduced to a very personable, young lady by my hostess. There will be many in the international oil business whose duties have required them to attend countless numbers of these uncivilized activities undertaken by long suffering managers who must 'show the flag'. They will recall how little attention is paid to the names of people to whom they are introduced, even though they may be very attractive brunettes. This is because they do not appear to be a threat to your company or a source of information for it. As a consequence, you barely pass the time of day with such people, as your eyes scan the assemblage with the hope of finding an individual that might reward you with a piece of information that could be of value in your day to day activities in the international oil business and maybe compensate for having to attend the primitive function in the first instance.

In this case, however, the introduction was performed right next to the buffet table that was loaded to overflowing with the most delicious, appetizing hors d'oeuvres for which the hostess was renown. As a result, I continued chatting to my charming, fellow guest with only half an ear tuned to the conversation, while I continued to enjoy, what I had decided, was such a delicious repast that it would serve as my dinner. As the conversation continued to ebb and flow between us, it suddenly dawned on me that it was going to very embarrassing for me when someone else at the party whom I knew joined us, and I would be unable to introduce the young lady. I took the plunge and enquired, "I'm sorry. I heard your name as Judy, but I didn't quite catch your last name," I confessed.

"Beckett," she replied. "My name is Judy Beckett."

All the little fragments of quite, idle chatter that experienced cocktail party goers hear, and which float around in their sub-conscious sometimes for days or weeks or months or perhaps for only the span of a minute, suddenly coalesced as she repeated, "My name is Judy Beckett." The bit about her being brought up in Northern Rhodesia. Her affection for her step-mother after her father remarried. The fact that her father had worked for the Northern Rhodesian Government. He had had an important job. He had been the Minster of Natural Resources, but had died of a heart attack shortly after retiring from Government Service. I gazed at her in startled amazement.

"You're Geoff Beckett's daughter," I blurted out.

She returned my stunned gaze as her mind did precisely what mine had done. She instantly put together all the little bits and pieces of inconsequential information that I had provided to keep our conversation flowing.

"You're the Palmer-Smith who killed my father," she spit out.

There are many who say there is no emotion in business. It is a cold blooded affair. There are no feelings. To those many, I would say they have never experienced having a lovely, personable, young woman tell you in the most bitter and devastating terms possible that you were responsible for her father's death.

If there are any women among those many who say there is no emotion in business, they would only have had to speak to my wife. She would refute the statement with intense feeling. She would recall the very special time, when she answered the telephone at six o'clock in the morning as it rang by her bedside. After listening to the caller, she turned to me with tears in her eyes. "It is Trudy Wuflson. She is crying. She said that Geoff Beckett, Harry's long time friend and business partner, punched Harry at an emergency board meeting of Barotseland Sawmills late last night. It was because of Harry's refusal to do anything about your putting the Zambezi River Transport Company into bankruptcy, which would jeopardize Geoff's life's savings in Barotseland Sawmills. She wants me to please ask you to do something before Geoff has a heart attack that will kill him."

17

Johannesburg, South Africa—Late 1965

In Rhodesia, the white government of Prime Minister Ian Smith followed the lead given by Great Britain and became independent. Great Britain had just bowed to the inevitable. She had granted independence to her two former colonies, Northern Rhodesia and Nyasaland. As was the prevalent fashion in that decade, the colonies promptly renamed themselves; Nyasaland became Malawi and Northern Rhodesia became Zambia.

There was a common usage difference between the names of the two Rhodesias, Southern and Northern. There had sprung up the habit of referring to them as Rhodesia and Northern Rhodesia prior to their independence to differentiate between them. Just as Queen Elizabeth signs her correspondence with a simple Royal 'E', and it is recognized as the only 'E' in the world, so in the same manner, the white settlers in Southern Rhodesia referred to their country as simply 'Rhodesia'. It was the only 'Rhodesia' in the world. White Rhodesians didn't have to geographically identify themselves. They left that necessity to their black neighbours. When you heard 'Rhodesia', the white settlers told the world that it was the only one that really mattered. It did not change its name immediately after independence. In fact, it was a long, twelve years later before Rhodesia became Zimbabwe, and its capital, Salisbury, became Harrari.

There was another, even greater, fundamental difference between the independence of Rhodesia and its two northern neighbors, Northern Rhodesia and Nyasaland. While Great Britain had granted independence to Northern Rhodesia and to Nyasaland, it had specifically withheld the granting of such a royal favour to Rhodesia until such time as Rhodesia had majority rule. While Northern Rhodesia and Nyasaland had 'Independence', Rhodesia had 'Unilateral Declaration of Independence' or 'UDI' as the acronym evolved. With the failure of their

Motherland to grant them independence, the white settlers of Rhodesia simply, unilaterally declared themselves independent of Great Britain.

The great Imperial British Lion had been having its tail twisted by many of its former subjects of all sorts of colours and hues throughout the world. In the climate of the times, it merely meowed and bowed to their demands. But when it was subjects of their own colour, white, who were twisting the lion's tail, it let out a roar for all the world to hear.

'We know how to handle white subjects who do not bow to our will,' the toothless lion roared. 'We will place an embargo on them,' the then shrinking, imperious power announced.

An embargo? An embargo that, although the subject was not specifically mentioned at that time, might include oil? At whose knee did the Arabs sit and learn their lessons?

During that era it was important to show the world that you only cared for those whose skin was a different colour than yours. As for the whites in Rhodesia, they were not only expendable, but by showing the world that you were willing to treat them less favourably than the blacks, you were able to wash away your prior sins with their blood.

November 11, 1965; Enter UDI. 'Unilateral Declaration of Independence'.

There was a tremendous 'hurrah' in everyone's heart as the news swept through all of Africa. That is to say, an 'hurrah' in everyone's red blooded heart who was white. There was a very soft spot in my heart for the Rhodesians. My younger son, at that time, had dual nationality, one of which was Rhodesian; he had been born there the year before UDI was declared.

Of all the 'white' colonies in Africa, Rhodesia actually was the least 'white'. There was a comradeship that existed between its white and black citizens that was nowhere to be found in the balance of Africa. Sadly, the hurrah was only in one's heart or just as in what one historian calls the 'last hurrah of a lost cause'[78], when referring to the German resistance against Hitler during the war.

Wherever your sympathies may lie, you could not but admire the courage that the Rhodesians were showing as they unflinchingly took an independent stand against all the remaining might of Great Britain. An hurrah in one's heart, yes, but in one's head, everyone knew that they didn't stand a chance. When their economy rapidly ground to a halt as a result of the sanctions, they would have to capitulate.

It subsequently turned out that they not only took on all the finale might of Great Britain, but, also, the force of all the great powers of the world. The great powers of the world who, eventually and collectively under the banner of the

United Nations, joined Great Britain in attempting to enforce the embargo with the help of the greatest of them all, the United States of America. This boded ill for the Americans, and it began an unfolding saga that was to end in a United States Government office in Manhattan seventeen years later, when the Treasury Department summoned me to New York from retirement in Florida.

The telephone rang from Salisbury. It was my long time colleague and close friend, Harry Bernard, whom I had met in Shanghai in 1948, and for whom I had worked as his Assistant Manager in Cairo and had been assigned to his staff as his special assistant in Nairobi. He had relieved me in Salisbury only a few months ago as a result of my transfer from Rhodesia to Johannesburg, South Africa. A transfer to South Africa and a responsibility that I was soon loath to have acquired. Unknown to all of us at the time of my transfer, Unilateral Declaration of Independence was looming on the horizon. Harry was unfortunate enough to have taken over the Salisbury office just prior to the momentous announcement of UDI.

Many times the sympathies and political loyalties of United States citizens have been suborned to that of the countries which they have adopted as their own, merely because they have taken up residence there while on an assignment for an international company or in the diplomatic service. Among the most important provisions of legislation that Secretary of State James F.Byrnes initiated in 1946 in his opinion, 'was one that called for more frequent and varied assignments in the United States of the State Department's foreign service. Its purpose was to prevent those 'sentinels' of the United States from losing touch with American life. As he recalled Woodrow Wilson saying, "It is easy to send an American to London or Paris, but it is hard to keep an *American* there". A man who represents his country abroad, no less than the man who represents his people in Congress, needs to return frequently to the "grass roots"'[79].

Possibly the reasons are complex in many instances as to why an individual's loyalties and sympathies can be swayed. In the case of the Rhodesians, it was very easy to pinpoint. The Rhodesians are a most hospitable people. They took you at face value and made no judgments until such time as you gave them cause. They welcomed you into their homes, and in many cases, into their hearts.

Throughout the world there are many people who do not view with favour the position that their own Governments take on certain international situations. Even more than their verbal disagreement with their government's position, they actively attempt to negate their government's stated policy and actions. In the case of the telephone caller, Harry Bernard, who was an American manager of an American international oil company, he was not presently going to propose to clandestinely oppose the policies and actions of his government. He was not going to do so at this time, only because the United States government had not yet taken a position on the embargo.

However, if there is one thing in the international oil business that no one should do, it is to prejudge a position. A position that may or may not be taken by your government; may or may not be taken by the country in which you are operating; may or may not be taken by your Arab supplier of crude oil; and last, but not least by any means, may or may not be taken by your own employer. Discretion being the better part of valour my Managing Director in Cape Town, Dick Wrigley, who had spent many, many years in the international arena, had informed my office that we were to observe the embargo until such time as the situation had been clarified.

'On 16 December 1965 ... the British Prime Minister was sitting in the elegance of the White House. Britain had already decided to introduce an oil embargo. But as Wilson later admitted, sanctions would only be effective if they were 'backed by other countries with big oil interests'. and the British Prime Minister therefore needed US support for his next move against the Smith regime.'[80]

There are a number of reasons given as to why the United States wasn't in favour of sanctions; the predominate one being that the United States Government believed that sanctions were almost impossible to enforce with any certainty. However, there was still another basic reason that the United States had not yet joined Great Britain in support of the general embargo. Many of our so called statesmen in the Senate and House of Representatives had not yet realized how many votes they could garner by 'bashing' helpless and expendable whites in a country whose name they probably had never heard until UDI hit the headlines. What a wonderful way to get votes from the blacks and from the ultra-liberal whites in their constituencies. Anything they did would never increase the loathing that the conservatives had for them anyway. Here was an opportunity fraught with no danger at all. The white settlers in the heart of Africa couldn't vote in the United States. There was no manner in which they could threaten to unseat any member of the Senate or the House.

So, off to the chamber where 'members often displayed a well-developed talent for hypocrisy'.[81] There, they would hold forth at great length and denounce the white settlers. They would tell the world (but it was only the world of their own constituents that they were really addressing—the ones who vote) that they were the great supporters of black aspirations, the great equalizers, the only bulwark against the racists, and they were the blacks only hope of emancipation. An emancipation that seems to have become derailed since the Emancipation Proclamation was first issued. They intended to make it clear that they were the only ones who could be trusted to reissue it. But, of course, only if you voted for them.

The only thing more cynical than the electioneering by these so called statesmen in the House and Senate was when 'America agreed to back the Rhodesian oil embargo in return for British political support for US policy towards Vietnam. President Johnson, a US diplomat commented, could now count on Wilson 'to curb the most extreme demands of Labour backbenchers who were now openly opposed to US policies in Vietnam.'[82]

It is, obviously, easy to see why a person, who is living side by side with those who are treated as expendable for no other reason than the opportunity to garner votes or because of a political trade off between world powers, can suddenly identify with their cause. Harry informed me over the telephone that he had received a delegation from the Government of Rhodesia. The purpose of the visit was to inquire as to how Caltex, in view of the embargo, was going to continue to make supplies of petroleum products available to Rhodesia. Rhodesia's normal means of supply through the port of Lourenço Marques in Mozambique had been shut off by the embargo. As history books inform us, Mozambique, at that time, was a Portuguese colony on the East coast of Africa.

Lourenço Marques was Mozambique's main commercial port and did a thriving business transshipping all kinds of goods to the inland land-locked countries of that part of east Africa. There had, also, been a pipeline built by Lonrho whose Managing Director, Tiny Rowland, was destined to become the subject of more yellow journalism over the years than any other business executive alive. This pipeline was to carry crude oil from Beria on the coast of Mozambique to Umtali in Rhodesia to supply the Central African Petroleum Refineries, Rhodesia's newly built refinery. As in the case of the Iraqi crisis, ports are the easiest means of enforcing embargoes, if one can safely assume that the countries that border its land boundaries also observe the embargo. Harry was inquiring as to how arrangements could be made through the Johannesburg office in South Africa to replace the port of Lourenço Marques as a supply source.

The geography of supplying Rhodesia from South Africa would be a very expensive substitution, indeed, for the Port of Lourenço Marques. It would consist of loading petroleum products such as gasoline, diesel oil and kerosene into large tank trucks in South Africa, after these products had already been transported from Lourenço Marques and then hauling the products overland by road all the way into Rhodesia. In the Port of Lourenço Marques, the giant ocean going tankers tied up along side the piers, and the petroleum products were pumped into huge storage tanks. From these storage tanks, enormous freight trains of tank cars would be filled, and the products would be hauled overland by rail, a very economical means of transporting petroleum products, as is done throughout the world on a daily basis.

However, the economics of 'war' are not cost effective. Although, such a substitution of means of supply would be exorbitantly expensive, no fuel at all would be even more prohibitive, as it would result in the downfall of the white government of Rhodesia. Harry was reluctantly informed that I had been personally advised on the telephone by Dick Wrigley in Cape Town to observe all terms of the embargo imposed by Great Britain on Rhodesia until further notice and clarification.

Harry announced that he would be on the next plane down to Johannesburg to personally discuss the matter. He was cautioned that he was always welcome, but until further instructions had been received from Dick Wrigley, there was no action that could be taken by me to substitute Johannesburg for Lourenço Marques as his source of supply.

He disdainfully informed me that his requirements were so insignificant compared to the volume of business done by the Johannesburg office that Cape Town would never know the difference. His comments were based on the fact that the Johannesburg office was responsible for over fifty percent of all the business handled in South Africa for THE COMPANY. The volume was tremendous. My reply to that statement was that, 'Cape Town may never know, but *I* would know'. That was enough for me to observe the instructions that had been verbally delivered to me over the telephone by Wrigley.

In addition to the fact that it was my Managing Director that had advised me so emphatically to observe the terms of the embargo, Wrigley was the very same individual to whom Harry reported from Salisbury through the principle of 'director-ships'. Here was a man that had already transferred his loyalties from his company and his superior to the white settlers of Rhodesia and had aligned himself with their cause.

In spite of my repeated attempts to convince him that his personal presence in Johannesburg would not alter my position, he dutifully arrived the next morning. There then ensued a long and rather acrimonious discussion regarding the stand that was being taken by me. He reiterated time and time again that my office was the only one in Johannesburg that was not cooperating with the Rhodesian government. The more he repeated this assertion, the more adamant I became that he was badly misinformed by the Rhodesian government.

He, then, told me that in spite of the assurances that he had given to his fellow oil company executives in Salisbury not to reveal the extent of their companies' involvement in supplying Rhodesia, he, reluctantly, would break his word to them. He would do so in order to convince me that my making supplies available to Rhodesia would not be contrary to the general practice that had evolved regarding the supply of petroleum products to Rhodesia subsequent to UDI.

Harry then proceeded to give a lengthy and involved description of just what the oil companies in South Africa were doing to break the embargo. I emphatically, again, assured him that he was entirely mistaken, inasmuch as I had been personally informed by all the oil company managers in Johannesburg that they were scrupulously observing the embargo. In particular, the two British companies, BP and Shell, were most adamant that they were observing the terms of the embargo.

He was, by now, convinced that there was no course of action that he could take to sway my decision. Having reached this conclusion, he carefully withdrew several hand drawn maps from his briefcase. In a lowered voice, he suggested that it might be in mine, as well in Cape Town's interest, to investigate the activities at certain designated areas on the maps. These areas had been pinpointed by what appeared to be newly laid down roads leading to isolated spots in the jungle. Isolated spots far removed not only from habitation of any kind, but also well off the heavily, traveled main roads. He was, again, assured by me that he was entirely mistaken. There was no evidence to doubt the veracity of the management of the other oil companies' statements to me regarding their non-involvement in supplying Rhodesia.

Although, he was issued the usual hospitable invitation of spending the night at my company house, he informed me that he felt there was no reason to take advantage of my offer. Would I please arrange to have him driven him back to the airport as he wanted to return as soon as possible to Salisbury. On arrival at the airport the chauffeur opened the door for my visitor, who then proceeded to disembark. I moved to follow him on to the pavement and into the terminal. "Don't bother," was his angry and deeply hurt response to my usual polite gesture of seeing my visitors off. He turned sharply and left me halfway between the car and the pavement.

This reaction was from a man whom I had met twenty years ago in Shanghai, when we were both very junior members of THE COMPANY. A man for whom I later worked as his second in command in Cairo under the most formidable circumstances, seven days a week and sometimes fifteen and twenty hours a day, finally culminating in an evacuation caused by the French, English and Israeli attack on Egypt. A friend and colleague for whom I thought there was no situation on earth that could break the bonds that had sprung up between us during those desperate times. Strange feelings, indeed, what the vagaries of the international oil business, and the loyalties and divided loyalties of your country and THE COMPANY can cause.

Immediately on returning to the office, a meeting was called of the senior staff members of the Johannesburg office. "Harry Bernard, the General Manager from Salisbury has given me information which is difficult to believe," I stated. "He has informed me that in spite of the assurances that I have received from my fellow managers here in Johannesburg that they are observing the embargo imposed by Great Britain, they are, in fact, breaking it. I find it hard to believe for two reasons. The managers of BP and Shell are personal friends of mine. In addition, not only are the companies British, but BP has a fifty-one percent interest in it owned by the British Government," I concluded naïvely.

"In order to prove that the General Manager of Rhodesia is mistaken, you are all to give priority to establishing that his information is false. And that he has been misled by his fellow oil company executives in Salisbury and by the Rhodesian Government," I instructed them. "Use what ever methods are appropriate in order to obtain the information and report back on a most urgent basis. The localities where you are to make your investigations are indicated here on these various maps. Have the necessary personnel proceed there immediately and report back as soon as they have collected, or not collected as I believe the case to be, the necessary evidence."

"I have repeatedly informed Cape Town that they can be assured that all concerned here in Johannesburg are observing the embargo to the letter of the law." There was one other admonishment. "Choose only your most loyal and experienced personnel. Impress on them the necessity of the fact that they are not to discuss any details of their activities with any of their colleagues in the other oil companies. If any correspondence has to be forwarded, it is to marked 'PERSONAL, PRIVATE and CONFIDENTIAL for the attention of R.PALMER-SMITH ONLY' and delivered by hand. The operation will be known as 'UNCOVER'."

Seventy two hours later. That was all that was necessary. It allowed for travel time, investigation of the sites, return to Johannesburg, development of the film and calling of the meeting to make a presentation of the findings of the select team sent out to investigate the information given to us by Harry. The team's efforts had produced a photographic indictment of the 'embargo busters'.

The pictures were not so remarkable for professionalism or for clarity. What was astounding was the fact that they had been shot in perfect sequence. Laid out in order of the timing with which they had been taken there appeared before your eyes a remarkable chronology of the perfidy of man.

On the one hand, there was a steady stream of tank trucks wending their way down a jungle trail totally hidden from all prying eyes that might have accidentally happened on the scene. All these tank trucks bore the names and trade marks of oil companies which were registered in South Africa. The tank trucks were driven up to the unloading ramps and parked. The ramps had been temporarily set up in the jungle and camouflaged to the best of the ability of the hastily assembled operating staff. The personnel could be seen in the photographs undertaking the various duties assigned to them. Even the still photos gave every indication of their extreme haste in completing their duties.

Coming in from the other direction was a corresponding flow of similar sized tank trucks. There was a striking difference in the appearance of these vehicles. They were totally unmarked, insofar as the names of any oil companies were concerned and painted a dull gray. They, eventually, became known as the 'gray ladies'. The only marks of identification were the Rhodesian license plates on each vehicle which were barely discernable. The unmarked vehicles drove up to the ramps, several loading hoses from the South African trucks were dropped into their manholes and heavy duty pumps commenced pumping immediately. When the unmarked tank trucks had been completely filled, they hastily left the area headed in the Northerly direction from which they had appeared and, quite obviously, returning to Rhodesia.

This then was the 'observance' of the embargo by the South African oil companies with which the company managers in Johannesburg had so emphatically stated to me that they were complying. To say that the evidence was shocking would be a master piece of understatement. As the compromising information lay spread out on my desk in full view of the members of the staff who had obtained it, the telephone rang. It was the Shell Manager. The call had been rung through by my secretary so that he knew to whom he was speaking. "My people have informed me that some members of your staff were seen to be taking pictures of one of our operations. Please be assured that arrangements are in hand for your company to obtain its share of 'the transfer'. There is no reason for you to be concerned," he hastened to assure me.

Fortunately, I was able to keep my voice on an even tone. "First of all let me tell you that my concern is not for 'my share'. We American companies have no such concept in our marketing endeavours. We have a law called the Sherman

Anti-Trust Act which forbids us under criminal penalties to engage in any such activities as you are suggesting," was my reply to his statement. "What concerns me is your outright prevarication that you were observing the embargo. It appears to me that was a deliberate lie. Could you please explain yourself?"

His immediate reaction was to take an offensive position. "You bloody Americans always retire behind some high sounding legal formula whenever there is an international situation on which your government doesn't seem to be able to make up its mind. If we had to wait for your cooperation before assisting our fellow brethren in Rhodesia, the government would have fallen while your bureaucracy still had the matter in committee".

"That statement has no relationship to the false information which you gave me regarding the fact that you were observing the embargo. In addition, the false information that you gave me was forwarded to Cape Town in good faith," was my response to his attempt to justify his actions. "I am requesting that a meeting be called in Cape Town by my Chairman of the Board. I will expect you, and all the other managers in Johannesburg to be there, as well as your superiors in Cape Town." I had no desire to continue the conversation and replaced the handset without even so much as a farewell. The next step was to inform Cape Town of the outcome of our investigations. And further request that an urgent meeting of all Managing Directors in Cape Town be called as soon as possible, with the added request that the Johannesburg managers be there in attendance. This was done and a time was set.

The Managing Directors of all those subsidiaries of the Seven Sisters who were represented in South Africa—Texaco, Chevron, BP, Shell, and Mobil, as well as Total who had a 40% share holding in it owned by the French Government, were present in the Caltex board room. As requested, the managers from Johannesburg had also been summoned by their superiors to be in attendance. Everyone took their places around the board room table and settled into their seats. I nodded my head to gain the attention of my Managing Director, who was chairing the meeting. "Before the meeting opens, and the proceedings are recorded, I would like to make a statement," I announced after being recognized by Dick Wrigley.

"My statement is very basic and very simple," was my beginning comment in a voice that seethed with controlled anger. "What I would like to make most emphatically clear to each and every member of this meeting is that.… there are a number of goddamn liars among you."

There was shocked reaction from everyone present and disbelief on the faces of most of the Cape Town Managing Directors. Before any one of them could regain his composure and attempt to either refute the statement or to justify his position, the Chairman opened the meeting. The opening of the meeting immediately after my accusation effectively ruled out any possible rebuttal. With the meeting now declared 'called to order' all statements made would be recorded. None of the individuals involved wished to have their answers to that particular accusation reproduced.

The pictures, which the Johannesburg staff had so carefully taken, were laid out in front of every member of the meeting. Enough copies had been reproduced to guarantee that the attention of everyone there would be riveted on them. The Chairman merely gestured towards the pictures and suggested, "Since every one at the meeting appears to be involved as can be seen from the pictures, why don't we just go clockwise around the table and listen to the explanations in that order." Needless to say there was considerable squirming and embarrassment on the part of all parties.

The Official Secrets Act of the South African Government was the opening gambit by the first speaker. As the conversation ebbed and flowed around the table, there was no doubt that this was the rationale of all concerned at the meeting. "The Official Secrets Act of the South African Government does not apply to American oil companies," asserted one of the Managing Directors supported in unison by all the other non-American oil company executives. "It is for this reason that the action taken by our Johannesburg managers was not made known to Mr.Palmer-Smith. You would have had to refer it to your government. We felt that it would be better for you to be unaware of the activities involving the supply of petroleum products to an embargoed country."

There were two fallacies in this reasoning. It is, generally, not known to the public (and perhaps consciously not to some of those in the international oil business) that in spite of the very prominent display of American trade marks in the foreign marketing of American products, the local company promoting those sales is a company which has all the characteristics of the nationality of the country in which it is operating. Although the company is known as American by its ancestry, is marketing American brand products and often supported by an even more visible means of identification, an American manager, the company is just as much South African as the South African Oil Company itself. The second, untenable position taken by the 'embargo busters' was that, at this time, the United States Government had not taken a position on the embargo. There was no necessity for us to report any information to the United States Government.

Caltex (Africa) Ltd. was registered in South Africa. It had to obey all South African Government laws, commercial as well as acts such as the Official Secrets

Act. This act is a 'law of survival'. All countries have such legislation under various disguises. It is a law which in effect says, 'It is not necessary for us to have grounds to justify our position. You will carry out our wishes merely because this is the way we want them to be carried out'.

'A Clear and Present Danger.' A black neighbour to the north of South Africa presented 'a clear and present danger'. The South African Government was determined to prevent such a possibility occurring at any cost. True, there were some of the Broderbund living there. Albeit few in number, there were many bonds remaining between them and the Broderbund in South Africa. 'The Broderbund, a group of nationalists, was a secret society which had been formed to counter the Englishmen's power establishment and its network was dedicated to Afrikanerdom. The society had been formed two years after General Hertzog, a hero of the Boer War, had formed his extreme National Party'[83]. There were many who said that it was only in support of the Broderbund that the South African Government decided to back the government of Ian Smith and UDI. The real reason was as clear as *black and white.*

The very well respected ECONOMIST of London had another theory, as they stated in their issue of 23 April 1966 under the caption of:

THE WORLD

International Report

What might make Verwoerd cry chicken

....

Somewhere, it is assumed in Pretoria there is a brink beyond which Mr. Wilson will not go in this game. But Dr. Verwoerd also has his scale of risks and costs. His commitment outside the lager is strictly limited and somewhere for him too there is a brink that he will stop short at. He very much wants Mr. Smith's rebellion to succeed, but not because he thinks this would give him a permanent buffer against the black north (Rhodesia does not follow a policy of true apartheid, so eventual black rule is regarded as inevitable). He wants it because this would permanently discredit sanctions as a method of bringing down unpopular regimes. Accordingly whatever assistance Dr. Verwoerd lends must stop short of placing his own country at risk. It is also very much in his interests to avoid making it apparent to everybody that Rhodesia is surviving only because of South African help. *Far better that the world should gain the impression that it requires only a few cunning businessmen to make sanctions fail.* (emphasis is mine). If Dr Verwoerd were ever to get the

impression that it is Mr. Wilson's intention to bring down the Smith regime at any cost, he would disengage rapidly and completely. He has no desire to involve South Africa in a Rhodesian failure, whatever principles may be at stake.

....

The ECONOMIST was not on the payroll of Dr. Verwoerd, as was the South African Afrikaner press. The ECONOMIST might have actively promoted the theory of *cunning businessmen* which they attributed to Dr. Verwoerd, because they actually believed it. There was nobody else who was involved in the activities, or were simply passive observers, of the 'embargo busting international subsidiaries' of the Seven Sisters that could possibly buy the theory that *cunning businessmen* were the reason that sanctions wouldn't work. Perhaps, in another part of the world, this theory might hold, but in a police state, such as South Africa, it just didn't hold water, or in this case, oil.

The Seven Sisters' subsidiaries were captives of the South African Government. Just as The Seven Sisters, themselves, were '… destined to become completely subservient to their host government,' as Walter Levy, an independent oil consultant in New York and later adviser to all Seven Sisters, pointed out when writing in *Foreign Affairs* in 1971[84]. Mr. Levy's comments were brought about by the necessity of The Seven Sisters being faced with the major decision of 'to what extent and for how long they can be held hostage by their resource interests in producing countries …'[85] At the time of the Arab oil embargo against the West in late 1973, 'the control of the producing countries over the international oil companies had become so complete that American and Dutch owned companies had no choice but to become the instruments for the embargo on oil shipments to their own home countries'[86].

In the case of the Seven Sisters, there may have been a place for them in the international oil business if they were to decide to confront their host governments in the producing countries. In the case of their subsidiaries in South Africa, there was no such choice. 'If you couldn't beat them, you *had* to join them' or perish, as the South African Government made quite clear in their application of the Official Secrets Act.

What ever the reason, Caltex was caught squarely in the middle of an international incident of blockade busting. This was amply evidenced by the assembled personage around the board room table. Caught in the middle, not on legal grounds since THE COMPANY was observing the embargo, but caught in the middle of what was already proving to be a marketing war. If Caltex did nothing to assist Rhodesia to obtain its supply of petroleum products during the embargo, THE COMPANY could be assured that after the embargo was over, they would never be allowed to regain their share of the market under the existing government. Undeniably, the likelihood was unmistakable that THE COMPANY would be de-registered by the Rhodesian Government if Ian Smith remained in power.

In all fairness to Harry Bernard, he repeatedly emphasized this point during our discussions. Also, in spite of the protestations of the Shell Manager in Johannesburg concerning his position that Caltex would have had to refer the proposed plan to break the embargo to the United States Government, it was now becoming very apparent that he was well aware of the increased market share in which his activities had resulted. It was only after he knew that his actions had been exposed that he had offered to share the so called 'transfer', but only on a 'post discovery' basis. By that time, he had acquired a substantial increase in market share as had BP also. Dick Wrigley in Cape Town had recognized this possibility immediately as an ancillary cause for the embargo busting in the first instance. By leaving Caltex out of their proposed plans, the embargo busters would guarantee they would enhance their market position by the amount lost by Caltex.

The finale speaker in the board room finished mumbling some vague reasons to defend himself as to why he had lied in his teeth about not breaking the embargo and the meeting closed. The board room door swung shut after the last member of the meeting had exited. By this time, Wrigley was seething with the same rage that had engulfed me, when I had first viewed the pictures taken by the Johannesburg team that had been sent out to investigate the sites pin-pointed on Harry's maps.

He turned to me and said savagely, "We'll put the sons of bitches of this goddamn, prevaricating oil industry in South Africa on notice that this will be the last time that they will ever attempt to screw Caltex. We'll do it in a way that will make them understand why we did it, and, also, we will do it where it will hurt them the most, or at least where they will *think* it is going to hurt them the most." He paused and in ominous tones continued, "We will make an offer to the Rhodesian Government at a below cost discount if the Rhodesian Government will agree to make Caltex their sole supplier," he stated.

Wrigley's tactics suited me perfectly, but I had been mad long enough now so that rage was not the only emotion governing me. I thought that 'reason' was an aspect that should be considered under the circumstances. I was afraid that Wrigley, on the spur of the moment, had allowed his emotions to overcome his reason and had let his anger run away with him. One should never make this kind of mistake in judgment, when dealing with your superior who had spent years in the international oil arena dueling with his competitors and various governments and was a canny and extremely skilled negotiator.

I jumped in with both feet. I attempted to caution him by stating that it would be a most unfortunate position in which to be identified, if Caltex were to be the sole supplier of petroleum products to an embargoed country. I got my just desserts for doubting his keen instincts with his immediate response.

"As usual Robert, you aren't listening. I said, 'where it will hurt them the most, *or at least where they will think it is going to hurt them the most*'. Within an hour after we make the offer, the moles that Shell and BP have in the government offices in Rhodesia will have reported the offer to their handlers in Shell and BP in Salisbury. They, in turn, will be on the telephone to their head offices in Cape Town and within minutes my phone will be ringing off the hook. When I decide to answer, I will let them know, in no uncertain terms, the reason for our offer. I will stall long enough to make them sweat and then, reluctantly, agree to withdraw the offer. By that time, the Rhodesian Government will have turned us down, but our friends in Shell and BP will believe that it was my agreement with them that terminated the offer."

Although, I had been bloodied because I hadn't been listening according to Dick, I again jumped in with both feet, and asked if it were possible that the Rhodesian Government might accept our offer and not turn it down. I got my just desserts again.

"You not only don't listen Robert, but you must be terribly naïve as well. You can't really believe that any government in its right mind would ever make itself hostage to a sole supplier and, particularly, a government in the world's spotlight such as Rhodesia is. No government ever puts all its eggs in one basket, no matter how much they might like the price. The Rhodesian Government will go through the polite procedure of telling us that they have seriously considered our offer, but under the present circumstances they are not in a position to accept it. By that time our goddamn, lying, fellow members of the oil industry will have received the message from me that Caltex is out of bounds when they next decide to screw someone. Call Harry when you get back to Johannesburg and tell him I want him in Cape Town immediately. As soon as we work out how we are going to handle the offer, either through him or your office, I'll have him stop off in Johannesburg on his way back to Salisbury and he can let you have all the details and the method we intend to use."

I may have been naïve when I posed the question to Dick as to the possibility that the Rhodesians might accept our offer. Never, in Dick's wildest imagination, could he have considered how desperate the Rhodesian Government was to cut the overwhelming costs of obtaining their petroleum products from South Africa. The first part of Dick's scenario ran exactly true to form. Within hours after our offer had been made to the Rhodesian Government, the telephone wires to Dick's office were burning up the atmosphere. When Dick was through delivering his message to the 'embargo busters', they were left with no illusions as to what would happen to them, if they ever again in the future tried to grab Caltex's share of the market through brazen lying.

Whoever coined the term 'embarrassment of riches' could not have, conceivably, been able to envisage what the depth of that embarrassment entailed when the Rhodesian Government seriously took our offer under consideration. The Bingham report covered this fiasco when it stated that, 'In June 1966 Caltex South Africa had apparently offered to supply Rhodesia with oil at a discount—on one condition that the company acquired a monopoly as Rhodesia's sole supplier (B5.92).... this offer was later withdrawn much to the anger of the Rhodesians....'[87]

There were only three people privy to the reason as to why the offer had been made; Dick, Harry and myself. Neither Mr.Bingham, QC, who had been commissioned by the English Parliament to investigate the sanctions busting, nor the Rhodesian Government were part of that trio.

There was no way that the Rhodesian Government could hold us to our offer under the circumstances which faced them as an outcast on the world scene. We were too horrified to even think about the consequences for us, if we were to honour our offer. Consequently, we choose the lesser of the two evils by forgetting our honour and reneging on our offer, rather than having to fulfill the obligations contained in it.

After the fact, there was considerable speculation that both the South African Government and the Rhodesian Government were, due to their commonwealth association, initially in discussions with the British companies and not the American ones. It was believed that the two governments were concerned, not with *who* supplied Rhodesia with petroleum products, but only *that it be supplied*. In addition, the speculation was rife that the original contacts had been by the South African and the Rhodesian Governments with BP and Shell in Salisbury. BP and Shell in Salisbury, in turn, contacted their respective offices in South Africa, just as Harry had contacted me after the Rhodesian Government made its desires clear to him.

It wasn't until it appeared that the embargo could be enforced by the principle of 'conditional selling' did the South African Government actually enter the scene on its own home turf. Had the South African Government decided that the embargo would be enforced, not one gallon of petroleum products would ever have crossed the border between South Africa and Rhodesia, no matter how many '*cunning businessmen*' were involved.

Such speculation carried ominous overtones. What position had the two British Government directors on BP's Board of Directors taken on a matter that, by any vestige of reasonable business acumen, had to be referred to the Board in London by their South African subsidiary? I was fully aware that Wrigley constantly consulted with the New York Board of Caltex Petroleum Corporation, inasmuch as he was repeatedly on the telephone with me in connection with those discussions.

It is possible, but extremely unlikely, that BP in South Africa did not inform their London board in the very beginning regarding the extent of their involvement. But after a very short time, when all the international press was reporting on the progress, or lack of progress, of the embargo, it would have been impossible not to have consulted with them. If they hadn't contacted them initially or even at a later date, then the BP Board in London, particularly the two Government Directors, was in serious dereliction of its duties. The Board should have demanded a full explanation of their subsidiary's position in South Africa vis-à-vis the embargo. Barring a satisfactory explanation, the Board should have sent its own representatives to South Africa to confirm or deny their subsidiary's reports.

When Churchill in 1914, through '... the Admiralty agreed to pay two million pounds for fifty-one percent of BP, the agreement stipulated that the Company must always remain an independent British concern, and that every director must be a British subject. The Government would appoint two directors who would have the right of veto, and they assured the company that the veto would only be exercised on questions of foreign or military policy, or on matters directly bearing on Admiralty contracts'[88]. Although BP, as one of The Seven Sisters, has been known by that name for decades, actually in 1914 'The British Government bought a controlling interest in Anglo-Persian Oil Company, which from then on operated in Iran on terms much more favourable to the British than to the Iranians'[89]

If ever that agreement should have been applied and that veto cast and sustained, it was during the British Government's embargo of Rhodesia. But then BP would have gone out of business in South Africa, a very, very, profitable market.

Where were the two British Government directors during the 'embargo busting'? Their appointment to the BP Board, as stipulated in the purchase agreement by the Admiralty in 1914, was made by the British Government for the express purpose of representing the British Government's interest on foreign or military policy. Very painfully and obviously, these two British Government Directors had abdicated that responsibility. And what was the background of the other twelve directors? And where did their basic loyalties lie?

'In 1974 the fourteen directors included six peers, including (as one of the government directors) the former head of the Foreign Office, Lord Greenhill; an ex-head of the Bank of England, Lord Cobbold, an ex-chief of the Defense Staff, Lord Elworthy, and an ex-ambassador to Moscow, Lord Trevelyan.' Some of these directors may not have been on the Board at the start of the embargo, although Lord Greenhill was, but their predecessors surely had the same look of 'a miniature House of Lords'[90].

None of the twelve non-government directors was bound to invoke the veto as laid down in the agreement at the time of the Admiralty's purchase of fifty-one percent of BP in 1914. Surely, however, there must have existed a remnant of loyalty by some of them to a government that had so richly rewarded them in public honours as well as remuneratively. Apparently not so. Here was a Board of Directors of a majority owned British Government oil company actively negating the stated political aims of its majority owner, the British Government.

In the case of the two Directors appointed by the British Government, they should have been brought to trial and accused of treason by the British Government. The outcome of any trial is always subject to the whims and whimsies of the jurors. However, the writer is well aware that, barring outright perjury by the employees of the South African subsidiary of BP, the only verdict the jury could find would have to be one of 'guilty', with a sentence of a jail term to be appropriately determined by the magistrate. In time of war, they would have been shot for their activities. Certainly, if the British Government for its own political reasons wished to avoid public disclosure of the activities of their two representatives, the very least they should have done was to strip them of their public honours and revoke their pensions.

During the meeting, there appeared to be no doubt in anyone's mind that the South African Government had indeed made its position clear to even the most faint hearted of the international oil company executives, particularly, the Americans. 'Rhodesia will be supplied with all its needs as far as petroleum products are concerned'.

If there had been any uncertainty in the Americans' minds before the meeting, the British managers delivered the South African Government's message to us personally. 'If you find it impossible to accommodate us in this way,' was the government's position, 'perhaps you will find a more hospitable country in which to continue your operations. This will leave the field to those who know and understand the meaning and the force of our Official Secrets Act.'

Just as the Seven Sisters were to fall captive to their producer countries in the future, their subsidiaries had now fallen captive to the South African Government.

And just as the Arabs had sat at the knee of their learned British masters to become proficient in the art of embargoes, so had the South Africans sat at the knee of their compatriots, the Americans, in order to understand the art of 'conditional selling'. Having understood it, they were prepared to defeat it. It was in World War II that 'conditional selling' first reared its ugly head. No doubt, a study of commercial history would show that other instances of conditional selling could be found. There is never a first time.

The commodity involved in conditional selling during World War II was much more plebeian, however, than petroleum products. Many will remember the atrocious quality, as well as the quantity (twelve bottles of vinegary wine) that had to be purchased as a 'condition' during the war years in order to enjoy one single bottle of Scotch. Scotch was in very short supply in the United States at that time. The Germans were no respecters of the discerning taste of the Americans. They continued to sink all shipping to and from Great Britain whatever the cargo the vessels carried, including that rare merchandise, excellent Scotch whiskey.

As soon as the art of 'conditional selling' became known to the American government during the war, it was immediately outlawed. Outlawed the world learned from the American's example. As an art, it was well remembered. The decision to outlaw it in the future, if circumstances ever required it, was, also, carefully recorded in many governments' archives throughout the world. It, certainly, was well remembered by the South African Government in connection with the sale of petroleum products in South Africa during the British, and later, the American and UN embargo of Rhodesia. This knowledge allowed the South African Government to pre-empt any attempt to invoke 'conditional selling' by any of the oil companies as a means of implementing the embargo.

'There will be no conditional selling,' trumpeted the South African Government.

Conditional selling, in spite of the fact that it is against the law, is allegedly a permanent marketing tool of the international oil companies and their subsidiaries. Wholesale customers, who enjoy huge discounts because of the large volume purchased by them, are forbidden to resell the products purchased by them to any outsider. Any fuels bought by them have to be consumed on their premises or by their company owned vehicles. They could sell to their own employees, but not to anyone not associated with their business. In the very beginning, it appeared to Wrigley that there existed a large loophole through which the South Africans could aid their brethren to the North. Those who intended to break the embargo could sell to South African companies, who in turn would resell to the Rhodesians.

Wrigley had initially discussed with me the possibility of using conditional selling as a means to enforce the embargo in South Africa. Our program envisaged limiting not only the quantity that could be bought, based on the history of the customer's previous volume of purchases, but the customer could not re-sell the product to anyone else after purchasing it from us. This prohibition on reselling would be in force, even if the history of the volume of prior purchases wasn't exceeded. Unfortunately for our plans, however, clear and concise instructions covering the meaning of the Official Secrets Act, in regard to conditional selling, were spelled out very meticulously by the South African Government.

Basically these instructions could be condensed into three articles of faith:

One: No oil company operating in South Africa will refuse to sell petroleum products to any South African company.

Two: There will be no restrictions on the amount of product to be sold to any South African company.

Three: There will be no conditions attached to the products delivered to such South African companies, particularly, with reference to any restrictions on resale or the finale destination of the products.

Unlike the BP Board in London, who allegedly turned a blind eye to their subsidiary's actions, the Caltex Board sent an independent team of their own to South Africa. The team's terms of reference were to personally discuss all aspects of the traffic of petroleum products between South Africa and Rhodesia. This team was sent out to South Africa in spite of the constant contact maintained with the Caltex Board in New York from South Africa by Wrigley on the telephone.

The decision by Caltex Petroleum Corporation in New York to have their own people personally review the matter was, undoubtedly, occasioned by a second article in the same issue of the Economist of April 23, 1966:

'… But there has been one significant change since March. Then most of the running was being made by the subsidiaries of two British oil companies and one French company. Though the tankers were repainted, their registration numbers showed that most of them belonged to British Petroleum, Shell or Total (and they were seen and photographed filling up at BP, Shell and Total depots in the Northern Transvaal). But this is no longer the case. The British companies seem to have fallen out of it now and been replaced mainly by the American company Caltex. The fact that there has been a change could indicate that there has been some successful persuasion exercised through the British companies.

The change in the 'visible' supply from the British companies to Caltex was, merely, due to our late arrival on the scene. It was in no way due to any 'successful persuasion' through the British companies. We were only picking up the inefficient and unwanted pieces of the operation occasioned by the South African Government's decree that no oil company in South Africa will refuse to sell to a South African company.

By this time, we knew that our sophisticated British friends had long since allegedly graduated back to the much more economical method of tank car loadings. Fred Hardy, the Caltex Manager from Lourenço Marques, was a frequent visitor to my office as he would often stop over en route to Cape Town or on his return from there. He related hair raising tales of clandestine activities in the rail yards in Lorenço Marques during the pitch of night, when the destination tank car loading documentation on the rail cars would be surreptitiously changed from South Africa to Rhodesia.

These tank car loadings take place well out of the causal public's eye on railroad sidings which, generally, can be securely barricaded with high fences and other security measures. Careful policing would make it difficult for anyone to accurately obtain information on such activities. In spite of all the security measures in South Africa, however, the enterprising London Sunday Telegraph headlined their findings on February 19, 1967 complete with a detailed map. They showed, not only the newly built Rhodesian Government depot, but, in addition, with irritating accuracy as well, they pin pointed the exact location of what they labeled as a *SECRET FARM* on the map, and which they said was a Caltex operation.

Rhodesia Builds Oil Depot in S.Africa

BY OUR COMMONWEALTH AFFAIRS STAFF

The South African Government has allowed the Smith regime to build its own oil supply depot on South African soil to beat the United Nations oil embargo. The huge depot, which was completed recently near Messina, a small town 10 miles from the Rhodesian border, is now supplying Rhodesia with over 700,000 gallons of petrol and other fuels a week. Bulk storage tanks are surrounded by security wire with a notice "The Swiftlee Depot, Box 15, Messina." This is a "front name" for Genta, the Rhodesian Government's organization responsible for oil supplies. On checking the postal address it was found that Box 15 is registered under the name Genta. Previously Caltex, an American oil company, had been supplying most of Rhodesia's petrol by road from a rendezvous on a lonely farm about 300 miles south of the border and 11 miles north of Pretoria. The transfer of oil from Caltex road tankers to unmarked 5,000-gallon road tankers under contract from South African transport firms to Genta, was planned like a military operation. Big underground tanks were sunk and camouflaged among thick trees off a sandy road about half a mile from the main road to Rhodesia.

Camp abandoned

Day and night the unmarked tankers pulled into the camp to rest crews, load and start the long costly journey of 600 miles to Bulawayo. At night marked Caltex tankers from the company's Pretoria depot would swing off the main road through trees and offload into the camp's underground tanks or transfer fuel directly into the waiting unmarked tankers. Aviation fuel, supplied by another American company, Mobil Oil, was run from the Mobil depot at Jan Smuts International airport Johannesburg, to storage tanks at Bulawayo. The oil camp was abandoned in recent weeks, and the South African unmarked tankers are now based at the new Rhodesian-owned depot at Messina. The new system will cut the high costs the Smith regime had to pay for road transport from Pretoria to Bulawayo.

Border survey

About 20 8,000 gallon railway tankers, dispatched from South African ports or the Johannesburg oil pipe-line outlet, are arriving daily at the Genta depot at Messina. The fuels are then pumped into Genta's huge static tanks and later loaded into the unmarked road tankers. From the depot the oil is carried by road 10 miles to the border post and then another 79 mile to the nearest Rhodesian railway siding at Rutenga, where it is again transferred into railway tankers. Tankers with Rhodesian registration numbers are also crossing the border to the Genta depot to supplement the oil lift. At least one belongs to the Shell Oil Co. A sur-

vey at the border shows about 21 tankers, carrying 110,000 gallons, are passing over Beit Bridge every 24 hours.

So much for the respected ECONOMIST's theory that Dr. Verwoerd was trying to promote the concept that only a few *'cunning businessmen'* are required to give the world the impression that sanctions can be made to fail. Perhaps, the ECONOMIST should have confirmed their theory with Dr. Verwoerd before rushing into print with an appearance of superior knowledge; an appearance of superior knowledge that they hoped would help to sell their publication.

"You can't be serious," was my comment to the South African Manager of Operations as the work order crossed my desk in Johannesburg. "You're telling me that a Johannesburg bus company customer, who owns three busses, has requested that we install one hundred thousand gallons of storage at his premises, and further more, those premises have been moved to a country farm?" A few rapid mental calculations, and it was obvious that the initial fill of one hundred thousand gallons after the installation was complete would last well over an entire year.

The name of the bus company suddenly set off bells clanging in my head. "Isn't that the same company whose checks for payment of their previous deliveries bounced, and not only bounced once, but the same check bounced a number of times?," was my query. The operations manager assured me that payment would present no problem. In support of his position, he had brought the Fiscal Manager with him, another South African.

The Fiscal Manager, a man not easily persuaded as to a customer's credit worthiness, lent his endorsement to the operations manager's. He very happily declared, "Not only is there no danger of not being paid for deliveries, but, in effect, they have already been paid for as we hold an unlimited, open letter of credit."

An open letter of credit is the dream of every oil company manager. It meant that for any and all deliveries payment would be made by the bank on which the letter of credit had been drawn. It meant no sleepless nights. The money was already there. It only remained to be drawn, when the value of the products delivered to the customer was verified to the bank's satisfaction by the confirmed invoices. The delight that such news evoked caused common sense to be submerged in the euphoria of having a doubtful customer to whom credit didn't have to be granted. The euphoria, also, left the most important question not asked, which common sense would have immediately dictated.

'Where did a company, that only a short time ago couldn't cover its checks sufficiently enough to keep them from bouncing several times, obtain the collateral to open an unlimited letter of credit for hundreds of thousands of gallons of gasoline?'

Perhaps, just as important in a different vein were the questions, 'what was a small bus company going to do with one hundred thousand gallons of storage, and why had they changed their basis of operation from their old bus depot in town to a country operation on a farm?'

Instinctively, it was better to avoid the latter questions. The Official Secrets Act and conditional selling were very raw nerves in our being at the time. However, in avoiding the questions of what was a small bus company going to do with one hundred thousand gallons of storage and, furthermore, such storage to be located in the country, neither was the former question posed. How did the same, small bus company produce the collateral necessary to open a letter of credit of the magnitude necessary to pay for these huge quantities? Not that the letter of credit was in doubt. After all, the Fiscal Manager had vouched for it. It was the sudden affluence of a doubtful payer that should have engendered questions as to from where his new found wealth had come.

If only that question had been asked. As it later transpired, the letter of credit had not been drawn by the bus company. Why didn't the Fiscal Manger point out who was paying for the products? In all the subsequent, legal maneuvering with the Treasury Department of the United States Government, the question always asked by them was, 'To whom were you selling the products?' Never was the question asked, 'Who was paying for the products?'

As white South Africans, whose sympathies lay with their white brethren to the North, the South African employees of Caltex, obviously, would never have made the point to an American manger of 'who was paying for the products'. The American manager would have had to refer the answer to that question to his superior in Cape Town, who, in turn, would have had to refer it to the United States Government, inasmuch as the United States had joined the UN on the embargo at that time. The entire case of the Treasury Department of the United States Government fell by the wayside, because they, also, did not ask that vitally important and fundamental question of 'who was paying for the products'. Seventeen years later in a Manhattan government office, the Treasury Department still had the opportunity to ask that question, but they didn't. The question of 'how the products were being paid for' did arise at one time.

Cape Town informed us that the company attorney from New York was arriving in Johannesburg, and we were to answer any questions he posed. At this time, the situation had become critical. The United States Government had informed the British Prime Minister that it was going to join Great Britain and the UN in enforcing the embargo and had done so. Just as United States citizens are subject to United States taxation in whatever country they are employed, so are they subject to the long arm of United States law no matter where they operate.

It was decided that clarification should be sought as to just what information should be given to the company attorney. Particularly in view of the fact that such information could possibly be in contravention of the Official Secrets Act, which specifically prohibited the passing of any information concerning the security of South Africa to non-South African nationals. Even though the United States Government had joined the embargo, to the best of my knowledge THE COMPANY was, technically, not in breach of any United States Government laws.

Caltex (Africa) Ltd., which was registered in South Africa, had to obey the South African Government's Official Secrets Act in regard to not refusing to sell petroleum products to any South African company. Considerable anxiety, however, was expressed by the South African executives on the staff over the visit of the New York attorney. They were extremely concerned that by giving information to an 'outsider', they, as South Africans, could conceivably be contravening that very same Official Secrets Act.

Clarification was sought by use of the telex, because long distance telephone connections in South Africa, at that time, were difficult to make on short notice. Even more importantly, the telex also provided a paper trail of all electronic conversations. A paper trail which acted as documentary evidence. Documentary evidence, also known as 'cover your ass', a most important ingredient during these perilous times. The question submitted to Cape Town was, "Should all, repeat, all information be made known to the company attorney in response to any questions that he may ask?".

The answer, as recorded by the telex, was in the affirmative. 'Yes, any and all information,' was the actual reply.

The company attorney arrived in the office after being picked up from the airport and checking into the President Hotel in Johannesburg. Surprisingly, he had a visitor with him whom he introduced as his personal attorney from an outside law firm; This is a nicety in the law. If a company attorney is made aware of certain information he has obtained from another company employee, it is not client-attorney privileged information, because the attorney works for THE COMPANY and not for his fellow employee. If, however, the company attorney has his personal attorney with him, then, the information is privileged and does not have to be divulged in a court of law. A fine point, and also the reason why it was possible to disclose all information regarding our activities. Activities, which I believed were, in essence, generally avoiding the contravention of the Official Secrets Act of the South African Government and still complying with the sanctions imposed by the United States Government through the UN.

After having tea served and making the visitors comfortable, they were queried about the purpose of their visit. The company attorney asked if he could see certain documents—if such documents actually existed. His tone of voice indicated that it was most unlikely that such pieces of paper could conceivably still exist at this time. Unfortunately, they did exist. There were no paper shredders in our Watergate complex. One of his requests was for the copies of the paid invoices of the bus company at whose premises we had installed the one hundred thousand gallons of storage at a outlying farm. The other was for the expense account of Wilhelm Loew, a South African employee of the Johannesburg branch. Both requests had an air of unreality about them, except for a very central theme.

The paid invoices, which had been settled by that infamous letter of credit, were the ones that represented the bus company's suddenly increased requirements of hundreds of thousands of gallons of fuel. The other was even more bizarre. Why would the expense account of a South African employee, Wilhelm Loew, of the Johannesburg office be of any interest to a New York attorney of Caltex Petroleum Corporation?

Could it be, perhaps, because the employee was on detached duty from the Johannesburg office in South Africa and was serving in Rhodesia? And half of his expenses were being paid by the Rhodesian Government and the balance by the Johannesburg office. Not necessarily 'embargo busting', but a very thin line of intent that might easily be breached.

It was still extremely nerve wracking to read, even though it was many, many years later that, 'Caltex Rhodesia, for instance, borrowed a District Manger from the Johannesburg office of Caltex South Africa who knew the Transvaal intimately and, speaking Afrikaans, was able to tap every possible source of supply in the area.' This disclosure was published in the Bingham Report and quoted by Martin Bailey in his book 'OILGATE, The Sanctions Scandal'[91]. No doubt Wilhem Loew, that very same district manager from Johannesburg to whom the reference was made, and whom I had personally released from his local duties, proudly showed his children the published accolades of his loyalty to the Broderbund in Rhodesia.

The requested pieces of paper were obtained by my secretary and handed by her to the company attorney. He and his personal attorney examined them in microscopic detail. When he was finished, he gestured toward the voluminous pile of paid invoices and causally commented that in view of the substantial sums of money involved with such a large customer had we ever experienced any difficulty with payment? He had seen many years of service with THE COMPANY and was fully aware of the frequent times that it was necessary for us to use legal action to effect payment from some of our larger and better customers.

With a certain degree of smugness, I informed him that we hadn't. We (although the royal 'we' was a bit of an ex-exaggeration as I had had nothing to do with it—but it never hurts to let the legal department know how smart you are), we had obtained an open, unlimited letter of credit from the customer. With a slight smile, he commented that was nice to know for a change. As an after thought, he suggested that just as a matter of curiosity, he would like to see the letter of credit. He commented that with all his years of pursuing delinquent customers he hadn't seen too many open, unlimited letters of credit. The fiscal director was telephoned and asked to procure it, which he did, and when he arrived he handed it to the company attorney.

He and his personal attorney again bent their efforts to examining it in microscopic detail. He politely returned it to the fiscal director, and asked if he could request a favour of my secretary. He was assured that he was perfectly free to do so, and she was dutifully called back. He handed her his airline ticket and that of his attorney's and requested her to change their departure from three days hence to the next morning. He also requested her to change their booking at the President Hotel from a three night stay to a departure in the morning. When she had left the room to carry out his requests, he was questioned as to what had precipitated his sudden change in arrangements. His reply was very short, but quite emphatic.

"I had expected the enquiry to take three days of investigation. It didn't seem possible that the documents for which I asked actually existed, as well as the letter of credit of which I was totally unaware. Since, however, they do exist, it is not necessary for me to do any further investigation. It would only represent overkill. There is, however, one very strong recommendation that I would make to you and your superior in Cape Town after seeing these documents. In the future, if you ever contemplate entering into an arrangement of this kind, hire an attorney first before you finalize any such commitment. Even more importantly, make sure that he is a crooked attorney, because no honest attorney would ever go along with it."

As he and his companion departed to return to their hotel, I turned to the Fiscal Manager and suggested in very deliberate tones that he might just enlighten me as to the exact significance of the letter of credit. The expense account of the employee from the Johannesburg branch, who was serving in Rhodesia, did not need any further lurid exposé of just what the implications of such a situation represented. And I was well aware of the gray area represented by the company's confirmed, paid invoices showing that we were delivering those immense quantities to a South African transport company which owned only three buses.

The Fiscal Manager handed me the letter of credit without so much as uttering a word. He, also, studiously avoided looking me in the eye. I glanced at the document. Again, as had happened before during crucial times of service in the international oil arena, my blood congealed as if I had suddenly become submerged in a sub-zero pool of liquid.

The letter of credit had not been drawn by the bus company. It had been drawn by the Government of Rhodesia.

The Fiscal Manager's face immediately, and in startling contrast, took prominence over the vision of all those senior officers of THE COMPANY. The ones who had convinced me during my pre-employment interviews that the life of an international oil executive was going to be one of 'ease and comfort'. I stared at him in total disbelief. It was he who, now, caused that constant, recurring thought to grip my whole being.

IS ASSASSINATION A VIABLE ALTERNATIVE!

For the entire period of time during which we had been making deliveries to the South African Bus Company, we had been receiving payment for the deliveries directly from the white government of Ian Smith in Rhodesia. Inconceivable? How can it happen? Happen it did. The whys and wherefores are now ancient history. Hopefully, we can learn from history, but if that famous saying is as true today as it was when it was first uttered, we know that 'the only thing we learn from history is that we learn nothing from history'.

With the Official Secrets Act firmly entrenched in our minds, and the illegality of conditional selling just as firmly ingrained in all oil company executives' minds, supplies to Rhodesia were put on a much more economical and rational basis. Freight car loadings ordered by South African companies had replaced to a great degree the fugitive operations in the jungle. The wild and exuberant buying by a three bus company operation slowly faded. That is not to say that the gray ladies disappeared altogether. There were service stations just across the border that profited handsomely by buying in South Africa at low prices and selling in Rhodesia at the higher prices mandated by the government.

The higher, government mandated prices had been averaged out to cover the cost of supplying even the most remote parts of Rhodesia. These high prices had been necessary in order to compensate for the greater cost of obtaining product through South Africa. They were universally set for the whole of Rhodesia. As always, there were profiteers on both sides of the border who were willing to capitalize on the 'war' conditions existing between Rhodesia and the rest of the world.

Life went on and Rhodesia was left to itself. UDI had made an indelible impact on the international community as well on the relationships of the white and black countries of Africa. It had, also, stretched the bonds of friendship of various individuals in the international oil business, some of which were never able to weather the strain. The 'old boy' affinity never did regain its solid standing. Rhodesia was something you read about in the newspapers now. It was not something that broke your day to day routine activities. Or so it seemed in the aftermath of that hectic transition from normal supply prior to UDI, to fugitive supply immediately subsequent to UDI, and finally to organized supply.

There was a call from Pretoria my secretary advised me breathlessly. Why breathlessly? A call from Pretoria was fairly routine. THE COMPANY had a rather large office and supply depot there. It was not unusual to hear from them. Perhaps, slightly unusual for the call to go directly to the manager's office, but, then, there were senior men there who were not adverse to speaking to the manager on the occasions that demanded it. Why 'breathlessly' was made clear in the next breath, because the call was not from the Caltex depot.

"The call is from the Minister of Justice's office in Pretoria. It is the Minister himself," she gasped. Was the secretary breathless? So was the manager. After making the usual polite, social exchanges, the Minister asked if it were possible for me to come to Pretoria. If so, when would it be convenient? In the army, the sergeant yells orders and the general makes requests, but the effect is the same. Everyone jumps.

It is difficult to explain to fellow Americans, one's reactions to a call from the Minister of Justice in a country where the Minister of Justice wields the power of life and death. That is not to say that the office of the Minister of Justice in South Africa was a junior KGB, but there would be many that would be hard put upon to tell you the difference. "Yes sir! Anytime you say sir! This afternoon sir! Now sir!"

"Well, if this afternoon isn't an imposition, it would be appreciated if you could arrange to be here immediately after lunch, say at one o'clock?" Whose lunch was he talking about? Certainly not mine. Pretoria was at least an hour's drive and to be there at one o'clock meant forgoing lunch entirely.

"Yes, sir! That would be most convenient."

If one is conditioned by the movie industry to expect certain impressions to be confirmed by real life when the situation arrives, it is only because the movie industry has gone to great pains to make its screen presentations as realistic as possible. The Minister's office, or to be more accurate the Minister's room, since it was no more than a room, conformed to exactly what you would expect of the KGB. There were only four pieces of furniture, the Minister's desk, two chairs—his and a visitor's—and a large wooden file cabinet which would have passed for a cupboard in the eighteen hundreds. The only window in the room was placed high in the wall directly behind the Minister, and as the movie establishment had accurately depicted, it was barred. The walls were white washed, slightly gray from neglect. The whole atmosphere made you wonder how in the world had you ever let THE COMPANY place you in such a forbidding atmosphere under such calamitous conditions.

Your mind was already running wild with the conviction that conditions were going to be calamitous. They had to be. Everything about the situation indicated that it was not normal for the Minister of Justice of a police state to request the presence of an American manger of an international oil company to come to his office on the spur of the moment. That it was not the spur of the moment only became very clear as the meeting progressed.

If ever that constant, recurring thought of assassination crossed my mind with profound implications, it certainly did now, as I envisaged that life of 'ease and comfort' that those senior officers of THE COMPANY had painted so vividly for my benefit. Not only that illusory life of 'ease and comfort' appeared to be fast disappearing, but even the ability to be at liberty to enjoy its non-existence seemed to be slipping dangerously out of my grasp.

The Minister attempted to put me at ease by inquiring if the drive to Pretoria had been uneventful and whether or not there had been any difficulty in finding his office. His attempt was entirely futile. It only served to induce me to think that he was preparing the way for some unheard of assault on my liberty.

On the contrary. He informed me that he would be very appreciative if I could do a personal favour for him. "Certainly," was my immediate response. "How is it possible for a poor, American manager of a small company in South Africa to be in a position to help one of the most powerful men in the Republic?" I asked. His response, under ordinary circumstances, would have caused the listener to assume that the request was the normal procedure of using one's influence to get jobs for the faithful. It appeared that he had two friends that were badly in need of employment. He thought that with my company being so large and employing so many people, he hoped that it would be possible for me to place them with Caltex.

The staff of the Johannesburg branch had shrunk from over six hundred to barely three hundred, just after my arrival, due to judicious pruning of deadwood ably assisted by a head hunting team from New York, plus early retirements and just plain firings under my tutorship. Nevertheless, there was always room for two more; certainly for two of the Minister's friends. "What are their names and what is the field of expertise of the Minister's friends," I respectfully inquired. To say that his answer astounded me would be an understatement of epic proportions. His response to the first part of the question was enough of a shock to make me think that I was back in the fantasy land of North China.

"Their names are John Ngono and James Dimouamoua." To the uninitiated, the names may make no impression whatsoever. To those who are familiar with that part of the world, the names told you, immediately and unequivocally, that the Minister's friends were black. Had the stress and strain of the job impaired my hearing? Had the Minister truly said that he had two black, that is to say, black friends? That he was using his official time and office in order to obtain jobs for them? A white Minister, in the South African Government, taking his official time to attempt to find jobs for blacks? My mind reeled with the incongruity of the situation. While I was still stunned, the Minister was in the process of dealing a finale blow to my already unbalanced state of mind.

"They are deck hands," he continued in explanation to the second part of my question concerning their field of expertise, "and it is very difficult to find employment of that kind in South Africa." I recovered enough to be able to assure him that I would do my best to place them and would definitely do so. However, since the Minister recognized that that type of employment was difficult to find in South Africa, perhaps not in their field.

Apparently, there is no end to the assaults on one's state of mind. His next statements were made in a matter of fact tone of voice. His expression gave no indication of what a tremendous impact he must have known they would have on the listener. "I wasn't thinking of your South African organization, but rather the Zambezi River Transport Company that Caltex owns in Zambia." It was not too much of a surprise to be made aware that the Minister knew of the operation. It was well known that one of the landing ports of ZRT, Katima Mulilo, on the river was in South West Africa, particularly well known after all the attendant publicity about the military air base. What, of course, was not well known at all, particularly in South Africa, was the fact that Caltex owned the operation having taken it over in the bankruptcy proceedings.

All South Africans knew that South West Africa was a mandate of the United Nations which South Africa had been appointed to administer. Certainly, it was part of the terms of reference for The Minister of Justice to know. The South Africans had been requested to relinquish the administration of the territory, but with the rising nationalism in Africa the South Africans had refused. They had no desire to have an independent, black neighbour on their front line of defense. The Zambezi River, however, was no respecter of man made national boundaries. It wandered all over that part of southern Africa. As has been documented, Zambezi River Transport Company's operation actually started in Livingstone, Zambia, going up river to Katima Mulilo in South West Africa in the Caprivi Strip where the river section terminated. Then, on again by road back to Zambia.

What was totally unnerving was his response to my immediate attempt to hedge my offer of employment for his two black, so called, friends. "But Zambia is not part of my South Africa operation Mister Minister," I hastened to explain.

"I'm aware of that," he affirmed, "but you managed the river company from the day that Caltex took it over in bankruptcy proceedings." There was beginning to be an icy feeling starting in the pit of my stomach. If his knowledge of my involvement in the river transport company was giving me qualms, his next response to my continued attempt to backtrack on my offer of employment for his two friends was absolutely spine chilling.

"Yes, Mister Minister, you are absolutely correct. That operation was managed by me when I was General Manager in Salisbury in charge of Rhodesia and responsible for Zambia as well. There is another General Manager there now. It would be necessary for me to request his cooperation in this matter, and that would be very, very difficult to guarantee."

Spine chilling? Were those the words used to describe his response to my attempt to backtrack on my offer of employment for his two black friends? His next statement, made in his usual matter of fact voice, told volumes about the work of the Ministry of Justice in South Africa. "Why would that be so difficult?" he inquired. "The General Manager of Caltex in Salisbury, Mr.Harry Bernard, is a long time friend of yours whom you met in Shanghai. You worked for him in Cairo and East Africa. In fact, he just relieved you not too long ago in Salisbury. I'm sure that he would be glad to cooperate with you on this small matter due to your relationship with him."

How do you impart to Americans, who have never left the shores of that great nation, how unnerving it is to realize that some government officials have the power and the means to know everything about certain foreigners that reside in their respective countries? The Minister of Justice in South Africa apparently had a 'file' on a certain American international oil executive in his country. At this moment, the subject of the file was in a state of shock, because of the implications behind such an exhaustive investigation. An investigation that, apparently, was made at the highest level of the government. And for what reason? To obtain employment for two friends of the Minister's? And two black friends at that?

Whatever the reasons, there appeared to be no doubt that there was no alternative to finding employment with Zambezi River Transport Company for the Minister's two friends. Upon returning to Johannesburg, a telephone call was placed to Salisbury. Since the operation was still losing money, it took considerable persuasion to convince Harry that it was imperative that the two friends of the Minister's be given employment. After the usual give and take, Harry reluctantly agreed to place the two friends on the payroll. Upon his agreement, the Minister was telephoned, as had been previously arranged with him, and given the name of the then manager of ZRT in order that his two friends would know whom to contact. Harry had, also, been given the names of the two friends to be relayed to the manager of ZRT to avoid having them turned away, as had so many other prospective job seekers in the past.

That Harry's reaction to the names of the two friends of the Minister's was one of total disbelief can be readily understood. It was not possible to discuss the matter on the telephone. Telephones in South Africa were not instruments of trust. As in all other countries, there were no such items as 'secure lines' available to lowly commercial executives in the oil business. All discussion had to be postponed until a face to face meeting ensued.

During a routine telephone conversation at a later date, Harry confirmed that Ngono and Dimouamoua had applied for jobs as deck hands in the river transport company. They had been duly hired. Nothing had been said to any other members of the staff in Johannesburg about the Minister's request. My secretary had been cautioned, also, to say nothing about his telephone call. In spite of the fact that the Minister's request was beginning to take on the air of what appeared to be 'jobs for the boys', there lurked in the back of my mind that constant, nagging doubt that told me ... no white Minister of Justice in South Africa had black friends.

Several weeks passed. The momentous meeting with the Minister of Justice faded into the background. More pressing matters than the selling of oil occupied our attention. It appeared that a delegation from the Wild Life Society in the

United States was due to arrive in Johannesburg. As was the customary proce-dure, the obligation of selling oil had to take second place. South Africa is a haven for wild life. Wild life represents a goodly portion of the gross national product because of tourism. As a consequence, the twenty-five delegates from the Society were being entertained by the Prime Minister.

THE COMPANY, recognizing the potential government relations value of such a group, had agreed to sponsor the visit to Johannesburg. Consequently, Caltex was on the invitation list to a cocktail party at the Prime Minister's home in Pretoria. The cocktail party was to be followed by a dinner which was to be hosted by THE COMPANY. This necessitated my wife, who had photographic recall, to commit to memory each of the twenty-five names of the representatives of the Wild Life Society, the cities from which they came and their business asso-ciation. On the hour's drive to Pretoria we went over the list name by name.

When we were introduced to each member of the delegation, my wife was able to relate some piece of information which she had retained in her memory in regard to either the city from which they came or their business association. To say that they were duly impressed would be putting it mildly. What they couldn't possibly have known, of course, was that the information was only a matter of minutes old. When the delegation had departed from Johannesburg, she would have replaced their names and the information with another list of visitors which THE COMPANY felt was a public relation's asset. In fact, after the departure of the group even the name of the society became a distant blur on the memory recall band.

During the preparation for these festivities, my mind was being lulled into a false sense of security, insofar as the Minister of Justice was concerned. I was relaxing during the usual Thursday morning staff meeting, as I wondered what my wife would order for dinner for the Wild Life Society. Perhaps venison would look good on the menu? No....! She wouldn't do that ...! Or would she ...? She had been known to get very annoyed with that benign dictatorship for which we both worked, I officially and she unofficially. She might just use this opportunity to make her annoyance known.

These weekly meetings didn't sell any oil, but they were considered a vital part of big oil's business. Each department head presented a brief review of what had transpired the previous week compared to what, at the prior week's meeting, he had forecasted. Then a projection of the activities for the ensuing week was pre-sented by each department head, which he fervently hoped he would be able to verify at the next meeting. And so it went on week after week. These meetings always gave me several hours relaxation, while the department heads did the talking, and my mind was free to peruse my own interests.

Why then did my heart stop beating? Was that the head of the Public Relations department's voice that I heard reporting his week's activities? Was he reading from a letter in Afrikaans and translating at the same time? He had an engaging, if that is what it could be called, sense of humour which he was apparently exercising as he opened his report with the comment, "Apparently you kept your staff under better control when you were running the Zambezi River Transport Company than the present General Manger in Salisbury."

He continued to translate the letter, which merely explained in matter of fact terms, that two deck hands of a river transport company on the Zambezi River had, apparently for no reason at all, suddenly machine-gunned several of the passengers. Having killed them, the two deck hands then threw the bodies into the Zambezi River, where it could be presumed that the crocodiles took care of the evidence. The letter went on to report that the two deck hands, who were both South Africans and recent hires of the river company, jumped overboard and swam towards the shoreline. With several bloody bodies in the water, the crocodiles were sure to feast on them first and leave the two swimmers to make their way safely to shore, or so the letter implied.

The guerilla warfare in South West Africa had been going on for a number of years. Guns, ammunition and *guerrillas* were being supplied from the sanctuary of the countries surrounding South West. There had been many suspicions voiced within THE COMPANY as to the means of conveyance of these instruments of terror. These suspicions had often been the subject of conjecture by those of us who were merely on-lookers to the vicious and deadly results of this particular guerrilla war.

The conclusion, universally reached, was that 'the need *not* to know' was of paramount importance if one were to keep a sense of equilibrium in the topsy turvy world of terrorism and counter-terrorism. Indisputably and understandably not so with the South African Government. It was the South African Government's citizens, both black and white, who were doing the fighting and dying in the war of attrition against the guerrillas in South West Africa. The South African Government had vowed to bring this terrorism to an end. They had announced they would use any means to stop the supply of guns, ammunition and, particularly, the *guerrillas* into the country.

The Zambezi River Transport Company manager's monthly fiscal reports indicated an alarming drop in income derived from passenger traffic in transit to South West Africa.

The Minister of Justice of the South African Government was pleased to announce that its counter-terrorist division had been eminently successful in stemming the flow of guerrillas into South West Africa.

For some strange reason, the subject of guerrilla warfare in South West Africa lost all sense of interest to those of us who had previously followed with avid preoccupation the details of the South African Government's effort to bring to a halt, what they termed to be an 'insurrection'.

The subject of the two black friends of the Minister's was never raised again by anyone in THE COMPANY.

18

New York, USA—1970

Home! After twenty-two years. Home? Where is home? They say 'home is where the heart is'. Surely New York couldn't be home to me. I choose to leave it twenty-two years ago. Never once in that twenty-two years had any yearnings been engendered in my heart to return to it. As far as I was concerned, now, I thought of it only as a way-station on my career progress to greater responsibility abroad.

There are a myriad number of New Yorkers who will tell you that the city is actually alive. That it pulses with buried emotions. That it is vibrant and moving. They will, also state, quite emphatically, that it is perfectly capable of having feelings which are normally only reserved for the human race. Just as 'it has become an automatic reflex for French writers to give their country human traits. She has an eternal soul'[92], they say.

New Yorkers will tell you, however, that among those traits would be the one of resentment. A feeling which would be brought about by having an intruder suddenly thrust upon it, who had no desire to live there. An interloper, who was anxiously looking forward to the day when he could, again, board some trans-Atlantic giant and escape from that consummate, concrete jungle. Although those faithful residents never articulated what action would result from that resentment, I was soon to learn the vengeful shape that that alienation would take.

Nevertheless, having been brought up in New York, and in spite of no desire to become a resident in that world famous metropolis again, I was acutely familiar with some of its wonderful elements. Elements which were unique to that one and only city which nine million other people called home. One of those pre-eminent aspects was a theater district that even New York's most severe critics will admit is not rivaled anywhere else in the world.

In my late teens and early twenties, I was privileged to have the unparalleled opportunity of seeing every great, near great, and just passable show on Broadway during my school years. Also, some which the critics lauded, such as "By the Skin of Your Teeth", but from which the public stayed away in droves. A show from which we walked out in the middle of the second act, sadly shaking our heads over the unanswerable question as to why we hadn't walked out during the first act. In addition to the great and near great, there were some that were just a pleasure to behold as master pieces of acting and simply pure entertainment.

"Life with Father" was one of those. It ran for so long that the young cast had to be replaced on a periodic basis, as the children outgrew their parts with startlingly regularity over a span of seven years. There was another play in that same category of just, simply, pure entertainment. To this day, the name of which eludes me. It escapes me if only for the fact that I never gave it another single thought for the entire thirty-five years that had passed after seeing it. This was rather unkind of me since I had so thoroughly enjoyed the masterful performance of its main character. But like "Life with Father", although it didn't approach that accomplished piece's longevity of enjoyment, it was just, simply, pure entertainment.

It was a mystery thriller. The leading character was a 'Lord of the Realm', who had inherited the family estate in Great Britain. The manor was replete with master pieces of oil paintings, objects d'art, hundred years old Persian carpets which the family lineage had garnered during its periods of service in the empire and other priceless relics of times long past. It, also, housed a host of faithful and long time, resident servants, who had nurtured its ancestry with the loving care that can only be found in one of those typically English manors.

Like so many heirs to those grand landmarks on the horizon of history, the liberals had taken a heavy toll on his financial and liquid resources. Inheritance taxes, income taxes, taxes enacted to ensure the redistribution of wealth had all become unbearable and impossible to meet. There was only the unthinkable and intolerable solution to which so many of the landed gentry in the British Isles had reluctantly succumbed, as they slowly wended their way in the deepest depths of despair to the auction rooms of Sotheby's. There, they would see their family heirlooms sold to the nouveau riche who had accumulated vast sums of capital in those oh-so-lowly endeavours of commerce and trade.

As you sat in the audience, you cringed at the obvious emotions passing through our hero's mind as he contemplated the thought of having to reduce the faithful and devoted staff. A dedicated and loyal staff who handed down their duties from father to son and who had ironed the wrinkles from the daily newspapers of generations of his ancestors and then warmed them in front of the fireplace before delivering them to their Lordships.

You could, almost, physically feel his revulsion, as he visualized the thought of those crass members of Sotheby's staff pawing over his beloved relics of another age, as they dutifully went about their task of attaching auction tags to a large number of items. Items from which he imagined he would soon have to part in order to meet the latest onslaught of the Socialist's insistence that he share his wealth with the great, unwashed masses of that embattled island called England. An island on which my illustrious father had been born and raised and which always induced in me longings to have been part of that great empire when it was at its peak. Even at this moment, as I watch 'Remains of the Day' for the fourth time, I think I would gladly give up my twentieth century, scientific wonders in order to be part of that glorious and never to be repeated past.

No!

Never would those priceless family heirlooms fall into the hands of lesser mortals as long as there was a conceivable solution to this agonizing dilemma. Nor would a single member of that long serving and faithful staff be sent out into the cold and forbidding world of unemployment.

His Lordship went about filling out various forms which the audience slowly, but surely, were privileged to learn were life insurance applications for policies on a near and reasonably, dear relative. With horrific suddenness, it dawned on all the onlookers to this heart rending drama what avenue his Lordship had chosen to avoid the inexorable onslaught of the social engineers of his generation and how he intended to meet their unprincipled demands on his wealth.

His Lordship's dinner guest arrived after a discrete telephone invitation, which had been initiated when Lloyds of London had confirmed the issuance of the life insurance policies. The audience watched in spellbound fixation in hope of being able to discern what means his Lordship would use to bring about the demise of his dinner companion. After the normal, delightful repast served by those dedicated servants of the household, his Lordship dismissed the staff after dinner. After all, it was Thursday. Their normal day off. So such action caused no suspicions to arise in their faithful minds.

As his Lordship, and his soon to be departed kin, sipped their after-dinner brandies in the library, the audience was entitled to surreptitiously view his Lordship slip the lethal dose into his guest's cognac. Then, as the onlookers' flesh chilled, the lights began to dim just after an overlarge steamer trunk had been dragged to the center of the stage by our soon to be beneficiary of the insurance policies. All the spectators were made vividly aware of in what activity his Lordship was engaged by the sounds emanating from the stage after the lights had faded. There was not a single doubt in the imagination of any one of the listeners that the body was being dismembered, reduced to manageable proportions, the pieces wrapped in water proof coverings and carefully stowed in the steamer trunk which occupied the front and center of the theater's stage. When the curtain was rung up for the second act, not a single eye in the audience could do anything but rivet itself on the steamer trunk with the absolute knowledge of what, and in what condition, the contents were.

As we all left the theater at the fall of the finale curtain, the atmosphere of the entire audience was one of congenial, good spirits after having enjoyed another masterful and artful serving up by that wonderful group of the theater world. Actors, actresses, directors, producers, stage hands, designers, they had all contributed to our spending another enchanting evening in that one and only area known as the 'Broadway Theater District'.

I made only one philosophical comment to my companion. "In real life, there is no one, *absolutely no one*, who would even think about, much less commit murder for the sake of continuing to enjoy privileges and a way of life that he was in danger of losing".

No …?????

Why was I so philosophically sure of that profound statement thirty-five years ago as we left the theater? It was now thirty-five years later. Thirty-five years later, almost to the very day. Thirty-five years during which I had not given that evening or the play an instant's thought. And, now, suddenly, those few short hours of thirty-five years ago were as large as life in my whole being. Figurative assassination had occupied my mind countless number of times over the past years.

But murder?

Into what manic-depressive, psychosomatic state had I fallen? Had I, inescapably, after thirty-five years, literally and absolutely found myself a complete soulmate of his Lordship? Had I, in stunning reality, actually grasped the soul destroying, inner feelings of a man, who was about to lose a way of life without which there was no longer life?

At exactly what point the suddenness of my descent from the heights of the royally privileged to the bottomless pit of lessor mortals was actually reached, I can not pin-point with accuracy. But descend I did, and with such a gut wrenching, painful abruptness that I was physically ill for weeks.

Perhaps, it was my daughter's tears. She had been quietly sobbing herself to sleep for a long time and refused to confess the reason. One night, as I was lovingly tucking her into bed, she could no longer contain herself, and with a heart bursting rush of tears she blurted out, "Why did you lose your job?"

I gazed at her in absolute astonishment. "What in heaven's name makes you think I lost my job?" I asked in total amazement. In between a continual barrage of sobs and tears, the story was painfully wrung out of the inner-most recesses of her very young heart.

"I got up early one morning to go to the bathroom and I heard you in the kitchen. I came out to say 'good morning' to you and..... ."

"And ...?", I queried. With a final rush of sobs and tears, she confessed to knowing with a certainty that I had lost my job. By this time, she was huddled in my arms with the painful moans wracking her small body and causing her to be almost breathless. In as gentle a voice as I could muster, because by now her distress had brought me almost to the verge of tears myself, I asked her how she could be so sure that I had lost my job.

"Because you were shining your own shoes yourself."

As long as she could remember over the years as she was growing up and if she were about the house in the very early morning, she would see the house-boy bring my carefully, polished riding boots to the bedroom. At the same time, the maid was bringing my bed tea, which served as a signal that it was time for me to get dressed in my riding habit and go to the club to exercise my polo ponies.

While she was getting ready for school with the help of the nanny, she would see that same maid bring my brightly, daily shined shoes to the summer-house by the pool and put them alongside my office clothes, which the house-boy was laying out. Since I always did twelve lengths of the heated swimming pool after exercising my polo ponies, the summer-house was an ideal place for me to shower and dress.

As she was leaving for school, she would kiss me goodbye at the breakfast table as the maid was serving me a rather large and welcome rasher of bacon that the cook had browned to the exact degree that I relished. A meal that was badly needed to replace all the energy used in exercising the ponies and swimming twelve lengths of the pool. She would wave a cheerful 'good morning' to the chauffeur in the driveway, who by now had had his breakfast after driving me to the club and back and was, therefore, ready to take me to the office and start the long day of waiting for me to decide when I would need his services again.

As she descended the steps of the house, she would, then, be assisted by the gardener to settle herself and her books on her bicycle, which was her mode of transportation to her school. The gardener had been standing there studiously awaiting her arrival and holding her bicycle in anticipation of her departure for school. As was his usual wont, he had polished the bicycle to a brilliant finish, which was his constant practice in catering for his young charge.

"Because you were shining your own shoes yourself."

She hadn't seen that masterful play on Broadway full of heart wracking, psychological drama, but she sensed that things were not as they should be. She and the other children use to love to have the chauffeur drive them to the office at the close of the working day, when we were going to take them out for an early evening in the city. Although they were all quite young, they could sense the deep deference that the office staff paid them, as the children of the all powerful head of one of the subsidiaries of two of The Seven Sisters.

They adored the breathtaking view of the city from my office on the sixteenth floor. An office, to which they had to gain access through my large and spacious waiting room with its hushed atmosphere of wall to wall carpeting that was so deeply napped that their small shoes almost disappeared in the lushness. They, also, had to pass an extremely, attractive, young secretary, who always had some appetizing tid-bits hidden in her desk for them.

One of them asked me, shortly after our arrival in New York, what my new office was like there, and when could they come and see me. I artfully explained that in New York the wall to wall carpeting wasn't quite as luxurious as that in Johannesburg, because we had a lot many more visitors and the carpeting had to endure considerably more wear and tear.

"Because you were shining your own shoes yourself."

The sins of omission and commission, particularly omission. How could I tell them that, although I had wall to wall carpeting, the walls didn't go all the way up to the ceiling? I was assigned to a windowless, door-less alcove on the inner side of the twelfth floor of the head office of Caltex Petroleum Corporation on 350 Madison Avenue in New York City. An alcove far removed from the windows and next to the niche which housed the secretary of the Regional Director for Africa. She made her displeasure and annoyance known very deliberately every time I had to request her to type a short letter, which I had hand written and on which I had worked for several days. A letter, that normally, I would have dictated to my secretary in about five minutes or even more likely, considering the contents of the letter, I would have delegated the subject to one of my many junior staff. The reason that it took several days to concoct the letter was because if I had finished it within a normal time frame of about fifteen minutes, I would then find myself with nothing to do for days on end.

The alcove was so small that it was impossible to even tilt the desk chair backwards, as it would hit the wall after moving only a few inches. I found it necessary to turn sideways every time I left my desk to exit the area, because the desk, although very small, occupied almost the entire space even though I had shoved it up against one of the moveable partitions on one side. In spite of this maneuver, I was still forced to employ the device of turning sideways as I passed the desk in order to leave through the door-less entrance to what would pass as a cell for solitary confinement in one of the penal hells of the colonialists in the middle ages.

My normal, previous practice in the field had been to have my secretary accumulate the day's publications or any voluminous reading material originating from the head office. She would send this material down to my chauffeur, via the office boy, at the close of the day. This signaled the chauffeur that I was on my way down, and he was to have the car ready with the engine running at the front door of the office. During the fifteen minute trip on the way home in the car, I would, then, glance through the material and segregate it so that after dinner and the children had retired, I could utilize my time to the best advantage. There was just insufficient opportunity during normal office hours to read and absorb all the material that crossed my desk. Now, I was aghast to learn that not only did I not have to accumulate the day's reading material in order to save time, but if I didn't read it in the office, there was absolutely nothing else to do.

Inasmuch as I was at a complete loss for something to do in the office and, consequently, nothing to do at home, it was decided that we would go to the theater one evening with the children to an early show. The children were very fond of the movies and had acquired the habit of often going to a Saturday matinée. At a young age, we had put them on a very strict, weekly allowance of US fifty-cents in equivalent local currency of the country in which we were resident at the time. Since the admission to the cinema for them had been only ten cents US in South African rand, they could indulge their liking for the movies without severely depleting their basic allowance.

I returned from the box-office with a rather dazed look on my face, and my wife anxiously asked me if the theater was sold out since I had no tickets in my hand. I replied that there were plenty of seats, but I hadn't purchased any. "For heaven's sake, why not?" she asked wonderingly.

"Because they want eighteen dollars and fifty cents for the six of us," I replied in an unbelieving voice. The 'Poseidon Adventure' had just been released and was commanding premium prices. I had read the review of the film and thought that the subject would just fit my frame of mind perfectly.

My eyes glazed over and my mind traveled back, not to the mystery thriller again to which I had not given thought for thirty-five years, but to another evening's dinner and theater party at which His Lordship would have felt perfectly at home. And to a way of life to which I had grown so accustomed that I, actually, had begun to believe that we, the chosen people, would always live in such a fashion.

As we were driven up to the steps of Government House, the chauffeur's back straightened almost imperceptibly as he assumed a position befitting his dignity. He knew from previous visits to Government House that it was not necessary for him to exit the car immediately on bringing the vehicle to a stop in order to open the door to allow us to alight. There were two lesser mortals standing there in the spotless full regalia of footmen, who were charged with that responsibility. Waiting at the head of the stairs was the Governor-General's aide de campe in his almost dazzlingly, splendid, white uniform with its masses of gold braid draped over his shoulder. He acknowledged our arrival with just enough of a bow to show the proper deference to those who were to dine with his Commander-in-Chief.

As we reached the top of the spacious staircase, the ADC produced a printed, glass covered, framed diagram of the seating arrangement for the evening's dinner. He had been holding it in his clasped hands behind his back, and he politely extended it just a few inches in front of him as we approached, which would allow us to glance at it without slowing our pace. In this manner, there would be no confusion or hesitation on the part of any guest as to where he or she were to be seated at the conclusion of the cocktails being served in the lounge.

In actuality, the first seating place that you glanced at immediately was to the right of the Governor-General. You, then knew, instantly, who were the guests of honour and to whom you had to exercise the utmost respect when engaging him or her in conversation. Next, you rapidly counted the number of places down from the Governor-General's position at the head of the table, and you were aware of two more most important and paramount features. Where you were to physically sit at the dinner table, and even more significantly, where you fitted in the hierarchy of the evening's gathering, inasmuch as the further away from the head of the table that you were, the further down the level of importance that you occupied.

The Governor-General abruptly rose from his seated position in the lounge. A signal, with which all present were aware, indicated that it was time to proceed to the dining room. If you hadn't finished your cocktail, that was your misfortune. You should have been quietly glancing at the Governor's glass, and, then, you would have known how much time you had to down the remains of your drink. You never, but never, gulped the remnants in your glass after the Governor-General had risen. Preceded by the Governor-General, the guests entered the dining room. They approached their places, whose exact position had been imbedded in their minds ever since they had apparently nonchalantly, but very knowingly, glanced at the seating arrangement which the ADC had produced from behind his back on their arrival.

As the gathering proceeded into the dining room, every footman standing behind each guest's chair lifted it fractionally to avoid any sound emanating from the legs of the chair as it was withdrawn from its close proximity to the table. All the guests took their positions at their appointed places and awaited the signal from the Governor-General that would allow them to take their seats. Without so much as a glance towards the assemblage, His Excellency sat down. It was, now, possible for the guests to assume their seats with which each footman standing behind them was ready to assist them to do so and prepare to engage each other in conversation. At the same time, every one kept a wary eye on the Governor-General in case he were to suddenly make a statement that was meant for all to hear and to which each and everyone present would be aware was the reason for their being there in the first instance.

No one was ever invited to Government House for the mere pleasure of enjoying a convivial evening and good food. These were occasions when a policy in the making was about to be floated, and the Governor-General was using the opportunity to run up a trial balloon. Alternatively, he wanted the top executives of the community to air their views on any recently promulgated laws and regulations and to hear unofficially, without the danger of being quoted, their reaction as to how the staff of their large organizations were bearing up under such recent proclamations.

As in all centers of government, Dar-es-Salaam was a tiny microcosm similar to that of the Beltway of Washington D.C. where '…. social life provides a mechanism for measuring intangibles and understanding nuances. Moods can be gauged by newspapermen and ambassadors and senior civil servants that are not discernible at formal meetings. It is at their dinner parties and receptions that the relationships are created without which the machinery of government would soon stalemate itself'[93].

As the dinner drew to a close, His Excellency casually mentioned that after dinner he had arranged for all his guests to proceed to the theater to see the opening of the latest play which was being produced at that time. For those of us who may have been watching the expressions on some of our fellow guests' faces, the almost, imperceptibly, raised eyebrows told you that the chances were very good that they had, actually, originally booked seats for the opening themselves. They very likely, also, had several invited guests or were invited guests themselves. Unfortunately for them and their guests or their respective hosts, an invitation from the Governor-General took precedence over all other such engagements. It was only necessary to tell your guests, or alternatively your hosts if you were an invited guest to a function, that such arrangements had been pre-empted by the issuance of an invitation to Government House.

Protocol was an absolutely, necessary ingredient for those of us who were privileged to be exposed to such a way of life. Even at home, when entertaining the Governor-General and there was slightly less formality than when attending a state dinner at Government House, you never lost sight of this most important factor as I was very forcibly reminded on one such occasion. Unknown to me and my wife at the time, the occasion happened to be the day of His Excellency's birthday when we were entertaining him at our home. As a result, although he never told us until some time later that it was his birthday, he relaxed to such an extent that he magnanimously suggested that we release the entire staff of servants, while we all enjoyed a finale nightcap at mid-night after dinner. Having dispensed with their services, we then finished our drinks.

My wife, who after dismissing the servants, took a place behind the bar in the salon and was chatting vivaciously with His Excellency. She suggested, that since His Excellency appeared to be in such a relaxed frame of mind, perhaps, he would enjoy another very, special nightcap based on her own personal recipe which she would fix personally for him. He very graciously agreed. As my wife was mixing His Excellency's drink, I took the opportunity to serve the other guests. As I approached the American Ambassador, I suddenly became aware that he was frowning rather deeply. When I got within earshot of him, he leaned forward slightly and whispered intently, "For Christ's sake Robert, would you please be so kind as to get Connie out from behind that bar so that His Excellency will go home. I've got an important meeting at nine o'clock in the morning, and I have to be in the office early to prepare for it, and I can't afford to be too tired."

American Ambassadors, heads of large international organizations, District Commissioners, visiting dignitaries, none of our guests and their wives could depart until His Excellency had taken his leave.

Just as the curtain could not be raised in the theater until His Excellency had arrived. After a leisurely dinner at Government House, we all joined each other at the theater more than twenty minutes after the curtain would normally have been raised. Being so late meant that everyone else had taken their seats and the theater was completely full. As we entered the hall, preceded by the Governor-General, every member of the audience instantly rose to their feet and remained standing until we had all taken our places and sat down in the very best orchestra seats of the house. As we settled into our places, the audience resumed their seats and the curtain was allowed to rise for the first act.

There are many theater goers who are painfully familiar with the unpleasant crush at the bar during intermission time, and the need to be alert to the passing of time so as not to miss the raising of the curtain for the next act. To avoid this discomfort, perhaps, they should take advantage of the next invitation from His Excellency.

As you leisurely strolled up the theater aisle after the curtain had fallen on the first act, none of the audience, who again had all assumed a standing position, makes a move until the Governor-General's party has exited the theater to the spacious garden surrounding the building. There you will find two bars. The public one and the one at which you will immediately recognize the head butler from Government House, who is holding reign over the two barmen and the two footmen who are manning His Excellency's private bar.

There is no need to constantly check your watch for the passage of time. The curtain will not rise again until the Governor-General and his company have finished their drinks and re-entered the theater to the same ritual of having the entire audience rise to their feet, while you assume your position in the front of the theater. An experience that does things to the ego: that makes one really believe that he is a member of the chosen race and far above the lesser mortals that inhabit the same planet as the royally privileged do.

"Because you were shining your own shoes yourself."

And, now, I had become a watcher of time or the train would leave without me. In the hot, sweaty crush of smelly bodies that make up the mass of commuters in Grand Central Station in New York City, people would push by me and then turn to stare at someone who seemed at a complete loss as to where he was going, or even in what world he was living. Never once, while headed for the platform from which my train would depart, did I fail to visualize another occasion when I was about to embark on a train journey.

The rail head of the Government owned railway line had been extended a number of miles into the interior of that vast jungle on the East coast of Africa. On the occasion of the first use of the extension, there was to be a formal celebration at the site of the new rail head. This function was the normal show of magnificence on the part of the colonial owners of the railway. Colonial masters, who not only owned the railway, but ruled the land with an iron hand as well—to say nothing of the people.

As we approached the railway station, the chauffeur had no difficulty recognizing the platform from which the Governor-General's private train would depart. Standing at the entrance to the railway station, and at the foot of the plat-form, were those same two footmen from His Excellency's staff. They each stood apart from one another separated by a wide, deep red carpet that ran from the entrance of the station up to the platform and then up to the door of His Excel-lency's private car. At the foot of the steps of the railway car stood that same aide de campe. This time, however, he was holding a framed diagram showing which compartment each guest would occupy on the overnight journey. Inasmuch as the roadbed was obviously quite new and had not settled properly onto its foun-dation, the trip of necessity was slow enough to allow all the guests' chauffeurs to race overnight to the site of the new rail head and, then, be in position to drive them back to the city at the completion of the ceremonies.

The men donned their evening clothes, and the women put on their full length gowns in the privacy of their compartments for the occasion of dinner in the dining car of His Excellency's private train. The servants were dressed in their immaculate, white uniforms with red sashes, tasseled fezzes and pure, white gloves. Nothing had really changed since 1900 except the color of the dress of the servants when "… aboard George Gould's private train of five palace cars, the ser-vants were dressed in black satin knee breeches and crimson tailcoats…. and guests were thus expected to dine in full evening dress".[94]

As the guests gathered in the dining car, neither was much thought given to the back breaking labour or even to the simple sweat and discomfort of those black hands that had made this journey possible. Certainly, no one even bothered to recall the horrible deaths of the workers brought about by marauding lions on another railway extension on that same coast of Africa. An onslaught that killed so many of the labourers, that the completion date of the extension had been drastically lengthened and threatened the professionalism of the English masters, who had been imported for the purpose of establishing their engineering superi-ority.

"Because you were shining your own shoes yourself."

My state of mind occupied so much of my selfish, inward and depressed feel-ings that I scarcely gave thought to what my family may have been going through. That very young daughter, that was so concerned over the obvious, out-ward manifestations of what, in her mind, gave credence to the indisputable fact that I had lost my job, had no doubt forgotten her first comment on arriving at Kennedy Airport in New York City.

As we exited the plane from the first class section of the aircraft, a means of travel to which she had grown so accustomed that she didn't realize that there were lesser mortals who didn't move around the world in the same fashion, we proceeded to the baggage area. A typical New York porter, huge, rotund, very knowledgeable and very, very black approached us. In the normal way of such individuals, he asked, "How many bags do you have? Do you want a taxi or do you have private transportation? Are you going into the city or are you in transit?"

On hearing these questions voiced by this large, very black individual of the type by whom she had been surrounded for almost the entire twelve years of her life, she turned to me. In that broad, English accent, which all of the children had acquired from having been brought up in British colonies and territories for, essentially, their entire lives, she asked, "I say, father, do all the natives speak English here?"

This from a twelve year old American child; Perhaps James Byrnes should have included the children of diplomats and expatriates in his legislation requiring that they return to their home country on a more frequent basis.

Fortunately, because of that broad English accent and the whine of the jets overhead, the object of her enquiry didn't understand the question she had posed to me. Also, fortunately, there were no hotel staff in the suite at the hotel where we were settling in after leaving the airport to hear our American son's comment after we had instructed him to wash up and take his bath before retiring to bed.

We looked up as we heard the bathroom door of the suite slam open and gazed upon an highly, indignant, stark naked, eleven year old citizen of the United States. He, then, proceeded to state, quite emphatically, in terms that left no doubt as to why he was so outraged, and with the same broad English accent that his sister had exhibited at the airport, "I say, nobody has drawn my bath!"

As to their school experiences, no doubt, to them, they were as traumatic in their way as my experiences were in the office. In its usual, benign, dictatorship manner, THE COMPANY had allowed me a number of days to settle in before requiring my presence in the office. As a result, I was at the house when our elder daughter, Lynn, arrived home in tears from her first day of attending an American school. Seeing her tears, I was instantly ready to proceed to the school and do battle with the school authorities, who in my mind could have been the only ones responsible for reducing my daughter to tears.

"What happened?" I demanded. "Who did this to you? Tell me their names. I'll go to the headmaster immediately and I assure you when I get through with him and whoever on the staff did it, they will never do it again."

"Oh," she wailed, "you will never believe it!"

Believe what?" I demanded again. This time with a strong note of anxiety creeping into my voice.

"I'm never going back to that class again", she said with a little more firmness as she began to get a grip on herself.

"Please tell me exactly what happened. If you don't give me some inkling of what happened I won't be able to do anything about it", I asked in a more gentle tone of voice.

With this, she burst into tears again and almost heart-brokenly said, "They all laughed at me."

"Who is *they* and why did *they* all laugh at you?" I questioned her now in absolute bewilderment.

"The whole class laughed at me," she sobbed.

"Why would they do that?" I asked. "What in the world did you do that made the whole class laugh at you?"

"It happened when the teacher came into the classroom", she continued. "I was the only one that stood up."

None of our children had ever attended an American school. All their school lives had been spent under that authoritative atmosphere of the English system, where every student was made aware, and truly believed, that their teachers were special people and deserved the utmost in respect, as they unquestionably did. In Lynn's case, which was for the entire eight years of her school life, she had stood up as a token of respect whenever the teacher entered the classroom. And now a gale of raucous laughter had shattered that image and reduced her to an object of ridicule. No wonder she was devastated.

At this moment, our elder son, James, arrived home from his first day at the same American school. His eyes were as big as saucers and he entered the house in a very hesitant manner as if he were unsure of his perquisites. He gazed at Lynn, who was still trying to dry the copious tears that had been flowing ever since she had explained her traumatic experience in school.

"What's wrong Lynn?" he asked in a quite and very subdued voice. We explained to him that the entire class had laughed at her, because she had stood up as a mark of respect for those wonderful people who dedicate their lives to the hopeful process of enriching the future of their charges.

"I can understand that," he volunteered, "because you won't believe what happened in my class either. I'm not sure that I really want to go back to that school." Apparently he, too, had undergone some emotionally and traumatic experience that was definitely upsetting him and had left him at a loss as to how to regard the previous values which he had held as sacrosanct all his school life.

For the moment, I put behind me my selfish feelings of thinking that I was the only mortal on earth that had wounded emotions and a sense of having been cast adrift in a sea of unknown and unfamiliar hazards. "Don't worry son. If it is bad as that, we will find another school, even if it has to be private, and we have to pay for it. I certainly don't want you going to a school that, obviously, leaves you with such a feeling of uncertainty. But tell us exactly what happened."

"You won't believe it," he repeated. "I, certainly, couldn't believe my ears. The students, actually, talk back to the teachers." Our children's introduction to the great, American school system.

A system that has been utterly demoralized and degraded by the social liberals of our times and aided and abetted by that greatest evil that the civilized world of respect and manners has ever known, The American Civil Liberties Union. Even the name is a contradiction of terms. Nothing they stand for has any relationship to being *civil* or respectful of your fellow citizens' rights or feelings. Although Bill and Hilary Clinton, Ted Kennedy and their many, Democratic, liberal colleagues may or may not (I do not have access to the membership roles of the ACLU) be card carrying members of that distasteful organization, there is no doubt that their collective philosophy, and that of the ACLU, can be viewed the way Soren Kierkegaard did in his criticism, in general, of the Idealistic philosophy. A philosophy, which the Clintons, the Clintonites, the Kennedys and the Democratic Party liberals so basically represent.

'Soren Kierkegaard put the criticism of the dominant Idealistic philosophy, with its incongruity between words and deeds, in another way: A thinker erects an immense building, a system, a system which embraces the whole of existence and world history, etc.—and if we contemplate his personal life, we discover to our astonishment this terrible and ludicrous fact, that he himself does not live in this immense high-vaulted palace, but in a barn alongside of it, or in a dog kennel, or at the most in the porter's lodge …'[95] or even in a more ludicrous residence such as in the White House from which you can send your only child to a private school or you live in a millionaire's estate in Nantucket.

As the days wore on in the office and I began to believe that there were no greater depths to which I could sink, I was summarily ordered to the office of the Vice-President, Legal. On my arrival, he indicated that I was to seat myself in the chair in front of his desk. Although, we had met a number of times in the past and were on a first name basis, he didn't bother to exchange any pleasantries. He merely stated that, "I understand that you were, somehow or other, connected with our operation in Rhodesia." Not being an attorney or having had any other similar training in double talk, I had no idea of what his statement meant. It was to remind me of nothing more than the definition which I read many years later of the word 'obfuscation'. 'As in they didn't really say what you heard, but you drew your own conclusions which they can reject at a later date. Therefore, whatever goes wrong is your fault, not theirs'[96] The entire, senior staff of THE COMPANY, all the Vice-Presidents and the President and Chairman as well, were aware that I had just returned from ten years in Africa with my two most recent assignments having been South Africa and Rhodesia.

"Frankly, I don't want to discuss it with you. I, most certainly, don't want to know any of the details. THE COMPANY has made arrangements for our outside attorneys to be present at your debriefing. Your first meeting with them will be in the law library tomorrow morning at 9:00 AM and there will be two company attorneys present. One is the regular attorney assigned to the African Division and the other is an experienced, recent hire that, hopefully, will be able to be as impartial as possible in the ensuing discussions."

Although, I was completely baffled by his attitude, my mind had retained enough resiliency to recognize the import of having the company's outside attorneys present. I was free to explain, in absolute detail, all that had transpired during the period of the 'embargo busting' by the subsidiaries of the other SEVEN SISTERS, because of the attorney-client privilege established by having the outside attorneys present.

He ended his very brusque meeting with me by stating, "Tomorrow morning will be the start of the preparation for your 'confrontation', if I may use the appropriate word in order to equip you psychologically, with the Treasury Department lawyers. You will be prepared for your discussions with them by the two outside attorneys and the two company attorneys. They are going to drill you and advise you of your rights, as far as your meeting with the Treasury Department lawyers is concerned."

Another sleepless night. When was this ordeal of my New York assignment going to end? In addition, how involved was I going to appear to be in the Treasury Department's eyes in the embargo busting? The next morning began the precursor '…. for the 'murder boards,' the mock trials at which candidate Justice Clarence Thomas would be grilled on his every speech and ruling'[97] for the Senate Committee hearings in 1991 on his nomination to the Supreme Court by President Bush. Although Justice Thomas' 'murder boards' were held in secret in the Old Executive Office Building, the ornate former War Department across from the White House, mine were held in the cramped law library on the thirteenth floor in the legal department. They were open to any one who wanted to or needed to use the library. After the first meeting, I was convinced that I could use a lot more secretiveness, if I were going to survive the ordeal that was being imposed on me.

Although, I was well aware of the attorney-client privilege, to be confronted with an array of outside legal talent that sometimes commanded fees in the neighborhood of $1000.00 per hour left me with the feeling that my days were numbered, to say the least. I had no idea of how to handle such a confrontational group that had been set up to prepare me for my meetings with the Treasury Department lawyers. The outside attorneys took the lead, when they stated that there were three principles by which I must be guided absolutely as I would be under oath;

> One: Do not lie! If you can not honestly remember, just state, 'I can not honestly remember', but do not lie.
>
> Two: Do not lie! But do not volunteer any information that is not directly requested of you. Answer the questions in as short a manner as possible with absolutely no additional information, but whatever you do say, do not lie.
>
> Three: Do not lie! If you can not answer the question with absolute assurance, because you feel that the question is ambiguous or vague, do not attempt to answer it. Ask them to rephrase the question. Let us impress upon you that under no circumstances should you ever use the phrases, 'I think' or 'I believe'. If you do make the mistake of answering a vague or ambiguous question, you are entitled to give a vague or ambiguous answer, but even under those circumstances remember the cardinal rule, do not lie.

Candidate Justice Thomas, in the days to come before his ordeal of facing the Senate hearings, was going to be briefed by Mike Luttig, an attorney in the Justice Department 'who had one of the sharpest legal minds in the administration. Before being elevated to the federal bench, he oversaw the Justice Department's Office of Legal Counsel, an elite corps of conservative lawyers that one Democratic Senate Judiciary Committee aide called 'the Green Berets of the Law.'[98] In the case of Justice Thomas, he had the Green Berets on his side. In my case, I was definitely convinced that they had been all convened to attack me.

As with Justice Thomas, when the fateful days of his confirmation hearings arrived, I passed muster. I can only say that it was because I knew that I had unfinished business. Unfinished business, which gave me the required strength to last throughout my torment. Unfinished business, which I intended to settle the moment the hearings were closed.

I was well aware that sitting below me, in their comfortable offices on the twelfth floor, were all those senior officers of THE COMPANY that had promised me a life of 'comfort and ease' as an international oil executive. I had to survive and conserve my strength at the same time, because I was going to go down to that twelfth floor. No longer was assassination going to be a figment of my imagination. It was going to be an actuality. I was going to strangle them with my bare hands in front of witnesses.

During the entire time that the United States Treasury Department attorneys were gathered in the law library on the thirteenth floor of Caltex Petroleum Corporation confronting me, I did not draw a single breath. Inasmuch as I survived, it appears that a human being can exist that long without breathing. I, consistently, held my breath waiting for that fateful and deadly, incriminating question, "Who was paying for the products?" It was never asked. I didn't volunteer the information.

19

Sydney, Australia—1971

"What did you say Gayle? You cocked a wog and you're crook." After attempting Sinhala, Tamil, Egyptian Arabic, Lebanese Arabic, French and Swahili and having grown up with German as the second language in her home, my wife had drawn the line about adding any more languages to her already impressive repertoire while we were in South Africa. There she was faced with the prospect of learning Afrikaans, but since all the population spoke English anyway she felt that she was quite justified in not attempting Afrikaans. In any case, now that we had been assigned to Australia, and it appeared that the Australians spoke the same language that we did, it wouldn't be necessary to study another foreign language. Our younger daughter, Gayle, who was calling us from her boarding school in Walla Walla in the South of Australia, however, was definitely not speaking the same language that we were. Furthermore, we couldn't blame it on a bad telephone connection.

"What do you mean Gayle, 'you cocked a wog and you're crook'?" I questioned her again.

Like all children who were entering the age where they felt that they could assert their independence, she immediately answered with the comment, "What is wrong with you Father, don't you speak English?"

"Yes, Gayle, *I* speak English, but *you* aren't. So please enlighten me as to exactly what it is that you mean by that expression."

"I caught a bug and I'm sick. I can't come home this weekend." Wog, crook, Sheilas, walkabouts, roos, the outback, dibs, tucker, jackeroos, a whole host of new words and expressions were about to be added to the lexicon of the same familiar language that we believed was English and which we thought the Australians employed in communicating with each other.

During the entire time that I had suffered the ignominy of having nothing to do in the African Division and being treated like the proverbial mushroom, 'kept in the dark and covered in—', no one had bothered to tell me the reason that I had nothing to do. It was because the machinery in the Board Room was grinding in its excruciatingly, usually, slow fashion. The Board had not wanted me to take up any responsibilities or start on any projects in the African Division, because my time was suppose to be extremely limited in that Division.

It had been proposed to the Board that after ten years in the field of the African Division I was be to transferred to the Australian Division on my return to New York. A transfer that the two divisions involved had expected to be accomplished in a matter of a few days or a week at the most instead of the months that it actually consumed. One of the reasons that I heard afterwards that had contributed to the extraordinary delay was when the Chevron Director questioned the advisability of such a transfer. He felt that an executive, with ten years experience in the field covering the area of the responsibilities of that particular division in New York, could best put that background to better advantage. By keeping me in the African division, he believed it made it possible for New York management to see the problems of the field through the eyes of one of their own New York staff who had just spent ten years in that very area.

There were two other, rather cynical, observations made by my colleagues, which they voiced when the announcement of my transfer from the African Division to the Australian Division was finally made through the usual 'PERSONNEL NOTICE—Distribution all Divisions'. 'We're no different than that other huge bureaucracy, the State Department. If you speak fluent French, you can be assured that you will be assigned to the embassy in Germany. On the other hand, if your German is so excellent that you are sometimes mistaken for a native, you can be guaranteed that you will end up in the embassy in Paris. After all, with ten years in the African division in the field, where else could you put all that experience to better advantage than in the Australian division? Actually, a good move, the two divisions begin with an 'A'.'

Far more cynical was the second comment made by one of my associates from the legal department. "They don't want any sanctions' busters in the African Division. They're going to bury you in the Australian Division. Mark my words, don't unpack all your personal belongings when you get there, because not only are you going to be buried in the Australian Division, but they will try to send you to the South Pole. Barring that, the closest that they can get you to the South Pole will be Australia."

And, sure enough, here I was in Sydney, Australia after only eleven months in New York. Unfortunately for me, they hadn't been able to get me out of New York before the Treasury Department had caught up with me, because of the snail's pace at which such immense bureaucracies move. I never really thought, or actually believed, that those cynical remarks about my being buried in the Australian Division had any basis in fact. However, at the time it suited my frame of mind, as I was quite prepared to believe the worst of those senior officers of THE COMPANY—the very ones who had convinced me when I was hired by Caltex that I was embarked on a 'life of ease and comfort' in the international oil business.

In any case, I just couldn't have cared less. I would, gladly, have gone to the South Pole just to get out of New York. Now, I was not only out of New York, but I was back to my huge office with its wall to wall carpeting, a waiting room and my own personal secretary who also had her own office with a window. There was an executive parking space reserved for me in the basement of Caltex House—as the building that housed its largest tenant was known. You simply drove up to the doors of the lift in the basement parking garage, alighted and the company parking attendant moved your vehicle to its reserved place. And most magnificent of all, there was an overpowering view of the Sydney harbour through my two picture windows.

In addition, there were three fully stocked bars in the executive suites. Dudley Braham, the Managing Director, had his own bar in his office. Dudley was a tall, physically fit, imposing figure with slight traces of graying hair which greatly added to his impressive appearance. In addition to Dudley's bar in his office, there was one in the ante-chamber adjoining the Board Room. The third was the most impressive of all; A complete lounge containing the third magnificent bar; an executive dining room attached to the lounge and all the furnishings necessary to support such luxurious living as well as a superb barman, stewards and a major domo, Charles. All of these individuals appeared miraculously when ever there were functions that involved opening the lounge for any occasion. Of course, they only miraculously appeared if the major domo, Charles, was informed that he and his staff's services were required.

The lounge had been designed for the reception of customers, visiting dignitaries, social get togethers for the staff and executive lunches when the occasion called for them. This stunning lounge was to be my nemesis on two occasions very shortly after my arrival, when I had barely become accustomed to some of the duties required of the Marketing Director by the Managing Director.

The Directors and the senior members of the staff, who were all very frequent visitors to that striking lounge, had a very strong personal dislike for it. What, under ordinary circumstances, would be considered a most prestigious perk caused them to grimace with almost physical pain when they were informed that their attendance was required in the executive lounge. On the other hand, when a junior member of the staff was invited to have cocktails in the lounge once a year, his chest swelled with pride when he telephoned his wife to tell her that he would be home late for dinner, because he was having drinks with the Managing Director and the other Directors of THE COMPANY.

Those very Directors and senior members of the staff who were such frequent visitors to the lounge and, particularly, their wives who were on the other end of the telephone, were tired of having to phone home once or twice a week to say that they had been summoned to Dudley's royal presence in the lounge and would be home late for dinner again. Although, they may have thoroughly enjoyed their first few visits to the lounge just after it had been completed, they soon realized that Dudley, being a bachelor, had no urgent desire to go home immediately after office hours. He much preferred to have a captive audience, who would have to listen to his pronouncements on world affairs and a detailed analysis of how well he was running THE COMPANY, rather than go home to his empty house.

Dudley stopped in my office one afternoon to inform me that he had invited his luncheon companions from the club, who were from overseas, to drinks in the lounge that evening after office hours. He said that he thought I would be most interested in meeting them as they were very knowledgeable, and he was sure that some of the other Directors would also be interested in meeting them if I would let them know about the arrangements.

I promptly telephoned the other Directors and advised them of the information that Dudley had given me and said that as this was my first visit to the lounge, I would look forward to seeing them there. I was so new to the experience that their almost audible groans of dismay didn't register on me as they were to do so at a later date when I, too, dreaded to have to phone my wife to say that, again as usual, I would be home late for dinner.

As we gathered in the lounge that evening and were individually introduced to Dudley's guests, I caught a questioning glance from Dudley shortly after the first few of the Directors had assembled. I immediately approached him to ascertain what the problem was as he was in the act of beginning to frown in my direction as well. "Why isn't the bar open and where are the barman and the stewards?" was his whispered question which, in reality, was in a tone of voice more resembling a command than a question. My mind, in turn, formed the question of 'How the hell would I know?' but my voice said, "I'm sorry, but I have no idea".

"Didn't you advise Charles that we would be using the bar this evening?"

'Oh my God, was I suppose to do that, just because Dudley had officially put me in charge of issuing the invitations?' Apparently so. Like Winston Churchill's comment over Britain's lack of preparation for Singapore's defense during the War sums it up: 'I did not know; I was not told; I should have asked.'[99]

With a lot of embarrassment and a few apologies to Dudley's guests, I ascertained from John, the Fiscal Director, that there was an extra set of keys to the bar in his office (inasmuch as Fiscal Director, John monitored the consumption of liquor in the lounge). He sympathetically offered to get them for me and said that he would help to set up the bar as it was now too late, he told me, to get Charles or the stewards as they had long since gone home.

The rest of the evening was a continuous, vague blur of embarrassment for me, between the sympathetic glances of my fellow directors and the continued frowns of Dudley as he assisted his guests in refilling their glasses, and I acted as barman, steward, and general factotum. I vowed to myself that I would never let that happen again. I prided myself on being a very quick learner. During my entire two year stay as Marketing Director, never again did I fail to advise Charles that his services were required after office hours in the lounge, when I was the one who was asked by Dudley to issue the invitations to the other Directors and staff members. At the very least, I never forgot to undertake that phase of my official duties concerning advice to Charles that his presence was required.

John, the Fiscal Director, was a very conscientious and hard working member of the Board of Directors. He had an inherent kindness which was reflected in his beaming smile and rotund figure which always seemed to be rolling along in pursuit of some unseen objective. In addition to his devotion to his work, he also subscribed to that long standing theory of Francis Bacon, 'For knowledge, too, is itself power'. As a result, he spent most of the official working day gleaning from casual conversations with his fellow directors that knowledge which he felt gave him the power and the impetus to remain at the top of the hierarchy of the Sydney office. As a result of his unofficial activities during normal working hours, he often had to spend his constructive time in his office after closing hours. This, also, necessitated his having to frequently retain the services of many of his senior and junior staff after office hours as they had been unable to contact him during his constant daily efforts to add to his arsenal of knowledge that he felt assured kept his hold on his power intact.

He had had no better example of how correct his philosophy was than the fact that his fellow Australian, the previous Marketing Director, whose title I had just assumed, had forgotten this maximum. As a result, Dudley demoted him to Sales Manager which had left the chair vacant that I was now occupying. I often relied on John for an unofficial consensus on what the staff felt about certain policy decisions that had been made. At other times, when policy decisions were in the formative stage and I needed input, I again relied on John's vast accumulation of knowledge as to how to shape them so that they would add, and not detract because of unintended consequences, from the efficiency of the marketing effort. An effort that was designed to keep ahead of the infamous Shell Company, that well known organization which had institutionalized the feeling that they were really an extension of the Foreign Office of Great Britain.

Dudley stuck his head in my office, again, one day just after lunch and, in his usual offhand manner, advised me that there were two advertising experts in town and that he had invited them to Caltex House for drinks. He suggested that, undoubtedly, the marketing senior staff and, certainly, the advertising department, would be interested in meeting them, as well as one or two of the other Directors. I immediately knew what my 'official' duties were.

Before Dudley's back was out of view on his return to his office, I was on my feet and headed down to the administration division where Charles held sway. I wasn't about to even trust the telephone with the message that Charles and his staff were required in the executive lounge for the evening's occasion. When I got there, I actually went over the kinds of hors d'oeuvres that Charles would be preparing for the guests. I ventured even further and suggested that Charles might try some unusually tasty ones on which my wife had often been complimented at the many dinner and cocktail parties that she had had to organize in the name of THE COMPANY over the years.

When I was sure that there was no misunderstanding as to the necessity of his, the barman and stewards' presence at the function that evening, I went back to my office. I drew my first deep breath of relief since Dudley had casually suggested that the senior marketing staff and the advertising department, as well as a few of the directors, would be most interested in joining his guests in the lounge that evening.

I knew that I wouldn't have to bear the sympathetic glances of my fellow directors that evening and I wouldn't have to rely on John again for his aid in opening the bar and assisting me in my menial duties of serving drinks and being general factotum. I made it a point to arrive first in the lounge that evening, now that I was fully aware of my official duties. My initial feelings were confirmed that all was well. Charles and his staff were outfitted in their immaculate steward's uniforms and the barman was ensconced behind the bar with its sparkling glasses adorning the shelves with a huge choice of alcoholic beverages surrounding them. A large number of trays of hors d'oeuvres were laid out on various tables within reach of the expected guests.

Dudley and his two visitors arrived after their initial brief conversation in Dudley's office and the introductions were acknowledged. I was totally relaxed. I knew that there would be no whispered commands from Dudley that would make this evening a shambles as the last one had been.

What was it, then, that made me begin to have such an uneasy feeling, if I were so sure of myself? Dudley was busy receiving compliments from his guests about the magnificent lounge in which they were being entertained. Now it was Charles' turn to cast a questioning, but respectful, glance in my direction. He had a large silver tray in his hands which was over flowing with the most unimaginable, hot, appetizing tidbits with which he had just finished serving Dudley and his guests of honour. Now, he was looking for someone else to whom to offer the delectable choices that he had so labouriously prepared for the evening. He approached me with the offering, still bearing that slight and respectful questioning air, but with no one else to whom to offer the delicacies residing on his tray.

'Oh my God' (a constant Deity upon whom I seemed to be forever calling)! Where were the other members of this gathering? There were enough drinks and food to supply a small battalion of thirsty and hungry people, but there was no one to take advantage of the offering, except four, lonely people; Dudley, his two guests and myself. Now I knew what had happened and why I had begun to have that anxious feeling. In my anxiety to ensure that Charles and his staff were in full control of servicing the occasion in their usual efficient manner, I had failed to issue any invitations to, either the senior marketing staff, the advertising department or to any of the other directors.

I frantically headed for the exit of the lounge in such haste that the other three individuals in the lounge, as well as Charles and the stewards, looked questionably in my direction. I made a half-hearted motion with my hand in the direction of my crotch as if to say that I had had a sudden and desperate urge to visit the rest rooms. Actually, I was headed for the floor on which John's fiscal division was housed. As I ran down the four flights of stairs, ignoring the obviously, glacial-like movement of the lifts, I voiced a silent prayer to myself, 'Oh Lord, let John and his staff be there. Surely this can't be the one day, among all others, of the year that he has decided to go home early. Yes, oh Lord. He must be there'.

And sure enough, John was there, just as if my prayer had been answered. He was there, if for no other reason than that he had spent well over an hour in my office that very morning, which was only one of his many stops on his quest for knowledge as I well knew by this time. He had been questioning me about how much information I had on the forthcoming visit of John McKinley, a Texaco Director, and about how much I may have known about his past history and, in particular, as to my feelings as to his possible future advancement in Texaco. I explained to him that I had no idea. I didn't even know who John McKinley was. However, if he really wanted some detailed information, I suggested that he contact my wife as she had originally worked for Texaco and, undoubtedly, would know where McKinley fitted in the hierarchy.

I burst into John's office with panic written all over my face. "What's wrong?" he questioned me immediately before I could utter a word as he recognized from the look of desperation on my face that I was in real trouble.

Without even attempting to answer him, as I was loath to lose not even a minute of valuable time, I burst out with the command, "John, get your coat and tie on this instant and get every one of your staff who has a coat and tie to put them on immediately and get upstairs to the executive lounge!"

John, being the wonderful sympathetic person that he was, was out his seat and reaching for his coat and tightening his tie against his collar as he headed for the door of his office without even waiting for an explanation in answer to his question. At the same time, he was shouting instructions to all his staff who had coats and ties to don them immediately and 'report' to the executive lounge without delay. He, further, advised them that whatever urgent requirements he had made on their efforts in the way of producing any pressing reports, they were to ignore them until further consultation in the morning.

On the way upstairs back to the lounge, I had to, shamefacedly, confess the reason for my unprecedented demands on him and his staff. He laughed uproariously. He laughed even more hilariously when I questioned him as to how observant Dudley would be in regard to the fact that there would be no senior marketing staff present, no advertising staff present and the only Director present would be the Fiscal Director, the least interested of all the Directors in meeting advertising experts.

"Hey! No problem. You should know by now that all Dudley requires is an audience. He doesn't care of what it is composed as long as he has a captive audience. Don't worry. He will never notice." John was correct as usual. Dudley was totally unaware of what the pattern of the gathering was and I inwardly wondered how I could ever have imagined that I wouldn't need John's assistance after the last fiasco of failing to notify Charles of the need for his services.

I never did get to see the 'Tasmanian Devil', inasmuch as I never found the time to get to Tasmania. Although, I traveled the length and breadth of Australia, it was such a large country that finding time to travel to an area that didn't have any problems from Caltex's point of view just wasn't in the cards. I did have to go to Papua New Guinea, however, as we had real problems there.

As far as I could see on my arrival, Papua New Guinea hadn't changed since the late 1930's when BP started exploring for oil there. Papua at that time was, and still '… is a land of swamp and jungle, a lusher, more humid and infinitely more menacing jungle than that of Trinidad. A cutting gang would do well if they hack 300 yards of narrow track in twenty-four hours and this will vanish in a matter of days if left alone. A man who steps off the track without leaving a companion may be irretrievably lost within a matter of yards. The jungle is a perpetual and unrelenting enemy'[100].

The jungle itself, for the purpose of my visit, was not so much of a problem in so far as the things that grew. What was a problem, even in the city of Port Moresby, were the things that crawled. We had been repeatedly warned not to sit on any public benches, including chairs at the airport, where the local population from the 'jungle' had taken the opportunity to occupy them prior to a European utilizing them. This was due to the fact that the prior occupants had left them infested with a vicious type of body lice that did irreparable harm to your blood stream if you were unfortunate enough to become host infested in the same manner that our jungle brethren were infected.

As I stood at the airport for several hours awaiting the delayed departure of my plane back to Sydney, unable to relax on any of the benches or chairs, I wondered if 'Willie, The Bastard' had been warned not to sit on any of the lounge chairs in his exclusive club in San Francisco.

Caltex's problem was that it was about to lose its main agent, whether by death or escape was what I had gone up to Papua to find out. The Papuans had a century's old tribal custom called 'payback'. Although they had never read the bible, strangely enough it was based on the same philosophy of '… an eye for an eye, a tooth for a tooth …' It appeared that coming home late one night from the club and negotiating the dimly lighted streets, our agent had failed to see the dark skinned pedestrian shuffling along the roadway as there were no such modern facilities called sidewalks in this ancient part of the world.

Unfortunately, when he did glimpse him it was too late to avoid hitting him and, very unfortunately, sufficiently hard enough to result in his death. His tribal brethren immediately insisted on 'payback', which in this case was a demand for the agent's life. 'Payback' in the jungle society in which THE COMPANY was operating, even in this so-called modern age, did not resemble the ancient, Chinese, civilized philosophy of demand of retribution for 'breaking a man's rice bowel'. The death of the perpetrator would only result in breaking another man's rice bowl which would horrify any right thinking individual in one of the oldest civilizations on earth.

I tentatively suggested to the agent that he might be able to utilize the age-old system of the Orient. I, further, inferred that THE COMPANY might even consider some sort of partial compensation if he were successful in his endeavours and, therefore, did not have to leave the island furtively in the dead of night. 'Willie the Bastard' not withstanding, those of us who served THE COMPANY loyally over the years were fully aware of the almost impossibility of finding Europeans who were willing to endure the primitive conditions existing in some of the areas in which Caltex operated and the amount of compensation required to keep them at their posts.

I took my leave after the discussions with the agent which had been conducted in his home with all the shutters closed, the lights extinguished and one small candle burning in the back room of his home. He was taking no chances on being surprised before the question of 'payback' had been successfully negotiated.

There was another new experience that was in store for me. In over twenty three years in the service of THE COMPANY, I had had the good fortune of not having to contend with the problem. I had heard many tales of the harrowing predicaments encountered by several of my fellow American directors, who had had the misfortune to be faced with reconciling the jurisdictional disputes formed by the ever evolving concept of 'American management' versus 'local management'.

In general, the philosophy of attempting to use as much local talent as possible was just beginning to be a noticeable part of the policy of the international oil companies. The unusual, heavy expense of maintaining American expatriates in the field was one of the major contributing reasons for this change in the corporate mentality of the board rooms of the head offices of the internationals. Another astounding discovery on their part was that there was a wealth of hidden talent in the local organizations that had for years remained untapped.

Like the pendulum of the clock, however, this philosophy swung between the extremes of allowing local management to entirely run the organization and the sudden realization that New York management may have abrogated its responsibilities. Sometimes, local management became so entrenched and threatening to the New York Director in charge of the area that he felt that the trend had to be completely and forcibly reversed.

Unfortunately for local management in many instances they, apparently, had not had the good fortune of having the very sage advice passed on to them that I had received from my father via my mother. She, invariably, seized the opportunity to quote to me that he had warned that you should,'Always be nice to the people you pass on the way up as you climb the ladder of success. They are the very, same ones you pass on the way down.' Unluckily for me, it was the latter situation that I found myself involved in when my Regional Director of the Australian Division, Bob McCoy, informed me that I was to be transferred to Sydney, Australia as Marketing Director.

Naturally, many young Americans, as part of their overseas career development, were assigned to the field. Sometimes in certain areas to which they were assigned, the management was entirely composed of the nationals of that country. In some instances, even very senior American personnel were, also, assigned to such organizations. However, they were always junior to the local Managing Director as in cases where the refinery manager was, obviously, a very senior position, but subordinate to the Managing Director who was a local. The national management seemed to have a blind spot in regard to the disdain with which they treated these young Americans and, even more seriously, how they treated the very senior American managers that reported to them.

The opportunity of being the Managing Director and the chance to show the bloody Americans how much smarter they were, blinded them to the fact that, in the finale analysis, those very Americans towards whom they were so contemptuous would, eventually, end up in New York. New York, which unfortunately for local management, was the place from which the world wide organization of THE COMPANY was ruled with a rod of iron; a strategy which Caltex had inherited from the Two Sisters.

More devastating to some of the local management, however, there were a select few of these Americans who were re-assigned as Chief Executive Officers to the very organizations in which they had been so arrogantly treated. That made it even more humiliating for the country management, because these Americans were re-assigned to those very same organizations in order to specifically reverse the abdication of New York's iron rule. This meant that the local Managing Director was now junior to the very same American that he had so scornfully treated when that American had been previously assigned to the organization. In the cardinal rules of human nature, these Americans, invariably, had very long memories.

In a few rare cases, however, a very senior American individual assigned to the field did not report to the national manager. This in no way changed the attitude of the local management. In fact, this senior American didn't report to anyone or have anyone reporting to him, even though his title was very impressive. He was known as the 'Shareholders Representative'. This was a face saving device produced by the geniuses that inhabited the Board Room in New York. It was a means that allowed them to 'show the flag' in those countries where they inwardly thought they may abrogated their responsibilities, but outwardly, actually, knew that they had revoked those responsibilities by allowing local management to entirely run the organization. They were fearful of possible questions that might be raised by the Directors of the Two Sisters on the Caltex Board, who had never abdicated any of the autocratic rule that they used to run their own organizations. They knew that the Directors of the Two Sisters on the Caltex Board would feel that local management, in charge of one of their far distant subsidiaries, somehow or other indicated that they too, by association, had given up that iron rule.

When the Shareholder's Representative wanted some information on certain aspects of the local company over whose shoulder he was, ostensibly, suppose to be only looking, not running, he would be met by indifference to his request. There would be long and frustrating delays before finally obtaining the details after repeated enquiries. If he called the Managing Director personally to ascertain why there were such inordinate delays to his requests, he would find himself having to suffer the indignity of being told by the Managing Director's secretary that the Managing Director was busy or in a meeting or just simply unavailable.

Inasmuch as the local Managing Director was a national of the country and Chief Executive Officer as well, this meant that the so-called very senior, on paper, American executive known as the 'Shareholder's Representative' was 'socially inferior' to the local manager, even though there was no direct line of chain of command. And he was treated just that way at the many social and official functions to which both he and the Managing Director were sometimes invited.

"Is there something bothering you?" my wife questioned me one evening as we sat in front of the roaring fire in our beautiful home in Pymble, the Scarsdale of Sydney. I had been gazing out the window at the immense swimming pool which was two levels below the living room. The pool was part of our superb, four level home which had been constructed entirely of sturdy, local, hard wood and built on a sloping hill. The hill led down to a wonderfully, noisy stream at the foot of our property with no other residences to obstruct our view of the surrounding hills. "You normally read that office material so rapidly that your constant turning of the pages annoys me intensely. You've been sitting there for twenty minutes and haven't even glanced at the page you are apparently suppose to be reading. What's wrong?"

"Loyalty," I replied.

My wife looked up from her book with considerable concern expressed on her face. "You've never had a problem of loyalty to THE COMPANY before. Neither have I, in spite of how annoyed I can get at them. What's happened to cause you to have doubts now after over twenty years?"

"Oh, no," I hastened to assure her, "it isn't THE COMPANY."

With an immediate air of relief, she questioned me about what problems I could possibly have with loyalty if they weren't associated with THE COMPANY. I, hesitantly, embarked on a brief résumé detailing what, to me, could only be considered a litany of horrors. "My real problem of loyalty lies in the fact that I'm caught in the middle between Dudley Braham and Ed Letscher." Ed was the Shareholders Representative and looked the part. Although not very tall, he was stockily built and he gave the appearance that he was quite willing and able to take on any and all comers.

My wife reacted immediately to the sound of Dudley's name. "Well, you can be sure I wouldn't have any problems of loyalty to that male, chauvinistic pig. I'd run him off the gangplank without a second's thought. I wouldn't be totally unkind, of course, because I'd help him to mount the steps leading to the gangplank. And you want to know something else? There isn't a company wife that I know that wouldn't be there to help me push him over the side."

Her emotional reaction was a result of an evening of being exposed to not only Dudley's normal chauvinism, but to what could only be called downright and deliberate rudeness.

The Public Relations Department in Sydney was holding its captivating, annual occasion for all of our prime customers and business contacts. There were, also, a number of key government people who were included as is, invariably, required in the international oil business.

This affair consisted of chartering a Boeing 727 for the evening. It would take off just before dinner after all the guests had taken their assigned seats and been served with excellent, chilled vintage champagne while we were still on the ground. Another serving of champagne was made when we reached cruising altitude. And then, the most elaborate meal that Quantas could dream up, including some of the best red and white Australian wines that Quantas provided from their extensive cellars. The meal ended with a mind boggling assortment of digestives from which to choose such as Remy Matin, Irish Whiskey, Port, Armagnac, Grand Marnier, Kirsch, Bénédictine and a host of others.

At the conclusion of the meal, and after everyone had settled back in their comfortable first class lounge chairs which occupied the entire 727, the door at the front of the plane opened. 'Was the pilot going to join us when he should be paying attention to flying the aircraft?' I'm not the normal, nervous type of passenger, but after all, we weren't on a trans-Pacific flight and he definitely wouldn't have put the aircraft on automatic pilot for the simple flight plan that we were following just for the evening.

No! It, certainly, was not the Captain!

No Captain had gorgeous, flowing, blond hair with a beautifully, bronzed skin that could only have been obtained by surfing on the fabulous beaches of Sydney. In addition, she was clad only in the latest model bikini. I have always marveled why it s that the less material a bikini contained the more expensive it was, and the price of this one must have been absolutely astronomical; as we later learned that it was when all of the guests were given the opportunity of purchasing any of the items which had been modeled. The entire balance of the evening, with drinks being served on a non-stop basis by the most delightful stewardesses that Quantas could provide, was in the form of a fashion show. The models, each more strikingly beautiful than the other, if such a thing were possible, marched up and down the aisle of the aircraft. They showed off not only the almost non-existent bikinis, but the latest haute couture of the world designers, Oscar de la Renta, Christian Lacroix, Pierre Cardin, Yves Saint Laurant. Our customers loved it. The government people loved it. So did we.

I'm absolutely convinced that the Texaco directors had no idea how the Public Relations Department functioned in Sydney.

Initially, my wife had been quite flattered that her seating companion on the plane was to be Dudley, the Managing Director. Since she was the wife of the Marketing Director, the 'senior service' in the organization, it appeared only natural that she would be accorded this honour. Dudley was a life-long bachelor, which may in some way have contributed to his basic chauvinism. However, from the moment we arrived to board the aircraft and she took her seat and the aircraft gained altitude, as well as throughout the entire evening until the aircraft landed, Dudley did not address a single word to her. He was totally oblivious to her presence. He occupied himself entirely with the business and government guests on the aircraft, even when the 'Fasten Your Seat Belt' sign was on. At that time, he continued to totally ignore his seating companion by engaging in conversation with the occupants of the seats just in front of him.

As I had learned earlier, bachelors are an abomination to company wives. In the case of Dudley, however, even some of his fellow bachelors on the staff, as well as many of the married male members of The COMPANY, agreed with the company wives.

It wasn't that he could possibly have been accused of buying the staff's loyalty with salary increases and the like, but then if he didn't buy it, he certainly rewarded it. The most outstanding award, just after my arrival, was allegedly made to the Manager of the Sydney branch in the form of a Mercedes Benz that was far and above the category for which the 'big black book' called as to the class of vehicle to which a Branch Manger was entitled. Almost immediately after that, and there were many, cynical observations made as to a startling coincidence (second purchases often command big discounts), Dudley bought a Mercedes Benz for himself as a company car. This category just happened to be the top-of-the-line Mercedes Benz and was, very definitely, above the category for which the Accounting Manual called.

The poor Mercedes Benz dealer from whom the vehicles were purchased, certainly, never realized at the time he delivered the vehicles to THE COMPANY that he had entered the world of revolving doors.

At the time the Sydney Branch Manager's Mercedes appeared in the basement of Caltex House, I scarcely noticed it. Even after the Branch Manager's Mercedes disappeared and Dudley's arrived and was parked in his specially reserved parking space, I didn't notice it, although, it was the kind of vehicle that drew admiring stares from pedestrians in town as they waited for the traffic light to change.

The uncomfortable reason that I didn't notice these luxurious cars was that I was always on the look-out for Ed or Dudley in the parking area. I didn't want to be seen talking to Ed alone, when Dudley arrived in the evening to take his departure.

When I first occupied the Marketing Director's office and leaned back in the big, over stuffed, reclining chair, I noticed that right across the hall was Dudley's office. His door was always open, which meant that he could see every visitor that I had. Since my philosophy in my business career had always been that of 'an open door', as far as my staff were concerned, this didn't give me any problem. However, what did give me a problem was when the Chairman visited my office. Whether from habit or because he didn't want Dudley seeing him in my office, which I later learned, much to my chagrin, was the actual reason, Ed always took the opportunity of closing my office door before sitting down in front of me at my desk.

Within minutes, without so much as a knock or a 'by your leave', the door opened. "Oh, sorry. Didn't know you had a visitor," was the salutation addressed to me by Dudley as he sat down in the chair next to Ed's.

'Didn't know I had a visitor? Hey, you've got to be putting me on Dudley. Your door was wide open just minutes before Ed arrived. You bloody well knew that Ed was in my office. That's why you're now sitting in front of me next to him.'

The conversation turned to the weather and to things like what preparations were in hand for the visit of John McKinley, that autocratic and extremely rude Texaco Director who was, eventually, to become Chairman of Texaco and 'who would perpetrate the self-contained rule of his many predecessors'. The subjects of over staffing, lax office routines, excessive expense accounts, declining market shares were never mentioned when I had the two of them in my office. On the phone with Ed or when I was in his office, these were the only subjects that Ed wanted to discuss.

Ed and I, eventually, worked out a series of verbal codes that told him whether or not Dudley was within earshot when he telephoned me or even if he was actually in my office. Even my secretary, unfortunately for her, had to be made aware of the necessity that under no condition was she to transfer Ed's calls to me when Dudley was in my office. As her position was below the necessity of Dudley having to 'buy' or 'reward' her loyalty, she had indicated much earlier that her loyalty was to the individual who occupied the Marketing Director's chair just past her office and to whom she reported on a daily basis.

There are very few articles that can be bought for THE COMPANY by the staff of Caltex that don't require two or more authorizing signatures. However, automobiles are most certainly not among those few that don't require at least two signatures. In fact, as far as The Three Horsemen of the Apocalypse—Company cars, Company Houses and Company Wives—are concerned, company cars not only require more than two signatures, but require the Managing Director's signature on each and every company car purchased by and for anyone throughout the entire organization.

How was it possible that an experienced Sydney Branch Manager purchased a company car for himself, just prior to his retirement, without the Managing Director's signature allegedly on the purchase order? Not only purchased a company car for himself without the Managing Director's signature on the purchase order, but purchased a car well above the class allowed for a Branch Manager? An experienced Branch Manager, who had been purchasing company cars for the many members of his staff that were entitled to them over the years and was intimately familiar with each and every class of vehicle to which each and every member of his staff was allowed. He was, obviously, well aware of the paperwork procedures involved in purchasing vehicles for company employees, including himself, particularly, the requirement of the Managing Director's signature.

Rumour had it that when Ed was leaving the office one evening and saw the Mercedes Benz in the Branch Manager's parking place, he immediately returned to his office and got out the big black book. He wanted to confirm that a Mercedes Benz was an authorized class of vehicle for the Sydney Branch Manager. Actually, he knew that it wasn't. He just wanted to be sure, when confronting Dudley, of the page and paragraph in the big black book where it stated what class of vehicle could be assigned to the Sydney Branch Manger. The page and paragraph that he was researching stated that 'NO BRANCH MANAGER IS ENTITLED TO A MERCEDES BENZ'. In fact, it actually stated that *'NO EMPLOYEE* OF CALTEX—WORLD WIDE—IS ENTITLED TO A MERCEDES BENZ'.

It took considerable digging to unearth the copy of the original purchase order that had gone to the Mercedes Benz dealer to determine who had actually signed the purchase order. Before the copy of the purchase order had been unearthed, however, Dudley made an unusual number of visits to the Sydney Branch Manager's office. This was the opposite of the normal routine as the Branch Manger usually spent his time in Dudley's office. Rumour had it, also, that observers noticed that the first time Dudley left the Branch Manager's office, after Ed had raised the question as to how a Mercedes Benz could have been purchased by the Sydney Branch Manager, there was an incredulous look on the Branch Manger's face.

The second time Dudley left the Branch Manger's office, the look had become defiant. The third time Dudley left, the Branch Manager appeared resigned. Eventually and until just before the copy of the 'original' purchase order surfaced, allegedly unsigned by the Managing Director, he, literally, appeared morose. If you consulted with his colleagues, they would the be the first to confirm that he was not only morose, but extremely despondent as well.

Rumour had it, also, that when Ed challenged Dudley on how a Branch Manager could possibly have purchased a Mercedes Benz for himself just prior to his retirement (which meant that under the rules of the Accounting Manual, he could take the company car with him into retirement), Dudley stated that he would look into it immediately.

The revolving door, at the entrance of the Mercedes Benz dealer's premises, opened and out of the slot shot the Mercedes Benz of the Sydney Branch Manager headed for the showroom sales floor.

The agenda every year in the invitations to the many, huge corporate, annual meetings in the United States is quite familiar to the scores of Americans who hold shares in those massive bureaucracies. The agenda, invariably, consists of only two main items and one other; unless, of course, some shareholder group feels the company is insulting the environment or is doing business in a politically incorrect country such as was the case for many years with South Africa, and then, there can be any number of items in addition to the standard normal three.

The two main items are 'The Election of Directors' and 'The Appointment of the Auditors'. The third item is the usual 'Any Other Business Which May Come Before the Meeting'. It is under this last item that disgruntled shareholders hold forth on the obscene, multi-million dollar bonuses given to the Chairmen of corporations which are constantly showing tremendous losses and decreases in the share value, while the remuneration to the Chairman progressively climbs to lofty, space age levels.

In the Board Rooms of the subsidiaries of these corporations, this item of 'Any Other Business Which May Come Before the Meeting' is reduced to a much more manageable phrase as in 'Any Other Business'. It is a mere formality. It is never expected that any captive director would have the audacity to raise any matter under this caption. However, by having it on the agenda, the autocratically ruled subsidiaries of The Seven Sisters can always claim that they are entirely democratic, and all the Directors are free to air any controversial views which they may be unfortunate enough to hold. Since the Chairman of the Board of these subsidiaries holds absolute authority, insofar as the preparation of the agenda for these meetings is concerned, he would, normally, never activate this item himself.

And so as the monthly Board Meeting drew to its quick and efficient close in Caltex House in Sydney, all the Directors started to shut their beautifully, embossed, board room, leather bound file holders. The meetings were always brisk and proficient, inasmuch as all the items on the Board agenda had been discussed by each director with his fellow directors before going into the meeting. In this way, complete unanimity could always be obtained and, as such, it reflected the hallmark of a competently run organization. In any case, moreover, New York had already told us how to vote in the majority of cases.

With the closing of their file holders, several of the directors had risen to their feet. They were just in the act of nudging their chairs back from the ornate, board room table in preparation to falling in line behind the Chairman as he headed towards the ante-chamber, where the stewards had already opened the bar and prepared the drinks and hors d'oeuvres. The Chairman, who hadn't closed his file holder, and who hadn't risen to his feet as was his usual custom, announced in a low voice that he had an item to raise under 'Any Other Business'.

There was an abrupt retreat of those directors who were standing, as they panic strickenly regained their seats. The Chairman, in a voice that could only be described as sad and melancholy, declared that he was sorry to have to raise a question which he felt affected each and every director of THE COMPANY in the way of putting their special privileges at risk. He went on to say that one of the directors was jeopardizing these allowances by a certain action that this particular director had taken.

Every eye darted frantically and fearfully around the board room table to ascertain who this absent director could be, although each and everyone of us knew, in our heads and in our hearts, that each and every director of THE COMPANY was sitting in that very board room at that very moment. No one knew in which direction to look. I, surreptitiously, stole a glance across the table at John who always sat opposite me at the board meetings. If anyone would have an inkling of what item the Chairman was going to raise, it would be John. I was convinced that with his 'power of knowledge' he must have been able to glean some morsel of information that was behind Ed's unthinkable break in tradition of raising an item under 'Any Other Business'. With an invisible shrug of his shoulders, and an even more invisible rolling of his eyes heavenward, he sent the message that he had absolutely no idea of what was behind the Chairman's unprecedented action.

In the same sad and melancholy tone of voice, Ed continued to say how unfortunate it was that a director would take an action that would reflect on the perquisites of his fellow directors. By this time, all the directors were squirming in their seats as if the plush, board room chairs had suddenly turned into scorching hot plates. Ed continued. "Yes," he said, "it appears that one of the Directors has purchased a company car for himself far above the allowed class of vehicle for his position".

Every director physically and visibly flinched. Every director, but one, then simultaneously glanced at the edge of the board room table to see if he could, in any way, get under that table without such action possibly being noticed by his fellow directors. I realized immediately that there wouldn't be room for all of us under the table at the same time. Instantaneously, every other director had come to the same conclusion and consequently we sat frozen in our seats. Dudley, who had recoiled violently after Ed's announcement, literally leapt out his chair with his face a flaming red, leaned over the Chairman and in a low voice, that could only be described as strangled, said, "I think we can better discuss this in your office Mr. Chairman".

The revolving door at the entrance of the Mercedes Benz dealer's premises opened, and out of the slot shot Dudley's Mercedes Benz headed for the showroom sales floor.

Ed had been appointed to Australia several years ago at an earlier date and had enjoyed that lofty title in Sydney of 'Shareholder's Representative' reporting to no one and having no one report to him. Subsequently, he had been appointed Chairman of Caltex Australia, Ltd. in order to reverse what New York had, finally, inwardly acknowledged to themselves and outwardly confirmed by the appointment; They had abdicated their responsibilities and iron clad rule by allowing local management to entirely run the organization. Ed, as with all human nature and, particularly his, had a very long memory.

Perhaps, it was just as well that those ostentatious Mercedes Benezs were not within view of the expected visitor John McKinley, the Texaco Director, who was on the usual familiarization tour after having been assigned the responsibility for the Australian area. As is the usual custom with the subsidiaries in the field when one of Directors of one of the Two Sisters is on a familiarization trip, countless hours are spent in preparing graphs, statistics and presentations by various senior members of the staff. Background information on the country, the people, their culture and dress and their habits was also supplied as well. In addition, countless social gatherings were scheduled which were very, much part of the visit. There are a number of arranged visits to the many activities of the subsidiary including refineries, depots, lubrication plants and any other facility that may exist in the country at that time or which is under construction.

These arranged visits to the various facilities resemble nothing more than the Admiral's inspection in the United States Navy. All hands fervently hope that the newly applied paint over the top molding of the doorways will be dry before the Admiral runs his white, gloved hands over it looking for dust.

By an unusual coincidence, however, this particular visit varied from the customary Admiral's inspection. Some MBA in Texaco (although it may have been highly unlikely that it was an MBA, probably just a normal bottom-liner, as Texaco would never pay the entry salary that those exalted MBA degree holders demanded) had established that no painting should take place for appearance only. Any piece of equipment that required painting should be painted only if the painting were to prevent corrosion, preserve the material or ensure that no further deterioration in the item would take place. This policy would add substantially to the bottom line of the balance sheet and further emphasize the axiom heard so often in the halls of Caltex at 350 Madison Avenue in New York. 'Work for Chevron, but own Texaco stock.'

In Texaco, this directive had been sent out to all facilities through their usual bureaucratic, distribution system. In the case of Caltex, the Texaco director on the Caltex board had made the new policy quite plain at one of the monthly board meetings. In any event, the policy had filtered its way 'down under' to Australia and no painting had been undertaken in anticipation of McKinley's visit. However, the usual tidying up had been zealously attempted, and the Australians were satisfied that, barring painting, everything had been done to satisfy the requirements of the Texaco director's visit.

Many American World War II veterans will recall the startling contrast between the appearance of their British allies and the appearance of their French allies. The English, with their baggy uniforms, slouched hats and ungainly appearing boots, were a remarkable contrast to the neat, creased trousers and firm, pill box hats of the French. The appearance of the British troops in no way affected their gallant and extraordinary courage that allowed them to take unbelievable punishment from Rommel's Afrika Corps and, at the same time, push Rommel out of North Africa. The French, on the other hand, started losing wars in 1870 and haven't won one since, in spite of their creased trousers and their pill box hats.

The Australians, because of their British ancestry, had a tendency to apply the same baggy trouser, slouched hat and ungainly appearance attitude of the military to their housekeeping at their industrial sites. The Caltex Australian staff were no different in this respect. McKinley, who in the usual autocratic and arrogant way of his predecessors, had probably failed to even bother reading the brief given to him as part of the background of the country that he was in the process of visiting. Consequently, he had no idea of any of the customs that the Australians had garnered from their British ancestors—not that this particular untidy item would have been mentioned in the brief. Just as likely, he was totally unaware of the tremendous contribution the Australians had made to the World War II effort, not only right on their doorstep where Darwin had been repeatedly bombed by the japs, but in Europe and the Far East as well, thousands of miles away from their homeland.

"What did you think of our terminal Mr. McKinley?" the Caltex Operations Manager asked. Without giving McKinley a chance to answer, the Operations Manager followed up his question with the proud comment, "You probably noticed that we have followed Texaco's policy of only painting for the sake of preservation and not for appearance."

The exposure to McKinley was, in many respects, the closest that the majority of the staff of Caltex came to being on speaking terms with 'god'. A god who ruled powerfully and autocratically. A god that used the tactics of creating fear and trepidation in his followers in order to sustain that power.

McKinley's answer to the Operations Manager's question left everyone in the room with a shocked recognition. Here was a member of the senior management of one of the Two Sisters that owned Caltex, marking out his turf like a bull pawing the ground around his harem, and serving notice that he was the one and only member of the herd that had any rights, and those rights could never be questioned.

"Just because you can't paint doesn't mean that you have to live in a pigsty," were the words that every director and senior member of the staff of Caltex (Australia) Ltd. heard coming from one of the directors of their American owners, whom they had always regarded with considerable awe.

There was one aspect of Caltex management that, without a doubt, contributed to the extraordinary loyalty that all Caltex employees displayed towards THE COMPANY. No matter how often THE COMPANY would force the wives—the unpaid members of the team of two—to pack up and move from one country to another with very little notice and with great disruption to their children's education, as well as exposing the wives to cultural changes that were as different as night and day, one thing they never, ever did was to be rude to those unpaid members of their staff.

In fact, they went out of their way on every occasion to make sure that the wives were informed that they had been considered on every occasion of a move and the company's only regret was that the demands of the service impacted on them so adversely. At all the never ending functions to which the company wives were invited, and which were undertaken on the part of THE COMPANY to ensure that the company's most important customers or government representatives were properly entertained, the American Caltex directors and the most senior management deliberately made every effort to treat the wives with utmost gallantry and politeness. Their chivalry was impeccable in this respect.

McKinley's devastating response to the Manager of Operations' question produced the exact result that he had intended. From that moment on, the entire group was cowed into submission and responded to his probing questions as if they were on trial for their lives and were facing the inquisition. On and on went the presentations, the showing of graphs, the reciting of statistics and the never ending questions from McKinley. I had seen Ed glance at his watch several times as the meeting dragged interminably on. I, too, had taken the opportunity to check my watch. I knew, that at the conclusion of the meeting, we were all suppose to join the wives at the American Club where a very special dinner had been laid on in honour of McKinley's visit.

By the time I had seen Ed glance at his watch for the third time, I knew we were already thirty minutes late for dinner. Even in Ed, however, who enjoyed the awe inspiring title of Chairman of Caltex Australia, Ltd. McKinley had produced the exact fearful and submissive mood that he had planned. Ed was petrified to even mention that we were already late for dinner. Another fifteen minutes passed and Ed finally and very reluctantly overcame his fear. In desperation, he raised the question regarding as to how late we were for dinner and how long the wives had been waiting in anticipation of our joining them for the special repast set up for the Texaco director.

McKinley looked up from one of the multitudinous reports that he had been looking at while listening to the explanation from the head of the department that had prepared it. A report that had been exhaustively generated in anticipation of his visit. Before responding to Ed's observation in regard as to how late it was becoming, and how very long the wives had been waiting, McKinley made sure that the speaker had interrupted his presentation and that there were no other voices to be heard in the room. He glanced in Ed's direction, with every eye in the room following his every motion and said in a tone of voice that virtually bordered on the deepest disgust, "I didn't come to Australia to have dinner. They can wait."

20

New York, USA—1972

Even if it only opened onto East 47th Street and looked across that narrow space to another typically, dingy, New York office building, at least it was a window. Back to New York again where this time I stayed in the division in which I had spent my field time. And most important of all, I was assigned an office with a window. Most field employees when they are promoted back to New York to an office with a window can rationalize that, at least, the promotion compensates in part for their one third reduction in pay.

Almost everyone to whom you tell that you have been promoted, and as a reward have received a one third reduction in income scoff at such a statement. They can not believe that a promotion and a reduction in pay can be mutually inclusive. Even more than that, they can not grasp that such a move can actually result in your losing one third of your income. You give them a quick review of several percentages, and it slowly sinks in that it is, actually, a fact. An employee of THE COMPANY transferred back to New York from the field with, and particularly without a promotion does, in reality, forego a minimum of thirty-three and a third percent of his earnings.

The seers of finance and budgeting estimate that a wage earner should spend 25% of his monthly income on housing and utilities. Inasmuch as THE COMPANY provided free housing and free utilities for expatriates, this item alone represented 25% of the expatriates' base pay. In addition, there was always the 20% bonus of an employee's salary as an overseas allowance. Estimating that owning and operating a vehicle in New York would consume 5% of an employee's income, the sum of these three percentages equals exactly 50%. With THE COMPANY providing free company housing and free utilities, a free company car and all expenses incurred in operating it, and the added sweetener of a 20% bonus, the loss of these three items as a result of being promoted to New York meant a reduction of one third of your income. In addition, all three of these overseas' allowances were tax free, and the tax advantage is not even included in this simplified calculation.

It is easy to understand why a field employee dreads being promoted back to New York. In my case, I was merely transferred back to New York without the compensating, psychological lift of consoling myself that at least I had been promoted. Anyway, I did have my window, and that was a great solace compared to my previous assignment to my solitary cell on Devil's Island which I had occupied two years ago on the twelfth floor of 350 Madison Avenue. I, also, comforted myself with the thought that I was no longer caught between the Chairman and the Managing Director as I had been in Australia. I could go about my business without having to worry about the personalities of the people to whom I reported and with whom I worked. And no more having to worry about whether I had forgotten to inform Charles about a forthcoming function and making sure that the right people were invited to those functions and that the menu was appropriate. No longer would I have to endure the endless rounds of constantly over drinking and overeating in that executive lounge in Caltex House in Australia. Those things just didn't happen in New York.

Just how naïve could I continue to be and still exist in this wonderful world which all humans inhabit?

With the usual arrogance of international companies, Caltex had divided the world in half. Each half had been assigned to its respective Senior Vice-President. No longer was I to be caught between two such personalities as I had been in Australia.

No! Not caught between them, but as it very shortly developed, I was caught under them.

One of them, Hal Lewis and his extremely charming and attractive wife Ruth, were just as much at home on Savile Row as they were on 550 Fifth Avenue in the French Building where THE COMPANY once had been headquartered before moving to Madison Avenue. Rumour had it that the other Senior Vice-president, known as 'The Gypsy' because his name literally translated as 'The Gypsy', had allegedly been turned down by the Mafia when he had originally applied to them for employment when just out of school. The Mafia felt that since they were such an urbane and gentlemanly organization, The Gypsy would present them with a bad public relations problem if he ever became their spokesman. This was due to the fact that four letter words were not part of the Mafia's vocabulary (witness the Moraldo brothers in one of the finale scenes in the Hollywood production of John Grisham's, 'The Firm').

I have never used four letter words since the first time that I made the fatal mistake, at the age of thirteen, of having used one where my mother over-heard me. I would, indeed, have welcomed and much preferred the thrashing that I so justly deserved. In retrospect, had I received it, I may have gone on using those very four letter words the rest of my life, but much more discreetly and well out of the hearing of my mother. However, instead of the proper thrashing, I was subjected to a heart to heart talk in which I was told that such conduct was a disgrace to the family. I was informed in no uncertain terms that my revered father never used four letter words as part of his vocabulary, because his command of English was so precise and his vocabulary so extensive that he never felt a need of such invective.

He claimed that only people who never had the ability to master the language of Shakespeare needed the crutch of four letter words, because there was such a huge void in their ability to express themselves coherently to their fellow men. As an after result of this exchange of views, my mother doing the talking and I doing the listening, I found my desk in my bedroom the next morning loaded down with required reading. This required reading included Tolstoy's War and Peace, Anna Karenina, Longfellow's poems, the complete works of Shakespeare and Edgar Allen Poe, plus a host of others, all of which were supported by Webster's Unabridged Edition and a time table set up for completion of the reading of this mass of material.

In addition to my inability to use four letter words when carrying on a discussion with my Senior Vice-President, the alleged reject from the Mafia, I had also developed some very negative, English, business habits over the many, many years that I had spent working in British colonies and territories. I could never put my feet up on my own desk, much less to my horror on anyone else's desk, as my Senior Vice-President was very often in the habit of so doing. I could never sit down in his office unless specifically invited to do so, which left him with the feeling that I was a wimp. There was no way that I could tell him, and wouldn't have in any event, that the wimp had actually pulled strings in the Navy Department in Washington D.C. during his period of shore duty in the Boston Navy Yard to get sea duty during the war. Sea duty, where he felt that every able bodied American should be; confronting the enemy from behind a gun and not from the comfortable and safe surroundings of shore based duty in a United States Navy Yard in Boston repairing those very vessels on which his fellow Americans had been torpedoed and killed.

It didn't take me very long to realize that I had a problem. I didn't know how serious it was until I was in the office of another Vice-President, Jim Wolahan.

Jim was Vice-President in charge of sales. This was another division that THE COMPANY had created in regard to the separation of functional duties. I was in the process of renewing the contract between Caltex and The Aluminum Company of America—ALCOA. I was too busy consulting about the terms of the contract with the TWO SISTERS that owned us to be able to take the time to examine my relations with my Senior Vice-President, who controlled my destiny. Another indication of how naïve I was in the allocation of priorities in the corporate power struggle to ensure that I would be a survivor.

Jim was a born and bred, jovial Irishman as his name so aptly described. He was always smiling and never was too busy to listen to the woes of a fellow employee. Broad shouldered, with a twinkle in his eye and a debonair attitude, he never let you leave his office without the feeling that you were glad that you had visited him. He greeted me with a very penetrating comment one morning when I was checking out his expertise on the market price for fuel oil and the transportation costs of this product. These were the two most important items, in fact they were the only items, that mattered in any contract that THE COMPANY drew up between itself and the customer. They had been particularly important in the original agreement that I had negotiated with ALCOA. At that time it had been a long term contract for the supply of heavy fuel oil to one of ALCOA's operations in Australia and it contained a fixed price for the fuel and a fixed price for the transportation for a period of five years. These two items, cost of product and cost of transportation, occupy about ten lines of double space typing in any contract between THE COMPANY and a customer. All the rest of the twenty five pages of the contract are a monument to the ability of the legal department to maintain their highly paid positions on the staff of THE COMPANY.

"What's with you and Zingaro?", was his opening question when I arrived in his office early on a Monday morning. I suddenly realized that I had been quite delinquent in failing to remember the details of the survivor course which all corporate executives surreptitiously read avidly when they join a huge corporation. It took a question from a Vice-President, who didn't control my destiny and must have, most obviously, been discussing the matter with my Senior Vice-President, to make me aware that, indeed, I did have a very, serious problem.

What was I going to do? I couldn't start using four letter words because my vocal cords were totally incapable of forming them. I couldn't put my feet up on my desk, or anyone's else's desk, inasmuch as during all those years in the staid and proper atmosphere of the English business atmosphere, the muscles that would have provided the motion for such an action had atrophied. After spending several sleepless nights, it became apparent to me that the best, immediate remedy for my quandary was to apply myself diligently to the preparation for the renewal of the contract with ALCOA. This would, hopefully, make me concentrate on duties for which I was being paid, and stop me wondering whether or not I was going to be able to feed my family in the near future.

It can, no doubt, be said that the vast majority of American citizens are in awe of those vast, monolithic, giant bureaucracies represented by the international oil companies. Because of what the general public believe to be the fabulous salaries paid by these dinosaurs to their over achieving and over educated staff, the impression is that those employees can not make mistakes.

The value of the original contract with ALCOA, which I had negotiated just before being transferred to Australia, was in the neighborhood of one hundred million dollars a year. The subsequent renewal, on which I was now working, was many times that amount in view of the escalating prices imposed by OPEC. The original contract contained a fixed price for the product and the transportation for a period of five years. In the case of ALCOA, who had their own tankers, the cost of transport was included in the contract for those voyages when their own vessels might be engaged elsewhere in their world trade and it was necessary to use one of ours.

Because of the fixed price for the product and the transportation, it behooved THE COMPANY to make sure that whatever terms we arrived at with ALCOA they had the blessings of the TWO SISTERS that owned us. In any event, as far as the cost of transportation was concerned, all of the massive, ocean going tankers that had been sailing with the Caltex logo embossed on their smoke stacks and had been controlled by THE COMPANY for many years had long ago been taken over by the shareholders. Consequently, it now required their concurrence to whatever cost of transportation was to be entered in the contract. This action of removing the control of our tankers and transferring the resultant income from THE COMPANY to our owners was the result of an embarrassing faux pas on the part of Caltex.

It is a lesson that all subsidiaries of major international, as well as domestic, corporations should take to heart. It was a bitter lesson that was painfully learned. In our haste and desire to continue our astonishing, headlong rush towards greater and greater market share and more and more revenue and higher and higher profit for our shareholders, we had failed to look over our shoulders. Had we done so, we would have immediately made a comparison with our massive increase in income and market share with that of the TWO SISTERS that owned us. We would have instantly recognized the danger signs. Their major operations were in a much more mature and slower growing market in the Western world rather than in The Third World one in which we were prospering so enormously. Consequently, we were becoming fatter, bigger and richer than either of the two of them without realizing it.

Fatal!

The first indication of our having made such a disastrous mistake was to lose control of our tanker fleet, which was their initial attempt to cut us down to size. Now we had to ask their indulgence and bow and scrape every time we wanted a tanker from either one of them to move the vast volume of product to the countries where we, the Step-Sister, had well and truly established ourselves beyond all the expectations and belief of our TWO SISTERS who owned us. Their sibling was putting them in the shadows.

The second indication was when they decided that they and their staff were much more entitled to enjoy the luxury and good living of Europe. 'Paris in the Spring', dining at Maxim's and Tour d'Argent, the Follies Bergères, the Louvre, and the Lido when entertaining, all of which we had taken as our divine right for many years because of the successful aggressive nature of our onslaught on our competitors.

Down came the Caltex signs in the service stations throughout Europe and up went the Texaco and Chevron logos. THE COMPANY was out of business in Europe. We were cut down to a size more resembling that of an unruly and rambunctious sibling than that of a rival for more and more coverage in their annual reports, and bigger and more overwhelming numbers in the balance sheet than they themselves commanded.

C'est la vie! We will address ourselves to our remaining empire. At the time, it didn't seem possible that we could possibly again become a thorn in their sides. But we so outdid ourselves that we, subsequently, through no fault of our own, became still another threat to our owners and to their oversize egos that said no Step-Sister could out-do either of two of the Seven Sisters.

Although, it might seem strange that a five year contract was being renewed after only two years, this was a result of the arrogant oil industry being abruptly brought to its senses by their Arab producing, host countries. No sooner had we mailed the five year contract to ALCOA with a fixed price for five years than an obscure, obscure at that time, oil minister by the name of Yamani had convinced his royal masters that they, the Arabs, owned the oil underneath their feet in the scorching desert—not those high and mighty white faces sitting in board rooms a half a world away. And if the Arabs owned it, it was they who would set the prices and control the volume of production, and not some faceless, non-believers living in the decadent Western, so called civilization.

Overnight our five year, fixed price contract was a nightmare. All motorists, who had to line up at service stations through out the world at that time, will well remember how the price of crude oil was escalating. It went from one US Dollar a barrel, on an almost monthly basis until it, eventually, reached thirty-four dollars a barrel with its subsequent impact on gasoline prices and no end in sight at that stage either.

We were aghast. How many times did we bless the fact that we had checked with our two owners on the price before embarking on this suicidal journey into bankruptcy? At the fixed price that we had offered to ALCOA for the fuel oil and the transportation, and extrapolating the increases in the price of crude oil and subsequent increased cost of transportation brought on by the increased cost of the fuel necessary to move those huge super tankers, we were stunned. We calculated that when the price had reached the level of thirty-four US dollars a barrel of crude oil that OPEC was enforcing on the international oil companies, every super-tanker that we loaded resulted in a loss of US$ 11,550,000/. Not even the obscenely, wealthy oil companies can support that kind of regular loss over a period of five years with deliveries averaging every two or three weeks.

All businessmen are thoroughly familiar with the terms 'offer' and 'counter-offer'. When a supplier offers a price and certain terms for delivery of a product, it is a good faith offer and if the customer accepts it, the supplier is bound by contract law to full-fill the terms of the contract. If, on the other hand, the customer believes he can make an improvement in the terms of the original offer and makes a counter-offer, the contract offer is no longer enforceable by the customer as he has chosen to try to better the terms of the offer in the contract. The supplier is now free to accept the counter-offer or declare that it is unacceptable, and his original contract is null and void and no longer valid. Never in ALCOA's wildest dreams did they ever envisage what Caltex would construe as a counter-offer.

ALCOA hurriedly signed the contract as they, too, had suddenly become aware of the stirs of ownership in the Arab's breasts. In their covering letter to the signed contract, they mentioned that in addition to their five vessels already named and listed in the contract, they wished to inform Caltex that they had purchased another tanker and would Caltex be so kind as to include it in the list of tankers that would augment those supplied by ALCOA and would be engaged in plying their trade between Saudi Arabia and Australia on behalf of ALCOA. An additional listing of a tanker in a contract would be as mundane as asking that the mailing address for invoices be altered from one post office box to another.

"COUNTER-OFFER", SCREAMED CALTEX!

ALCOA's contract negotiator, Emile, a soft spoken, honest man of diminutive statue was on the next plane to New York where his consuming rage made him seem gigantic compared to his human physical form. He left no doubt in anyone's mind what his opinion was of the sons of bitches that ran THE COMPANY. Over the period of the company's negotiations with ALCOA, Emile and I had become very good friends. When his fury had subsided to a level in which he felt that he could talk to me on the basis of our long standing friendship, he asked me how it was possible that I could have been a party to such an outrageous interpretation of 'counter-offer'.

I had to confess to him that before he had ever gotten on the plane to confront us, I had stormed into the office of the attorney for the Australian division with the same anger that he must have felt when he first read our interpretation of his desire to include another vessel in the listing in the contract as a counter-offer. I told him how shameful I felt about the whole sordid affair and that I had pounded on the attorney's desk and demanded where in the hell the goddamn morals of THE COMPANY were. The attorney replied politely that I was in the legal department. The moral's department was down the hall in the Chairman's office.

In the midst of this chaos, I had had to take my departure for Australia because of my transfer which, hopefully, would keep me out of the further clutches of the Treasury Department. I learned later that a meeting of the minds had been reached and Emile had agreed to an increase in the fixed price. An increase which, to THE COMPANY, seemed substantial at that time and satisfactory enough to cover any subsequent increases in the posted prices by the Arabs. Little did we realize the rapacious appetites of the Arabs. It was not long before we were again on that suicidal decent into bankruptcy as OPEC kept raising the price ad infinitum. Eventually, THE COMPANY again took matters into its own hands and unilaterally canceled the contract and requested that it be re-negotiated on the basis of a variable price instead of a fixed price.

ALCOA agreed and Emile was again the contract negotiator. Why ALCOA agreed to re-negotiate a legal and binding contract will always remain a mystery. Shell, another one of those organizations staffed by highly paid over-achievers, had made the same fatal error of consummating a five year contract with a fixed price with a customer in Australia. Too many years of being the unofficial, reigning, royal masters of the desert tribes and controlling the Arabs' destiny through setting the crude oil prices of their natural resources had left the internationals with a mind set that would not allow them to accept the most unpleasant truth that they had been dethroned. Shell followed Caltex's lead and allegedly cancelled their contract. The Australians, however, were not as docile as ALCOA and promptly took Shell to court. The court handed Shell its just desserts by deciding against Shell and, to add insult to injury, allegedly awarded the customer $25,000,000.00 in punitive damages.

All of this unpleasantness was long forgotten two years later when I arrived back in New York for my second tour. It was contract renewal time. Emile was anxious to start negotiations before it got too close to the expiration date, where he felt that he would be negotiating from under the guns of those sons of bitches that ran THE COMPANY. He, also, wanted plenty of time to find another supplier, if Caltex did not appear amenable to his proposed terms of the new contract. He was able to take this stand because the oil industry was awash in heavy fuel oil. It was being discounted heavily throughout the trade, because without moving all that heavy fuel oil it would be impossible to manufacture and store the highly profitable gasoline and other high priced, refined products.

He had, in addition, become more sure of his ability as a negotiator. No doubt he had, as well, established himself firmly in the hierarchy of ALCOA and was able to speak with a lot more authority now than he had in the past. There was no uncertainty in my mind about the second assumption when he telephoned me and announced that he, the customer, was tired of commuting from San Francisco to his supplier's office in New York. The negotiations were going to be held on his home turf. I assumed that he meant that to be San Francisco. Imagine my surprise and pleasure when he announced in no uncertain terms that the negotiations would held in Las Vegas at the MGM Grand Hotel.

I was out of my chair in an instant and sprinted upstairs to Jim Wolahan's office, my friendly VP who was to be part of the negotiating team, with the great news of where our negotiations were going to take place. Although, I was well aware of Texaco's narrow view of the sinful world in which they felt they had to exist, I was still amazed by Jim's reaction. He was dismayed. His face fell and I could almost feel an invisible flinch.

"That is out the question," he stated emphatically. "Texaco would never stand still for Caltex going to Las Vegas to negotiate a contract, even a multi-million dollar one."

"Jim," I said, "this is the customer talking. This is not Caltex's idea. This is ALCOA, one of the world's largest, if not the largest, aluminum company in the world. This is the twentieth century Jim. Emile is not some WOG in one of the colonies. This customer wants to buy several hundred million dollars worth of our fuel oil. He wants to negotiate the contract in Las Vegas, and you're afraid of Texaco's reaction to THE COMPANY going to Las Vegas for the purpose of negotiating a multi-million dollar contract?".

He was adamant. There was no way that I could sway him. He was just downright fearful of Texaco's reaction to such a bizarre location for contract negotiations. And the fear that Texaco would frown on what activities in which the employees of their Step-Sister might engage when they were not in the conference room negotiating.

Jim and I had become good friends over the time that I had been in New York. We had been on several pub crawls together. Therefore, I felt free to make a suggestion that I would never have voiced to my allegedly, mafia VP. I leaned across his desk and whispered, "Don't tell them." He was even more aghast and nervously looked over his shoulder as if an incarnation of Gus Long were standing there behind him listening to the entire conversation.

"My God," he said, "do you realize how many moles the goddamn shareholders have in THE COMPANY? They would know where we were going before we even bought the tickets."

"OK Jim, with no disrespect to a Vice-President of this God-fearing, non-drinking, non-gambling organization of pious individuals known as The Caltex Family, you stay put! I will keep you advised of our progress on the negotiations by telephone on a minute by minute basis from Las Vegas. I have no intention of telling my customer that you are so bloody scared of those puritanical, autocratic, goddamn shareholders that you would rather lose a multi-million dollar customer than risk their wrath that you might stray off the straight and narrow by drinking. In fact, heaven forbid, you might possibly gamble with Emile and put your losses on your expense account if you went to Las Vegas on an airline ticket for which THE COMPANY had paid."

Jim blinked. My determination had left him in a quandary. Here was a junior officer of THE COMPANY telling him in no uncertain terms that the age of the monolithic, arrogant dinosaur was over. Texaco could no longer impose its will on Caltex when it came to matters of operating. THE COMPANY had gotten where it was by flaunting such insidious thought control by the shareholders very often over the years. Admittedly, it was always in very out of the way places and strange countries and never in so vividly a context as negotiating a contract with ALCOA in Las Vegas in the United States.

Jim never told me how he resolved his conflict. I suspected that he didn't consult with Texaco, but he surely sought out the advice of our Chairman, Jim Voss. Inasmuch as Jim Voss had grown up in Caltex before he became chairman and, therefore, didn't have the brain washing that so many of his predecessors had had when they were part of one of the Two Sisters, particularly Texaco. He, undoubtedly, told Jim to bury his fears. After we had sewed up the contract, we could worry about the fall out from Texaco when we confronted them with a multi-million dollar, signed contract negotiated in that city of sin and degradation that the customer had chosen in which to immerse himself and his fellow sinners.

As Texaco would have suspected of the employees of its Step-Sister, we did everything that would have brought frowns to their ascetic faces. We gambled. We drank untold, extra dry, gin martinis—not vodka. We stayed up late at night. We downed gallons of wine poured from leather wine bags slung over the shoulders of the slave girls at Ceaser's Palace and we successfully renegotiated the contract.

Emile may have been a multi-million dollar customer and he could rightly have expected the red carpet treatment, but fortunately for him he was in the dirty end of the oil business. He was a buyer of heavy fuel oil which is known as a 'dirty product'. He was concerned with price, tanker loadings, demurrage costs and all those down to earth items that can be measured in dollars and cents, and which had a finite and discernable influence on the bottom line of the shareholders' balance sheets. He couldn't influence governments or public bodies, and he wasn't a practitioner of government relations, public relations or press relations. Consequently, we never had to subject him to one of those interminable, drawn out, speech making dinners at the Plaza Hotel. He never knew how fortunate he was.

I must confess that I was very impressed the first time my wife and I were 'included' at one of these grand functions at the one of the world's most prestigious hotels. The word is 'included' not 'invited'. We were included, because we had had some distant relationship with the guest of honour having served in his country and possibly even attended the independence celebrations when they ran the royal colours down for the last time. THE COMPANY wanted him to feel comfortable by having some familiar faces around.

The ornate, private dining room in the Plaza, with its walls lined by highly polished book shelves made of burled-walnut with their intricate, lead lined, glass doors to protect the valuable collection of rare editions, gave every indication of decadent, obscene wealth. Of course, that was exactly what it was. One had to assume that the books were rare editions behind those lead lined glass doors or else why this secure method of protecting them from any prying hands? The security method also guaranteed that they could never be read on a current basis or, probably, never initially read either.

There was the usual, matching burled-walnut, huge, oval dining table with the high backed chairs, so typical of the style of the carriage trade at the time that the Plaza burst onto the New York scene. No! Not burst, but emerged. The Plaza would never burst onto any scene. It was almost awe inspiring to a first time diner and, particularly, to me as impressionable as I was.

At this stage, I can not remember if the main course of the dinner was roast beef or roast chicken. It doesn't really matter, because on the innumerable occasions at which my wife and I attended these functions the routine was 'writ in stone'; Cocktails in the lounge for a fixed period of forty-five minutes exactly. Then a jovial invitation from the host, whether he was the Chairman or the President or a lowly Vice-president depending on the guest of honour, to enter the dining room and take our seats and start working our jaws through one of the two main courses that was always served, rubbery chicken or the overdone roast beef. By the time desert and coffee had arrived, there were the usual, ominous indications that the host was ready to introduce the guest of honour and the speeches were about to begin.

We could make ready to steel ourselves for the ordeal of hearing how wonderful the relationship was between THE COMPANY and the guest of honour's country, or between THE COMPANY and the decades' long relationship of the franchise holder. A franchise holder whom we had inadvertently made a millionaire, or between some US Government official that we had long been lobbying from our fully staffed, permanent, Washington D.C. office.

During the polite applause acknowledging the introduction of the guest of honour, my wife leaned over and whispered in my ear, "Did you have anything to do with these arrangements?" she asked.

"No. Why?"

"It seems to me that it is an exact replica of the arrangements that you and Charles always made in Australia, and you promised me, that after Australia, that we wouldn't have to endure anymore of these ordeals," she almost hissed.

"A fluke. Once in a lifetime. Don't worry."

Naïvety! Naïvety! Naïvety! I was still cursed with that failing. Not only were we included in any number of these functions, but it wasn't long before I was yearning for the ever-ready presence of Charles who was always close at hand in Australia and able to work miracles when the occasion demanded it. Now in New York, it was I alone that had to arrange a dinner for thirty people in the appropriate restaurant; pick out a menu that would satisfy everyone; choose the proper vintage wine and make sure that there was sufficient transportation so that every-one arrived on time and that the limousines were at the door at the instant that the dinner was declared finished and the guests were ready to depart. It was more of a nightmare than I ever thought could possibly surpass the two horrific moments of my initial introduction to the Executive Lounge in Caltex House in Sydney, Australia.

There was no aide de camp to show the guests where they were to be seated at the dinner that I was arranging. If only there were, I could have avoided the embarrassing moment of having to tell Mrs. Vice-President, Jim Wolahan's wife, that she was going to have to sit opposite me, the lowest figure on the totem pole at this particular gathering. The whole affair had started off with the usual miscal-culation on my part that time would have mellowed my wife as far as the guest of honour was concerned.

She had moved to Florida where we were building our retirement home, but even at that distance she remained her usual, accommodating self when my, and the company's, interest required her participation in functions in which I had now become the main participant. No longer was I just 'included'. I was the mover and shaker. I picked the local. I choose the menu. I selected the wines. I made up the seating arrangements after being told who was the guest of honour for the particular function which I had been asked, as in the general requests, to set up.

My arrangements with my wife had reached a perfect routine. As soon as I was made aware of the date for the particular function that I was to arrange and that would require her presence, I would telephone her in Florida. I would advise her of the location, that her airline ticket would be ready at the airport for her to pick up and on her arrival the limousine would take her to one of the company suites in New York and that an appointment had been made with her favourite hair-dresser close to the hotel. From there on, I would be available to pick her up, have her chauffeured to the dinner and after that she was free to spend the rest of her time shopping in New York until the time for departure back to Florida.

After almost thirty years of married life, I still harboured the forlorn feeling that perhaps I might come out ahead in a no-win situation. Why is naïvety such a strong part of my character or perhaps lack of character? If I got her to New York without her knowing who was the guest of honour, she couldn't fail to concede that being there already she would have to participate in the evening's festivities. I based that assumption on the fact that many times she would wait to be briefed after she got to New York as to whom and why THE COMPANY was entertaining some figure important to its interests. Not this time. Her inherent instincts must have told her that she should ask before she got on the plane.

"What's the occasion?" she queried. "I have a duplicate bridge tournament this week and would hate to miss it, but if you feel that I have to be there I'll postpone it to the following week."

"Oh, just the usual. He and his wife are on a retirement tour and we are rolling out the red carpet in recognition of almost forty years of service," was my ambiguous reply. Thirty years is a long time to be married.

"Don't be evasive. Just tell me who it is and have I met his wife before? There is only one person that I could imagine you being so circumspect about, but he isn't married."

"Well, actually, I understand that she is charming and since being married he apparently has become a changed man. She has made such a difference in him I've been told that nobody recognizes him."

"That chauvinistic pig would never get married, but something tells me that, if he has, she has lots of money and something else tells me that you are trying to get me to New York before you tell me that it is Dudley whom you going to wine and dine without the able assistance of your 'ever-lovin' wife. The answer is, *no!* I am playing a duplicate bridge tournament this week and you can offer my apologies to Ray and Barber and tell them how disappointed I am that I will be unable to join them for dinner. Oh, and if Dudley should ask for me, which I doubt, tell him I'm attending a fashion show." Men will never understand women.

The absence of one guest can be explained without too much embarrassment. After all, Florida is a long way from New York, but I should have known that my abortive attempt to mislead my wife into coming to New York for Dudley's retirement dinner was a harbinger of even more embarrassment—like as in the absence of the host.

"What did you say Ray?" as I gazed at the phone with that sinking feeling in the pit of my stomach which told me that the coming evening was going to be a disaster with no Charles to work miracles and no John to fill in for the absent guests. "You can't make the dinner on Friday night? What happened?" His answer didn't really make any difference. I was now faced with a dinner party that had no host, my wife was not there to give me moral support and do her usual, fine supporting function of seeing that the guests mixed comfortably and the conversation flowed. I was thoroughly convinced that the food would be uneatable, the wine corked and the limousines late in picking up the guests.

When I asked Ray who should take his place, his immediate suggestion was to ask Jim Wolahan, but before I did so I was to be sure to check with Barbara to see if that substitution was satisfactory to her. Ray had just celebrated his thirty-fifth wedding anniversary, but he was miles ahead of me in the feelings of marital sensitivity. Barbara agreed and Jim, with his usual good humour and willingness to help out during a major problem, said he would be delighted to play host. And there-in lay the problem.

Jim was delighted to play host, but there was no mention of hostess. From the look on his wife's face when I indicated where she was to sit at this important function, I swiftly came to the conclusion that Jim had successfully pulled my stunt on his wife that I had been so unsuccessful in trying on my wife. He hadn't told her that she wasn't going to be the hostess. He had, apparently, only told her that he was going to be the host and let her assume that she was going to be the hostess. Having gotten her there under false pretenses, just as I had hoped to get my wife to New York where it would be too late to back out of any arrangements, she was now at the dinner and couldn't very well leave, but she sure could make my life and the dinner conversation miserable.

Fortunately, the food was more than eatable, it was delicious. The vintage wine wasn't corked and the superb soufflé desert that I had personally chosen as I well knew the reputation of the chef came to the table at the peak of its fluffiness. As usual, my astute wife was absolutely correct. Dudley's wife reeked of money, but in spite of this she was charming and had, as we had been informed, worked miracles on Dudley to such an extent that he almost resembled a human being. In all the times that I continued to make arrangements for these functions a la Charles and Australia, I never choose the Plaza.

We all believed that the two senior vice-presidents allegedly loathed each other if for no other reason than the fact that both of them wanted to be Chairman and only one of them was going to make it. It all depended, of course, on whom Jim Voss was going to anoint and that depended on how well each of them performed their duties. In addition, their personalities were so different that there just had to be a fundamental dislike between them. Neither one of them said anything or ever indicated the depth of their contempt for each other, but it was easy to see in the way in which they regarded each other. Jim had a habit of rotating them between their two halves of the world as an inducement to have them out perform each other when they took over the other's half of the world. That was how I, so very unfortunately, went out from under Hal Lewis' wing and ended up under Zingaro's claws when Jim made one of his half-world responsibilities' changes.

I was still under Hal when Jim had the usual dinner at the Plaza to entertain some very important Australian government visitors. I wondered why Zingaoro and several of his senior staff had been invited to the dinner as it was not in anyway part of his area. Unknown to me, of course, the invitation was part of the familiarization program which all senior executives undergo when they take over a new area, à la the Texaco and Chevron directors, and which Jim was initiating in anticipation of the transfer of powers from Hal to Zingaro. Had I but known that the change-over was to take place, I would never have visibly laughed so uproariously at Jim's after dinner ethnic story. Normally, I have no liking for ethnic stories and I often wondered why Jim would tell them, but in this case it was directed against Zingaro and I couldn't help but enjoy it.

Jim's story consisted of describing the traffic situation on a four corner intersection in California. Apparently in some parts of California at a change in the traffic lights, there are crossings which are totally allocated to traffic free crossing by pedestrians. This is accomplished by turning all vehicular lights from all four directions red. This allows the pedestrian to cross at any angle he or she wishes; either directly from one side of the street to the other or diagonally across the intersection. Jim further explained that a Brinks truck had just crossed the intersection before the lights changed and a ten thousand dollar bill had fallen out of the back door and was lying exactly in the middle of the intersection.

Among the many pedestrians waiting to cross in anticipation of the traffic lights turning red for all the vehicular traffic, there were four in particular. It appeared that on one corner of the four corners of the intersection there was a Tooth Fairy, on another corner stood Santa Claus, on another corner stood a smart Italian and on the fourth corner stood a dumb Polack. All four of these individuals had their eyes glued on the ten thousand dollar bill lying in the center of the four corner intersection. Each was poised to take off immediately the traffic came to a halt.

When Jim had finished his description of what the situation was at this particular crossing with the four main characters identified and the location of the ten-thousand dollar bill marked, there was no doubt in any one's mind what his question was going to be. "Well," he said as he looked around the room at the guests and, particularly, at Zingaro for some, unobvious reason at that stage, "Which of the four characters that I've described recovered the ten thousand dollar bill when the vehicular traffic came to a stand-still?"

There was a lot of good natured laughter and some boisterous shouting from some of the heavy drinkers. One of the ladies suggested that it was the Tooth Fairy, as he was going to use the money to reward all those trusting children who over the years had hidden their teeth under their pillows. Another endorsed Santa Claus, because of the increased cost of living he needed the money to feed his reindeer. Some self-serving, smart survivor who lived under Zingaro's half of the world piped up and said that it had to be the smart Italian. No one suggested that it might be the dumb Polack. Dumb Polack stories are too numerous to count and, of course, the dumb Polack is always the loser.

To everyone's surprise, Jim announced that it was the dumb Polack who retrieved the ten thousand dollar note. There was a chorus of shouts of 'no way', 'not possible', 'you have got to be kidding', and the final one from Zingaro who said, "There are millions of dumb Polacks, but there is not one that could out smart a smart Italian".

Jim laughed and turned toward Zingaro and said, "That's where you are wrong my friend. Everybody knows there is no Tooth Fairy and although Santa Claus is a living legend, once you are six years of age you realize that there is no Santa Claus. That leaves the last two characters to compete for the chance to retrieve the ten thousand dollar bill and while the whole world knows that there is no Tooth Fairy and no Santa Claus, God knows there is no such thing as a smart Italian either, so that leaves our friend, the dumb Polack as the winner".

The room exploded in hilarious laughter at Zingaro's expense. As the laughter subsided, Ruth Lewis' voice could be heard with indignant over-tones as she directed her comment towards Jim. A comment made because of her inherent kindness and decency. "I don't think that's a particularly nice story to tell Jim and, most certainly, not in front of Zingaro". Whatever lingering sounds of laughter were still to be heard ceased instantly.

I immediately looked at Hal who was sitting opposite me. The look on his face was almost comical. He appeared to be trying by ESP to ask Ruth whose side she was on. He had pushed himself back from the table enough so that if Jim had glanced down in his direction, he would not be able to see him trying to get her attention and get her to affect some kind of damage control. He was finally successful and, if anyone doubted it, they had only to look at Ruth's face. She was aghast. Hal's look had immediately told her that she had committed two unpardonable sins. She had publicly criticized the Chairman and as far as Hal was concerned, she had committed an even greater sin. She had sided with Zingaro.

Although kindness and decency were deep, inherent qualities in Ruth, her love and support of her husband took priority. She immediately turned and addressed Jim, "What I meant to say Jim was that it's a cute story and no doubt Zingaro enjoyed it as much as we did, as I am sure he knew you were pulling his leg". I had known Ruth a number of years and had been a guest in her home so I could sense, through association, that having to reverse herself must have really been a distressing effort. Sitting next to her, I could almost hear her gagging over her damage control. I saw Hal relax partially and the rest of the room suddenly came alive with subdued conversation. Zingaro had been at the forefront of the laughter when Jim had finished his story. It didn't matter to Zingaro what or how often Jim made him the butt of his stories as long as he thought he had a chance at the Chairmanship. And so ended another Plaza dinner.

Dinner after dinner, luncheon after luncheon, expense account after expense account and my stay in New York lengthened into years until one day I found sitting in front of me a young, personable, well dressed MBA. He had been sent up to me from the Personal Department, because I had now reached that lofty position known as a 'senior international oil executive'. I was a Regional Director. The areas for which I was charged were Australia, Papua New Guinea and New Zealand. In addition to these physical areas, as a senior international oil executive, the same type who had interviewed me when I had first applied to THE COMPANY, I was charged with interviewing prospective employees who had lost all perception of common sense and wanted to join an international oil company.

I could not believe what I was telling this young man who had a life time of business experience ahead of him, 'As an international oil executive you will see the world, enjoy a substantial income and live a life of comfort and ease'. Had I really said that? Had I sold my soul to the devil? Was I another Dorian Grey? What moral corruption had I undergone in the New York office of THE COMPANY? Did I have no sense of decency left?

A LIFE OF EASE AND COMFORT????

It was time for me to retire.

21

The Treasury Department—1984

All of you who are looking forward to retirement with such great longing and anticipation had better have second thoughts. Do you realize that you will be leaving a highly exciting and energized environment to which you have been subjected for countless years? Do you realize that you are suddenly going to be exposed to a morale destroying, sedimentary way of life in which you know exactly what each day is going to bring?

On your first day after you have retired the reality of your retirement sinks in. You suddenly grasp the fact that you do not have to get up in the morning; you do not have to be ready to answer the boss' questions; you do not have to do anything including being answerable to your wife's queries on the telephone as to whether or not you are going to be home for dinner or whether you will be stuck in the office for an indeterminate length of time. You are not going to be stuck in the office, because you no longer have an office. You are not going to be home late for dinner because you are already home. Your relationship with your wife has instantly started to undergo a metamorphosis. Her marriage vows have suddenly taken on a different meaning, 'For better or worse, but not for lunch'.

Retirement for me was a repeat of the nightmare that I experienced when I left the Navy and entered civilian life. From the day that I had been born I had been 'subject' to the will and fancy of various adults most of whom were, obviously, my superiors. In my formative years it was my mother. When I entered The Polytechnic Institute of New York, it was my professors. When I graduated from The Polytechnic and left home and joined the Navy, it was my commanding officers. When I was discharged from the Navy at the cessation of hostilities I had no one to whom I had to be subservient. I was twenty-seven years old; twenty-seven years old and during that entire twenty-seven year period I had never been in a position where I could make the decision that I wasn't going to do what was expected of me. Suddenly I could do, or not do, anything if I so chose; nothing, including earning a living.

I was aghast. I use to wake up in the middle of the night in a cold sweat and toss and turn for hours on end because I realized that soon dawn was going to break on the horizon and when it did I didn't have to get up in the morning. I didn't have to report to anyone; be it my mother, my professors, my superior officers or even some unknown character that represented a boss in my new employment, because I didn't have any new employment. I didn't have a boss. I didn't have a job. I didn't have any safe anchor that told me that I had better do this or that or the consequences would be disastrous for me as a result of my not doing as I had been told. There was no one to tell me what I should do. I longed for those days when I had railed against those in power who had the authority to direct my life.

I had been raised during that period of the great depression in the 1930's. On my way to school commuting to Brooklyn Technical High School and after graduation from there to The Polytechnic Institute of New York, I had climbed over the many bodies of those homeless who slept on newspapers under the protection of the overhead tracks at the Kings Highway Station of the New York Subway system in Brooklyn. It was a bitter memory that I bore throughout my life.

It was the constant source of never ending accusations from my wife that I thought more of my job than I did of her and our children. I never wavered from stating that it was because of my concern for them and the need to feed and house them that I spent so much of my energies on ensuring that I would always be in a position to have an income which guaranteed that I would never become one of those hopeless people sleeping on newspapers or selling apples on the corners of the streets of the City of New York.

Suddenly in the midst of all this trauma as I returned home for lunch from The Yacht Club where I had been commiserating with the barman and consuming an unwarranted amount of alcohol to ease the pain of my dilemma, my wife announced that THE COMPANY had telephoned from Dallas. Caltex had joined the great migration and had moved its corporate headquarters from New York to Dallas, Texas.

Oh, yes, apropos of the Harvard Business Review article, the chairman lived in Austin, Texas.

THE COMPANY wanted me. My prayers had been answered. They needed me and were going to call me back from retirement. Who says there is no Santa Claus, Tooth Fairy or Smart Italians?

"You are to call them the moment you get home", my wife announced. "They wouldn't tell me what it was all about", she continued in a suspicious voice. I could tell from her tone that she too had visions of THE COMPANY again intruding on a life to which she had only so recently come to the conclusion would no longer consist of constant up-rooting, packing the household belongings and saying goodbye to friends only too recently made. I also had the same visions, but with an entirely different reaction to what she now dreaded and for which I was longing.

I was on the telephone before the echo of her voice had died away. I was so enthralled with the thought that I imagined that I was about to get back into harness that her added comment that I was to call an attorney in the legal department hadn't registered on my mind. While the telephone was ringing in Dallas, the fact that I had been requested to call the legal department and that I had actually dialed the number without a second's thought, suddenly sank in. Not the Chairman or the Personnel Department or one of my previous Vice-Presidents; even The Gypsy appeared to be wearing a halo at this stage, but the legal department!

Yes! On serious and measured reflection, it is true and very sad to relate. There is no Santa Claus, Tooth Fairy or even Smart Italians wearing halos.

"We're Federal Expressing you your airline ticket to New York. You will arrive in New York Sunday night which will allow you to be in our New York attorneys' office at nine o'clock on Monday morning. You will be briefed by them during the entire day and a finale review on Tuesday morning. Your appointment with the Treasury Department is at 2:30 PM on Tuesday afternoon which should allow you sufficient time to reassess all aspects of the period covered during your stay in Johannesburg. Unfortunately, the two New York, outside attorneys who handled your briefing for your initial meeting with the Treasury Department are no longer with the firm so you will have to be prepared to review the entire case history of the embargo busting by our competitors." Whether or not it was a memory lapse or that seventeen years had induced a mind set in the company attorney to whom I was talking that it was our competitors who were responsible for the embargo busting, I didn't question. Although this particular attorney had not been part of the two man company team that had been my 'antagonists' during the prior inquisition and 'murder boards', he was fully aware from contact with his colleagues of all aspects of the company's involvement in the supply of petroleum products to Rhodesia during the embargo.

I had escaped unscathed from my previous encounters with The Treasury Department. I, also, had the rather comforting feeling that the statue of limitations must surely apply after a period of seventeen years. I assuaged my disappointment at not being called back to work by deciding that I would enjoy myself as much as possible before being subjected to another inquisition and to the 'murder boards'.

I immediately booked a suite at the Helmsley Palace Hotel. I had often entertained visiting dignitaries there, as well as my Vice-President Ray Johnson, in the most luxurious dinning facilities of that historical site. While dining there, I had often wondered if the accommodations were equal to the efforts put forward by the hotel's chef. I also called the London Towne Car Company which had always provided me with excellent limousine service over the many years that I had commuted from New York to Australia, New Zealand and London. Even if I were not going to get back in harness, at least I would have all the outward trappings of power.

As I finished making these arrangements on the telephone my wife, who had been reading the latest issue of 'Gourmet' magazine, had correctly interpreted my feelings from listening to the arrangements I had made to ensure that I would have all the illusions of being back at work. She suggested that I might be interested in an article which she had just finished. She said that there were three restaurants listed in the article which claimed that they were the three best French ones in New York. "Interestingly enough," she said, "You and I have been to two of the three. The only one that we missed is the Lutetia. Perhaps it will help to ease the pain and give you a psychological lift for your confrontation on Tuesday if you dine there on Monday night. You can give me a plate by plate description of the menu and how you enjoyed it by calling me after dinner." It was, indeed, an excellent suggestion for a morale boaster, but it also gave me just a little bit of an embarrassing feeling at a later date when I hesitated over putting $350.00 on my expense account for a dinner. Three hundred and fifty dollars and sometimes $1000/for dinner or lunch were no strangers to my previous expense accounts for those times when I had been the host, but $350.00 for dinner for myself was unique.

At the time, I didn't know that 'Lutetia' was the name that the Romans had given the present site of Paris in the middle of the third century when they had first settled in that area. Since The Lutetia had been listed in the 'Gourmet' magazine as one of the three best French restaurants in New York I should have stirred myself to enquire as to the origin of the restaurant's name. It was, indeed, a very strange coincidence that many years later after retirement the first place in Paris that I lived was just across the street from one of the oldest and most prestigious hotels in Paris called, of course, The Lutetia. It was at that time that I learned how the name had come about.

In addition to all this old world charm of the Lutetia Hotel so near to me, the name of the street just across from The Lutetia and on which my apartment was located was rue Recamier. There are many readers who are familiar with the various mistresses of the royals. And, also, of the simply great figures of France from the ancient days down to the present time when François Mitterand's mistress attracted so much publicity when she and her daughter—sired by Mittererand—were invited to his funeral by his widow. Madame Recamier was the mistress of Chateau Briand, the famous French writer. Rumour had it that she had, as a permanent vantage point, the front window of her bedroom which over looked rue Recamier which was supposed to have been named after her. From here she could watch Chateau Briand as he left and arrived from his apartments on the same street and could see whether or not there were any other female companions in attendance besides his wife. From this vantage point she was thus able to determine if any one was infringing on her position as the second most important woman in Chateau Briand's life

The Beluga Caviar and Absolut Vodka at the Lutetia were superb appetizers and an excellent starter. It brought back very fond memories of the visit to that port city in Iran on the Caspian Sea. As was usual, I had been unfortunate enough to be in Iran during one of their religious holidays which were as frequent as the drenching showers during the monsoon season. The only compensating feature was that my good friend and colleague and competitor from Mobil, Don Speilman, was also stuck there with nothing to do as well as all business was at a standstill during the festivities. He suggested that perhaps it would be an ideal time to visit the Caspian Sea and perhaps taste some caviar right at the source. Since Mobil already had an active agent in Iran, while I was only trying to set one up, Don had his agent's transportation facilities at his command. It was a hair raising ride over the country roads of Iran as we wended our way North from Tehran to the Caspian Sea. The City of Resht was actually located on the river close to the Caspian.

We checked into our hotel and washed the grime of our dusty voyage off our faces and clothes and dressed appropriately for a dinner that was going to begin with that ultimate luxury known around the world as 'food fit for a king'. After ordering the caviar as an appetizer, the waiter asked what we would like as a second course. Both Don and I without consulting with each other told the waiter simultaneously that we would wait until we had consumed our appetizer before we decided on our second course. We must have had the same unconscious thoughts because after savouring the most delicious caviar either one of us had ever had the pleasure of eating, we both blurted out to each other, "Since we are on the Caspian sea, why not have something to do with fish?" After some great discussion, it was decided that the only thing that had to do with fish was caviar. And so our second course consisted of a repeat of the first. However, when we told our waiter that our main course was going to be caviar, he just shook his head in disbelief. He was absolutely convinced that these non-believers from the Western World had taken leave of their senses. He was further assured of his conclusion about the non-believers when we ordered caviar for desert.

Well, I obviously couldn't repeat that performance here in New York, but certainly Canard à l'Orange with champigions and a purée accompanied by a vintage bottle of St.Emillion would be appropriate for a restaurant listed as one of the best three French restaurants in New York. I also had remembered that Champagne was the choice of a dessert wine. Not too sweet so as to offset the sweetness of the soufflé. Going down memory lane again I thought of all the Môet et Chandon that THE COMPANY had supplied for those glorious weekends in Hong Kong when we were using the company tug and the customer couldn't be fueled on a Sunday. It didn't take much of an effort to decide to repeat those glorious Hong Kong days, particularly, when the sommelier informed me that he had one of the best vintage years of Môet et Chandon in the Lutetia cellars.

Monday morning arrived and I presented myself at the office of the company's New York attorneys. We immediately started with the three articles of faith. *DO NOT LIE! DO NOT LIE! DO NOT LIE!* They, then, insisted that we review every piece of information that I had given to the previous 'murder boards' seventeen years ago. Although, I had written copious notes on the plane from Florida to New York, I found that I didn't have to refer to them once when presenting the information to the outside attorneys. The facts had been indelibly burned into my mind seventeen years ago where they had lain dormant waiting for some idiot bureaucrat to rub the genie's bottle seventeen years later. What kind of file system and follow up procedures did The Treasury department have that allowed a dormant case, seventeen years old, to suddenly surface? I would never know the answer to these questions, but both the questions and the non-existent answers were academic. The genie was loose.

We spent the whole day taking turns at confrontational interrogation. By the end of the day, I was exhausted as expected. I had been informed by the attorneys that I was to get a good night's rest. In addition, I had no desire to repeat last nights gourmet repast. In the short time since retirement, my stomach had grown unaccustomed to the level of rich and calorie laden fare supplied by the normal Caltex expense account. I had no desire to be at anything but my best for Tuesday afternoon's clash with the United States Government in the form of The Treasury Department.

Although my intentions were of the best, I would be the first to admit that I didn't spend a restful night. Tuesday morning was no help to my frame of mind as the murder boards were intensified and the confrontational attitudes became more and more antagonistic. By lunch time, I felt that I was entitled to a good, extra, dry gin, not vodka, martini, and I so informed the waiter. To my utmost surprise, my order was countermanded by the outside attorneys who advised me that Dallas had told them that under no condition was The Treasury Department to elicit any additional information from me than they had seventeen years ago and, certainly, not because I couldn't wait until after the meeting to enjoy one of Texaco's forbidden gin martinis. The preparation for the meeting and the cost of it must have paid off, because The Treasury Department was left exactly where it was at the close of the previous meetings seventeen years before.

They didn't ask who was paying for the product. I didn't volunteer the information.

22

Paris—2007

Caltex Petroleum Corporation

It was a marvelous company and unique among the internationals. There were many wonderful people that were part of the company and it was an honour and a privilege to work for them and with them. I would not change a minute of the thirty-four years.

R. Palmer Smith
Regional Director (Ret.)

Epilogue

'Nos moritores te salutamus'

The greatest democracy in the world, past and present, is the United States of America. The third is Great Britain. There is no second. A distant fourth is France. There are many that follow closely in the footsteps of these three great nations. Nonetheless, as those who frequent the wagering windows of the fleet footed genus Equus know, there is no pay off after the third runner comes home.

The Archbishop of Canterbury is wrong. "It is better to be *dead*, than *Red*." He has never lived under an oppressive, soul destroying, morally corrupting regime governed by those individuals who are committed to obliterating any vestige of independent thought by their subjects. If he had, he would never have made that world wide, well known statement with which he has been credited, rightly or wrongly, "It is better to be *Red*, than *dead*".

There may be some who would challenge the premiss that there is no greater democracy than the United States. More importantly, their real challenge is not which country occupies first place in the hierarchy, but whether or not democracy is the arena for man's endless search to find the ultimate rational for his being. I would suggest to them that they become citizens under some of the kind of regimes which are represented in the list of contents of this chronology or even some that are not listed. Perhaps, they would care to take up residence in Bosnia or in Rwanda or in the streets of North Korea or even, conceivably, in Havana just across the water from the shores of the United States.

If they are honest searchers, they will accept the gauntlet. If they are members of that world wide conspiracy dedicated to perpetuating themselves and their power in pursuit of the total domination of humanity with the intent of enslaving them, the invitation is academic. They are too perceptive to rise to such a challenge. They are fully determined, and they intend to remain so in those societies which they so despotically rule, that man will not even be permitted to think, much less be allowed to embark on a philosophical journey.

There are no greater, supporting, economic systems for safeguarding democracy and the consequent betterment of man, spiritually and materially, than the free market and free trade. The international oil companies with their global system of interchange of market intelligence allows them to react instantaneously to a change in even the remotest parts of the world. There is no requirement to have those commercial decisions referred to a government controlled, central planning committee before they can be implemented.

That is not to say they are entitled to carte blanche in pursuit of their profit oriented goals. Nor is it to say that the international oil business is or should be a completely free market, that is 'totally free' of government influence or control.

As far as the international oil companies' continuing efforts to shift their profits to those countries with the lowest tax base, it behooves the world to follow the example of the European Community and create a level playing field in so far as the rate of taxation is concerned. The oil accounting systems are intricate enough to thoroughly confuse any layman. In the words of Les Aspin, the then Democrat Congressman from Wisconsin, 'no serious students of business could adequately compare the relative financial positions of any of the thirty (oil) corporations'[101]. With no tax haven to which to shift their profits, the international oil companies will self-righteously pay their taxes to that country which is entitled to them. Whether it be the crude producing countries, the oil transiting countries or those countries that now seem to generate the maximum profit for the oil companies, the 'end users'. Without a level playing field for the payment of taxes, there is no government bureaucracy big enough or with the huge talent required to police the tax-avoidance power of the international companies.

The international oil companies operate under extremely unusual conditions, hostage as they are and completely subservient to their producing host governments. Because the product they supply has such vast implications to the security and defense, as well as the comfort of the world's populations, it remains an open question as to how free the oil market should be. Just how much influence governments will have in the future on the conduct of this unique, vitally necessary, commercial endeavor is entirely dependent on how moral or determined the world governments of today are.

In the case of the embargo of Rhodesia by Great Britain, the position taken in the body of this text was that the two Government Directors of BP had to have known that BP was breaking the embargo and they did not bring this knowledge to the attention of their own government. Even if they had done so, there is another valid scenario. The British Government was in desperate need of the trade of South Africa. Therefore, they turned a blind eye to the activities of their majority owned oil company. There is no doubt in the author's mind that the gravest possibility exists that the factor that allowed a British Government, majority owned oil company to continue to supply petroleum products to a country, a country that had been embargoed by that very same majority owner, was the British Government's need for the economic impetus represented by the South African economy.

It is only necessary to examine the record of the history of the U.N. Security Council. 'In the December 1966 debate George Brown made it clear that Britain would resist any proposal to amend its draft so as to commit the UN to take action against South Africa or Portugal if they violated the Charter (as both did) by refusing to comply with the Council's mandatory decisions'.[102] 'Caradon expounded his government's view that Britain could not stand the economic shock of a break with South Africa; and he reminded the Council that using British force against Rhodesia was not a matter of maintaining order in a colony where Britain had troops, but one of invading a territory which had been self-governing, controlling its own armed forces for half a century, and where there had never been a British army or a British administration'.[103]

Anyone that had even a passing acquaintance with the activities of the international oil companies, and the British Government had very much more than a passing acquaintance with 'the Frankenstein syndrome of BP which they had created',[104] knew that it was impossible for Rhodesia to be supplied with its petroleum requirements without the international oil companies being the source of that supply. After all, to slightly paraphrase a hackneyed expression, 'If it walks like a duck, swims like a duck, flies like a duck, smells like duck, looks like a duck, quacks like a duck and fornicates like a duck, by god it is a duck'.

Winston Churchill's comment over Britain's lack of preparation for Singapore's defense during the War sums it up: 'I did not know; I was not told; I should have asked.'[105] It wasn't necessary for the British Government to ask. They had only to look. In addition, there is another well grounded, cynical theory. That is, that having made the grand, public gesture for world consumption of backing the independent aspirations of the blacks in Rhodesia, Great Britain then merely sat back on its haunches and let the international oil companies, and in particular the one of which they were the majority owner, take over its real basic foreign policy; that policy was the protection of their domestic economy.

Detailed examination of Hansard of the Commons appears to indicate that at no time was there any serious consideration ever given to embargoing South Africa. An embargo which could have been a serious threat, indeed, to the British economy if prolonged. Yet one that it seems would have spelled the downfall of Ian Smith's white government quicker than it would have taken the British Navy to get into position to enforce the blockade. 'It is true to say that, following an International Conference on Sanctions in London, the world community was able to exert sufficient pressure on the South African regime to prevent the death sentences on Mandela and his colleagues in the Rivonia trial of 1964. And so, right through the 60's, 70's and the 80's *the effectiveness of sanctions were proved* ... (emphasis is mine).'[106]

In addition, how many in Parliament really cared about their previous black subjects? How many in the Cabinet were truly concerned about that far and distant land that was now in the process of being divorced from the Empire? Certainly the British never hesitated to shoot thousands and thousands of Indians when it suited the demands of preserving their empire. They never shrank from starving hundreds and hundreds of innocent women and children in their concentration camps in South Africa during the Boer War, as well as leaving those same women and children open to ghastly, death dealing diseases. All done in protection of that same empire.

Even as recently as 1945 at Yalta when Churchill was faced with, what he believed to be, the threat of trusteeships being placed over parts of the British Empire by the United Nations through Dumbarton Oaks, he vehemently stated, "I absolutely disagree. I will not have one scrap of British territory flung into that area."[107] Why should the British politicians really care about a few misguided blacks in what was soon to be a former territory?

As Martin Bailey ends his devastating chronology in 'OILGATE, The Sanctions Scandal', he asks a dreadfully and morally disturbing and penetrating question, "... is ... it ... a more dramatic and well-documented example of the political process in Britain today?"

It is self evident that all companies, domestic and inter-national, are run by human beings. Human beings who, at one time or another, are susceptible to temptation. Whether that temptation be monetary or the self destroying grasp for personal power is a fault of the individuals, not the fault of the system of a free market. It is in this respect that government responsibility becomes manifest. It is the duty of government 'to govern and to police'. The government's checks and balances in a democracy prohibit the kind of excesses which the people of totalitarian regimes regularly endure as a routine measure of the inherent nature of such powers. That same atmosphere created by the checks and balances of a democratically, governing body will prohibit economic brutality, such as exercised by Mr. Putin against his political adversaries in the oil industry, by the policing department of a democracy.

Ever since leaving university and becoming an officer in the United States Navy, I have sat on management's side of the table across from labour. From this secure vantage point, I was privileged to learn a vital lesson concerning the free market. With man's penchant for exorbitant, personal, monetary gain or a plain and simple grab for absolute power, the free market place needs still another bulwark to keep it that way. *Unions!*

To paraphrase Voltaire's biographer who wrote, 'If Voltaire's philosophy could be summed up in one sentence it would be', "I disagree with what you say, but I will defend to the death your right to say it", I say to the unions, "I believe your actions are detrimental to the well being of the corporation, but I will defend to the death your right to exist".

Let us not too soon forget that without Solidarity, Poland might still be enslaved to its Board of Directors, the previous 'Union of Soviet Socialist Republics'.

With the God given opportunity of having lived, seen and been part of almost half the known world for well over half a century, I say to my fellow Americans, "Get down on your knees and thank your God, whoever HE may be, that in spite of all of its faults, you are a citizen of the greatest democracy the world has ever known."

GLOSSARY

Afrikanner: South Africa had four 'classes' of people. The main two categories were white and black. Within the white group were two subdivisions, the English Speakers as the descendants from Great Britain were known and the Afrikanners, the Dutch descendants. Within the black division there were actually three subdivisions, the Indians, the coloured (mixed races), and then there were the blacks.

AFRA: **A**verage **F**reight **R**ate **A**ssessment. **AFRA**. This number was as inviolable as the posted price of crude oil. It was the basis for all freight calculations by the international oil companies.

Bookera: The transliteration for the Arabic word tomorrow. (See 'Ins'Allah' also).

Bruderbund: The political organization of the Afrikanners of South Africa was known as the 'Bruderbund'.

Bucsheese: Transliteration of the Chinese word for tip or bribe given for special services.

Channel Fever: Expatriates as they reach the end of their tour of duty, whether it be three years as in the case of the Caltex employees or seven to ten years as in the case of the old colonial rulers, they begin to count the number of days left of their tour. They begin to long to be rid of 'the chains that bound them' to whatever country they happen to be resident at the moment. They look across the water to imagined freedom, and their eyes become glazed. It is at this time that they are diagnosed as to be afflicted with 'channel fever'.

Chummery: A British expression denoting bachelors' quarters.

Clean or dirty: A clean product is one in which the carrying vessel doesn't have to be cleaned before it can carry its new cargo, ie: Gasoline, kerosene, gasoil, etc. A dirty product is one in which the vessel has to be cleaned if it carried crude oil,

493

heavy fuel oil or any 'black oil' and it is intended to use the vessel to carry a clean product. The terminology is also applied to the vessel itself that has carried 'clean' or 'dirty' cargoes.

Da beze: Transliteration of the Chinese phrase for foreigner. In the inimitable way of the Chinese whose language, particularly the written language, is a graphic description of the object or event, 'da' is big and 'beze' is nose. There are no other human beings in the universe except the Chinese, and those others with big noses.

Demurrage: Each size vessel has a standard loading time. If the loading time is exceeded through the fault of the vessel (slow pumps, vessel not clean, etc.) the vessel incurs 'demurrage' which is payable by the owner. If the vessel is unable to enter the port because of the failure of the 'supplier' to have made the necessary arrangements or the product is not ready for loading, 'demurrage' is, also, incurred by the vessel, but in this case it is payable by the supplier and not by the vessel's owner.

Ding hao: Transliteration of the Chinese phrase for the word 'excellent'.

Distressed vessel: A vessel that has no cargo and no contract to pick up a cargo.

Extra-Territorial: The Western powers never 'colonized' China as so many of them 'colonized' the lands of Africa and the peoples of the Middle East. Nevertheless, they did set up their own courts, staked out certain areas over which they flew their imperial flags and tried their own citizens in these courts.

Grandfathered: A very common expression used in several languages. It indicates that although the rules were changed, those who had operated previously under the old rules were allowed to continue under them, hence, 'grandfathered'.

Grunts: This was the terminology applied to the foot soldiers of World War II

Gymkhana: This is an all encompassing term for sporting events. It is mainly dedicated to competition between horses and their riders, but in general it is one in which horses are the main attraction.

Harrari: Harrari in the local dialect means freedom and was 'shouted from the roof tops' during the transition from colonial rule to independence in all African colonies. It became the name that replaced the name of the capital of Rhodesia, Salisbury, which was symbolic of the times.

Ins'Allah:'God (Allah) willing!' Every moment of everyone's existence in the Middle East or wherever the Muslim religion reigns, Allah's will controls everything. A farewell of, 'Bookera Ins'Allah' would translate to 'see you soon'—not the actual translation of 'tomorrow', and would only occur—Ins'Allah—God willing. Do you think it will rain tomorrow? Ins'Allah! Maybe it will be sunny tomorrow. Ins'Allah! Perhaps it will be cold tomorrow. Ins'Allah. Bon voyage! Ins'Allah! There should be many tourists on the weekend to help the economy. Ins'Allah!

Maalish: Next to 'bookera', this has to be the most frustrating Arabic expression to Westerners. 'Maalish! Never mind! It's not important! Forget it!, ie: I just had an accident, and my car is a total loss! 'Maalish!'

Mazbout: This is a thick (and to Westerners—sickeningly sweet) Arabic cup of coffee. To the Arabs it is just the right or correct mixture. Hence, you can order 'mazbout' in a cafe or in conversation you can agree with the correctness of the statement as in "Mazbout". "I agree", or "You are correct".

Ming tien: Transliteration of the Chinese phrase for 'au revoir'.

MTC: Military **T**ransport **C**ommand. There was a very large fleet of civilian manned, transport vessels which were utilized by the Army. By having them manned by civilian merchant marine personnel, the military could concentrate its efforts on training and keeping their troops in combat readiness instead of attempting to provide personnel to man ships for which the merchant marine already had a sufficient complement.

OPEC: The Organization of **P**etroleum **E**xporting **C**ountries. As the name implies, this cartel is composed of those countries who have crude oil as an indigenous raw material which they export.

POSH: There are many people who frequently use this acronym when referring to a matter about which they are slightly envious, (although they may not admit it). POSH designates a very special place in the hierarchy of the pecking order. While many people use the expression quite correctly, there are few, if any, that recall its origin. Long before the days of air conditioning, the voyage for the British colonialist was hot, humid and unending on the way East. Those who had influence or the rank that entitled them to avoid the sun and the heat always booked their passage on the port side of the vessel when going to the far flung outposts of the empire to help rule the King's subjects. After their tour of duty ended and they began the same interminable voyage home many years later, they also avoided the sun by booking their passage on the starboard side of the vessel. Hence:"*P*ort *O*utwards *S*tarboard *H*omewards".

Purple heart: An award made by the American military to those who were wounded in action.

Roll the Bones: As in any game of chance, a variety of items are thrown at random. The resultant position in which these items come to rest after the 'throw' determines the outcome of the 'game'. In the case of witch doctors, the items thrown are human bones. The position in which they come to rest after being thrown by the witch doctor forecasts how successful the spell he is conjuring up is going to be.

Roughneck: The terminology applied to those individuals that physically, and with great manual effort and dexterity, handled all the drilling equipment and heavy machinery on a drilling site or platform.

Seven Sisters: This was a derisive term applied to the seven major international oil companies, Esso, Mobil, Texaco, Standard Oil of California (SOCAL or Chevron) Shell, BP and Gulf.

Sampan: A small Chinese boat propelled by sculling with an oar from the stern.

Sisal: A very tough fibrous plant whose fibers were used in the manufacture of rope, particularly rope or ships' lines used for tying up vessels.

Spot charter: A one voyage contract as opposed to a long time charter of a year or more. Mainly used to fill an immediate need and completed 'on the spot'. Hence, 'Spot Charter'.

Taipan: Transliteration of the Chinese word used to describe the head or Chief Executive officer of any large organization.

WOG: **W**esternized **O**riental **G**entleman. A very derogatory term applied to those residents of the Middle and Far East, in particular those that had acquired not only the ability to converse in the language of the Westerners, but had acquired their habits of dress and mannerisms as well.

END NOTES

Chapter 1

[1] Anthony Sampson, **The Seven Sisters**, (Great Britain: Hodder and Stoughton Limited, 1988), p.162

[2] Anthony Sampson, **Black & Gold**, (Great Britain: Hodder and Stoughton Limited, 1987), p.129,130.

[3] Carl Mydans & Shelly Mydans, **The Violent Peace**, (Canada: McClelland and Stewart Ltd., 1968), p.169

[4] George F.Will, **The Leveling Wind,** (Viking, New York, N.Y. 1994), p 345

[5] Bevin Alexander, **How Great Generals Win,** (W.W.Norton & Company, Inc. 1993), p.235

Chapter 2

[6] Carl Mydans & Shelly Mydans, **The Violent Peace**, (Canada: McClelland and Stewart Ltd., 1968), p.49

Chapter 3

[7] John A.Pugsley, **The Alpha Strategy**, (Los Angeles: Harper & Row, 1980), p.30

[8] Peter F.Drucker, **Managing in Turbulent Times**, (New York, Harper & Row Publishers, 1980), p.10

[9] James F.Byrnes, **Speaking Frankly**, (New York: Harper & Brothers Publishers, 1947), p.18

[10] John Prados, **Combined Fleet Decoded,** (Random House, New York 1995) p.297

[11] Pugsley, p.17

[12] **The Wall Street Journal**, May 4, 1993.

[13] P.J O'Rourke, **Parliament of Whores**, (New York, N.Y. Atlantic Monthly Press, 1991)

[14] Kenneth Memories and Alan M.Siegel, **Guide to Understanding Money & Investing,** (The Wall Street Journal, Lightbulb Press, Inc.,1993) p.7

[15.] Martin Caidin, **A Torch to the Enemy,** (Bantam Books, New York, NY 1992) p.42

Chapter 5

[16.] Vol.182, No.5, NOVEMBER 1992, **National Geographic,**p.79,85

Chapter 7

[17.] Carl Mydans & Shelly Mydans, **The Violent Peace,** (Canada: McClelland and Stewart Ltd. 1968) p.61
[18.] Carl Mydans & Shelly Mydans, p.61-62
[19.] Anthony Sampson, **The Seven Sisters**, (Great Britain: Hodder and Stoughton Limited, 1988), p.209
[20.] Sampson, p.209
[21.] Sampson, p.209
[22.] Sampson, p.209
[23.] John Prados, **COMBINED FLEET DECODED,** (Random House, New York 1995) p.17

Chapter 8

[24.] Robert Standish, **Elephant Walk**, (Great Britain: Peter Davis Limited, 1948)

Chapter 9

[25.] Anthony Sampson, **The Seven Sisters**, (Great Britain: Hodder and Stoughton Limited, 1988), p.85
[26.] Mohamed Heikal, **Autumn of Fury**, (Great Britain: Andre Deutsch Limited, 1983), p.91
[27.] Keith Wheelock, **Nasser's New Egypt**, (New York, N.Y.: Frederick A. Prager, 1960), p.58

Chapter 10

[28.] Keith Wheelock, **Nasser's New Egypt**, (New York, N.Y.: Frederick A.Prager, 1960), p.58
[29.] Henry Longhurst, **Adventure in Oil,** (Sidgwick and Jackson, 1959, London) p.32
[30.] Miles Copeland, **The Game of Nations**, (Birkenhead, London: Willmer Brothers limited, 1969), p.81
[31.] Wheelock, p.239

[32.] Wheelock, p.57

[33.] John G.Stoessinger, **Why Nations Go To War**, (New York, N.Y.: St.Martin's Press, Inc., 1982), p.156

[34.] Mohamed Heikal, **Autumn of Fury**, (Great Britain: Andre Deutsch Limited, 1983), p.77

[35.] Stewart Steven, **The Spymasters of Israel,** (New York, Ballaltine Books, 1980) pg 82*

Chapter 11

[36.] Keith Wheelock, **Nasser's New Egypt**, (New York, N.Y.: Frederick A.Prager, 1960, p.250

[37.] Miles Copeland, **The Game of Nations**, (Birkenhead, London: Willmer Brothers Limited, 1969), p.220

[38.] Wheelock, p.250

Chapter 12

[39.] **Newsweek**, December 3, 1956, refer Keith Wheelock, **Nasser's New Egypt**, (New York, N.Y.: Frederick A.Prager, 1960), p.248

[40.] James F.Byrnes, **Speaking Frankly**, (New York, N.Y.: Harper & Brothers, 1947), p.292

[41.] Martin Caidin, **A TORCH TO THE ENEMY,** (New York, N.Y., Bantam Books, 1992) p.167

[42.] Lt.(jg) Bowles, USNR, Lt.(jg) Carter, USNR, Chief Ship's Clerk Forde, USN, **U.S.S.CORE, A History,** (Tacoma, Washington: Aboard ship), p.38

[43.] John G.Stoessinger, **Why Nations Go To War**, (New York, N.Y.: St.Martin's Press. 1982) p.170

[44.] Anthony Sampson, **The Seven Sisters**, (Great Britain: Hodder and Stoughton Limited, 1988), p. 152

Chapter 13

[45.] Miles Copeland, **The Game of Nations**, (Birkenhead, London: Wilmer Brothers Limited, 1969), p. 194

[46.] Anthony Sampson, **The Seven Sisters**, (Great Britain: Hodder and Stoughton Limited 1988), p.104

[47.] Sampson, p.85

[48.] **The Wall Street Journal**, '137 Cases of Executive Action', January 16, 1987

[49.] James B.Stewart, **Den of Thieves**, (New York, N.Y.:

Simon & Schuster, 1991), p.346

50. Sampson, p.114

51. Copeland, p.192

52. Copeland, p.196, 197

53. Oleg Penkovskiy, **The Penkovskiy Papers,** (Avon Books, Doubleday & Company, Inc. 1965), p.354

54. Copeland, p.197

55. Tom Clancy, **Red Storm Rising**, (New York, New York: G.P.Putnam's Sons, August 1986) p.170

56. Copeland, p.197

57. Copeland, p.197

Chapter 14

58. Carl Midas & Shelly Midas, **The Violent Peace**, (Canada: McClelland and Stewart Ltd., 1968), p.102,103,104

59. Anthony Sampson, **The Seven Sisters**, (Great Britain: Hotter and Stoughton Limited, 1988), p.125

60. Sampson, p.125

61. Sampson, p.159

Chapter 15

62. NEWSWEEK, **Herd of White Elephants,** The bank has plenty of boondoggles to answer for, October 9, 1995 p. 43

63. Anthony Sampson, **The Seven Sisters**, (Great Britain: Hodder and Stoughton Limited, 1988), p.346

64. Sampson, p.164

65. **International Herald Tribune**, November 27, 1991

67. Noel Barber, **The War of the Running Dogs**, (Great Britain: Wm. Collins, 1971), p.247

68. Joseph C. Grew, **Ten Years in Japan,** (New York: Simon and Schuster, 1944), p.376

Chapter 16

69. Ronald Segal & Ruth First—edited by, South West Africa: **Travesty of Trust**, (London: Andre Deutsch Limited, 1967), p.254

70. Anthony Sampson, **The Seven Sisters**, (Great Britain: Hodder and Stoughton Limited, 1988), p.348

71. Sampson, p.349

72. Nicholas Tomalin, **The Sunday Times**, 19 December 1965

73. Ronald Segal & Ruth First, p.254

74. Ronald Segal & Ruth First, p.254

75. **Guardian**, 22 November 1965.

76. Ronald Segal & Ruth First, p. 255

77. Ronald Segal & Ruth First, p.254

78. Ronald Segal & Ruth First, p.255

Chapter 17

79. **Plotting Hitler's Death**, Joachim Fest, (Weidenfeld & Nicolson, Great Britain, 1996) p. 339

80. James F.Byrnes, **Speaking Frankly**, (New York, N.Y.: Harper & Brothers, 1947), p.248

81. Martin Bailey, **OILGATE, The Sanctions Scandal,** (Great Britain: Hodder and Stoughton Limited, 1979), p.124

82. Colin L.Powell, **MY AMERICAN JOURNEY,** (Random House, New York 1995) p.296

83. Martin Baily, **OILGATE, The Sanctions Scandal,** (Great Britain; Hodder and Stoughton Limited, 1997), p.124

84. Anthony Sampson, **Black & Gold**, (Great Britain: Hodder and Stoughton Limited, 1987), p.79

85. Anthony Sampson, **The Seven Sisters**, (Great Britain: Hodder and Stoughton Limited, 1988), p.246

86. Sampson, **The Seven Sisters**, p.247

87. John G.Stoessinger, **Why Nations Go To War**, (New York, N.Y.: St.Martin's Press, Inc., 1982), p.182

88. Martin Baily, **OILGATE, The Sanctions Scandal**, (Great Britain; Hodder and Stoughton Limited, 1979), p. 167

89. Sampson, **The Seven Sisters**, p.72

90. **THE SHAH'S LAST RIDE**, William Shawcross, (Simon and Schuster, New York, New York 1988) p.52

91. Sampson, **The Seven Sisters**, p.212

92. Martin Bailey, **OILGATE, The Sanctions Scandal**, (Great Britain: Hodder and Stoughton Limited, 1979), p.137

Chapter 18

[93.] Sanche de Gramont, **THE FRENCH, Portrait of a People,** (G.P.Putnam's, New York), p.16

[94.] The White House Years, **Henry Kissinger,** (George Weidenfeld & Nicolson Ltd. Great Britain, 1979) p. 20

[95.] The Rainbow People, **Richard Collier** (Weidenfeld and Nicolson, London, 1984) p.35

[96.] Franklin Hamlin Littell, **The German Phoenix,** (Doubleday & Company, Inc., Garden City, New York 1960), p. 45

[97.] Robert Ludlum, **The Scorpio Illusion,** (Great Britain: Harper Collins Publishers, 1993), p.243

[98.] Jane Mayer & Jill Abramson, **Strange Justice,** (Houghton Mifflin Company, 1994) p. 211

[99.] Jane Mayer & Jill Abramson, p. 211

Chapter 19

[100.] Martin Bailey, **OILGATE …, The Sanctions Scandal**, (Great Britain: Coronet Books, 1979), p.214

[101.] Henry Longhurst, **ADVENTURES IN OIL,** (Sedgwick and Jackson Ltd. 1959) pg. 256

Epilogue

[102.] Anthony Sampson, **The Seven Sisters**, (Great Britain: Hodder and Stoughton Limited, 1988), p.217

[103.] Andrew Boyd, **Fifteen Men on a Powder Keg**, (Methuen & Co. Ltd.1971) p.228

[104.] Andrew Boyd, p.255

[105.] Sampson, p.73

[106.] Martin Bailey, **OILGATE, The Sanctions Scandal**, (Great Britain: Coronet Books, 1979), p.214

[107.] Trevor Huddleston, **Return to South Africa, The Ecstasy and the Agony,**(Hammersmith, London: Harper Collins **Publishers**, 1991),p.16

[108.] James F. Byrnes, **Speaking Frankly**, (New York, N.Y.: Harper & Brothers, 1947), Short hand notes taken by Mr. Byrnes at Yalta on February 9, 1945.

978-0-595-42597-6
0-595-42597-6

Printed in the United States
86162LV00003B/16/A